Wine
Report
2009
Tom Stevenson

LONDON NEW YORK MUNICH
MELBOURNE DELHI

FOR DORLING KINDERSLEY
Managing Editor Dawn Henderson
Managing Art Editor Christine Keilty
Production Editor Ben Marcus
US Editor Christine Heilman

PRODUCED FOR DORLING KINDERSLEY BY
Sands Publishing Solutions
4 Jenner Way, Eccles, Aylesford, Kent ME20 7SQ
Project Editors David & Sylvia Tombesi-Walton
Project Art Editor Simon Murrell

FOR TOM STEVENSON
Editor Pat Carroll
Tasting Logistics Jeff Porter, Evenlode Press

First American Edition, 2008

Published in the United States by
DK Publishing
375 Hudson Street
New York, New York 10014

08 09 10 11   10 9 8 7 6 5 4 3 2 1

WD180—10/2008

Published in Great Britain by
Dorling Kindersley Limited.

A catalog record for this book is available from
the Library of Congress.

ISBN 978-0-7566-3983-9

DK books are available at special discounts when
purchased in bulk for sales promotions, premiums,
fund-raising, or educational use. For details,
contact: DK Publishing Special Markets, 375 Hudson Street, New York, New York 10014
or SpecialSales@dk.com.

Printed and bound in China by
Leo Paper

Discover more at

www.dk.com

CONTENTS

Introduction 4

FRANCE

Bordeaux
DAVID PEPPERCORN MW 10

Burgundy
CLIVE COATES MW 19

Champagne
TOM STEVENSON 29

Alsace
TOM STEVENSON 38

Loire Valley
CHARLES SYDNEY 47

Rhône Valley
OLIVIER POELS 56

Jura & Savoie
WINK LORCH 62

Southwest France
PAUL STRANG 72

Languedoc-Roussillon
ROSEMARY GEORGE MW 80

Vins de Pays & Vins de Table
ROSEMARY GEORGE MW 89

GERMANY

Germany
MICHAEL SCHMIDT 97

ITALY

Italy overview
NICOLAS BELFRAGE MW
& FRANCO ZILIANI 107

Northern Italy
NICOLAS BELFRAGE MW
& FRANCO ZILIANI 111

Central & Southern Italy
NICOLAS BELFRAGE MW
& FRANCO ZILIANI 120

SPAIN

Spain
JOHN RADFORD 128

Sherry
JULIAN JEFFS QC 137

PORTUGAL

Portugal
CHARLES METCALFE 144

Port & Madeira
RICHARD MAYSON 152

GREAT BRITAIN

Great Britain
STEPHEN SKELTON MW 160

BELGIUM, NETHERLANDS & SCANDINAVIA

Belgium, Netherlands & Scandinavia
FIONA MORRISON MW & RONALD DE GROOT 168

LUXEMBOURG

Luxembourg
DAVID FURER 177

SWITZERLAND

Switzerland
CHANDRA KURT 185

AUSTRIA

Austria
PHILIPP BLOM 192

EASTERN & SOUTHEASTERN EUROPE

Eastern & Southeastern Europe
DR. CAROLINE GILBY MW 200

Greece
NICO MANESSIS 213

MIDDLE EAST

Lebanon
MICHAEL KARAM 221

Israel
DANIEL ROGOV 230

SOUTH AFRICA

South Africa
CATHY VAN ZYL MW & TIM JAMES 237

NORTH AMERICA

California
DAN BERGER 247

Pacific Northwest
PAUL GREGUTT 254

Atlantic Northeast
SANDRA SILFVEN 265

Other US States
DOUG FROST MW 273

Canada
TONY ASPLER 283

SOUTH & CENTRAL AMERICA

Chile
PETER RICHARDS 292

Argentina
TIM ATKIN MW 300

AUSTRALASIA

Australia
HUON HOOKE 308

New Zealand
BOB CAMPBELL MW 319

Asia
DENIS GASTIN 328

NON-REGIONAL REPORTS

Organic & Biodynamic Wines
MONTY WALDIN 338

Wine & Health
BEVERLEY BLANNING MW 349

Grape Varieties
DR. FRANÇOIS LEFORT 355

Classic Wine Vintage Guide
SERENA SUTCLIFFE MW 365

Wine Auctions & Investment
ANTHONY ROSE 373

Viticulture
DR. RICHARD SMART &
DR. CAROLINE GILBY MW 381

Wine Science 388
DR. RONALD JACKSON

Wine on the Web
TOM CANNAVAN 396

The 100 Most Exciting
Wine Finds 404

INDEX 418

Introduction
Best in the world

Wine Report's often obscure and bizarre insights into the world of wine have earned it a third Best in World prize at the Gourmand International Awards.

No other book has won two such awards, let alone three, and it was the first and only wine book in Gourmand's Hall of Fame until it was joined by *The World Atlas of Wine* in April 2008. I constantly meet people in the wine trade who have never heard of *Wine Report*, but anyone who has is so hooked that he or she cannot wait for the next edition. This includes me, because I write just two contributions (Champagne and Alsace) and, like everybody else, I look forward to reading all the other reports.

This year, Clive Coates slams Beaujolais Nouveau, and I reveal the truth behind Champagne's expansion, while Olivier Poels applauds the intentions of "zero-sulfite" wine producers in the Rhône but is dubious about their results. The EU-law-breaking Vin de Pays des Vignobles de France is up and running, but the Eurocrats prevent Spain from going ahead with its proposed Viñedos de España appellation. What's going on there?

Michael Schmidt reports from Germany on vineyard gazumping in the Rheinhessen, and John Radford digs out a delicious, glugging Spanish white wine for just €2.50! Nicolas Belfrage and Franco Ziliani investigate yet more fraud in the Italian wine trade, while Julian Jeffs reveals that sherry vinegar has become more profitable than wine in Jerez.

Stephen Skelton explains why he wonders whether the UK's sparkling-wine boom will "all end in tears"; Nico Manessis reports on the explosion of quality driven by Greece's boutique wineries; and Caroline Gilby tells us how Russia's tightening of the economic screw on Moldova has all but destroyed that country's wine industry.

We learn that István Szepsy has released single-vineyard Tokajis, Parker has discovered Israeli wine, and Asia now has in excess of 800 wineries.

There are swings and roundabouts in the alcohol debate, as Beverley Blanning reveals that, while it can increase the risk of breast cancer, it can also reduce the risk of kidney cancer. Last but not least: Paul Gregutt has had a haircut and a shave!

Tom Stevenson

About This Guide

This is not so much a "How to Use" section as an explanation of the brief that I gave to contributors and the parameters they applied (or did not!).

Contributors

Every contributor to *Wine Report* was my personal choice. For the most part, they are the expert's experts in their various specialty areas. For some regions there are no experts, and I had to twist the arm of the most strategically placed professionals to tackle such reports. There have been small changes in contributors since the first edition, and I imagine there will be more in the future. *Wine Report* has very specific needs, so if some contributors come and go, the going has nothing to do with their expertise on the subject and everything to do with how I expect it to be applied. Ideally, I would like to see no more than one report per contributor, since this would project the desired specialist ambience, but it will take time to achieve.

Opinions expressed by contributors

These are, of course, their own. I am not referring specifically to the Opinion section of each report (which is dealt with separately below), but rather the more general way in which they report a story. For example, the way that François Lefort (Grape Varieties) writes about GMOs could not be further from the way that Monty Waldin (Organic & Biodynamic Wines) covers the subject. I respect both of these contributors' opinions, although I do not completely agree with either of them. (Anyone interested in my view should look at www.wine-pages.com/guests/tom/gm.htm.)

Reader's knowledge level

Unlike most other wine books, *Wine Report* assumes a certain level of knowledge. Therefore, there are rarely any explanations of technical terms or even references to historical incidents. Readers are expected to know what these terms mean and what the references refer to, or at least have the intelligence and curiosity to look them up.

News and Grapevine items

Regional reports include news affecting the region and its producers, wines, and consumers. This may incorporate gossip and rumor but not marketing or sales stories unless they are of an exceptional or very hot nature. Nonregional reports have their own structure. It should be noted that, for Wine & Health, Beverley Blanning has been specifically commissioned to report the bad news as well as the good and, if anything, to err on the side of the former rather than the latter. I want to give readers as much good health news as possible, but *Wine Report* is for wine enthusiasts and cannot afford to be vulnerable to accusations of selective reporting of this sensitive issue.

Opinion

Contributors have quite a free hand to spout off about anything they feel strongly about, but there are certain categories of opinion that are obligatory. These are, essentially, anything that is currently practiced, legally or not, that the contributor believes should not be, and anything that the contributor believes should be happening, but is not. Contributors should always attempt to balance their criticisms with practical solutions. Readers should expect to see the same opinions repeated or refined in each edition, unless the situation changes, which would be news in itself.

Vintage Reports

Each regional contributor provides an advance report on the very latest harvest (the year before date of publication for the Northern Hemisphere, the actual year of publication for the Southern Hemisphere), plus brief updates on the previous five vintages. In the first edition, it was difficult enough to get some contributors to rate vintages on a 100-point scale, but most toed the line. However, everyone was using a different yardstick, so, from the second edition, all vintage ratings conform to the following definitions.

100	No vintage can be accurately described as perfect, but those achieving a maximum score must be truly great vintages.
90–99	Excellent to superb.
80–89	Good to very good.
70–79	Average to good.
60–69	Disappointing.
40–59	Very bad.
0–39	Disastrous.

Vintage ratings should merely be seen as "betting odds." They express the likelihood of what might be reasonably expected from a wine of a given year. The higher the rating, the fewer the exceptions; quality and consistency do, to some extent, go hand in hand.

Top 10s

If percentile ratings for vintages did not set the cat among the pigeons, then these Top 10s of producers and wines certainly did. Very few contributors were worried about listing the 10 best of anything, but several were extremely reluctant to put that list in order of preference. Eventually most agreed to do this, but readers might come across the odd list that looks suspiciously as if it is in alphabetical order...

There was no requirement for each Top 10 to be fully utilized. If a contributor truly believes that, for example, only five or six producers or wines deserve a place in a particular Top 10, then that is perfectly acceptable. Furthermore, it was permitted to place the same producer or wine in more than one list. Such coexistence could even apply to the Greatest and Best-Value Producers or Best Bargain Top 10s.

Prices

All prices in this guide are average retail prices, including tax, per bottle, expressed in the local currency of the country of origin. This is not a buyer's guide; the wines listed are supposed to be the greatest, best-bargain, or most exciting or unusual, without restricting the choice to those that happen to be available on any specific market.

Greatest Wine Producers

My guidelines to the contributors made it clear that their choice should be "regardless of status." In other words, even if there is some sort of acknowledged hierarchy, such as Bordeaux's *cru classé* system, the contributor should not feel restrained by it. On the other hand, if a contributor agrees entirely with a perceived hierarchy, there is nothing preventing him or her from following it slavishly. Some contributors set themselves their own criteria. Dan Berger, for example, told me that for his greatest producers he had decided: (a) the winery had to be in business for at least 10 years, and production over that period had to have remained substantially the same; (b) the winery had to use substantially the same fruit sources, mainly from owned or leased vineyards, for the last 10 years, and not deviate from a house style; (c) the ownership and winemaking had to be consistent over the last 10 years; and (d) the winery must make at least two wines that have achieved the highest levels of quality without ever deviating from that level, even in a mediocre vintage.

Dan's criteria represent a very professional way of ascertaining greatness, but they are not ones that I would impose on all contributors. Furthermore, the term "greatest" is relative: it does not necessarily mean that the producer is intrinsically great. The best producer in California should be intrinsically great, but although the greatest producer in Belgium must, by definition, be its greatest, in practice it will be no more than "interesting." Readers should expect the Greatest Producers list to change the least of all the Top 10s from year to year.

Fastest-Improving Producers

Whether good or bad, reputations tend to stick well beyond their shelf life, which is why this particular Top 10 is probably the most useful. While the rest of the market lags behind, you can benefit from the insider knowledge of *Wine Report*, buying up top-performing wines long before others cotton on and prices increase.

New Up-and-Coming Producers

While Fastest-Improving Producers will probably be well-established wineries that have perked up, this Top 10 focuses on the newer producers that are the ones to watch. In some of the more conservative traditional areas, "new" will be relative and should perhaps be taken to mean newer, or a producer whose wines used to be sold only from the cellar door but have recently become more widely available.

Best-Value Producers

This is self-explanatory.

Greatest-Quality Wines

Each contributor has his or her own method for determining their greatest wines. I am sure that many do as I tend to do, and that is to list the greatest I have tasted within the last 12 months, rather than the greatest wines per se. True experts in classic areas will probably have notes on thousands of wines tasted in the last 12 months, and of these there could be 50-plus wines that would justifiably achieve a top score. Most contributors could probably fill their Top 10 Greatest Wines several times over. (Most years I could fill the Top 10 Greatest Alsace Wines twice over with just Zind Humbrecht's wines.) Thus realistically this should be viewed as merely "10 of the greatest." Then, of course, we have to put them in order of preference, which can be a real pain. How, for example, is it possible to say whether the greatest red bordeaux is better than the greatest Sauternes, or the greatest Alsace Gewurztraminer better than the greatest Alsace Pinot Gris? If David Peppercorn and I find this difficult, what about Nick Belfrage and Franco Ziliani? The range of wines in Italy is far more complex. So, what most contributors end up with is "10 of the greatest in a less-than-logical order of preference." This would worry me in any other book, but readers of *Wine Report* are supposed to be sophisticated enough to understand that this is fascinating enough in its own right.

Best Bargains

Although most will be relatively inexpensive, bargains do not necessarily have to be cheap. It is easier to find bargains at lower prices, just as it is easier to find great wines at higher prices, but it is possible to find relative bargains at any price point. In theory, the greatest, most expensive bordeaux could be the number-one Best Bargain.

Most Exciting or Unusual Finds

This could be an unusually fine wine from what is normally a below-standard region, winery, or grape. It might be an atypical wine, or the first of a certain variety or style. Each wine listed will carry a brief explanation of why it is so exciting and/or unusual.

The 100 Most Exciting Wine Finds

Each contributor was asked to submit four wines for consideration for this section of the book, which meant approximately 150 wines. Only contributors for the emerging or more obscure wine regions were allowed to proffer wines from their Greatest Wines. The rest had to select wines from either their Best Bargains or Most Exciting or Unusual Finds, otherwise this section would be stacked with Pétrus, Krug, Romanée-Conti, the quality of which most readers will be aware of, but few can afford. I then tasted the wines blind, grouped by variety or style, culling almost 40 percent (which is why I limited myself to two wines from Champagne and one from Alsace). Contributors also provided a tasting note, which is followed by my own comment.

Bordeaux

David Peppercorn MW

Looking back, 2007 could be the year when Bordeaux's top elite finally disconnected with the rest of the market.

DAVID PEPPERCORN MW

I have been studying the monthly bulletins put out by Liv-ex (the London International Vintners Exchange). They use a sophisticated system to rank each wine based on average prices from 2000 onward; the notional availability, based on the château's production; the monetary value of wine traded through the exchange; and Parker points. Here are their top 32 in 2007, together with their ranking for 2006 (November to November).

2007 ranking	Château	2006 ranking
1	Lafite	1
2	Latour	2
3	Ausone	5
4	Margaux	3
5	Mouton Rothschild	7
6	Haut-Brion	6
7	La Mission Haut-Brion	15
8	Pétrus	4
9	Cheval Blanc	8
10	Le Pin	11

DAVID PEPPERCORN MW When David Peppercorn went to Bordeaux as a Cambridge undergraduate in September 1953, it was the beginning of a lifelong love affair. He became a Master of Wine in 1962 and was chairman of the Institute of Masters of Wine from 1968 to 1970. It was while David was a buyer for IDV (International Distillers & Vintners) in the 1970s that he started writing about wine, making his debut as an author with the award-winning *Bordeaux* (Faber & Faber, 1982). His *Wines of Bordeaux* (Mitchell Beazley) has been updated regularly since 1986 (2004 being the latest edition). David now spends his time traveling, writing, consulting, and lecturing. He is married to Serena Sutcliffe MW.

2007 ranking	Château	2006 ranking
11	Lafleur	13
12	Léoville-Las-Cases	9
13	Yquem	10
14	Montrose	17
15	Les Forts de Latour	New
16	Pichon-Lalande	14
17	Palmer	16
18	Pavie	23
19	Cos d'Estournel	12
20	Carruades de Lafite	24
21	Léoville Barton	19
22	Léoville Poyferré	20
23	Ducru-Beaucaillou	22
24	Angélus	21
25	Lynch-Bages	18
26	Pichon-Baron	25
27	Vieux Château Certan	30
28	Pavillon Blanc	New
29	La Fleur-Pétrus	New
30	Pape Clément	New
31	Troplong Mondot	29
32	Pavie Macquin	New

The most spectacular increase in rating is for La Mission Haut-Brion, from 15 to 7, immediately behind its Domaine Dillon partner Haut-Brion, and above Pétrus and Cheval Blanc—confirmation, perhaps, of the market's agreement with the Domaine's re-rating of La Mission in the 2006 *primeurs*. Ausone and Mouton both climb two places, while Pétrus drops four places. Montrose climbs three places, while Léoville-Las-Cases and Yquem drop three places. The most startling performance of all is the arrival of Les Forts de Latour from nowhere to 15th place, ahead of Super-Seconds such as Pichon-Lalande, Palmer, and Cos d'Estournel, all of whom fell, while Carruades moved up on the coattails of Lafite, above Léoville Barton, Léoville Poyferré, Ducru-Beaucaillou, and Lynch-Bages. The prevailing wisdom until very recently was that second wines had no investment value, so watch out for Pavillon Rouge next!

Another point to notice is that the price difference *en primeur*, and on the secondary market, between the Firsts and the Super-Seconds has widened significantly, a case of more money chasing fewer cases. I can remember (just!) the days when many English wine lovers mostly drank First Growths, and at £1 a bottle who could blame them? But the first impact of the opening up of the US market in the mid-1950s was a 50 percent increase in the prices of the Firsts, so buyers started to look around for value. The same thing will continue to happen now.

Why have Pétrus, with its small production, and Cheval Blanc, with its much higher production and high profile, fallen behind the Left Bank Firsts? I suspect that the principal answer is connected with their very high *en primeur prices*. Since Cheval Blanc has been under the commercial control of LVMH, the aim has been to come out at a higher price than the Left Bank Firsts, based on the premise that the production is lower. But the market has noticed that its price is static for the first three or four years, while the Left Bank Firsts still show healthy premiums in that initial period. The new Pétrus is now Ausone—even smaller production and on the open market—while Pétrus is distributed via its owners, JP Moueix's exclusive agents.

Another pointer in the same direction is the juxtaposition of Montrose and Cos d'Estournel. Cos makes a point of coming out at a higher price than Montrose, but investors make more money out of Montrose, so Montrose now stands at five places above Cos in the index. Last year, Cos was five places ahead of Montrose. Buyers are not fools!

The Chinese have arrived!

In January 2008, Longhai International completed the purchase of Château Latour-Laguens in Entre-Deux-Mers, the first Chinese purchase in Bordeaux. It is a 60-ha property with 30 ha under vine. The red is sold as Bordeaux Supérieur, and 160,000 bottles are produced. The price was not disclosed, but with an average price of €18,000–20,000 per hectare, prices here are among the lowest in Bordeaux.

I wonder if the Latour name could have anything to do with the Chinese choice of property? One feels sure François Pinault will be watching future labeling with great interest!

Drama in St-Emilion

St-Emilion had a year full of drama in 2007. Although the classification system had worked perfectly well for 50 years, some demoted châteaux challenged the result of the reclassification and went to court. When the Bordeaux court suspended the entire classification, St-Emilion was in uproar and appealed to the Conseil d'Etat in Paris, which fortunately has confirmed and reinstated the classification as printed in *Wine Report 2008*.

Opinion:
The Bordeaux market

The Bordeaux *place* is the largest wine market in the world. Its demise is constantly being predicted, but the most powerful châteaux regard it as essential and irreplaceable. Why?

Most of the criticism I hear clearly shows that many commentators do not understand how the market operates and why small châteaux may not need it if they have a powerful image—but First Growth Médocs certainly do. The market works on the simple principle of supply and demand. So, if an owner pitches his price too high, buyers sit on their hands. If the market thinks the price is a bargain, the orders flood in, and supplies run short—so the price rises. You only have to realize that the big Médoc châteaux often have between 15,000 and 30,000 cases to sell in a vintage. There is no other system where such quantities can be sold in a matter of hours.

The people making these decisions are the Bordeaux *négociants*, and sometimes they get it wrong, typically by paying too much for a lesser vintage, as in 1997. The mistake is made usually because there is a shortage of stock following two successive good years, when enthusiastic buyers have, in the heat of the moment, pushed prices high for excellent wines, so stocks are at a premium. This also happened most famously in 1972 after the scramble for 1970 and 1971.

After the record prices for the fabulous 2005, many buyers were nervous about the less consistent 2006. In fact, the wines sold better than many expected, including myself. This was largely fueled by new markets, especially China, and also a handful of super-rich Russians. So what will happen with 2007? Clearly, the quality and consistency are below 2006, but the best wines are very attractive for early drinking, as were the 2004s and indeed the 1997s. This time, the situation is complicated by the strength of the euro against other currencies, especially the US dollar and the pound sterling, which fell by 18 percent between January and late April 2008. So the *négociants* have a difficult judgment to make—and will the châteaux owners follow the advice anyway? Hardest of all, how will buyers react if prices stay at 2006 levels? In the end, no doubt, some will gain and others will lose.

Vintage Report

Advance report on the latest harvest

2007

Another nail-biting season for growers—like 2002, only worse. One grower told me that by the end of August it looked like a disaster. After the warmest April for 100 years, unsettled weather in May and June spun out the flowering, leading to widespread *coulure* and mildew, and July was drizzly. The final straw was a cool, showery second half of August. Then, after heavy rain on August 29, a classic high-pressure system arrived the following day, and it was the driest September since 1985. The other remarkable figure was the longest hang ever—in some cases 140 days from flowering to harvest, though 125 to 130 was more usual. The Left Bank has produced easy, medium-textured, charming wines with real breed. They will be drinkable before 2006 and remind me of both 1997 and 2004. There are very good Pomerols with a lovely freshness to the fruit. The more variable St-Emilions are at their best wonderfully succulent and flattering, again for early drinking. The dry whites are beautifully fresh and tangy— some of the best I have ever seen—and this is the best Sauternes vintage since 2001. To cap it all, the pound sterling has fallen significantly against the euro since the last campaign; the situation for the dollar is even worse.

Updates on the previous five vintages

2006

Vintage rating: *Left Bank—Red: 92, White: 90, Sweet: 93; Right Bank—Red: 90*

After the *primeur* tastings and during the campaign, there were growing differences of opinion as to the quality of the red wines. Very good in Pomerol: closer to 2001 than 2004; more mixed in St-Emilion—as usual. But the Left Bank (Médoc and Pessac-Léognan) was more consistently successful overall, again closer to 2001 than 2004, and prices reflected this. But those few who suggested that 2006 would prove the equal of 2005 are, I believe, wide of the mark. What can be said with some certainty is that they are likely to be enjoyable to drink before the 2005s, thus mirroring the 2001/2000 situation. The dry whites are now giving great pleasure. The Sauternes are evolving very well indeed.

2005

Vintage rating: *Left Bank—Red: 99, White: 90, Sweet: 95; Right Bank—Red: 98*

Yes, the wines do live up to the hype! The weather cycle was as near perfection as can be imagined in an imperfect world, with drought the key factor. One general rule is that the greatest wines come from the greatest vineyards, and if you want to discover what any of the First Growths are capable of, you will find it in 2005. It is in this sense that arguments as to whether Lafite is better than Latour, or Margaux than Mouton, or Haut-Brion than La Mission really miss the point in this vintage. Each is a profound expression of the character of each *cru*. The only caveat is that there are, as usual, some overextracted wines, mostly in St-Emilion, at properties that harvested overripe Merlots. The other problem is that you are likely to have to wait a very long time—20 to 30 years—to see these wines at their peak. But, on the positive side, there are many wonderful lesser and middle-ranking wines, to say nothing of second wines, which will give immense pleasure after 5–10 years, and at moderate prices. While prices overall were 30 percent higher than in 2000, many wines showed only 10–15 percent increases, so top wines have correspondingly much higher increases. Again, the marvelous Sauternes are great value and will be enjoyable, if not at their peak, in five to seven years. And don't forget the lovely fruity dry whites!

2004

Vintage rating: *Left Bank—Red: 92, White: 90, Sweet: 93; Right Bank—Red: 92*

After the very small crop of 2003, the vines were raring to go in 2004, and with much stricter limits on yields now being imposed by INAO, most vineyards had to work hard to keep their production within the prescribed limits. Damp August conditions tested growers' nerves, but then the hoped-for high-pressure system kicked in on August 31 and stayed in control until October 10, with most picking concentrated between September 27 and October 14. This is a year of consistent quality across the region, with wines showing lovely harmony with beautiful fruit flavors and rich, ripe, well-integrated tannins, with a freshness that enhances the flavors and is developing real complexity. The Sauternes have a lovely freshness, which balances the fruity richness of wines that have real character and are classic after the exceptional sugar levels of 2003. This is a vintage that, overall, will give much pleasure.

2003

Vintage rating: *Left Bank—Red: 93, White: 80, Sweet: 98; Right Bank—Red: 82*

The extreme heat of June, July, and August caused growers many problems. Those who delayed picking until September were rewarded by more moderate conditions. The more vulnerable Merlots on the Right Bank suffered most and are very uneven. But great wines with a markedly exotic character were made in St-Estèphe especially, but also in Pauillac and St-Julien. Margaux, surprisingly, produced some wines of great breed and typicity. Pessac-Léognan is less good. The crop was half the normal size or less. Sauternes had an exceptional year with good yields and even richer wines than 2001.

2002

Vintage rating: *Left Bank—Red: 92, White: 90, Sweet: 88; Right Bank—Red: 86*

Very nearly a disaster, this year was saved by a classic high-pressure system in September. The Left Bank Cabernets took full advantage, and very fine wines resulted in Pauillac, St-Julien, and St-Estèphe. The first tastings in bottle showed Margaux doing better than expected, while the general level in the Médoc was high. Excellent botrytis in Sauternes also means another fine vintage there. But *coulure* had already accounted for much of the old-vine Merlot on the Right Bank, and the weather change was just too late to help the Merlots produce top quality. Those with good levels of Cabernet Franc benefited. The dry whites have an attractive fresh fruitiness.

Grapevine

• **Unfortunately for the Crus Bourgeois of the Médoc,** their legal wars were not assisted by the St-Emilion decision. Their classification was made under different rules, so it's back to the drawing board for them.

• **Following the declassification** of the Château La Tour du Pin Figeac belonging to the other branch of the Moueix family, the vineyard was bought in June 2006 by the owners of Cheval Blanc, just across the road. Now simply called La Tour du Pin, the 2006 showed favorably during the *primeur* tastings at Cheval Blanc. There are 8 ha planted with 75 percent Merlot and 25 percent Cabernet Franc. Watch this space!

• **The Cuvelier family** of Clos Fourtet, 1er Cru Classé of St-Emilion, has bought Château Poujeaux, one of the leading *crus* of Moulis, together with Chasse-Spleen. It is sad to see the Thiel family leave, but recently there had been family problems and quality was affected. Poujeaux should have a bright future under the dynamic Cuveliers.

• **If you have followed** the Tribaie story (see *Wine Report 2006*), you will be interested to know that, following its success in the new installation at Château Rochemorin, André Lurton has now reorganized the harvest reception area at La Louvière around a Tribaie sorting machine.

GREATEST WINE PRODUCERS

1. Château Lafite
2. Château d'Yquem
3. Château Ausone
4. Château Pétrus
5. Château Margaux
6. Château Léoville-Las-Cases
7. Château Lafleur
8. Château Latour
9. Château Haut-Brion/ La Mission Haut-Brion
10. Château Pichon-Longueville Lalande

FASTEST-IMPROVING PRODUCERS

1. Château Lafite *Very good from 1982 to 1990 but has moved into another gear as of 1996.*
2. Château Ausone *Some of the greatest wines in Bordeaux since 1998; more sensual and just more of everything—look out for 2002!*
3. Château Pontet-Canet *Outstanding since 1996 and up another gear with 2005.*
4. Château Pavie Macquin *Since Thienpont and Derenoncourt took charge in 1995, progress has been continuous and consistent. Promoted to Premier Grand Cru in 2006.*
5. Château Calon-Ségur *A new generation has forgotten that this used to be one of the Médoc's most sought-after crus. The climb-back was at first steady (1995, 1996) and is now spectacular (2000, 2002, 2003, 2004, 2005).*
6. Château du Tertre *The real potential is now being realized, especially since the marvelous 2000.*
8. Château Malartic-Lagravière *The investment and commitment of the new owners here are now paying off. The 2002 is outstanding.*
9. Château Berliquet *Since Patrick Valette began consulting, the class of this cru is shining through.*

NEW UP-AND-COMING PRODUCERS

1. Château Pontac-Lynch (Margaux)
2. Château La Fleur Morange (St-Emilion)
3. Château Bellevue (St-Emilion)
4. Château Clauzet (St-Estèphe)
5. Château Mille Roses (Haut-Médoc)
6. Château Loudenne (Médoc)
7. Château Séguin (Pessac-Léognan)
8. Château Sénéjac (Haut-Médoc)
9. Château Joanin-Bécot (Côtes de Castillon)
10. Providence (Pomerol)

BEST-VALUE PRODUCERS

1. Château Sénéjac (Haut-Médoc)
2. Château Doisy-Védrines (Barsac)
3. Château de Malle (Sauternes)
4. Clos Floridène (Graves Blanc)
5. Château Tour de Mirambeau (Bordeaux Blanc Cuvée Passion)
6. Château Potensac (Médoc)
7. Château Matras (St-Emilion Cru Classé)
8. Château Berliquet (St-Emilion Cru Classé)
9. Château Beauregard (Pomerol)
10. Château Rouget (Pomerol)

GREATEST-QUALITY WINES

1. **Château Lafite 1982** (€1,520)
2. **Château Canon 1982** (€116)
3. **Château Pichon-Longueville Lalande 1966** (€88)
4. **Château Pétrus 1964** (€963)
5. **Château Figeac 1983** (€62)
6. **Château Haut-Bailly 1985** (€36)
7. **Château La Mission Haut-Brion 1995** (€142)
8. **Château Cheval Blanc 1990** (€1,682)
9. **Château Mouton Rothschild 2000** (€570)
10. **Château Rauzan-Ségla 1986** (€88)

BEST BARGAINS

1. **Clos Floridène Graves Blanc 2005** (€12)

2. **L'Enclos du Château Lezongars Premières Côtes de Bordeaux 2001** (€10)

3. **Château Sénéjac Haut-Médoc 2005** (€13)

4. **Château Loudenne Médoc 2005** (€8)

5. **Château Tour de Mirambeau Bordeaux Blanc Cuvée Passion 2006** (€15)

6. **Château Preuillac Médoc 2005** (€12.50)

7. **Château Hostens-Picant Ste-Foy Bordeaux Blanc 2006** (€15)

8. **Château Ste-Marie Entre Deux Mers 2006** (€10)

9. **Château Doisy-Védrines Barsac 2004** (€22)

10. **Château Thieuley Bordeaux Blanc Cuvée Francis Courselle 2006** (€10)

MOST EXCITING OR UNUSUAL FINDS

1. **Château La Prade Côtes de Francs 2004** (€17) *This 90 percent Merlot vineyard was bought by Nicolas Thienpont from Patrick Valette in 2001. This is a great success in the context of 2004, with vivid, pure fruit and an intensity that will ensure good aging potential.*

2. **Château Séguin Pessac-Léognan 2005** (€16.50) *This vineyard lies in the commune of Canéjan, just to the west of Léognan, and has been gradually reconstructed during the 1990s. This is perhaps the first vintage to demonstrate what the vineyard is capable of: rich, juicy fruit with a robust extrovert character. Still quite tight tannins, but there is lovely fruit and elegance with breed. A fine wine of real promise.*

3. **Château Bellegrave Pauillac 2005** (€16) *This property, sunk in obscurity for most of the 20th century, has been gradually reconstructed by the Meffre family of Château Glana. This is the most successful vintage yet, with real Pauillac character and power.*

4. **Château Pontac-Lynch Margaux 2005** (€13) *The first time I have tasted a really good wine from this property. I noted very perfumed fruit with great succulence. Well structured, both beautiful and serious—a wine of real class.*

5. **Château La Fleur Morange St-Emilion 2005** (€65) *This newcomer was a wild card when tasted blind at Decanter. It was very scented and dense-textured, enormously rich, and powerful. It is either overdone or a great wine. Certainly worth waiting and watching.*

6. **Providence Pomerol 2005** (€56) *In the center of the Pomerol plateau next to Hosanna, this vineyard was bought by JP Moueix in 2005. This first vintage is a remarkable wine with a terrific bouquet, massive flavor, and complexity. A new jewel in the Moueix crown.*

Grapevine

• Following Château Bellevue's **demotion** in the 2006 St-Emilion classification, its owners have sold a 50 percent stake to neighbor Château Angélus. The Bellevue vineyard lies just across the road from the entrance to Angélus, on rising ground. Since Nicolas Thienpont took over management of the vineyard in 2000, great progress has been made, but unfortunately the vintages judged were 1994 and 2003, and the pre-Thienpont years clearly told against them. First indications are that Nicolas Thienpont will continue to have an input.

Burgundy

Clive Coates MW

What is the point of Beaujolais Nouveau?

CLIVE COATES MW

Many years ago, at the height of the popularity of Beaujolais Nouveau, I posed the following: in a bad vintage, Beaujolais Nouveau is sour and unpleasant; in a good year, it is a waste of excellent wine, for proper Beaujolais of Villages and *cru* status can be delicious indeed, as the 2005s have shown.

Nouveau, by its very nature, can only be artificial. You have to use artificial yeasts to ensure a quick and efficient fermentation; ditto bacterium for the malolactic. The poor wine is strangulated at birth and straitjacketed so that it can be ready for bottling early in November. In some late vintages the fruit is not collected until October 1, so that is a month for what takes other wines a year and a half. No wonder we find strange flavors of banana, bubblegum, and the rest in the wine.

Now fashion has turned its back on this objectionable beast, at least in the UK. The Americans continue to order the wine by the truckload, if with a little less enthusiasm than hitherto, and the Japanese still adore it. The 2007 vintage is light and fruity, without a lot of acidity—perfect for drinking with a picnic in the summer of 2008. But not in November 2007. I've tasted a few from so-called authoritative sources. I was not inspired.

CLIVE COATES MW is the author of *The Wines of Burgundy* (University of California Press, 2008), as well as a number of other prize-winning books on wine. The most recent include *The Great Wines of France* (Mitchell Beazley, 2005) and *The Wines of Bordeaux* (Weidenfeld & Nicolson and the University of California Press, 2004). As well as a number of other awards, his previous book on Burgundy, *Côte d'Or* (Weidenfeld & Nicolson, 1997), uniquely won the Prix des Arts et des Lettres from the Confrérie de Tastevin. This was the first time the prize had been awarded to a book on wine and a non-Burgundian.

Cream of the south

The Côte Chalonnaise has been underappreciated for far too long. For many years it has been producing affordable burgundy, both red and white, at prices little more than that asked for generic wine. Since at least the late 1970s, when I first started prospecting in the region, individual growers have been rearing and bottling their own produce, long before the majority of their peers started domaine-bottling in the Côte d'Or.

There are five main communes: from north to south, Bouzeron, Rully, Mercurey, Givry, and Montagny. Bouzeron is famous for its Aligoté, the best examples of which are produced from the Aligoté Doré, which seems to thrive on the marny slopes above the village. Rully, historically a prime source of raw material for the local sparkling wine, is now renowned for its whites. Mercurey, the largest of the villages, mainly makes red wine, as does Givry. It is only since the 2004 vintage that the small proportion of Chardonnay from these two appellations has become serious. Finally, there is Montagny: white wines only, of which 75 percent issues from the admirable cooperative at Buxy.

There has been much progress here in recent years. Today everyone with aspirations of quality picks by hand (still only about six domaines in Rully, sadly), prunes to produce wines of character and concentration, sorts out the bad from the good before vinification, and has a cellar with all the necessary temperature-control mechanisms. The dedication obvious at the top domaines has been rewarded with a splendid 2005 vintage for red wines and an equally fine 2006 vintage for whites. The absolute crème de la crème of the Côte Chalonnaise are:

Bouzeron: A&P de Villaine
Rully: Jean-Claude Brelière; Vincent Dureuil-Janthial; Henri & Paul Jacqueson; Christophe-Jean Grandmougin
Mercurey: Michel Juillot; Bruno Lorenzon; L Menand Père & Fils
Givry: Joblot; François Lumpp
Montagny: Stéphane Aladame.

Grapevine

• **Domaine Anne Gros,** in Vosne-Romanée, produced its first Echézeaux, from two-thirds of a hectare, in 2007. This parcel was formerly exploited by Anne's cousin Bernard of Gros Frère & Sœur under a 20-year lease taken up before the Anne Gros domaine was launched.

• **Nicky Potel** is gradually acquiring a wine domaine to supplement his merchant's business in Nuits-St-Georges. There are now 12 ha, mainly leased, mainly in the Côte de Beaune, including a number of *premiers crus* in Beaune and Savigny-lès-Beaune.

Why do prices rise?

The 2006s have left Burgundy at more or less the same prices as the 2005s. However, such was the demand for the 2005s that some wholesalers and retailers imposed higher margins than usual. Perhaps they were speculating that there would be thinner profits on the 2006s and any unsold 2004s. Moreover, both the pound (marginally) and the dollar (substantially) have lost value against the euro, forcing retail prices up in those countries. Certainly the result was that the superstars of 2005 wound up very expensive in the US. How much will the same-price 2006s cost customers?

In living memory

Fondation Pinot Noir is an idea of Aubert de Villaine, codirector of the Domaine de la Romanée-Conti. When an estate has to replace venerable old vines, it is proposed that cuttings be taken from the highest-quality plants before the old vine is consigned to the bonfire. These will be planted in an experimental vineyard and will be available for reproduction by future generations, thus serving as a continual memory of the best of Burgundy. A fine and original idea. Other vineyard areas please copy.

Grapevine

- **Maurice Ecard,** on his retirement, has sold his Savigny-lès-Beaune domaine to merchants Béjot of Meursault, who will continue to bottle the wines under the Maurice Ecard label. Meanwhile, Ecard's son Michel has launched his own estate with the 4 ha he has inherited. This includes five Savigny *premiers crus*.

- **Domaines des Estournelles** (Frédéric Esmonin) of Gevrey-Chambertin has sold half its holding in the excellent *premier cru* of Estournelles-St-Jacques to fellow Gevrey domaine Philippe Rossignol.

- **Following the sale** of the Charles Thomas estate (see *Wine Report 2007*), the Nuits-St-Georges *premier cru* Clos de Thorey, a *monopole*, has been acquired by Maison Rodet of Mercurey. Rodet has also taken over Maison Dufouleur Père & Fils and its subsidiary Domaine Guy Dufouleur, based in Nuits-St-Georges.

- **Maison Faiveley** of Nuits-St-Georges has bought two small estates in the Côte de Beaune: Matrot-Wittersheim in Meursault, and Annick Parent in Monthélie. This will give them six *premiers crus* in Meursault, Monthélie, Volnay, and Pommard.

- **The up-and-coming** Domaine Arlaud of Morey-St-Denis has taken over half (2.5 ha) of the estate of the now-retired Guy Coquard, also of Morey. Watch out for new *premiers crus* from Blanchards in Morey, and Chatelots and Noirots in neighboring Chambolle-Musigny.

- **Chanson Père & Fils,** one of the oldest merchants in Beaune and now owned by Champagne Bollinger, has acquired 7.35 ha of vines in the southern Côte de Beaune, including parcels in Puligny-Montrachet Les Folatières, Chassagne-Montrachet Les Chenevottes, and Santenay Le Beauregard, all *premiers crus*.

Opinion:
Never finer, but could do better

Burgundy has not had a bad vintage since 1984. It is as if Le Bon Dieu is smiling on the region and rewarding the growers for their dedication and individualism, their refusal to submit to uniformity and indulge in petty jealousies, and their reasonableness with prices. The standard of the wines and the very large number of praiseworthy domaines and merchants are far higher than they have ever been. Yet things can only get better— much better. While everyone is well equipped in their cellars, is as exigent about dispensing with herbicides and systemic sprays, and is, indeed, as biological if not as biodynamic as one would wish, the raw material—the vines themselves—leaves much to be desired.

Authentic "old vines" no longer exist, for the most part. Sadly, those that date back to the 1900s, 1910s, and 1920s (that is, the first generation of grafted vines planted after the *vignes françaises* died out) are very rare indeed. Today's so-called old vines are more likely to be the infamous Pinots Droits planted in the 1960s or the first generation of clones, reared for quantity as much as for disease resistance. Neither, of themselves, produces fine quality. Nor, for the most part, were the rootstocks they were grafted onto—for instance, the SO4—the most desirable. A vine on SO4 tends to race to maturity as September evolves, rendering the window of perfect opportunity very small indeed.

Moreover, there is still much of the Burgundy vineyard, overfertilized in the 1960s and 1970s, that is today, 40 years on, overburdened with potassium, resulting in wines with a deficiency of acidity.

So, if you find your 1999s delicious and are licking your lips in anticipation over the white 2002s and red 2005s, just think how brilliant burgundies are going to be in 2029, 2032, and 2035! Of course, some of us may no longer be around, and there is the threat of climate change, but it's a nice thought nonetheless.

Grapevine

• **Burgundians in the Languedoc.** Following the Mongeards and Jean-Marc Boillot, the latest Burgundians to set up in the Languedoc are Anne Gros and her partner Jean-Paul Tollot, who have bought a much-morcellated estate of old vines in the Minervois.

• **Domaine Hubert Lignier** in Morey-St-Denis has been split following disagreements between Kellen Lignier, widow of Romain, and the rest of the family. Kellen's inheritance is roughly two-thirds of the 7.7-ha estate.

Vintage Report

Advance report on the latest harvest

2007

One of the most climatically curious vintages has ended happily. Up to the end of August, growers were anticipating a disaster. The sun then started shining, and 10 weeks of the most spectacular fall followed. The leaves did not begin to fall until Hospices time, the first really proper frost being on the night of November 12, and the resulting color in the interim was truly magnificent. Sadly, it was a very early harvest, so not all could fully benefit. But there was nevertheless much early satisfaction with 2007 to be discerned as buyers and journalists toured Burgundy to sample the 2006s.

After a mild, dry winter—only one severe frost at the end of January—Burgundy enjoyed summer in April, with temperatures into the 80s (30+°C) and four weeks of abundant sun. Thereafter, apart from a week in mid-May, when the vines flowered some three weeks early, the weather was wet, cold, and miserable for two and a half months. Even after July 14 it was patchy, with more days of cloud and rain than days of sun. Unsettled weather persisted until the end of August, when clouds cleared and temperatures rose.

Overall it was a very wet summer. Mildew and rot remained a constant threat. With hindsight it became clear that, even more than usual, it was crucial not to overcrop, dangerous not to pay daily attention to the state of health of the vines, and advantageous, if possible, to delay the harvest.

Every year there is hail somewhere; in 2007 the *climat* of Charmes-Chambertin bore the brunt. There were three hailstorms in Chablis, variously ravaging the village of Chichée and the *premiers crus* of Montée de Tonnerre and Mont de Milieu and, later, Vaillons.

Early on the authorities announced that the *ban des vendanges* would be August 18, to give total liberty to each domaine to choose its own picking date. The vintage started first in the Côte de Beaune, around September 3. This was followed a week or so later by the Côte de Nuits, Chablis, and the Mâconnais and Beaujolais. Normally the latter two regions commence a good 10 days, and in the case of the Beaujolais, two weeks, before the Côte d'Or. The late pickers, the Côte Chalonnaise and the Hautes-Côtes, had the best of it, being able to profit more from the return to fine weather.

It was, it hardly needs to be said, essential to *tri*—to eliminate substandard fruit before fermentation—so most estates have produced a reduced crop, up to 25 percent less than 2006 (which was by no means large).

The Chablis results are variable. Alcohol levels are reasonable, but acidities are low. Many wines will be rather soft and ephemeral. Growers producing whites in the Côte de Beaune, especially those who picked later than most, are rather more enthusiastic, considering 2007 better than 2006. As far as reds are concerned, the vintage is considered superior in the Côte de Nuits to the Côte de Beaune, with *vignerons* in Gevrey-Chambertin even prepared to compare their 2007s with their 2005s. In the Mâconnais and the Beaujolais, the 2007 vintage is said to be good (better than 2006) but not great.

Updates on the previous five vintages

2006

Vintage rating: *Red: 85, White: 85*

This is a very variable vintage, even harder to generalize about than usual. Normally in "difficult" years the wines are proportionately better as one climbs the hierarchy—that is, the rating of both the estate and the vineyard. In 2006 there are some very successful generic wines and disappointing *grands crus* even in the cellars of the most highly regarded domaines. In general, however, the Chablis are very good (better than the 2005s), as are the whites of the Côte Chalonnaise, while the whites of the Mâconnais and the Côte d'Or are more variable, some being quite high in alcohol while weak in acidity, and therefore lacking bite as a result. The best are superior to the 2005s; the less good are not as interesting as the previous vintage. The reds are better in the Côte de Nuits than the Côte de Beaune, best of all in Nuits-St-Georges and Vosne-Romanée. Here the hail in July, experienced in Gevrey-Chambertin, has, apart from the yield, done no harm. The hail that followed in Chambolle in August, however, has left its effect. Some wines are tainted. In general, the red wines have turned out better than the growers expected just after the harvest. They are not up to the famous 2005s but have a decent color and show attractive fruit and ripe tannins, if, for the most part, not being very high in acidity. They will evolve in the medium term. And there are plenty of most agreeable wines to be found at the best cellars in Savigny, Pommard, and Volnay.

The 2006 vintage is good in the Beaujolais, with some very pleasant fruity wines having been produced, but it is not up to the standard of 2005.

2005

Vintage rating: *Red: 95, White: 85*

A magnificent red-wine vintage, but whites have failed to live up to their early promise. Now in bottle, the red wines, though they have begun to shut down a bit, are well deserving of all the ballyhoo they engendered at the outset. The vintage is consistently good (except in Santenay and Chassagne-Montrachet, where there was hail) from Marsannay to Maranges, and proportionately so from *grand cru* to humble generic. Few past vintages come close; perhaps the nearest is 1999, but this was a much more generous harvest. The relative shortness of the 2005 crop can be seen in the concentration of the wines. They also have depth, finesse, harmony, and the potential to last. What more do you want? Lay them down and throw away the key.

The white wines are variable. Those from the Mâconnais and Côte Chalonnaise are delicious and are beginning to drink well now. In both the Côte d'Or and Chablis, there is more variation. We have in both these regions the size and the concentration. In some cases, however, there is a lack of zip and finesse. This applies particularly in Chassagne-Montrachet and Santenay. But it can be found in the Meursaults and Pulignys, too. Many in the Côte d'Or cite 2004 over both 2005 and 2006.

A classic vintage for Beaujolais, the best only just now coming around.

2004

Vintage rating: *Red: 82, White: 85*

The summer of 2004 was inauspicious, with problems of oidium (powdery mildew) added to concerns about preventing vines from compensating for having produced only half a normal crop in 2003. The latter was resolved by an even more draconian approach to debudding and deflowering than usual (plus green-harvesting for those too lazy to attack the vines at the outset). The former was to have its effect on the cleanliness of the lees, so compromising the *élevage*. The quality of the vintage was much improved by a return to fine weather in September.

This resulted in many (but sadly not overall) white wines of real fragrance, delicious perfumes, only medium body, but with good acidities. There are some (Roulot, Château de Maltroye) who consider their 2004 whites to be the best of the 2003–07 half-decade; they are beginning to drink well now. The reds took their time; first in finishing their malos (it is only after this that you can assess the physical aspect of a wine—its mouthfeel), and generally getting their act together. At the outset the mood was glum; a year later, opinions had been revised; and now that a proper assessment in bottle is possible, the wines show even better. This is a medium-weight vintage—the lesser wines are now ready—of clean, stylish wines. They have less fruity charm but better balance than the 2006s. The Côte de Nuits produced better wines than the Côte de Beaune.

This is a very good year in Chablis and the Côte Chalonnaise, though not up to 2002 and 2005, and the wines are now ready. It is a good but not inspired vintage in the Mâconnais and the Beaujolais. Again, now fully mature.

2003

Vintage rating: *Red: 80 (but see below), White: 60*

This was the year of the *canicule* (heat wave). Logically, but paradoxically, as far as the white wines are concerned, the best-exposed vines on the best sites suffered more than those in generally cooler areas. And the standard of the resulting wines was affected likewise. Equally, the younger vines were under more stress than those with mature root systems. This puts the normal assessment on its head. There were some very successful Aligotés and generic wines from obscure vineyards such as the Couchois (west of the Côte Chalonnaise). But in general the vast majority of the whites, all the way from Chablis to Pouilly-Fuissé, are rather flat. They lack burgundy's usual refreshing elegance.

The reds are better, though hardly typical. Many taste as though they have had a dollop of Midi added to the blend. Some, even among the growers themselves, like their 2003s a lot more than I do. They have huge color for a Pinot Noir wine, rich, concentrated fruit, and no lack of weight. Not surprisingly, acidities are low but in most instances not too low, merely indicating, like the 1997s, they will not make old bones. In some cases— but much less than, say, bordeaux—there are some rather astringent tannins. Drink them quite soon. The lesser wines are at their best already.

Meanwhile the Beaujolais, magnificent a year or two ago, are beginning to coarsen. Finish them up.

2002

Vintage rating: *Red: 90, White: 93*

The more the 2002s evolve, the more I like them. Last year I made my usual four-year-on tasting and have extensively followed this up this year by sampling the produce of those domaines that were not on the table in July 2006. We have whites that are better than 1995, 1999, 2000, and 2005, the standouts of the decade, and have more structure than the best of 2004 and 2006; and red wines that, if lacking the succulent flair of 1999 or the sheer brilliance of 2005, are a close third. All this was due to a splendid September—warm, sunny, and windy—that had the effect of concentrating not only sugars and flavor, but acidities at the same time.

The whites are excellent all the way from Chablis to the Côte Chalonnaise, and the lesser examples are delicious now. The *premiers crus* and *grands crus* of the Côte de Beaune should still be kept. Some of the Mâconnais whites are a little too rich and should be drunk soon. The reds, for once, are equally successful in the Côte de Nuits, the Côte de Beaune, and the Côte Chalonnaise. The lesser wines are drinking well now.

The Beaujolais are good but beginning to show age.

GREATEST WINE PRODUCERS

1. Denis Bachelet (Gevrey-Chambertin)
2. Sylvain Cathiard (Vosne-Romanée)
3. Jean Grivot (Vosne-Romanée)
4. Anne Gros (Vosne-Romanée)
5. Comtes Lafon (Meursault)
6. Leflaive (Puligny-Montrachet)
7. Romanée-Conti (Vosne-Romanée)
8. Guy Roulot (Meursault)
9. Armand Rousseau (Gevrey-Chambertin)
10. Comte Georges de Vogüé (Chambolle-Musigny)

FASTEST-IMPROVING PRODUCERS

1. Louis Boillot (Chambolle-Musigny)
2. Chevalier (Ladoix)
3. Drouhin-Laroze (Gevrey-Chambertin)
4. Humbert Frères (Gevrey-Chambertin)
5. Lamarche (Vosne-Romanée)
6. Jean-Marc Millot (Nuits-St-Georges)
7. Nudant (Ladoix)
8. Louis Rémy (Morey-St-Denis)
9. Rossignol-Jeanniard (Volnay)
10. Taupenot-Merme (Morey-St-Denis)

NEW UP-AND-COMING PRODUCERS

1. Jean-Marie Burgaud (Morgon)
2. Pierre-Yves Colin-Morey (Chassagne-Montrachet)
3. David Croix (Maison Camille Giraud & Domaine des Croix, Beaune)
4. Michel Digoia-Royer (Chambolle-Musigny)
5. Benjamin Leroux (Domaine de Comte Armand, Pommard)
6. Louis-Michel Liger-Belair (Vosne-Romanée)
7. Alix de Montille (Les Deux Montilles, Volnay)
8. Antoine Olivier (Santenay)
9. Sylvain Pataille (Marsannay)
10. Carel Voorhuis (Domaine d'Ardhuy, Corgoloin)

BEST-VALUE PRODUCERS

1. Stéphane Aladame (Montagny)
2. Christophe & Fils (Fyé, Chablis)
3. Anita & Jean-Pierre Colinot (Irancy)
4. Ghislaine & Jean-Hugues Goisot (St-Bris)
5. Christophe-Jean Grandmougin (Rully)
6. Henri & Paul Jacqueson (Rully)
7. Giles Jourdan (Comblanchien, for Côte de Nuits-Villages)
8. Menand Père & Fils (Mercurey)
9. Lucien Muzard Père & Fils (Santenay)
10. Jacques & Nathalie Saumaize (Vergisson, for Mâcon & Pouilly-Fuissé)

GREATEST-QUALITY WINES

Ten fantastic 2005 reds for laying down.

1. **Bonnes-Mares** Georges Roumier (€175) *2020–40.*
2. **Chambertin Clos de Bèze** Louis Jadot (€200) *2020–40.*
3. **Chambertin** Armand Rousseau (€180) *2020–40.*
4. **Charmes-Chambertin** Denis Bachelet (€150) *2020–40.*
5. **Clos de Tart** Domaine du Clos de Tart (€175) *2020–40.*
6. **Mazis-Chambertin** Bernard Dugat-Py (€180) *2020–40.*
7. **Richebourg** Anne Gros (€250) *2020–40.*
8. **Romanée-St-Vivant** Sylvain Cathiard (€180) *2020–40.*
9. **Romanée-St-Vivant** Jean Grivot (€180) *2020–40.*
10. **La Tâche** Domaine de la Romanée-Conti (€400) *2020–40.*

BEST BARGAINS

1. **Mercurey Blanc 2006** Château de Chamirey (€8)
2. **Bourgogne Blanc 2006** Guy Roulot (€10)
3. **St-Véran La Côte Rôtie 2006** Bret Bros (€10)

④ **Pouilly-Fuissé La Roche 2006**
Jacques & Nathalie Saumaize
(€12.50)

⑤ **Rully La Pucelle 2006**
Henri & Paul Jacqueson (€13)

⑥ **Meursault Tessons 2006**
Les Deux Montilles (€18)

⑦ **Marsannay Rosé 2006**
Bruno Clair (€12)

⑧ **Côte de Brouilly Cuvée de la Chapelle 2005** Château Thivin
Claude Geoffray (€12)

⑨ **Fleurie La Madonne Vieilles Vignes 2005** Jean-Marc Déprés
(€12.50)

⑩ **Côte de Beaune-Villages 2005**
Louis Jadot (€12)

MOST EXCITING OR UNUSUAL FINDS

① **Givry Blanc Clos de la Servoisine 2006** Domaine Joblot
(€12.50) *Only since 2004 have the white wines of Givry and Montagny been acceptable. This is the best Givry Blanc of 2006, and it is delicious.*

② **Saint-Romain Blanc 2006**
Alain Gras (€10) *Most Saint-Romain whites (and all the reds) do not merit village appellation and should be downgraded to Bourgogne Hautes-Côtes de Beaune. Alain Gras's wine is the exception. Cheap, lots of character, plenty of style.*

③ **Santenay Blanc Beaurepaire 2006** Vincent Girardin (€13.50)
White Santenay is now easier to find. It is quite a different wine from Chassagne-Montrachet, less expensive, and, at its best, just as good. This is the most widely available and very reliable. I drink it every time I lunch at the local restaurant Le Terroir.

④ **Moulin-à-Vent Clos de Rochegrès 2006** Château des Jacques (€12) *This is a marvelous*

Beaujolais for keeping. It won't taste like Pinot Noir after five years, as some of the books would have you believe, but it will be full, creamy, and rich—a million miles away from Beaujolais Nouveau.

⑤ **Vosne-Romanée Les Beaumonts 2005** Jean Grivot
(€70) *Every year I am asked to recommend premier cru burgundies of grand cru standard. This is my favorite example. Drink 2017–35.*

⑥ **Volnay Clos de Chênes 2005**
Michel Lafarge (€40) *The best part of the best vineyard (arguably) for red wines in the Côte de Beaune; plus the best producer and the finest of recent vintages. Drink 2015–35.*

⑦ **Pommard Clos des Epeneaux 2005** Domaine de Comte Armand
(€40) *If there is one wine in the Côte de Beaune to rank alongside the entry above, this is it. Drink 2015–35.*

⑧ **Puligny-Montrachet Les Perrières 2006** Louis Carillon
(€40) *Carillon's wines are all about purity, grace, understatement, and subtlety. This is a wine that would wipe away most grands crus. Drink 2010–20.*

⑨ **Chablis Clos des Hospices 2006**
Christian Moreau (€40) *Perhaps the most exciting site in Chablis (a corner of the grand cru Les Clos, Chablis's best vineyard). 2006 is a very fine year here. Drink 2010–20.*

⑩ **Clos des Lambrays 2005**
Domaine des Lambrays (€70)
Cheap by grand cru standards, but what a lot of delicious wine you will get in your bottle if you are prepared to wait. All silk and finesse, potentially. Drink 2012–27.

Champagne

Tom Stevenson

Champagne's proposed expansion could create
€12 billion of new wealth for lucky landowners and
absolutely nothing for neighbors a stone's throw away.

TOM STEVENSON

On March 14, 2008, INAO approved the
village-level recommendations of its committee
of experts: Claudine Wolikow (historian),
Dominique Moncomble (agronomist), Stéphane
Thévenin (phytosociologist), Marcel Bazin
(geographer), and Michel Laurain (geologist).
INAO's decision is currently going through a
legal inquiry, which, with €12 billion at stake,
could turn into a wingding, since other
villages want a piece of the pie.

The experts examined two zones of
Champagne—the Zone de l'Elaboration and the Zone de Production.
The Zone de l'Elaboration marks the outer limits of the region, which
currently comprises 637 communes, covering in excess of 600,000 ha,
where grapes, clear wines, and bottled champagne may be freely
transported. It is also the only part of the region where it is legal to vinify
champagne. Within the Zone de l'Elaboration is the Zone de Production,
which currently consists of 319 communes, covering approximately
300,000 ha. Each of these 319 villages contains a small lacework of land

TOM STEVENSON has specialized in champagne for almost 30 years. *Champagne*
(Sotheby's Publications, 1986) was the first wine book to win four awards, and
it quickly established Tom's credentials as a leading expert in this field. In 1998,
his *Christie's World Encyclopedia of Champagne & Sparkling Wine* (Absolute Press, revised
2003) made history by being the only wine book ever to warrant a leader in any
national newspaper (*The Guardian*) when it published a 17th-century document
proving beyond doubt that the English used a second fermentation to convert
still wine into sparkling at least six years before Dom Pérignon even set foot in
the Abbey of Hautvillers. Tom has judged in France, Germany, Greece, the US,
and Australia, and he is chairman of the Champagne panel at the *Decanter* World
Wine Awards. His annual Champagne masterclass for Christie's is always a sellout.

that has been classified on a parcel-by-parcel basis as AOC Champagne, currently extending to 35,200 ha.

The proposals approved by INAO are: Zone de l'Elaboration extended to 675 communes (deletion of 119 villages, addition of 157) and Zone de Production extended to 357 communes (deletion of two villages, addition of 40). The village-level expansion of the Zone de l'Elaboration is very satisfactory for two reasons: the villages to be removed have no logistical rhyme or reason to be part of the region (for example, the northwestern extremity around Soissons and various remote areas between the Marne and Aube), and the additions envelop the proposed enlarged Zone de Production one commune deep in most parts, easing the necessary movements between vineyards, press-houses, wineries, and warehouses.

The village-level additions proposed for the Zone de Production are also mostly satisfactory. They do not represent an expansion outward as much as a consolidation inward, filling gaps between or adjacent to existing villages, where an impartial expert might reasonably expect vineyards should exist. In fact, there are at least another half-dozen equally deserving villages that have not been included—to demonstrate that the inquiry is not simply rubber-stamping INAO's proposals, perhaps? If some additional villages are admitted on the basis of well-supported arguments, it would pull the rug from beneath the rants and raves of demonstrably inferior villages. However, the two villages that the experts propose to remove from the Zone de Production (Germaine and Orbais l'Abbaye) are much less convincing. They are insignificant and farmed by three of the largest producers (Moët, Vranken, and Laurent-Perrier), who all have more to gain from any expansion than they could possibly lose from being denied access to such modest growths (for which, no doubt, they will be compensated).

But the *champenois* have not been strategically clever in timing this expansion. With almost every square inch of AOC land cultivated, and unprecedented pressure on stocks from record sales despite increasing prices, it looks as if they are merely milking every penny they can from an expanding market. They have been talking about an expansion for at least 30 years, and an announcement during either of the two major slumps—when they had thousands of unplanted hectares, cellars overflowing with stock, and prices were dropping—would have been ideal, since it would have been seen as an academic exercise and not drawn any flak. There is now only one get-out clause available to the *champenois*: to demonstrate transparently that all proposed new vineyards are superior to the average- (not lowest-) level vineyards currently classified. All this can be achieved by the experts with little more than the data accumulated by Champagne's five-year zonage project. Classifying only superior land makes an infallible argument, because to deny such an expansion would be to condemn Champagne to an intrinsically inferior future potential. However, to set out the parameters of vineyard quality and to demonstrate their application transparently will inevitably result in the declassification of some of the poorest currently classified AOC land. This would entail scrapping the Echelle des Crus, which is nothing more than a defunct, politically biased shopping list, and replacing it with a Côte d'Or-style parcel-by-parcel classification, which Champagne deserves.

If the *champenois* are hopeless at strategic thinking, they are even worse at damage control, otherwise they would have explained that in 1951 they asked for a reduction in the region from 46,000 ha spread over 407 villages to 34,000 ha in 302 villages. The committee of experts will take at least five years to do its work at vineyard level, so we won't know how many hectares or where until 2015, which is the earliest that any proposals agreed by INAO can be put to another public inquiry. In the meantime, someone in Champagne's bureaucracy should learn the meaning of damage control, because they could classify an additional 10,000 ha and end up with a smaller region!

Anyone for bling?

Krug's €3,000 Clos d'Ambonnay 1995 was released in May 2008. This extremely rich and intense wine is every bit as special as Clos du Mesnil, but neither *clos* is intrinsically superior to Krug Vintage. Occasionally a particular vintage of one or the other might be better than most Krug Vintage years, and Clos du Mesnil 1996 is one such wine, but I'm not convinced that even that wine will, over time, prove superior to all and every Krug Vintage. So how can the price be justified? Krug CEO Panos Sarantopoulos explained that Clos d'Ambonnay is not priced according to perceptions of quality, but like all Krug champagne, the price is proportionate to size of production. Although Krug has no control over its retail prices, he said that Clos d'Ambonnay was one-third the size of Clos du Mesnil, thus rarity makes it three times the price. Actually, at 0.685 ha compared to Clos du Mesnil's 1.85 ha, it is more than one-third the size—it is closer to 40 percent; and the price that Krug does control, the price under bond, was £1,150 to the UK trade, compared to £295 for Clos du Mesnil—closer to four times the price. However, with only 3,000 bottles produced, and 800 of those sold to Krug's best customers, invited to taste the wine at the *clos* in October 2007, it does not look as if Panos will have trouble shifting such an expensive *cuvée*. A couple of "rogue" six-bottle cases from the Oktoberfest surfaced at the Zachys auction in Las Vegas on February 8, 2008, three months before the official launch. They fetched $26,180 per lot (equivalent to €2,836, or £2,234, per bottle). Personally, I would prefer 12 bottles of Krug Vintage!

Opinion:
Sugar-coated?

Brut Nature (0–3 g/l residual sugar) and Extra Brut (0–6 g/l) seem to be flavor of the month in Champagne these days, and for devotees of mature champagne this is bad news indeed. I don't want to taste sugar in a brut-style champagne, but the lower the *dosage*, the more coarse and aldehydic it evolves following the oxidative shock of disgorgement. For a champagne to age smoothly in its post-disgorgement phase, it has to contain a certain minimum residual-sugar content. Why? We wine hacks talk blithely about sugar's general preservative qualities, but at concentrations found in champagne, it really has no preservative property at all. So it is not that. Sugars have several alcohol or hydroxyl groups that could, I suppose, react with the carbonyl group of acetaldehyde, and sugars can react with amino acids, potentially forming heterocycle compounds, which could also bind acetaldehyde. But do these things happen in champagne? And if they do, would they be sufficient to reduce aldehydic aromas and enable champagne to age gracefully? Having tasted tens of thousands of champagnes over 30 years, I can say categorically that *dosages* above 6 g/l have a smoothing effect on the aromatic development of champagne and that the increase and decrease in finesse above and below this minimum level are proportionate to the amount of residual sugar. However, empirical evidence is not pure science, so I turned to the greatest scientific expert I know on the chemistry of champagne: Bertrand Robillard. I asked him whether sugar could mask aldehydic aromas and was amused by his part-empirical response. To cut a long reply short, he told me, "A lot of people who make a low-*dosage* or no-*dosage* champagne do not add SO_2 at the time of disgorgement, and these wines show a high oxydability level. [And yes,] sugar is a good compound for screening some aromas." When I asked him to elaborate on the last sentence, he confessed, "I've never read of any experiments on the influence of sugar on aromas, but I have noticed this effect. I know that some people consider this to be a fact, and we can imagine that some aldehydes could be sensitive to this phenomenon." Robillard has introduced another important factor, SO_2, but if one of the world's leading scientists in champagne chemistry believes sugar affects positively the smooth and graceful post-disgorgement aging of champagne, that's good enough for me. However, it should not be good enough for the champagne industry. If ever there was a subject ripe for a doctorate, surely this is it. I know a bright young Australian lady who has put her doctorate on hold and would love to research this subject. Any takers?

Vintage Report

Advance report on the latest harvest
2007

A curious year, with the first buds appearing as early as April 5, and a very hot spring encouraging some observers to think that picking could commence on August 14, seven days earlier than 2003, the earliest harvest on record. July, however, saw strange weather: dark and brooding one moment, followed by an expected heavy downpour, then completely unexpected bright sunshine, and it seemed to rain all night, every night. Even while it was sunny, there was an almost electric tension in the air. Spring frost is usually Champagne's most dangerous meteorological threat, but in 2007 it was summer hail. On July 4, hail destroyed between 10 and 40 percent of the potential crop in Chigny, Rilly, Ludes, Taissy, Cormontreuil, and Montbré. The summer was relatively cold, dragging out the *véraison* and putting back the harvest to August 28. Tasting the *vins clairs*, the biggest problem was a reductive tendency in some of the Chardonnay. This is generally a non-vintage year that turned out better than hoped, with Mesnil, Avize, and Villers-Marmery among the most successful villages for Chardonnay; Aÿ, Mareuil-sur-Aÿ, Bouzy, and Verzy showing well for Pinot Noir; and Cumières and Villedommange for Meunier. Some producers will declare a vintage, and Roederer was among the best of these.

Updates on the previous five vintages
2006

Vintage rating: *85*

Definitely a "Chardonnay vintage," with some excellent base wines produced on the Côte des Blancs, but the Pinot Noir suffered rather more rot in 2006 than most producers were inclined to admit, and the Meunier was even worse. With nearly 16 percent affected, the normally hardy Meunier was exceptionally rot-prone for the second year running. This does not mean that some fine-quality champagnes won't be produced from black grapes, just that selection will very much be the key to this vintage. The Aube produced the most interesting Pinot Noir, although some grapes were overripe.

2005

Vintage rating: *85*

With about 14 percent gray rot in the black varieties, particularly Meunier, 2005 cannot be classified as a true or great vintage. Definitely not in the class of 2002; probably on par or just below 2004, although some producers may make better 2005s. This is a winemaker's year. Jean-Baptiste Lecaillon, the *chef de caves* at Roederer, told me: "If you are a good blender, one plus one can often equal three, but in 2005 one plus one equals four!" From tasting the *vins clairs*, I found Chardonnay overwhelmingly the best variety, with Le Mesnil-sur-Oger the most successful *cru*. As far as black varieties are concerned, Pinot Noir has the edge over Meunier, with Verzy and Verzenay standing out.

2004

Vintage rating: *85–88*

This is a vintage on steroids: huge and yet boosted by an injection of exceptional sunshine. The quality is good to very good, with excellent acids and purity. It is very early days, but the best so far appear to be the Clos des Goisses, Belle Epoque Brut, Comtes de Champagne Blanc de Blancs, Cristal, Dom Ruinart, Grande Dame, Brut, and Blanc de Blancs Brut from Deutz; Gastronome Brut from Pierre Gimonnet & Fils; and Cuvée Deluxe Blanc de Blancs Grand Cru from André Jacquart.

2003

Vintage rating: *50–90*

Frost destroyed 50 percent of the potential crop, then a pan-European heat wave ripened the grapes at an extraordinarily fast rate, resulting in the earliest harvest since 1822 (when records began), with high, but not excessively high, natural alcohol levels (an average of 10.6 percent ABV). The speed at which the grapes went through *véraison* produced the lowest acidity and highest pH on record. It is therefore not another 1976, 1959, or 1947, as some *champenois* would have us believe. Considering the small size of the crop and proportionately greater scarcity of Chardonnay, a number of houses might not release a standard vintage, but any producer who has not produced at least a small amount of pure 2003, even if only for in-house use, will regret it, since they will have no library bottles to consult if climate change continues. Most commercial 2003s are dismal, but the best are very special and include Clos des Goisses and 2003 by Bollinger; Paradox from Pierre Gimonnet & Fils; Célébris Extra Brut Rosé, Grand Vintage Brut, and Grand Vintage Brut Rosé from Moët & Chandon; and Cuvée de Prestige from JM Gobillard. Even Sainsbury's Taste the Difference isn't bad!

2002

Vintage rating: *90*

This is without doubt a vintage year, and a very special one, too, marked by the *passerillage* that reduced the crop in some vineyards by up to 40 percent and endowed the wines with the highest natural alcohol level since 1990 (which itself was the highest since 1959). It is definitely a Pinot Noir year, with Aÿ-Champagne the most successful village. There are some fine Chardonnays, but in general they are less impressively structured and lack acidity. Not that the Pinot Noirs are overblessed with acidity. Low acidity is a key feature of this vintage, with *vins clairs* tasting much softer than their analyses would have us believe. Many of the earliest 2002s to appear on the shelf have been disappointing, but the best are years away from release. Virtually everything with 2002 on the label is exciting—from Veuve Clicquot, which was released too early but hit a truly sweet spot by April 2008 and will stay there for years, to Dom Ruinart, the greatest 2002 I have tasted so far, although all the prestige *cuvées* from this vintage stand out.

Grapevine

• **At the** *Decanter* **World Wine Awards,** Taittinger's Les Folies de la Marquetterie won the Non-Vintage Champagne trophy, Charles Heidsieck's 1999 Brut Rosé Millésimé won the Rosé Champagne trophy, and Waitrose's own-label 1996 toughed out some very classy competition to win the Vintage Champagne trophy.

• **Perlage:** the perfect way to serve mature and prestige champagnes by the glass? I am putting the Perlage system to the test by letting my local wine bar, the Summertown Wine Café, play with it. I will report back next year. In the meantime, for details about this system, which has already been adopted by Dom Pérignon, see www.perlagesystems.com/About/.

• **Grower champagnes** are available by the glass seven days a week at a new bar-cum-*caviste*, C Comme Champagne, at 8 Rue Gambetta in Epernay. Up to 250 different champagnes from 45 growers are listed, but only five *cuvées* (on a rotating basis) are offered by the glass, although you should be able to manage a full bottle of the others over a coarse-pâté platter in the bar.

• **Two bottles of 1959 Dom Pérignon Rosé** went for $85,000 at an Acker Merrall & Condit auction in New York in April 2008. That's $42,500 each for bottles that are probably oxidized! I confess that I have never tasted the 1959 DPR, but I have tasted the straight 1959 DP many times, and most of those bottles and magnums have been oxidized. There is a flaw on the inner surface of the neck of the 1959 DP. It's well known. Whenever I have tasted this vintage with Richard Geoffroy, he always has two backups ready and waiting at the correct temperature. The last time all three were oxidized and had to be thrown away. I assume that they must have used the same bottles for the 1959 DPR…

GREATEST WINE PRODUCERS

1. Krug
2. Pol Roger
3. Louis Roederer
4. Billecart-Salmon
5. Bollinger
6. Deutz
7. Jacquesson
8. Gosset
9. Pierre Gimonnet & Fils
10. Vilmart

FASTEST-IMPROVING PRODUCERS

1. Lanson
2. Taittinger
3. Heidsieck & Co Monopole
4. Piper-Heidsieck
5. De Saint Gall
6. J Dumangin
7. Moët & Chandon
8. Mumm
9. Jacquart
10. Ayala

NEW UP-AND-COMING PRODUCERS

1. Jean-Noël Haton
2. Louis Barthelemy
3. Serge Mathieu
4. Henri Mandois
5. Fluteau
6. Bruno Paillard
7. Chanoine's Tsarine range
8. Henri Giraud
9. Audoin de Dampierre
10. Chapuy

BEST-VALUE PRODUCERS

1. Palmer
2. Piper-Heidsieck
3. Charles Heidsieck
4. Serge Mathieu
5. Henri Mandois
6. Jacquart
7. Lanson
8. Louis Roederer
9. Drappier
10. Heidsieck & Co Monopole

GREATEST-QUALITY WINES

1. **Cuvée R Lalou 1998**
   Mumm (€120)
2. **Les Folies de la Marquetterie NV** Taittinger (€41)
3. **Belle Epoque Rosé 2002**
   Perrier-Jouët (€200)
4. **Dom Pérignon 2000**
   Moët & Chandon (€95)
5. **Noble Cuvée Brut 1998**
   Lanson (€86.87)
6. **Vintage Brut 2002**
   Veuve Clicquot (€40)
7. **Brut Millésime 2000**
   Piper-Heidsieck (€39)
8. **Clos des Goisses 1998**
   Philipponnat (€86)
9. **Blanc de Blancs Fleuron 2002**
   Pierre Gimonnet & Fils (€26)
10. **Brut Réserve Dégorgement 2007 Mis en Cave en 2004 NV**
    Charles Heidsieck (€30)

BEST BARGAINS

1. **Grand Cellier Brut NV**
   Vilmart (€22)
2. **Brut NV** Palmer (€16.50)
3. **Brut 2000** J Dumangin (€22)
4. **Brut 2000** Jacquart (€22)
5. **Blanc de Blancs Brut 2002**
   Palmer (€24.90)
6. **Grand Sendrée 2000**
   Drappier (€30)
7. **Brut Réserve Dégorgement 2007 Mis en Cave en 2004 NV**
   Charles Heidsieck (€30)
8. **Blanc de Blancs Brut 2002**
   Chapuy (€21.90)
9. **Cuvée Prestige NV**
   Dumenil (€19.10)
10. **Silver Top 2002** Heidsieck & Co Monopole (€29.55)

MOST EXCITING OR UNUSUAL FINDS

1. **"Single-cask" Ratafia 2005** Janisson Baradon (€19) *The first ever Ratafia recommended in Wine Report, this pure Pinot Noir nectar really tastes as if it has been made from chocolate.*

2. **Pure Brut Nature NV** Pol Roger (€34) *The finest brut nature I've ever tasted.*

3. **Cordon Rouge Brut Millésimé 2002** Mumm (€31) *Mumm's best vintage since 1955!*

4. **Clos des Goisses Juste Rosé 1999** Philipponnat (€86) *Champagne's most exceptional terroir gets just a touch of color for its first-ever rosé. Look out for the 2000 vintage.*

5. **Brut Rosé Millésimé 1999** Charles Heidsieck (€75) *Buy this sumptuous rosé in so-called "rip-off Britain" for only £42 (€53), where the mousse is much softer and silkier due to its longer post-disgorgement aging.*

6. **Black Label Brut NV** Lanson (€24) *For the past two years this has been the best and most consistent non-vintage from any of the big grandes marques.*

7. **Rosé Brut NV** Bollinger (€65) *Although this is so Bollinger on the nose—that is, oxidative—this firm's first non-vintage rosé has an immaculate mousse and classy, focused fruit on the palate.*

8. **Millésime de Collection 1999** Pierre Gimonnet & Fils (€85 per magnum) *Minerality magnified by the magnum effect. Just starting to drink well.*

9. **Femme 1996** Duval-Leroy (€220 per magnum) *So much better in magnum. Cellar it for a decade!*

10. **Brut 2000** J Dumangin (€22) *With Gilles Dumangin's 2000 even better than his 1999, it looks as if quality and consistency are really starting to kick in.*

Grapevine

• **Hervé Jestin,** the former *chef de cave* at Duval-Leroy, has entered into a partnership with young Benoît Marguet of Ambonnay to produce a very special champagne for release in 2010. I cannot reveal any details, since that information was given to me confidentially, but I can say that I caught up with Hervé in Marguet's cellar, just around the corner from Krug's illustrious Clos d'Ambonnay. Marguet's vineyard is, in fact, just above the now famous *clos*, 30 ft (10 m) higher, but not benefiting from the protection of a wall. I tasted the wine in barrel, and it's outstanding. Almost too good for champagne, although both Benoît and Hervé have overoaked champagnes in the past, so I will wait until I taste it in bottle before passing judgment.

• **Fredrik Wikingsson,** a Swedish television host, paid £1,450 ($2,870) for a bottle of 1937 Champagne Moët & Chandon. Believed to have come from Hitler's private cellar, and rumored to have been injected with cyanide, the bottle will feature in a documentary about dictators, after which Wikingsson said he "might sell it off and donate the money to a Jewish charity."

Alsace

Tom Stevenson

Is René Muré's rejection of so-called physiological ripeness the start of a welcome trend or a glitch on the radar screen?

TOM STEVENSON

On my last visit to Muré, René told me that he had been harvesting grapes three days earlier since 2005. When I asked him why, he said that although he had been pleased with the wines he had been making, he wanted more freshness in the fruit. He wanted crisper wines. He wanted to make dry wines that could be enjoyed every day, not just on a special occasion. I thought back to the first discussion on so-called physiological ripeness I had launched into at this establishment. It was not that long ago. René had been picking riper and riper, and it was difficult to find a dry wine at Muré. To drive home the point I had been making, I had asked René what the oldest dry Riesling was in his cellar that was still drinking nicely. I forget the actual vintage, but when he told me, I remember asking what the potential alcohol would have been. "Eleven degrees, perhaps. Maybe only 10.5," he reckoned, and I responded, "Not bad, then, for physiologically unripe grapes."

That was in February 2006, months after René's first earlier harvest. Obviously I was preaching to the converted.

TOM STEVENSON specializes in champagne, but he is equally passionate about Alsace. In 1987, he was elected a *confrère oenophile* of the Confrérie Saint-Etienne, when he was the sole person to identify a 50-year-old wine made from Sylvaner. In 1994, his 600-page tome *The Wines of Alsace* (Faber & Faber, 1993) won the Veuve Clicquot Book of the Year award in the US and attracted the mother of all reviews in the UK from Malcolm Gluck, who declared: "It is not simply the best book about Alsace wines ever written, or the most penetrating book about a French wine region ever written; it is the greatest wine book ever written, period." A revision is in the pipeline but more than a few years away. Tom is chairman of the Alsace panel at the *Decanter* World Wine Awards.

Muré's 2005s show an increased freshness of fruit, with a crisper finish, but it is the 2006s that demonstrate the most dramatic change in quality and style. The fact that 2006 was a poor year (see Vintage Report) and 2005 a truly excellent one should illustrate just how influential Muré's earlier harvesting has been. Nowhere is this more evident than in the Pinot Noirs. Muré's vineyards on the Vorbourg include prime sites for red wine. So much so, in fact, that René has applied for permission to grow Syrah! The Vorbourg catches the full glare of the sun from dawn to dusk; consequently, René Muré's high-density Pinot Noir vines (10,000 vines per hectare) develop grapes with thick skins that are exceptionally heavy with pigment. The Clos St-Landelin Pinot Noir is located at the foot of the Vorbourg and usually makes the darkest Pinot Noir. The 2006 Clos St-Landelin is indeed darker than the "V" Pinot Noir (from the non-*clos* part of the Vorbourg, just 1,640 ft [500 m] above), but it is not as dark as the 2005 Clos St-Landelin, also picked early but from a much riper vintage. However, these two 2006s certainly do not lack richness or ripeness; they are just more clearly defined, with such beautiful fruit and finesse that they are in a completely different class. As far as the dry whites are concerned, even the generic Côtes de Rouffach Riesling has lovely fruit, despite having only 2.5 g of residual sugar. Not all of his 2006s are dry, of course, but the ones that are suggest this could be a watershed vintage for Muré. It took another year for René's changes to affect his truly sweet wines in an equally radical fashion. If bottling has no

Grapevine

● **Is the Flûte d'Alsace doomed?**
While fine for most Alsace varietals, the tall and slender Flûte d'Alsace bottle has always been a bizarre choice for red wines, but producers have had no choice in the matter, since this bottle was forced on them by law in 1959. So when Jean-Michel Deiss jumped the gun and used a semi-burgundian bottle for his Burlenberg before it was legally permitted, it was very welcome. Sometimes laws have to be broken for progress to be made, and in this instance the ends justified Deiss's means—but now we have another shape bottle. The bottle is one of two shapes that Willm has used to launch its NOW Pinot Gris. NOW stands for New Old World, and not unsurprisingly it is very oaky, but one of the bottles used tapers from a bordeaux-like shoulder to a significantly narrower base. It looks neither New nor Old World and does nothing for Alsace other than further erode the 1959 law.

● **Good totally Sylvaner** is hard to find in the year of the mushroom. Sylvaner 2006 Domaine Weinbach might be the most exquisite example of this grape I have tasted, but the basic Sylvaner 2006 Léon Beyer is a pretty smart wine, and at only 4 g of residual sugar, it is the best, driest Sylvaner I have tasted in years. I much preferred this wine to the "special" Sylvaner that Léon Beyer sold to The Wine Society.

detrimental effect, then his 2007 Muscat Clos St-Landelin SGN promises to be the first truly successful botrytized Muscat from Alsace, while his 2007 Riesling SGN is stunning, with 212 g residual sugar put on a knife edge by 16 g of acidity (expressed as tartaric).

My fear is that René will relent—or that no one else will be brave enough to renounce the false god of physiological ripeness and join him. But if Muré's earlier harvesting is the start of a trend to rediscover Alsace's dry-wine roots, relegating sweet styles to a tiny proportion of very special SGN or VT, then it could attract back this region's formerly most loyal consumers and appeal to new dry wine consumers.

Alsace gradually gets screwed

In *Wine Report 2007* I maintained that Alsace wines are ideal for screwcaps, but apart from Blanck, Willm, Jean-Pierre Frick, and Gustave Lorentz, most Alsace producers have failed to take advantage of this technology. A big stumbling block is that, apart from the *grands maisons*, relatively few Alsace producers are seriously involved in export markets, where the benefits of these closures are widely accepted by large and increasing numbers of fine-wine consumers. The French are not persuaded, even though Stelvin is a French invention. I mentioned that although Trimbach is one of Alsace's most widely exported brands, this firm won't invest in the technology until it is accepted in the US. I have since heard from JB Adam that its screwcap-bottling line was set up (for both Adam and Kuentz-Bas) in 2005 specifically to accommodate the US and Scandinavian markets. Talking about screwcaps to Marc Hugel, he gave me five reasons why he would not use screwcaps, only one of which I had not heard and dismissed before: they are easily damaged when moving bottles around by forklift trucks. I sent this to half a dozen of the most experienced screwcap winemakers in Australia and New Zealand, and they all came back with the same two comments: if he's that clumsy he shouldn't be driving a forklift truck; and if he made the same contact against a corked bottle, the glass would crack or shatter. Come on, guys—if Trimbach and Hugel went screwcap, Alsace would convert overnight. You do know the world is not flat, don't you?

Grapevine

• **Muré** might have made exceptional Pinot Noir in 2006, but his vines of the Vorbourg were unaffected by rot, while many producers had such huge problems that they did not dare macerate their wines on such rotten skins. Most who did must have regretted the decision (just five "passable" 2006 Pinot Noirs out of 70-odd tasted at CIVA), but the only alternative—to make a *blanc de noirs*— was equally disastrous. Beware the flood of orange wines, because I have yet to taste one that was enjoyable.

Opinion:
Sugar can kill!

In this year's edition of *Wine Report*, I seem to be arguing for more sugar in Champagne and less in Alsace, but of course neither argument is about sugar per se. Both arguments are based on what is necessary for their respective styles of wine. For Alsace, this not only concerns being true to the dry-wine image of Alsace wine for historical reasons, it also concerns reassuring consumers with a reasonably consistent style of wine, and then labeling it in such a way that consumers are not confused by anything as basic as whether it's dry or sweet.

There is no room for sweet wine in Alsace other than *vendanges tardives*, *sélection de grains nobles*, and maybe the occasional *vin de glace*. These are specialty wines and, as such, are expected to be rarities, prized and expensive, but they are devalued by the increasing sweetness of all other Alsace wines. A combination of seeking out the hottest, most expressive terroir (can be good), lower yields (good), biodynamics (good), so-called physiological ripeness (bad), and allowing wines to ferment as much or as little as "they want" (can be good or bad) has been responsible for the increasing number of inconsistently sweet Alsace wines, particularly among the *grands crus* and *lieux-dits*. Because of different vintage conditions and the tendency by some producers to allow wines to do their own thing during fermentation, it is impossible for experts, let alone consumers, to know whether the same wine is dry, medium sweet, or intensely sweet from year to year. And because there is no obligatory designation for all dry wines, consumers have absolutely no idea whether the wine they would like to order with their fish is going to be dry or sweet. This has been eroding consumer confidence in the wines of Alsace for the past 10 years or so, and that has harmed the hard-earned reputation of Alsace as a dry varietal-wine region. Not all biodynamic wines are sweet, but not all biodynamic wines are good, either. Some biodynamic wines are great and dry, but many biodynamic producers believe in physiological ripeness, even though Rudolf Steiner never proposed this concept.

With the exception of *vendanges tardives* and *sélection de grains nobles*, which should be produced in the most limited quantities to preserve their value, sugar is the long-term enemy in Alsace. But in the short term, once again, I ask whether it is too much to ask for an obligatory dry-wine designation to help consumers make a choice.

Vintage Report

Advance report on the latest harvest
2007

As in Champagne, a fantastically hot spring pushed the vines on one month in advance of their normal growth, but the weather started to fall apart in June. April and May were exceptionally hot and sunny, but on June 15 a hailstorm devastated up to 150 ha in the villages of Ammerschwihr, Sigolsheim, Kientzheim, Bennwihr, and Kaysersberg. I was dining at Bernard Trimbach's home the following week (June 20), when the telephone rang to say that a narrow band of fierce hail had struck their vines in Mittelwihr. Pierre and I went for a midnight drive in the wake of the storm to find 50 percent of the potential crop had been destroyed. Mid-August rains encouraged the most meticulous growers to remove the leaves above bunches to help avoid a repeat of the previous year's rampant rot. Despite these climatic difficulties, the harvest took place under ideal conditions throughout a typically sunny Alsatian September, and many great white and sweet white wines have been produced, with Pinot Blanc, Riesling, and Gewurztraminer the most successful grape varieties. Pinot Gris also excelled. As for the reds, opinion is divided.

Updates on the previous five vintages
2006

Vintage rating: *Red: 75, White: 75*

The year of the mushroom! Over the past 20 years, only 2003 and 1996 yielded worse wines, but unlike those two years, this was neither an unpleasant nor difficult year to taste. While the dead fruit and lack of acidity made the 2003s hard-going and the malic (not malolactic) stink of the 1996 was (and still is) repulsive, the mushroom aroma pervading most 2006s was not at all offensive. It is the result of rot, but it is just boring and even had a silver lining because it made tasting my way through 470 2006s much easier—particularly the 380 wines at my centralized tasting at CIVA. While I have to give the best wines my undivided attention in any year, as soon as I hit a 2006 with mushroom on the nose or palate, I moved on. What would be the point of any further consideration? I'm not going to recommend such wines, although one producer told me that his American importer told him to send over as much "risotto wine" as possible, because since he told his customers to drink it with mushroom risotto it's been flying off the shelf! No less than 12.6 percent of the 2006s I tasted at CIVA were mushroom-affected, and when each producer is restricted to a maximum of four wines, presumably they are showing me their very best. Putting the all-pervading mushroom problem to one side, the worst varietal performance was *blanc de noirs* from Pinot Noir that was not fit for red wine. Many did not bother with red wine, yet some like René Muré made the best red wine of their lives. There are some excellent 2006s, but this is not a vintage to buy on spec. Every producer was affected. You must be very picky.

2005

Vintage rating: *Red: 88, White: 90*

Overall, 2005 is better than 2004, with brighter fruit flavors, and it vies with 2001 and 2002, but the wines need time to confirm their precise qualities. Gewurztraminer was the best all-around performer, while Riesling was the most variable (although some Rieslings were as good as the best Gewurztraminers) and the Pinot Gris was excellent. All other varieties were good to very good. Ideal conditions for botrytis suggest excellent botrytized (as opposed to *passerillé*) VT and SGN.

Grapevine

- **Trimbach wins the *Decanter* Trophy again** with its Riesling Cuvée Frédéric Emile. Last year the 2001 vintage collected the trophy, this year it is the 2002. Domaine Schoffit's 2005 Gewurztraminer Harth Cuvée Caroline picked up the Dry Aromatic trophy, and Pierre Sparr's 2005 Gewurztraminer Sélection de Grains Nobles won the Sweet Alsace trophy. The 2008 competition received the highest number of Alsace wines, with 83 entered, up from 46 in 2007. The *Decanter* World Wine Awards (DWWA) is the only terroir-driven international wine competition where the chairmen and chairwomen are selected for their knowledge and experience of their respective regions and are given the freedom to choose and tweak the judges on the panel based on their individual expertise of the wines in question. All medals and regional trophies are judged not on a universal basis but on the variety or style as grown and produced in a specific region. In 2008 this resulted in eight gold medals (three of which were awarded regional trophies), 13 silver medals, and 21 bronze medals. The wines entered do not have to be available on the UK market. In fact, the DWWA is an ideal platform for producers not represented in the UK, since *Decanter* actively promotes successful wines that are not available to the UK trade. Contact worldwineawards@decanter.com in any language for details.

2004

Vintage rating: *Red: 86, White: 87*

Definitely a more classic vintage, with good fruit and excellent acidity levels. Not in the same class as 2002 or 2001, but it has a distinct edge over 2000 and is certainly fresher, fruitier, and more classic than 2003.

2003

Vintage rating: *Red: 93, White: 65*

There is no doubt that the oppressively hot year of 2003 provided an exceptional and extraordinary growing season, but apart from—potentially— Pinot Noir and a handful of anomalies, the quality is neither exceptional nor extraordinary. Plowing through 350 wines from this vintage in March 2005 was one of the hardest, most unenjoyable, but most instructive tasting experiences of my life. Acidification was allowed by special dispensation, but not everyone took advantage; of those who did, very few got it right, whereas many of those who did not acidify failed to produce wines of any elegance. Most are ugly with a deadness of fruit. Pinot Noir should be the star, but I have not yet tasted a glut of great Pinot Noir, although the optimist in me hopes that I will have more exciting news in the next edition of *Wine Report*. Putting to one side Pinot Noir, the most expressive 2003 grapes were Pinot Gris, which in fact looked as black as Pinot Noir on the vine and were made with a natural *vin gris* color.

2002

Vintage rating: *Red: 85, White: 89*

Although there is some variability in quality, the best 2002s have the weight of the 2000s but with far more focus and finesse. Riesling definitely fared best and will benefit from several years' bottle-age, but Gewurztraminer and Muscat also performed well. The Gewurztraminers are very aromatic, with broad spice notes, whereas the Muscats are exceptionally fresh and floral. Pinot Gris was less successful. Some extraordinary SGNs have been produced.

Grapevine

• At my annual tasting at CIVA, I tasted 57 Muscat d'Alsace, but only one stood out—the deliciously off-dry Muscat Tradition 2006 J-M & F Bernhard, which earned itself the number-three slot in Best Bargains. Of the dry style there were just three that passed muster. That evening I dined at the Brasserie l'Auberge, which was serving an excellent Muscat by the glass: Muscat Réserve 2006 Paul Buecher. I taste my way through nearly 60 Muscat wines that it is reasonable to assume were submitted to impress, then stumble across something much better by accident!

GREATEST WINE PRODUCERS

1. JosMeyer
2. Domaine Weinbach
3. Domaine Zind Humbrecht
4. Trimbach (Réserve and above)
5. René Muré
6. Schlumberger
7. Hugel (Jubilée and above)
8. Domaine Ostertag
9. André Kientzler
10. Léon Beyer (Réserve and above)

FASTEST-IMPROVING PRODUCERS

1. René Muré
2. Eric Rominger
3. Cave Vinicole de Hunawihr
4. Kuentz-Bas
5. Schlumberger
6. Jean Becker
7. Hugel
8. Robert Faller
9. Lucien Albrecht
10. Paul Blanck

NEW UP-AND-COMING PRODUCERS

1. Laurent Barth
2. André Kleinknecht
3. Leipp-Leininger
4. Gruss
5. Yves Amberg
6. Domaine Stirn
7. Jean & Daniel Klack
8. Schoenheitz
9. Clément Klur
10. Fernand Engel

BEST-VALUE PRODUCERS

1. JosMeyer
2. Jean Becker
3. Lucien Albrecht
4. Cave Vinicole de Hunawihr
5. Jean-Louis Schoepfer
6. René Muré

7. Schoffit
8. Laurent Barth
9. Meyer-Fonné
10. Paul Blanck

GREATEST-QUALITY WINES

1. *Riesling Cuvée Frédéric Emile 2002 Trimbach (€30)
2. Riesling Grand Cru Muenchberg 2006 Domaine Ostertag (€31.25)
3. *Pinot Noir Clos St-Landelin 2006 René Muré (€31.60)
4. Gewurztraminer Sélection de Grains Nobles 2005 Pierre Sparr (€34.40 per 50-cl bottle)
5. **Riesling Grand Cru Altenberg de Bergheim 1995 Gustave Lorentz (€30)
6. Grand Cru Altenberg de Bergheim 2006 Marcel Deiss (€54)
7. **Riesling Grand Cru Altenberg de Bergheim 1999 Gustave Lorentz (€23.40)
8. *Gewurztraminer Herrenweg 2006 Domaine Zind Humbrecht (€20)
9. *Riesling Les Escaliers 2004 Léon Beyer (€24.10)
10. *Riesling Grand Cru Furstentum 2006 Paul Blanck (€25)

BEST BARGAINS

1. *Gewurztraminer 2006 Jean-Louis Schoepfer (€5.80)
2. **Riesling Grand Cru Wineck-Schlossberg 2006 J-M & F Bernhard (€10)
3. **Muscat Tradition 2006 J-M & F Bernhard (€6)
4. Riesling Vendanges Tardives 1997 Lichtlé & Fils (€19.10)
5. *Riesling Turckheim 2006 Domaine Zind Humbrecht (€17.90)
6. **Gewurztraminer Grand Cru Sonnenglanz 2006 Jean Becker (€18.90)
7. *Riesling Grand Cru Sommerberg 2006 Albert Boxler (€18)

⑧ ***Riesling Grand Cru Froehn 2006** Philippe & François Becker (€18.50)

⑨ **Jubilée Pinot Noir 2006** Hugel (€19.50)

⑩ ***Riesling Réserve 2006** Trimbach (€19.60)

MOST EXCITING OR UNUSUAL FINDS

① ***Sylvaner 2006** Domaine Weinbach (€11.10) *I cannot remember a better, more exquisite Sylvaner than this, and from the 2006 vintage too!*

② ***Pinot Gris Calcaire 2006** Domaine Zind Humbrecht (€20) *Lovely acidity, sumptuous sweetness. A blend of 50 percent Heimbourg, 40 percent Clos Windsbuhl, and 10 percent Rotenberg.*

③ ****Riesling Cuvée Albert 2006** Albert Mann (€12.50) *Squeezed between two grands crus of the same residual sugar (11 g), and it was this wine that showed the class and finesse.*

④ **Le Zinn 2006** Eric Rominger (€24) *This assemblage of 45 percent Gewurztraminer, 30 percent Pinot Gris, and 25 percent Riesling is the finest Alsace classic blend I have tasted for two decades!*

⑤ ***Andlau Riesling 2006** Marc Kreydenweiss (€12) *Kreydenweiss's malolactic style is not for me—normally—but there are always exceptions, and this elegantly perfumed, soft, delicious wine is certainly one.*

⑥ ***Pinot Noir "V" 2006** René Muré (€25.60) *It's not certain whether this or the Clos St-Landelin is the better 2006 Pinot Noir.*

⑦ ***Riesling 1989** Léon Beyer (€55) *Amazing elegance for a vintage like this more than 20 years on.*

⑧ ***Riesling Grand Cru Kirchberg de Ribeauvillé 1978** Louis Sipp (€60) *Totally dry and honeyed, yet it still has another 10 years of positive development ahead of it.*

⑨ ***Pinot Blanc 2006** Domaine Weinbach (€16.60) *It is hard to imagine a more polished and poised Pinot Blanc than this 50/50 Pinot Blanc/Auxerrois blend.*

⑩ ****Klevener de Heiligenstein L'Opaline 2006** Zeyssolf (€10.50) *Not a grand vin, but this is the first Klevener de Heiligenstein I have encountered that has a sense of both variety and place.*

Notes: *Dry, **Off-dry

Grapevine

• At the 11th World Riesling Competition in Strasbourg on January 28, 2008, 514 wines were tasted from over 300 producers in 13 countries. Alsace scooped five of the nine trophies awarded: Riesling Vieilles Vignes Glintzberg 2006 Anstotz, Riesling Grand Cru Wineck-Schlossberg 2005 Cave Vinicole d'Ingersheim, Riesling Cuvée Daphné VT 2005 Vorburger-Meyer, Riesling Grand Cru Mandelberg 2002 Hartweg, and Riesling Grand Cru

Bruderthal 2000 Bernard Weber. With just 10 wines fewer than in 2007, it was very noticeable that the proportion of gold and silver medals had changed radically, from an even 79 golds and 79 silvers in 2007, each representing 15 percent of the total wines submitted, to no fewer than 124 golds and 19 silvers in 2008. That's a staggering 24 percent gold and a minuscule 3.6 percent silver! Alsace won 77 of the 124 gold medals, and 7 of the 19 silver medals.

Loire Valley

Charles Sydney

You've heard of Steven Spurrier's 1972 Judgment of Paris, which pitted top California reds against the greatest clarets.

CHARLES SYDNEY

Well, this time the Loire won the hat-trick at a blind tasting I organized during the Salon des Vins de Loire at Angers in February 2008. Three Loire *moelleux*—Château de Fesles Bonnezeaux, Domaine de la Taille aux Loups Montlouis Romulus, and Domaine des Forges Quarts de Chaume 2003—all came out ahead of the great Château d'Yquem 2003. Sixteen tasters were on the panel, which was composed of buyers from a range of leading UK and Swedish importers. Yquem was not listed first by anyone, and nine tasters listed it last.

Consolidation, consolidation, consolidation

Just four years after merging to create the giant Loire Propriétés, Touraine *négociant* Pierre Chainier and the Caves de la Loire group have split.

Pierre Chainier (which had already effectively taken over the local Oisly-Thésée cooperative) and Caves de la Loire (which includes the Anjou cooperative at Brissac) could potentially make a nice target for one of the surviving trio of Castel, Grands Chais de France, and Alliance Loire.

Grand Chais de France's appetite is clearly as great as ever. After buying out Nantes group Vinival in 2004, sparkling-wine specialist Lacheteau in

CHARLES SYDNEY has spent 20 years in Chinon as a *courtier en vins*—a wine broker—specializing in the Loire Valley. Based at the heart of the region, he works exclusively on the export market, creating a partnership between the leading producers and the more forward-looking importers. He has an almost evangelical desire to encourage growers to make wines that appeal to the public, at the same time leaning on the specialist press to understand the sometimes dramatic changes happening in one of the world's richest and most diverse wine regions.

November 2006, and Vouvray's Roger Felicien Brou early in 2007, Grands Chais de France has now taken over local *négociant* Sauvion & Fils at Château du Cléray—though oenologist Pierre Sauvion (nephew of the lovely Jean-Ernest) is staying at the helm. This means that they are still France's second-biggest group, just behind the competing house of Castel…

… who just happen to have bought out Nantes *négociant* Sautejeau-Beauquin (making it the largest producer of Muscadet) and Friedrich, the region's bag-in-box specialist.

Fortunately, there are still some 7,000 wine growers along the Loire. Of these, a high percentage sell their grapes or finished wine to the *négoce*, and an equally high percentage are members of the nine cooperative cellars that have joined together to create behemoth Alliance Loire.

All of which doesn't seem to leave much room for the small independent producers—are they being squeezed out? The answer is emphatically no: despite difficult conditions on local and export markets, the region's better producers are thriving (several domaines now reaching an impressive 100 ha or more) and are offering both quality and value of a level never before seen in the region.

Changes in Chenonceaux

Up in Chenonceaux (note the "x"—this is the village, not the château), they've decided that the red should be a blend of Cabernet Franc and Malbec (Cot to us locals), with Gamay an optional extra. Sounds a bit like that old but happily defunct and totally unsellable disaster, Touraine Tradition, a Cab-Cot-Gamay blend that was so awful no one would buy it. All the more similar when you think that there are no plans to limit the wines under the village appellation to wines actually grown in the village!

After that great success story, there's now talk of Chenonceaux white. Surprise, surprise—this is Sauvignon Blanc (they got that one right), not necessarily from Chenonceaux, but heck, this is France we're talking about. But it does have to go through a tasting panel. The only worry is that one of the best growers of the appellation has been refused *cru* status because his wines are too *fruité* and Sauvignon-styled!

Grapevine

• **After a disagreement** with his financial backer over winemaking and the commercialization of recently acquired Château de Chamboreau, gentle giant Jo Pithon and his equally gentle (if headstrong) wife Isabelle have left their domaine, leaving their name with it. Here's hoping they can pick things up and start again, since their dry Chenins have to be some of the purest and most ethereal wines of the Loire—and proof (whatever I may say) that organic wine growing really can make quality wines.

Opinion:
Force fed

Dramatic gestures being at the heart of French politics, Le Grenelle de l'Environnement forcibly pushes sustainability, enforcing quotas of organic food in school meals, apparently without questioning the basis of the Ayatollah-esque preachings of the "bio" lobby. At least the best *vignerons* understand the long-term benefits to the land and to the consumer of using the reasoned winemaking approach of *lutte raisonnée*. Still, it could be worse: they could be enforcing the lunatic fringe of biodynamists with their loony preparations. (Have you heard about the one made by fermenting oak bark in the skull of a domestic animal?)

Sweet and sour

Naturally ripe grapes not only give balanced wines but are also evidence of a certain honesty that the consumer really ought to have the right to expect. So the fact that a shrinking but still substantial percentage of *demi-sec* and *moelleux* wines with residual sugar (and not only the cheaper ones) have had sugar added during the fermentation process does make me cringe.

Unfortunately, chaptalization—the addition of sugar (usually from beets) to grape juice to increase the potential alcohol of the resultant mix—is not only legal but common practice.

If the aim is to improve structure and balance in a wine in a difficult vintage, I guess that's fine. When the practice is commonplace, it does leave two questions: first, is the *vigneron* actually capable of growing grapes to make wine? If the answer to that is yes, then is the grape variety suited to the local soil and microclimate?

Part of the problem is "the market." There is a demand, especially in the US but also from larger chains across the UK, for *demi-sec* Vouvrays with 25 g/l residual sugar to sell at a critical price point. But to make a wine with 12.5 percent ABV and 25 g/l residual sugar requires grapes with a natural potential of 14°. And that don't often happen naturally at $8.99! Since the wines are so much nicer dry (*demi-sec* can push the grapes to an unhealthy level of rot), wouldn't it be nice to see them taking a leaf out of Anjou's book and making high-quality dry whites by *tri* selective picking?

Currently this style is very much the realm of leading Saumur producers such as Thierry Germain and Edouard Pisani-Ferry and of Montlouis star Jacky Blot—and in Montlouis it is great to see them being followed by a handful of youngsters. Recently establishing themselves in this much-overlooked and underrated appellation, they've used the region's lower price per hectare to set up their own domaines and to prove a point qualitatively by making crisply pure dry whites with intensity and finesse.

Over in the Layon, chaptalization is a problem too, though less of one since the local *syndicat* introduced random analyses, sending any wine found to have been chaptalized over the legal 2° off to be distilled—a radical but effective deterrent that has accompanied a *prise de conscience* over the past 20 years that has seen the practice of enriching grape juice by anything up to a potential 10° (that's around 170 g of sugar per liter!) disappear among this region's generally brilliant and dedicated growers.

A more recent question here, though, is the use of cryoextraction, the more modern version of chaptalization. With this system, instead of adding sugar, the juice is frozen and the ice removed. The process makes wines with great sweet concentration (and can give the growers an equally wonderful reputation), but I just can't see 60 hl/ha (or more, according to some growers) giving the same quality and complexity of carefully managed vines being picked with successive selective *tris* and yields of 25 hl/ha or less.

This question is all the more vexing when one of the practitioners is among the handful of Quarts de Chaume producers to have opposed neighboring Chaume's claim to *premier cru* status.

Grapevine

• **Nice to see** people thinking quality, though perhaps the president of Touraine's St-Aignan region should realize that bringing yields for Sauvignon Blanc down to 40 hl/ha from the current 65 isn't going to improve quality but will push prices up and drive yet more hard-pressed *vignerons* to the wall.

• **The new Vin de Pays du Val de Loire** has at last replaced that awful Jardin de la France label. At least you now know where the stuff comes from—and growers are united in their belief in its potential, so there are some good wines from small domaines to be found, as well as the less exciting *négoce* blends.

• **Interloire,** the regional interprofessional organization, has grown, finally bringing Muscadet's CIVN into the fold as it joins Anjou and Touraine in a union representing (and I quote) 46 appellations running from Nantes to Blois. Good news upstream, too, as holdout Pouilly-Fumé has now joined Sancerre et al. in the Central Vineyards' BIVC. Are wedding bells expected soon?

• **Phylloxera it's not,** but since the government banned the use of sodium arsenite without offering any alternative cure, the fungus esca is wreaking havoc across France's vineyards, and the Loire is not immune. Although some varieties seem more resistant than others, growers of Cabernet Sauvignon and Sauvignon Blanc report between 20 and 30 percent of vines being affected. Maybe we should be looking hard at genetically modified vines sooner rather than later!

• **Wonders will never cease:** Anjou is finally allowing growers to put the grape variety on the label!

Vintage Report

Advance report on the latest harvest
2007

After a wonderful spring, 2007 was marked by an awful summer; then the sun came out, and the harvest was saved by weeks of excellent sunny, windy weather that held on until the last grapes were picked. A little like 2002 revisited, but actually rather better—and some compensation for quite dramatically low yields. It's fair to say that all the dry wines are fresh, aromatic, and intense, though there was perhaps some dilution in Sancerre compared with neighboring Pouilly. The reds are fine—fresh, fruity, and quite intense, really for early drinking. As for the Chenins: all that work in the vineyards paid off, and in the Layon the wines are really intense, concentrated, and fresh. Buy them and drink them—some will keep, but that's really missing the point of these wonderfully vibrant wines.

Muscadet—Lovely fruit, freshness, and intensity.

Sauvignon Blanc—*Typé*, aromatic, and crunchy.

Reds—Fruit and freshness (again!).

Dry Chenins—Balanced, aromatic, and intense.

Moelleux Chenins—Excellent in Layon; virtually non-existent in Vouvray.

Updates on the previous five vintages
2006

Vintage rating: *Red: 85, Muscadet: 70, Sauvignon: 95, Dry Chenin: 85, Moelleux Chenin: 75*

A great vintage for Sauvignons, with Sancerre and Pouilly even better than 2005, but the vintage was spoiled in the west by heavy rain in September (during harvest in Muscadet), making conditions difficult from Anjou through to Chinon and Vouvray. There are some great dry Chenins and fine, balanced reds from growers using the latest vineyard-management techniques, grassing through the vineyards, debudding in the spring, and—particularly—leaf plucking around the bunches to keep the grapes healthy.

2005

Vintage rating: *Red: 95, Muscadet: 95, Sauvignon: 95, Dry Chenin: 95, Moelleux Chenin: 95*

A great vintage—at least on a par with the wonderful 2003 for reds and sweet whites, but with more freshness and fruit for the dry whites from Muscadet through to Sancerre. And the wines have structure, too—making for some finely balanced reds and wonderfully intense sweet Chenins that are great now but will improve nicely over the next 5–10 years. This is certainly the best vintage ever for the new-wave barrel-fermented dry Chenins.

2004

Vintage rating: *Red: 85, Muscadet: 95, Sauvignon: 80, Dry Chenin: 80, Moelleux Chenin: 80*

Unusually uneven, though the best dry Chenins of Saumur and Anjou are still delightful. The reds are balanced and fresh, fine from the better producers, but to be avoided elsewhere. Farther east, things were more difficult, with high yields for the Sauvignons, so drink up and stick to the good growers!

2003

Vintage rating: *Red: 95, Muscadet: 95, Sauvignon: 85, Dry Chenin: 90, Moelleux Chenin: 95*

One of the great Loire vintages. Despite worries from outside the region that wines may be lacking in acidity, the Chenins and the reds have concentration, fruit, and balance that surpass 1990 and 1997. Okay, so the Sauvignons weren't as aromatic as we'd have liked, but the top *cuvées* are lovely. Prices are still more than reasonable.

2002

Vintage rating: *Red: 85, Muscadet: 95, Sauvignon: 90, Dry Chenin: 90, Moelleux Chenin: 85*

Sauvignons are quite ripe, the Muscadets are of rare exception, and there are great Chenins: this is a superb year for dry whites—better than 1996. These are excellent wines for aging. The reds, which are healthy, solid, and lively, are equal to the 1996s or slightly lower in quality. Their limiting factor is, sometimes, reduced potential longevity, yet they are better than the average quality of the reds produced farther south in France.

GREATEST WINE PRODUCERS

1. *Jacky Blot, Domaine de la Taille aux Loups (Montlouis, Vouvray), Domaine de la Butte (Bourgueil)
2. *Claude Papin, Château Pierre-Bise (Anjou, Savennières, Coteaux du Layon)
3. *Didier Dagueneau (Pouilly-Fumé)
4. *Vincent Pinard (Sancerre)
5. *Philippe Vatan, Château du Hureau (Saumur-Champigny)
6. Alphonse Mellot (Sancerre)
7. *Château de Fesles (Anjou, Bonnezeaux)
8. *Domaine Charles Joguet (Chinon)
9. Jean-Pierre Chevalier, Château de Villeneuve (Saumur-Champigny)
10. Domaine Vacheron (Sancerre)

FASTEST-IMPROVING PRODUCERS

1. *Domaine Henri Bourgeois (Sancerre)
2. Château de Passavant (Anjou)
3. Philippe Pichard (Chinon)
4. *Couly-Dutheil (Chinon)
5. Domaine de la Paleine (Saumur)
6. *Denis Goizil, Domaine du Petit Val (Coteaux du Layon)
7. *Domaine André & Edmond Figeat (Pouilly-Fumé)
8. *Domaine Henry Marionnet (Touraine)
9. Joël Mesnard, Domaine des Sablonettes (Anjou, Coteaux du Layon)
10. Les Frères Couillaud (Muscadet Sèvre & Maine)

NEW UP-AND-COMING PRODUCERS

1. *Jérémie Huchet, Domaine de la Chauvinière (Muscadet)
2. *Damien Delecheneau, Domaine La Grange Tiphaine (Touraine)
3. *Ampelidae (Haut-Poitou)
4. Domaine Valéry Renaudat (Reuilly)
5. Sébastien Redde, Domaine Michel Redde (Pouilly-Fumé)
6. Vincent Ricard (Touraine)
7. *Château de l'Aulée (Crémant de Loire, Touraine Azay-le-Rideau)
8. Stéphane Sérol (Côtes Roannaises)
9. Stéphane Cossais (Montlouis)
10. *Gérald Vallée, Domaine de la Cotelleraie (St-Nicolas de Bourgueil)

BEST-VALUE PRODUCERS

1. *Union des Vignerons de St-Pourçain (St-Pourçain)
2. *Rémi & Jean-Jacques Bonnet, Château la Tarcière (Muscadet Sèvre & Maine)
3. *Luc & Jérôme Choblet, Domaine des Herbauges (Muscadet Côtes de Grandlieu)
4. Les Frères Couillaud (Muscadet Sèvre & Maine)
5. *Quintin Frères (Coteaux du Giennois)
6. Cave du Haut-Poitou (Haut-Poitou)
7. *Stéphane Branchereau, Domaine des Forges (Anjou, Savennières, Coteaux du Layon)
8. *Jacky Marteau, Domaine de la Bergerie (Touraine)
9. Cave des Vignerons de Saumur (Saumur)
10. *Claude Papin, Château Pierre-Bise (Anjou, Savennières, Coteaux du Layon)

GREATEST-QUALITY WINES

1. ***Bonnezeaux 2003** Château de Fesles (€27 per 50-cl bottle)
2. ***Montlouis Romulus 2003** Jacky Blot, Domaine de la Taille aux Loups (€100)
3. ***Quarts de Chaume 2003** Stéphane Branchereau, Domaine des Forges (€20 per 50-cl bottle)

④ **Saumur-Champigny Le Grand Clos 2003** Jean-Pierre Chevalier, Château de Villeneuve (€14.50)

⑤ ***Pouilly-Fumé Silex 2006** Didier Dagueneau (€50)

⑥ ***Coteaux du Layon Beaulieu Les Rouannières 2005** Claude Papin, Château Pierre-Bise (€15 per 50-cl bottle)

⑦ ***Saumur-Champigny Lisagathe 2005** Philippe Vatan, Château du Hureau (€15)

⑧ **Sancerre Rouge La Belle Dame 2005** Domaine Vacheron (€23)

⑨ ***Anjou-Villages Brissac Les Millerits 2005** Jean-Yves & Jean-Hubert Lebreton, Domaine des Rochelles (€17)

⑩ **Saumur-Champigny Marginale 2005** Thierry Germain, Domaine des Roches Neuves (€17)

BEST BARGAINS

① **Saumur Rouge Réserve des Vignerons 2006** Cave des Vignerons de Saumur (€3.95)

② **VDQS Haut-Poitou Sauvignon 2007** Cave du Haut-Poitou (€3.75)

③ ***VDQS St-Pourçain Pinot Noir 2006** Union des Vignerons de St-Pourçain (€3.90)

④ ***Touraine Sauvignon 2007** Jacky Marteau, Domaine de la Bergerie (€4.20)

⑤ ***Pouilly-Fumé Les Chaumiennes 2007** Domaine André & Edmond Figeat (€8.50)

⑥ ***Coteaux du Layon Cuvée Simon 2005** Denis Goizil, Domaine du Petit Val (€9.50)

⑦ ***Vin de Pays du Val de Loire Chardonnay Elégance 2007** Luc & Jérôme Choblet, Domaine des Herbauges (€3.35)

⑧ All single-estate Muscadets.

⑨ All barrel-fermented dry Chenins.

⑩ All 2003, 2005, and 2007 Coteaux du Layons.

MOST EXCITING OR UNUSUAL FINDS

① **Melon de Bourgogne Jus de Raisin NV** Nelly Marcelleau-Couprie, Les Grands Presbytères (€3) *Grape juice "récolté sur les coteaux de St Fiacre": 0 percent ABV Melon de Bourgogne grapes that have been picked, pressed, and cold-settled for two days, then sterile-filtered and pasteurized to prevent fermenting in bottle. Refreshing, sufficiently complex to be interesting, and no problems with France's increasingly draconian drink-driving laws. And my 10-year-old loved it!*

② **VdP du Jardin de la France Pinot Gris Le Blanc 2006** Bonnet-Huteau (€5) *To keep his brain working, every sane wine grower needs to do something just a little different. Brothers Rémi and Jean-Jacques Bonnet's secret is their plot of Pinot Gris. At 30 g natural residual sugar per liter, it's perhaps a bit high for everyday drinking—but a great change from those bone-dry Muscadets!*

③ ***Touraine-Amboise Bécarre 2006** Damien Delecheneau, Domaine La Grange Tiphaine (€9.50) *Touraine-Amboise is one of those micro-appellations that you nearly give up on and which then surprise you with a real gem. Made by rising star Damien Delecheneau and his other half, Coralie Demeure, this pure Cabernet Franc is way riper than any I've tasted elsewhere in the Touraine. Matured for a year in oak, and its nose has all those violets you never find. Bagfuls of very, very ripe wild-cherry flavors.*

④ **Vin de Table Pinot Noir Blanc [2007]** Alphonse Mellot (€26) *There are only three barrels, but if you grovel you may get a taste!*

Alphonse senior and Alphonse junior seem to have a never-ending selection of oddities hidden away in their cellars. This year's special is a barrel-fermented Pinot Noir, pressed and vinified as a white. Tasted in cask just after fermentation, it was full of fresh fruit and intensity, promising greater things to come.

⑤ Pouilly-sur-Loire Gustave Daudin 2007 Domaine Michel Redde (€15) Sauvignon Blanc has taken over Pouilly-Fumé to such an extent that the often unexciting Chasselas has been steadily uprooted, so any surviving vines are as old as Methuselah, which, in the right hands, does give extra layers of complexity. At this old-established estate, son Sébastien has vinified this in 600-liter tonne casks. With just 11.7 percent ABV and 4.2 g acidity, it's full and fine, with the wine nicely balancing the oak.

⑥ Anjou-Villages Brissac Les Millerits 2005 Jean-Yves & Jean-Hubert Lebreton, Domaine des Rochelles (€17) Generally Anjou reds have such a whack of tannins that they are normally best avoided, all the more so if made from later-ripening Cabernet Sauvignon. But here, on slate and schist slopes at the top of the Aubance tributary, Jean-Hubert pushes the ripeness of his Cab Sauv grapes to an extreme, using the particularities of soil and microclimate to make one of the Loire Valley's greatest reds. The 2005's nose of licorice and black-currant gumdrops and the huge ripeness make the oak influence nicely discreet.

⑦ *Muscadet Sèvre & Maine Sur Lie Clos des Montys Vieilles Vignes 1914 2006 Jérémie Huchet, Domaine de la Chauvinière (€6.50) Jérémie took over from his father just six years ago and has already increased the size of the estate to 50 ha, which included a 1-ha plot of vines planted in 1914. This was hand-picked with yields of just 30 hl/ha, giving a Muscadet with concentration and character and perhaps the potential to age.

⑧ *Touraine Azay-le-Rideau Vieilles Vignes 2005 Château de l'Aulée (€7) Marielle Henrion and her husband took over the virtually abandoned vineyards of this château in 2004 and have since made a specialty of producing excellent sparkling wines. In the exceptional 2005 vintage, they also made a dry, barrel-fermented, old-vine Chenin Blanc of a quality that makes you wonder why other growers in this offbeat appellation are so stuck on respecting "tradition."

⑨ Reuilly Rouge Les Grandes Vignes 2007 Domaine Claude Lafond (€7) Nathalie Lafond is taking over from father Claude, and she's emphasizing vineyard management—in particular getting riper, richer reds. She's sussed that the first step with Pinot Noir is to reduce yields, though 30 hl/ha in 2007 was perhaps unnecessarily low! Using a cold pre-fermentation to bring out fruit and color, she's made a lovely, intense, balanced red to outsmart many a Sancerre Rouge.

⑩ Valençay Blanc Le Clos Delorme 2007 Bertrand Minchin (€6) I normally think blending Chardonnay with Sauvignon is catastrophic, and Valençay white is generally no exception—but again I've been proved wrong by Bertrand Minchin, who's expanded his Menetou-Salon-based estate by buying vines here on the Cher. The wine is fresh, grapefruity, and delicious, with that hit of Chardonnay adding just enough weight to the Sauvignon.

Rhône Valley

Olivier Poels

Marcel Richaud didn't get his *agrément*, and Marcel Richaud is fuming.

OLIVIER POELS

After being refused the *agrément* for his *primeur* wine because it was considered "atypical," the Cairanne flagship wine grower has decided to fight the decision— a decision that reflects the absurdity of the suicidal policy affecting this wine region. He is not the only one facing rejection: Domaine de la Janasse has also been refused. The decision taken by the *agrément* committee, however, does not reflect on the quality of the wine or harm the reputation of either producer. Some very ordinary *cuvées* have achieved *agréés* despite their "averageness," and we can only endorse Marcel Richaud's bitterness.

The INAO must address this ludicrous situation urgently, since it makes the *agrément* procedure look ridiculous. A situation cannot be justified where poor, flavorless wines have passed, while fruity, well-made wines have been rejected. This failing must be addressed by reform, but it's a reform that the French administration is a long way from implementing.

Jaboulet Aîné reorganizes

Two years after the acquisition of the Jaboulet domaine by the Frey family, reorganization and investment are continuing. Bordeaux oenologist Denis Dubourdieu has been hired to advise. Notably, the famous white Hermitage from La Chapelle that disappeared in 1962 will be revived from the 2006 vintage and positioned above the Chevalier de Stérimberg, due to its achieving a very high standard. Jaboulet has just bought a small plot in Côte Rôtie and is targeting more acquisitions in the Châteauneuf-du-Pape region.

OLIVIER POELS is a journalist at *La Revue du Vin de France* and a member of the Comité de Dégustation. He also produces wine programs for French TV channel LCI and is coauthor of the *Guide Malesan des Vins de France* and *Classement des Meilleurs Vins de France*.

Opinion:
The "zero-sulfite" debate

For some years the trend toward "zero sulfites" in wine has been growing among producers in all parts of France, and the Rhône Valley is no exception. Many domaines—such as Thierry Allemand from Cornas, Dard et Ribo in St-Joseph, and Gramenon in Côtes du Rhône—have adopted the creed. Although this approach is laudable in its intentions, its results are questionable. The use of sulfur was one of the most important advances in oenology in the 20th century. Nowadays, the proper use of sulfur ensures that wines are properly stabilized, clean, and protected. Although overuse was seen in some cellars where winemakers were heavy-handed with SO_2 dosage, its proper use has led to significant improvements in quality and better aromatic clarity in wines.

Wishing to produce "zero-sulfite" wine exposes producers to major risks. A lack of precision and aromatic deviation are very common in so-called natural *cuvées*. The oxidized tastes present in these bottles are often justified by the producers as a sign of great "terroir." The conservation of these extremely fragile wines poses real problems: exposing "zero-sulfite" bottles to temperatures over 68°F (20°C) will irreparably damage the quality of the contents. Well-controlled "zero-sulfite" winemaking may lead to interesting wines, but unfortunately the few good examples are overshadowed by the flood of poor-quality wines.

Grapevine

• **José Bento Dos Santos** and Michel Chapoutier have selected some of the oldest Syrah vines from parcels of L'Hermite (Hermitage) and Côte Rôtie. These will be used for grafting vines in the Quinta do Monte d'Oiro vineyard in Portugal to improve vine quality. The first vintage was 2007.

• **A comic book** starring the Guigal family has been published. The 64-page book, which features the members of the Guigal family, was released in early 2008. Published by Olmi, the story describes the life of this successful family, which has built a thriving wine business in only two generations, an outstanding example of entrepreneurship in winemaking.

• **An urban development project** is threatening part of the Cornas vineyard, since 3.4 ha of vines, representing production of 15,000 bottles, could disappear and be replaced by a housing development. Local wine growers are organizing resistance and have already launched a series of actions to oppose the project's implementation.

Vintage Report

Advance report on the latest harvest

2007

This year the Rhône Valley benefited from very favorable weather conditions, unlike many other French wine regions. Rhône producers suspect that the bad weather that affected many French regions will reflect on the 2007 vintage in their region. In the Rhône Valley, however, the summer was quite sunny, with optimal rainfall. The harvest took place during a bright and dry September, and the high quality of the juice portends a very good, classic, balanced vintage.

Updates on the previous five vintages

2006

Vintage rating: *Red: 88 (North: 87, South: 90), White: 87 (North: 85, South: 89)*

French vineyards had mixed experiences in 2006, but the Rhône Valley was rather privileged. August was, as everywhere else, very "moody," but it didn't affect the maturity of the vines. By contrast, September was superb. It gave the grapes optimal weather conditions to mature, and with no rainfall, there was no trace of rot. The grapes were very healthy in both northern and southern regions. The wines show nice fruit, density, and good balance. The overall quality level is expected to be high.

2005

Vintage rating: *Red: 96 (North: 92–98, South: 90–98), White: 93 (North: 90–95, South: 90–94)*

A rainy spring, a dry summer, and a bright, sunny September gave a winning ticket to the Rhône Valley in 2005. With a maturity that came early, this vintage has produced rich though extremely balanced wines. In the north (Hermitage, Côte Rôtie), the 2005s could match the excellent 1990s. In the south, the same conditions produced the same results: the Grenache is stunning, with a remarkable balance between alcohol, fruit, and acidity. Yields were generous, so wines will be widely available.

2004

Vintage rating: *Red: 91 (North: 82–90, South: 90–98), White: 88 (North: 80–90, South: 89–95)*

After the 2002 rains and the heat wave of 2003, 2004 marked a return to a classic vintage in the Rhône Valley. Very favorable weather conditions during September produced healthy, ripe grapes. The harvest schedule was normal: between September 6 and mid-October. Concentration is remarkable and alcohol levels are quite high, but the consequences of 2003 are still visible: yields are 20 percent lower than normal. In the south, the 2004s seem better balanced than the 2003s.

2003

Vintage rating: *Red: 95 (North: 90–97, South: 88–93), White: 89 (North: 83–90, South: 85–90)*

The north had one of its earliest vintages. The south needed more patience, since drought delayed ripening. The grapes were perfectly healthy, and quality was exceptional, despite a slight lack of acidity. The wines have high alcohol levels and very rich, mature tannins: the 2003s will keep for a very long time.

2002

Vintage rating: *Red: 70 (North: 70–75, South: 55–60), White: 73 (North: 70–75, South: 60–65)*

Dramatic rainfall destroyed a large part of the harvest, especially in the Vaucluse region. An average vintage in the north.

GREATEST WINE PRODUCERS

1. Domaine Jean-Louis Chave (Hermitage)
2. Château d'Ampuis (Côte Rôtie, Hermitage)
3. Michel Chapoutier (Hermitage, Châteauneuf-du-Pape)
4. Maison Tardieu-Laurent (Cuvées Vieilles Vignes)
5. Domaine Jamet (Côte Rôtie)
6. Château de Beaucastel (Châteauneuf-du-Pape)
7. Château Rayas (Châteauneuf-du-Pape)
8. Domaine de la Janasse (Châteauneuf-du-Pape)
9. Clos des Papes (Châteauneuf-du-Pape)
10. Domaine du Vieux Télégraphe (Châteauneuf-du-Pape)

FASTEST-IMPROVING PRODUCERS

1. Domaine Auguste Clape (Cornas)
2. Domaine de Marcoux (Châteauneuf-du-Pape)
3. Domaine Pierre Gaillard (Northern Rhône)
4. Domaine Charvin (Châteauneuf-du-Pape)
5. Maison Tardieu-Laurent (Rhône Valley)
6. Domaine François Villard (Northern Rhône)
7. Domaine Renouard (Costières de Nîmes)
8. Domaine Eric & Joël Durand (St-Joseph)
9. Domaine du Cayron (Gigondas)
10. Château La Verrerie (Côtes du Lubéron)

NEW UP-AND-COMING PRODUCERS

1. Domaine Montirius (Vacqueyras)
2. La Bastide du Claux (Côtes du Lubéron)
3. Domaine Matthieu Dumarcher (Côtes du Rhône)
4. Domaine Johann Michel (Cornas)
5. Domaine de la Roquète (Châteauneuf-du-Pape)
6. Domaine des Amadieu (Côtes du Rhône-Villages Cairanne)
7. Domaine des Entrefeaux (Crozes-Hermitage)
8. Domaine Les Pallières (Gigondas)
9. Domaine Pierre Finon (Northern Rhône)
10. Château de l'Amarine (Costières de Nîmes)

BEST-VALUE PRODUCERS

1. Domaine du Tunnel (Cornas)
2. Caves des Vignerons d'Estézargues (Côtes du Rhône)
3. Domaine des Hauts-Chassis (Crozes-Hermitage)
4. Domaine des Amouriers (Vacqueyras)
5. Domaine de Champal (St-Joseph)
6. Domaine du Cayron (Gigondas)
7. Domaine des Amadieu (Côtes du Rhône-Villages Cairanne)
8. Domaine Les Gouberts (Gigondas)
9. Domaine de la Monardière (Vacqueyras)
10. Château Mourgues du Grès (Costières de Nîmes)

GREATEST-QUALITY WINES

1. **Hermitage 2004** Domaine Jean-Louis Chave (€150)
2. **Côte Rôtie La Landonne 2003** Domaine Guigal (€250)
3. **Châteauneuf-du-Pape Roussanne Vieilles Vignes 2005** Château de Beaucastel (€70)
4. **Châteauneuf-du-Pape 2003** Château Rayas (€120)
5. **Côte Rôtie 2005** Domaine Jamet (€60)
6. **Hermitage Le Pavillon 2005** Michel Chapoutier (€200)
7. **Côte Rôtie La Landonne 2005** Jean-Michel Gérin (€90)
8. **Châteauneuf-du-Pape 2005** Domaine Charvin (€35)
9. **Côte Rôtie Maison Rouge 2005** Domaine Georges Vernay (€50)
10. **Châteauneuf-du-Pape 2005** Domaine du Vieux Télégraphe (€40)

BEST BARGAINS

1. **Gigondas 2005** Domaine du Cayron (€13)
2. **Crozes-Hermitage Champs Fourné 2006** Domaine des Entrefeaux (€8.50)
3. **Châteauneuf-du-Pape Réserve 2005** Domaine Roger Sabon (€16.70)
4. **Costières de Nîmes Réserve 2005** Château des Nages (€5.95)

⑤ **St-Joseph Les Rocailles 2005**
Domaine Pierre Finon (€11.20)

⑥ **St-Joseph 2006** Domaine de la
Côte Ste-Epine (€12)

⑦ **Côtes du Rhône-Villages
Cairanne Garrigue 2005**
Domaine des Amadieu (€6.80)

⑧ **Vacqueyras Signature 2005**
Domaine des Amouriers (€8.50)

⑨ **Cornas 2005** Domaine du Tunnel
(€18)

⑩ **Côtes du Ventoux Xavier 2005**
Xavier Vignon (€6.90)

MOST EXCITING OR UNUSUAL FINDS

① **Côte Rôtie La Landonne 2003**
Domaine Guigal (€250) *The style
of the great Guigal wines gives La
Landonne an incredible character
with perfect freshness.*

② **Château Grillet 2004** Château
Grillet (€70) *We are happy to see
this small appellation performing
so well. Famous Bordeaux
oenologist Denis Dubourdieu is
now consultant at the domaine.*

③ **Châteauneuf-du-Pape
Roussanne Vieilles Vignes 2005**
Château de Beaucastel (€70) *White
wine represents a very small part
of the production in Châteauneuf-
du-Pape. This fantastic* cuvée,
made with very old Roussanne,
is one of the most exciting white
wines in the world.

④ **Côtes du Lubéron Grand
Deffand 2003** Château La Verrerie
(€30) *This is not a very popular
appellation, but it can produce
wonderful wines. This Syrah shows
great personality.*

⑤ **Châteauneuf-du-Pape 2003**
Château Rayas (€120)
*Old Grenache vines on a terroir
of sand make very typical
Châteauneuf-du-Pape. This vintage
is a great success for the domaine.*

⑥ **Cornas 2005** Domaine Auguste
Clape (€52) *Cornas is one of the
most dynamic appellations in the
Rhône Valley, and this is a top
cuvée—much better than many
a Hermitage or Côte Rôtie.*

⑦ **Gigondas 2005** Domaine du
Cayron (€13) *Near Châteauneuf-
du-Pape, this appellation produces
very exciting wines; this is a very
classic* cuvée.

⑧ **St-Joseph Les Granits 2005**
Michel Chapoutier (€50) *Very
famous for his Hermitage* cuvées,
*Michel Chapoutier produces one
of the most exciting St-Josephs
from very old vineyards.*

Grapevine

• **Vinisud,** the major meeting place
for wine producers and professionals
in southern France, was host to
some interesting new *cuvées* in 2008.
Epsilon, a Hermitage from La Cave
de Tain, is one example. Another
discovery was the Crozes-Hermitage
from Domaine des Grands Chemins,
produced by Delas Frères.

• **Michel Chapoutier** has decided to
open a wine school. The winemaker
and wine lover wants to make the
world of great wines accessible
and will open the school in Tain
l'Hermitage. Classes will be held
for groups of up to 20 people.

Jura & Savoie

Wink Lorch

DNA testing on Savoie grape varieties has revealed some surprises and finally laid to rest the myths surrounding the origins of certain varieties deemed unique to Savoie.

WINK LORCH

Ampelographer Dr. José Vouillamoz of the University of Neuchâtel, Switzerland, gave a sneak preview of the results from recent DNA research when he spoke at the first general meeting of the new Centre d'Ampélographie Alpine Pierre Galet (the Pierre Galet Center for Alpine Ampelography) in Cevins on December 8, 2007.

It has been known for a few years that Mondeuse Blanche, a rare white Savoie variety, was one of the parents of the Rhône Valley's Syrah grape. Now Vouillamoz, an expert on alpine varieties, has proved a genetic link with the black Savoie variety Mondeuse Noire and the northern Rhône's white variety Viognier. It transpires that both Mondeuse Noire and Viognier are closely related to Mondeuse Blanche, as either a parent or an offspring. Exactly which is impossible to prove, since there is a missing link, likely to be a grape variety that no longer exists. However, this revelation means that both Viognier and Mondeuse are relatives of Syrah, one as a half-sibling and the other as a grandparent.

WINK LORCH is a wine writer and educator with a passion for the mountains. In 2007, she launched www.winetravelguides.com—a website with online guides for independent wine travelers, initially covering France. She is a past chairman of the Association of Wine Educators and has contributed to several books, including Jancis Robinson's *Oxford Companion to Wine*, Time-Life's *The Wine Guide*, and Le Cordon Bleu's *Wine Essentials*. Wink particularly enjoys enthusing about wines from vineyards in sight of snowcapped mountains, whether the Andes, the Alps, or the Jura. She divides her time between London and the French Alps.

DNA testing was also carried out on various white grape varieties, including Jacquère and Altesse (used to make Roussette de Savoie), both planted throughout Savoie. Jacquère has been confirmed as an offspring of a formerly very common grape variety, Gouais Blanc (known to ampelographers as the "Casanova of grape varieties"). Altesse is described in Savoie history books as having come from Cyprus and, more recently, was thought by Galet and others to be related to Hungary's Furmint. Vouillamoz rejects this hypothesis and suggests a relationship with Chasselas, both grapes being of western European origin. Testing was also carried out on Gringet, which grows only in the tiny *cru* of Ayze, near Bonneville in Haute Savoie. Until now, Gringet was believed to be a member of the Traminer family and related to Jura's Savagnin variety. DNA testing has proved that this is not the case; in fact, the variety is unique to Savoie and is probably related to Molette, which is grown mainly in Seyssel.

The famous ampelographer Professor Pierre Galet (now 86) also attended the meeting in Savoie and was unperturbed that modern DNA techniques refute some of the older thinking on these varieties. He has donated his vast collection of research documents to the new center, which bears his name and has the aim of preserving ancient alpine varieties. Both Galet and Vouillamoz confirmed the genetic importance of Savoie grape varieties. Wine producer Michel Grisard, one of the figures behind the creation of the center and co-owner of Domaine de l'Ardoisières in Cevins, hopes that funding will be forthcoming to create an experimental conservatory of alpine grape varieties.

Vin jaune to have taste profile

As part of AOC reforms, the Société du Viticulture du Jura, which is charged with liaising with the INAO (Institut National de l'Origine et de la Qualité), has initiated a study in conjunction with the Institut des Vin du Jura to establish an official taste profile for *vin jaune*. This is mainly in preparation for stricter controls being introduced on a national basis from July 2008 for the *agrément* (testing) carried out as part of Appellation Contrôlée rules. One of the study's key challenges is to differentiate between the taste profile of a white Jura Savagnin wine that has been aged oxidatively and that of a "real" *vin jaune*. Once the profiling has been completed during 2008, the institute plans to train professional tasters to use the profile to judge whether a *vin jaune* may be allowed to carry the label.

The *crise* begins to bite

As indicated in *Wine Report 2008*, all is not well in some sectors of Jura and Savoie due to the national downturn in wine buying, especially in the restaurant sector, so important to these two tourist-driven regions. The victims are relatively small *vignerons*, who fall primarily into two categories: first, those who make and market their own wine but whose quality falls well short of the mark, mainly due to lack of technological equipment and know-how (a particular problem in Savoie); second, those who sell their grapes primarily to *négociants*. This concerns the Jura in particular, where the dominant Henri Maire company announced dramatic cuts in wine purchases two months before the start of the 2007 harvest. The company used to purchase from 130 growers, but in 2007 they bought from only 30. Some of the remaining growers managed to find buyers, but many left their grapes unpicked.

Bugey has no choice

For several years, Vins de Bugey has tried without success to gain AOC status. With the VDQS category being abolished by 2010, promotion should finally become a reality. VDQS wine areas may choose to apply for AOC status or for the more flexible *vin de pays* category. The Syndicat des Vins de Bugey has been working on the required changes needed for elevation to AOC for some years; since over 60 percent of its production is sparkling wine, AOC is the only sensible choice. Volumes of the sparkling pink Cerdon VDQS, made by the *méthode ancestrale*, and white and rosé Vin de Bugey Mousseux VDQS, made by the *méthode traditionnelle*, have increased by more than 50 percent in the past decade, and demoting them to *vin de table* would be a severe blow to the region. Bugey is more than ready to adopt the AOC regime and hopes that it will receive approval in time for the 2009 vintage.

Grapevine

• **The Maison du Vin de Savoie** in Apremont finally opened in February 2008 after several years of planning. The official wine organizations have moved their offices and laboratories into the new building, which is in the heart of the wine area; however, there are administrative delays concerning the creation of a consumer visitor information center and shop: this will not open before summer 2009.

• **A heritage center** (Centre d'Interpretation du Patrimoine) opened in Château-Chalon in April 2008. Combining displays about the geology and history of this classic hilltop village with comprehensive background information on the wines, this will make a highly educational visit for tourists. The cellar area will also be used for wine tastings presented by the growers.

Opinion:
Jura: seize this opportunity!

In every appellation of France, committees have been meeting, commitments made, and papers written in time for the July 2008 deadline for AOC reform. The priority is to put in place all manner of checks—from the pruning of the vines, to the bottling of the wine—to be conducted by exterior independent inspection committees. This system will replace the existing compulsory *agrément* (taste test), although certain taste tests will still take place.

In the Jura, they are well advanced with plans to comply with the reform, knowing that—for the sake of the growers, who face substantial cost increases to pay for this—they must create an efficient and effective system. This is all well and good, and I applaud it. However, by focusing so much energy on compliance with the new regulations, the region is missing an important opportunity to market its wines better. Compliance with the AOC labeling system means labels that are woefully uninformative. The region's producers should introduce compulsory back labels that explain to the consumer what is in the bottle. This tiny region offers a bewildering choice of wine styles, and often the same label is used for a fresh, fruity style of Côtes du Jura Chardonnay as for a rich, barrel-fermented one or an oxidative, nutty style that tastes nothing like its grape variety. If Jura wants to combat falling local consumption by seeking sales outside the region and indeed outside the country, it must address this issue at the earliest possible opportunity.

Savoie producers must embrace wine tourism

In Savoie, too, there is an opportunity to combat falling sales. Encouraged by the Rhône-Alpes administrative region, a committee has been set up to examine the possibilities of promoting wine tourism in Savoie. This is so obvious that one wonders why it needs a committee, but Savoyards are notoriously slow to embrace change and opportunity. And they are loners too—*vignerons* want to plow their own metaphorical vineyard furrows. There are some plans being made now, but they are going to concentrate on visitors from the local region; the millions of foreigners they could welcome are not even being considered.

The Savoie vineyards are in one of the most beautiful regions in the world, with a benign climate, spectacular mountains, beautiful lakes, and historic cities (Annecy, Chambéry, Aix-les-Bains). The region welcomes millions of tourists every year—the majority come for ski vacations, but a significant number visit in summer as well. The wine industry is woefully late in getting on the tourist bandwagon. Even if wine routes are mapped out, there is little information about which *vignerons* are open for visits, and there has been no encouragement for hotels and restaurants to work with wine producers to encourage visits. Even if few direct purchases would be made, it would open doors for the Savoyard wine producers to sell more wine outside the region. They must consider this issue urgently.

Caution needed with "natural" wines

Jura has a higher proportion of organic vineyards than other French wine regions, which is great news. However, owners of organic vineyards in particular, but also of some conventionally farmed vineyards, seem under pressure from a fashion in France and, to an extent, North America for so-called "natural" wines. The main requirement of "natural" wines is that they should have no added SO_2. This is a dangerous move. Although I have been surprised by the good quality of a few no-sulfur wines I have tasted, there are many that disappoint. Keep levels as low as possible by all means, but eliminating SO_2 presents great risks. It would be a shame to see a region where quality is increasing risk its reputation with substandard wines made to feed a fashion.

Grapevine

• **Domaine Opus Vinum,** a tiny Arbois producer established in 2005, has been forced to change its name by California winery Opus One (owned by the giant Constellation group and Domaines Rothschild). Owners Alice Bouvot and Charles Dagand, who originally chose Opus Vinum for its musical reference, had not envisaged any possible conflict of interest between a small Jura domaine and a Napa Valley giant. It transpires that the name Opus has been registered by Opus One. In March 2008, the new name of Les Vins d'Alice was chosen after a competition among friends and customers.

• **La Savoie Viticole Authentique** was the name of a trade tasting staged by 20 renegade producers in Paris in November 2007. Concerned by the lack of opportunities provided by the official Savoie body, the producers joined forces to present their wines in the Aux Zingots restaurant. All 11 of the main organic/biodynamic producers of Savoie were present, and they had invited "similar-thinking" colleagues representing all the different geographical sectors to join them. More than half the producers are those listed in *Wine Report*. The tasting gave a rare opportunity for the trade to taste the wines from top producers side by side.

• **The release** of the 2001 vintage of *vin jaune* in 2008 will be somewhat muted. No Château-Chalon 2001 was allowed to be produced due to poor grape quality. Several producers of *vin jaune* have also decided to skip a year, hoping their stocks of the 2000 vintage will last until the 2002 can be released in 2009.

Vintage Report

Advance report on the latest harvest
2007

Jura—A strange year, when growers suffered hail attacks, excess heat, and heavy rainfall that led to outbreaks of mildew, which were often impossible to treat, since there were no gaps in the rainfall to allow spraying. The very warm April gave an even earlier flowering than 2003, but it was followed by rain for most of the summer. Catastrophe was avoided when the fine weather finally broke through at the end of August. By September, three weeks of north winds and sunshine dried out any gray rot and turned it into noble rot, giving good sugar concentration. The most successful wines are likely to be from those growers who dared to wait the longest to harvest. Late-ripening varieties did best, notably Savagnin and Trousseau.

Savoie—Toward the end of August, growers feared the worst vintage for some time. An unusually hot spring gave flowering five to six weeks earlier than an average year, but this was followed by a really wet summer, with severe outbreaks of mildew that were almost impossible to control. The fine weather in September with a dry north wind turned this into what most growers are describing as a "miracle vintage." It took place on average around a week earlier than normal, but with crops reduced by around 30 percent due to mildew and hail damage. Many growers are describing quality as exceptional, due to a complete absence of rot, and it looks like being particularly successful for the late-ripening Mondeuse.

Updates on the previous five vintages
Ratings for vin jaune *and* vin de paille *are included in the scores for white wines.*

2006

Vintage rating: *Jura—Red: 79, White: 83;*
Savoie—Red: 78, White: 81

Jura—A record-breaking, extremely hot July was followed by a very wet, cool August. A warm, sunny September saved what could have been a disastrous vintage. Rot was a problem for some, and the harvest was small overall. Decent reds were made by those producers who acted quickly and were selective, though some are quite light and should be drunk before the 2005s. Whites are generally of better quality, with good fruit though relatively soft acidity, and are also for drinking early.

Savoie—After a very hot July and a very cold, wet August, it was never going to be easy. September was a big improvement, but rainstorms hit in late September and early October. Rot of various types was the biggest problem, and for black grapes there was a level of underripeness, too. The producers who really took care in the vineyard and made a rigorous selection at harvest were the winners, though it is a relatively lightweight year for both whites and reds.

2005

Vintage rating: *Jura—Red: 90, White: 92; Savoie—Red: 88, White: 85*

Jura—A classic year throughout the region. There were high sugar levels, but acidity was maintained, and this, combined with good concentration and modest yields, produced successful wines from all varieties. The best wines show excellent balance of flavors and structure. Many wines have been released, but the wines can be kept for future drinking.

Savoie—Overall a good growing season, and it was a year when there should be no excuse for bad wines. Most whites made from Bergeron (Roussanne) and Altesse did not need any chaptalization, and the best show attractive flavors, balance, and length. Mondeuse reds are the real stars: lovely fruit flavors and ripe tannins resulting from better vineyard methods in combination with the weather.

2004

Vintage rating: *Jura—Red: 80, White: 82; Savoie—Red: 76, White: 78*

Jura—After a wet summer, September was dry and warm. Crop levels were high, and selection was essential. Much Crémant du Jura was made from Chardonnay. Savagnins were picked at good sugar and acidity levels, crucial for *vin jaune*. Trousseau was the most successful black variety.

Savoie—Excess quantity was the biggest problem in this year of variable weather, but the grapes were generally healthy. Growers who were selective produced reasonably concentrated Roussette de Savoie whites from Altesse, and the finest producers of Mondeuse did well.

2003

Vintage rating: *Jura—Red: 86, White: 76; Savoie—Red: 83, White: 81*

Jura—A very early and small harvest. Dealing with low acidity was a big challenge, especially for wines destined for *vin jaune*. Some interesting

Savagnin wines have been released, but most Chardonnays are a little too soft for keeping. Reds, for once, are actually red in color and taste of ripe fruit! **Savoie**—Low quantities in this unusually hot, dry year mean that few wines are still available. However, the best producers made deliciously fruity whites and some structured reds.

2002

Vintage rating: *Jura—Red: 86, White: 90; Savoie—Red: 79, White: 77*

Jura—Overall, good quality with fine potential for *vin jaune*. Chardonnays and some Trousseau reds are excellent still, with good weight and balance. **Savoie**—Wines are mainly sold and drunk. Mondeuse can still be good.

GREATEST WINE PRODUCERS

Jura
1. Domaine André & Mireille Tissot
2. Jacques Puffeney
3. Domaine Labet Père & Fils
4. Domaine Ganevat
5. Jean Rijckaert

Savoie
1. Domaine Dupasquier
2. André & Michel Quenard
3. Denis & Didier Berthollier
4. Domaine Louis Magnin
5. Pascal & Annick Quenard

FASTEST-IMPROVING PRODUCERS

Jura
1. Domaine Pignier
2. Domaine Ligier Père & Fils
3. Château d'Arlay
4. Domaine Berthet-Bondet
5. Domaine de la Tournelle

Savoie
1. La Cave du Prieuré
2. Domaine Belluard
3. Jean-Pierre & Philippe Grisard
4. Jean-Pierre & Jean-François Quenard
5. Domaine Delalex

NEW UP-AND-COMING PRODUCERS

Jura
1. Julien Labet
2. Les Vins d'Alice
3. Rémi Treuvey
4. Julien Maréchal
5. Domaine Cybelline

Savoie
1. Gilles Berlioz
2. Domaine de l'Ardoisières
3. Frédéric & David Giachino
4. Bruno Lupin
5. EARL La Gerbelle

BEST-VALUE PRODUCERS

Jura
1. Daniel Dugois
2. Frédéric Lornet
3. Domaine Baud Père & Fils
4. Domaine Jacques Tissot
5. Domaine Rolet Père & Fils

Savoie
1. Domaine de l'Idylle
2. Domaine St-Germain
3. Edmond Jacquin & Fils
4. Le Cellier du Palais
5. Domaine Jean Vullien & Fils

GREATEST-QUALITY WINES

Jura

1 **Château-Chalon 1999** Jean Macle (€28)

2 **Arbois Vin Jaune 1999** Jacques Puffeney (€29)

3 **Côtes du Jura Chardonnay Les Grandes Teppes Vieilles Vignes 2005** Domaine Ganevat (€14.50)

4 **Côtes du Jura Chardonnay Fleur de Marne La Bardette 2005** Domaine Labet Père & Fils (€12)

5 **Arbois Chardonnay La Mailloche 2005** Domaine André & Mireille Tissot (€15)

Savoie

1 **Vin de Table Son Altesse le Refus NV** Domaine Prieuré St-Christophe (€15)

2 **Roussette de Savoie Marestel 2005** Domaine Dupasquier (€7.50)

3 **Vin de Savoie Chignin Bergeron Cuvée Noé 2006** Pascal & Annick Quenard (€11)

4 **Vin de Savoie Chignin Bergeron Les Terrasses 2005** André & Michel Quenard (€8)

5 **Roussette de Savoie Baron Decouz 2006** Denis & Didier Berthollier (€6.25)

BEST BARGAINS

Jura

Note that wines 3 and 4 are both Savagnin Ouillé—that is, non-oxidative fresh, dry whites.

1 **Arbois Poulsard 2005** Jacques Puffeney (€6)

2 **Côtes du Jura Chardonnay à la Percenette 2006** Domaine Pignier (€12)

3 **Arbois Cuvée des Poètes 2005** Domaine Ligier Père & Fils (€10)

4 **Arbois Naturé 2005** Frédéric Lornet (€9.50)

5 **Côtes du Jura Trousseau 2006** Domaine Baud Père & Fils (€8.50)

Savoie

1 **Vin de Savoie Pinot Noir Cuvée Jeanine 2006** Domaine Jean Vullien & Fils (€5.70)

2 **Roussette de Savoie 2006** Domaine St-Germain (€7)

3 **Vin de Savoie Mondeuse 2006** Pascal & Annick Quenard (€7)

4 **Vin de Savoie Chignin Vieilles Vignes 2006** Denis & Didier Berthollier (€4.90)

5 **Vin de Savoie Jongieux Mondeuse 2006** La Cave du Prieuré (€5.80)

MOST EXCITING OR UNUSUAL FINDS

Jura

1 **Côtes du Jura Grains Nobles de Savagnin 2002** Domaine Labet Père & Fils (€20) *This is the first vintage the Labets have made a wine from a selection of nobly rotted grapes—and it's a great success. It was aged for three years in old demi-muids (600-liter barrels). A touch of residual sugar is balanced by high alcohol and acidity, yet it remains supremely elegant, with honey, lemon, and spicy flavors.*

2 **Arbois L'Opportun Trousseau Liquoreux 2006** Domaine André & Mireille Tissot (€42 per half-bottle) *Stéphane Tissot has turned out yet another experimental sweet marvel. From a berry selection of black Trousseau grapes that were either raisined or affected by noble rot, it was pressed and vinified as a white wine. It has a wonderful honey and black-grape-juice nose, and is sweet but not cloying, with a delicate Mirabelle plum character. With only 10.5 percent alcohol, it is nevertheless weighty in body and flavor.*

❸ **Arbois Savagnin Vendange de Novembre 2005** Domaine Jacques Tissot (€17.50 per half-bottle) *Each year, this large Jura domaine saves a few rows of its 50-year-old Savagnin vines to harvest when overripe in November. The result is this delicately sweet white wine, full of spicy, heady flavors. The naturally high acidity of Savagnin makes a good foil for the sweetness. Delicious!*

❹ **Côtes du Jura Rouge 2003** Château d'Arlay (€12) *Made almost entirely from Pinot Noir and aged for more than three years in old oak barrels. The unusually hot 2003 vintage conveyed extra-ripe, sweet berry-fruit flavors to this burgundian-style Pinot. It has the potential to age for several years.*

❺ **Crémant du Jura Brut Sauvage NV** Domaine Baud Père & Fils (€9) *Alain Baud does not believe his Pinot Noir makes a good red wine on its own, and as well as using it for a blended red, he has put it to excellent use in this sparkling wine, where, blended with Chardonnay, it forms 30 percent of the base wine.*

Savoie

❶ **Vin de Savoie Apremont Vieilles Vignes 2006** Domaine Jean Masson & Fils (white label) (€6.80) *This unusual producer makes at least six Apremont cuvées. This is one of two Vieilles Vignes versions— a traditionnelle and this one, which is in a burgundy-shaped bottle. It's made from 100-year-old vines—officially Jacquère, but one wonders… This is the most unusual Apremont I've ever tasted, with a richness and structure to age for a decade or more.*

❷ **Vin de Savoie Vendanges d'Exception 2005** Domaine de l'Idylle (€12 per 50-cl bottle) *Just 700 half-liter bottles were made of this exceptional Jacquère. It was made as a vin de paille, and the grapes were dried for two months, pressed in December, and the wine then matured in an old 600-liter barrel. Medium-sweet, with a delicate honeyed lemon character and good freshness, with some spiced peach character.*

❸ **Vin de Savoie Primitif NV** Frédéric & David Giachino (€5.50) *With organic vineyards covering both Apremont and Abymes crus known for their light, fresh whites, the Giachino brothers decided to make this cuvée without any chaptalization and minimal handling. The delightful result has just 9.2 percent alcohol and packs in more flavor than many Apremonts with 2 degrees more.*

❹ **Vin de Savoie Mondeuse Blanche 2006** Jean-Pierre & Philippe Grisard (€9.50) *The 2006 vintage really showed what this unusual variety can do when handled correctly. It is supremely herbal in flavor, both on nose and palate, reminiscent of a Rhône or Provence dry white, but with much higher acidity.*

❺ **Vin de Savoie Marin Clos du Pont 2006** Domaine Delalex (€6) *From a spectacular vineyard bowl with a view of Lac Léman, this Chasselas is made without malolactic fermentation (unlike other Chasselas from Haute Savoie or Switzerland). The result is a food-friendly, dry, and ageworthy wine that is an excellent buy.*

Southwest France

Paul Strang

According to Professor Roger Corder, the "French paradox" is no longer a mystery.

PAUL STRANG

Corder has at last published the results (*The Wine Diet*; Sphere, London, 2007), partly trailed earlier but now fully documented, of his investigation into the health-giving properties of wine. The so-called "French paradox" (low levels of heart disease in France despite high consumption of saturated fats) has been familiar to most of us for some time, but one of Corder's concerns was to find out why older men in southwest France survived to such an extraordinarily old age compared with those living elsewhere in France. The number of Gascons from the Gers, for example, living beyond the age of 90 is double the national average. The diet is heavy with fat, such as is found in cassoulet, foie gras, sausage, and cheese. The same pattern occurs also, but to a lesser degree, in the Lot. The first-named area is of course home to the wines of Madiran and the second to Cahors. Corder has put forth some conclusions that will come as a shot in the arm for both appellations. He establishes that it is largely down to the grape varieties

PAUL STRANG is recognized as one of the leading authorities on the wines of southwest France, where he has had a home for many years. A colleague describes him as "knowing every centimeter of the region." His first book on the area, *Wines of South West France* (Kyle Cathie, 1994) was short-listed for the Drink Book of the Year in the Glenfiddich awards. His *Languedoc-Roussillon: The Wines & Winemakers* (Mitchell Beazley, 2002) was the first groundbreaking book in recent years on that region. Paul has contributed the chapters on his specialist regions of southwest France and Languedoc-Roussillon to *Larousse des Vins* (2006). His new illustrated *South-West France: The Wines & Winemakers* is expected to appear at the same time as *Wine Report* in an English/French-language coedition from the University of California Press and Les Editions du Rouergue.

used there: in Madiran's case Tannat, and in Cahors's Malbec. The inherent virtues of the *cépages*, coupled with the benefits of the terroirs, the altitude of the vineyards, and the traditional methods of vinification result in wines high in procyanidins, substances that are strongly antioxidant and therefore likely to minimize the danger of thickening of the blood, leading to a lower incidence of heart disease and longer life-expectancy.

According to Corder, Madiran typically contains more than three to four times more protective procyanidins than his benchmark Argentine Cabernet Sauvignon. One small glass of Madiran, he says, can provide more benefit than two whole bottles of Australian wine. He claims that the high Madiran tannins become hardly noticeable when taken with food. Then comes the medical conclusion: "The winemakers of this region should be encouraged to resist all pressure to move toward modern tastes of berry fruits and soft ripe tannins. Theirs is genuine heart-protecting wine, and this is the real French paradox."

Sadly, the growers are not heeding this message; in Madiran they are trying to make wine with virtually no tannins, while in Cahors many producers are trying to make a *primeur*-type wine from Malbec. In neither case do the wines much resemble the real thing, and purists reel in horror.

Incidentally, Corder has been unable to find the French virtues in most Uruguayan Tannat or Argentine Malbec.

Grapevine

• **Romania beckons Yves Grassa,** head of the family that owns the 900-ha Domaine du Tariquet in the Côtes de Gascogne. Yves has bought several hundred hectares of land in Romania. He says he is diversifying into cereals, but how long will it be before he plants vines?

• **Mathieu Cosse,** the cult winemaker from Cahors, and one of the few new-wave growers to understand what Cahors is all about (see above), has taken charge of 150 ha of vines at Château La Coste near Aix-en-Provence, which has been acquired by Irishman Patrick MacKillen.

• **Fabrice de Suyrot,** a wealthy businessman, seems to have tired of his wine estate, Clos des Terrasses, in southern Bergerac, on which he spared no expense in replanting and cellar improvement. After only five years, de Suyrot is off to Majorca, and the vineyard is up for sale.

• **White Armagnac** now has its own AOC. When newly distilled, Armagnac is colorless, and its hue as a mature brandy is (or should be) derived entirely from the barrels in which it is matured. For many years there was a clandestine trade in the new white spirit, which you could buy from a few small distilleries if you brought your own opaque container.

GOODBYE AUXERROIS, HELLO MALBEC

Cahors has woken up to the fact that Argentina is stealing its clothes. The town is seeking a twinning with Mendoza, and the authorities in France are gradually abandoning the traditional name of their grape (Auxerrois) in favor of the now-chic Malbec. Twenty years ago no one used the name Malbec in the Lot. Having originally exported the grape to South America when thousands of French people emigrated to escape the economic disaster of phylloxera, they are now rechristening it. There is today a Compagnie France Malbec, located in Cahors. The proprietors, Ghislaine Baltenweck and her husband, own a small vineyard, but their main activity is as *négociants*, where they buy grapes from 400 other producers and sell mainly for export.

FRONTON MUST BE BLENDED

In its passion for insisting on blends of different grapes, the INAO has decreed that henceforth there can be no Fronton from 100 percent Négrette. To qualify for AOC status, the wines in bottle (not just in the vineyard) must contain at least two other authorized grape varieties, such as Syrah, Cabernets, Malbec, or Fer Servadou. Many growers are already producing blended wines, but others, notably Bellevue-la-Forêt (Ce Vin), Domaine de Joliet, and Château Baudare, have been producing some of the most original, characteristic, and interesting wines of the appellation from Négrette alone. Fronton owes its distinctiveness—even its very existence—to the Négrette grape. Why not allow growers the right to express its individuality in a mono-*cépage*, as they have done for so long?

Grapevine

• **The Cazottes family** in Gaillac has established a new artisanal distillery. Laurent Cazottes is making waves with his ultra-pure *eaux de vie*, notably but not exclusively made from pears. A biodynamic production, it is made from an old-fashioned artisanal still. No copper is used in the plumbing because it affects the taste, and their own fruit is picked off the ground just after it has fallen, involving several pickings each day.

• **The handsome Robert Schulte** and his lovely wife Agnes have been accused by the *Revue du Vin de France* of not being "sexy" enough. In a hurt response, they have produced Le Bel Insolent, a quaffing Marmandais from their beautiful Château de Beaulieu.

It is made from young vines and is "intended to wean the young off Coca-Cola and onto something more healthy." It is to be hoped that this is no replacement for their excellent Galipian, one of the best picnic reds to come out of the southwest.

• **The English have landed** in Madiran, hitherto an exclusively French bastion of viticulture. Domaine Pichard, one of the oldest and most respected estates in the area but rather disappointing in recent years, has been acquired by an Anglo-French partnership: Rod Cork and Jean Sentilles. The pair have had the good sense to retain Bernard Tachouères from the *ancien régime* to teach them the ropes.

Opinion:
Cahors is this year's black

As the phoenix of Cahors at last shows some signs of rising from the ashes of its troubled recent history, the latest publicity move prompts one to ask what the strategists in the appellation think Cahors is all about. Suddenly websites with addresses like frenchblackwine.com and blackisphere.fr proclaim, "Cahors is back, Cahors is black, Cahors is Malbec." Have they never thought of going back to the basic question, "What is the real character of Malbec in this terroir?" The table wines of Cahors were never black, and those that are black today owe their color to neither the grape nor the terroir but to modern methods of vinification. Historically, wine that was black and produced in Cahors was used only for blending, not for drinking; it was to beef up and blend with weaker wines from other areas. The blackness came from cooking the must and adding spirits.

This blackness was the principal cause of the decline in the popularity of Cahors wines in export markets, particularly Britain. People began to think that all Cahors was black and thus dense, thick, and forbidding in character. One wonders therefore whether the promoting bodies in Cahors have adopted a somewhat dubious marketing strategy and could be shooting themselves in the foot. Why should blackness be a virtue, unless the idea is to create the image that all Cahors is now in the style of the old black wine, which nobody ever drank on its own? If so, that is not only flying in the face of public taste for lighter, fruitier wines but against the true character of the Malbec grape, at least as it is grown in the Lot Valley.

Even as recently as 1971, when the present AOC came into being, no grower produced more than one *cuvée*; it corresponded to what they now call their "Tradition." Even today, their Prestige and other micro-*cuvée* wines rarely exceed a quarter of their output. The Tradition wines are often more representative of Malbec than the more ambitious wines, many of which are from too-ripe fruit, overextracted, excessive in alcohol, and overoaked.

So, what is the true Cahors character? Malbec, at least in the Lot, does produce dark-colored juice that is bright, clear, and transparent—the antithesis of "black." In its first years, the wine has strong aromas of red and black fruits and sometimes hints of almonds. As it matures, it develops flavors of the forest floor, game, leather, and truffles. This subtle wine should be elegant and fine, its style restrained rather than powerful. Cahors is an appellation torn between its true nature and the need to please a market with which it is largely out of tune.

Vintage Report

Advance report on the latest harvest

2007

Growers claim they have been saved by an Indian summer, but they would, wouldn't they? After a fairly normal winter, the spring was abnormally hot and sunny, with budburst and vine development much earlier than usual, bringing forward picking at the end of the season by an average of two weeks. The good weather was not to last: hail hit many areas in late April/early May, notably in Montravel, Madiran, and Gaillac. In St-Mont, 500 ha were devastated—about a quarter of the total crop. The rest of May was wet; and in mid-June, Gascony had 5 in (13 cm) of rain over a single weekend, bringing to all areas mildew and disease on a scale not seen for many years. The ensuing summer months were notable for an almost total absence of sun, just the occasional hot burst never lasting more than a couple of days. The summer was marked by the constant threat of mildew. Suddenly, in early September, the sun came out and shone for a couple of months. This enabled growers to harvest in much better conditions than they had feared, and late pickers such as in Monbazillac and Jurançon were anticipating a fine vintage. Optimism replaced objective judgment, and the true quality of what wine was made is anybody's guess. Pessimists say they lost most of their crop or declassified it; others may have been persuaded to give up permanently; but most were just keeping their fingers crossed as the fermentation tanks bubbled away. Overall quantity is down from between 15 to 50 percent, and the southwest has had a far more difficult year than any other part of France.

Updates on the previous five vintages

2006

Vintage rating: *White and red: 75*

A patchy year in which few really outstanding wines will have been made. Hail destroyed much of the crop in St-Mont, and Jurançon had a poor *arrière-saison*. Red and white wines fared equally, but production levels were on a par with 2005.

2005

Vintage rating: *Red: 93; Dry white: 90;*
Sweet white—Jurançon: 95; Monbazillac, Saussignac,
and Gaillac: 90; others: 87

Drought without excessive heat produced the best wines since 2001.
Growers in Jurançon have revised their opinion, claiming an equal success
with that of the previous year. Production down slightly on 2004.

2004

Vintage rating: *Red: 88, Dry white: 85,*
Sweet white: 86 (93 in Jurançon)

The whites show some acidity and, unless raised in oak, should be drunk
now. The reds are *à point*, though Cahors and Madirans will keep. Jurançon
was the success story, and both dry and sweet wines will age well.

2003

Vintage rating: *Red and dry white—east: 68, farther west: 85;*
Sweet white: 92

The reds are fruit-laden and for early drinking; most have little acidity and
some tannins are stalky. Better from Madiran and Irouléguy. Dry whites
should be drunk if not drunk already, but the sweet wines are much better
and the best will keep. The grilling of the grapes by the sun reduced
production levels drastically.

2002

Vintage rating: *Red and white Cahors and westward: 85,*
eastwards: 75, Sweet white: 89

The farther west, the better the wines. Lighter and more delicate than the
years before and after.

Grapevine

• **Robert Parker** seems to have lost
his balance. His guide to the wines of
France runs to 1,600-odd pages, but
he devotes just five of them to the
southwest.

GREATEST WINE PRODUCERS

1. Domaine Robert & Bernard Plageoles (Gaillac)
2. Clos de Gamot (Cahors)
3. La Tour des Gendres (Bergerac)
4. Domaine Tirecul-la-Gravière (Monbazillac)
5. Domaine de la Ramaye (Gaillac)
6. Domaine Causse-Maisonneuve (Cahors)
7. Les Jardins de Babylone (Jurançon)
8. Domaine Elian Da Ros (Marmandais)
9. Domaine Arretzea (Irouléguy)
10. Domaine Berthoumieu (Madiran)

FASTEST-IMPROVING PRODUCERS

1. Domaine Mouthes-le-Bihan (Côtes de Duras)
2. Domaine Causse-Marines (Gaillac)
3. Château La Reyne (Cahors)
4. Domaine du Souch (Jurançon)
5. Les Hauts de Caillevel (Monbazillac)
6. Clos d'un Jour (Cahors)
7. Clos des Verdots (Bergerac)
8. Domaine de la Bérengeraie (Cahors)
9. Domaine Ameztia (Irouléguy)
10. Clos Basté (Madiran)

NEW UP-AND-COMING PRODUCERS

1. Château Bovila (Cahors) (new owners)
2. Château Bourguet (Gaillac)
3. Château de Mazelières (Buzet)
4. Domaine Barbazon (Madiran)
5. Château de Cabidos (Pyrénées-Atlantiques)
6. Domaine Laurent Mousset (Entraygues-et-le-Fel)
7. Domaine Mourguy (Irouléguy)
8. Domaine Lauroux (Côtes de Gascogne)
9. Domaine Pichard (Madiran) (new owners)
10. Domaine Belmon (Vin de Pays du Lot)

BEST-VALUE PRODUCERS

1. Clos Lapeyre (Jurançon)
2. Château de Beaulieu (Marmandais)
3. Domaine Jonc Blanc (Montravel)
4. Château Laffitte-Teston (Madiran)
5. Les Vignerons d'Irouléguy (Irouléguy)
6. Château Plaisance (Fronton)
7. Domaine Bordenave (Jurançon)
8. Château de Saurs (Gaillac)
9. Domaine Labranche-Laffont (Madiran)
10. Château d'Arlus (Gaillac)

GREATEST-QUALITY WINES

1. **Monbazillac Clos Fontindoule 1976** G Cros (€25)
2. **Jurançon Quintessence 1989** Domaine Cauhapé (€50)
3. **Jurançon Les Jardins de Babylone 2005** Didier Dagueneau (€50)
4. **Jurançon Cuvée Kattila 1994** Domaine du Souch (€30)
5. **Cahors Clos de Gamot Cuvée Vignes Centenaires 2002** Jouffreau (€18)
6. **Vin de Table Vin de Voile 1989** Domaine Robert & Bernard Plageoles (€30)
7. **Gaillac Combe d'Avès Rouge 1998** Domaine de la Ramaye (€20)
8. **Madiran 1995** Château d'Aydie (€25)
9. **Marmandais Clos Baquey 2000** Domaine Elian Da Ros (€20)
10. **Bergerac Le Vin Muscadelle 2005** Château Les Tours des Verdots (€30)

BEST BARGAINS

① **Vin de Pays du Lot Cabernet Franc 2005** Domaine de Merchien (€7)

② **Vin de Pays des Côtes de Gascogne Moelleux 2005** Domaine Lauroux (€7)

③ **Côtes de Buzet 2002** Domaine du Pech (€12)

④ **Madiran Rouge Tradition 2005** Château Barréjat (€6)

⑤ **Côtes de Saint-Mont Les Vignes Retrouvées Blanc 2006** Plaimont Producteurs (€6)

⑥ **Fronton Rouge Tradition 2005** Château Baudare (€5)

⑦ **Cahors Rouge Tradition 2005** Château Latuc (€7)

⑧ **Vin de Pays des Côtes de Gascogne Blanc Sec 2006** Domaine San de Guilhem (€6)

⑨ **VDQS Entraygues-et-le-Fel Blanc Sec 2006** Domaine Méjanasserre (€5)

⑩ **Vin de Pays des Côtes de Gascogne Chardonnay/ Sauvignon 2006** Domaine du Tariquet (€6)

MOST EXCITING OR UNUSUAL FINDS

① **Vin de Pays du Lot Rouge 2006** Domaine de Sully (€16) *No other vineyards within 40 miles (65 km), a lovely micro-vineyard near Figeac producing just the one stylish red much sought after in local restaurants.*

② **VDQS Entraygues-le-Fel La Pauca 2005** Domaine Laurent Mousset (€8) *The best red in a rather exciting rebirth of these remote Aveyron vineyards. A collaboration between Mousset and Philippe Gard, winemaker at La Coume du Roy in Roussillon. Enhanced by partial gentle oaking.*

③ **Vin de Table Présambulle NV** Domaine Causse-Marines (€8) *Single continuous fermentation by the Gaillacois method (no added sugar or yeasts), unusual not only because it is sealed with a beer-bottle cap. Lovely with apple-and-blackberry crumble.*

④ **Bergerac Blanc 1996** Château La Jaubertie (€8) *Exciting because this Ryman property is now back on form after a disappointing patch. The Sauvignon/Semillon/Muscadelle (60/30/10) is a delicious blend.*

⑤ **Gaillac Moelleux 2006** Château Touny-les-Roses (€10) *Aiming-for-the-top wines in a modern style that corresponds with the deluxe château where it is made.*

⑥ **Eau-de-Vie de Poire NV** Laurent Cazottes (€58) *Diversifying from their good Gaillac wines (see above).*

⑦ **Vin de Pays des Côtes du Tarn Sauvignon d'Or 2006** Domaine D'en Ségur (€8) *Unusually rich and deep example of this grape. Southern without being heavy.*

⑧ **Marmandais Le Bel Insolent 2006** Château de Beaulieu (€6) *Specifically intended to appeal to younger drinkers (see above).*

⑨ **Vin de Pays des Côtes de Gascogne Rouge 2006** Domaine San de Guilhem (€6) *Well-made quaffing wine, spiked with a good dose of the Egiodola grape.*

⑩ **Vin de Pays du Lot Malbec 2006** Château de Caminade (€7) *One of many growers trying for a Malbec nouveau. A fair example of this controversial style.*

Languedoc-Roussillon

Rosemary George MW

The appellation of the Coteaux du Languedoc is in a
state of flux, supposedly for the benefit of consumers,
but more than likely it will add to their confusion.

ROSEMARY GEORGE MW

The appellation Coteaux du Languedoc was
created in 1985 and incorporated the two
existing AOCs of Faugères and St-Chinian,
as well as several VDQSs, such as La Clape,
Quatourze, St-Saturnin, as *crus*, with
vineyards stretching from the outskirts of
Narbonne all the way round to Nîmes in the
Gard. And ever since then, the INAO has
been tinkering with the appellation,
introducing new areas, which they call
terroirs, such as Terrasses du Larzac, which
covers the vineyards of St-Saturnin and Montpeyroux and the hills around
the Lac de Salagou. Next came Grès de Montpellier, covering most of the
vineyards behind Montpellier and the *crus* of St-Georges d'Orques,
St-Drézery, and Méjanelle. The latest is Pézenas, for vineyards in villages
around the historic town of Molière, toward Faugères and Clermont
l'Hérault in the north, while the nearby *cru* of Cabrières wishes to remain
separate from Pézenas. There are all sorts of regulations about permitted
percentages of grape varieties for Pézenas. Suffice it to say that Grenache
Noir, Mourvèdre, and Syrah are the dominant varieties, and no one variety

ROSEMARY GEORGE MW was lured into the wine trade by a glass of the
Wine Society's champagne at a job interview. Realizing that secretarial work
was not for her, she took the wine-trade exams, becoming one of the first
women to qualify as a Master of Wine in 1979. She has been a freelance wine
writer since 1981 and is the author of 10 books, including *Chablis* (Sotheby
Publications, 1984), *French Country Wines* (Faber & Faber, 1990), *The Wines of
New Zealand* (Faber & Faber, 1996), *The Wines of the South of France* (Faber & Faber,
2001), and *Walking Through the Vineyards of Tuscany* (Bantam Press, 2004). Her
most recent book, *The Wines of Chablis and the Grand Auxerrois* (Segrave Foulkes),
was published in November 2007.

should exceed 70 percent. At the same time, there have been some changes in the delimitation of the vineyards, with growers on the edge of the Vin de Pays des Côtes de Thongue, such as Domaine Monplézy, having some vineyards reclassified as Pézenas. Pézenas was agreed in 2007, with a retrospective use for the 2006 vintage—and only for red wine. The white wines were not deemed serious enough for a supposedly more prestigious appellation. And two more *crus* are in the pipeline: Sommières to the east of Montpellier, and possibly Terrasses de Béziers.

Meanwhile, the new appellation of Languedoc became official in May 2007. The authorities say that they are aiming for a Bordeaux model, so that Languedoc will become the basic appellation for the whole of Languedoc-Roussillon. The criteria for AOC Languedoc are the same as for AOC Coteaux du Languedoc, and eventually AOC Coteaux du Languedoc will disappear. However, they say that Languedoc is not a replacement for Coteaux du Languedoc but an enlargement, for it will incorporate the whole of Languedoc-Roussillon, with the aim of giving greater visibility to the image of Languedoc, grouping all the vineyards that overlook the Mediterranean from the Spanish border almost to the banks of the Rhône. AOC Languedoc will form the base of the pyramid, and the next layer will include AOCs such as Côtes du Roussillon, Minervois, Pézenas, and Terrasses du Larzac, with some of the *crus*, such as Pic St-Loup, La Clape, and Picpoul de Pinet aiming for their own individual appellation, to provide the pinnacle to the pyramid. Corbières and Minervois already have the two *crus* of Boutenac and La Livinière, respectively, and there are moves afoot for the implementation of others, such as Les Aspres in the Côtes du Roussillon. The pyramid of appellations means, for instance, that if your Minervois does not pass the *labelle* tasting to qualify for that appellation, you can resubmit it for the less stringent Languedoc.

Producers of Coteaux du Languedoc who are not part of a terroir or *cru*, such as the talented Dutch winemaker Lidewej Kuijper at Mas des Dames, are dismayed. Her vineyards are on the edge of St-Chinian, and yet her neighbor, with less satisfactory terroir, qualifies for St-Chinian. It would seem that the difference between the two has more to do with politics than quality. When the vineyards were classified an owner or two ago, her neighbor had more clout, while the previous owner of her land was not interested in an appellation. So she will find herself forced to use an appellation with no specific regionality. Marlène Soria of Domaine Peyre-Rose is another producer who will find herself outside a specific *cru*. Apparently the long-term plan is that every producer will become part of a *cru* above the basic AOC Languedoc, but there are numerous individual anomalies that will need to be addressed.

The producers of Coteaux du Languedoc have five years to make the transition to Languedoc *tout court*. A straw poll of producers from the region at the annual Paris Salon des Vignerons Indépendants produced the fairly universal reaction of "Bof!"—a French expression that says everything and nothing, in this instance implying that this particular piece of bureaucratic idiocy is "nothing to do with us." Most see it as something that the bigger players, *négociants*, and cooperatives might benefit from, but not them. Meanwhile, the hapless consumer is best advised to choose wine according to the reputation of the producer rather than the appellation.

Organic vineyards

Perpignan is home to the annual Millésime Bio, an annual wine fair for organic wine. The venue is entirely appropriate, since Languedoc-Roussillon is the region of France with the greatest number of organic vineyards, with 359 producers accounting for 5,290 ha. However, that represents only 2 percent of production, in contrast with Corsica, where 16 producers account for 231 ha and 18 percent of production and the region of Provence-Alpes-Côte d'Azur (PACA), with 289 producers covering 4,276 ha and 12 percent of production. The regional authorities of PACA are offering €1,000 to producers who convert to organic viticulture, as part of the region's aim to increase the percentage of organic vineyards within the next few years. There is no doubt that the whole of the south of France has an unqualified advantage for organic, and indeed biodynamic, growers: the prevailing dry north wind, the

Grapevine

• **Village cooperatives,** which are such a fundamental part of the fabric of villages in the Midi, are not in a happy situation. They suffer the effects of the economic crisis, acting as a weather vane to the vagaries of the market. The only constant seems to be their decline, from 160 to 80 over the past 15 years, with a further decline to 50 predicted within five years. Some, however, do continue to flourish and, indeed, have money to invest. The two cooperatives of Sales and Rivesaltes have combined to form Arnaud de Villeneuve, named after the 13th-century doctor who effectively invented VDN by

discovering that alcohol stopped grape juice from fermenting. They have invested £1.5 million in a high-tech winery on the site of an old fruit-juice factory.

• **The required percentages** of grape varieties for Côtes du Roussillon Blanc have been tweaked so that Vermentino, Marsanne, and Roussanne, either together or singly, must represent a minimum of 20 percent in the blend. Previously there was no minimum requirement and you could make Côtes du Roussillon from just two less distinguished varieties: Macabeu and Malvoisie de Roussillon.

Mistral. Any rain will quickly be followed by dry, clear days, with the accompanying wind eliminating any possibility of disease and rot.

Back to the future

The economic situation is far from satisfactory; 2007 was the 100th anniversary of the riots in the Midi, which were sparked by demands for viticultural reform and led by Marcellin Albert. They were prompted by an economic crisis of overproduction; some reforms were effected and comparisons have been drawn with the present-day situation. The Comité Régional d'Action Viticole (CRAV), which represents the most militant groups among the Midi winemakers, has been responsible for some unlawful acts of protest. Meanwhile, the EU is looking for a reduction of 200,000 ha in the European vineyard area. Inevitably, Languedoc-Roussillon will be one of the regions most affected by this.

Stringent measures are also needed on a smaller, individual scale to address the problems; one informed *vigneron* outlined the steps taken by his own family: pulling vines that were planted on less satisfactory land to concentrate on better vineyard sites, with reinvestment in cellars in order to improve quality and sales.

Much hope is put in the new brand Sud de France, which is not only for wine, both appellation and *vins de pays*, but also for other agricultural products, such as cheese and oysters, with an emphasis on southern French provenance. For many consumers the south of France is a much more vivid image than Languedoc.

Grapevine

- **Château La Roque,** an important Pic St-Loup property, has been sold to a retired industrialist from Normandy, Jacques Rivette. This is an example of the lure of the Midi for people with money to spend, looking for a second career in wine.

- **AOC Côtes de Provence** is also developing *crus*. The first was Côtes de Provence St-Victoire, for the vineyards at the foot of the dramatic Mont St-Victoire outside Aix-en-Provence; and more recent is Côtes de Provence Fréjus, covering the eastern part of the appellation in the hinterland of the port. The *crus* are for red and rosé, but not white wine.

- **Plans to build a new power station** at Beaucaire in the heart of Costières de Nîmes are being energetically opposed by local growers, with the support of the INAO. The authorities are being urged to revert to a previous plan for a site that will not involve any vineyards.

- **Gérard Bertrand** of Domaine de l'Hospitalet in La Clape continues to expand his activities with the purchase of Domaine de l'Aigle, one of the leading Limoux estates, which was originally the property of Jean-Louis Denois and then the Burgundian *négociants* Antonin Rodet.

Opinion:

Oak or no oak?

Am I alone in avoiding wines that boldly state "Vieilli en fût de chêne" when they come from the Languedoc? In a region where the key grape varieties— Syrah, Grenache, Mourvèdre, Carignan, and Cinsault—are packed with flavor and ripened by warm sunshine, why do you need the extra dimension of oak? Don't get me wrong: when a wine is vinified with care, so that the use of oak is subtle and understated, it can undoubtedly add an extra layer of quality, but so often the oak is clumsy and heavy-handed, with the result that the taste of toasted new oak and vanilla, at best, or dried-out fruit that has been leached by the oak completely overwhelms the intrinsic flavors of the wine. Heavy oak often goes hand in hand with high alcohol, but that is another problem. The wines of the Midi are produced from some wonderful terroir; you should only have to taste them to envisage the summer warmth on the wild hillsides of the Languedoc—hillsides that are covered in wild herbs, thyme, laurel, rosemary, juniper, scented pines, and cistus flowers. In so many instances I opt for the *cuvée tradition* rather than the *grand vin*. And there is another advantage: it's usually cheaper!

A good year for the south

The 2007 harvest in Languedoc-Roussillon is a wonderful vintage of exceptional quality—quite unlike the rest of France. I have never spoken to so many happy, smiling winemakers, all of whom are thrilled by the quality of their grapes in 2007 and are very anxious that their wines should not be judged under the umbrella opinion that France has had a bad vintage in 2007, just because Bordeaux and Burgundy have had problems. The cooler-than-average summer greatly benefited the quality of the grapes from Perpignan to Nice, and it cannot be emphasized enough that 2007 shows tremendous potential in the south and will provide wonderful wines for both early consumption and laying down.

Grapevine

● **Château Pennautier,** one of Cabardès's leading estates, is expanding outside its appellation and has just bought the St-Chinian and Faugères property of Moulin de Ciffre. Sadly, the previous owner, Jacques Lésineau, a *bordelais* who had worked hard to establish the reputation of Moulin de Ciffre, was killed in a car accident in 2006. It is unique for being the only estate to encompass the two adjoining appellations.

Vintage Report

Advance report on the latest harvest

2007

The spring was dull and wet; June was warm and sunny, with good weather at flowering, which was later than usual as a result of the cool spring. The summer was generally dry, with temperatures in August well below average, so that the vines did not suffer excessively from drought and the vintage took place in fine, sunny weather. Faugères, for example, had 30 percent lower production as a result of the drought, but the cool August made for a fine vintage. The results are excellent, with promises of some beautifully balanced wines throughout the region. Eloi Dürrbach of Domaine Trévallon says that 2007 is his best vintage since 1982. For Catherine Roque of Domaine du Clovallon, it is "one of the best vintages ever."

Updates on the previous five vintages

2006

Vintage rating: Red: 85, White: 85

A cool spring delayed budbreak. Good weather at flowering; a hot July and cooler August, with some rain. A year that depends on the talent of the winemaker.

2005

Vintage rating: Red: 90, White: 88

A wet winter made for good water levels; the spring was late and the summer warm, with rainfall at the appropriate moment. Some heavy rain just before the harvest caused a few problems for Syrah, but the ensuing Indian summer produced some ripe fruit, resulting in well-balanced wines and some particularly fine whites.

2004

Vintage rating: *Red: 90, White: 88*

Some nicely balanced wines—a relief after the heat of 2003. The best will continue to develop and provide some excellent drinking.

2003

Vintage rating: *Red: 78, White: 80*

The year of the heat wave, inevitably producing wines that lack acidity and are high in alcohol but are not necessarily with ripe tannins, since the vines suffered stress from the drought. Cooler areas such as Pic St-Loup and Terrasses du Larzac fared better. Not wines to keep.

2002

Vintage rating: *Red: 83, White: 80*
(60 for both east of Montpellier)

A problematic year dominated by the cool, wet summer and floods in the eastern Languedoc and into Provence. Pic St-Loup and environs are unexciting; by contrast, the Minervois and surrounding areas are excellent and continue to provide rewarding drinking.

GREATEST WINE PRODUCERS

I have chosen estates with a history, rather than properties developed over the past decade.

1. Domaine Gauby
   (Côtes du Roussillon Villages)
2. Château Simone (Palette)
3. Domaine Tempier (Bandol)
4. Domaine Jean-Michel Alquier
   (Faugères)
5. Clos Centeilles
   (Minervois-La Livinière)
6. Domaine de la Rectorie (Banyuls)
7. Prieuré de St-Jean de Bébian
   (Coteaux du Languedoc)
8. Domaine de l'Hortus (Pic St-Loup)
9. Domaine de Nouvelles
   (Fitou/Rivesaltes)
10. Domaine Antoine Arena
    (Patrimonio)

FASTEST-IMPROVING PRODUCERS

1. Domaine Le Conte des Floris
   (Coteaux du Languedoc)
2. Domaine Laguerre
   (Côtes du Roussillon)
3. Château de Valflaunès (Pic St-Loup)
4. Château de Nizas
   (Coteaux du Languedoc)
5. Domaine La Tour Vieille
   (Collioure/Banyuls)
6. Domaine Navarre (St-Chinian)
7. Mas Amiel
   (Maury/Côtes du Roussillon)
8. Domaine Ollier-Taillefer (Faugères)
9. Mas Champart (St-Chinian)
10. Mas de la Séranne
    (Terrasses du Larzac)

NEW UP-AND-COMING PRODUCERS

1. Mas des Dames
   (Coteaux du Languedoc)
2. Domaine Virgile Joly (St-Saturnin)
3. Mas de l'Ecriture
   (Coteaux du Languedoc)
4. Domaine La Sauvageonne (Coteaux du Languedoc/Terrasses du Larzac)
5. Domaine St Jacques d'Albas
   (Minervois)
6. Mas Cal Demoura
   (Coteaux du Languedoc)
7. Mas d'Auzières (Grès de Montpellier)
8. Domaine La Croix Vanel (Coteaux du Languedoc/Pézenas)
9. Domaine Stella Nova
   (Coteaux du Languedoc/Pézenas)
10. Domaine Rocaudy
    (Coteaux du Languedoc)

BEST-VALUE PRODUCERS

1. Cave Coopérative de Mont Tauch
   (Fitou/Corbières)
2. Domaine Clavel
   (Coteaux du Languedoc)
3. Domaine La Sauvageonne
   (Coteaux du Languedoc)
4. Cave Coopérative de Cabrières
   (Coteaux du Languedoc/Clairette du Languedoc)
5. Mas Montel
   (Coteaux du Languedoc)
6. Château de Gourgazaud (Minervois)

7. Cave Coopérative de Camplong
   (Corbières)
8. Mas d'Auzières
   (Grès de Montpellier)
9. Mas de Bressades
   (Costières de Gard)
10. Domaine de Barroubio
    (St-Jean de Minervois)

GREATEST-QUALITY WINES

1. **Côtes du Roussillon Villages Calcinaires 1998** Domaine Gauby (€20)
2. **Bandol Cuvée Classique 2004** Domaine Tempier (€21)
3. **Coteaux du Languedoc 2001** Prieuré de St-Jean de Bébian (€29)
4. **Pic St-Loup Grande Réserve 2004** Domaine de l'Hortus (€15.10)
5. **Minervois-La Livinière 2002** Clos Centeilles (€14.50)
6. **Coteaux du Languedoc Villafranchien 2003** Domaine Le Conte des Floris (€11)
7. **Banyuls 1952 Solera** Domaine La Tour Vieille (€50 per 50-cl bottle)
8. **Coteaux du Languedoc Terrasses du Larzac l'Infidèle 2005** Mas Cal Demoura (€12.80)
9. **Banyuls Prestige 15 Ans** Mas Amiel (€22.50)
10. **Coteaux du Languedoc Roc d'Anglade 2001** SCEA Pedréno & Rostaing (€40)

Grapevine

• **The regulations for Rivesaltes** have been modified: the minimum aging period has been increased from 24 to 36 months.

• **The Mont Tauch cooperative** in the village of Tuchan is already the biggest producer of Fitou and has joined forces with the cooperative in the village of Fitou, as well as that of Lapalme. Mont Tauch is helping with viticulture and sales advice, and it benefits from an even greater area from which to select grapes. Similarly, it is working with the cooperative in Maury and has thus added that appellation to its repertoire. This makes sense, since the vineyards adjoin each other, even though one is in Roussillon and the other in the Languedoc.

BEST BARGAINS

① **Coteaux du Languedoc 2005**
Mas des Dames (€6.30)

② **Minervois 2005**
Domaine St Jacques d'Albas (€5)

③ **Faugères Les Collines 2006**
Domaine Ollier-Taillefer (€5.50)

④ **Coteaux du Languedoc Campredon 2006**
Domaine Chabanon (€11)

⑤ **Coteaux du Languedoc Les Ruffes 2005** Domaine La Sauvageonne (€5.50)

⑥ **Grès de Montpellier Le Mas 2006** Domaine Clavel (€5.30)

⑦ **Cabardès Classique 2006**
Château Pennautier (€4.70)

⑧ **Coteaux du Languedoc Le Joly Rouge 2006** Domaine Virgile Joly (€6.50)

⑨ **St-Chinian Cuvée Ancestra 2005** Domaine Jougla (€6.75)

⑩ **St-Chinian Fleur de Cynanque Rosé 2006** Mas de Cynanque (€5)

MOST EXCITING OR UNUSUAL FINDS

Focusing mainly but not exclusively on estates that are relatively new to me.

① **Limoux Rouge Grande Cuvée 2004** Domaine Jean-Louis Denois (€10) *The first red Limoux that I have enjoyed: a blend of Cabernet Sauvignon, Merlot, and Grenache, aged for 18 months in 500-liter barrels. Elegant and harmonious fruit, with balanced tannins.*

② **St-Saturnin Saturne 2005**
Domaine Virgile Joly (€13)
Virgile Joly created the first new independent estate in St-Saturnin for 50 years. This is a satisfying blend of Grenache, Carignan, and Cinsault, and refreshingly matured in vat, not barrel.

③ **Côtes du Roussillon L'Envie 2006** Mas Crémat (€8.50)
A wonderfully ripe, spicy wine without a trace of oak. From Grenache, Syrah, and a little Carignan.

④ **Coteaux du Languedoc Rouge 2004** Domaine du Montcalmès (€18) *From vineyards that were in the village cooperative for the two previous generations. The first vintage of the new generation was produced in 1999.*

⑤ **Coteaux du Languedoc 1999**
Mas Julien (€39) *This is an example of how well the wines of the Languedoc age.*

⑥ **Collioure Blanc Les Canadells 2006** Domaine La Tour Vieille (€13)
A relatively new appellation and a blend of Grenache Gris, Blanc, and Macabeu. Some lovely herbal notes and a hint of oak, balanced with good acidity.

⑦ **Minervois 2002** Château Villerambert-Julien (€13.90) *Shows how successful this much-decried vintage was in the Minervois.*

⑧ **Minervois Cambosc 2005**
Domaine Prieuré St Martin de Laure (€15) *The first vintage of this new Minervois estate was in 2002. This is the top cuvée—an elegant Syrah/Grenache/Carignan blend.*

⑨ **Bandol Rouge 2004** Domaine La Bastide Blanche (€15) *I couldn't resist straying into Provence for a great vintage in Bandol. Mainly Mourvèdre, with 13 percent Grenache Noir. Combines elegance and power.*

⑩ **Pézenas Pléiades 2003** Domaine Stella Nova (€16.50) *The first vintage of this new estate was 2001. A classic Midi blend of Grenache, Syrah, Carignan, and Mourvèdre.*

Vins de Pays & Vins de Table

Rosemary George MW

The new Vin de Pays des Vignobles de France, which was recognized as *Wine Report 2008* went to press, is now up and running.

ROSEMARY GEORGE MW

The decree allows winemakers to blend varietal wines from the 64 denominations of *vin de pays* based on *départements*. I will spare you the list of all 64 and merely cite an example or two, from areas as diverse as the Loire-Atlantique, the Hérault, and the Tarn. Smaller areas such as Côtes de Thongue or Vallée de Paradis are not included. The emphasis is on grape variety, or grape varieties, with as many as three allowed on the label.

This is obviously seen as a key move to help develop the export market, and the potential volume is expected to represent between 5 and 10 percent of total *vin de pays* production. The mention of France on the label will be an obvious attraction for new, growing markets such as China or Russia, with new consumers recognizing the quality of France as a wine-producing country, whereas they would be challenged to know where Ile de Beauté or Comté Tolosan were.

The great advantage from the winemaking point of view is the flexibility that it allows, making it possible to blend, for example, a riper, more full-bodied Sauvignon from the Midi with some fresh, pithy wine from the

ROSEMARY GEORGE MW was lured into the wine trade by a glass of the Wine Society's champagne at a job interview. Realizing that secretarial work was not for her, she took the wine-trade exams, becoming one of the first women to qualify as a Master of Wine in 1979. She has been a freelance wine writer since 1981 and is the author of 10 books, including *Chablis* (Sotheby Publications, 1984), *French Country Wines* (Faber & Faber, 1990), *The Wines of New Zealand* (Faber & Faber, 1996), *The Wines of the South of France* (Faber & Faber, 2001), and *Walking Through the Vineyards of Tuscany* (Bantam Press, 2004). *The Wines of Chablis and the Grand Auxerrois* (Segrave Foulkes) was published in November 2007.

Loire, and maybe even to add a dash of wine from Bordeaux for extra aroma. Valerie Pajotin, the bright director of Onivins, the organization responsible for *vins de pays*, sees this as an exciting opportunity to create new wines and new tastes. The blending could potentially be very ambitious and innovative—for example, a Syrah from the Rhône Valley could be blended with Cabernet Sauvignon from the Gironde, and if you can't afford oak barrels, there is nothing to stop you from using oak chips, or *copeaux*. It can also circumvent problems of small crops in one part of the country, maintaining continuity of supply. Naturally it is the big players, the *négociants* with a broad international perspective, who will benefit, rather than smaller producers who concentrate on their own locality. So far a dozen producers have asked for an *agrément* for Vin de Pays des Vignobles de France. The first on the market is Chamarré for three wines— Pinot Noir, Chardonnay, and Cabernet Sauvignon, which they were already selling in the United States as *vin de table*. The blend was already in place; all they had to do was change the label.

There is one dissenter, the biggest *vin de pays* of all, Vin de Pays d'Oc, whose president Jacques Gravegeal was the lone voice voting against the creation of Vin de Pays des Vignobles de France. It is, of course, a question of vested interests. At the moment Vin de Pays d'Oc is by far the biggest producer of varietal wines in France. However, that may change, not only with the creation of Vin de Pays des Vignobles de France, but because the EU has just agreed that plain *vin de table* from France can now indicate a grape variety and the vintage on the label. They were hitherto condemned to anonymity.

There was an initial problem with Vignobles de France. The EU refused to publish the decree in its official journal because a wine cannot bear the name of an entire country. The French authorities argue that it does not represent the totality of France's vineyard area, since there are vineyards that produce only appellation wines and not *vins de pays*. The two other new *vins de pays*—Vin de Pays de l'Atlantique (covering a large part of southwest France, including the Gironde and neighboring *départements*) and Vin de Pays des Gaules (encompassing the 95 Beaujolais villages)—also encountered a similar problem: Atlantique is not deemed to be a place in terms of viticulture, and Gaul ceased to exist a few centuries ago. This had repercussions on the export market in that the US refused to accept the wines in question, but the French government negotiated and the problem was solved. Sarkozy may have a reputation as a teetotaler, but he was the one presidential candidate to show any interest in wine at all, recognizing its importance as France's largest agricultural export.

Both Vin de Pays de l'Atlantique and des Gaules are beginning to appear on the market. The first harvest of Vin de Pays de l'Atlantique amounted to 17,500 hl, reduced from an original 33,052 hl after the enforcement of strict quality criteria, split 66 percent red, 24 percent white, and 10 percent pink. The Bordeaux *négociants* Ginestet have launched Cap 270 Vin de Pays des Gaules, which was first released in time for Christmas 2007. The total harvest, just 4,000 hl, was composed almost entirely of Gamay, even though 18 other grape varieties are permitted.

Celebrating Carignan

John Bojanowski of Clos de Gravillas, and the driving force behind the move to revive Carignan, continues his crusade, with a Fête du Vieux Carignan organized for 15 November, to compete with Beaujolais Nouveau. Carignan plays an important part in the *vins de pays* of the south; any pure Carignan must of necessity be *vin de pays*, since the permitted percentage for Carignan in the appellations of the Midi is strictly limited to a minority role. However, it is now possible to plant Carignan with the help of *primes de plantation*, or subsidies. As far as Bojanowski is concerned, this is definitely a step in the right direction. And there is a steadily growing number of varietal Carignan wines.

Ports and gardens closed

Vin de Pays des Portes de la Méditerranée has been shortened to simple Vin de Pays de Méditerranée. The area covers the *départements* of the region Provence-Alpes-Côte d'Azur, the two *départements* of Corsica, and two *départements* of the Rhône-Alpes, namely the Ardèche and the Drôme. The color breakdown for the wine is 56 percent red, 27 percent rosé, and 17 percent white, with a 14 percent increase in crop declaration for the first year of the new name.

The other more significant change is the replacement of the picturesque Vin de Pays du Jardin de la France with the more obvious Vin de Pays du Val de Loire, which will be a help for those who are geographically challenged. Apparently, many French people confused it with Ile de France, which is the area around Paris and not usually known for its vineyards. Some of the small producers fear that the image of Vin de Pays du Val de Loire will be tarnished by large producers concentrating on quantity rather than quality, since 80 percent of Vin de Pays du Val de Loire production lies in the hands of three big players.

Opinion:
Spoiled for choice

The diversity of *vins de pays* never ceases to delight me, nor does the plethora of reasons as to why a wine is a *vin de pays* rather than an appellation, or indeed a *vin de table* rather than a *vin de pays*. Much stems from the individuality of the average French winemaker. The standard cliché is that Italians are individualists—but so are the French, especially in winemaking communities in some of the more off-the-beaten-track vineyards of France. One of the most obvious sources of experimentation is sweet wine. AOC legislation in many parts of France often does not include sweet wine; or if it does, such as the various *vins doux naturels* of Roussillon, it does not allow for late-harvest wines. Consequently, the variety of dessert wines is amazing.

In the space of a few hours at the Salon des Vignerons Indépendants in Paris, I tasted an extraordinary array of different wines. There was a Vin de Pays de la Côte Vermeille *rancio sec*, made from Grenache Blanc and Grenache Gris, aged in barrel for four years, which completely contradicted the appellation rules for white Banyuls; Domaine des Henrys in the Côtes de Thongue produces a *moelleux* Muscat by cryoextraction, whereby the grapes are frozen and then pressed, and fermentation stopped by chilling. It is a simple *vin de table*, since M. Bouchard cannot be bothered with the bureaucratic hassle of the *labelle* tasting. At Château Pennautier in Cabardès, they make a late-harvest Chardonnay, Vendange d'après Vin de Table, with some peachy fruit and a streak of oak.

Picturesque names indicate a late-harvest wine, such as Vin d'Automne from Domaine Camp Galhan in the Cévennes, which is a Vin de Pays d'Oc made from Viognier, Roussanne, and Chardonnay. Domaine Orviel, also in the Cévennes, produces Barriques Oubliées, an intriguing blend of three vintages and three grape varieties: Chardonnay, Sauvignon, and Viognier. Again, the grapes are harvested late and the wine fermented in oak.

At Domaine de l'Engarran in the Grès de Montpellier they make two Vins de Pays d'Oc Doux, one from pure Grenache Noir and the other from Sauvignon, called Caprice and Folie de l'Engarran, respectively. In both instances, the fermentation is stopped by chilling. While I am familiar with dry Picpoul de Pinet, the Midi's traditional accompaniment to an oyster, a late-harvest Picpoul was a new experience. Les Oréades, a *vin de table doux* from Domaine Gaujal de Saint Bon, is made only in the best years, from grapes picked in November with a yield of barely 5 hl/ha. It was deliciously honeyed. When I asked why it wasn't *vin de pays*, the response was the French equivalent of "So what?"

Côtes de Gascogne allows for the categories of *moelleux*, *doux*, and *demi-sec* in its decree, and many producers take advantage of them, notably Domaine de Tariquet with Premières and Dernières Grives, and Domaine de St Lannes with an evocative Prélude d'Hiver. Vin de Pays d'Oc also permits the category Vendanges Surmûries, which implies a late harvest of grapes that are *passerillé* or dried on the vine, and may have some noble rot. Chateau de Stony is known normally for the Vin Doux Naturel of Muscat de Frontignan, but for sweet wines that are not muted by the addition of alcohol, *vin de pays* is the appropriate category, with Lumière d'Automne for a late-harvest, barrel-aged Muscat. One of the most original is Cazes Frères Libre Expression, a pure Macabeu *vin de table*. The grapes are picked late and the juice fermented slowly in vat, and the resulting wine is not dissimilar to Tuscany's Vin Santo.

The permutations are infinite and rewarding to explore.

Grapevine

• **The Vins de Pays d'Oc** have created a three-tier quality structure with names to tempt the wine drinker. The base of the pyramid is Séduction, with Style forming the middle range, and the pinnacle is Collection, for which the wines have to meet quality criteria decided by a tasting. So far, 16 producers have joined the Club des Marques, representing 70 percent of total production, including most of the large players such as Vignerons Val d'Orbieu, Sieur d'Arques, Jeanjean, and so on, as well as medium-sized producers such as Domaines Paul Mas and smaller wine estates like Domaine Condamine-Bertrand. And, like the appellations of the Midi, they support the umbrella brand Sud de France.

• **The sources** of *vins de pays* are inexhaustible. One of the newest vineyards, Vin de Pays Charentais, is in a dramatic position overlooking the estuary of the Gironde on the cliffs at Talmont-sur-Gironde, where no vines have been planted before. Three associates, including talented young winemaker Lionel Gardrat, have joined forces to produce a pure Colombard, Vin de Pays Charentais Les Hauts de Talmont. They planted 2.5 ha in 2003 on limestone and clay soil in a site that claims as much sunshine as Nice. Their first vintage was in 2005. Colombard was once planted extensively for cognac but now accounts for only about 10 percent of the vineyards of the Charente. They are hoping to instigate a revival. Meanwhile, Vin de Pays Charentais is declining in production as cognac sales soar. Vineyards of Sauvignon are even being replaced by Ugni Blanc.

• **About a hundred estates** now exist in the Fenouillèdes, the corner of Roussillon that focuses on Maury and the Agly Valley, with wonderful old Grenache vines. The area continues to attract interest and investment, with a Mexican and three American importers following the example of the *bordelais* and buying vineyards. South African Jeff Grier has had a successful first vintage with Jean-Louis Denois.

Many vin de pays producers also make appellation wines in Languedoc-Roussillon. I have tried to opt for one or other category but have not always succeeded, so there is inevitable overlap. A great vin de pays producer is likely also to be a great appellation producer, and great quality and good value will apply in both instances.

GREATEST WINE PRODUCERS

1. Domaine de Trévallon (Bouches du Rhône)
2. Domaine de Clovallon (Oc/Haute Vallée de l'Orb)
3. Domaine Gauby (Côtes Catalanes) (whites)
4. Domaine de la Grange des Pères (Hérault)
5. Domaine Chabanon (Oc)
6. Mas des Chimères (Coteaux du Salagou)
7. Mas de Daumas Gassac (Hérault)
8. Producteurs Plaimont (Côtes de Gascogne)
9. Domaine Jean-Louis Denois (Oc)
10. Domaine La Croix-Belle (Côtes de Thongue)

FASTEST-IMPROVING PRODUCERS

1. Domaine des Soulanes (Côtes Catalanes)
2. Domaine Le Soula (Côtes Catalanes)
3. Mas Conscience (Oc)
4. Domaine de Magellan (Côtes de Thongue)
5. Domaine de Vignelaure (Coteaux du Verdon)
6. Ampelidae (Val de Loire)
7. Domaine Gravillas (Côtes du Brian)
8. Domaine de Puechamp (Cévennes)
9. Domaine de Ravanès (Coteaux de Murviel)
10. Domaine de Perdiguier (Coteaux d'Enserune)

NEW UP-AND-COMING PRODUCERS

1. Domaine des Vents (Côtes Catalanes)
2. Mas Laval (Hérault)
3. Domaine de Ribonnet (Comté Tolosan)
4. Domaine Canteperdrix (Cassan)
5. Domaine des Tremières (Oc)
6. Les Trois Poules (Côtes de Thongue)
7. Les Trois Terres (Oc)
8. Domaine de la Fontaine aux Muses (Yonne)
9. Domaine des Conquêtes (Hérault)
10. Les Hauts de Talmont (Charentais)

BEST-VALUE PRODUCERS

1. Producteurs Plaimont (Côtes de Gascogne)
2. Domaine de Perdiguier (Coteaux d'Enserune)
3. Domaine des Tremières (Oc)
4. Domaine Camp Galhan (Duché d'Uzès)
5. Domaine de Granoupiac (Oc)
6. Domaine de St Lannes (Côtes de Gascogne)
7. Domaine Cazes (Côtes Catalanes)
8. Domaine de l'Orviel (Oc, Cévennes, Duché d'Uzès)
9. Domaines Paul Mas (Oc)
10. Les Trois Poules (Côtes de Thongue)

Grapevine

• **Foster's,** after ruining the James Herrick Chardonnay brand it bought in 1999, is rumored to be selling the La Motte vineyard—the backbone of what was once one of the best Chardonnays from the south of France.

GREATEST-QUALITY WINES

1. **Vin de Pays des Bouches du Rhône Rouge 2004** Domaine de Trévallon (€39)
2. **Vin de Pays des Bouches du Rhône Blanc 2005** Domaine de Trévallon (€47)
3. **Vin de Pays de l'Hérault Rouge 2004** Domaine de la Grange des Pères (€39)
4. **Vin de Pays des Côtes Catalanes Vieilles Vignes 2005** Domaine Gauby (€27)
5. **Vin de Pays de la Haute Vallée de l'Orb Pinot Noir Les Pomarèdes 2006** Domaine de Clovallon (€14)
6. **Vin de Pays d'Oc Blanc 2004** Domaine Chabanon (€23)
7. **Vin de Pays des Coteaux du Verdon La Colline de Vignelaure 2001** Domaine Vignelaure (€32)
8. **Vin de Pays des Coteaux de Murviel L'Omega 2005** Domaine de Ravanès (€32)
9. **Vin de Pays de l'Hérault Rouge 2006** Mas de Daumas Gassac (€30)
10. **Vin de Pays des Côtes Catalanes Le Credo 1996** Domaine Cazes (€36.80 per 150-cl bottle)

BEST BARGAINS

1. **Vin de Pays d'Oc Viognier 2006** Domaine de Gourgazaud (€7.80)
2. **Vin de Pays des Côtes Catalanes Cuvée Jean Pull 2005** Domaine des Soulanes (€7)
3. **Vin de Pays des Côtes Catalanes Aquilon 2005** Domaine des Vents (€7.50)
4. **Vin de Pays des Côtes de Gascogne Colombelle 2006** Producteurs Plaimont (€2.90)
5. **Vin de Pays du Val de Montferrand La Loup dans la Bergerie NV** Domaine de l'Hortus (€5.10)
6. **Vin de Pays des Coteaux d'Enserune Cuvée d'en Auger 2005** Domaine de Perdiguier (€9)
7. **Vin de Pays d'Oc Rouge 2005** Domaine de l'Engarran (€7.40)
8. **Vin de Pays de l'Hérault Rigoletto 2006** Domaine de Granoupiac (€5.50)
9. **Vin de Pays des Côtes de Thau Rosé 2006** Domaine Gaujal de Saint Bon (€4.10)
10. **Vin de Pays du Val de Loire Cépage Cabernet Sauvignon 2006** Domaine de la Hardonnière (€4.70)

Grapevine

• **Interest in the annual competition** Top 100 Vins de Pays continues to grow. In 2007 there were a record-breaking 1,115 entrants, and the final 100 included wines as diverse as Sauvignon Gris from the Loire Valley (Domaine de l'Aujardière), Pinot Noir from Franche-Comté (Vignobles Guillaume), an Aleatico from Corsica (Domaine du Mont St Jean), and a Braucol from the Tarn (Domaine Chaumet Lagrange), as well as a strong selection of international varieties, such as Chardonnay, Sauvignon, Roussanne, and Syrah, to mention just a few.

• **Domaine de la Colombette's** imaginative attempt to combat the ever-rising alcohol levels coming from the south of France has had a setback: 25,000 bottles of their brand Plume, at a modest 9 percent ABV, had to be withdrawn from the shelves of Tesco, since the osmosis technique that is used to remove the alcohol from the wine is not allowed under EU law. Illogically, the same technique is permitted for Australian and US wines, so there are no prizes for guessing what has filled Plume's place on Tesco's shelves.

MOST EXCITING OR UNUSUAL FINDS

❶ Vin de Table Le Villard NV Domaine Chabanon (€25) *The Midi's answer to Tuscan Vin Santo! Rich, long, and intense, with a flavor of dry raisins and figs. Pure Chenin Blanc, passerillé grapes, and 48 months' élevage. A blend of 2001 and 2003. No wonder it can't be anything other than vin de table!*

❷ Vin de Pays d'Oc Réserve 2004 Domaine de Nizas (€25) *A satisfying and successful blend of 50 percent Petit Verdot, 30 percent Cabernet Sauvignon, and 20 percent Syrah. This is the first vintage.*

❸ Vin de Pays d'Oc Les Souls 2005 Mas Laval (€15) *A southern Chardonnay of surprising elegance, with good acidity and well-integrated oak.*

❹ Vin de Pays de l'Hérault 2004 Domaine des Conquêtes (€9) *An intriguing blend of Chenin Blanc, Chardonnay, Grenache Blanc, and Vermentino.*

❺ Vin de Pays de la Cité de Carcassonne Le 100% d'Oustric 2005 Domaine d'Oustric (€10) *Another successful example of a* pure Carignan: a long fermentation and 18 months in barrel.*

❻ Vin de Pays du Comté Tolosan Cépage Chenin Blanc 2005 Domaine de Ribonnet (€7) *A surprise to find Chenin Blanc in vineyards south of Toulouse.*

❼ Vin de Pays Charentais Le Colombard 2006 Les Hauts de Talmont (€6.75) *From new vineyards overlooking the Gironde estuary, with sunshine levels as high as Nice!*

❽ Vin de Table Rosé Renaissance [2006] Domaine Cransac (€7.50) *A blend of Négrette and Cabernet Sauvignon produced in Fronton, but rosé is not included in the appellation. A vin de table rather than a vin de pays in order to avoid bureaucratic hassle.*

❾ Vin de Table Blanc Doux Les Oréades [2002] Domaine Gaujal de Saint Bon (€13) *This is the first time I have ever encountered late-harvest Picpoul.*

❿ Vin de Pays des Côtes Catalanes Trigone 2006 Domaine Le Soula (€9) *A new cuvée: a cheaper "second" wine from a leading Côtes Catalanes producer.*

Grapevine

• **Vin de Pays** accounts for about a third of French wine production, with a 2007 crop of 14.5 million hl, showing a 2 percent decrease on the previous vintage. However, permitted yields have just been increased for the 2007 vintage, after the harvest, to a permitted yield of 105 hl/ha for red wine and 110 hl/ha for white. If you produce *vin de table* as well as *vin de pays*, your *vin de table* crop is limited to 130 hl/ha, but if you produce only *vin de table*, the sky is the limit. Given that *vin de pays* yields were always fixed at 80 hl/ha for strict quality reasons, this appears to be complete idiocy, and, as one informed commentator observed, it makes even less sense in a year when the increased yields are impossible to meet. France has had a short harvest and there is pressure on prices, with the result that the big players exporting to the opening markets such as China and Russia are short of wine.

• **Michel Laroche** of Chablis fame celebrated 10 years of wine production in the Languedoc at Mas de la Chevalière in September 2007.

Germany

Michael Schmidt

What some see as the unacceptable face of capitalism was spotted behind the mask of benefaction in 2007.

MICHAEL SCHMIDT

A local businessman backed by multimillionaire investor Detlev Meyer paid three times the going rate for the purchase of 1.6 ha of the Rheinhessen premium vineyard Niersteiner Pettenthal, shutting out any interested local growers. Leaseholders at the time were Agnes and Fritz Hasselbach from the highly esteemed Gunderloch estate. They had spent five years of hard graft and lots of money to restore the run-down site, only to be unceremoniously dumped just as they had achieved their goal. Before this takeover, Meyer's reputation was more that of a savior, having injected large amounts of capital into the two reputable but financially troubled Nierstein estates St Antony and Heyl zu Herrnsheim.

In from the cold

An area that once had 16,000 ha of vines and today boasts a history of more than 1,000 years of wine growing has gone unnoticed by most of the world's prominent wine magazines, but the little-known eastern German regions of Saale-Unstrut and Sachsen deserve a higher profile.

MICHAEL SCHMIDT says his passion for the wines of his country started with a few bottles of the legendary 1959 vintage, given to him and his wife as a wedding present in 1969. Today they live in the Ahr Valley region in a house surrounded by vineyards. From here, Michael keeps a close eye on the latest developments on the German wine scene. Over the years he has worked as a consultant for a number of publications, from the early editions of the *Sunday Telegraph Good Wine Guide* to his continuing role as adviser for the German section of *The Sotheby's Wine Encyclopedia* (Dorling Kindersley). For the past two decades Michael has been involved as a tutor in wine education and as a judge at the International Wine & Spirit Competition. He is also a contributor to German wine publications *Wein Plus* and *Vinum*.

Though vineyards in the region can be traced back to 998, it was the arrival of Cistercian monks 150 years later that started the expansion. By the 14th century, 6,000 ha of vines had been established on the banks of the Elbe River and another 10,000 along its two smaller tributaries. Wine production made a significant contribution to the local economy until phylloxera in the 19th century left just 100 ha of vines standing. In the fightback against the dreaded plague, the small Saale-Unstrut region became Germany's central station of command when the government set up the country's first viticultural research institute at Naumburg in 1899 and, a year later, the first nursery dedicated exclusively to the propagation of grafted vines in Freyburg. World War I and the subsequent economic crisis, however, did not allow for a return to profitable production levels. Local growers pooled resources and founded the cooperatives of Freyburg (Saale-Unstrut) and Meissen (Sachsen) in the mid-1930s. Both organizations survived the radical changes in political systems that were to follow and are by far the largest producers in their respective regions today. During the Communist days of the German Democratic Republic they churned out millions of liters of wine, the vast majority of which was imported in bulk from countries as varied as Bulgaria and Algeria. This fate as supplier of dubious foreign plonk was shared by Kloster Pforta and Schloss Wackerbarth, the state-owned wine institutes of Sachsen Anhalt and Sachsen, respectively. A bottle of indigenous origin would have been available only on the black market at a price not affordable by your average comrade.

In the mid-1980s, the East German economy began to head for meltdown and there were many shortages, which sometimes evoked some ingenious responses from producers. Even today the cooperative at Freyburg sports a large array of glass pipes supplied by the famous Carl Zeiss works of Jena in times when stainless steel was simply not available. Disused railroad ties were employed in the vineyard as anchors for wire training. A complete lack of cultured yeasts also forced growers to familiarize themselves with the intricacies of spontaneous fermentation. In the winter of 1986/87, another severe blow was dealt to domestic production when temperatures plummeted to −27.4°F (−33°C) and almost completely wiped out Müller-Thurgau, which accounted for 60 percent of the vines in the GDR. With hard currency in desperately short supply, the Politburo might have been excused for ignoring the plight of a minute niche industry, but a close friendship between the country's most preeminent (and wine-loving) painter and the president saw a miraculous release of funds to replenish depleted vineyards. Choice of material, however, was limited to what was instantly available from eastern neighbors, leading to the appearance of such unlikely contenders as Blauer Zweigelt, André, and Morio Muskat.

Though the northeasterly location does have its drawbacks, with both late spring and early fall frosts, there are also some advantages. The Harz and Thüringen mountain ranges provide an effective cloud barrier, and the yearly average of 20 in (500 mm) precipitation is among the lowest of any of the German regions. The hot days and cool nights of a truly continental summer with an annual 1,600 hours of sunshine provide optimal ripening conditions. Yields of around 50 hl/ha are virtually half that of the national average, and grapes benefit, with greater concentration of fruit and aromas. Prices are relatively high, but there is strong loyalty among local consumers. Most of the wines from Saale-Unstrut's 650 ha are (and always have been) vinified in the *Trocken* fashion, whereas the majority of Sachsen's 410 ha still provides for the off-dry to medium-sweet taste. Müller-Thurgau continues to lead, ahead of Weisser and Grauer Burgunder, Riesling, Silvaner, and Traminer. Black varieties have trebled their share over the past 20 years to 20 percent of the total area under vine, and Blauer Zweigelt has been joined by significant plantings of Spätburgunder and Dornfelder.

Since the political unification of the country in 1990, the vineyards of the two regions have been returned to private ownership, but whereas the Freyburg-Unstrut cooperative received more than €10 million for a complete overhaul of operations and will remain on the European drip until 2013, the largest private producer, Prinz zu Lippe, had to invest €8 million of his own money to buy back and modernize his family's former ancestral estate, Schloss Proschwitz, at Zadel. These two producers, plus the Meissen cooperative and the state domaines of Kloster Pforta and Schloss Wackerbarth, account for more than 70 percent of east German vineyard holdings. Though all five have benefited from large capital injections in one way or another, only Schloss Proschwitz can challenge for the lead in quality that has been taken by a few small private growers. Lützkendorf and Pawis emerged as the early contenders in the mid-90s, but in my recent journey of discovery I was even more impressed by the stunning wines of Gussek in Naumburg and Zimmerling of Dresden (!).

It is exciting to observe how, after many years of enforced stagnation, newly found enthusiasm and energy express themselves in interesting experiments and innovative projects. East Germany's first cooperage was opened in 2006 in the village of Grosswillsdorf, with the 700-liter maiden cask made from Spessart oak going to the Freyburg cooperative. On the vine front, Kloster Pforta of Bad Kösen is using parts of one of the district's oldest vineyards, the Köppelberg site, to study the viability of reintroducing historic but almost extinct varieties such as Elbling, Roter Riesling, and Heunisch. The east Germans are coming!

Opinion:
How great are the Great Growths?

Steffen Christmann, the new president of the VDP (association of premium wine growers) has made it clear that there can be no more change in direction from the agreement reached by all members in the so-called Marienthal resolutions with regard to the association's classification system, and that the main task now has to be to push for official recognition of the concept and its terminology by the country's wine laws. Some success has already been achieved, with the VDP being allowed to identify wines from its most highly ranked vineyards with a logo depicting a cluster of grapes paired with the number one, either on the label or embossed on the bottle. Wines from these *Erste Lagen*, the term chosen by the VDP for its premier sites, can be dry or sweet. The dry wines, whose upper limit of residual sugar has been reduced to 9 g/l, are called *Große Gewächse* (*grands crus*) and, in addition to the logo, may display the letters GG after the vineyard name. Noble sweet wines from *Erste Lagen* carry the traditional distinctions from *Spätlese* to *Trockenbeerenauslese* plus the logo. A grace period until 2015 has been granted to members who are presently circumventing some of the association's rules and directives.

Grapevine

- **The celebrated Jordan wine estate** in the Palatinate, which was split into three independent domaines because of inheritance issues 149 years ago, was reunited under one ownership in November 2007. Local business magnate Joachim Niederberger, who in recent years acquired the estates of Bassermann-Jordan and von Buhl, completed the set with the purchase of the house of Dr. Deinhard in Deidesheim, making him Germany's largest private wine producer in the process. He now owns 150 ha of prime vineyard sites in the prestigious locations of Deidesheim, Forst, and Ruppertsberg. According to a company spokesperson, the three estates will continue to be run independently.

- **The Mosel** is happy to oblige with proof of global warming. Once renowned as the only German region to forbid the planting of black grape varieties, today almost 10 percent of its vineyards have been handed over to such obvious candidates as Spätburgunder and Dornfelder, but even Merlot, Cabernet Sauvignon, and Pinot Meunier (Schwarzriesling) are getting a look-in. Riesling's share in the area has slipped to an all-time low of 58 percent.

- **Straw wine** could soon become a new addition to the German wine portfolio after a Mosel grower's successful appeal to the European Commission against a ban by the local courts.

The growers of the Rheingau VDP are allowed to continue with the term *Erstes Gewächs* and 12 g/l for dry wines from their premium sites. Having attended one of their press conferences, it is clear that they feel very strongly about this exception and the parent organization will have its work cut out to make them fall in line by 2015 or at any time in the future. While the rules followed by Rheingau producers are legal, it is totally unacceptable to allow variations from the agreed VDP regulations if the VDP wishes its classification to get the recognition enjoyed by established *cru classé* systems in other countries.

The VDP has put tremendous effort into the creation and promotion of its grading system and cannot afford to turn a blind eye to members who continue to flout the rules. Some of them sell *Gutswein Trocken* (dry wine from the lowest of the three classification tiers) at higher prices than their *Große Gewächse*; others go even further by offering *Tafelwein Trocken* at twice or three times the going rate of their *grands crus*. Great growths not so great? The credibility of the classification is at stake.

Another contentious issue concerns the proliferation of sites classified as *Erste Lagen*, with 347 vineyards awarded this designation by August 2007. The VDP insists that it has very stringent practical controls in place and that it refuses *grand cru* status to a substantial number of entries from *Erste Lagen* sites every year. Some doubt is thrown on this assertion by the fact that, at the 2007 preview, the modest 2006 vintage was represented by 240 white wines as opposed to about 190 from the far superior 2005 the previous year. One senior German wine critic put it in a nutshell when he mischievously called the 2006 *grands crus* "*ernste Lage*" (serious state of affairs) instead of *Erste Lage*. The steadfast refusal to allow any external experts on the VDP's assessment panels does nothing to defuse rumors of amicable arrangements on the odd occasion.

Grapevine

• **Planting ungrafted vines** in German vineyards became illegal in 2007, but a good number of plots still sport original rootstocks, sometimes over 100 years old. They can mainly be found in the Mosel and Ahr regions, since phylloxera appears to have an aversion to the highly acidic slate soils. Molitor, Mönchhof, and Gutzler in Rheinhessen and Kesseler in the Rheingau still produce separate parcels of the "real thing."

• **Does Riesling have more colors** than any other variety? After Weisser Riesling and its suspected predecessor Roter Riesling, there is of course the unrelated Schwarzriesling (Pinot Meunier). Goldriesling, a crossing of Riesling × Courtellier originating from Alsace, can be added to the list, but nowadays it's found only in the Elbe Valley.

Vintage Report

Advance report on the latest harvest

2007

After a mild winter, an extraordinarily warm spring pushed flowering three weeks ahead of the long-term average. This early vegetation lead was maintained well into the fall. Summer rains came at the right time to replenish water tables without causing rot or mildew. Even a small amount of grape sunburn across the regions caused by a short period of extreme heat in July did not manage to put the proverbial fly in the ointment, since it helped the more ambitious growers with their green harvest. Relatively modest temperatures in August facilitated a slower and more even ripening process than 2003, preventing a premature drop of acidity levels. The traditional enemies of pests, diseases, and hail made hardly any appearance at all, allowing grapes to reach harvesting dates in exceptionally rude health. Sunny days and cool nights in the fall played right into the hands of Riesling. A large harvest of 11 million hl compensated for the shortfall of the previous two years, though an average of more than 100 hl/ha is likely to result in some dilution in the lower spheres of the market. At the opposite end we can expect some very fine wines indeed.

Grapevine

• *Wine Report* can now reveal that it was only by a lucky twist of fate that Georg Friedrich Händel became a great composer instead of an inferior wine grower. Documents found in the archives of the state of Sachsen-Anhalt reveal that, in 1624, Händel's grandfather Valentin owned a vineyard in the village of Zappendorf, near Halle, but this was sold by the composer's father Georg in 1649. In 1998, preparations began for a symbolic restoration of a small parcel of the original site, and in 2001 the first grapes were gathered from the two varieties Weisser and Roter Gutedel. The wine from the "Händel" vineyard has been made by the Freyburg cooperative in the Saale-Unstrut region since 2004.

• **Germany's most northerly wine estate** lies on the Schwarze Elster River in Sachsen, only a few miles short of 52° north. Twelve hectares of vineyards are owned by the Franke family in the villages of Jessen and Schweinitz, and in centuries past, wine from this area could claim a number of celebrities among its imbibers. Records show that Martin Luther was an avid fan of wine from the Jessener Gorrenberg, gifted to him regularly in large quantities by Duke Johann Friedrich. Johann Sebastian Bach appears to have been slightly more discerning: years later, he described the Gorrenberger as a "sour drop of wine."

Updates on the previous five vintages

2006

Vintage rating: *Red: 78, White 80*

A year of extreme changes in terms of weather and vegetation presented growers with the most challenging conditions for many a vintage. Following a long winter, a cold and wet spring delayed development of the vines but topped off water levels to an optimum degree. May was warm and dry, June and July hot with occasional showers, and vines were two weeks ahead in annual average vegetation until they were slowed down by a cool, rainy August. Indian-summer conditions in September resulted in fully ripe and healthy grapes, raising hopes for an excellent vintage. These expectations were dashed by the arrival of floodlike rains from late September. Not all grapes were brought in before serious damage was done. Top producers applied stringent selection procedures, and their efforts were rewarded with some respectable results. The overall standard of wines from this vintage has turned out to be somewhere between modest and poor. Exceptions can be found in the smaller and more northerly regions (Ahr!). Adding insult to injury, quantity was well below average for the second year running.

2005

Vintage rating: *Red: 89, Dry white: 89, Sweet white: 97*

Early predictions for 2005 raised expectations of another vintage of the century, combining the fruit of 2004 with the body and power of 2003, comparisons being drawn with the great 1959 and 1947 vintages. Warm weeks in the spring facilitated a problem-free flowering period. Despite ample rainfall in the summer, almost uninterrupted sunshine in the fall led to an early ripening of the grapes. All 13 regions were unanimous in reporting excellent physiological ripeness with an optimum ratio of sugar and acids. However, incidents of rot caused by humid conditions led to a few problems in the Pfalz and Rheinhessen. Stringent selection procedures proved the saving grace for quality-conscious growers, though even some of their wines fell just short of top marks. Mosel, Nahe, Mittelrhein, and Franken excelled. A below-average crop of 9 million hl put many smaller estates under financial pressure.

2004

Vintage rating: *Red: 85, White: 91*

Squeezed between two hyped-up vintages, 2004 is beginning to get the credit it deserves. Refreshing, lively whites, with an excellent balance of fruit, body, and acidity, and reds with a sensible degree of alcohol and supple tannins were the results of an even ripening period with ample precipitation, warm rather than hot temperatures in July and August, and a gentle Indian summer. There was a bountiful harvest of healthy grapes, and 10–11 million hl of wine were produced. The wines were at first more appreciated by the growers than their customers.

2003

Vintage rating: *Red: 94, Dry white: 85, Sweet white: 96*
A record-breaking vintage with the driest and warmest growing conditions in Germany since 1540. The starting gun for the harvest was fired in early August, and by the end of September the first *Trockenbeerenauslese* grapes were gathered. Several growers reported must weights of over 300° *Oechsle*. Harvest conditions were ideal, and most grapes achieved at least *Spätlese* level. Mainly due to the lack of precipitation, quantity was down by 20 percent, with an estimated total of 8 million hl. Expectations of a vintage of the century did not materialize, as many producers struggled to find the right balance between alcohol, fruit, and acidity.

2002

Vintage rating: *Red: 81, White: 92*
An even growing season with an almost perfect balance of sunshine and precipitation was spoiled somewhat by heavy rains from the end of September onward. Low fall temperatures prevented the spread of rot seen in the warmer and more humid conditions of October 2000. Patient growers were rewarded with grapes of *Auslese*, *Eiswein*, and *Trockenbeerenauslese* quality.

GREATEST WINE PRODUCERS

1. Keller (Rheinhessen)
2. Dönnhoff (Nahe)
3. Fürst (Franken)
4. Emrich-Schönleber (Nahe)
5. Geltz-Zilliken (Saar)
6. Schäfer-Fröhlich (Nahe)
7. Knipser (Pfalz)
8. Wittmann (Rheinhessen)
9. Huber (Baden)
10. Reinhold Haart (Mosel)

FASTEST-IMPROVING PRODUCERS

1. Schnaitmann (Württemberg)
2. Mosbacher (Pfalz)
3. Philipp Kuhn (Pfalz)
4. KF Groebe (Rheinhessen)
5. Clemens Busch (Mosel)
6. Adeneuer (Ahr)
7. van Volxem (Saar)
8. Wirsching (Franken)
9. J Ellwanger (Württemberg)
10. Klaus Zimmerling (Sachsen)

NEW UP-AND-COMING PRODUCERS

1. Gutzler (Rheinhessen)
2. Martin Waßmer (Baden)
3. Winter (Rheinhessen)
4. Fritz Waßmer (Baden)
5. Melsheimer (Mosel)
6. Gussek (Saale-Unstrut)
7. Weiser-Künstler (Mosel)
8. Philipps-Eckstein (Mosel)
9. Trenz (Rheingau)
10. Weingut Schloss Wackerbarth (Sachsen)

BEST-VALUE PRODUCERS

1. Merkelbach (Mosel)
2. August & Thomas Perll (Mittelrhein)
3. Didinger (Mittelrhein)
4. Weingart (Mittelrhein)
5. Manz (Rheinhessen)
6. Trenz (Rheingau)
7. Benderhof (Pfalz)
8. Knab (Baden)
9. Sermann-Kreuzberg (Ahr)
10. Wachtstetter (Württemberg)

GREATEST-QUALITY WINES

1. **Kiedricher Gräfenberg Riesling Trockenbeerenauslese 2006** Weil, Rheingau (€250)
2. **Bockenauer Felseneck Riesling Auslese Goldkapsel 2006** Schäfer-Fröhlich, Nahe (to be auctioned; est €100 per half-bottle)
3. **Hunsrück Spätburgunder Trocken "R" Großes Gewächs 2005** Fürst, Franken (€85)
4. **Niederhäuser Hermannshöhle Riesling Großes Gewächs 2006** Dönnhoff, Nahe (€29.50)
5. **Chardonnay Spätlese Trocken "R" 2006** Rebholz, Pfalz (€22)
6. **Birkweiler Mandelberg Weißer Burgunder Spätlese Großes Gewächs 2006** Dr Wehrheim, Pfalz (€24.50)

7. **Kirschgarten Frühburgunder Qualitätswein Trocken 2005** Philipp Kuhn, Pfalz (€19.80)
8. **Burkheimer Schlossgarten Grauer Burgunder Großes Gewächs 2006** Bercher, Baden (€17)
9. **Iphöfer Julius-Echterberg Silvaner Großes Gewächs 2006** Wirsching, Franken (€19.50)
10. **Hades Lemberger Qualitätswein Trocken 2005** J Ellwanger, Württemberg (€20)

BEST BARGAINS

1. **Dürkheimer Schenkenböhl Riesling Auslese 2006** Vier Jahreszeiten Winzer EG, Pfalz (€5.30)
2. **Sylvaner Classic 2006** Teschke, Rheinhessen (€3.40)
3. **Bopparder Hamm Riesling Spätlese Trocken 2006** Didinger, Mittelrhein (€6)
4. **Wollmersheimer Mütterle Gewürztraminer Spätlese 2006** Leiner, Pfalz (€5.20)
5. **Achkarrener Castellberg Weißburgunder Qualitätswein Trocken 2006** Michel, Baden (€6.10)
6. **Spätburgunder Qualitätswein Trocken 2005** Trenz, Rheingau (€6.60)
7. **Grauer Burgunder Kabinett Trocken 2006** Bernhart, Pfalz (€5.50)
8. **Lemberger Qualitätswein Trocken 2005** Wachtstetter, Württemberg (€5.80)
9. **Detzemer Würzgarten Riesling Kabinett Halbtrocken 2006** Walter Rauen, Mosel (€4.90)
10. **Dernauer Hardtberg Frühburgunder Trocken 2006** Sermann-Kreuzberg, Ahr (€7)

MOST EXCITING OR UNUSUAL FINDS

❶ Kerner R Sächsischer Landwein 2006 Klaus Zimmerling, Sachsen (€11 per 50-cl bottle) *Incredibly low yields reveal an essence of apricots, cloves, and bitter almonds hitherto unknown to me from this variety. A Viognier lookalike from the outskirts of Dresden.*

❷ Kaatschener Dachsberg Silvaner Bin 80 Spätlese 2006 Gussek, Saale-Unstrut (€12.50) *Eighty-year-old vines extract fantastic minerality from Sachsen's steepest terraced vineyard. Delicate notes of golden apple and guava complement a slightly spicy and vegetal flavor. The epitome of Silvaner.*

❸ Mandelberg Sangiovese Trocken Barrique Aged 2005 Philip Kuhn, Pfalz (€32) *Hand-harvested from 10-year-old vines; 20 months in predominantly new French oak provide a firm backbone to this vinous rarity, which combines fruit and spices in equal measure.*

❹ Mußbacher Kurfürst Gänsfüßer Qualitätswein Trocken 2005 Staatsweingut mit Johannitergut, Pfalz (€10) *Very popular in the Palatinate five centuries ago, this black grape is now grown only by the Neustadt state domaine. Fruity, spicy, and full-bodied, backed up by firm tannins.*

❺ Cuvée Luitmar Trocken Barrique Aged 2005 Philip Kuhn, Pfalz (€19.20) *A "Euroblend" powerhouse of Blaufränkisch, Cabernet Sauvignon, St Laurent, and Sangiovese from a young winemaker who scooped two first and two second prizes at Germany's premier red-wine competition in 2007. Fruits of the forest mingle with notes of coffee and spices.*

❻ Grossjenaer Blütengrund André Qualitätswein Trocken 2005 Landesweingut Kloster-Pforta, Saale-Unstrut (€9.50) *With its dark color and aromas of cherries, herbs, and spices, this could almost be considered as Germany's answer to Syrah. This impression is backed up by sound acidity and peppery aftertaste, but not the mercifully modest alcohol of 12.5 percent.*

❼ Nebbiolo Qualitätswein Trocken 2003 Brenneis-Koch, Pfalz (€16.80) *Aromas of dark berries and herbs are backed up with spicy nuances and a gentle aftertaste of fine bitter chocolate. Impressive first attempt from young vines.*

❽ Mandelberg Viognier Qualitätswein Trocken 2005 Philipp Kuhn, Pfalz (€12.60) *Kuhn's third exotic entry, though it would be wrong to assume that he can't handle the classics. His Viognier combines the German virtues of minerality and acidity with the grape's concentrated apricot aromas so well known from the northern Rhône.*

❾ Hölder Qualitätswein Trocken 2006 Winzervereinigung Freyburg-Unstrut, Saale-Unstrut (€5.50) *With only 12 ha countrywide, this Riesling x Grauburgunder crossing is an absolute rarity. It combines the fruit of one with the body of the other and has been known to reach Eiswein quality.*

❿ Jessener Gorrenberg Spätburgunder Qualitätswein Trocken 2006 Weingut Hanke, Sachsen (€7) *This qualifies as exotic, since it is probably Europe's most northerly expression of Pinot Noir awarded an official quality designation. What does it taste like? Would I lie to you?*

Italy overview

Nicolas Belfrage MW & Franco Ziliani

Alas, fraud in the wine sector remains as prevalent in Italy as it does even in France, although Italians are not so clever at covering it up.

The Italians do, however, have a nicer word for it—"sophistication"— and the many honest growers and merchants are let down badly by the "sophisticated" few.

In Germany, units from the Nucleo Anti-Sofisticazione (NAS) have uncovered phony bottles of Barolo, Brunello, and Chianti. In the province of Siena, 47 ha of vineyard and 800,000 liters of wine "suitable for making Chianti" have been sequestered by the fiscal police in Operation Clean Wine, preventing up to 3 million bottles (after blending with the not so suitable) of "Chianti Classico" from being marketed through the doubtless innocent offices of three well-known, indeed "leading," wine merchants.

Up in the Veneto, the finance police trumped this with the sequestration of 900,000 fake bottles and, indeed, of an entire "laboratory" in which the phony liquid was apparently put together from the cheapest ingredients. Eleven people were arrested for their part in the scam. Among the labels found were DOC(G)s such as Prosecco, Amarone, and Chianti, and the destination of the wines was intended to be the supermarket chains of Germany. Meanwhile, following Italy's lowest harvest for 50 years, rumors are flying that the late fall months of 2007 have seen droves of Italian bulk merchants roaming the *bodegas* of Spain, buying up dry white Airén like there was no tomorrow. So that's what cheap "Pinot Grigio" will be tasting of next year…

The police, however, are fighting back, not just with raids on vineyards and wineries but with their taste buds, in a tacit admission that they could not tell the difference between Pinot Grigio and Airén (or Sangiovese and Garnacha) if it smacked them in the chops. Yes, the *carabinieri* are sending their lads to wine school, which in Italy means the course of the Association of Sommeliers. That distinctive red stripe down the side of the trousers will soon no doubt become as much a part of the sommelier's uniform as the *tastevin* they wear around their necks and never use (who would?).

Italian wine exports are in rude health

With news of Italian wine exports soaring and new markets opening up, Andrea Sartori of the Unione Italiana Vini commented: "This is the umpteenth indication that the attraction of our wines abroad is confirmed and growing. However, we must not forget that matters are very different concerning the home market. Consumption is stagnant—indeed, in constant decline over the past few years—and the specter hangs over us of various legislative changes that risk compromising the image of a product that is the patrimony of all Italians and that provides work for thousands of people, creates wealth and at the same time profit for the treasury, and contributes to the safeguarding of our lands."

In other words, dear reader, Italian wine, like that of other countries in our civilized world, is well on the road to those big black letters on the label reading: ALCOHOL KILLS.

Short price

Last year we predicted that wine prices in Italy would rise, and they did, in what now seems a modest way. Who was to foretell then that 2007 would prove to be one of the hottest and driest vintages ever, leading to the shortest crop for 50 years? This seems to have been the catalyst for some truly draconian increases at source, due to a variety of factors: the weather; the fact that increases in dry materials, utilities, and labor have been steadily piling up since 2003, while prices have remained largely stagnant; that producers have been cutting profit margins year after year in order to keep up with the challenge from the New World; that the authorities have been clamping down ever more heavily on fraudulent production…

But the main reason that it seems just about everybody in Italy is putting up prices this year—and not by just a few cents—is psychological. There is a renewed confidence in the Italian wine business today that had been eroded following the crisis of the early years of the century. No longer are producers frightened to lose market share; instead they are saying, "We have a good, indeed unique, product; we have certain costs and profit requirements; and we are going to damn well sell our goods at a level that makes us feel we are working for ourselves and not just for the banks." Nor is this phenomenon to be confused with the recklessness of the late 1990s, when Super-Tuscan makers and other fanaticists thought they could think of a price and double it. No, these increases seem more based on realism. And what better time to raise prices than when the market is strong and supply is diminished?

The screw tightens

Two of Italy's most powerful wine groupings, UIV (Unione Italiana Vini) and Federvini, have joined the battle against the politicians in favor of relaxing the currently heavy-handed regulations against alternative closures in DOC and DOCG wines. Rome having answered, in effect, "Computer says no" (except, according to Paolo Castelletti of the UIV, for certain DOCs, excluding Riserva and Superiore categories), the government has come under attack from various influential sources calling for exactly what *Wine Report* suggested last year, namely greater freedom for the producer to choose the closure according to the requirements of the market. Entering the debate on the same side is Ernesto Abbona of the prestigious Piedmontese producer Marchesi di Barolo, who is quoted as saying, "This position puts us in conflict with world distribution, which is complaining about our insistence on using cork." On the conservative side is the AIS (Associazione Italiana Sommeliers—sommeliers' association), which defends the cork as "traditional since the 18th century." The issue, presumably, will run and run all the way up through the channels of the EU, where Portugal (not to mention Italy, on behalf of its Sardinian cork manufacturers) will presumably ensure that nothing changes.

Opinion:
An atypical nation

The possible introduction of IGT Italia is getting Italians up and down the land in a bit of a lather. The overall EU situation is somewhat confused, since Spain's Viñedos de España was passed, despite local objections, only to be refused by the EU on the grounds that classifications must be regional, not countrywide. Meanwhile, France's Vin de Pays des Vignobles de France has gone ahead, but nobody is holding their breath. This perfectly reflects the ambivalent attitude of Italians, a number of big names having voiced their disquiet at the proposal, including Maurizio Zanella of Ca' del Bosco and Marco Caprai of the eponymous *azienda*. The loudest and internationally best recognized voice, however, has been that of Angelo Gaja, who comments, "I recognize that the IGT category has allowed producers to express their creativity, indeed fantasy. Frankly, though, it seems to me that a 'typical' geographic indication applying to all of Italy is just too much."

We couldn't agree more. Indeed the proposition would appear absurd, given, as Gaja points out, that the T in IGT stands for "typical." How on earth can anything from such a diverse country, where just about every region—not to say every district—has its own grape variety and/or style of winemaking, be described as "typical"? Or are we, as Gaja wonders, only talking about non-indigenous ("international") varieties, in which case perhaps one could talk semi-justifiably of a "typical" Italian Cabernet or Chardonnay (we already have the example of Pinot Grigio, which international consumers seem persuaded has a certain Italian typicity). But how "typical" of Italy is Merlot?

Admittedly the Sicilia and Toscana IGTs have been a commercial success, and in a way we are bound to approve of them, since they reduce the confusion of nomenclature that hangs over Italian wines internationally like a curse. But that has nothing to do with "typicity." Perhaps the answer is to create a new category altogether, which recognizes that the real problem is not one of local politics but of marketing. Let the DOC(G) system, like AOC or DO, take care of the "typical." And give to those who don't care about typicity a denomination that does not make them appear faintly ridiculous. Why not "Vigneti d'Italia," indeed? Or just plain "Italia," with no mention of typicity?

Northern Italy

Nicolas Belfrage MW & Franco Ziliani

Transparency has been the buzzword in Eurospeak
for more than a decade, but transparency requires
honesty, and regulators need to be equipped to deal
with the tiny minority of dishonest producers.

Academics in Emilia-Romagna
seem to be taking the lead in
this quest, via chemistry and
geology, to render wine
traceable from the bottle all
the way back to the soil from
which it originated.

Carmela Vaccari, professor of
petrography at the University
of Ferrara, has stated that
within a couple of years it will

NICOLAS BELFRAGE MW   FRANCO ZILIANI

be possible to "identify the area of provenance of a wine, combining the
data from the isotopes of soil samples taken from vineyard plots with the

NICOLAS BELFRAGE MW was born in Los Angeles and raised in New York and
England. He studied in Paris, Siena, and London, earning a degree at University
College London in French and Italian. Nick has been specializing in Italian wines
since the 1970s and became a Master of Wine in 1980, the first American citizen
to do so. He is the author of the double-award-winning *Life Beyond Lambrusco*
(Sidgwick & Jackson, 1985), *Barolo to Valpolicella* (Mitchell Beazley, 1999), and
Brunello to Zibibbo (Mitchell Beazley, 2001). Nick is a regular contributor to
Harpers Wine and Spirit Weekly and *The World of Fine Wine*.

FRANCO ZILIANI is a freelance writer who has specialized in Italian wines
since 1985. He is a regular contributor to the English periodicals *Harpers Wine
and Spirit Weekly*, *Decanter*, and *The World of Fine Wine* (where he is also a member
of the editorial board), the California magazine *Wine Business Monthly*, the Italian
periodicals *Il Sommelier Italiano*, *AIS Lombardia News*, *LaVINIum*, and *VQ*, and the Italian
weekly magazine *Il Corriere Vinicolo* (the official organ of Unione Italiana Vini).
Franco publishes a weekly wine newsletter, *Bvino*, which is mailed to 28,000
wine enthusiasts, and a wine blog, *Vino al Vino* (www.vinoalvino.org).

results of chemical analysis of the contents of a bottle. It will be necessary, though," she continues, "to distinguish between the substances that derive directly from the original composition of the land in question and those that have been added through cultivation practices."

However, as Paolo Barbieri of the Environmental Radioactivity section of Bologna's ENEA (Ente per le Nuove tecnologie, l'Energia e l'Ambiente) explains, this system of analysis is more complicated for wine than for other products to which it might be applied. "Theoretically," he comments, "with chemical analysis it should be possible to understand where a wine comes from: if we have a bottle of unknown provenance, we ought to be able to establish its 'isotope fingerprints' and to verify what zone they correspond to. For wine, however, given the variety not just of provenances but also of grape types having particular characteristics, the research requires a greater period of time."

Over at the University of Piacenza, Professor Mario Fregoni is inching ever nearer to a system of determining the grape varieties contained in a bottle of wine. The problem to date has been that, while the DNA of unfermented grape must be readily established, that of wine is more difficult to ascertain due to the destructive effect, after a short time (two months), of alcohol on the strands of DNA. Professor Fregoni is confident that science will soon overcome this barrier, using not just DNA analysis but also that of aromatic substances and trace elements.

"But," he asks, "what problems might this cause the Italian wine industry, 96 percent of whose wines have been shown by my researches to be blends, properly or illicitly?"

Grapevine

• **MiWine,** the Milan-based biennial wine fair, is to have another go in 2009 despite failing badly in 2004 and worse in 2006. Set up as a rival to Verona's annual Vinitaly, it was wished godspeed by numerous producers and wine professionals, who thought the idea of skipping the odd year was a good one and of not allowing the great unwashed through the doors even better. The result was to spur Vinitaly to even greater heights of arrogance and, alas, success. MiWine has decided to run parallel with a food fair called Tuttofood on June 10–13, 2009. It won't be easy. Following the dismal first attempts, many will be wary of wasting their time and money. And this time MiWine, which previously happened only in years when Bordeaux slept, will fall between Vinitaly and Vinexpo.

Chicken feed

The giant American wine producer Gallo has, it is rumored, teamed up with a couple of large Trentino-Alto Adige producers to supply its Italian brands. For the Ecco Domani brand the lucky supplier will be the Trentino cooperative Mezzacorona (35 million bottles per annum, €120 million turnover, 1,500 grower members with 2,600 ha, plus another 1,000 ha in Sicily). Wines of the Bella Sera mark will instead be furnished by the Swiss-owned Schenk corporation of Alto Adige. Between them, the two producers have, it is said, received commissions for a total of up to 30 million bottles a year, representing turnover of several million euros.

Skin deep

The two regions growing what we, following a ruling by the European Court, are no longer allowed to call "Tocai" have gone their separate ways. The description "Friulano," chosen by Friuli-Venezia Giulia producers, would seem out of place or even improper in the Veneto, since the Veneto grape is not necessarily related that closely to the Friuli version. The solution on the part of the *veneti* has been to excise two letters from the accursed word, reducing it to "Tai." In the case of what was Tocai Rosso, the new name will be Tai Rosso. To celebrate the new moniker, the Colli Berici producers are aiming to take a leaf from neighboring Valpolicella producers and make a fuller, more concentrated version in the *ripasso* style via a light surmaturation of the grapes and a longer period of skin contact.

Back to Friuli, and just to make matters more complicated, it appears that growers have won the right to call their wine "Tocai Friulano" as in the good old days—but only if sold within the confines of Italy.

Grapevine

• **Raise a glass** to world-conquering Oltrepò Pavese Metodo Classico, which, from 2007, has been elevated to the heady heights of DOCG-dom. Long noted for the quality of its Pinot Nero, which must underpin the blend at a minimum of 70 percent, OP Metodo Classico may also contain 30 percent of other Pinot grapes (Bianco, Grigio, and Chardonnay).

Opinion:
The Piedmontese identity

We read with surprise that the Piedmontese don't seem to know in which direction they are headed. Mino Taricco, regional agricultural minister, expressed these doubts during a recent meeting called Vigneto Piemonte ("Piedmontese Vineyard"): "We must find an identity in the briefest time," he said. "The system is sound but is in need of a new impulse, otherwise we risk losing entire agricultural areas and seeing many businesses close as the young fail to replace the old. And we must decide whether we should aim at high quality or lower our sights somewhat to meet the demands of the ordinary consumer, bearing in mind that great wines are not always associated with the region from which they come. We need to work together as a team, not separately as a bunch of prima donnas. And we need," he added, "to realize that fragmentation of wine producers may be a good thing from one point of view but can also constitute a limitation if the *aziende* lack a common strategy for raising the profile of the region in general."

Is this the Piedmont we know and love—the region of supreme Barolo and majestic Barbaresco, of magical Barbera and Dolcetto and a variety of others, not to mention truffles, chocolates, and world-class cuisine? The Piedmont of 28,500 *aziende* cultivating 53,000 ha of vineyard and producing 3 million hl of wine, worth a cool €1 billion in turnover? Where 80 percent of wines are DOC or DOCG? Is this Piedmont now to start worrying about the rest of the world? Let the rest of the world worry about fragmentation—about Piedmont if you like—and let Piedmont carry on doing what it does best, creating art in oenological and gastronomic form. Can we believe that Piedmont is in danger of being broken? If not, let's not try to fix it.

Vintage Report

Advance report on the latest harvest

2007

The most spectacular fact about the 2007 vintage in Italy, nationally, was that it was the shortest since 1948, with just 40.5 million hl nationwide—a reduction of 18 percent against 2006 and some 16 percent in comparison with the average for the past five years. Although the north suffered less in terms of quantity than the south, it was still well short of the average.

The winter of 2006/07 was unusually warm in the north, as well as being extremely dry. Normally, when winter doesn't happen, spring is cold and wet, but April was positively summery in the best touristic sense. There was some rain in May and June, but July and August brought more stifling heat and lack of precipitation except, in some cases, for hail.

Despite the problems, 2007 has turned out positively in most of the north. Nebbiolos (Barolo, Barbaresco, Roero, Gattinara/Ghemme, Valtellina) all fared well, especially from mature vineyards with developed root systems, so we can look forward to some excellent Barolos from 2011 on (2010 for Barbarescos), full of color and concentration, with surprisingly little of that jamminess that afflicted the 2003s. Dolcetto and Barbera seem to have come out well, too, if a little on the alcoholic side. Whites such as Gavi and Arneis are less convincing.

Alto Adige and Trentino had an excellent time of it in 2007, weather conditions in August and September providing warm days and cool nights suitable for balance in whites. Friuli, also predominantly a white-wine area (at least as far as the market is concerned), not only pulled off good quality but went against the national trend, increasing production over 2006 by about 10 percent. In the Veneto, however, there were some deadly hailstorms badly affecting whites in Soave and Valdobbiadene; as a result, prices from both of those areas, especially for Prosecco, can be expected to rise steeply in coming months. Valpolicella was another partial victim of hail, but those who were not hit are talking about excellent quality if reduced quantity.

Updates on the previous five vintages

2006

Vintage rating: Red: 92, White: 93

This was a positive year for northern Italy in terms of both quality and quantity. In Piedmont, June was very hot but July brought less baking temperatures and some rain. August was unusually cool, and there were doubts whether the late ripeners would make it, but September was fine until mid-month, when there were three days of heavy rainfall. Despite more rain falling the following week, the grapes had developed thick skins and there was little or no rot; nor did rain recur until after the harvest. In short, it was a year of balance and complexity, giving wines of good ageability.

Conditions and results in Lombardy resembled those of Piedmont, and white wines in particular were successful. As indeed was the case in Alto Adige and Trentino, where volume was up 10 percent, and quality, apart from odd patches of rot, was good to excellent.

Producers in Veneto and Friuli were also very pleased with the quality of whites and reds alike, although quantity in Friuli was down about 10 percent year on year. In Emilia-Romagna, quantity was steady and quality good to very good, especially for Sangiovese di Romagna.

2005

Vintage rating: Red: 87, White: 89

Not a bad year; a number of good wines have emerged, though little of great note. The biggest problem, perhaps, was the fall in quantity compared with 2004: in the north, between 10 and 25 percent. Quality, however, was also down on 2004, with wines just that bit more diluted and less complex, without being bad. As a matter of fact, there were some quite good drinking wines, but nothing much that you'd be inclined to lay down.

2004

Vintage rating: Red: 92, White: 90

This vintage has largely lived up to its promise as (with 2001) one of the best of the century, not that that's saying too much (yet). Following two difficult years, 2004—a year of measured heat and rainfall, with the added bonus of fine weather at harvest time—came up trumps for both quantity and quality, whites as well as reds. The whites of Friuli, Alto Adige, Trentino, Veneto, Lombardy, and Piedmont show great finesse and brightness, with rich, intense fragrances and aromas. Reds are marked by solid structure, good varietal characteristics, balance, and excellent aging potential. Piedmontese reds Nebbiolo, Dolcetto, and Barbera showed a significant increase in sugar levels, and acid levels were ideal, the wines combining the best of traditional structure with modern roundness, fruit, and balance.

2003

Vintage rating: *Red: 88, White: 82*

This was one of the shortest harvests in the past 50 years, following the absolute shortest, 2002. The year was marked by high temperatures and drought, the good news being that grapes remained universally healthy; the bad being that many were raisined, baked, or overconcentrated. A very early harvest, whites being picked in many cases in the first half of August, reds not much later. Those who go in for mega-wines will like the 2003s, but balance was not easy to come by and was achieved, when it was achieved, in well-tended, deep-rooted vineyards. Barolo and Barbaresco attracted some raves, as did Valpolicella and other reds, but it was a year, when all is said and done, for careful selection.

2002

Vintage rating: *Red: 70, White: 80*

In retrospect, from certain points of view, not as bad as we thought at the time, and certainly not as bad as the international pundits have painted it. In Piedmont, it's true, many Barolos/Barbarescos were produced in tiny quantities or not at all, due to hail damage or general lack of ripeness, but Nebbiolos of lesser denominations, as well as Barberas and Dolcettos, often benefited from the addition of grapes from great vineyards normally reserved for the *crus*. A similar comment could be made in Valpolicella— wines not as big as usual but drinking nicely now. As for whites, some growers in Soave were declaring 2002 to be the best year for a decade, and indeed there was plenty of freshness and nerve, if less alcohol, in whites of other northern zones: Gavi, Alto Adige, and Friuli.

Lists compiled by Franco Ziliani

GREATEST WINE PRODUCERS

1. Bruno Giacosa
   (Barolo & Barbaresco)
2. Cavallotto (Barolo)
3. Giacomo Conterno (Barolo)
4. Giuseppe Mascarello (Barolo)
5. Marchesi Cisa Asinari di Gresy
   (Barbaresco)
6. Rinaldi Giuseppe (Barolo)
7. Ca' del Bosco (Franciacorta)
8. Quintarelli (Valpolicella)
9. Arpepe (Valtellina)
10. Borgo del Tiglio (Friuli)

FASTEST-IMPROVING PRODUCERS

1. Les Crêtes (Aosta Valley)
2. Castello di Neive (Barbaresco)
3. Rizzi (Barbaresco)
4. Brovia (Barolo)
5. Gagliasso (Barolo)
6. Comm. GB Burlotto (Barolo)
7. Walter Massa (Colli Tortonesi)
8. Cavalleri (Franciacorta)
9. Le Salette (Valpolicella)
10. Tedeschi (Valpolicella)

NEW UP-AND-COMING PRODUCERS

1. Adriano Marco & Vittorio (Barbaresco)
2. Ugo Lequio (Barbaresco)
3. Giuseppe Cortese (Barbaresco)
4. Edoardo Sobrino (Barolo)
5. Lo Triolet (Aosta Valley)
6. Les Granges (Aosta Valley)
7. Dirupi (Valtellina)
8. Colline della Stella (Franciacorta)
9. Ferghettina (Franciacorta)
10. Carlo Boscaini (Valpolicella)

BEST-VALUE PRODUCERS

1. Cave des Onze Communes Aymavilles (Aosta Valley)
2. Cave Coopérative de Donnas (Aosta Valley)
3. Piazzo Armando (Barolo & Barbaresco)
4. Produttori del Barbaresco (Barbaresco)
5. Cascina Luisin (Barbaresco)
6. Comm. GB Burlotto (Barolo)
7. Brezza (Barolo)
8. San Cristoforo (Franciacorta)
9. Paolo Rodaro (Friuli)
10. Cantina Produttori Terlano (South Tyrol)

GREATEST-QUALITY WINES

1. **Barbaresco Pajoré Suran 2004** Rizzi, Piedmont (€27)
2. **Barolo Le Rocche del Falletto Riserva 2001** Bruno Giacosa, Piedmont (€110)
3. **Barolo Cascina Francia 2003** Giacomo Conterno, Piedmont (€85)
4. **Barolo Rocche dei Brovia 2001** Brovia, Piedmont (€45)
5. **Barolo Bricco Boschis Vigna San Giuseppe Riserva 2001** Cavallotto, Piedmont (€45)
6. **Barolo Monvigliero 1999** Comm. GB Burlotto, Piedmont (€45)
7. **Amarone della Valpolicella Classico La Marega 2003** Le Salette, Valpolicella (€35)
8. **Franciacorta Brut Blanc de Blancs Collezione 2001** Cavalleri, Franciacorta (€35)
9. **Collio Bianco Vecchie Vigne 2004** Il Roncus, Friuli-Venezia Giulia (€30)
10. **Valtellina Superiore Sassella Riserva 1995** Arpepe, Valtellina (€40)

BEST BARGAINS

1. **Barbaresco Rabajà 2004** Giuseppe Cortese, Piedmont (€25)
2. **Barbaresco Borgese 2004** Piero Busso, Piedmont (€30)
3. **Barbaresco Sorì Loreto 2004** Varaldo, Piedmont (€25)
4. **Barolo Ginestra Casa Maté 2003** Elio Grasso, Piedmont (€35)
5. **Barolo Torriglione 2003** Mario Gagliasso, Piedmont (€30)
6. **Barolo Sarmassa 2003** Brezza, Piedmont (€30)
7. **Dolcetto d'Alba 2005** Luigi Baudana, Piedmont (€10)
8. **Franciacorta Dosaggio Zero NV** Colline della Stella, Franciacorta (€20)
9. **Franciacorta Brut NV** San Cristoforo, Franciacorta (€20)
10. **Garda Marzemino 2005** Cascina Belmonte, Lombardy (€10)

MOST EXCITING OR UNUSUAL FINDS

1 **Vallée d'Aoste Petite Arvine Vigne Champorette 2006** Les Crêtes, Aosta Valley (€13) *Great wines can also be produced from this Swiss variety in neighboring Switzerland. Here's the proof, from Aosta's number-one producer: a wine of outstanding personality and character.*

2 **Vallée d'Aoste Nus Malvoisie Flétrie 2005** La Crotta di Vegneron, Aosta Valley (€22) *Aosta sweet wines are mainly associated with Muscat de Chambave Passito, but this Malvoisie (local biotype of Pinot Gris) is, from this vintage, a wine of more elegance than ever—clean and pure and aromatically complex.*

3 **Barbaresco Basarin 2004** Adriano Marco & Vittorio, Piedmont (€20) *A great vineyard, a great year for Barbaresco, proposed by a small, as yet little-known grower for €20.*

4 **Barolo Santo Stefano di Perno 2000** Giuseppe Mascarello, Piedmont (€40) *Santo Stefano di Perno has been somewhat forgotten among the great vineyards between Castiglione Falletto and Monforte d'Alba, but this outstanding 2000 shows that it is a terroir to be given serious consideration.*

5 **Langhe Bianco Anascetta 2006** Elvio Cogno, Piedmont (€12) *The rarest and least-known vine variety of the Barolo zone is Nas-cetta or Anascetta from Novello. A unique white wine, with incredible aging potential, almost as tannic as a red.*

6 **Langhe Bianco Riesling 2006** GD Vajra, Piedmont (€25) *One of Italy's best Rieslings, this demonstrates the potential for whites at an altitude of 1,300 ft (400 m) in the village of Vergne, just north of Barolo. Still very young, but already excellent, this wine should be purchased and left to age a good while.*

7 **Terrazze Retiche di Sondrio Pignola 2004** Triacca-Marchiopolo, Valtellina (€35) *An authentic oenological rarity, the Pignola grape variety is native to Valtellina (on the border between Lombardy and Switzerland). It resembles Nebbiolo in its aromatic complexity and Pinot Noir in its elegance.*

8 **Valtellina Superiore Grumello Rocca De Piro 2002** Arpepe, Valtellina (€15) *The 2002 vintage was supposed to be the annus horribilis, but it was a great year in Valtellina. This Grumello is the proof: 95 percent Nebbiolo with a splash of local varieties like Brugnola and Rossola.*

9 **Franciacorta Extra Brut Millesimato 2000** Ferghettina, Franciacorta (€25) *Six years on the yeasts, this champagne-style wine combines complexity and structure with great freshness and drinkability.*

10 **Franciacorta Brut Blanc de Blancs Collezione 2001** Cavalleri, Franciacorta (€35) *A great vintage; one of the outstanding producers of Franciacorta; a wine of superior elegance and class that remains splendidly drinkable. Almost on a par with the best champagne.*

Central & Southern Italy

Nicolas Belfrage MW & Franco Ziliani

Consorzio promises to clean up Chianti's act now that it is in full control.

NICOLAS BELFRAGE MW   FRANCO ZILIANI

The Consorzio del Vino Chianti received official authorization from the government as the "authentic controller" of the denomination. The Consorzio is the most recent consortium to be given such powers. Its duty is to define a precise and meticulous plan of controls, approved by the Ministry, for the production of Chianti and to provide itself with an efficient inspectorate to verify this process has been adhered to. All Chianti producers are now subject to the *consorzio*'s authority, whether or not they are members. The inspectorate's task will be to ensure the genuineness and quality of any generic Chianti or Chianti from any of the seven subzones (Colli Aretini, Colli Fiorentini, Colli Senesi, Colline Pisane, Montalbano, Rufina, and Montespertoli) but

NICOLAS BELFRAGE MW was born in Los Angeles and raised in New York and England. He studied in Paris, Siena, and London, earning a degree at University College London in French and Italian. Nick has been specializing in Italian wines since the 1970s and became a Master of Wine in 1980, the first American citizen to do so. He is the author of the double-award-winning *Life Beyond Lambrusco* (Sidgwick & Jackson, 1985), *Barolo to Valpolicella* (Mitchell Beazley, 1999), and *Brunello to Zibibbo* (Mitchell Beazley, 2001). Nick is a regular contributor to *Harpers Wine and Spirit Weekly* and *The World of Fine Wine*.

FRANCO ZILIANI is a freelance writer who has specialized in Italian wines since 1985. He is a regular contributor to the English periodicals *Harpers Wine and Spirit Weekly*, *Decanter*, and *The World of Fine Wine* (where he is also a member of the editorial board), the California magazine *Wine Business Monthly*, the Italian periodicals *Il Sommelier Italiano*, *AIS Lombardia News*, *LaVINIum*, and *VQ*, and the Italian weekly magazine *Il Corriere Vinicolo* (the official organ of Unione Italiana Vini). Franco publishes a weekly wine newsletter, *Bvino*, which is mailed to 28,000 wine enthusiasts, and a wine blog, *Vino al Vino* (www.vinoalvino.org).

not, it should be noted, Chianti Classico. The historic *classico* heartland is not included because the Consorzio del Vino Chianti Classico broke with the general Chianti *consorzio* several years ago. However, Chianti Classico is not the problem; cheap so-called Chianti DOCG is.

It is the Consorzio del Vino Chianti that will, in future, certify that a Chianti is what it says it is, verifying this by a strip of paper over the bottle's neck. The president of the Consorzio, Nunzio Capurso, commented that "with these controls we will be able to intervene to 'cut off' anything that doesn't measure up. Our objective is to maintain the high quality level of the final product." There are those who consider that plain Chianti, which sells in some quarters at remarkably low prices (and is sometimes clearly not what it purports to be) should be demoted to DOC. They believe that a cheap Chianti is an insult to the august DOCG initials. No doubt Signor Capurso would argue the point, claiming that, now that all powers of reward and punishment rest with the *consorzio*, it will be able to put Chianti DOCG back where it belongs. This won't be easy, and we wish them luck—there are a lot of powerful interests vested in inexpensive Chianti.

Cinzano takes over Brunello di Montalcino

Count Francesco Marone Cinzano, owner of Tenuta Col d'Orcia, one of Montalcino's historic wineries, has succeeded Fillippo Baldassarre Fanti as the new president of the Consorzio del Brunello, the organ responsible for the protection and promotion of one of Italy's most famous wines. Francesco Cinzano can be described as "the vine grower of two worlds," since as well as being in charge for over 30 years at Col d'Orcia (142 ha of vineyard, of which 106 are inscribed to Brunello), he has been responsible for another wine estate in Chile. Cinzano was quoted as saying, "I am happy with the honor bestowed on me by the new council and will work to uphold the image and integrity of the terroir-brand Brunello di Montalcino."

Sardinia's golden oldies

Antonio Argiolas, titular head of the firm of Argiolas, sometimes cited as Sardinia's best, having reached the 100 mark with all his faculties intact, is being held up as a prime example of the "fact"—according to a program aired on Italian television's RAI1 channel—that people live longer in Sardinia than in any other part of Italy. Apparently there are 16 centenarians for every 100,000 inhabitants in Sardinia, compared to 4.4 across the entire Italian population. The secret? "The satisfactions that come from working in a prestigious Italian winery ... and, above all [you guessed it], a good glass of wine at mealtimes." The adjective "good" is taken to refer not only to the quality, but also the quantity.

Opinion:
Climate change threatens vineyards

Within a century, some of central and southern Italy's most famous wines, including Brunello di Montalcino, Vino Nobile di Montepulciano, and Chianti Classico, could be extinct. Such is the apocalyptic vision of a study carried out by the University of Florence. According to the authors, the conditions that currently characterize the relevant growing zones could cease to produce grapes of a composition necessary for making fine wines at these latitudes, and they would have to move to the north. The study projects a rise in temperature brought about by "greenhouse gases" largely caused by human activity, of 3.2–7.2°F (1.8–4°C) by the year 2100. Are we to imagine Sangiovese instead of Nebbiolo in Alba, and Nebbiolo instead of Pinot Noir in Burgundy? But such a thing is ridiculous: "terroir" consists of more than just climatic conditions. Extinction, then, would appear inevitable for our greatest wines.

Denomination proliferation

Two new DOCs of central Italy have brought the total number up to 350, an exponential increase over the previous year, with another 35 DOCGs, not to mention the 120 IGTs we complained about last year, raising the total of Italian denominations of one sort or another to over 500. Congratulations are no doubt in order for the good folks in Lazio, whose Moscato di Terracina Spumante Dolce is no doubt set to take the wine world by storm, as, surely, is the amazing Terre di Casole Rosso from Tuscany's province of Siena. But the very obscurity of the wines in question underlines the absurdity of that *campanilismo* we wrote about last year that lies at the heart of Italian wine-naming "policy." Wake up, Italy, and start thinking about the consumer! Yes, we know that we are declaiming in a void, and that no one in Rome is listening, because they know where the votes lie.

Grapevine

• **Carlo Corino,** who died recently at age 68, was a Piedmontese who transformed Sicilian oenology. This technician of great experience and skill was linked with Planeta from the time when, in 1989, Diego Planeta involved him in one of the projects that was to relaunch Sicilian wine. He introduced techniques and systems that, at that time, were innovative and unthinkable in a land still mired in the past. He also played an important role as a consultant, working, among others, for D'Amico and Castel de Paolis in Lazio, Frescobaldi in Tuscany, and Cavit in Trentino.

Vintage Report

Advance report on the latest harvest
2007

If 2007 was short volume-wise in northern Italy, in parts of the center and south it was practically a disaster—especially in Sicily, where the harvest was down 50 percent in places on 2006. It was also one of the earliest harvests ever, with picking beginning in several places in the first third of August. In terms of overall quality, according to Giuseppe Martelli of the Italian Oenologists Union, results were "heterogeneous, with very interesting wines coming from the precocious varieties." The 2006/07 winter was one of the warmest and driest on record. July and August were stiflingly hot, but some longed-for rain arrived in August. September brought generally fine weather and some helpful day–night temperature variations, which enhanced quality considerably.

Tuscany was down 10 percent on 2006. Quality is seen as generally very good, with some points of excellence. Brunello producers are looking forward to some outstanding wines for the third year in four, with more body and extract perhaps than in the more restrained 2004 and 2006 vintages but less elegance. From Montepulciano (Vino Nobile) and Chianti Classico the message is similar. The big problem is prices, which, following several years of restraint and a good but short vintage, are set to rise substantially.

Along the east coast—from the Marche, south to Puglia—volumes were down 15–25 percent, partly due to drought. This has particularly hit the Marche's Verdicchio, but wines should be concentrated and reasonably balanced with high sugar content and adequate acidity. For whites, this will be a year when those who took proper care of their vineyards came out distinctly on top, so careful selection is needed.

Abruzzo is one of the hardest-hit regions in 2007 volume-wise (at least 20 percent down), although the quality of certain Montepulciano-based wines can be expected to be exceptional, with deep colors and rich, structured wines. In Puglia, also some 20 percent down, large swaths of vineyard were left unpicked due to peronospera. Those vineyards that were well tended brought forth some exemplary wines of rich (perhaps slightly jammy) easy-drinking fruitiness. It should be a great year for the Primitivos and Negroamaros of the Salento peninsula, though prices will surely rise.

Sicily was, as indicated, the region most affected by weather conditions in 2007, with some eastern zones down 50 percent. Here, too, with rains alternating with periods of high heat and humidity, peronospera caused havoc, treatment coming at such a cost compared with revenue that many plots were left unpicked. Pantelleria was down 30 percent, but grapes were of great concentration. Generally, in Sicily, quality will be high where growers were willing and able to look after their vineyards properly.

Sardinia distinguished itself from the rest of the south by equaling its 2006 production levels and benefiting from less torrid temperatures. Wines of good character and balance are expected.

Updates on the previous five vintages

2006

Vintage rating: *Red: 95, White: 93*

A year of good quantity and very good to excellent quality in most parts of the center and south. The Tuscan classics—Chianti, Vino Nobile, and Brunello—emerged as wines of complexity and elegance, and even Tuscan whites were unusually balanced. West of the Apennines quantity was down somewhat, but quality was excellent. There are some very good Verdicchios from the Marche and Pecorinos from Abruzzo, suitable for aging. Reds based on Sangiovese and Montepulciano are showing splendidly.

Campania enjoyed a bumper harvest in both senses, increased volume (around 10 percent) being matched by an even higher percentage increase in quality, if such things can be quantified. Poor old Puglia, which used to pride itself on its fine September weather, had yet another rainy one, and while Salento's Primitivo and Negroamaro are reasonably good quality, quantities are down. Sicily and Sardinia were hit by heat and drought and consequently suffered a somewhat short harvest, though the wines have proved to have good perfume and body.

2005

Vintage rating: *Red: 86, White: 88*

This was a year for early pickers. After a less-than-ideal September, conditions worsened considerably in October. The first 10 days were wet, and anything picked after that time was compromised. There are some decent wines, mainly from early-gathered grapes, but they are not of the long-lived variety, more for drinking up. A similar picture prevailed east of the Apennines in the Marche and Abruzzo, where the 30 percent of wines that are good all come from early-picked grapes. Farther south, the picture was brighter, with some very agreeable reds and whites from Puglia and Campania. Sicily and Sardinia, on the other hand, fared very well, with points of excellence.

2004

Vintage rating: *Red: 95, White: 90*

In central Italy and most of the south, all the factors for exceptional wine were in place: growth stages all normal, slow and gradual sugar accumulation, good balance of components in the fruit, and appropriate yield ratio between grapes and wine. What was needed was an exemplary September, bestowing sunny days, a touch of rain, and good diurnal temperature differences. Which was precisely what central viticultural areas west of the Apennines, and some southern areas, received.

In Tuscany, Brunello di Montalcino was given the first maximum rating of five stars since 1997, and it was a similar story in Chianti Classico and Montepulciano. In Tuscany, Romagna, the Marche, Lazio, Campania, and Sardinia, the judgment was "exceptional." Only along the eastern coast, toward the south—in Abruzzo, Molise, and especially Puglia—was quality compromised to some extent by vintage-time rain.

2003

Vintage rating: *Red: 88, White: 80*

A year of drought and very high temperatures, with little relief in the evenings. Vineyards worst affected were toward the center, these conditions being more normal in the south—for example, Puglia's principal reds, Negroamaro and Primitivo, especially those planted to *alberello*, thrived in the conditions. But it was too much for most whites, which tended to emerge flabby and overweight, and many reds, especially those lacking deep roots or planted in well-drained soil. Sugar ripening was very advanced in many places, but it was not necessarily accompanied by polyphenolic ripeness, which made for too many unbalanced wines. As in the north, the classic wines will need careful selection.

2002

Vintage rating: *Red: 67, White: 79*

The shortest vintage in quantity for 50 years, qualitatively 2002 has proved not as bad as predicted. White wines like Verdicchio are fresh and fragrant, with plenty of nerve. Sangiovese in Tuscany had a poor time of it, but there is so much Merlot and Cabernet these days that they can compensate. Lower-than-average temperatures, plenty of rain, and freak weather conditions made a mess of things along the east coast, but modern techniques saved a lot that would have gone down the pan in 1992.

GREATEST WINE PRODUCERS

1. Fattoria di Felsina (Chianti Classico)
2. Montevertine (Chianti Classico)
3. Fontodi (Chianti Classico)
4. Biondi Santi (Montalcino)
5. Case Basse Soldera (Montalcino)
6. Lisini (Montalcino)
7. Fattoria Poggio di Sotto (Montalcino)
8. Valentini (Abruzzo)
9. Agricole Vallone (Puglia)
10. Cantina Santadi (Sardinia)

FASTEST-IMPROVING PRODUCERS

1. Montenidoli (San Gimignano)
2. Frascole (Chianti Rufina)
3. Marchesi Gondi Tenuta Bossi (Chianti Rufina)
4. Il Marroneto (Montalcino)
5. Mormoraia (San Gimignano)
6. Panizzi (San Gimignano)
7. Gorelli Le Potazzine (Montalcino)
8. Podere San Lorenzo (Montalcino)
9. Antonelli San Marco (Umbria)
10. Cataldi Madonna (Abruzzo)

NEW UP-AND-COMING PRODUCERS

1. Castello del Trebbio (Chianti Rufina)
2. Cupano (Montalcino)
3. Stella di Campalto (Montalcino)
4. Le Chiuse (Montalcino)
5. Tenuta Le Calcinaie (San Gimignano)
6. Poggio Argentiera (Morellino di Scansano)
7. La Distesa (Marche)
8. Polvanera (Puglia)
9. Villa Diamante (Campania)
10. Feudo Montoni (Sicily)

BEST-VALUE PRODUCERS

1. Fratelli Vagnoni (San Gimignano)
2. Capanna (Montalcino)
3. Crociani (Montepulciano)
4. Antica Masseria Venditti (Campania)
5. Vadiaperti (Campania)
6. D'Angelo (Basilicata)
7. Candido (Puglia)
8. Fatalone (Puglia)
9. Cantine Due Palme (Puglia)
10. Valle dell'Asso (Puglia)

GREATEST-QUALITY WINES

1. **Brunello di Montalcino Ugolaia 2001** Lisini, Tuscany (€70)
2. **Brunello di Montalcino Riserva 2001** Il Poggione, Tuscany (€40)
3. **Percarlo 2004** San Giusto a Rentennano, Tuscany (€40)
4. **Flaccianello della Pieve 2004** Fontodi, Tuscany (€35)
5. **Chianti Classico 2005** Ormanni, Tuscany (€12)
6. **Vin Santo di Carmignano Riserva 2001** Tenuta di Capezzana, Tuscany (€40)
7. **Vin Santo di Montepulciano 1997** Crociani, Tuscany (€20)
8. **IGT Salento Le Braci 2004** Azienda Monaci, Puglia (€30)
9. **IGT Salento Graticciaia 2003** Agricole Vallone, Puglia (€40)
10. **IGT Val di Neto Gravello 2005** Librandi, Calabria (€25)

BEST BARGAINS

1. **Vernaccia di San Gimignano Vigna ai Sassi 2004** Tenuta Le Calcinaie, Tuscany (€12)
2. **Vernaccia di San Gimignano 2006** Panizzi, Tuscany (€10)
3. **IGT Toscana Rosato Pancolino 2006** Fratelli Vagnoni, Tuscany (€6)

④ **Chianti Classico 2004**
Villa Calcinaia, Tuscany (€10)

⑤ **Fontalloro 2004**
Fattoria di Felsina, Tuscany (€30)

⑥ **Chianti Classico 2005** San Giusto
a Rentennano, Tuscany (€12)

⑦ **Verdicchio dei Castelli di Jesi
Classico Superiore Conscio
2006** Accadia, Marche (€8)

⑧ **Montepulciano d'Abruzzo
Cerasuolo Cerano 2006**
Pietrantonj, Abruzzo (€12)

⑨ **Montepulciano d'Abruzzo 2005**
Nestore Bosco, Abruzzo (€8)

⑩ **Salice Salentino Rosato Le
Pozzelle 2006** Candido, Puglia (€8)

MOST EXCITING OR UNUSUAL FINDS

① **Vernaccia di San Gimignano
Tradizionale 2005** Montenidoli,
Tuscany (€13) *The purest,
most elegant, most enjoyable
interpretation of Vernaccia di
San Gimignano existing today.
A wine unforgettable for its
purity and style.*

② **Vernaccia di San Gimignano
Riserva Isabella 2001** San Quirico,
Tuscany (€12) *Fermented and aged
in oval 23-hl Slavonian oak barrels,
with regular bâtonnage, this
Riserva is surprising for its fullness
and variety of flavor, and richness
of body combined with liveliness
of acidity.*

③ **IGT Toscana Trebbiano 2004**
Tenuta di Capezzana, Tuscany (€18)
*This is what happens when the
lowly Trebbiano Toscano is subject
to massal selection, short pruning,
bunch-thinning, and late picking.
The result is almost burgundian.*

④ **Brunello di Montalcino Riserva
2001** Caprili, Tuscany (€40)
*Everything you could ask of a
Brunello: clean, austere, but with
great aging potential and a real
sense of terroir.*

⑤ **Rosso di Montalcino 2005**
Tenuta di Sesta, Tuscany (€12)
*The 2005 vintage was splendid
for the "second" wine of
Montalcino, when much of what
would normally go to Brunello
ends up as Rosso, as in the case
of this wine from Tenuta di Sesta.*

⑥ **Salento IGT Rosato Magilda
2006** Barsento, Puglia (€10)
*This is a wine dedicated to those
who consider that rosés ought to
have the character and structure
of a red. Unusually, made entirely
from Malvasia Nera as distinct
from Negroamaro, Primitivo, or
Montepulciano.*

⑦ **Murgia IGT Gravisano 2001**
Botromagno, Puglia (€15)
*A passito wine from Puglia, made
from Malvasia Bianca grapes
allowed to dry for about a month.
Complex perfumes, sweet without
being sticky.*

⑧ **IGT Toscana Salvino 2005** Podere
Erbolo, Tuscany (€10) *Virtually a
Chianti Classico even though, by
Italian law, it is only Tuscany IGT
because the Sangiovese is blended
with white grapes, as Chianti
invariably once did but may no
longer. Displays the freshness and
perfumes of traditional Chianti.*

⑨ **Brunello di Montalcino Poggio
al Vento Riserva 1999** Col
d'Orcia, Tuscany (€65) *Suffice it to
say that this is one of the greatest
Brunello di Montalcinos we have
tasted in the past 10 years: a
classic wine of outstanding quality.*

⑩ **Marche Bianco IGT Pecorino
2006** Velenosi, Marche (€8)
*A variety indigenous to northern
Abruzzo and the southern Marche,
Pecorino was in danger of
becoming extinct until rediscovered
about five years ago. This version
demonstrates the potential of the
grape in careful hands.*

Spain

John Radford

The Viñedos de España classification has been rejected by the EU.

JOHN RADFORD

Last year I reported cheerfully that the new classification Viñedos de España would be on the market from the 2006 vintage. In case you missed it, this would have allowed customers to buy a Spanish Tempranillo 2007 or Spanish Garnacha 2007, blended from most of the country (excluding the northwest; a full list appeared in *Wine Report 2008*). France had a similar project called Vignobles de France, and the idea behind them both was to give retail parity with such New World classics as Australian Chardonnay, California Cabernet, and Chilean Sauvignon. The project fell at the last fence when Brussels decreed that you can have a regional wine only if it comes from a specific region, and Spain and France are not regions, but countries. At the time of writing, the original idea is back in the design software but, this being Spain, there are some wines already on local markets calling themselves Viñedos de España, which is legal under Spanish law for sale within Spain. Whether the category will continue is unsure, because Madrid is awaiting a response from Brussels. Meanwhile the French are pressing ahead regardless (see the "Vins de Pays & Vins de Table" report).

JOHN RADFORD is a writer and broadcaster with more than 30 years' experience of the culture, landscapes, architecture, food, and wine of Spain. He is the author of *The New Spain* (Mitchell Beazley), which won four international awards, a new edition of which was published in September 2004; and *The Wines of Rioja* (Mitchell Beazley Classic Wine Series), which was published in November 2004 and won the Livre Gourmand Best European Wine Book award at Barcelona in 2005. He was awarded the Premio Especial Alimentos de España in 2006 by the Spanish government for his coverage of Spanish wines. He co-wrote *Cook España, Drink España!* with Spanish celebrity chef Mario Sandoval, published in 2007, which won the Livre Gourmand Best Wine Book in the World award in 2008. He is also the chairman of the Spanish committee of the *Decanter* World Wine Awards.

Brussels got better press over the new proposals from the Organisation Commune du Marché Vitivinicole (OCM-Vin), at least from the Federación Español del Vino (FEV), which gave the proposals "a cautious welcome." The new regulations include a ban on chaptalization (not a problem in Spain since it's illegal here already), abandonment of the demand for planting rights, abolishing government subsidies for distillation of bulk wines, and quite a few other things. Deals have been done to provide a four-year delay for the distillation program, and the planting-rights legislation has been delayed until 2015. The proposals do, however, provide for grape variety and vintage date to be put on the label of Vino de Mesa, mooted last year, and this has been welcomed by most regions, though not Rioja. The OIPVR is worried that it will chip away at the whole edifice of the DO system (more Rioja news below).

Rioja rules

In addition to mounting its opposition against some of the OCM proposals, Rioja has extended its ban on oak chips (as reported in *Wine Report 2008*) to oak staves and has also made slight changes to other regulations, including a small reduction in the *rendimiento*, probably aimed at demonstrating to the outside world that the OIPVR really is serious about driving up quality.

Grapevine

• **Of the original five** VCPRD zones "promoted" from VdlT under the 2003 wine law, four have leapfrogged the five-year rule to become DO on the grounds that they were already reporting to DO standards in the hope of promotion before the law was changed. They are Tierras de León (2005), Arlanza (2007), Arribes (2007), and Tierra del Vino de Zamora (2007). Benavente remains VCPRD and Valtiendas also became VCPRD in 2007. All are in Castilla y León.

• **There is still no confirmation** of the date when the DOs Ribera del Duero and Cava will become DOCa/DOQ. Cava has been on the stocks since 2003, and Ribera del Duero confirmed in 2007 that it had met all the necessary criteria and was waiting for official confirmation.

• **The Balearic Islands** held their first wine convention in 2007 to pull together ideas for promotion and marketing to the outside world. All the main islands now have some kind of official recognition: Mallorca has two DOs and one VdlT, Menorca, Eivissa, and Formentera all have their own island-wide VdlT, and there's a VdlT Illes Balears that covers the whole archipelago. The wines, particularly on Mallorca, are of vastly improving quality, but it's still cheaper to import Rioja.

• **Spain now has 75 QWPSR zones,** including 5 DO Pago, 2 DOCa/DOQ, 66 DO, and 2 VCPRD. There are 38 "official" VdlT zones, with a further 20 using their own names locally but without, as yet, official sanction nationally.

Unity is strength

The success of the organization Grandes Pagos de España seems to have encouraged other independent producers to band together and share marketing costs and expertise. One of the most recent is Vinos Singulares de Pagos Andaluces (VSPA), with five founder *bodegas*: Marenas (tiny estate in Córdoba), Vetas (even tinier estate in Málaga), Barranco Oscuro (mainland Spain's highest vineyards, in Granada—see "Most Exciting or Unusual Finds" list), Naranjuez (another tiny estate, Sierra Nevada, Granada), and Cauzón (a small estate in Granada). They farm 28 ha between them, of which Barranco Oscuro has 15. As well as the producers, membership of the organization is open to other companies working in the wine business, including retailers. For more details, see vinossingulares.com, but see "What's a pago?" below for confusion over the term "pago."

What's a pago?

Opinion is divided over the use of the word "pago" since it became enshrined in national law in 2003. The term, meaning "vineyard" in this context, has been used in sherry country for centuries, and in recent years a fair number of brand names have been registered using the word—for example, Pago de los Capellanes (DO Ribera del Duero) and Pago del Vicario (VdlT Castilla). These are not to be confused with "DO Pago," which is an appellation reserved for single estates of international significance that have achieved what we might describe as *grand cru* status, beyond the normal DO system. To make matters even more complicated, members of the organization Grandes Pagos de España (GPE; grandespagos.com) use the term to describe their estates, and many, if not most of them, are generally seen as angling for eventual "promotion" to DO Pago status. In general, however, the DO Pago estates don't use the term on their labels, simply describing themselves as "DO Dehesa del Carrizal," etc.

New DO Pago in Navarra

In December 2007, the Señorío de Arínzano, a single-vineyard estate belonging to Bodegas Chivite, was confirmed as Spain's fifth DO Pago, and the first outside Castilla-La Mancha. Although DO Pago legislation is part of national wine law, each regional government has to ratify it before an estate can become its own DO. Until 2005, Navarra had vigorously opposed any fragmentation of the region-wide DO Navarra, but wine surpluses have meant massive declassification and distillation—300,000 hl in 2006. The new law allows for the ad hoc possibility of diversification into subzones or even, in the future, a Vino de la Tierra—something that has been the subject of so-far unsuccessful lobbying for many years by neighboring Aragón. The change in the law may also open the door to DO Pago status for Bodegas Guelbenzu, which seceded from DO Navarra a few years ago.

Back to nature

One of the criteria for membership of GPE, according to the organization's manifesto, is "to defend and promote the culture of single-estate wines, produced in specific vineyards and reflecting the unique personality of their soils, subsoils and climate." This seems to be something of a prevailing philosophy among Spain's winemakers (as witness the new VSPA, above), with an increasing interest in organic and biodynamic viticulture. Encouragingly, exports of Spanish wine in the past year have grown, but the increase in value has been greater than the increase in quantity, which seems to indicate that the market is interested in better-quality wines and is willing to pay for them. It is likely that more and more producers will be looking at the opportunities to improve their wines, and this is very much to be welcomed.

Grapevine

• **Although DO La Mancha** has had sparkling wine on its *reglamento* since 1995, very little happened until the early 2000s when trial and error finally sorted out the wines that were actually salable outside the area. In 2004, four *bodegas* produced about 300,000 bottles. In 2007, there were 20 *bodegas* involved that, between them, broke the million-bottle barrier. Sales are particularly strong in Madrid: possibly a distant echo of the Cava boycott of 2004/05.

• **Mariano García** made his name as winemaker of Vega Sicilia for 30 years and has always been active in the family's Bodegas Mauro (VdlT Castilla y León) and, latterly, Aalto (DO Ribera del Duero) and Maurodós (DO Toro). His son Eduardo is now making wine at Bodegas Astrales (DO Ribera del Duero; see "Most Exciting or Unusual Finds"), as well as at the private *bodega* that makes the house wine for Jesús Ramiro's restaurant at the Science Museum in Valladolid.

• **A small group of** *bodegas* in the province of Palencia has started a campaign for a VdlT Palencia to differentiate the area from neighboring DO Arlanza and the region-wide VdlT Castilla y León. The quality of the wines is high, and the prices are low, so we may see some inward investment from the "big boys" in Ribera del Duero.

• **Capitalizing on its plantations** of old Garnacha on the steep *laderas* (slopes) of the zone, the CRDO Calatayud has created a new classification, Calatayud Superior, for wines made from a minimum of 85 percent Garnacha from vines at least 50 years old and yielding no more than 1.5 kg (3.3 lb) per vine. The wine will carry a special stamp, and the 2005 vintage was launched in 2008. The style is described as having "high color" and a richer concentration of polyphenols.

Opinion:
The usual rants

Still too much irrigation. Still too many "prairie wines," typically made from Chardonnay, Cabernet, and the usual suspects, which show no regional or national character. Still too many cynical supermarket buyers driving down prices (and therefore quality) by profiteering at the expense of the wine producers; one export manager told me she'd received a call from a buyer asking for Crianza Rioja for €1 a bottle ex cellars. She directed him to the exit, but sadly there are still those producers who think they can get a look-in at a low price and crank it up later. They're wrong, of course.

OCM—planting rights and distillation

I believe these proposals are to be welcomed, as well as being inextricably linked. The planting-rights legislation was designed to restrict new plantings to drain the European "wine lake," but the effect has been simply to hand over a large chunk of the market to the New World, which faces no such restrictions. It also means that valuable and perhaps potentially excellent vineyard land is being wasted because it's planted with the wrong vines or is being mismanaged, or because good vineyard land lies fallow while poor vineyards hog the rights. Those private *bodegas* that buy in grapes have always paid on a sliding scale according to grape quality, with the ultimate sanction of rejecting grapes if the quality is not good enough. The co-ops don't have that luxury: they must take everything their members produce, but they, too, are now paying on a sliding scale, with the worst grapes bought in at the "distillation" rate. There will be substandard grapes in any year, from any grower, but there are some growers who produce the lowest common denominator in quality most, if not all, years and are quite happy to take the distillation price. These people should be encouraged to give up grape-growing and do something else. In the short term (until 2015), that would free up planting rights for someone who cares about the grapes they produce. In the longer term, when planting rights go out the window, there will be no market at all for these poor-quality grapes. I wrote a piece for a Catalan newspaper last year welcoming the OCM proposals under the headline "Nobody Wants Crap Wine." I believe this to be truer than ever, given the increased quality focus in Spain. Anything that drives quality up and yields down is to be welcomed. There will always be forces of reaction, and it's up to the *bodegas* (and the co-ops) either to offer them advice on vine husbandry or to show them the door.

Vintage Report

Advance report on the latest harvest

2007

Overall, the summer of 2007 was cool and wet, and sugar levels were reduced in most areas, although many producers welcomed the opportunity to make lower-strength wines with fresher acidity and, making a virtue of necessity, predicting "very good" wines as a result. Nevertheless, the vintage started as early as August 20 in some areas and extended to November 5 in others. A lot of reports speak of "slow ripening" as a positive aspect of all this, but yields are generally down slightly on 2006. The Levant suffered poor weather during the ripening season, with generally average or slightly below-average yields, and most areas had rain during the harvest, which slowed things down. The Upper Ebro (Rioja, Navarra, Aragón) had similarly cool temperatures, as well as high humidity, which brought some problems with fungal diseases in lowland vineyards. The Duero Valley had frost in late September, and producers are predicting an "average" vintage at this stage. Winners in all this were in La Mancha, where Valdepeñas in particular escaped frost, hail, and storms and had a vintage that was two weeks late but nevertheless yielded a bigger harvest than 2006, described by the CRDO as "lower strength but fresher acidity." Overall this does not have the hallmarks of a great vintage, but it may very well be a "useful" vintage: modestly priced and early-drinking.

Updates on the previous five vintages

2006

Vintage rating: *Red: 85 (Valdepeñas: 90), White: 80*
These are proving to be good to very good early-drinking wines. Rioja and Ribera del Duero made a smaller quantity of "aging" wines, and the first of these were released just before Christmas 2008. The style is lighter than previous years and (they hope!) that this will make them salable earlier.

2005

Vintage rating: *Red—Rioja: 95, others: 90; White: 90*
Beginning to drink very well, fulfilling the promise of the *excelente* vintage. Great estates will live for 10 years or more; everyday wines will start to drink in 2009 and have lovely, vibrant fruit and freshness. When the *gran reservas* are released (earliest date October 1, 2009), they should be spectacular.

2004

Vintage rating: *Red—Rioja: 90, others: 80; White: 90*

This was an "isometric" split, with the northwest and south-central doing well and the north-central and northeast having a fair amount of dull and cloudy weather, although the latter part of the ripening season was warm and sunny in most areas. Rioja, particularly, came through with its second *excelente* year of the century.

2003

Vintage rating: *Red: 90, White: 90*

High levels of summer heat right across Spain brought the harvest forward by anything up to 10 days. Parts of Rioja suffered very badly, and vineyards with irrigation survived the best. Penedès harvested excellent reds with the exception of Syrah, which had suffered from the heat, and quantity was down almost everywhere. Most wines are now drinking well.

2002

Vintage rating: *Northeast—Red: 60, White: 60; Southwest—Red: 80, White: 70*

The 2002 vintage in Spain divided roughly into a southwest/northeast divide, with the former having the better time of it. Rioja *gran reservas* are a bit unexciting, although *reservas* from Rioja, Ribera del Duero, and the emerging regions of Castilla y León are drinking well but will probably need decanting, as will any wines older than this.

GREATEST WINE PRODUCERS

1. Alvaro Palacios
   (Priorat, Bierzo, Rioja)
2. Mariano García (Ribera del Duero, Toro, Rioja, Castilla y León)
3. Peter Sisseck (Ribera del Duero)
4. Xavier Ausás, Vega Sicilia
   (Ribera del Duero, Toro)
5. Alejandro Fernández
   (Ribera del Duero, Toro, La Mancha)
6. Carlos Falcó (Dominio de
   Valdepusa, Pagos de Familia)
7. Miguel Torres (Penedès/Catalunya)
8. Marcos Eguren (Rioja, Toro)
9. Telmo Rodríguez (ubique)
10. Benjamín Romeo (Rioja)

FASTEST-IMPROVING PRODUCERS

1. Bentomiz (Málaga)
2. La Setera (Arribes)
3. Gordonzello
   (Tierra de León)
4. Rejadorada (Toro)
5. Otero (Benavente)
6. Huerta de Albalá (Cádiz)
7. Peique (Bierzo)
8. Viyuela (Ribera del Duero)
9. Frutos Villar
   (Cigales, Toro, Ribera del Duero)
10. Barranco Oscuro
    (Contraviesa-Alpujarra)

NEW UP-AND-COMING PRODUCERS

1. O Fournier (Ribera del Duero)
2. Abad (Bierzo)
3. Buezo (Arlanza)
4. Los Astrales (Ribera del Duero)
5. Palacio Quemado (Ribera del Guadiana)
6. Los Aguilares (Sierras de Málaga)
7. Peique (Bierzo)
8. Finca Anfora (Ribera del Andarax)
9. Pagos del Rey (Rioja)
10. Benito Urbina (La Rioja)

BEST-VALUE PRODUCERS

1. Pago de Larrainzar (Navarra)
2. Fernandez de Manzanos (Rioja)
3. Casa de La Viña (Castilla)
4. As Laxas (Rías Baixas)
5. Casa de la Ermita (Jumilla)
6. Agustí Torelló (Cava)
7. Felix Solís (Valdepeñas)
8. Palacio de Bornos (Rueda)
9. Muruve (Toro)
10. Señorío de los Llanos (Valdepeñas)

GREATEST-QUALITY WINES

1. **Ribera del Duero Unico 1982**
   Vega Sicilia (€395)
2. **Ribera del Duero Pingus 1999**
   Dominio de Pingus (€485)
3. **Priorat L'Ermita 2002**
   Alvaro Palacios (€395)
4. **Rioja Contador 2003**
   Benjamín Romeo (€350)
5. **Penedès Dominio Cusiné 2003**
   Parés Baltà (€270)
6. **Toro Termanthia 2004**
   Eguren (€126.70)
7. **Bierzo Moncerbal 2003**
   Descendientes de J Palacios (€92.30)
8. **Arribes Bruñal 2004**
   Ribera de Palazas (€112.21)
9. **Bierzo Pieros 2001** Estefanía (€67)
10. **Ribera del Duero 2004**
    O Fournier (€35)

BEST BARGAINS

1. **Tierra del Vino de Zamora Brochero 2006**
   Teso Blanco (€2.50)
2. **Toro Muruve Joven 2006**
   Frutos Villar (€2.50)
3. **Cigales Calderona Joven 2005**
   Frutos Villar (€2.50)
4. **Almansa Higueruela 2006**
   Tintoralba (€3)
5. **Bierzo Joven 2006**
   Peique (€3.40)
6. **Arribes Joven 2005**
   La Setera (€4)
7. **VdlT Castilla Infinitus Tempranillo 2006**
   Martínez Bujanda (€4.25)
8. **Ribera del Duero Joven 2005**
   Viyuela (€5)
9. **Bierzo Tilenus Joven 2006**
   Estefanía (€5)
10. **Tierra de León Peregrino 2004**
    Gordonzello (€6)

MOST EXCITING OR UNUSUAL FINDS

1. **Vino de Mesa Blancos Nobles Clásico 2005** Barranco Oscuro (€8.93) *From Contraviesa-Alpujarra, the main grape is the Vijiriega, extinct elsewhere on the peninsula, with some Riesling, Sauvignon Blanc, Vermentino, and others. Winemaker Javier Valenzuela's vineyards are at an altitude of 4,200–4,430 ft (1,280–1,350 m) and have few problems with insect pests and cryptogams. Javier believes that the wild herbs that surround the vineyard affect the microflora on the grape and, because he ferments with natural yeasts, add to the character of the wine.*

❷ **Sierras de Málaga Ariyanas Tinto 2006** Bentomiz (€12.50) *I discovered this bodega about four years ago, when it was making sweet whites from Malvasia and Moscatel (which it still does), but this is its first venture into red. It's made from 40 percent Tempranillo, 40 percent Cabernet Sauvignon, and 20 percent Romé, a grape local to the Málaga area. The wine has six months in new French and American oak barricas.*

❸ **Monterrei Godello 2006** Crego e Monaguillo (€9.50) *Proving that there is life beyond Albariño and it's alive and kicking in Galicia's smallest DO. The Godello is coming into its own, here helped by a little Treixadura from a small family firm, whose first vintage was in 2003. The name means "Priest and Altar-Boy" in Galego.*

❹ **Arlanza Varietales 2004** Buezo (€13) *The 2004 was the first vintage from this new company, in a brand-new bodega in the wilds of Arlanza. They make three wines with varying grape mixes, but this one is 50 percent Tempranillo and 25 percent each of Cabernet Sauvignon and Merlot, with 12 months in predominantly French oak.*

❺ **Ribera del Duero Astrales 2005** Los Astrales (€24) *The next generation of the García dynasty makes its mark: Eduardo, son of Mariano and grandson of Mauro García, is the winemaker at this new bodega, founded in 2000, with 29 ha of vines, of which 15 ha are old, some as old as 70 years.*

❻ **Tierra del Vino de Zamora Brochero 2006** Teso Blanco (€2.50) *Founded in 1999, this is another improving bodega in a new DO zone with 45 ha of Tinto*

Fino, an average age of 45 years, and some 150-year-old vines. The top wine, Sexmil Edición Summa, sells for €60, but Brochero is a bargain at €2.50.

❼ **Illes Baleares Pessigolles dels Cavallers 2005** Galmes i Ribot (€14.88 per 50-cl bottle) *The name means "Ticklishness of the Horsemen," and it's a beguiling late-harvest Chardonnay from Mallorca, usually served with the traditional ensaimada pastry.*

❽ **Vino de Mesa Plot 2006** Benito Urbina, La Rioja (€8) *This is made from Tempranillo in a single-vineyard "plot" of this respected Riojano producer, but it's not Rioja, because the winemaker might want to buy in Tempranillo grapes from elsewhere in dodgy years. He didn't have to do so in 2006, but he still badged the wine as Vino de Mesa, just in case.*

❾ **Ribera del Duero Parcela El Nogal 2003** Pago de los Capellanes (€35) *This is one of the best individual vineyards within the estate of the Pago de los Capellanes and, according to the winemaker, made only in the best years. It's pure Tempranillo and aged in new French oak for 22 months. Quite outstanding.*

❿ **Priorat Oli Verge 2007** Alvaro Palacios *This was a Christmas embarrassment for me last year. Alvaro sent me a bottle as a gift, and I told the assembled family to assume the genuflect position as I opened it to try with roast goose. Catalan speakers will be ahead of me, of course, as I poured the fabulous, light-green, cold-pressed virgin olive oil. It was wonderful on the roast potatoes. If only it had been labeled "Aceite Virgen"…*

Sherry

Julian Jeffs QC

Global sales of sherry increased in 2007, indicating that the tide might be turning at last.

JULIAN JEFFS QC

In 2006, sales of sherry were slightly down, yet again, as the export market continued its decline, although the domestic market was very slowly rising. In 2007, however, sales increased, albeit by a modest 2.8 percent. The trend is upward this time, and export markets would have been even better if sales had not declined in the Netherlands and Germany. Although traditional sherry drinkers are beginning to fall off the perch, their place is slowly being filled by younger drinkers, helped by the rise of tapas bars.

The enthusiasm of young people when they are given the chance to try the finest wines is impressive. They are even beginning to say that sherry is "cool"—as it should be, of course. There is a continuing shift from cheap wines to those of top quality, and these are themselves absurdly cheap for what they are, though prices are rightly rising. They remain the best-value mature wines obtainable anywhere. Some at least have been

JULIAN JEFFS QC became a Gray's Inn barrister in 1958, attained Queen's Counsel in 1975, and retired from practice in 1991, although he continued as a Deputy High Court Judge until 1996. His love of sherry began in 1956, when he was a sherry shipper's assistant in Spain, and this led to a passion for writing when his book *Sherry* (Faber & Faber) was published in 1961. He began a two-year stint as editor of *Wine and Food* in 1965, and in 1971 he created Faber & Faber's radically new Wine Series. Over the next 40-plus years he commissioned many of the most respected, long-lasting, and definitive works on wine. He held this position until 2002, when Faber & Faber sold the Wine Series to Mitchell Beazley. Julian has been chairman (1970–72), vice president (1975–91), and president (1992–96) of the Circle of Wine Writers, winning the Glenfiddich Wine Writer award in 1974 and 1978. His books include *The Wines of Europe* (Faber & Faber, 1971), *The Little Dictionary of Drink* (Pelham, 1973), and *The Wines of Spain* (Faber & Faber, 1999).

recognized as such, to the extent that they are on allocation, and one specialist *bodega* actually sold out in 2007. Their shippers sound very happy, and more become available each year.

It has been very difficult indeed to limit the "Greatest-Quality Wines" to 10, since there are at least three times as many, while the list of "Best Bargains" has been just as difficult; it is hard to find a sherry that is not a bargain. It is the shippers of the cheaper ones who are suffering, while supermarkets use their muscle. There is little if any profit at this end of the trade. So I would advise anyone to make the most of the finest wines before their prices inevitably rise. Another success area is sherry vinegar—a very fine condiment that is finding favor with all the best chefs and is a useful sideline.

Age-dated wines

Although still accounting for a very small proportion of total production, this is an area that is on the up. At the last count it had increased by 172 percent. An up-to-date list was published in *Wine Report 2008*, and there have not been many changes. CAYDSA, the shipping arm of the big cooperative in Sanlúcar de Barrameda, has entered the list with a VORS palo cortado, San Griel. Other shippers in this town have been active, too. Gaspar Florido is marketing a VOS palo cortado and a VORS oloroso, while the renowned Pedro Romero has added a VOS palo cortado, Old Pedro Romero Prestige, to its impressive list of three VORS wines. One name has disappeared—Gil Luque—but this can be regarded as temporary, since the company has been taken over and is being reorganized. The wines are still there and are being cherished.

More acquisitions

Consolidation continues and makes good sense. The latest has been the purchase by the burgeoning business José Estévez of the long-established and excellent Sanlúcar *bodega* Hijos de Rainera Perez Marín, taking with it the Jerez subsidiary M Gil Luque, specializing in age-dated wines. The Gil Luque wines are being relocated in a fine old *bodega* owned by Perez Marín in El Puerto de Santa María, where they will be carefully tended. Some time ago, Estévez bought the oldest and one of the finest *bodegas*, Valdespino. Its wines have been continued and are as good as ever, so the new takeover can be regarded only with approbation.

Opinion:
The way ahead

There are clearly two ways ahead: to concentrate on quality, and to explore new markets. Quality wines are not necessarily expensive. Finos and manzanillas do not require, and cannot have, great aging. They are also extremely versatile. Now that they are being shipped at 15 percent ABV, people are beginning to see how well they go with food, and one only has to compare their prices with those of alternative white table wines to get the point. At the other end of the scale, the fine dessert olorosos are superb with cheese. Here the comparison in price is with very old tawny and vintage port. As for the export markets, sherry is beginning to catch on in East Asia. In Japan there is an exotic taste for sherry cocktails, and why not? To make a cocktail with an age-dated sherry would be as ill-inspired as to make one with a VSOP brandy or a malt whiskey, but that leaves plenty to choose from. And how about sherry with Chinese food?

Grapevine

• **Reduced crops in central Spain** and in some parts of France have resulted in a substantial increase in the price of alcohol used for fortification. This will have little or no impact on top-quality wines but is a misfortune to the shippers of cheap, especially BOB, wines. Since these were making little or no profit before, prices will simply have to go up, and it could be a body blow to some of their shippers. The situation is exacerbated by an increase in the price of fuel.

• **Moving with the times** (or perhaps a little ahead of them), there is a private initiative to install a new high-resolution satellite-based vineyard-control system, devised by the Spanish astronaut Pedro Duque, for the vineyards. This is expected to give early warning of vine diseases and to monitor crop ripeness and yield.

• **Sherry vinegar** is now well established. It has become a favorite with French chefs and is even being promoted in Italy. This is a profitable sideline for nearly all the sherry shippers, and some companies have been established to make nothing else. There is now a new category of "Reserva"—vinegars of great concentration that may only be sold bottled.

• **Table wines made from grapes** grown in the sherry vineyards, which were successfully pioneered by Barbadillo and are now made by several of the shippers, were prohibited from putting "Jerez" on their labels. Under new rules likely to come into being very soon, this prohibition will go, but they will definitely fall outside the Sherry DO and will not be sold as sherry.

Vintage Report

Advance report on the latest harvest

2007

After some short harvests, things could hardly have gone better. Following several years of drought and early harvests, rainfall was 24.4 in (620 mm) and, more importantly, was ideally distributed throughout the growing period. Temperatures in July and August were mild. Harvesting was back to the traditional time, the end of August and the beginning of September, but it rained heavily on September 12–13, by which time many grapes had been gathered, but this caused a few minor outbreaks of botrytis in some areas, and big logistical problems. A total of 10,078 ha of vineyards were in production, yielding 251,749,440 lb (114,191,625 kg) of grapes, 32 percent more than in 2006 (though this was an unusually short vintage). *Baumé* levels were on the low side at under 11 degrees. The maximum qualification per hectare was set at 66.5 hl/ha, giving 126,000 butts of qualified must, making up somewhat for the shortfall in the two previous years. Despite the slightly low strength, good wines will be made, and the yield was a great relief.

Updates on the previous five vintages

2006

Vintage rating: *98*

The consistently high ratings of sherry vintages must be the envy of nearly all wine growers in other places. The vintage began early, on August 14, and was rather low in quantity owing to drought—though not as low as had been feared because a storm just before the vintage (not an unusual occurrence) helped the grapes; but it was of very good quality. The average *Baumé* was 12.1 degrees. Production was 66.3 hl/ha, giving 113,295 butts that qualified for the DO. There was plenty of free-run juice.

2005

Vintage rating: *98*

After some abundant vintages, the small quantity of top-quality must came as a relief to the shippers if not to the growers. Very ripe, small, healthy grapes gave an average *Baumé* of 11.93 degrees with a yield of 66 hl/ha; 97,000 butts qualified for the DO, but there was not a lot of free-run juice for finos.

2004

Vintage rating: *90*

A wet year but with the rain well distributed. A damp spring caused mildew in a few areas, though it was dry before the vintage and the grapes were harvested in excellent conditions. Production was 81.62 hl/ha, with 138,244 butts qualifying for the DO. The *Baumé* was 11.3 degrees.

2003

Vintage rating: *95*

A yield of 64 hl/ha provided 138,000 butts of DO-qualified wine. After a hot summer, some of the grapes were overripe but very mature, giving a *Baumé* of 12 degrees.

2002

Vintage rating: *95*

A yield of 64 hl/ha provided 137,888 butts of DO wine. Quality: excellent—good maturity with 11 degrees *Baumé*.

Grapevine

• **Fears expressed** that the beautiful old *bodegas* of Argüeso near the waterfront at Sanlúcar, having been bought by a rich property developer, would be razed have proved groundless. They are untouched, and the old team is in place, continuing to make their excellent wines.

• **New categories** of "fino superior" and "manzanilla superior" are being actively planned, but regulations are not yet in place.

• **The *cupo*** is currently set at 37 percent. That is, no *bodega* will be able to sell more than 37 percent of stocks held on September 1.

• **A team from the University of Seville** has published a paper in the *Journal of the Science of Food and Agriculture* showing that a moderate consumption of biologically aged sherries (finos and manzanillas) can reduce by a third the bad cholesterol in the bloodstream, has an anti-carcinogenic effect, slows down the development of senile dementia, and has other health-giving properties. It is pleasant to have confirmation of what one always knew.

• **Valdivia,** the premium bodega established in 2006 by outside investors (construction industry), has been bought by Garvey.

• **Domecq brands** have been sold by Pernod Ricard to Osborne. (NB: not the Domecq or John Harvey brands, but individual brands Amontillado 51-1ª, Botaina, Capuchino, La Ina, Rio Viejo, Sibarita, Venerable, and Viña 25, which will now appear under the Osborne umbrella brand.)

• **Marqués del Real Tesoro** (José Estévez) has bought La Guita, which was apparently suffering from financial problems and quality-control issues.

GREATEST WINE PRODUCERS

1. González Byass (including Croft and Wisdom & Warter)
2. Beam Global España (Domecq, Harveys)
3. Osborne
4. José Estévez (including Valdespino, Perez Marín, Gil Luque, and Real Tesoro)
5. Hidalgo-La Gitana
6. Barbadillo
7. Garvey (including de Soto and Sandeman)
8. Emilio Lustau/Luis Caballero
9. Williams & Humbert
10. Sánchez Romate

FASTEST-IMPROVING PRODUCERS

1. José Estévez
2. Alvaro Domecq
3. Pedro Romero
4. Dios Baco
5. Pilar Plá Pechovierto
6. Bodegas 501
7. Emilio Hidalgo
8. Williams & Humbert
9. Delgado Zuleta

NEW UP-AND-COMING PRODUCERS

1. Alvaro Domecq
2. Tradición
3. Rey Fernando de Castilla
4. Pilar Plá Pechovierto
5. Gutiérrez Colosia
6. Ferris
7. Dios Baco
8. Valdivia

BEST-VALUE PRODUCERS

1. González Byass/Wisdom & Warter
2. Beam Global España
3. Williams & Humbert
4. Emilio Lustau
5. José Estévez
6. Bodegas 501
7. Gutiérrez Colosia
8. Federico Paternina
9. Herederos de Argüeso
10. Delgado Zuleta

GREATEST-QUALITY WINES

This selection has been hard to make, since there are now so many top-quality wines, but I have aimed to include wines of every style and age, which are listed in order of price, bearing in mind that a good age-dated wine must necessarily be more expensive than a good fino.

1. **San Léon Manzanilla** Herederos de Argüeso (€5.10)
2. **Tio Pepe** González Byass (€7.60)
3. **Pastrana Manzanilla Pasada** Hidalgo-La Gitana (€11)
4. **Noé Pedro Ximénez Muy Viejo VORS** González Byass (€36)
5. **Amontillado del Duque VORS** González Byass (€20 per half-bottle)
6. **Amontillado 51-1ª VORS** Domecq (€50)
7. **Sibarita Oloroso VORS** Domecq (€50)
8. **Palo Cortado VOS** Emilio Lustau (€95)
9. **Cardenal Palo Cortado VORS** Valdespino (€150)
10. **Solera PΔP Palo Cortado** Osborne (€150)

BEST BARGAINS

What is a bargain? Generally, with sherry as with everything else, you get what you pay for, but often you are surprised and would have expected to pay more. This applies to the first five "Greatest-Quality Wines." Happily, there are a great many sherries that could be counted as bargains. Those that follow are just a selection.

1. **Las Medallas Manzanilla** Herederos de Argüeso (€3.60)
2. **La Gitana Manzanilla** Hidalgo-La Gitana (€4.65)
3. **Antique Oloroso** Rey Fernando de Castilla (€28)
4. **Royal Corregidor VOS** Sandeman (€29.99)
5. **Palo Cortado VORS** Barbadillo (€30.40)
6. **Sacromonte Amontillado** Valdivia (€32.50)
7. **Sacromonte 15 Year Old Oloroso Seco** Valdivia (€33.50)
8. **Noé Pedro Ximénez Muy Viejo VORS** González Byass (€36)
9. **Dos Cortados** Williams & Humbert (€36.50)
10. **Palo Cortado de Bandera VORS** Gil Luque (€60)

MOST EXCITING OR UNUSUAL FINDS

1. **La Goya Manzanilla Pasada** Delgado Zuleta (€5) *Sometimes one meets an old friend and finds that with the passage of time he has become more elegant. This is just such a case, and I was delighted to find it again.*
2. **Inocente Fino** Valdespino (€10) *This has long been one of my favorite finos, but of late it has changed. It used to have so much age that it was really a fino-amontillado. Under Valdespino's new ownership it still*

has ample age but is definitely a fino—and a very good one.

3. **El Maestro Sierra Viñas Viejas Oloroso** Pilar Plá Pechovierto (€68) *A classic oloroso, generous but not sweet, with a fine nose and great length, made in the only bodega in Jerez run entirely by women.*
4. **Amontillado Prestige 50 Don VORS** Pedro Romero (€40.37 per 50-cl bottle) *Delicate nose, with the austerity of a true Sanlúcar amontillado, complexity, and great length.*
5. **Palo Cortado** Harveys (€50) *A delightful example of this elegant style of wine. Not age-dated but fully mature, with a fine nose, complexity, and length. A wine to drink with infinite pleasure—and that, after all, is what it is all about.*
6. **Oloroso** Harveys (€50) *This is a delightful mature oloroso with fine mouthfeel and excellent length. An oloroso companion for the palo cortado, and what is written above equally applies.*
7. **Amontillado Navazos** Sánchez Ayala (€50) *A completely new discovery from a small bodega in Sanlúcar whose wines I have never tried before. Sanlúcar amontillados are lighter than those from Jerez. A perfect example of its kind.*
8. **Lustau Oloroso VOS** Emilio Lustau (€95) *VOS wines are more approachable than VORS, and this one is just the right age for easy drinking, with more than enough age to give it excellence.*
9. **Palo Cortado Añada 1978** González Byass (€120) *Vintage wines are always fascinating to try, and González Byass has a fine line in them. This is the latest that has come my way and is a wonderful example, well worth seeking out—and paying for.*

Portugal

Charles Metcalfe

In 2007, Portuguese wine sales to the United States grew by 34 percent in value, while sales to the UK increased by 6 percent.

CHARLES METCALFE

This has handsomely repaid the investment recommended by the American management and economic consultant Michael Porter, who was commissioned to write a report on Portuguese export potential by the Portuguese government in the early 1990s. One of his key recommendations, delivered in 2003, was that Portugal should put significant funds into developing wine sales in the United States and the UK. Sales in the UK responded more quickly than in the States, but last year the latter came good.

Another Porter suggestion was the establishment of the Fine Wines Board, a panel to recommend wines particularly suited for certain export markets. This met for the first time in Lisbon in February 2007. There were judges from three target markets—the US, the UK, and Germany. A total of 27 Seals of Merit were awarded. Each panel had two judges from the target market and one Portuguese judge, and it seemed to

CHARLES METCALFE's latest book, *The Wine and Food Lover's Guide to Portugal*, was published in 2007 (Inn House Publishing). Past careers as an opera singer, investment analyst, tour guide, security guard, and freelance cook provided the perfect preparation for founding Britain's second consumer wine magazine (*Wine International*) and the International Wine Challenge. Having served a 12-year term as drinks expert on Richard and Judy's *This Morning*, Charles will talk to anybody and everybody about wine—from vast corporations to local wine societies. His palate is much in demand in tasting competitions, and he has judged in Australia, France, Germany, Italy, New Zealand, Portugal, South Africa, and Spain, as well as being co-chairman of the International Wine Challenge, the biggest wine competition in the world. He writes sporadically for a number of publications and occasionally embarrasses his children by popping up on TV programs as a drinks presenter.

the non-Portuguese judges that the Portuguese judge on each panel marked the wines much less generously than the foreigners. The result is that the final awards are more of a reflection of a rather restricted Portuguese view of what should be rewarded than the views of the judges from the target markets.

Alentejo expansion

After all the takeovers and changes of ownership of 2006, 2007 was a year of consolidation in the Portuguese unfortified-wine industry. The one region that continues to grow apace is the Alentejo, where plantings have risen over 50 percent in the past 10 years. The varietal profile of the Alentejo vineyards is changing, too. Although 2007 was a fantastic year for it, Aragonez is not an obvious variety to grow in the Alentejo. In normal (hot and dry) years, Aragonez gets high sugar readings way before the tannins are anywhere near ripe. Trincadeira, another of the main grapes planted, is very prone to rot if there's any rain. More and more growers are turning to Touriga Nacional, which makes delicious wine in the Alentejo, or to French varieties. One of these, Alicante Bouschet, despised in its native France, is an honorary Portuguese national. The varieties of the northern Rhône are also increasingly popular with growers, particularly Syrah. And 2007 saw the release of Portugal's first pure Viognier (see Most Exciting list).

Estremadura no longer

In *Wine Report 2008* we mentioned rumors that Estremadura and Ribatejo were courting, with the intention of merging into one VR region, probably to be called Lisboa. Well, we do have a new VR region, and it is called Lisboa, but it is the old Estremadura VR region renamed. Estremadura has scooped the name, and the VR Ribatejano is still separate and called by its old name. What went wrong? Apparently, the two regions could not decide which would provide the president of the new, enlarged VR Lisboa region, and Ribatejo went off in a huff. This is something that they may regret…

Grapevine

• **The Sala Ogival** in the Praça do Comércio in Lisbon has a sibling in Porto. Porto already has the Solar do Vinho do Porto, where you can taste a phenomenal range of ports. Now it has its own Sala Ogival, in the magnificent Palacio da Bolsa, where an ever-changing range of unfortified wines from all over Portugal is on show. And it's all free. ViniPortugal, which runs both these tasting centers, is looking for the right site in the Algarve. That would really bring wines to British visitors.

Opinion:
Staying unique

Portugal has to put some effort into promoting its great native grapes. If Portugal has one true USP, it is these local varieties. Of course, there are other reasons why Portuguese wines are so full of character, including the variety of terroir: old sandy soils, rich alluvial earth, steep granite mountains, winding schist terraces. But you can find all these in other countries as well. Okay, the splendid vineyards of the Douro are an exception, but you can't promote a whole country's wines on the basis of one region. The star local grapes are all over the country, more so today than ever. Now that growers and producers have realized how much more flexibility and choice are offered by VR (*vinho regional*) rules than by DOC (*denominação de origem*), they are grubbing up or grafting over some of the less successful local grapes in their regions and replacing them with top varieties such as Alvarinho, Arinto, Touriga Nacional, Touriga Franca, Aragonez, and Alfrocheiro. And since Portuguese wines have no prohibitions on using grape names on labels, in contrast with most French AOCs, producers can use these grape names bold and clear to give the drinker an idea of the style of wine inside the bottle. But outside Portugal this is no use, unless non-Portuguese drinkers have some idea of the flavor and style of wines from these wonderful grapes. So the Portuguese should tell them! Otherwise, with the increasing internationalization of wine, there is a risk that other countries will discover these vine jewels, plant them, and shout about them—and the USP for Portuguese wines will be unique no longer.

Grapevine

• **Luís Pato,** the doyen of Bairrada, stopped using "Bairrada" on his labels some years ago, after disagreements with the local regulatory authorities. After considerable local pressure, he has relented and returned to the Bairrada fold, but with only one wine. He has made it with his daughter Filipa, also a skilled winemaker, and it is (shock, horror) a sweet white, made by cryoextraction. This is not something they'd ever seen in Bairrada before, and it took three tries before it was approved by the local tasting panel.

• **Portuguese wine producers** had gotten used to doing their own thing after years of rather half-hearted promotion through government agencies. First out as a marketing group was G7, consisting of seven of the large, well-established exporting companies. Last year, Sogrape left G7, citing a need to follow its own star. For just over a year now, G7 has had six members but gives no sign that the name is going to change.

Vintage Report

Advance report on the latest harvest

2007

This year, the north of Portugal saw an end to the depletion of water reserves caused by the last four dry years, with enough rain in October, November, and February to restore the balance. Much of the rest of the year was damp, too, and these unusual conditions favored the spread of fungal diseases such as mildew. For conscientious grape growers who treated their vines, this caused no real problems. But for part-time growers, or those who had seen two very dry years with no disease risk and had done no treatments, mildew caused large reductions in quantity, with no corresponding quality increase.

For most of Portugal, 2007 was an unusually cool vintage. Poor fruit set in June and disease pressure resulted in quantities about 20 percent down, with the Minho, Beiras, and Alentejo particularly hard hit. But after a long, cool summer and rain around the fall equinox, the skies cleared and conditions were ideal for harvest. The lack of blazing heat has meant an excellent year for whites and sparklers, with fresh acidities and lots of aromatics. It has also favored black grapes that need longer to arrive at phenolic maturity, such as Aragonez, Touriga Franca, Touriga Nacional, and Cabernet Sauvignon.

In Vinho Verde, average quantities were down 30 percent, and for some growers down by as much as 70 percent. But the wines that were made are "expressive and balanced," according to Helder Cunha of Vinhos Borges, with grapes much riper than usual. The Douro was hit by mildew in June and July, but growers who had treated their vines sailed through a long, cool, damp summer, and made fantastic whites and elegant, aromatic reds.

The Beiras was hardest hit by the wet summer, with Dão quantities down 40 percent on average. But the later-ripening Tinta Roriz and Touriga Nacional were helped by a dry, warm fall and made lovely, aromatic wines of good color. Touriga Nacional was also a star in Bairrada, although the Baga wines were more aromatic as well. Bairrada whites should be excellent. In Estremadura, quantities were down about 20 percent, but successful wines are aromatic and balanced. The Ribatejo was not as hard hit on quantities and has made very aromatic wines. The story is similar in the Terras do Sado: fresh, aromatic whites and reds, but quantities down by about 15 percent. In the Alentejo, it was the late-ripening Aragonez, Alicante Bouschet, Cabernet Sauvignon, and Touriga Nacional that shone, and the cool summer has given reds of expressive elegance and balance. The same goes for the Algarve.

Updates on the previous five vintages

2006

Vintage rating: *73*

After good rains in winter, Portugal had a hot, dry summer. In Bairrada, the Alentejo, and the Douro Superior, the heat was too much for the vines and ripening was delayed by vines shutting down. Bairrada reds were hit by rain and rot. Douro grapes survived better, with some raisining, but most wines lack structure, although they are aromatic. Aragonez in the Alentejo never really ripened properly after the heat-stressed shutdown, but some good wines were made from earlier-ripening varieties. In Dão, good wines were made from the early-ripening Alfrocheiro and Jaen, but the later-ripening Aragonez, Touriga Nacional, and Tinto Cão never quite made the grade. In the Minho, Dão, Terras de Sado, and Ribatejo, early-picked grapes made good, if not great, wines. Good white wines were made in the Minho, Bairrada, Dão, Ribatejo, and Terras de Sado before the rain. Moscatels in the Setúbal peninsula have been particularly successful.

2005

Vintage rating: *83*

The winter of 2004/05 was the driest on record. The summer months (especially July) were warmer than average, and by early August many vines were losing their leaves, and grapes were drying up on the vine. However, rain at the end of August and the beginning of September helped swell the grapes, especially in the north. For the Alentejo and the south, this was too little too late, since the harvest was already well under way. Cool, clear weather continued into October, but with production down by as much as 30 percent, some concentrated but often fiercely alcoholic and unbalanced wines have been made. Farther north and toward the coast, some excellent wines have been made by quality-conscious producers in Dão, Bairrada, and the Douro. At 7.5 million hl, overall production was just above the 10-year average.

2004

Vintage rating: *88*

Rain in August and early September caused sporadic outbreaks of rot, but the weather took a significant turn for the better just before the harvest. Some fantastic wines have been made. In Dão and the Douro, Touriga Nacional has performed especially well. Overall, 2004 has produced some wonderfully well-balanced reds with alcohol, intensity, and acidity, which should hold them in good stead for years.

2003

Vintage rating: *85*

At the end of July, the entire country sustained nearly three weeks of extreme heat. Photosynthesis slowed, and the maturation process came to a standstill. By the start of September, the harvest was under way throughout much of southern Portugal, but sugar readings remained unusually low. However, as the warm weather continued, *Baumés* suddenly rose. Those who got their timing wrong made unbalanced wines with high pH and surprisingly low alcohol. The Alentejo, Dão, and parts of the Douro suffered most heat damage, whereas Bairrada enjoyed its best and most trouble-free vintage for a decade. The best wines are those from late-ripening varieties. With the exception of reds from Bairrada and parts of the Douro, wines from 2003 are forward and early maturing.

2002

Vintage rating: *65*

By early September, the grapes were generally in good condition, but it rained for five full days in the middle of the month. The unsettled weather continued into October, spelling disaster for Bairrada and Vinho Verde, where many growers watched their grapes rotting on the vine. Some excellent wines were made in the Douro by those who harvested early, and there are small quantities of good wine from the south. But for most producers, 2002 is a vintage they would rather forget.

GREATEST WINE PRODUCERS

1. Quinta da Pellada (Dão)
2. Niepoort (Douro)
3. Quinta do Crasto (Douro)
4. Wine & Soul (Douro)
5. Luís Pato (Beiras)
6. Quinta dos Roques (Dão)
7. Quinta do Vale Meão (Douro)
8. Quinta do Vallado (Douro)
9. Herdade do Mouchão (Alentejo)
10. Quinta do Monte d'Oiro (Estremadura)

FASTEST-IMPROVING PRODUCERS

1. Herdade de Malhadinha Nova (Alentejo)
2. Vinhos Borges (Douro, Dão, Vinho Verde)
3. PROVAM (Vinho Verde)
4. Quinta de la Rosa (Douro)
5. Quinta de Macedos (Douro)
6. Quinta da Covela (Minho)
7. Manuel dos Santos Campolargo (Bairrada)
8. Quinta da Falorca (Dão)
9. Quinta da Revolta (Douro)
10. Quinta do Barranco Longo (Algarve)

NEW UP-AND-COMING PRODUCERS

1. Fita Preta (Alentejo)
2. Paulo Laureano Vinus (Alentejo)
3. Anselmo Mendes (Vinho Verde)
4. Casa Santa Vitória (Alentejo)

⑤ Quinta da Maritávora (Douro)
⑥ Herdade Paço de Camões (Alentejo)
⑦ Muxagat (Douro)
⑧ Azamor (Alentejo)
⑨ Momentos do Douro (Douro)
⑩ Terras de Alter (Alentejo)

BEST-VALUE PRODUCERS

① Adega Cooperativa Regional de Monção (Minho)
② Casa Santos Lima (Estremadura)
③ J Portugal Ramos (Alentejo)
④ Vinhos do Douro Superior (Douro)
⑤ Adega Cooperativa de Borba (Alentejo)
⑥ Sogrape (Vinho Verde, Douro, Dão, Alentejo)
⑦ Casa Ermelinda Freitas (Terras do Sado)
⑧ Falua (Ribatejo)
⑨ Adega Cooperativa San Isidro de Pegões (Terras do Sado)
⑩ Esporão (Alentejo)

GREATEST-QUALITY WINES

① **Dão Carrocel 2006**
Quinta da Pellada (€40)
② **Douro Vinha Maria Teresa 2005**
Quinta do Crasto (€110)
③ **Douro Granja 2005**
Quinta do Vallado (€90)
④ **Douro 2003**
Quinta de Macedos (€28)
⑤ **Beiras Vinhas Velhas de Santa Maria 2005** Quinta de Foz d'Arouce (€55)
⑥ **Douro 2005**
Quinta do Vale Meão (€60)
⑦ **Douro Batuta 2005** Niepoort (€63)
⑧ **Dão Garrafeira 2003**
Quinta da Falorca (€29.50)
⑨ **Alentejo Marias da Malhadinha 2004** Herdade da Malhadinha Nova (€60)
⑩ **Douro VT 2005** PV (€35)

BEST BARGAINS

① **Alentejo adegaborba.pt Tinto 2004** Adega Cooperativa de Borda (€4)
② **Douro Castello d'Alba Branco Reserva 2006** Vinhos do Douro Superior (€5)
③ **Setúbal JP Moscatel 2001** Bacalhôa Vinhos de Portugal (€5)
④ **Alentejano Santa Vitória Rosé 2007** Casa Santa Vitória (€4)
⑤ **Beiras Irreverente 2004** UDACA (€5)
⑥ **Vinho Verde 2006** Quinta de Azevedo (€4.25)
⑦ **Ribatejano Tagus Creek Reserve Cabernet Sauvignon Touriga Nacional 2006** Falua (€6.50)
⑧ **Alentejano Hot Spot Reserva 2005** Caves Vidigal (€4)
⑨ **Alentejano Fado Tinto 2006** Terras de Alter (€5)
⑩ **Douro Colheita Seleccionada 2004** Quinta do Margarido (€4)

MOST EXCITING OR UNUSUAL FINDS

① **Dão Primus Branco Reserva 2006** Quinta da Pellada (€26) *Alvaro de Castro is a great maverick of Portuguese winemaking, though faithful to the best of his terroir, his high sites in the foothills of the Serra da Estrela. He has made white wines before but never released one named after his top estate, Quinta da Pellada. This is a blend of old-vine Encruzado, Bical, Cerceal, and a touch of Terrantez. It begins and ends its cellar life in stainless steel, but spends the latter part of fermentation and about three months after in new François Frères barrels.*
② **Alentejano Alicante Bouschet 2005** Paulo Laureano Vinus (€58) *Paulo Laureano has been one of*

the winemaking champions of the Alentejo for years, a fierce advocate of local grapes and winemaking guru behind some of the region's top wines, including Mouchão. The eponymous company name is a recent development, coinciding with the purchase of a 75-ha estate and winery near Vidigueira. This Alicante Bouschet is the cuckoo in his Portuguese nest, accepted as an honorary refugee from his native France.

③ **Vinho Verde Espumante Côto de Mamoelas Alvarinho Brut 2005** PROVAM (€11) *Another region, another star winemaker. This time, the Monção subregion within the DOC Vinho Verde, and Anselmo Mendes. Sparkling Vinho Verde has had its own legislation for less than 10 years, and producers are only now beginning to explore the potential of the style.*

④ **Bairrada FLP 2005** Luís & Filipa Pato (€16 per 50-cl bottle) *Pato and daughter Filipa hatched this wine to test the extent to which the locals wanted him back under the Bairrada umbrella, which has never before allowed sweet wines. It's the second vintage released, a blend of Bical, Sercealinho, and Maria Gomes, and the juice is treated by cryoextraction to give a richer must than normal.*

⑤ **Alentejano Branco Reserva 2006** Casa Santa Vitória (€10) *The Vila Galé hotel group owns this winery, not far from Beja in the southern Alentejo. This wine is a recent addition to the range: 60 percent Chardonnay and 40 percent Arinto, cold-macerated for 48 hours, then fermented half and half in steel and new oak. It has the richness of barrel-fermented Chardonnay, with the lean backbone of Arinto—creamy but crisp.*

⑥ **Douro Pintas Character 2005** Wine & Soul (€36) *The baby brother of the wonderful Douro red, Pintas. Jorge and Sandra Borges' idea here is to create another label that allows them to expand their production to include grapes from other growers. The criterion is still old-vine grapes.*

⑦ **Algarve Vida Nova Verdelho 2007** Adega do Cantor (€7.50) *Congratulations to this Algarve partnership between Sir Cliff and two other families! This is the second version of the Vida Nova white, made from 100 percent Verdelho, in stainless steel, and reminiscent of a good Tuscan Vermentino. Crisp, herby, and dry.*

⑧ **Alentejano Zéfyro Branco 2006** Herdade Paço de Camões (€12) *This Viognier is the first effort from a hectare of vines at the estate owned by the Pinsent family. It's barrel-fermented but left in barrel for only two months, allowing aromas of citrus, peaches, and flowers to emerge unsmothered.*

⑨ **Douro Touriga Fêmea 2006** Quinta da Revolta (€12) *Nobody had heard of this grape, but it's on the official list and is different from Touriga Franca. The wines of this Lower Corgo estate have taken a recent upward turn. This is foot-trodden in lagares, then spends five months in new French oak.*

⑩ **Beira Interior Bonjardim Tinto 2005** Quinta do Albergue do Bonjardim (€26) *The grapes are organically certified, and only wild yeasts are used for fermentation. It's not quite right yet, and it has to be decanted and aerated to rid it of smelly "off" notes. Underneath, though, it has bright, intensely aromatic Touriga Nacional raspberry and herb flavors and terrific length. Worth watching.*

Port & Madeira

Richard Mayson

Calls for the scrapping of the *benefício*—the complex system of licensing and production rights that underpins the port industry—have come from two major shippers.

RICHARD MAYSON

The *benefício* originated in response to overproduction in the 1930s. However, Adrian Bridge, managing director of the Fladgate Partnership (which includes Taylor, Fonseca, Croft, and Delaforce), believes that the *benefício* is now "illogical and outdated." In an article for Portugal's *Revista de Vinhos*, he says, "This system, which sets the amount of must that can be made into port in any one year and is distributed by means of production rights to thousands of small growers, does not pay attention to the quality of the grapes." He describes the *benefício* as a "structural constraint" creating an "artificial market" in which the port industry is effectively "cross-subsidizing the production of Douro wine"—that is, unfortified wine. This is reflected in grape prices. Grapes with the license to produce port fetch around

RICHARD MAYSON writes and lectures on wine, dividing his time between London, Portugal, and a family business in England's Peak District. He speaks fluent Portuguese, having been brought up in Portugal, and is regarded as one of the most respected authorities on port, sherry, madeira, and the wines of Spain and Portugal. His interest in the subject goes back to his university days, when he wrote a thesis on the microclimates of the vineyards of the Douro Valley. His books include *Portugal's Wines and Wine Makers* (Ebury Press, 1992), *Port and the Douro* (Faber & Faber, 1999), and *The Wines and Vineyards of Portugal* (Mitchell Beazley), which won the André Simon award for the best drinks book published in 2003. A second, fully revised edition of *Port and the Douro* was published by Mitchell Beazley in 2004, and Richard is currently preparing a book on the wines of Madeira and a third edition of *Portugal's Wines and Wine Makers*. He also owns a vineyard in the Alto Alentejo region of Portugal and launched his first wine, Pedra Basta, in 2007.

€1,000 a ton, whereas the same grapes, without *beneficio*, are sold for just €200. "In my view," says Bridge, "it is urgent that we eliminate the distortion and asymmetry caused by this antiquated system." He proposes that the *beneficio* should either be applied to Douro wine or "abandoned completely, creating a free market in which each producer chooses a strategy according to their economic needs."

Rupert Symington, a director of Symington Family Estates (which includes Dow, Graham, and Warre), agrees that the production of low-quality grapes has to be drastically reduced to keep the port industry healthy. Symington argues for reform of the present system, where owners of A-grade vineyards with excess production are able to buy up production rights from producers of low-quality grapes. This, he advocates, could be done through an auction and would be beneficial to the entire region.

At 125,000 pipes, the 2007 *beneficio* represents a 1 percent increase on 2006.

Unlimited partnership

The Fladgate Partnership, owner of Taylor, Fonseca, Croft, Delaforce, and Romariz, has taken a 17 percent stake in the Portuguese family-owned port shipper Messias. This is a strategic move to secure the ownership of Quinta do Cachão, the Messias-owned property that adjoins Quinta de Vargellas and São Xisto in the Douro Superior. The Fladgate Partnership has also bought the 50-ha Quinta da Eira Velha from the Newman family. The Newmans have been involved in the port trade since the 17th century, having been owners of Hunt Roope, subsequently sold to Ferreira. Since the late 1970s, Eira Velha has been managed by Cockburn's and the wine sold under the Martinez label. All Cockburn's assets in the Douro and Vila Nova de Gaia (including the Martinez brand) were sold to the Symington family in 2006. The Newmans have strong links with Newfoundland through their historic trade in *bacalhau* (salt cod). Their brand, Newman's Celebrated Port, will continue to be produced and shipped by the Fladgate Partnership.

Grapevine

• **The EU is supporting growers** of rare Madeira grapes by increasing structural funds. From 2007 to 2010, growers of Sercial, Verdelho, Terrantez, Malvasia Cândida, Malvasia Roxa, Bastardo, and Listrão will receive €500 for every ton of grapes they produce.

• **The Cockburn's Port brand** has been retained by Fortune amid the sale of most of their wine assets.

• **Dow's 1996 Quinta do Bomfim** has been released with a centennial label to mark the company's purchase of the estate in 1896.

GRAN CRUZ GETS GRANDER

French-owned Gran Cruz, currently the second-largest port shipper with 17 percent of the market, is looking to expand by buying up smaller port shippers. According to the Portuguese newspaper *Diário Economico*, Cruz is believed to have bid for Poças, Andresen, and Wiese & Krohn and is considering a takeover of the Companhia Comercial de Vinhos do Porto, which includes Castelinho Vinhos.

PLACES TO STAY

The Fladgate Partnership has announced the construction of the Yeatman Hotel. This five-star hotel, with 85 bedrooms, two restaurants, and a spa, will be built on land behind the Croft lodges in the historic *entreposto* of Vila Nova de Gaia. The investment, which also includes a housing development, is expected to be €30 million. The Yeatman is expected to open in 2009.

Several other hotels have opened in the Douro in 2007, including Quinta da Romaneira, which was built by a group of French and English investors led by Christian Seeley, managing director of AXA Millésimes, which owns neighboring Quinta do Noval. Quinta do Crasto and port shippers Rozès are also planning hotels in the Douro Valley. The annual number of tourist nights currently spent in the Douro is 180,000—a figure the government expects to triple by 2015.

GOLDEN JOE EYES SOGRAPE

Salvador Guedes, president of Portugal's largest wine company Sogrape, which includes port shippers Ferreira, Offley, and Sandeman, has described the purchase of 33 percent of the company by Joe Berardo as "uncomfortable and hostile." Berardo (nicknamed "Golden Joe") is one of Portugal's wealthiest businessmen and also owns Bacalhoa Vinhos, 60 percent of Caves Aliança, and Philip Shaw in Australia. He is trying to put together a package to rescue the debt-laden Casa do Douro.

CHURCHILL REFINANCED

Churchill Graham, the port shipper founded by brothers Johnny, Anthony, and William Graham in 1981, has been recapitalized with an additional €4 million investment from Phipps and Company, a private family business with interests ranging from oil exploration to manufacturing and distribution. Dr. Colin Phipps, chairman of Phipps and Company, said, "My longstanding interest in vintage port has led me to seek investment opportunities in the Douro." Work has already started to double the capacity of Churchill's principal vineyard, Quinta da Gricha.

2005 DECLARED

The 2005 vintage has been declared by a number of shippers. Kopke, Niepoort, Barros, Burmester, Cálem, and Ramos Pinto made full declarations, whereas the majority of shippers opted for single-*quinta* or second-label wines. Dirk Niepoort is particularly effusive about the 2005 vintage, describing it as "the best I have made and probably the best Niepoort since 1945. The brilliance of the 2005 vintage is its harmony and balance."

Opinion:
What should happen next?

The attack on the *benefício* system (see main news story) is well timed. Some radical initiatives are needed to correct the structural imbalances that have grown up in the port trade. With 88 percent of the Douro's growers still owning less than 2 ha, the complicated system of production rights devised by Alvaro Moreira da Fonseca in the 1940s has become little more than a social subsidy for small farmers. The problem for the government is that these small farmers, excluding family and dependants, represent nearly 35,000 votes. Although the larger farmers may have a louder voice, growers with more than 8 ha represent just 810 votes at election time.

The free-market alternative to the *benefício* advocated by Adrian Bridge would be a catastrophe for the region. With the Casa do Douro debacle still fresh in everyone's minds and not yet resolved, self-regulation would bring anarchy to the Douro, not to mention immediate hardship for thousands of small growers. Despite its contradictions, the *benefício* has served the port region reasonably well, keeping supply and demand in check and preventing the "boom and bust" crises that have befallen the sherry industry. There is an excess of regulation in the port industry, but gradual reform from within would serve the trade industry much better than the overthrow of the entire system.

The government must start by incentivizing the uprooting of vineyards and the merger of small, uneconomic vineyard holdings. Over the past 10 years there has been a 24 percent increase in the area of vineyard with the right to *benefício*, while global sales of port have been virtually static. Port sales currently represent 10.3 million cases a year, sales of Douro wine 3 million, yet the entire region can produce the equivalent of 20 million cases. This excess represents a potential flood of port and has to be reduced before the *benefício* can be radically reformed, let alone abolished.

Grapevine

- **Quinta do Zimbro,** an A-grade estate in the Ribalonga Valley that belonged to the Symington family until the 1950s, has been bought by Manuel Pinto Hespanhol, producer of Douro red Calços da Tanha. Hespanhol intends to produce port and develop the estate for tourism.

- **The Symington family** will invest €5 million in the vineyards and wineries that used to belong to Cockburn's before 2012. This will include the introduction of robotic *lagares*.

Vintage Report

Advance report on the latest harvest
2007

Port—Not since 1994 have the port shippers been so bullish so early about a vintage. The fall and winter were mild but wet, which helped replenish the water table after four hot, dry years. Budburst and flowering were early. June was abnormally wet, and with many smaller growers unable to keep on top of oidium, overall yields were significantly down. The summer was not excessively hot but there was plenty of sunshine. Heavy rain fell in early September, but when picking began in the Cima Corgo subregion around the 17th, the weather was cool and clear. Conditions were perfect and stayed that way for the rest of the harvest. Touriga Franca and Tinta Roriz, the two most widely planted Douro varieties, performed particularly well. Adrian Bridge, MD of the Fladgate Partnership, said, "If wines deliver on their early promise, collectors will be well advised to set aside funds for 2007 ports, which will be released in 2009." This is a sure sign that a full-fledged vintage declaration is looming.

Madeira—An unusually wet July was followed by more rain during the harvest. Some very good Verdelho and Malvasia were produced. Other varieties (including Tinta Negra Mole, which represents more than 80 percent of production) were much less successful.

Updates on the previous five vintages
2006

Vintage rating: *Port: 70, Madeira: 95*

Port—Following the extreme drought of 2005, heavy winter rain went some way toward replenishing groundwater reserves. Hail in June caused much damage in the Pinhão and Torto valleys. July was very hot and another burst of heat at the start of September damaged grapes, some of which shriveled on the vine. Picking began early in the Douro Superior, but the weather broke in the middle of September and much of the region picked in the rain. As a result, 2006 is extremely variable in the Douro, with the best wines produced from older vineyards and warmer sites where picking took place early.

Madeira—The best harvest in over a decade for the island's principal grape variety, Tinta Negra Mole. With production up by 18 percent on 2005, quality was matched by quantity.

2005

Vintage rating: *Port: 80, Madeira: 95*

Port—The harvest was one of the earliest on record, after one of the driest and warmest growing seasons in living memory. There was a high incidence of raisined berries in younger vineyards, which produced unbalanced wines. Yields were significantly down in some parts of the region. Despite the challenging conditions, small quantities of good, concentrated wine have been made from the older vineyards best placed to withstand the drought.

Madeira—The island enjoyed an outstanding harvest with no shortage of high-quality fruit. The shippers have already set aside their best *lotes* for colheitas and vintage madeiras, the latter to be released in 20 years' time. Expect some outstanding Verdelho and Bual.

2004

Vintage rating: *Port: 87, Madeira: 88*

Port—After rain in early and mid-September, the sunshine returned just in time. Sugar levels rose suddenly, taking many by surprise, and continued to rise as temperatures exceeded 86°F (30°C). With yields down slightly on the previous year, the overriding feature of 2004 is the balance of the musts. Some fine single-*quinta* ports have been declared.

Madeira—Some fine wines were made from all parts of the island. This was another dry year, with the hottest temperatures for nearly 30 years at the end of July. Vineyards on the north side suffered from excess humidity in August, but well-ventilated sites on the south side yielded the best grapes. Bual (of which there was no shortage) proved to be outstanding.

2003

Vintage rating: *Port: 94, Madeira: 90*

Port—An abnormally hot growing season produced some very promising wines. Yields were above average, and ports of a very high standard were made throughout the Douro region. One leading shipper has already stated that 2003 could be considered "a textbook year." A vintage was unanimously declared in the spring and summer of 2005.

Madeira—An exceptional year with a large production of healthy, generally disease-free grapes. This was an excellent year for Tinta Negra Mole and Verdelho, both of which registered good levels of ripeness. For Verdelho it was the best harvest for 10 years. Both Sercial and Bual produced some good wines, but for Malvasia it was a year with low production and some localized disease problems.

2002

Vintage rating: *Port: 70, Madeira: 85*

Port—Bouts of torrential rain from mid-September made it a stop–start vintage. Growers who picked before the rain have small quantities of good wine. A few single *quintas* declared, but for most, 2002 was a damp squib.

Madeira—Large production and particularly good-quality Tinta Negra Mole in the south, and excellent quality with large volumes of Bual from Calheta at the extreme west. Bual and Tinta Negra Mole in the Campanário district suffered due to fog in the four weeks or so before the vintage. Malmsey and Sercial were inconsistent. Verdelho was excellent but limited in volume.

GREATEST WINE PRODUCERS

1. Fonseca
2. Graham
3. Dow
4. Quinta do Noval
5. Taylor
6. Blandy (madeira)
7. Barbeito (madeira)
8. Niepoort
9. Henriques & Henriques (madeira)
10. Warre

FASTEST-IMPROVING PRODUCERS

1. Croft
2. Quinta de la Rosa
3. Delaforce
4. Cockburn
5. Quinta do Portal
6. Quinta do Passadouro
7. Andresen
8. Quinta do Ventozelo
9. Poças
10. Cálem

NEW UP-AND-COMING PRODUCERS

1. Quinta de Roriz
2. Quinta da Prelada
3. Quinta do Portal
4. Quinta do Passadouro
5. Quinta Nova (de Nossa Senhora do Carmo)
6. Quinta do Ventozelo
7. Quinta Vale Dona Maria
8. Quinta do Vallado
9. Wine & Soul
10. Quinta do Tedo

BEST-VALUE PRODUCERS

1. Smith Woodhouse
2. Cruz
3. Croft
4. Gould Campbell
5. Warre

GREATEST-QUALITY WINES

1. **Taylor's Vintage Port 1945** (€1,160)
2. **Blandy's 1920 Bual** (€276)
3. **Croft Vintage Port 1955** (€180)
4. **Fonseca Vintage Port 1977** (€120)
5. **Quinta do Noval Vintage Port 2004** (€50)
6. **Dow's Quinta Senhora da Ribeira Vintage Port 2005** (€40)
7. **Ramos Pinto Quinta do Bom Retiro Twenty Year Old Tawny Port** (€40)
8. **Blandy's 1977 Bual** (€60)
9. **Quinta do Vesúvio Vintage Port 2005** (€45)
10. **Quinta de Roriz Vintage Port 2003** (€45)

BEST BARGAINS

1. **Graham's Crusted Port** (bottled 2001) (€20)
2. **Porto Cruz Tribute Ruby Reserve NV** (€8)
3. **Warre's 1999 LBV** (€17.50)
4. **Croft Quinta da Roeda Vintage Port 2005** (€30)
5. **Graham's Six Grapes Reserve Port NV** (€12)
6. **Graham's LBV 2001** (€15)
7. **Sandeman LBV 2001** (€15)
8. **Cockburn's 20 Year Old Tawny Port** (€16 per half-bottle)
9. **Warre's Warrior Reserve Port NV** (€12)

MOST EXCITING OR UNUSUAL FINDS

1. **D'Oliveira's Terrantez 1977** (bottled 2007) (€50) *Near-perfect expression of one of Madeira's rarest grapes: mid-mahogany color, the nose sings from the glass; lovely bittersweet fruit, powerful with a dry citrus finish that goes on and on.*
2. **Quinta do Noval Vintage Port 2004** (€50) *One of very few houses to declare outright in 2004: dense, sullen on the nose yet with plenty underlying; fine, tight-knit on the palate, ripe and focused with lovely purity of fruit. Will be very fine in 15 years.*
3. **Quinta de Vargellas Vinha Velha Vintage Port 1995** (€160) *The first vintage of this wine, made from the oldest vines on the property (early 20th century). Still opaque—black in color, closed but just beginning to reveal wonderful underlying perfume; rich, multilayered, power offset by great elegance and length. Only 250 cases made.*
4. **Pintas Vintage Port 2005** Wine & Soul (€35) *Very fine, rich, powerful vintage port from a hot, dry year. Made by husband-and-wife team Jorge Borges and Sandra Tavares da Silva, it comes from a plot of old vines in the Pinhão Valley.*
5. **Smith Woodhouse Vintage Port 1977** (€55) *Still one of the most impressive wines of 1977 in a 30th-anniversary lineup: very deep in color, ripe, opulent aromas, retaining power and concentration, sweet and focused with firm tannic backbone. Drink now to 2020+.*
6. **HM Borges 40 Year Old** (€100) *Mid-mahogany color, figs, raisins, and prunes, the richness of age in cask offset by typically refreshing fresh acidity. Wonderful texture and length of flavor. Few wines make it to this category, most having been bottled at 20 years or so as vintage madeira.*
7. **Barbeito Colheita Cask 8a & d 1999** (€15 per 50-cl bottle) *Grapes from São Vicente on the north side of the island, aged in two separate lodges in Funchal: very fine pure Boal character, dried apricots with delicate, steely acidity.*
8. **Croft Vintage Port 1994** (€45) *Representing the renaissance of one of the great names of port after two decades in the doldrums: powerful, ripe, fleshy fruit supported by bold tannins. Impressive. Drink 2012–30+.*
9. **Cockburn's 20 Year Old Tawny Port** (€16 per half-bottle) *A fine, seductive 20-year-old from an underperforming shipper whose wines are now made by the Symington family. Deservedly won a gold in the Decanter World Wine Awards. Full yet supremely elegant—and good value, too.*
10. **Andresen 10 Year Old Dry White Port** (€12 per 50-cl bottle) *The first white port to be bottled with an indication of age: dried apricots and figs with nutty complexity from aging in cask. Worlds away in character and style from bland dry white port.*

Great Britain

Stephen Skelton MW

The vine-planting boom in the UK seems unstoppable, but will it all end in tears?

STEPHEN SKELTON MW

The official figures show that, by mid-2007, out of the 998 ha planted, 275 ha (28 percent) were occupied by champagne varieties. The official figures tend to lag behind reality, and I estimate that the area planted to sparkling varieties is now somewhere north of 375 ha. EWP (English Wine Producers) chairman Mike Roberts did a guesstimate to convince DEFRA that we needed the 25,000-hl annual production limit raised and came up with a figure of 1,478 ha for the total area under vine by the end of 2008, more than 50 percent of which would be sparkling varieties. In any other wine-growing region where this sort of expansion has taken place, the result has been overproduction, leading to dramatic falls in grape and wine prices. Although I accept that the UK is very different, in that the overall scale of planting is still minute, we are surely not immune to the law of supply and demand, and with a 15- to 20-fold increase in supply on the horizon, things are bound to get interesting.

STEPHEN SKELTON MW established the award-winning Tenterden Vineyards in 1977 and made wine there for 22 years. His wines have won the Gore-Browne Trophy for the Best UK Wine on three occasions. He is currently a consultant to a number of UK vineyards and wineries. Stephen was a director of the United Kingdom Vineyards Association (UKVA) between 1982 and 1998 and chairman from 1998 until 2003. Having written on wine, winemaking, and viticulture since 1986, he published *The Vineyards of England* in 1989 and rewrote and updated this work under the new title of *The Wines of Britain and Ireland* (Faber & Faber, 2001). This book won the André Simon Award in 2002. Stephen became a Master of Wine in 2003, also winning the Mondavi prize, which is awarded to the candidate gaining the highest marks in the written part of the examination.

Despite what I fear will be some fairly hefty discounting on the part of some wineries, I am more optimistic about the future of the UK wine-growing industry than ever before. The reason is simple: in sparkling wine based on champagne varieties, we have a good product—sometimes even very good—and as the vines, the viticulturists, and the winemakers mature, the quality can only get better. The interest shown by some Champagne houses is genuine and based on a realization that the UK could be the next up-and-coming wine region.

Planting ban banned

The EU has extended the general planting ban until 2015, but in countries where there is no existing ban (the UK and the other small producer countries: Belgium, Denmark, Netherlands, etc.), there will be no planting ban in the future, and so we are free to expand our vineyards to our hearts' (and our market's) content.

The EU reformers also agreed to reduce the enrichment (aka chaptalization) allowance to 3 percent (down from 3.5 percent), with an additional 0.5 percent available in "difficult" years. This is as much as UK producers ever hoped for and is about the only really good news I can ever remember coming out of Brussels.

Grapevine

• **Denbies was crowned** IWSC UK Wine Producer of the Year in 2007 in the International Wine and Spirit Competition's tastings and won a silver medal and Best in Class for its 2003 Greenfields Sparkling Cuvée. At the International Wine Challenge (IWC), it picked up a gold medal for the same wine, the only one awarded to a UK-grown wine.

• **Chapel Down** has moved from a policy of not owning its own vineyards (apart from the 8 ha surrounding the winery) and has bought just over 40 ha of prime chalk-rich downland just north of Maidstone. It plans to establish around 24 ha of champagne varieties in 2008, with a further 10 ha in 2009. This site will bring its total vineyard area up to almost 121 ha, confirming its position as the UK's largest producer.

• **Nyetimber's** excellent 2003 Pinot Meunier Cuvée, which won a gold medal in the 2006 UKVA competition and then disappeared, is now back in circulation and on sale at Harvey Nichols for £37.50 a bottle.

• **Sharpham Vineyard** picked up a prize for Best Soft Cheese!

• **Jancis Robinson MW** cut the ribbon on the new teaching winery at Plumpton College near Lewes, East Sussex, on June 29, 2007. Her speech of welcome was briefly interrupted when a bottle of bottle-fermented (fermenting?) sparkling wine decided to pop its cork, but this was taken as a good omen. The winery is well equipped with a warm room for MLF, a cold room for cold stabilization, and a very-cozy-temperature vintner's room for tastings, receptions, and other wine-related events.

MERRETOCRACY

When Mike Roberts and wife Christine started RidgeView Estate in 1995, I am sure they never expected to get to where they are today so quickly. From small beginnings, based on the 6.5 ha at their Ditchling Common base, they have now expanded, with the help of son, daughter, and daughter-in-law, to encompass a business that aims to press 200 tons of sparkling-wine grapes in 2008, rising to 400 tons in 2014. To do this, they have encouraged other growers to plant vineyards and become suppliers to their RidgeView Merret Sparkling Wines empire, and by 2009 around 91 ha of vines will be dedicated to supply fruit to the winery. In 2007 they sold 25 percent of the company to the Tukker family for £600,000. The Tukkers, who are among the largest growers of lettuces and salad crops in the UK, planted an 11-ha vineyard at their Tinwood farm in Halnaker just outside Chichester, West Sussex, and plan a further 8 ha in 2008. This is a win–win investment: it gives the Roberts family an injection of cash with which to improve facilities and build up stocks, and gives the Tukkers a home for their grapes, as well as an involvement in the UK's premier sparkling-wine producer.

For RidgeView the past 12 months have been another period of expansion and success. Two gold medals in the UK Vineyards Association's annual competition for its 2004 Bloomsbury and 2004 Fitzrovia, and the Best International Rosé in the Le Mondial de Rosé competition were topped by winning Egon Ronay's Grand Prix of Gastronomy for the "person, venture, or product that has done most for UK gastronomy in the last 12 months." The impressive range of wines—whites Bloomsbury, Cavendish, and Grosvenor and rosé Fitzrovia—has won a huge clutch of awards and has the most consistent quality of all UK producers.

Another feature that lifts RidgeView to the top of the tree is its pricing policy. Current prices (ex vineyard) are £18.95–19.95 for the Bloomsbury, Cavendish, and Fitzrovia labels, with a modest £21.95 for the Grosvenor blend. The wines sell for the same prices in retailers such as Waitrose. Compare this to the other major UK producers. Nyetimber's Première Cuvée and Blanc de Blancs both have a recommended retail price of £24.99 but usually sell for more—its wines are currently £26–27.50 in Fortnum & Mason. The 2001 Première Cuvée, due for release in spring 2008, will go out at £25.99 but, according to sales manager Nina Walters, will sell for "between £24 and £32, depending on the retailer." Chapel Down, while having a basic, non-champagne-variety-based wine at £14.99, sells its champagne-variety-based sparkling wines from £24.99 to £30. These are serious prices that put these wines directly in competition with the prestige brands. At present, UK-produced champagne-variety-based sparkling wine is in short supply with retailers. If you can get these prices, well and good, but when supply exceeds demand, which must happen in the next few years, my guess is that RidgeView will be better placed to increase its sales without having to drop prices too much.

GOLD FOUND IN THEALE HILL

Not content with dominating the mail-order business in the UK, Tony Laithwaite, via his latest "undiscovered" vineyard region, has produced one of the world's top 10 sparkling wines— at least as judged at the Effervescents du Monde competition held in Dijon in November 2007, where 408 wines from 24 countries were put to the test. Although France dominated the medal-winners with six out of the top 10 wines, the UK was in good company with wines from Australia, Argentina, and Italy.

Laithwaites's bijou vineyard—all 700 vines of it—was planted on a patch of spare ground just outside the company's new offices in Theale, near Reading. The land, which had been a dumping ground for building debris, was shaped into a mini-south-facing hill, covered with suitable topsoil and planted with Chardonnay vines in spring 2000. The 2003 Theale Vineyard Sparkling Chardonnay, which retails for £22.99, won not only a gold medal at the Dijon event, but also silver at the International Wine Challenge, as well as coming equal first at *Decanter*'s March 2008 tasting of (almost) every UK-grown sparkling wine. The wine is made by RidgeView Wine Estate, which also looks after the vineyard.

CAMEL VALLEY WINS EVERYTHING!

Bob Lindo's son Sam was anointed Winemaker of the Year at the UK Vineyards Association's annual awards by winning gold medals for three wines: the 2004 and 2005 Sparkling Pinot Noir Rosé and the 2005 Sparkling Pinot Noir. Camel Valley also picked up the Gore-Browne Trophy for the best large-production wine and the Vintner's Trophy for best sparkling—both with the Pinot Noir Rosé 2004. Another of Sam's wines, the delicious Polgoon Rosé 2006, won a silver medal and the Waitrose Best Rosé trophy. Camel Valley also picked up a silver medal in the Japan Wine Challenge.

NYETIMBER UPS PRODUCTION

Despite the generally poor weather during the summer of 2007, Nyetimber harvested 103 tons of grapes from its 14.6 ha, which is about normal. From 2008, the first of its big new plantations will come on stream, and it will be harvesting from 77 ha. From 2009, this will rise to a grand total of 105 ha, which will put it right into the (very) big time. With a potential crop of maybe 1,000 tons to handle, their new winery will need to be commissioned fairly soon. In 2007, some inconsistencies in batches of both its wines were noticed, and several bottles were far too oxidized. Perhaps this was just down to the changeover in winemakers; I hope that the quality for which Nyetimber has become renowned will return with the next vintage.

Opinion:
Distilling wine reforms

Since I first became interested in growing vines in 1973, EU wine reform has been a constant topic. The EU still produces more wine than it can sell, and almost every year around 15–20 percent of total production is distilled. The latest attempt to curb overproduction focused on the usual proposals: pay growers to tear out vines, reduce the amount of money paid for distillation, and try to curb overproduction. For many growers, however, vines are their only crop and they rely on the distillation money. Overproduction always seems to center on half-hearted attempts to reduce yield levels in regions where yield is not really the problem and to stop the northern growing regions from using sugar to chaptalize. The trouble is that the "sugarers" are mostly in the wealthy northern states such as Germany and France, whereas the "distillers" are in the poorer southern parts of the EU. The original—extremely laudable—proposals have been watered down—sorry, amended—by 795 different amendments, taking much of the sting out of the original proposals. Most in the industry are convinced that the nuclear option of removing all subsidies and all support, letting the market decide which wines it wants to drink, is the only long-term solution, but hey, this is Europe, and that's rather a New World solution, isn't it?

Grapevine

• **Plumpton College's** 2006 Cloudy Ridge won a gold medal in the South East Vineyards Association's wine competition. This wine is now sold at the Michelin-starred Hakkasan restaurant in London.

• **Yearlstone Vineyard in Devon** continues to create a whirlwind of publicity, with Oz Clarke declaring its 2004 Vintage Brut sparkling wine "magic" and "more like champagne than champagne itself" on BBC1. This wine was judged equal to Montana's Pinot Noir and sold out in six months at £15 a bottle. After a bumper crop in 2006 that saw the winery handle 51 tons of its own and contract growers' fruit, the poor summer weather in 2007 cut the throughput to 21 tons. Sales continue to increase, however, with 20,000 bottles sold in the year. Yearlstone wines continue to win medals in the UKVA competition, but the company's refusal to put them through the Regional or Quality Wine Schemes means they cannot carry a vintage or varietal name. It's a pity, and I wish Roger and Juliet White would review this decision.

• **Buzzard Valley,** Staffordshire's newest wine producer, has recently set up a new winery with a semi-automated bottling and labeling line and is producing a big range of wines. Curiously, some wines are labeled Buzzard Valley and others Buzzards Valley.

Vintage Report

Advance report on the latest harvest

2007

Whatever the gods were doing in the summer of 2007, it's for sure they were not looking down on the UK's vineyards. After an exceptionally hot April, the weather deteriorated, and by mid-May the wet weather had set in and continued in fits and starts until the end of August. September and October were dry, but by then the damage had been done. What had been one of the best shows of flower trusses turned into a wet, late flowering, with most crops averaging 50 percent or less than those in the previous few years. In some cases, downy mildew caused significant—and even complete—crop loss. As for quality, we will see; I am not predicting anything until I taste a few more. Acids were high, which might mean some long-lived whites and sparklers, but reds, in all but the most favored vineyards, could be weak. I just hope that winemakers decide to take the rosé option.

Updates on the previous five vintages

2006

Vintage rating: *Red: 80, White: 88, Sparkling: 87*
Although overshadowed by the 2004s and 05s, there were some good 2006 wines produced in UK vineyards, with rosés shining through and wines made from Bacchus also showing well. Reds are less successful. As for sparkling wines, it's too early to tell, although on paper the sugar/acid balances were good and yields not too high. As ever, it's the good growers and winemakers that make the difference and the cowboys who fall by the wayside.

2005

Vintage rating: *Red: 86, White: 90, Sparkling: 86*
Yet another strange year for UK growers. Despite what felt like a cool, somewhat damp summer with on/off sun and rain, September and October turned into very good months, and sugar levels ended up even better than those achieved in 2003, the hottest year on record. A few vineyards got caught by frost in May, but in general the yields were above average, very clean, and certainly better-than-average quality. Sugar/acid balances seem to be perfect.

2004

Vintage rating: *Red: 85, White: 89, Sparkling: 88*

Despite the large yields, many of the 2004s have turned into really typical UK-grown wines, with a good balance of fruit and acidity. A high proportion of the silver medals awarded in the 2005 UKVA Wine of the Year competition went to 2004s. The best wines made from Bacchus have good flavor with sufficient length for their style and have the typical freshness and fragrance this variety brings.

2003

Vintage rating: *Red: 92, White: 90, Sparkling: 93*

An amazing year for UK winemakers. A trouble-free spring was followed by great summer weather, with temperatures hitting the high 90s (35+°C), but the fall was the clincher. September and October were very warm, sunny, and almost completely dry. Grapes were harvested at unheard-of sugar levels, with potential alcohol levels of 11–13 percent in many vineyards. All competent growers have made extremely good wines, with reds and sparklings from traditional varieties (that is, traditional champagne varieties) the stars. It was certainly the best year for black varieties that anyone can remember. In general, the 2003s are very good, with some in the "excellent" category.

2002

Vintage rating: *Red: 82, White: 85, Sparkling: 90*

The overall crop was smaller than average, but an Indian summer resulted in exceptional quality, especially with the harder-to-ripen varieties, such as Chardonnay, and the successful black varieties: Pinot Noir, Rondo, Regent, and Dornfelder. Natural sugar levels, which usually languish around 7–9 percent, were well into double figures in many cases. Several winemakers made completely natural wines—that is, without chaptalization.

GREATEST WINE PRODUCERS

Still wines
1 Chapel Down
2 Camel Valley
3 Denbies Wine Estate
4 Sharpham
5 Stanlake Park

Sparkling wines
1 RidgeView Estate
2 Nyetimber
3 Camel Valley
4 Chapel Down
5 Denbies Wine Estate

FASTEST-IMPROVING PRODUCERS

1. Polgoon
2. a'Beckett's
3. Yearlstone
4. Ludlow
5. Meopham Valley
6. Bookers
7. Bothy
8. Parva Farm
9. Wyken
10. Wroxeter Roman

NEW UP-AND-COMING PRODUCERS

1. Somborne Valley
2. Polgoon
3. Parva Farm
4. Sherborne Castle
5. Lulham Court
6. Brightwell
7. Pheasants Ridge
8. Sandyford
9. Childrey Manor
10. Welland Valley

BEST-VALUE PRODUCERS

1. RidgeView Estate
2. Chapel Down
3. Denbies Wine Estate
4. Three Choirs
5. Camel Valley
6. Stanlake Park

GREATEST-QUALITY WINES

1. **Fitzrovia Rosé Sparkling 2004** RidgeView Estate (£19.95)
2. **English Rosé 2006** Chapel Down (£9.99)
3. **Bacchus 2006** Camel Valley (£10.95)
4. **Tenterden Bacchus Reserve 2005** Chapel Down (£12.99)
5. **Cornwall Pinot Noir Brut Rosé Sparkling 2004** Camel Valley (£22.95)
6. **Coopers Brook 2004** Denbies Wine Estate (£6.25)
7. **Ortega 2004** Denbies Wine Estate (£11.99)
8. **Premium Selection Rosé 2006** Three Choirs (£5.80)
9. **Classic Cuvée Sparkling 2000** Nyetimber (£25)
10. **Pinot Noir 2004** Sandhurst (£10.99)

BEST BARGAINS

1. **Brut Sparkling NV** Chapel Down (£14.99)
2. **Coopers Brook 2004** Denbies Wine Estate (£6.25)
3. **Pinot Noir 2004** Sandhurst (£10.99)
4. **Premium Selection Rosé 2006** Three Choirs (£5.80)
5. **Fitzrovia Rosé Sparkling 2004** RidgeView Estate (£19.95)
6. **Estate Selection 2006** Sharpham (£9)
7. **Bacchus 2005** Chapel Down (£9.99)

MOST EXCITING OR UNUSUAL FINDS

1. **Rosé 2006** Polgoon (£8.80) *Great fruit—really refreshing. This is what the UK should be producing.*
2. **Walled Garden White 2005** Ickworth (£8.50) *A worthy gold-medal winner with length and elegance.*
3. **Estate Sparkling 2005** a'Beckett's (£12.95) *Crisp with a slightly spicy finish.*
4. **Pinot Reserve Sparkling 2002** Chapel Down (£29.99) *Full with a great yeasty nose and long finish.*
5. **Coopers Brook 2004** Denbies Wine Estate (£6.25) *Just off-dry and very well balanced.*

Belgium, Netherlands & Scandinavia

Fiona Morrison MW & Ronald de Groot

This year finds Belgian wine producers in an optimistic mood.

FIONA MORRISON MW   RONALD DE GROOT

BELGIUM

After a decade or so of cottage winemaking, several producers have begun to receive real acclaim for their wines. Sommeliers and specialty stores are paying more attention to local wines, and a website dedicated exclusively to Belgian wines is helping spread the word among the wine-drinking public. Indeed, several producers contacted this year for tasting samples had completely sold out.

Kasteel Genoels-Elderen, the largest Belgian winery, celebrated its 15th anniversary in great style, and there are several new producers, such as Clos des Agaises and Vidaigne, who are making some very attractive, fruity wines.

The quality of wines made by Peter Colemont in his tiny 1-ha Clos d'Opleeuw vineyard is the pinnacle of Belgian capability: at a blind tasting with Jancis Robinson MW, we both pronounced his Chardonnay to be a very good Puligny. Colemont has now achieved international recognition, making the front page of the *Financial Times*. However, most wine producers continue to grow grapes as a hobby.

FIONA MORRISON MW has spent more than 20 years in the wine trade around the world and speaks several languages. She became a Master of Wine in 1994 and is now a freelance wine journalist and lecturer. She is married to Jacques Thienpont, a wine *négociant* and owner of Le Pin in Pomerol, and together they divide their time between Bordeaux and Belgium, making, tasting, and promoting wine.
RONALD DE GROOT is owner and editor of the leading Dutch wine magazine *Perswijn*. He organizes tasting events for professionals and consumers and is a freelance contributor to various media. As a wine consultant, he is a member of the KLM Royal Dutch Airlines tasting panel. He is also a member of one of Europe's leading tasting panels, the Grand Jury Européen.

Beginning to sparkle

Sparkling wines have been the most improved category this year, with around 10 producers making decent commercial wines. This type of wine appeals to the Belgian public, and spurred on by the success of their English neighbors, they look set to increase both production and sales. Several sparkling-wine appellations were created recently, but consumers don't seem too concerned about classifications. One of the newly recognized areas, Heuvelland, in the hills near Ypres, has seen considerable success and is the most northerly wine region in Belgium (most of the other regions are located south of Brussels and toward the Dutch border in the region of Limburg).

Noble grapes on the increase

As producer confidence increases, plantings of Chardonnay and Pinot Noir spread in the south, although most growers still plant hybrids. Encouraged by the success of Belgian sparkling wines, made almost entirely from Chardonnay and Pinot Noir, growers are taking advantage of rising temperatures and better viticultural methods to plant these varieties.

THE NETHERLANDS

New vineyards are being planted in every province of the Netherlands, and the vineyard area is expanding by about 15–20 percent per year. The most important provinces for wine are Limburg in the south, Gelderland in the east, and Zeeland in the southwest.

Total vineyard area has increased from about 100 ha in recent years to 175 ha. Production is too small for EU regulations to limit planting, so growth will continue for the foreseeable future. There are now 100 professional wine growers, and the total number of bottles produced per year is nearing a million. Only the biggest producers work on a national basis. The largest producers, such as Apostelhoeve (Limburg), Kleine Schorre (Zeeland), and Hof van Twente (Overijssel), have around 6 ha of vineyard.

Self-sufficiency

Until now, the best Dutch wines have been made by producers trained outside the Netherlands, but courses are now being developed to improve Dutch winemakers' skills. This will help producers avoid the problems of "foxy" odors and harsh tannins in wines made from hybrid varieties.

Seminars are also being organized on organic wine growing and vinification. Organic wine growing is quite a challenge in the Dutch climate. Because of the difficulties of treating mildew organically, only hybrid grapes are suitable for organic treatment. Despite these obstacles, 25 percent of all professional winemakers are expected to be working organically by 2009.

SCANDINAVIA

Climate change has increased interest in northern grape growing. The key selling point of growing wines so far north is that they benefit from the "white nights"—the long summer days that bring extra sunlight, giving a longer but sunnier growing season than most regions.

In Sweden, 24 wineries are registered in the official growers' association, mainly in the southern part of Sweden on the two big islands in Ostersjön (Gotland and Oland). The group has a website (in Swedish) that offers advice and news to members: www.svenskavinodlare.se. The most famous winery is the Blaxa Vineyard (see www.blaxstawine.com), which claims to be Europe's most northerly estate. Making wines from fruit grown on the estate, one of the earliest wines is an apple icewine made from Akerö apples. The vineyard is 2.5 ha and is planted with Vidal (80 percent), Chardonnay, and Merlot, although they are currently experimenting with Cabernet Franc. The vineyard was planted in 2000 and is expanding each year. The wines received several awards, including a bronze for the Vidal icewine 2005, at the 2007 International Wine Challenge in London.

The second-best-known Swedish estate is Gutevin AB (www.gutevin.se), situated on Gotland. A TV documentary shown in Germany has led to considerable interest from that country, and the wines are now exported there. The estate specializes in growing 50 different grape varieties, including Bacchus, Léon Millot, Domina, and Orion. See their website for the full list: www.gutevin.se/vinodling/sorter.html.

On the whole, Swedish wines remain very expensive and attract more curiosity than commerce. The same goes for Denmark, where permission to establish commercial wine production was granted by the EU in 2000. The vineyards are located mainly along the coastal areas of Zealand, Bornholm, Lolland, and Jutland. The best-known growers are Sven Moesgaard, whose vineyard, Skaersoegaard, produces red and white table wines as well as a sparkling wine called Dons, and Jens Michael Gundersen, whose Nordlund winery produces full-bodied reds in Avedøre, south of Copenhagen. Gundersen is also chairman of the Danish growers' association and recently launched a website—http://www.vinavl.dk—for members.

There is talk of a new vineyard project in Norway. Klaus Peter Keller of Weingut Keller in the Rheinhessen has singled out a granite vineyard site near Kristiansand in southern Norway and intends to plant Riesling. If the climate is too cold to ripen Riesling successfully, Keller hopes to make some *Eiswein*, which is becoming increasingly difficult to make in Germany.

Opinion:
Belgians over a barrel

For most of the past year, Belgium has survived without a government, which has brought to the world's attention the problems it faces in being divided into Dutch-speaking Flanders and French-speaking Walloon. Belgian wine growing also remains fragmented, with many small growers surviving with no growers' association or regional grouping. Apart from the larger regions of Haspengouw, Hageland, and, increasingly, Heuvelland, there is no organization to promote quality, cooperation, or ambition.

Recently, however, there has been growing interest in Belgian wines, with most of the country's newspapers now conducting tastings and comparing leading producers, and many restaurants carrying one or two selections. There are about five table-wine producers and four sparkling-wine producers who are making interesting wines. Their efforts are being increasingly rewarded by good press reviews and an enthusiastic response from sommeliers. However, even these successful producers seem to have no desire to expand beyond the limited confines of their small estates.

The biggest winemaking error is the use of too much oak for aging Chardonnay. Most Belgian wines are tank fermented with no oak, but growers seem to think wines aged in French oak are taken more seriously. In the future, perhaps, they will learn to make more balanced wines.

Going Dutch

With the growth in vineyard plantings, the gap between the best and the rest seems to be increasing. And it isn't always the professionals who shine. Even some "professional" growers lack the skills to make good wines.

Quality winemakers are on the rise, but no cohesive group has yet been formed. The Netherlands lags behind Belgium, which has created several denominations and has established wine regulations. Although production in the Netherlands is higher and growing faster than in Belgium, no denominations exist. This matter is urgent, since there is a clear distinction between vineyards in the southern part of the country, with the southern part of Limburg as the best example, and the middle and eastern parts of the country. Farmers in Limburg, with vineyards on rolling hills with loam soils, rely mostly on *Vitis vinifera* grapes. In the new vineyards in Gelderland, however, planting is dominated by hybrids, especially Regent, Rondo, Merzling, and Solaris. Delimiting areas of wine production, specifying varieties for each denomination, would benefit growers and consumers alike.

Vintage Report

Advance report on the latest harvest

2007

Belgium—Excellent weather during April led to early flowering under perfect conditions. The grapes ripened well throughout the summer, although the weather was rather dull and mixed during most of June, July, and August. Rain in early fall led to frantic treatments to prevent rot from spreading, but the weather improved slightly in early October. The wines will be light, fruity, and with good acidity, but perhaps lacking the concentration found in 2005 and 2006.

Netherlands—This was a difficult year from the start. Early budding was followed by a severe spring frost, which caused a lot of damage in the east in April, reducing potential yield. Flowering in June was hampered by rain and cold. Summer was cool and wet, but growth was about a week ahead at the beginning of fall. Unfortunately, there was no Indian summer, only persistent rain, which caused widespread rot. This is a real winemakers' vintage. The grapes had to be harvested at the right moment, between the showers, avoiding rot and reaching as much ripeness as possible under the circumstances.

Updates on the previous five vintages

2006

Vintage rating: *Belgium—Red: 87, White: 90; Netherlands—Red: 85, White: 84*

Belgium—Perfect summer weather at the beginning of June and through most of July gave a great boost to the grapes during flowering. By the time the dull August weather came along, the vines were well advanced and the lack of sunshine did no harm. Quantities were up slightly on 2005 for white grapes and quality is good for red wines and very good for whites.

Netherlands—An extremely wet August, in contrast to a hot July, led to a lot of disease. Relief came in the fall, with splendid weather in September and October. Early-ripening grapes did not benefit, but later-ripening ones, such as Riesling and Pinot Gris, are showing very well now. The hybrid grape Regent also did quite well. Red wines are better in general because of their later ripening. In our tasting, the wines showed better than expected.

2005

Vintage rating: *Belgium—Red: 89, White: 86; Netherlands—Red: 83, White: 85*

Belgium—A wonderful spring resulted in an exceptional flowering. The summer, however, was disappointing; from mid-July until the end of August the weather was wet and cloudy, with relatively little sunshine. Luckily, the end of August and all of September were excellent, turning the harvest from an average one to one of very good potential.

Netherlands—A slightly cooler summer forced producers to harvest a bit later than normal, but the grapes were generally ripe. Sugar and acidity were well balanced, producing quite powerful wines. The harvest was down by 20 percent because of weather problems in the fall. In general, it was quite a good vintage for Dutch growers.

2004

Vintage rating: *Belgium—Red: 87, White: 83; Netherlands—Red: 80, White: 82*

Belgium—A mild winter and an unsettled spring, but good weather during flowering. The summer was disappointing, with dull weather and quite a lot of rain. However, the Indian summer in September and October brought a fairly abundant crop of decent quality.

Netherlands—The season was cool, making it difficult for grapes to ripen. In September and October the grapes caught up to some extent, but rain disturbed the harvest. The wet weather contributed to a larger harvest than normal. Wines are more elegant in character, more "nervous," with higher acidity, but quality is quite acceptable. A vintage for lovers of a fresher style.

2003

Vintage rating: *Belgium—Red: 81, White: 85; Netherlands—Red: 83, White: 86*

Belgium—A wonderful vintage on paper because of the high amount of sunshine during summer and fall. However, northern grape varieties are used to dealing with excess water, and several vineyards suffered from hydric stress. The wines are not as concentrated and rich as the summer heat might have suggested, but there are some very good ones.

Netherlands—This was a very good vintage with a few exceptions. The wonderful summer and fall brought powerful wines, with some excellent examples with real complexity and more alcohol than usual. Vines on sandy soils suffered from drought, which stressed the vines, so there were some mixed results here. In general, as in other countries, there is less acidity, so wines are ripening faster.

2002

Vintage rating: *Belgium—Red: 79, White: 81;*
Netherlands; Red: 82, White: 84

Belgium—Another vintage saved by the sunny late-summer weather after mixed weather during a long growing season. Some attractive wines made people sit up and take notice of Belgian wines.

Netherlands—Quite a good vintage, with well-balanced wines, good acidity, and nice power. Saved by good fall weather.

GREATEST WINE PRODUCERS

1. Clos d'Opleeuw (Gors-Opleeuw, Belgium)
2. Apostelhoeve (Maastricht, Netherlands)
3. Genoels-Elderen (Riemst, Belgium)
4. Kleine Schorre (Schouwen-Duivenland, Netherlands)
5. Wijngaard Wageningse Berg (Wageningen, Netherlands)
6. Fromberg (Valkenberg, Netherlands)
7. Pietershof (Teuven, Belgium)
8. Wijnhoeve de Colonjes (Groesbeek, Netherlands)
9. Hof van Twente (Bentelo, Netherlands)
10. Clos des Agaises (Haulchin, Belgium)

FASTEST-IMPROVING PRODUCERS

1. Peter Colemont, Clos d'Opleeuw (Gors-Opleeuw, Belgium)
2. Kleine Schorre (Schouwen-Duivenland, Netherlands)
3. Clos des Agaises (Haulchin, Belgium)
4. Betuws Wijndomein (Erichem, Netherlands)
5. Verenigde Achterhoekse Wijnbouwers (Lievelde, Netherlands)
6. Wijngaard Karthuizerhof (Kortessem, Belgium)
7. Pietershof (Teuven, Belgium)

8. Wijngaard Wageningse Berg (Wageningen, Netherlands)
9. Hof van Twente (Bentelo, Netherlands)
10. Monteberg (Dranouter, Belgium)

NEW UP-AND-COMING PRODUCERS

1. Pietershof (Teuven, Belgium)
2. Kleine Schorre (Schouwen-Duivenland, Netherlands)
3. Meerdaal (Oud-Heverlee, Belgium)
4. Sint-Mauritius (Schin-op-Geul, Netherlands)
5. Verenigde Achterhoekse Wijnbouwers (Lievelde, Netherlands)
6. Wijngaard Karthuizerhof (Kortessem, Belgium)
7. Domein Vidaigne (Westouter, Belgium)
8. Monteberg (Dranouter, Belgium)
9. Clos des Agaises (Haulchin, Belgium)
10. Hof van Twente (Bentelo, Netherlands)

BEST-VALUE PRODUCERS

1. Aldenyck (Maasvallei, Belgium)
2. Kleine Schorre (Schouwen-Duivenland, Netherlands)
3. Wijnhoeve de Colonjes (Groesbeek, Netherlands)
4. Fromberg (Valkenberg, Netherlands)
5. Meerdaal (Oud-Heverlee, Belgium)

6 Pietershof (Teuven, Belgium)
7 Elzenbosch (Assent, Belgium)
8 Genoels-Elderen (Riemst, Belgium)
9 Verenigde Achterhoekse Wijnbouwers (Lievelde, Netherlands)
10 Wijngaard Wageningse Berg (Wageningen, Netherlands)

GREATEST-QUALITY WINES

1 **Chardonnay 2005** Clos d'Opleeuw, Belgium (€20)
2 **Chardonnay Goud 2004** Genoels-Elderen, Belgium (€25)
3 **Pinot Gris 2006** Apostelhoeve, Netherlands (€9)
4 **Louwberg Maastricht Riesling 2006** Apostelhoeve, Netherlands (€9)
5 **Auxerrois+ 2006** Kleine Schorre, Netherlands (€8.95)
6 **Ruffus Chardonnay Brut Méthode Traditionnelle NV** Clos des Agaises, Belgium (€15)
7 **Vidaigne 2006** Domein Vidaigne, Belgium (€8)
8 **Chardonnay Crindaeler 2005** Pietershof, Belgium (€15.50)
9 **Regent Barrique 2006** Wijngaard Wageningse Berg, Netherlands (€12)
10 **Nederlandse Landwijn QV 2006** Fromberg, Netherlands (€8.95)

BEST BARGAINS

1 **Auxerrois 2006** Apostelhoeve, Netherlands (€9)
2 **Auxerrois+ 2006** Kleine Schorre, Netherlands (€8.95)
3 **Chardonnay Wit 2004** Genoels-Elderen, Belgium (€7.50)
4 **Regent Fruitig 2006** Wijngaard Wageningse Berg, Netherlands (€12)
5 **Nederlandse Landwijn Merzling/Johanniter 2006** Wijngaard Wageningse Berg, Netherlands (€12)

6 **Müller-Thurgau 2005** Apostelhoeve, Netherlands (€9)
7 **Regent Barrique 2005** Wijnhoeve de Colonjes, Netherlands (€10.50)
8 **Nederlandse Landwijn QV 2006** Fromberg, Netherlands (€8.95)

MOST EXCITING OR UNUSUAL FINDS

1 **Chardonnay 2006** Clos d'Opleeuw, Belgium (€20) *Slightly less deep and concentrated than the outstanding 2005, but still a very good wine. Well balanced, some nice wood. In a league of its own.*
2 **Auxerrois+ 2006** Kleine Schorre, Netherlands (€8.95) *The discussion about hybrids and "the real stuff" continues, but wines like this prove that, for white wines, the classic grapes are generally doing better. Auxerrois combined with some Pinot Blanc results in lots of white fruit, elegance, and freshness.*
3 **Ruffus Chardonnay Brut Méthode Traditionnelle NV** Clos des Agaises, Belgium (€15) *Sparkling wines of high quality are quite rare in the Benelux countries, but this is a surprisingly good example. In blind tastings with champagne, people thought it was the real thing.*
4 **Louwberg Maastricht Riesling 2006** Apostelhoeve, Netherlands (€9) *Riesling is not very successful in the Benelux countries, being difficult to ripen. This is the exception, made by the Netherlands' top producer, with the help of an Indian summer. Elegant and fresh, very Riesling, in a dry style.*
5 **Chardonnay 2005** Sint-Mauritius, Netherlands (€15) *Available only from the vineyard or top restaurants—5,000 bottles made per year: a hidden secret found*

down south in Limburg, near Belgium. Spectacular fruit and subtle wood, fat and fresh.

⑥ **Regent Barrique 2006** Wijngaard Wageningse Berg, Netherlands (€12) *The hybrid Regent and the barrique are not always best friends, since the wood is inclined to dry out Regent's strong tannins. Jan Oude Voshaar married both well in the 2006 vintage, thanks to an abundance of fruit.*

⑦ **Chardonnay Goud 2004** Genoels-Elderen, Belgium (€25) *There is always discussion at tastings about the use of wood in Genoels-Elderen wines. Sometimes it is really excessive, but the 2004 vintage has enough freshness and fruit to handle it.*

⑧ **Pinot Noir Crindaeler 2006** Pietershof, Belgium (€15) *With climate change, it is becoming possible to grow Pinot Noir in northerly regions. This is a good example, with its nice fruit: it's elegant, fresh, très Pinot.*

⑨ **Solaris 2006** Verenigde Achterhoekse Wijnbouwers, Netherlands (€13.50) *New dynamic cooperative with 11 members in Gelderland, the region with most vineyards in the Netherlands. This is their best wine, with mouth-filling exotic fruit and good freshness.*

⑩ **Nederlandse Landwijn QV 2006** Fromberg, Netherlands (€8.95) *The best wine from this producer—one of the best in the Netherlands, making light, elegant, fresh wines.*

Grapevine

• **Belgian producer** Genoels-Elderen celebrated its 15th anniversary with the launch of Zilveren Parel Brut 2003. Limburg governor Steve Stevaert opened the first bottle using the traditional saber method.

• **The first Belgian Wine Fair,** organized by young sommelier Vincent De Coninck, was held in October 2007. Eleven of the top producers, including Clos d'Opleeuw, Les Vins de Roisin, and Clos des Agaises, poured their wines for a packed crowd of consumers at Kastel Van Horst near Leuven.

• **Sugar still allowed:** In 2007, the European Commission proposed a plan that included a ban on chaptalization in wine production throughout the EU. There was widespread panic at this announcement, since it would be a severe blow for Dutch wine growers: sugar levels are practically never high enough for serious winemaking. Strong lobbying from the Dutch Ministry of Agriculture could prevent this.

• **No restrictions, no submissions:** With the level of wine production in the Low Countries at such a tiny level, there is no EU intervention. This is an ideal situation for the EU, because it means that there are no submissions for uprooting or for improvement—in fact, nothing at all. The growers have to respond to the market to sell their wines. In an ideal world, this would be the situation for the whole EU, but it will not be a reality in the near future.

• **Gelderland won more prizes** than ever in the 2008 Dutch Wine Selection, held every year in September. With the new cooperative De Achterhoekse Wijnbouwers now active in the eastern part of the province, 32 out of 56 awards went to wine growers in Gelderland: silver medals were awarded to Betuws Domein, Wageningse Berg, De Colonjes, and the Achterhoekse Wijnbouwers.

Luxembourg

David Furer

Slow progress is being made on the viticultural and export fronts. Experimentation in vineyards is the buzz, with adjustments to winery techniques trailing behind.

DAVID FURER

The availability of wines from all over the globe has stimulated Luxembourg consumers' interest in varieties and styles. Growers are consequently being spurred on to plant new varieties that can withstand the effects of climate change.

The problem for Luxembourg exports, according to fourth-generation winemaker Mathis Bastian, continues to be its "cheap Rivaner" image and correspondingly low prices. In a move to promote exports, a tour by wine journalists and writers from the UK, Norway, Italy, Germany, and Belgium was organized by this writer in September 2007 on behalf of the wine marketing and promotions board. A busy schedule in the fine fall weather yielded many great tastings, with the highlight a comparison of old and young vintages of Riesling, Pinot Gris, and Auxerrois held by neighbor wineries Mme Aly Duhr and Clos Mon Vieux Moulin. A stunning bottle of Aly Duhr Riesling Palmberg 1959 laid to rest the notion that top Luxembourg wines should necessarily be consumed in their youth.

DAVID FURER is the author of *Wine Places* (Mitchell Beazley, 2005), a contributor to the *Which? Wine Guide*, and a contributing editor to *Santé*. He also writes for *Decanter*, *Harpers Wine and Spirit Weekly*, *Imbibe*, *Revija Vino*, *Sommelier Journal*, *Vinforum*, *Vinum*, wein.pur, www.matchingfoodandwine.com, www.bkwine.com, *Eat Sussex*, and Merrick's Media travel titles. He has led wine classes and guest lectured at the University of Chicago, California's Professional Culinary Institute, Oxford and Cambridge universities, and at Volkshochschulen in Germany. Generic trade organizations throughout Europe and restaurants in London, Vienna, and Chicago have retained his services as a consultant. He is a Certified Wine Educator, an Advanced Sommelier, and a Certified Sherry Educator and has had the pleasure of working at five wineries.

All the old vineyards love Alice

Alice Hartmann has turned history upside down. Until 1945, the Germans, along with the French, dominated Luxembourg wine-grape production by importing much of the produce for use in their anonymous blends. Now there is at least one Luxembourg winery making German and French wines. This small Wormeldange domaine has produced a 2006 Spätlese *feinherb* and a 2006 Auslese from the German Mosel's famed Trittenheimer Apotheke vineyard, to join its St-Aubin (Burgundy) white. Native Trittenheimer and Hartmann winemaker Hans-Jörg Befort snagged a parcel in the heart of the vineyard immediately below its cheesy name sign and fashioned two Rieslings that are as good as any from this vineyard.

That's the best they could do?

The fall 2007 issue of *Télécran* magazine published a story by its wine critic Claude François on a blind tasting of Luxembourg wines he arranged with several of the country's qualified wine judges. The results, while reflecting much of the best of what the country has to offer, were topped out by the 2005 vintage of Domaine St Martin's Crémant Rosé. Owner Marc Gales is, of course, thrilled with the results and has publicized them to good effect. While this bubbly represents very good value (see "Best Bargains"), it's hardly an expression of what Luxembourg in general, and the three Gales labels in particular, offer as the best in their bubblies, let alone its many great Rieslings and Pinot Gris. Every wine judge has his or her off-days, but this ranking certainly raised my eyebrow.

Grapevine

• **Henri Ruppert** began construction of a new, 6,500-sq-ft (600-sq-m), partially gravity-fed cellar in April 2007 below the north end of Schengen. Heating will be provided by a wood pellet furnace, which has near-neutral CO_2 emissions. Guy Krier of Krier-Welbes has received dispensation for, and has integrated into his tanks, an experimental system that monitors the volume of CO_2 expulsion and automatically adjusts the temperature accordingly. The Sunnen-Hoffman winery is reported to be doing something similar. Is it only coincidence that these three growers are located in the south?

• **St Laurent**—an early-ripening variety of disputed origin but probably from a Pinot Noir seedling—has taken up residence in Luxembourg for the first time since 1911. Named after the patron saint of cooks, this black variety has been planted by growers L&R Kox for a red, Krier-Welbes for a *barrique*-aged red, and Kohll-Leuck for a rosé, all with reasonably good results. To celebrate its rebirth, the growers were joined by various Luxembourg and German luminaries, along with noted Austrian winemaker Helmut Gangl, who himself has made a few successful bottlings with the grape.

Opinion:
New varieties, new styles

Spurred by climate change, individual curiosity, and the slowly changing Luxembourg palate, the willingness to experiment with new varieties now seen in Luxembourg's wine growers is to be heartily commended. There also seems to be a trend toward greater style experimentation and more severe clonal selection. What's still lacking is attention to getting greater concentration of flavors in the source material through tighter vine spacing, organic viticultural practices, the use of native yeasts when possible, and more green pruning. Hope springs in this writer's heart with the purchase at Clos des Rochers of three new 3,000-liter wooden vats in time for the 2007 harvest to hold Riesling and Pinot Gris. The results of this have yet to be determined.

Opportunities for *crémant*

An appreciation of the quality of their *crémants* is growing among Luxembourgers. With the shortage of, and high prices for, champagne, this remains this country's best opportunity to export its wines to a curious wine public thirsty for quality bubbles. Reflecting this attitude, grower Laurent Kox said, "Luxembourg's white-wine drinkers are getting older … so we must find a way to adapt to the tastes of younger drinkers and those who prefer sweeter and more carbonic drinks such as colas, tequila-based drinks, and mixers. That is the question for the next 10–20 years." Seems to me that naturally off-dry *crémants* are the answer. Young *vigneron* Henri Ruppert, now making his mark with heavily extracted Pinot Noir rather than with his country's traditional wines, thinks that "we must make wines more to the pleasure of changing palates, both for wines and for food such as white meats and Asian food."

Grapevine

• **A group of producers,** including Vinsmoselle, Legill, Schumacher, and Ruppert, has agreed to limit yields and to focus on south-facing vineyards in an effort billed "Chart de Schengen," beginning with the 2007 vintage. Henri Ruppert may have the first release—his Wintranfe Felsberg Pinot Gris. Guy Krier, along with his colleagues, will start to sell his 2007 vintage in November 2008, a full year after the vintage, to ensure greater appreciation for these wines, which are very often sold and consumed too quickly.

Vintage Report

Advance report on the latest harvest

2007

The warm March/April weather accelerated budbreak by two to three weeks and bloom by as much as four in some vineyards. Flowering conditions were less than ideal for many varieties, with scarcer clusters than normal found throughout the region. During June the wet weather increased the occurrence of downy mildew, with some infections reported just after bloom in mid-June, but they had abated long before the relatively early harvest. Picking of sparkling-wine grapes began in mid-September, one to two weeks earlier than usual, with Pinots Blanc/Gris and Chardonnay soon following. September was generally sunny and mild, which made for a long, slow ripening period for most whites and reds. These nearly ideal weather conditions enabled growers to harvest their crops at optimal sugar and phenolic ripeness levels. Leading grower Mathis Bastian said, "2007 will have the power of 2005 coupled with the finesse of 2006." This will surely be a vintage of great quality, with slightly less quantity than normal.

Updates on the previous five vintages

2006

Vintage rating: Red (Pinot Noir and its cousins Frühburgunder and St Laurent): 84, White: 89

A relatively dry winter with no spring frost. Heavy rains came at the end of May/early June, with patchy hailstorms destroying up to 60 percent of some crops in Remerschen and Wormeldange. Muscat and Gewürztraminer were affected by relatively humid conditions later in June, but a dry July stopped the development of powdery mildew; however, weather conditions were perfect for downy mildew. Although August saw three times the normal rainfall, September weather was great, with the harvest beginning on September 21. Rivaner saw some rot. For those who employ it, skin contact was limited because, in some cases, 30–60 percent of the grapes were affected by mold. Even being harvested on average two weeks earlier than usual, Riesling possessed a higher-than-normal level of acidity, and serious selection was required. Pinot Gris showed high acidity and possibly some green notes due to an earlyish harvest. Pinot Noir was solid, not outstanding, for both still and *crémant* wines, with a decrease of as much as 25 percent in Pinot Noir and Riesling as growers scrambled to separate healthy grapes from rotten ones. Musts of botrytized grapes often required clarification to minimize the risk of the development of vinegar. Nearly all grapes were harvested by October 18 in what IVV viticulturist Serge Fischer describes as "one of the shortest harvests of the last decade," down about 9 percent from normal.

2005

Vintage rating: *Red (Pinot Noir): 88, White: 93*
Spring frosts and later hail damaged berries in the north, lowering yields by up to 40 percent. July was wet, August cool and cloudy. An almost perfect harvest began on September 19. Mildew didn't pose major problems, and most growers used pheromones against moth infestation, limiting the need for spraying pesticides. Musty notes from the mold esca and from a bit of botrytis have found their way into a few Pinots Blanc and Gris, though most are terrific. Nearly all whites are showing well, with excellent balance; many have good-to-great aging potential. Best are Riesling and Gewürztraminer. The Pinot Noirs are eclipsed by those from 2003 and will probably be outshone by the 2007s. *Crémants*, most on the market by now, are excellent value. Many good-to-great icewines are now available or soon will be.

2004

Vintage rating: *Red (Pinot Noir): 85, White: 88*
Overall, a good year both for quantity and quality, comparable to the excellent 1998. IVV reported above-average health for grapes. A dry fall with cool nights and warm days followed a fairly dry summer, ensuring a classic vintage. Bad weather during blooming caused *coulure* in many Riesling vineyards, lowering yields. Pinots were less affected, though autumn hail and late frost caused damage in scattered vineyards, mostly in the north. The harvest began on October 4 for *crémant* base wines. Chilly nights supported retention of acidity and aromatic complexity. The high levels of malic versus tartaric acid in many whites may ensure a reasonably long life, though with an excessively sour character. Those who left Riesling on the vine to mature fully have been rewarded with great wines. Gewürztraminers are very good across the board—the best since 2001. Pinot Noirs range from average to good quality.

2003

Vintage rating: *Red (Pinot Noir): 90, White: 85*

A long, hot, dry summer meant very ripe grapes with low natural acidity, particularly for those who did not take care in the vineyard. This was the first year Luxembourg was allowed to acidify, so inexperienced producers made disharmonious wines. Auxerrois was harvested by the end of September, allowing for some acid retention. There are a few difficult Pinot Blancs and many difficult Pinot Gris due to excessive residual sugar coupled with high alcohol, but most will offer pleasure for the near- to mid-term. Riesling and Pinot Noir can be excellent, maintaining regional character despite the intense summer heat. Rieslings often have a bit of residual sugar, but those with enough balancing acidity should age well. There are many expressive *vendanges tardives* and *vins de paille*, and some terrific icewines from Riesling and Auxerrois for the short to mid-term. This vintage puts Luxembourg Pinot Noir on the map, if you can find any. With their atypically heavy fruit nose and palate, *crémants* made from this vintage are best avoided.

2002

Vintage rating: *Red (Pinot Noir): 83, White: 92*

Although the harvested grapes were sugar-ripe, the high acidity levels of many 2002 wines meant longer fermentation periods for grapes from the more northerly, limestone-influenced soils. Since nearly all work in Luxembourg is done in steel tank, this translated to what are now very reduced wines. The best dry wines will take several years to open. Pinot Blanc, Riesling, Auxerrois, Gewürztraminer, and Chardonnay are all interesting to great, with many Pinot Blancs now showing generously. Most Pinot Gris and Pinot Noirs rank as only okay, since they tend toward leanness without corresponding fruit concentration. Good icewines were harvested in early January. A few fine *crémants* are still available.

Grapevine

- **Bernard-Massard's** new export manager is Jonathan Lyddon, formerly of Belgium's Fourcroy and Burgundy's Patriarche. Lyddon is attempting to grow niche markets in the English-speaking countries of the US, the UK, and Canada. "They are unfamiliar with the styles and varieties Luxembourg produces," the Brit laments, but he adds that "people seem to like these wines." To its amazement, B-M introduced an Auxerrois to Finland with great success and now has the positive problem of having to contend with a short supply.

- **Rumors abound** of a forthcoming initiative to encourage Luxembourg's growers to withhold wines until ready to drink and for keen Luxembourg restaurateurs to stock and promote them as such.

GREATEST WINE PRODUCERS

1. Alice Hartmann
2. Mathis Bastian
3. Mme Aly Duhr & Fils
4. Charles Decker
5. Clos des Rochers
6. Gales
7. Château Pauqué
8. Clos Mon Vieux Moulin
9. Cep d'Or
10. Schumacher-Knepper

FASTEST-IMPROVING PRODUCERS

1. Schumacher-Knepper
2. Sunnen-Hoffmann
3. A Gloden & Fils
4. Cep d'Or
5. Vinsmoselle
6. Häremillen
7. Kohll-Leuck
8. Henri Ruppert
9. Clos des Rochers

NEW UP-AND-COMING PRODUCERS

1. Kayl
2. Schumacher-Knepper
3. Krier-Welbes
4. Mesenburg-Sadler
5. Henri Ruppert
6. Kohll-Reuland
7. Häremillen
8. Kohll-Leuck
9. Paul Legill

BEST-VALUE PRODUCERS

1. Gales
2. Mme Aly Duhr & Fils
3. Cep d'Or
4. Mathis Bastian
5. Vinsmoselle
6. A Gloden & Fils
7. Schumacher-Knepper
8. Krier-Welbes
9. Kohll-Leuck
10. Linden-Heinisch

Grapevine

• **The fourth edition** of the annual Festival Vins & Crémants was held at Luxembourg City's Place Guillaume. It's the largest so far for both attendance and participating wineries. On hand was the country's most notable *enfant* (not so) *terrible* Charles Decker, who finally joined in because "I wanted to know what I was missing." In response to the October 1 countrywide lowering of the permitted blood-alcohol limit for drivers from .08 to .05, organizer Nathalie Reckinger arranged for a free taxi service for attendees leaving the gathering.

• **Wellenstein's Gloden guys** have found success with their growing plantings of Frühburgunder (an early-ripening and closely related cousin of Pinot Noir) so will continue to use it in their Pinot Noir blends. Frühburgunder, or Pinot Noir Précoce, is considered a subvariety of Pinot Noir, so blending with "standard" Pinot Noir is possible.

• **Vinsmoselle's Constant Infalt** is leaving his position as managing director to oversee its sales in China. With the Olympics fast approaching, this bodes well for the cooperative's efforts to find a wider audience, and whither goest Vinsmoselle goes Luxembourg as a whole.

• **Chateau Pauqué's Abi Duhr** has purchased 1 ha of unplanted vineyard land near the Schengen Fels, claiming it's the only Luxembourg vineyard dominated by sandstone.

• **Hermann Tapp,** former vineyard manager at Germany's Van Volxem winery, has been hired by Mathis Bastian.

GREATEST-QUALITY WINES

1. **Pinot Gris Vin de Paille 2006** Charles Decker (€35 per half-bottle)
2. **Riesling Vin de Glace 2006** Alice Hartmann (€68 per half-bottle)
3. **Riesling Wormeldange Koeppchen *** 2006** Alice Hartmann (€14)
4. **Riesling Wormeldange Koeppchen Les Terrasses 2006** Alice Hartmann (€11)
5. **Gewürztraminer Vendange Tardive Wellenstein Foulschette 2005** Mathis Bastian (€15)
6. **Auxerrois Vin de Paille 2006** Charles Decker (€35 per half-bottle)
7. **Pinot Blanc Vin de Paille 2006** Charles Decker (€35 per half-bottle)
8. **Riesling Domaine & Tradition 2005** Mathis Bastian (€9)
9. **Riesling Domaine & Tradition 2005** Mme Aly Duhr & Fils (€8)
10. **Pinot Gris Domaine & Tradition 2006** Clos Mon Vieux Moulin (€10)

BEST BARGAINS

1. **Crémant Riesling 2002** A Gloden & Fils (€7)
2. **Crémant Rosé Brut 2005** Caves St Martin (€5)
3. **Auxerrois 2005** Mathis Bastian (€5)
4. **Riesling Domaine & Tradition 2005** Mathis Bastian (€9)
5. **Riesling Füt 50 2006** Schumacher-Knepper (€7)
6. **Riesling Wormeldange Koeppchen *** 2006** Alice Hartmann (€14)
7. **Riesling Wormeldange Nussbaum 2006** Krier-Welbes (€7)
8. **Riesling Wormeldange Nussbaum 2006** Mme Aly Duhr & Fils (€7)
9. **Riesling Domaine & Tradition 2005** Mme Aly Duhr & Fils (€8)

MOST EXCITING OR UNUSUAL FINDS

1. **Hommage Vin de Mousseux NV** Cep d'Or (€7) *In 2007 Johnny Vesque and nephew released a mousseux of 90 percent Elbling and 10 percent Pinot Blanc and a bold initiative to age it for four-and-a-half years on the lees. Terrific!*
2. **Riesling Crémant 2002** A Gloden & Fils (€7) *Tasted à point, one month from disgorgement. It's both great value and speaks to what most crémants should strive to be.*
3. **Regent 2006** Ries (€6) *Surprisingly palatable, and certified organic.*
4. **Crémant Blanc de Noirs NV** Charles Decker (€9) *A blend of vintages 2002–05 in a country where single- or double-vintage bottlings are the norm.*
5. **Spirit of Schengen Crémant 2005** Vinsmoselle (€9) *Agreeable quaff made with grapes from France, Germany, and Luxembourg but, due to grandfathered-in vineyards, entitled to a "Luxembourg" label.*
6. **Crémant 2005** Schmit-Fohl (€9) *Mostly Chardonnay with some Auxerrois, and aged exclusively in second-year barriques.*
7. **Crémant 2005** Linden-Heinisch (€8) *Jean's been tinkering with botrytized grapes in wines not accustomed to them. Hints at noble rot without it dominating.*
8. **Riesling Vin de Glace 2006** Alice Hartmann (€68 per half-bottle) *Harvested mid-December, so has clear varietal character and great length. Absurdly expensive but equal to Germany's finest of the type.*
9. **Riesling Selection 2006** A Gloden & Fils (€9) *One degree too dry for a vendange tardive, yet too sweet to receive a Grand Premier Cru certificate—a classic example of the failings of the Luxembourg classification system.*

Switzerland

Chandra Kurt

There have been some exciting developments in this small wine country.

CHANDRA KURT

Experiments with newly developed or newly discovered varieties such as Vidal, Johanitter, Blaufränkisch, and Cabernet Dorsat are taking place throughout the country and are finding favor with consumers. The warmer climate is also having an impact on the wine industry: in general, red wines are becoming fuller-bodied and fruitier, and there are fewer thin, insipid wines. The parallel evolution of terroir and commercial wines goes on, creating a range of classic wine styles for both reds and whites that focus on structure, elegance, and complexity. On the other hand, the number of New World–style consumer-friendly fruit bombs with lots of residual sugar is increasing as well.

"Swissness" has become a very fashionable term, and local products are enjoying a positive image. A number of new restaurants serving only Swiss products have opened, so traditional wines such as Chasselas and Müller-Thurgau profit from this ethnological boom. Retail chains are giving more shelf space to Swiss wines, and wine clubs are also very popular.

CHANDRA KURT is the author of several wine books, including the bestseller *Weinseller*, which she has been publishing for nine years. Chandra is a freelance wine writer and contributes on a regular basis to leading newspapers such as *Cash*, *Al dente*, and *Schweizer Familie*, as well as leading wine publications such as *Hugh Johnson's Pocket Wine Book*. In 2004, her first fiction book, *Wine Tales* (Orell Füssli), was published; it was translated into Italian in 2005. In 2006, she won three awards: the Lanson prize for originality for the book *Weintipps* (Werd-Verlag, 2006); the Swiss government's Goldene Rebschere 2006 award for her work in the wine business; and Best Book of the Year 2006 from the Italian sommeliers' association for *Racconti del Vino*. Chandra works as a wine consultant for Swiss International Airlines and several Swiss retail institutions. Chandra's website is www.chandrakurt.com.

The older the better

There is some truth in the belief that older rootstocks produce better wines. This was confirmed by scientists of the viticulture research station Agroscope Changins-Wädenswil (ACW). In a four-year trial, they compared wines made from vines with older rootstocks with four- to eight-year-old vines. The study investigated Syrah, Humagne Rouge, Gamay, Chasselas, Petite Arvine, and Pinot Blanc vines.

One of the main differences between young and old vines is the rootstock. Young plants tend to suffer from water shortages because of their shallower root systems. They are also weaker in physiological values. Although both young and old plants had the same amount of sugar and almost the same amount of polyphenols, older plants showed a higher amount of total acidity and formol index. The tasting showed that the "age bonus" had a stronger effect on Syrah, Humagne Rouge, and Pinot Blanc. Chasselas and Petite Arvine were judged to be the same, whether old or young.

Ladybird threat

Two major Asian lady beetle infestations were discovered in sunflower and corn fields on the shores of Lake Geneva in the Vaud region. So far no vineyard has been affected. If Asian lady beetles (a.k.a. ladybugs or ladybirds) are present when grapes are crushed, they can contaminate large quantities of wine. When crushed or scared, the insect secretes a yellow alkaloid that, while harmless to humans, produces the distinctive aroma of peanuts in wine.

Grapevine

• **The first Lötschberg wine bar** has opened in Bern. In cooperation with the AOC producers of Switzerland, only Swiss wine and AOC products such as Raclette, dried meat, sausages, cheese, and bread are sold (www.loetschberg-aoc.ch).

• **The area devoted to Chasselas** has shrunk again. In the past year, 140 ha were replanted with other grape varieties. The main variety is still Pinot Noir, with 4,490 ha.

• **An Agroscope student** has discovered that wine aged in barrels develops a strong taste of cloves, while wine aged with oak chips contains more vanillin.

• **The wine village of Salgesch** will be part of the European educational project Eurovinq. The project has been put together by a consortium of institutions from Germany, Italy, Spain, Hungary, Poland, France, and Switzerland. Its main objective is the development of a training program for continuing vocational qualifications in the field of wine.

• **The newly developed yeast** Fructoferm W3, which was developed by Swiss research institute Agroscope, has won the Innovation prize for 2007 at the Intervitis Interfructa. Using Fructoferm W3 helps prevent stopped fermentations.

Opinion:
Thinking internationally

The federalist system in Switzerland sometimes brings more disadvantages than advantages in the area of wine. The wine regions work independently, with no national consensus. A high-level row has emphasized this trend: the Valais canton has left the national wine growers' association after a disagreement over the new agrarian politics. Export subsidies will disappear by 2011, and import restrictions will cease. These policies will encourage Swiss growers to produce only top-quality products that can compete in an international market. The downside, however, is that competition will be much fiercer at home. There is also disagreement over the use of oak chips, which have been permitted since 2007, but many wine growers are opposed to their use. Some would like to see a declaration on the wine label, while others don't think it is necessary.

It is also difficult to describe a typical Swiss wine. Chasselas and Pinot Noir are the main varieties, but next to them lots of newly created or rediscovered old varieties are popping up. It will be interesting to see how long they survive on the market and whether they will become a serious part of the Swiss wine industry.

One positive development is that a growing appreciation of "Swissness" means that local products are in vogue.

Grapevine

• **The Volg Winery** (Winterthur) has had its first harvest of newly planted varieties Elbling and Blaufränkisch. A limited number of bottles were launched at the end of 2007 and sold out immediately.

• **The Filtrox company** (St Gallen) has developed a filter that can effectively remove compounds like trichloranisole (TCA) from wine. The filter, Fibrafix TX-R, was developed in partnership with a California company for wine producer Gallo.

• **The European Court of Justice** has ruled that winemakers in the Swiss village of Champagne cannot use the town's name on their wine labels.

• **Diego Mathier** from the Valais winery Nouveau Salquenen (Salgesch) was chosen as Winegrower of the Year 2007 at the official competition Grand Prix du Vin Suisse 2007.

• **The wine university** of Wädenswil (Hochschule Wädenswil) has become part of the Zürcher Hochschule für Angewandte Wissenschaften (www.zhaw.ch). The merger should create more opportunities for international cooperation and research programs.

• **Carrefour** has closed its doors in Switzerland for the second time. The wine department will be replaced by the wines of Coop, the country's biggest retailer (www.coop.ch).

Vintage Report

Advance report on the latest harvest

2007

Right to the end, this was a most unpredictable year. Winter was unusually mild, and April's sudden heat wave led growers to believe that the harvest would be unusually early. This prediction turned out to be wrong after cold weather in May stopped growth. May, June, and July were rather chilly, with lots of rain and some hail. In mid-July, temperatures jumped suddenly from 55°F (13°C) to 91°F (33°C), and grapes were almost sunburned. Beautiful weather in September and October raised sugar levels, with the result that the vintage is considered very good but rather low in quantity.

Updates on the previous five vintages

2006

Vintage rating: *Red: 90, White: 86*

Quality is similar to the rather good 2005s, especially for reds; very good results in the Valais, the Ticino, and the Bündner Herrschaft (Grisons). In the Grisons, main grape Pinot Noir reached an average 100° *Oechsle*. In the Ticino, Merlot (85 percent of production) reached an average of 89° *Oechsle*, 0.4 up on 2005. The main white grape became Chardonnay.

The Valais, the biggest canton in terms of production, harvested 40.9 million liters. With 10.2 million liters, Chasselas made up a quarter of the total harvest there. Despite a lot of rain at the end of August in the Valais, the fall was long and warm. There was no rot, and black varieties were mature and healthy at harvest. Late-harvest wines are very interesting, since they reached an *Oechsle* level of 200°. The Waadt harvest was the smallest for 25 years. Quality-wise, 2006 is being compared to 2002.

2005

Vintage rating: *Red: 92, White: 91*

As in most of Europe, 2005 was a very special vintage. The overall quality is very good but quite limited, so wines sold more quickly than usual. Unlike 2003, higher-quality wines (especially reds) show good aging potential and are marked by elegance and balance. In 2004, wines were generally delicate, fruity, and lively, whereas in 2003 they showed concentration and maturity: 2005 seems to have taken the best out of these two vintages.

2004

Vintage rating: *Red: 90, White: 90*

Most producers were happy that 2004 was not as hot as 2003. Though similar in quantity to 1998 and 2001, quality was far better, and wines were more balanced. In the Valais, red wines have very good structure and balance. In the Vaud, the Chasselas had a lively, fruity freshness. Red wines in Geneva appear to have the edge on quality: the Pinot Noirs of the Drei-Seen-Region reached 90° *Oechsle*, while Chasselas was lower at 72°. The wines from Bündner Herrschaft had higher sugar levels due to the Föhn (the region's warm fall wind): 98° *Oechsle* for Pinot Noir and 73–78° for Müller-Thurgau. In general, reds and whites are harmonious and balanced. In the Ticino, Merlot reached an average of 86.6° *Oechsle*.

2003

Vintage rating: *Red: 91, White: 88*

Although many of the 2003 results are outstanding in quality and aroma, cellar work needed flexibility and skill. Wine quality is extraordinary. Pinot Noir reached an average 106° *Oechsle*, Müller-Thurgau 83°. In general, most of the varieties had *Oechsles* over 100°, a quality level not seen since 1947. It was also a very early harvest—a month earlier than usual in the Grisons. Due to a difficult, very hot summer, there are two types of quality. Wine growers with more experience knew how to manage the high sugar levels, but many smaller growers produced overalcoholic wines with an overcooked taste. When buying wine, you have to know who did a good job in the cellar.

2002

Vintage rating: *Red: 90, White: 85*

Quality varies from good to excellent, with wines that are more elegant than full-bodied. In some regions, quantity dropped by as much as 30 percent over 2001, showing that growers reduced quantity to increase quality.

GREATEST WINE PRODUCERS

1. Daniel & Martha Gantenbein (Fläsch)
2. Jean-René Germanier, Bon Père, Germanier (Vétroz)
3. Hans Ulrich Kesselring, Schlossgut Bachtobel (Ottoberg)
4. Fromm Weingut (Malans)
5. Luigi Zanini (Besazio)
6. Werner Stucky (Rivera)
7. Didier Joris (Chamoson)
8. Raymond Paccot (Féchy)
9. Daniel Huber (Monteggio)
10. Anne-Catherine & Denis Mercier (Sierre)

FASTEST-IMPROVING PRODUCERS

1. Domaine du Daley (Lutry)
2. Cave du Rhodan (Salgesch)
3. Grillette Domaine de Cressier (Cressier)
4. Mario Chanton, Chanton Weine (Visp)
5. Stéphane Reynard & Dany Varone, Domaine Cornulus (Sierre)
6. Robert Gaillard (Sion)
7. Jacques Tatasciere, Domaine de la Rochette (Cressier)
8. Weingut Donatsch (Malans)
9. Volg Weinkellereien (Winterthur)
10. Provins (Sion)

NEW UP-AND-COMING PRODUCERS

1. Mario Chanton, Chanton Weine (Visp)
2. Pierre & Jean Hutin (Dardagny)
3. Weingut Mürset (Twann)
4. Weingut Bisang (Dagmersellen)
5. Weingut Reblaube (Uetikon am See)
6. Nicolas Bonnet, Domaine de la Comtesse Eldegarde (Satigny)
7. Christian Obrecht, Weingut zur Sonne (Jenins)
8. Jürg Saxer, Weingut Bruppach (Neftenbach)
9. Weingut Umbricht (Untersiggenthal)
10. Philippe Darioli (Martigny)

BEST-VALUE PRODUCERS

1. Provins (Sion)
2. Volg Weinkellereien (Winterthur)
3. Domaine du Centaure (Dardagny)
4. Zweifel & Co. (Zürich)
5. Vins Rouvinez (Sierre)
6. Jean-René Germanier, Bon Père, Germanier (Vétroz)
7. Henri Cruchon (Echichens)
8. Raymond Paccot (Féchy)
9. Hermann Schwarzenbach (Meilen)
10. Rimuss- und Weinkellerei Rahm (Hallau)

GREATEST-QUALITY WINES

1. **Pinot Noir 2005** Daniel & Martha Gantenbein, Fläsch (SF 52)
2. **Pinot Noir Nr. 3 Der Andere 2005** Schlossgut Bachtobel, Ottoberg (SF 29)
3. **Pinot Noir Uris 2006** Davaz, Fläsch (SF 32)
4. **Bianco del Ticino 2005** Castello Luigi, Luigi Zanini, Besazio (SF 95)
5. **Heida Spätlese 2005** Mario Chanton, Chanton Weine, Visp (SF 35 per half-bottle)
6. **Müller-Thurgau 2006** Schlossgut Bachtobel, Ottoberg (SF 15)
7. **Pinot Noir Malanser Barrique 2005** Fromm Weingut, Malans (SF 30)
8. **Sauvignon Blanc 2006** Grillette Domaine de Cressier, Cressier (SF 21)
9. **Cayas 2005** Jean-René Germanier, Bon Père, Germanier, Vétroz (SF 33)
10. **Cornalin 2005** Anne-Catherine & Denis Mercier, Sierre (SF 36)

BEST BARGAINS

1. **Féchy Le Brez 2006** Raymond Paccot, Féchy (SF 12.75)
2. **Vétroz Grand Cru 2006** André Fontannaz, Cave de la Madeleine, Vétroz (SF 15)
3. **Rosé de Pinot Noir 2006** Domaine du Daley, Lutry (SF 15)
4. **Muscat Petit Grain 2006** Robert Gaillard, Sion (SF 19.90)
5. **Riesling x Sylvaner 2006** Turmgut Erlenbach, Erlenbach (SF 14)
6. **Fendant Vétroz Les Terrasses 2006** Jean-René Germanier, Bon Père, Germanier, Vétroz (SF 13)
7. **Blauburgunder 2006** Weingut Pircher, Eglisau (SF 14.50)
8. **Le Chasselas Grand Cru Vilette 2006** Domaine du Daley, Lutry (SF 14.20)

⑨ **Federweisser 2006** Weingut Baumann, Oberhallau (SF 13.80)

⑩ **Riesling x Sylvaner Goldbeere 2006** Volg Weinkellereien, Winterthur (SF 10.50)

MOST EXCITING OR UNUSUAL FINDS

① **Grillette Brut Absolu G Méthode Traditionnelle NV** Grillette Domaine de Cressier, Cressier (SF 26) *What freshness and minerality! For me, this is the most exciting Swiss sparkling wine today, showing lots of finesse and length. Seventy percent Pinot Noir and 30 percent Chardonnay.*
I could name a lot of champagnes that do not taste as good. There is no liqueur de dosage. Brrr... only for hard-core Ultra Brut lovers.

② **Heida Spätlese 2005** Mario Chanton, Chanton Weine, Visp (SF 35 per half-bottle) *The aromatics of this wine are new to me—even the variety is an old grape of the Valais (Heida). Honey, lime, and fleur de sel, very intense, mark the main characteristics. Absolutely impressive and full of passion. A new level of Helvetic sweet-wine pleasure.*

③ **Müller-Thurgau 2006** Schlossgut Bachtobel, Ottoberg (SF 15) *As in Germany, Hans Ulrich Kesselring doesn't do a malolactic fermentation with this wine (most other Swiss producers do). The result is an ultra-crisp white wine with marvelous acidity and freshness and wonderful sweet-sour aromatic seduction on the palate.*

④ **Pinot Noir 2005** Mario Chanton, Chanton Weine, Visp (SF 28) *Unlike his father, Chosy Chanton, who is known for cultivating old Valais grape varieties, Mario has been growing classic varieties such as Pinot Noir. His new release is very dense, concentrated, and opulent.*
The tannins are very fine and the fruit is ripe and marked by strawberries and black currants.

⑤ **Amigné de Vétroz flétrie sur souche 2005** André Fontannaz, Cave de la Madeleine, Vétroz (SF 34) *A perfect example of Swiss wine culture, loaded with notes of honey, caramel, dried apricots, balsamic vinegar, and raisins. A Valais classic.*

⑥ **Domaine du Chapitre 2005** Provins, Sion (SF 39) *Arvine, Amigne, and Humagne Blanche are the varieties in this new white wine, which shows another step in the quality development of the biggest cooperative in Switzerland. The opposite of rather neutral Chasselas wines or Müller-Thurgau from Schlossgut Bachtobel (see above). As good as it gets.*

⑦ **Strohwein Barrique 2004** Volg Weinkellereien, Winterthur (SF 33.50) *Sweet, ripe aromatics, some woody notes, velvety, smooth taste. An Amarone-style red made from Pinot Noir. A specialty from east Switzerland. Warm, dense finish. Some cooked fruit but very soft and elegant.*

⑧ **Sauvignon Blanc 2006** Lattenberg, Zweifel & Co., Zürich (SF 25) *Crisp, elegant, and highly perfumed. Modern winemaking from a traditional Zürich producer.*

⑨ **Pinot Noir Graf Zeppelin Réserve 2005** Grillette Domaine de Cressier, Cressier (SF 36) *A wine that improves every year. Complex and heavy in body, with lots of ripe fruit expression. One of the 10 best Pinot Noirs in Switzerland.*

⑩ **Pinot Noir Premium 2005** Landolt Weine, Zürich (SF 40) *This newly launched velvety, full-bodied Pinot Noir speaks a new language—maybe one of a warmer climate in Zürich. Modern, jammy taste with a charming finish.*

Austria

Philipp Blom

The most significant recent indicator of change is a surprising one: Austria produces increasingly good Pinot Noirs.

PHILIPP BLOM

Why is that important? Because Pinot only ever has a chance of becoming great if it is made with transparency and terroir character in mind, if it is made in the vineyard rather than in the cellar. In Austria, where "cellar-heavy" red and white wines have been much in evidence in recent years, the emergence of good Pinot is both the result of a stylistic rethink and a beacon driving wine styles forward.

Producers such as Willi Bründlmayer, Schloss Gobelsburg, Fred Loimer, Schloss Halbturn, and Claus Preisinger have led the way here, though others are following with plenty of initiative and increasingly defined stylistic concepts. These wines have occasioned heated discussions among producers. A great deal is going to happen over the next decade. Notoriously delicate, Pinot needs the right clones, the right density of vines per hectare, and, crucially, the right age. Once new plantings come into production and reach maturity in the coming years, it will become clear what the real potential for this variety is in Austria, where it has been present since the Middle Ages.

Another aspect of this increasing discussion about wine styles and regional identity is the changing face of Blaufränkisch, Austria's best indigenous black variety. The heartland of this grape is the Middle and South Burgenland, and it is becoming more obvious that the big, soupy,

PHILIPP BLOM is a writer and journalist (*Wine & Spirits* magazine, *Hugh Johnson's Pocket Wine Book*). His book *The Wines of Austria* was published by Faber & Faber in 2000 and appeared in a revised and extended edition in 2006. His other books include *The Vertigo Years: Change and Culture in the West, 1900–1914* (London, 2008). He lives in Vienna.

alcohol-rich monsters of the early 2000s are a thing of the past. The most significant initiative came from Roland Velich's Moric project—a range of Blaufränkisch wines from old vines in the Middle Burgenland vinified without new wood and with a very burgundian style in mind. These wines have opened up a new dimension of this variety. Now other growers are pursuing this vision of Blaufränkisch as a regionally typical cool-climate red wine with great aging potential and an emphasis on balance and elegance, and not a style from hotter climes with the help of cellar technology. This new wave, it seems to me, is the future for Austrian reds.

Death of Alois Kracher

The most shocking news of the year was the sudden death, in late 2007, of Alois Kracher, sweet-wine champion, wine pioneer, and winemaker extraordinaire, as well as unofficial ambassador of his country, from New York to Tokyo. He was 48. The Kracher winery is now led by his son Gerhard.

Boost for Stift Göttweig

The venerable Stift Göttweig, a monastery founded in the Middle Ages and commanding the eastern entrance to the Wachau, has put the vinification of its hitherto thoroughly unremarkable wines into the very capable hands of Fritz Miesbauer, ex-Freie Weingärtner Wachau, who has already transformed the Weingut der Stadt Krems, of which he remains director.

Positive moves in Vienna

As part of the renaissance of Viennese wines, the traditional Viennese estate and *Heurige* Mayer am Pfarrplatz, so far synonymous with old-fashioned wine in the worst sense of the word, has been purchased by financier Hans Schmidt, who has put Willi Balaniuk in charge of winemaking, with predictably positive results. Wines from Vienna are beginning to shape up in earnest.

Grapevine

• **Peter Veyder-Malberg** has decided to strike out on his own as a wine consultant, planning eventually to have an estate somewhere in Austria. He spent 14 years as winemaker at Schloss Hardegg, which pioneered a new quality wave in the northern Weinviertel.

• **The DAC initiative in Austria** (controlled districts similar to the French AOC) is continuing apace, with two new DACs—Traisental and Kremstal—as of the 2007 vintage.

Opinion:
Striving for improvements

After years of stunning success internationally as well as nationally, Austria's top producers are finding that it is not enough to stand still and keep the quality level: things have to evolve, styles have to be redefined. Having been the darling of the press, the prestigious Wachau growers suddenly found fickle media attention drifting to Germany's Rheingau and Rheinhessen areas for Riesling and searching for clearer, more mineral wines, away from the often botrytis-laced top wines of some well-known Wachau estates. Also, the absence of true contenders in the international mass market and the influx of cheap and reliably made foreign wines into Austrian supermarkets meant that redefinition was necessary.

On a broad level, the DAC initiative is proof of a search for quality and regional character for the more everyday wines, and improvements are evident, even if—particularly in the Weinviertel—the great jump in quality that had been envisaged for large parts of the region's production has so far been only partly realized. The Weinviertel has therefore started "Weinviertel Plus," another quality-control mechanism, using outside experts to consult on vineyard and cellar work, as well as to taste the finished wines.

On a more individual level, quality initiatives are sprouting everywhere, be it the Leithaberg initiative in Neusiedlersee-Hügelland or the involvement of Australian wine consultant Mac Forbes in Carnuntum. By far the most significant change, however, has been a move to organic and even biodynamic winemaking. Whatever one may think of the ideology behind biodynamic winemaking, it does deliver the goods. The Swiss-American consultant Andrew Lorrand has become the biodynamic guide to a substantial group of elite wine growers, including Judith Beck, Fred Loimer, Bernhard Ott, John Nittnaus, and Franz Weninger. Many others are experimenting with biodynamic methods.

Another move is away from modern, technologically based vinification methods and international varieties and clones, and back to old vines (Prager/Bodenstein, Velich, Gebelshuber) and old methods, including fermentation with wild yeasts, more oxidative styles of vinification, and large used barrels. The results so far—first and foremost Gobelsburg's consistently delicious and fascinating Tradition Riesling and Grüner Veltliner—are most encouraging, and it seems that Austrian winemakers are on the way to forging a more focused, regionally based identity for themselves.

Vintage Report

Advance report on the latest harvest
2007

This was a year of two halves. After a mild winter and a fine spring with early warm days and brilliant April sunshine, vegetation was well in advance of average years. Flowering started in May, and June continued sunny and almost ideal, despite hailstorms damaging some vineyards around Krems and the Thermenregion. Amid the July heat, with the first signs of sunburn on the grapes, one of the earliest harvests on record seemed a certainty, and early varieties for Sekt and simple wines were beginning to be picked in August, but rain later in the month and a cool, wet September suddenly changed everything and split the harvest in half. October and November proved unreliable, with short sunny periods alternating with rain. Harvesting well was a question of choosing exactly the right days, long enough after the rains to allow the grapes to dry off without being drenched once again.

Patience was a great advantage in 2007. In many areas the wet September meant that most harvesting was done by mid-October, with only a few growers in Lower Austria holding out for their top wines until well into November. The resulting wines often show good fruit but rarely very high sugar levels, and the Wachau in particular will struggle to produce the same amount of Smaragd wines as usual. Favoring elegant acidity and balanced aromas over power and exuberance, 2007 may be compared to 2002. Yields were average to good, particularly for Grüner Veltliner, whose thicker skins withstood the moisture better than many Rieslings. Red wines are showing good color and structure.

Updates on the previous five vintages
2006

Vintage rating: *Red: 97, White: 93, Sweet: 93*

A great year by any standard—the best in two decades. Initially, things looked bleak. A long, cold, snowy winter turned into a cool, wet spring. In June, the summer finally arrived with a heat wave and warm winds. July was fine, but August was cool and exceptionally rainy, and only the radiant September and October brought relief and provided perfect ripening conditions. Yields were generally low, but quality was exceptional.

Black varieties reached full maturity without losing acidity, and Pinot Noir, Blaufränkisch, and St Laurent showed beautiful fruit and balanced structure with excellent aging potential. Among the whites, Rieslings performed very well and Grüner Veltliner possibly set new quality standards for the variety in terms of fruit, maturity, and acidity. Some great wines can be expected here. Other grapes, such as Chardonnay and Sauvignon Blanc, also did very well. Only sweet wines were more difficult, since the warm and dry fall did little to help the development of botrytis, a boon for all dry wines. This is a classic vintage, and the prospects for aging both red and white wines are excellent.

2005

Vintage rating: *Red: 91, White: 86, Sweet: 92*
As ever, the scores are misleading, since they ignore the great quality differences in this vintage, ranging from very mediocre to outstanding, especially for dry whites. After an endlessly rainy fall, some top growers had to accept yields of only 30 percent of normal in order to ensure perfectly ripe and healthy material, producing some exceptional wines.

Expect pure fruit, elegant acidity, and good ripeness for leading white wines in Lower Austria. Reds from early-ripening varieties have done well here, too. In Styria, vineyards suffered from Mediterranean low-pressure systems more than the rest of Austria, but with equivalent quantitative losses, producers were able to achieve full ripeness and good fruit for their wines. It is certainly a vintage that emphasizes terroir over sheer fruit extract. For once, early ripeness was not an advantage in the Burgenland, where growers had to wait for harvesting and also had to deal with substantial botrytis infections. This was good news for sweet wines, and there are outstanding TBAs, if only in very small quantities.

2004

Vintage rating: *Red: 84, White: 88, Sweet: 87*
Simple scores misrepresent 2004, since the quality of wines depended on individual producers' care in the vineyard, and results vary widely. In general, though, this is the weakest of the past 10 years, and while there are successful wines, they should not be laid down for too long.

The weather was far from ideal, even if a beautiful August and early September rescued much of what had been written off. Only the grapes of those producers relying on low yields from the start could achieve full physiological ripeness, and these produced clean and strongly varietal wines with pronounced acidity. It was a particularly elegant vintage for Grüner Veltliner and Riesling, but quantities were small. Among the black grapes, early ripeners like Zweigelt had a clear advantage, but these will not be wines for aging. Varieties such as Blaufränkisch often benefit from good acidity, while other, hotter grapes such as Cabernet Sauvignon and Syrah had trouble achieving full ripeness.

2003

Vintage rating: Red: 94, White: 92, Sweet: 85

Marked by two heat waves, in May and late summer, this was an exceptional year. Harvests began in August, the earliest recorded date, and under ideal conditions, though younger vines especially suffered from drought. Growers who dealt well with the excessive heat (by leaving leaf canopies, etc.) could bring in a dream harvest.

This is a perfect year for red wines, and while conditions would have allowed another charge of blockbusters, many producers opted for denser, more structured wines. Growers who protected their grapes from sun stress also harvested white wines of astonishing freshness with beautiful acidity and great aging potential.

2002

Vintage rating: Red: 89, White: 91, Sweet: 97

In Lower Austria this year will be remembered for its fall rains and floods that made many terraced vineyards collapse. Red wines are well balanced with ripe tannins, and the prevalent botrytis was good news for nobly sweet wines.

Styrian growers made expressive Sauvignon Blancs and Chardonnays, and in Lower Austria this difficult vintage proved to possess the seeds of true greatness for producers who practiced rigorous grape selection and who harvested late. Wonderfully balanced Rieslings and, to a lesser extent, Grüner Veltliners, especially in the Wachau and the Kamptal, show great elegance, depth, and potential.

GREATEST WINE PRODUCERS

1. Alzinger (Wachau)
2. Bründlmayer (Kamptal)
3. Gross (South Styria)
4. Hirtzberger (Wachau)
5. Knoll (Wachau)
6. Kracher (Neusiedlersee)
7. FX Pichler (Wachau)
8. Prager (Wachau)
9. Tement (South Styria)
10. Ernst Triebaumer (Neusiedlersee-Hügelland)

FASTEST-IMPROVING PRODUCERS

1. Stift Göttweig (Kremstal)
2. Judith Beck (Burgenland)
3. Sax (Kamptal)
4. Geyerhof (Wachau)
5. Mayer am Pfarrplatz (Vienna)
6. Platzer (South Styria)
7. Rudi Rabl (Kamptal)
8. Summerer (Kamptal)
9. Hermann Moser (Weinviertel)
10. Wachter-Wiesler (South Burgenland)

NEW UP-AND-COMING PRODUCERS

1. Josef Bauer (Donauland)
2. Franz Gruber (Weinviertel)
3. Anton & Ulrike Hagen (Kremstal)
4. Markus Huber (Traisental)
5. Jalits (Südburgenland)
6. Daniel Jaunegg (South Styria)
7. Heinrich Sigl (Wachau)
8. Franz Schneider (Donauland)
9. Hannes Trappel (Carnuntum)
10. Familie Rosner (Kamptal)

BEST-VALUE PRODUCERS

1. Günter Brandl (Kamptal)
2. Buchegger (Kamptal)
3. Schloss Gobelsburg (Kamptal)
4. Roman Pfaffl (Weinviertel)

5. Peter Schandl (Neusiedlersee-Hügelland)
6. Heidi Schröck (Neusiedlersee-Hügelland)
7. Anton & Ulrike Hagen (Kremstal)
8. Markus Huber (Traisental)
9. Undhof Salomon (Kremstal)
10. Wachter-Wiesler (South Burgenland)

GREATEST-QUALITY WINES

1. **Riesling Heiligenstein Lyra 2006** Bründlmayer, Kamptal (€25)
2. **Riesling Smaragd Wachstum Bodenstein 2006** Prager, Wachau (€30)
3. **Grüner Veltliner Lamm 2006** Schloss Gobelsburg, Kamptal (€24)
4. **Riesling Beerenauslese 2005** Hirtzberger, Wachau (€38)
5. **Blaufränkisch 2005** Moric, Neckenmarkt, Middle Burgenland (€25)
6. **Grüner Veltliner Smaragd Kellerberg 2004** FX Pichler, Wachau (€30)
7. **Blaufränkisch Cupido 2004** J Heinrich, Middle Burgenland (€40)
8. **Riesling Smaragd Steinertal 2003** Alzinger, Wachau (€15.50)
9. **Sauvignon Blanc Zieregg 2003** Tement, South Styria (€28)
10. **Nouvelle Vague Chardonnay TBA Nr. 8 2002** Kracher, Neusiedlersee (€39)

BEST BARGAINS

1. **Grüner Veltliner Tradition 2006** Schloss Gobelsburg, Kamptal (€14)
2. **Grüner Veltliner Vinum Optimum 2006** Rudi Rabl, Kamptal (€7.50)
3. **Riesling Urgestein 2006** Summerer, Kamptal (€7.50)
4. **Riesling Moosburgerin 2006** Buchegger, Kremstal (€16)

⑤ **Blaufränkisch Hochberg 2006**
Wellanschitz, Mittelburgenland (€8)

⑥ **Cuvée Julia 2005** Wachter-Wiesler,
South Burgenland (€18)

⑦ **Pinot Noir 2005**
Judith Beck, Burgenland (€20)

⑧ **Blaufränkisch Umriss 2004**
Feiler Artinger, Neusiedlersee-
Hügelland (€12.50)

⑨ **Riesling Galgenberg 2005**
Schneider, Weinviertel (€5.50)

⑩ **Nouvelle Vague Chardonnay TBA
Nr. 8 2002** Kracher, Neusiedlersee
(€39)

MOST EXCITING OR UNUSUAL FINDS

① **Blaufränkisch Cupido 2004**
J Heinrich, Middle Burgenland (€40)
*This was a difficult year, yet Sylvia
Heinrich produced this marvel of
a wine—perfectly balanced and
sophisticated, a true new-generation
Blaufränkisch with ripe tannins,
well-integrated wood, a touch of
salty fruit, and plenty of potential.*

② **Pinot Noir 2005** Judith Beck,
Burgenland (€20) *Oh, what a
lovely Pinot! Part of Austria's Pinot
renaissance, it shows a real search
for finesse and individuality, with
beautiful aromas of red fruit and
autumn leaves. This is definitely
the right idea.*

③ **Blaufränkisch 2005** Moric,
Neckenmarkt, Middle Burgenland
(€25) *Deep concentration and
delicate structure, a wine with a
clearly burgundian style and real
terroir character made from
50-year-old Blaufränkisch vines.
Great definition and fine fruit—
a wine that looks into the future.*

④ **Grüner Veltliner Achleiten
Smaragd 2006** Prager, Wachau
(€25) *Concentration and vibrant
mineral notes, citrus and pear
aromas, smoky depth. Every whiff*

*brings new nuances—a wine of
immense length and clarity, with
great aging potential.*

⑤ **Grüner Veltliner Tradition 2005**
Schloss Gobelsburg, Kamptal (€14)
*At once focused and generous, with
great freshness and wonderful
potential for development. Made
with pre-modern techniques; the
initially slightly yeasty, oxidative
aromas are translated into depth
and creamy complexity.*

⑥ **Grüner Veltliner Berg 2006**
Markus Huber, Traisental (€14)
*A new name in Austria, and a
Grüner Veltliner with plenty of
personality and finesse from one
of the lesser-known regions. I was
impressed by the focus and style.*

⑦ **Roter Veltliner Scheiben 2006**
Leth, Wagram (€15) *An unusual wine
from an unusual variety: generous
and mature. Residual sweetness
gives it opulence and exotic charm.*

⑧ **Gelber Muskateller Klassik 2006**
Daniel Jaunegg, South Styria (€7)
*A young winemaker created this
perfect, fragrant summer wine.
In recent years there have been
few new names coming out of this
region, but Mr. Jaunegg shows that
he has the right ideas.*

⑨ **Grüner Veltliner Alte Reben
2006** Bründlmayer, Kamptal (€20)
*Depth and complexity combined
with unforced expression. Blossoms,
lemony acidity, and smoky mineral
tones. Profound and long, with
evolving aromas. Cellar this wine,
watch it evolve, and marvel.*

⑩ **Grüner Veltliner Smaragd
Berglage Loiben 2006** Donabaum,
Wachau (€18) *Clear, deep, and
fragrant, combining the mineral
clarity of the western Wachau with
floral complexity, never losing its
focus and finesse. Beautiful balance
and great potential.*

Eastern & Southeastern Europe

Dr. Caroline Gilby MW

Last year's ban by Russia (see *Wine Report 2008*) on all wine from Georgia and Moldova has had a disastrous effect on both countries.

DR CAROLINE GILBY MW

Both countries were hugely dependent both on wine and on Russia for export earnings. After 18 months of intense negotiations, Moldova finally saw the first shipments heading back to Russia in November 2007. The industry has been barely clinging on, with losses reaching US$180 million by January 2007 and numerous reports of bankruptcies and layoffs. The ban, imposed in March 2006 with claims that Moldovan wine was contaminated (though no proof has ever emerged), was a calamity for such a desperately poor country whose biggest export earner (28 percent) was its wines. Estimates suggest that a quarter of the population have links with the wine industry. One source said, "People are starving in the countryside." The knock-on effects across the economy are huge, with all the banks reported to be hit: buying grapes with loans secured against Russian sales was normal practice.

Russia has imposed very strict conditions for Moldova's return to the market, including 52 analyses carried out by the single state-owned lab. Unfortunately this is underequipped, and the Moldovan authorities have been seeking donor aid for adequate modern equipment. Shipments also

DR. CAROLINE GILBY MW is a freelance writer specializing in Eastern Europe and viticulture. She contributed to *Wines of the World* and *The Oxford Companion to Wine* and writes for *Decanter, Harpers Wine and Spirit Weekly,* wine-pages.com, and *Drinks International.* She is also on the editorial board of the *Journal of Wine Research.* She has a PhD in plant sciences but left science to become senior wine buyer for a major UK retail chain. She lectures for the WSET Diploma and judges the *Decanter* World Wine Awards as well as international wine shows. Caroline also works as an independent consultant to the wine trade.

have to go through a single point of entry controlled by a Russian agency, which takes a levy for marketing and promotions. This is causing delays, and there is concern that the system is open to corruption. In addition, a team of Russian officials has inspected all the wineries that have been approved to export again: currently around 17 have approval, and many of these, coincidentally, are Russian-owned.

A key question, however, is whether Russian consumers will return to buying Moldovan wine, or has its reputation been irreparably damaged? Moldova had nearly 50 percent market share before the ban, but much of this has been filled by so-called "Russian" wine made with imported winemaking materials and cheap bulk wine (especially from Spain and South America), which is finished locally.

Georgia

Sadly, the ban remains firmly in place in Georgia, and while the country was not as dependent on wine sales to Russia as Moldova, wine exports accounted for nearly 10 percent of export earnings, over 80 percent of which went to Russia. There's no sign of any change in status, since, according to one source, "Georgia has made it clear that it does not intend to turn back politically." Georgia also needs to reform its industry and has put the task of writing a new national wine strategy out to tender.

On the positive side, there are several wineries (such as Chandrebi's Orovela, GWS, and Telavi) demonstrating that Georgia has the potential to make internationally appealing yet uniquely Georgian wines from grapes such as Saperavi and Mtsvane. Georgia's historical legacy as the birthplace of wine, as well as its many unique grape varieties (up to 500, of which around 40 are in commercial production), helps create a point of difference. It also has a distinctive cuisine and a culture of wine drinking. Many wineries in Georgia were founded on the model that they could sell anything to the former Soviet countries, and it is these companies, lacking the skill or mindset to change direction, that are suffering most, along with the small farmers who supplied them. There are rumors of numerous bankruptcies. However, the domestic market is reported to be booming, while exports to Poland and the former Soviet satellites are improving—not yet enough to fill the hole, though.

Slovenia shows its mettle

The 2007 *Decanter* World Wine Awards showed that Slovenia is really starting to hit the high notes in terms of quality and exciting unique wines. There were three gold medals for sweet wines, including a stunning Šipon icewine from PraVino that audaciously whisked the regional trophy from under the noses of some superb Tokajis. Even more exciting was the award of two golds to dry whites for the first time (Jakončič and Sutor) and a raft of well-deserved silvers, too.

Slovenia's leading producers aren't resting on their laurels either: Primoz Lavrenčič at Sutor has just made his first Pinot Noir from Burgundy clones. In spite of power outages in the winery and the youth of his vines, the wine seems stunning from barrel—silky and elegant. His 2006 Chardonnay looks like his best ever. Aleks Simčič, winemaker at Edi Simčič, has taken his range up to a new level of quality (and price, too) with two impressive single-vineyard releases: Kosana Chardonnay 2005 and Kolos 2003 (a red blend). The charismatic Ales Kristančič at Movia has installed a new fermentation vat with oak "windows" to develop further his own ideas on biodynamics—while his Puro sparkling wine goes underground for three years for aging and *remuage*. Western Slovenia has created a niche for macerated white wines with long skin contact, influenced by producers in Italy's Collio such as Gravner and Radikon. Not all are done well, but the best are impressive, powerful, and distinctive wines, including Marjan Simčič's Rebula, Sutor's Burja, and Blazic's Sauvignonasse.

On with the EU

The EU continues to exert major influence across the region. Bulgaria and Romania are settling into their membership and have brought wine laws up to EU norms. Bulgaria has completed its vineyard register, though the process is still ongoing in Romania. Even Slovenia (joined in 2004) has not filled the gap between 17,000 ha registered compared to 23,000 ha of vines that show up on aerial images. There are also EU subsidies available for vineyard restructuring in 2007/08, including €18 million to Bulgaria, €11 million to the Czech Republic, €2.2 million to Cyprus, €12 million to Hungary, €25 million to Romania, and €2.7 million to Slovenia.

Croatia is making progress with its accession negotiations and hopes to join by 2009. Grapes are Croatia's most important fruit crop, and the industry hopes to benefit from Instrument for Pre-Accession funding. Macedonia has also been accepted formally as a candidate country, and agreements are in place with other Balkan nations and Turkey.

Grapevine

- **German producer** Henkell & Söhnlein (also owners of Torley in Hungary and Bohemia Sekt in the Czech Republic) acquired a majority shareholding in Ukraine's Kyiv Stolichny Sparkling Wine Plant in October 2007. Major investments are planned in the factory, which produced 16 million bottles of sparkling wine in 2006 and held 23 percent local market share.

Opinion:
Quality does count

Both Moldova and Georgia need to reinvent themselves and get away from their dependence on Russia. Moldova, in particular, should not be lulled into believing all is well again by the trickle of wines going back into Russia. It's highly unlikely that sales will recover to anything like their previous level. The country needs a fundamental reform of the wine sector at all levels, including removal of overly bureaucratic and restrictive wine regulations. This includes seven official agencies involved in wine and 150,000 pages of often conflicting legislation, with more than 4,000 different technological instructions. Moldova must switch from its production-led emphasis on selling wine as a commodity as cheaply as possible.

Unfortunately, lessons do not appear to have been learned from the crisis with Russia. Although Romania is now one of Moldova's biggest customers, the Romanian consumer protection office (ANPC) has recently highlighted cases of Moldovan wine containing banned hybrids and so-called quality wines with too low a level of extract, implying "stretching" of the product. One source mentioned seeing wine vats used for mixing agrochemicals, and there are several wineries where the state of hygiene would give any Western quality controller a heart attack. This kind of attitude has to be stamped out. Also, wineries need a scheme to clear old stocks, perhaps through distillation.

Education is vital—from modern viticulture, to consumer-focused marketing and branding—as well as ensuring that what is in the bottle is correct, legal, and drinkable. Moldovan authorities need to remove their heads from the sand. Instead of talking about doubling yields by 2015 and increasing vineyard area, they should work out where their customers are and what sort of wines they need to produce. The country should also take the opportunity to learn from its neighbors, several of whom have been through similar issues before, and where improved viticulture, foreign investment, stronger domestic markets, and the rise of small boutique-type wineries are all starting to pay dividends.

Burn the barrels

A surprisingly large number of producers across the region remain wedded to the idea that old oak barrels are essential for winemaking if they have any pretensions to quality. My heart sinks at the reek of volatile acidity, mold, and who knows what other microbial infections in so many wineries as they proudly show off their barrel room. It seems almost miraculous when anything survives this treatment to be halfway drinkable; more often than not, whatever fruit was there has been killed off. There's no place for this in modern winemaking, and any oak (old or new) must be scrupulously clean. At the same time, many wineries should replace their pipes and learn to hang them up instead of leaving them to fester in pools of stale wine. Basic hygiene procedures, such as cleaning tanks properly, sealing damaged rusty surfaces, and topping off, are not difficult and make a huge impact for a small investment. This makes the situation sound very grim in this part of Europe, but there are enough wineries doing it right to demonstrate that there's great potential—with both old and new equipment.

Create a wine culture

With global oversupply and more efficient and aggressive exporters claiming market share at the expense of Eastern Europe, it's essential that countries in this region look to their domestic markets. Moldovans drink 40 million bottles of vodka to 2 million bottles of commercial wine. Switching to wine drinking would be better for the economy and for people's health, as well as soaking up some of the vast stocks sitting in winery vats. Similarly, *rakia* still has pride of place on Bulgarian dining tables. In Cyprus, locals need to learn about the rapid improvements in wine quality on their own island (and the opportunity of 3 million tourists as ambassadors) and develop a sense of pride. Both Slovenia and Hungary have strong domestic markets and a growing culture of food and wine, allowing the development of high-quality individual estates and good high-volume producers. Both countries could do more by clamping down on the gray market, which undermines quality developments. Romania, too, has such a buoyant domestic wine market that prices are high and wineries are pulling out of export contracts to meet demand.

The march of the supermarkets continues

Western supermarkets continue to expand into the booming retail markets across Eastern and Southeastern Europe. Producers claim ever-greater demands for listing fees and rebates, while there are also concerns about cheap imports and hard discounters selling only a limited range of private labels. More positively, some producers see the benefits of bringing commercial wine to the public via supermarkets, with their responsibility to their customers, and switching drinkers from homemade or black-market wines sold through kiosks and at the roadside.

Vintage Report

Advance report on the latest harvest

2007

As ever across such a geographically diverse region, opinions vary on the quality of 2007. For some producers it is superb, while others complain of drought stress and burned-out fruit. Most countries suffered from lack of rainfall and report an early start to the harvest. Winter was mild, with little frost (except Romania) and low rainfall, meaning dry soils at the start of the growing season and early flowering. The summer was hot and dry, in places hitting 104°F (40°C) in July, though short spells of rain in August or September rescued the ripening process in most places.

In Slovenia, the harvest was very early and very good, though not quite as good as 2006, especially for whites, where there are some problems with low acidity. The best whites were picked up to a month early to retain acidity. Reds seem to be very successful, and there are also hopes that it will be an excellent year for sweet late-harvest and botrytis wines. In Hungary, 2007 looks like another great Tokaji vintage, with very intense botrytis and also very good results for dry wines. Elsewhere, producers in Villány rate the vintage very highly for reds. Good results for reds in Sopron, too, subject to careful selection to remove botrytis. In Romania, there was little disease and good sugar accumulation, though acidity levels were on the low side. Overall it was good to very good, but with small quantities of good reds. Total harvest volume was up by 4 percent to nearly 900,000 tons, but this is not enough to meet booming demand. In neighboring Moldova, quality is well regarded, especially in whites, though a lot of producers needed to acidify, and aromatics in Sauvignon have suffered in the heat. Fruit was healthy and gave good color in reds, but yields suffered due to the drought.

In Bulgaria, some producers found the summer too hot and have reported burned-out fruit characters. Others are claiming the best vintage since 2000, especially for reds, with good colors, high alcohols, and ripe, concentrated flavors, though whites are more variable. Young vineyards with irrigation survived the drought best, and in the southwest there were life-saving rains in August. Georgia also reports a good, even great year, with few problems during the season. Whites are complex and expressive, while reds are concentrated, with soft tannins and good acid balance and harmony. Reds show potential for longevity, too.

Cyprus also had a dry winter and hot summer, which lowered yields by 10–20 percent. Hot summer temperatures are not unusual here and the harvest was only a few days early. Reds are deep-colored with lots of extract, while whites, especially Xynisteri, did best at higher altitudes.

Updates on the previous five vintages

2006

Vintage rating: *Red: 65 (Moldova), 77 (Georgia, Cyprus), 90 (Romania, Bulgaria), 95 (Slovenia, Hungary), White: 70 (Moldova, Croatia, Georgia), 90 (Romania, Bulgaria, Cyprus), 95 (Slovenia, Hungary), Sweet: 97*

A substantial improvement in quality over 2005. Most areas experienced a cool August, retaining good acidity, followed by a warm September bringing good ripeness levels.

Slovenia had an excellent year, with fruit showing good sugar levels, body, and balanced acidities, though quantities are down by 25–50 percent. Neighboring Croatia did less well, producing mediocre results due to hot spells and rain before and during harvest. Hungary also produced excellent quality due to the warm September and October, accompanied

Grapevine

• **István Szepsy** has launched an impressive range of single-vineyard and dry Tokajis in 2006, from what he reckons to be the most exciting vintage so far for dry wines.

• In the Tokaj village of Mád, 15 producers (Arvay, Barta, DemeterVin, Bodvin, Budaházy, Gergely, Lenkey, Orosz, Royal Tokaj, Galambosi, Tokaj Classic, Matisa Carlo, Gundel, Török, and Szepsy) have formed an association to develop a program of controlled origin and improved quality. There will be three quality levels, including regional wines, village wines, historical classified-growth sites, and *kert* ("garden") wines from individual sites.

• **Belvedere's** new €12-million Katarzyna Winery in the south of Bulgaria was opened officially in September 2007, though its first vintage, made elsewhere by consultant Marc Dworkin, had been released six

months earlier. So far, 600 ha have been planted, and the aim is over 1,000 ha by 2009. The best wine so far is Contemplation, a stylish blend of Cabernet, Merlot, Mavrud, and Syrah.

• **Telish Wine Cellars** in Bulgaria is continuing to work with Michel Rolland. The 2007 vintage was made in the new winery, and the winemaking team will travel to Argentina to work with Rolland and gain more international experience.

• **Leading Bulgarian winemaker** Ognyan Tzvetanov (owner of Valley Vintners and producer of Sensum) has made his first vintage in his own winery at Borovitza in northwestern Bulgaria (bought jointly with Adriana Srebinova of Maxxima). The winery has planted its first 15,000 vines and plans another 8 ha in spring 2008, although fruit will continue to be sourced from selected 40-year-old vineyards in the northwest.

by cool nights, giving fruit with excellent body, ripe flavors, and plenty of acidity. In Tokaj, *aszú* formation is good, but low in quantity due to drought. Quality already seems much better than 2005 for dry, late-harvest, and *aszú* styles. In Bulgaria, quality is very good on the whole, with some producers claiming the best vintage in the past decade. In Romania, 2006 is a significant improvement over 2005; grapes are very healthy, with good sugar levels and little rot.

Moldova, southern Ukraine, and Russia were hit badly by severe winter cold, with temperatures dropping to −22°F (−30°C), damaging up to 80 percent of vines in some places. In Moldova, sugar levels were very high, but lack of spraying meant problems with disease. Georgia, too, had high disease pressure, and in some areas black grapes are showing green acidity. In Russia, the growing season was hot and dry, so the limited crop was very high in quality. The Czech Republic was also hit by severe winter cold and poor fruit set, but a warm September rescued the season, and the result is very high-quality, healthy fruit with good acidity. Terrific results are reported in Slovakia. The crop in Cyprus suffered from drought, giving very small berries and high tannin levels, as well as ripening problems in black varieties where vines shut down. Whites fared better overall.

Grapevine

• **Georgia's** first super-premium Saperavi, Orovela, has been released. It was made by consultant winemaker Lado Uzunashvili from selected grapes picked from the 40-ha Chandrebi estate in the Kakheti region.

• **The new wine office** in Hungary may finally have some funds to start promoting Hungarian wine. The first installment of the levy of HUF 8 per liter, previously paid as excise duty, was due to be collected in December 2007. It plans to do more strategic promotions rather than ad hoc events and will work with other agencies, such as the tourist office and Agricultural Marketing Centrum.

• **Weninger & Gere Winery** in Villány, Hungary, has released its first Pinot Noir from the 2006 vintage. Gere also harvested the first crop from young Tempranillo and Barbera plots in 2006, though volumes are not yet commercial. The winery is

also developing a wine hotel with 25 rooms: it will have a high-quality restaurant and spa facilities.

• **Dveri Pax,** in Slovenia, opened its dramatic new winery, which cost around €2.7 million, in June 2007. The winery, owned by Austrian Benedictine monks, is investing €10 million and has 56 ha planted so far.

• **Chateau de Val** in Bulgaria has planted a new 30-ha vineyard, which will be managed organically, and includes Petit Verdot, Viognier, Cabernet Sauvignon, and Merlot.

• **New Slovenian producer** Verus Estate made its first wines in 2007, which looked very promising at an early tasting in November 2007. It was founded by three former employees of Jeruzalem-Ormož wine cellars. The winemaker is Danilo Snajder, and Angela Muir MW is a non-executive director.

2005

Vintage rating: *Red: 75 (Bulgaria, Romania, Turkey),
85 (Slovenia, Hungary, Georgia, Cyprus, Moldova),
White: 80, Sweet: 85*

A variable year, with producers in most countries reporting a late and
difficult year with a cool summer and damp August.

In Hungary, quality was satisfactory, though in the south, later varieties
were better, giving slow-maturing but potentially long-lived reds. Szekszárd
and Sopron also produced some very good reds, while in Tokaj a warm
fall rescued a poor season. This allowed botrytis development for producers
in the north of the region, who are very optimistic about the quality of
aszú wines. In Romania, the vintage was disappointing, with low sugars
and high acid, and whites fared better than reds. In Bulgaria, quality was
below 2004. Where wineries own vineyards, there were some nicely
balanced wines, and there were good results in the south. Western Slovenia
saw a harvest similar to 2004, with better-than-expected quality in the
reds, and whites are ripe but fresh. Eastern Slovenia had problems with
achieving full ripeness. Croatia had rains mid-harvest, so wines will be
mediocre overall, especially whites.

Both Macedonia and Moldova had a much better season than 2004.
Clean, healthy fruit, with good natural sugar, flavor development, and
acidity—similar to 2003—are reported. In the Czech Republic, the damp
summer was rescued by a warm fall, giving good sugars and plenty of
aromatics. Cyprus produced a small harvest but with fresh aromatic whites
and promising reds. In Turkey, quality was low due to downy mildew and
picking too early. In Georgia, careful fruit selection was essential due to
heavy rain and hailstorms in late August, but overall quality is promising,
especially for Saperavi, which is showing excellent varietal character.

2004

Vintage rating: *Red: 75, White: 80 (Slovenia & Hungary
best producers: 85), Sweet: 80*

A late and cool vintage, where low yields were crucial to achieve full
ripeness in many areas. In Hungary, whites and rosés showed good fruit
levels and crisp acidity. Reds ripened well only on favored sites and
gave decent results only with ultra-low yields and meticulous selection.
However, the best are showing lovely elegance and finesse. In Romania,

reds are lighter than 2003, but whites are fresh with good aromatics. The Bulgarian harvest was smaller than 2003, and reds are less ripe, though notable for fresh whites. In Tokaj, there were good levels of botrytis but without great concentration, so wines are elegant and fruity, but mainly at lower *puttonyos* levels.

In the west of Slovenia, whites are fruity and fresh, while reds have good color and fruit, except for some green tannins in Cabernet. In the east, grapes were low in sugar with high acid, except where yields were severely reduced. Croatia reported a slightly better-than-average vintage, though less tannic than normal, with some botrytis development for sweet wines, with a similar picture in the Czech Republic and Slovakia.

Farther east, Georgia had a very good vintage, with expressive and well-balanced whites, and reds with fine, well-matured tannins. However, both Moldova and Russia had a difficult year due to high disease pressure and very high acid levels.

2003

Vintage rating: *Red: 95 (except Ukraine & SE Romania: 75), White: 90, Sweet: 95*

The hot, dry summer across Europe meant most countries reported particularly good results for reds and a very early start to the harvest.

In Bulgaria, quality was very good, with high levels of sugar and polyphenols at harvest, but with unusually high acidity levels. In Romania, the western areas reported a warm, dry summer, and quality was very good. In Moldova, the 2003 harvest was generous and of high quality— the best vintage in the previous five years. Slovenia had a very early vintage with extremely high-quality reds (the best ever for some producers), though some whites suffered from low acidity. Tokaj in Hungary saw a lower *aszú* yield than expected. The first releases of 2003 *aszú* wines look excellent, though perhaps lacking a little of the balancing acidity of 1999 and not as rich in sugar as 2000. Very good to outstanding results for dry and late-harvest wines. The rest of Hungary reports excellent reds and intense fruit flavors in whites, though low acidity in some varieties. In Croatia, 2003 is a year with lots of extract, alcohol, and excellent quality. Cyprus also reports one of the best vintages in recent years and good quantities. In Slovakia, picking of Riesling was delayed until October but with excellent results.

2002

Vintage rating: *Red: 75, White: 80 (Slovenia & Hungary: 90), Sweet: 90*

A mixed year, ranging from outstanding in Transylvania to below average in areas such as northern Bulgaria and southeastern Romania, which were hit by heavy rains.

In Hungary, wines are very concentrated. Reds, especially from the south, continue to show well. In Tokaj, hopes for a great *aszú* vintage were dashed by some rain in October, but wines are nicely balanced, especially for fruit harvested early. Slovenian production was down 20–30 percent, but overall quality was high in both reds and whites. In Romania, most areas are showing very good quality but heavily reduced yields due to drought at flowering. Not a successful year for either Bulgaria or Macedonia. In Cyprus, quality was good, though low in quantity.

GREATEST WINE PRODUCERS

1. Szepsy (Hungary)
2. Királyudvar (Hungary)
3. Domaine de Disznókő (Hungary)
4. Oremus (Hungary)
5. Edi Simčič (Slovenia)
6. Marjan Simčič (Slovenia)
7. Gere Atila/Weninger & Gere (Hungary)
8. Malatinszky Kúria (Hungary)
9. Weninger (Hungary)
10. Movia (Slovenia)

FASTEST-IMPROVING PRODUCERS

1. Sutor (Slovenia)
2. PraVino (Slovenia)
3. Dobogó Winery (Hungary)
4. Recaş Winery (Romania)
5. Carl Reh Winery (Romania)
6. Santa Sarah Winery (Bulgaria)
7. Casa Davino (Romania)
8. Vlassides (Cyprus)
9. Kyperounda (Cyprus)
10. Pendits Winery (Hungary)

NEW UP-AND-COMING PRODUCERS

1. Verus (Slovenia)
2. Katarzyna Estate (Bulgaria)
3. Borovitza (Valley Vintners) (Bulgaria)
4. Dveri Pax (Slovenia)
5. Arvay & Co (Hungary)
6. Patricius Winery (Hungary)
7. Bessa Valley (Bulgaria)
8. Miroglio (Bulgaria)
9. Terra Tangra (Bulgaria)
10. Chandrebi Estate (Orovela) (Georgia)

BEST-VALUE PRODUCERS

1. Pannonhalmi Apátsági Pincészet (Hungary)
2. Chateau Vincent (Hungary)
3. Telish Wine Cellar (Bulgaria)
4. Recaş Winery (Romania)
5. Carl Reh Winery (Romania)
6. Nyakas Winery (Budai) (Hungary)
7. Maxxima (Bulgaria)
8. Goriska Brda (Slovenia)
9. Miro Mundo (Slovenia)
10. Torley Wines (Hungary)

GREATEST-QUALITY WINES

1. **Tokaji Cuvée Botond 2006** Szepsy, Hungary (HUF 9,360)
2. **Tokaji Aszú 6 Puttonyos 2003** Szepsy, Hungary (HUF 19,500)
3. **Tokaji Aszú 6 Puttonyos 2000** Királyudvar, Hungary (HUF 18,900)
4. **Šipon Ledeno Vino 2004** (icewine) PraVino, Slovenia (€100)
5. **Tokaji Aszú Esszencia 1996** Royal Tokaji Wine Co, Hungary (HUF 27,000)
6. **Kolos 2003** Edi Simčič, Slovenia (€66)
7. **Cabernet Franc Selection 2004** Weninger & Gere, Hungary (HUF 6,900)
8. **Kékfrankos Spern Steiner Selection 2004** Weninger & Gere, Hungary (HUF 5,600)
9. **Villány Cabernet Franc 2006** Malatinszky Kúria, Hungary (HUF 13,000)
10. **Teodor Rdece Reserve 2003** Marjan Simčič, Slovenia (€30)

BEST BARGAINS

1. **Terase 2006** Jeruzalem-Ormož, Slovenia (€3)
2. **Tramini 2006** Pannonhalmi Apátsági Pincészet, Hungary (HUF 1,350)
3. **Extra Brut 2000** Chateau Vincent (HUF 2,900)
4. **Budai Pinot Gris 2005** Nyakas Winery, Hungary (HUF 1,440)
5. **Quercus Beli Pinot 2006** Goriska Brda (€4.50)
6. **Petritis 2006** Kyperounda, Cyprus (€5.70)
7. **Šipon 2006** Miro Mundo, Slovenia (€4.75)
8. **Cabernet Sauvignon 2006** Telish Wine Cellar, Bulgaria (BGN 6)
9. **Sensum 2004** Valley Vintners, Bulgaria (BGN 12)

10. **Kemendy Cabernet Franc Barrique 2003** Gyorgy Villa, Hungary (HUF 1,800)

MOST EXCITING OR UNUSUAL FINDS

1. **Tokaji Mylitta Alma 2005** Dobogó Winery, Hungary (HUF 13,300) *Simply a gorgeous example of modern Tokaji, produced by the tiny Dobogó winery from first-growth vineyards. It's lusciously sweet but superbly clean and pure, and with the Tokaji hallmark of great acid balance.*
2. **Pinot Noir 2006** Sutor, Slovenia (€19.20) *Primoz Lavrenčič's first Pinot Noir from his young plot of Burgundy clones. The winemaking may not have gone according to plan due to power outages in the winery, but it doesn't matter when you can get lovely fruit like this, with fine-textured tannins and great finesse. Definitely a young winemaker to watch.*
3. **Laški Rizling Ledeno Vino 2005** PraVino, Slovenia (€120) *I don't normally have much time for Laški Rizling, but this is a wine to change my mind. Undoubtedly the best wine from the grape I've ever tasted, with immense presence and excellent balance. A labor of love to produce, too, since it was picked at 6.8°F (−14°C) in January.*
4. **Carolina Bela 2004** Jakončič, Slovenia (€20) *A beautifully made and harmonious blend of Chardonnay with Rebula, which gives the wine a real sense of place. This small family winery in Slovenian Collio is really on top form and deserved its trophy at the Decanter World Wine Awards.*

⑤ Tokaji Hárslevelű Király 2006 Szepsy, Hungary (HUF 5,800) *It may be Furmint that has been getting all the attention as Tokaji's great dry white hope, but this stunning example from István Szepsy shows that Hárslevelű from really great sites like Király can certainly make the grade as a top-quality dry wine, too.*

⑥ Rebula 2004 Marjan Simčič, Slovenia (€16.50) *An excellent example of the unique Collio approach to making white wines: this is macerated white wine done superbly. It spends six months on skins in wooden vats, resulting in a golden tawny wine that is uniquely powerful, complex, and structured, with notes of quince, orange peel, and acacia.*

⑦ Muscat 2004 Ayia Mavri, Cyprus (€6) *It's perhaps not surprising that the heat of Cyprus suits Muscat, but this wine, made by a husband-and-wife team from their family vineyards at over 3,300 ft (1,000 m), is a revelation. It has an amazing nose, excellent intensity, and great purity.*

⑧ Šipon Chardonnay TBA 2005 Dveri Pax, Slovenia (€60) *Dveri Pax is owned by Austrian Benedictine monks and has just opened a brand-new winery on the site of an ancient monastery. This part of Slovenia is best known for whites with vivid fruit and crisp acids. The combination of Šipon (Furmint) and Chardonnay is unusual, but it works well in this elegant, velvety, sweet wine.*

⑨ Domaine Ceptura White 2006 Casa Davino, Romania (RON 70) *A blend of Sauvignon Blanc, Fetească Alba, and Riesling Italico from a small winery with big ambitions: to be the best in Romania. This is a fine and graceful wine, with delicate, fresh, yet exotic fruit notes supported by mineral undertones.*

⑩ Le Sommelier Kékfrankos Rosé 2006 Malatinszky Kúria, Hungary (HUF 1,790) *Rosé as it should be, though the choice of Kékfrankos (Blaufränkisch) is not so common. This is perfect rose pink, with vibrant, fresh fruit and a surprisingly long, clean finish.*

Grapevine

• **The Cyprus Vine Commission** has announced EU funds of around €2.2 million for grubbing up and restructuring, including planting better varieties like Maratheftiko (up 11.5 percent), Lefkada (up 4 percent), and Shiraz (up 18 percent).

• **In Turkey,** a group of 10 producers has agreed to work together and market their wines internationally under the brand "Anatolian Wines." Turkish authorities clamped down on black-market wines starting in fall 2007 by imposing official stamps on all bottles sold. The Wine Industrialists' Association estimates that only 30 million liters, out of a total 110 million liters of wine, are produced by registered growers. The rest is illegally produced and often of very poor quality.

• **Leading Cyprus producer** Sophocles Vlassides is continuing his work with the local Maratheftiko grape variety by planting three different vineyard plots at altitudes ranging from 2,300 ft (700 m) to 3,600 ft (1,100 m) with temperature and humidity probes. He aims to research the effects of weather conditions on flowering, since the variety is prone to uneven berry set.

Greece

Nico Manessis

A shift in strategy has occurred in the country's creaking cooperative movement as the best and most profitable cooperatives are cherry-picked.

NICO MANESSIS

In a unique change of policy, the well-managed and profitable Zitsa Wine Cooperative has been spun off from the Union of Ioannina Cooperatives, which includes food and supermarket outlets. The new name is Zoinos. In a novel arrangement, the new company has awarded a small number of shares to a group of growers who have been farming some of the better Debina vineyards organically. The 35-year-old winery will be decked out with the latest technology. If the new company is successful, other chronically mismanaged co-ops—nearly 20 percent of Greek wine production—will have to take notice. Political handouts have been reduced, so co-ops will have to stand on their own two feet or wither.

NICO MANESSIS is the author of *The Illustrated Greek Wine Book* (Olive Press, 2000) and the three editions of *The Greek Wine Guide* (Olive Press, 1994, 1995, 1996). He is currently working on a new book. He lectures on Greece in a variety of fora, such as the Université du Vin in France, the Ecole du Vin de Changins in Switzerland, and the Le Monde Institute in Greece. He has been writing articles on the wines of his native Greece in the international press for more than 14 years. During the Athens 2004 Olympics he presented a program on Greek vineyards and wines for NBC TV. Nico is a contributor to *The Oxford Companion to Wine* and editor at large of the Greek magazine *Wine & Pleasures*. He judges at international wine competitions and is regional chair of Greece at the *Decanter* World Wine Awards. He is based in Geneva, where he is a member of the Académie Internationale du Vin. In 2007, Nico was honored for his past and ongoing international contribution to Greek wine by the Wine Producers' Association of the Northern Greece Vineyard (ENOABE; for more information, see www.wineroads.gr). Nico's website is greekwineworld.com.

The next generation

The long-awaited shift in the home market is finally happening. Younger, curious, open-minded, and ultimately more demanding consumers have moved away from the larger producers. New to wine and better traveled, these sophisticated consumers are searching elsewhere for broader taste horizons. The market shift is real and has far-reaching ramifications.

Boutique estates have been rewarded for moving Greek wine into the modern age and encouraged to go further. They are exploring the character and nuances of the national vineyard, saving dozens of indigenous grapes from near-extinction. Many—such as Santameriana, the fragrant Malagousia, or the Ionian island specialties Vardea and Vertzami—have much to offer. These developments are a triumph for diversity, but, more important, they are a fundamental part of Greek wine's coming of age.

Samos must do better

For more than 300 years, Samos Muscat has been one of Greece's two most famous sweet wines, with Vinsanto from Santorini. It was appreciated at Versailles and in the Nordic countries and is still appreciated in France; nearly half the island's production is exported in bulk and bottled in Paris.

The Samos Union of Cooperatives was created by an emergency decree in 1934 to stop the civil war that erupted due to merchants' exploitation of farmers. Over the past 20 years it has been a paragon of high quality and good value, winning many medals and awards. More recently the wines have been lackluster. An inertia-ridden complacency is now setting in. Samos is a priceless treasure, but it urgently needs to modernize its antiquated approach and bring these wines, among the finest of their kind, into the 21st century. The island-bottled wines need to be fresher; and when they are, selling in bulk must be stopped. Some styles should have less residual sugar. Packaging needs a makeover. It's high time that a private concern invested in these old terraced vines, to provide some healthy competition.

Greek escapades

Evangelos Gerovassiliou and Vasilis Tsaktsarlis are two of the most gifted and successful winemakers of their generation. They have now joined forces with Stockholm-based wine merchant Takis Soldatos, a marketing maverick with worldwide interests, notably in Tuscany. Their joint venture, Escapades, has invested in Stellenbosch in the Cape and has released a Sauvignon Blanc, a Shiraz, a Pinotage, a Merlot, and a Cabernet Sauvignon. The older vines have been replanted. Gerovassiliou says, "It is great to be working on a different terroir with grapes we know, and we look forward in the near future to introducing Assyrtiko to the Cape."

Opinion:
To respect and protect

Investment in new wineries and vineyards has not been matched by the way wine is treated after it leaves the winery. It takes only a few hours to destroy a year's work. I have seen wines with protruding corks due to "storage" near the radiator. Poor glassware is often used. White wine is served too cold, red wines too warm, and so on. There is a litany of unprofessional practices.

Fifteen million tourists visit our country annually. The customer at the restaurant, café, bar, beach, or mountain resort is not interested in feeble excuses. There has been some progress: there are some gifted, hard-working cooks out there and, more than ever, wine is part of their creativity. Wherever there are sommeliers, they are doing a sterling job. Many cafés now sell screwcapped quarter-bottles or bag-in-box wine, an improvement on carafes of oxidized wine.

But education and training have yet to make their impact. Both the WSET local offshoot and the sommeliers' association have people who can provide invaluable leadership. Wine and its service are now on the curriculum of hospitality service colleges. Graduates are coming into the market, but their expertise has yet to trickle down to grassroots level. Until storage conditions, service, and all the missing links are in place, wine will not be treated with the respect it deserves. Unprofessional practices also do a great disservice to Greek wine prospects abroad. The number of visitors going out of their way to discover indigenous varieties and the diversity Greek wines offer is an opportunity not to be missed.

Grapevine

• **Assyrtiko is on the move** outside its home borders. The latest to plant, albeit on an experimental basis, is the forward-thinking Alois Lageder, a leading producer in Italy's Alto Adige. It will be fascinating to watch how the high-acid, mineral-charged grape will perform at this latitude and altitude.

• **Thirty-four wineries** on 19 Aegean islands have grouped together under a new promotional organization, Aegean Wine Roads. This novel approach offers visitors an insider's view of wine, local food, and culture. With diverse soils and viticultural methods, these island vineyards are home to star indigenous white grapes such as Athiri and Assyrtiko. For more details see aegeanwineroads.gr.

• **Rebuilding has begun** at Tetramythos, the up-and-coming Peloponnesian boutique producer that was burned to the ground during the 2007 fires. The scattered vineyards survived.

Vintage Report

Advance report on the latest harvest

2007

There hasn't been a vintage quite like it in living memory. A lack of winter rainfall and three successive heat waves in June and July reduced berry size, and the crop was down by 20–45 percent. The much-reported fires were at their worst in the northern Peloponnese. Two of the six wine-producing Aighialia subregions were destroyed, representing 20 percent of land. One winery was burned to the ground (see Grapevine). An estimated 60 ha of vines were lost, mostly rows adjacent to the conifer forests. These are being replanted.

Both colors are concentrated and rich-tasting, though not always balanced, since water-stressed vines were widespread. With the exception of volcanic Santorini, where the hallmark minerality is intact, white wines have power, but with less florality and minerality. With such a fragmented vineyard, there are exceptions. Mantinia's grapey wines are aromatically intense, as are central Crete's Vilana wines.

Red wines are stylistically all over the place. Crete struggled with heat stress, and black varieties had the earliest harvest on record. The largest single appellation, Nemea, is most atypical. Beyond deep colors, their aromatic complexity has been replaced by vinous intensity.

The success story is the great Xinomavro grape, with the finest vintage since 1990, and in several instances the finest to date. Naoussa and Amyndeo excelled. Goumenissa and Rapsani, which also blend in Xinomavro with other indigenous black varieties, are also of star quality.

Updates on the previous five vintages

2006

Vintage rating: *Red: 88, White: 87*

A year of unusually extreme weather patterns. June was sunny and warm, but July was one of the coolest on record. August was hot and dry, with excellent conditions, although black grapes were two weeks behind average, and some suffered vine stress due to drought. After timely winter rains, Santorini managed a record-breaking fourth vintage of exceptional quality. September was cool with intermittent showers, heavier in Naoussa and Goumenissa. Hailstorms struck high Aighialia in late September. On the islands, whites were harvested a week later than usual, and black grapes two to three weeks later. Mantinia's Moschophilero is less aromatic than 2005. Amyndeo benefited from the slow maturity cycle, which added fragrance to both colors. On Crete, the tougher-skinned Mandelari grape rather outperformed the softer-tannined Kotsifali. Wines are not as uniform as the splendid 2005s. There are, however, exceptions in many regions, highlighting the levels of high quality now attained by the top names, even in a year of such climatic contrasts.

2005

Vintage rating: *Red: 90, White: 89*

After the abundance of the two previous vintages, nature corrected itself with a yield drop of up to 15 percent. Summer had no extreme weather, and sunny days with cool nights produced ripe, healthy grapes. Conditions during picking were textbook, with the exception of Nemea, which experienced heavy rain toward the end of harvesting. The northern vineyards of Naoussa, Amyndeo, Epanomi, Kavala, and Drama did particularly well in reds and whites. In the Peloponnese Patra, Mantinia did best. The dessert Muscats of Rio Patra are among the most fragrant and balanced in recent years. In the upper part of Nemea, wines harvested prior to the rain have deep color, with more body than the more delicate 2004s. Santorini made super-concentrated, bone-dry whites. Cretan dry whites, especially those made with central Crete's spicy Vilana grape, are astonishing for their levels of ripeness and freshness. Samos Muscats are perfumed and have real backbone, and they should age magnificently.

2004

Vintage rating: *Red: 88, White: 92*

Harvest started a week later than average for white grapes, and two or three weeks later for black. White grapes ripened fully. International grape varieties were of a rarely seen homogeneous quality. Delicate indigenous whites are more concentrated, with natural high acidity. It is a rare and outstanding vintage for all white wines, including the sweet specialties. A dry and sunny October saved the red-wine harvest. Reds have good color and elegant tannins and are very fragrant. Across the board there is a more northern-latitude climatic imprint, not unlike the 1997 vintage, though with far more complete and distinctive wines.

2003

Vintage rating: *Red: 90, White: 88*

A good vintage with successes in most regions, especially where yields were lower. Whites were in a generous style, but are not for keeping, except for Santorini, which is very good. Nemea did not turn out to be as great as we initially thought and proved the saying that "wine has the last word." The fruit is not as vibrant as in other top years. They are holding, however. Time will tell us more about the aging potential of wines from this charismatic region. Naoussa and Goumenissa's high yields of Xinomavro did no one a service. Amyndeo gave notice of the sheer potential of Xinomavro in this reenergized region. The island Muscats of Limnos and Samos are richly flavored but are not for the long term.

2002

Vintage rating: *Red: 75, White: 85*

With rare exceptions, a vintage to forget. Whites fared better, though they were short-lived. Most red-wine regions were plagued by rain. Nemea experienced almost unprecedented daily afternoon showers from mid-July to the end of harvest. There was widespread rot.

In Naoussa, rainfall was nearly incessant, even worse than the previous disastrous year back in 1983. The only beneficial outcome of this painful vintage was that nature replenished its water reserves.

Grapevine

• **Karanika Wines** (see *Wine Report 2007*) has changed its name to Ktima Karanika. The estate has opened its doors to wine tourism in the revitalized Amyndeo region. Owner Laurens Hartmann is the first to have a new vertical champagne press (PAI horizontal press Coquard) in this cool-climate region, which is planted with the high-potential Xinomavro.

• **Mediterra Winery,** the new name of Creta Olympias, has new red wines in the pipeline. The potential for red wines from Crete has been only recently realized.

• **DNA analysis** has confirmed that Tsabournakos, brought out of obscurity by Ktima Voyatzis at Velvendo's lakeshore vineyards is … Cabernet Franc! Nobody knows how or when it arrived. Historians assume it was introduced by French soldiers in 1918, or earlier by 18th- or 19th-century travelers.

GREATEST WINE PRODUCERS

1. Ktima Gerovassiliou
2. Gaia Wines
3. Alpha Estate
4. Tselepos
5. Biblia Chora
6. Ktima Mercouri
7. Antonopoulos
8. Sigalas
9. Ktima Kosta Lazaridi
10. Parparoussis

FASTEST-IMPROVING PRODUCERS

1. Avantis Mountrihas
2. Lyrarakis
3. Ktima Voyatzis
4. Karipidis
5. Kefalonia Cooperative
6. SantoWines
7. Tatsis Bros
8. Papaggianakos
9. Vertzamo (Lefkada)
10. Douloufakis

NEW UP-AND-COMING PRODUCERS

1. Dryopi
2. Ampelones Zafiraki
3. Kikones
4. Ktima Karanika
5. Ktima Vassiliou Nemea
6. Ktima Vourvoukeli
7. Palivos
8. Tetramythos
9. Nassiakos
10. Kokkalis

BEST-VALUE PRODUCERS

1. Semeli Nemea
2. Mitravelas
3. Lyrarakis
4. Meditterra Winery
5. Oenoforos
6. Katogi-Strofilia
7. Avantis Mountrihas
8. Emery
9. Tsantalis
10. Boutaris

GREATEST-QUALITY WINES

1. **Gerovassiliou 2004** Ktima Gerovassiliou (€16)
2. **Gaia Estate 2006** Gaia Wines (€20)
3. **Ghi ke Uranos 2006** Thimiopoulos (€16)
4. **Xinomavro 2005** Alpha Estate (€20.50)
5. **Adoli Ghis 2007** Antonopoulos (€11)
6. **Santorini 2007** Hatzidakis (€10)
7. **Mantinia 2007** Tselepos (€8)
8. **Villaré 2007** Emery (€8)
9. **Foloi 2007** Ktima Mercouri (€6.50)
10. **Robola 2007** Gentilini (€11)

BEST BARGAINS

1. **Kokkino se Mavro 2007** Mitravelas (€6)
2. **Robola 2007** Kefaliona Cooperative (€6)
3. **Foloi 2007** Ktima Mercouri (€6.50)
4. **Epiloges Debina 2007** Zitsa Co-operative (€6.50)
5. **Xerolithia 2007** Mediterra Winery (€7.50)
6. **Assyrtiko 2007** SantoWines (€8)
7. **Averoff White 2007** Katogi (€8)
8. **XM Rosé 2007** Ktima Karanika (€8.50)
9. **Armyra 2006** Skouras (€9)
10. **Samaropetra 2007** Kyr Yianni (€9.50)

MOST EXCITING OR UNUSUAL FINDS

1. **Gaia S 2006** Gaia Wines (€18)
   This compellingly different, skillfully crafted, stylish newcomer from this

trailblazing address continues pushing the Nemea(-based) envelope to new heights. A rule-breaker, since the 30 percent Syrah here grown on marl (limestone) was a gamble. What a match to the supple and multidimensional Aghiorghitiko, which continues to show us how little we really know about it.

② **Antares 2005** Ktima Mercouri (€15) Now that the vines (15+ years) have "settled," what a great offbeat wine this has grown up to be. Phenolically ripened Mourvèdre (60 percent) and the dark, higher-acidity Avgoustiatis (40 percent)—dark, dense, and succulent warm fruit that continues across the palate with mouthwatering, intense vinosity.

③ **Morpheas 2005** Antonopoulos (€13) A rarely seen varietal (dry) Mavrodaphne from 40-year-old vines with southwesterly exposure above Patra. Sour cherries and raspberries and, thanks to lees stirring, a crème patisserie tease on the palate that follows on with coffee and chocolate.

④ **Syrah 2004** Kikones (€15) From the deep-red soils of Maronia, Thrace comes one of the most astonishing varietals to emerge in years—further proof of how many other great terroirs await (re)discovery. Think of the northern Rhône with Greek minerality. Made by young Melina Tassou, who will be much talked about.

⑤ **Muscat La Terra 2006** Limnos Organic Wines (€11 per 50-cl bottle) From the eponymous volcanic island in the northern Aegean, and made by the island's articulate and restless top producer. Packed with lemony Muscat of Alexandria fragrance. Grapey, layered, and balanced.

⑥ **Chardonnay 2007** Ampelones Zafiraki (€9.50) Who needs a Greek Chardonnay? Well, the home market. From recently established modern vineyards in Tyrnavo. Made with three clones and wild yeast and fermented in acacia and French oak. Buttercup yellow, viscous, nutty, yeasty-textured finish. Not short of character.

⑦ **Cabernet Sauvignon Aghiorghitiko 2005** Oenotria Ghi Kosta Lazaridi (€18) From the recent sprawling estate in Kapandriti (see Wine Report 2006) planted to black grapes around Lake Marathon. Tobacco leaf, cocoa, fine-grained tannins. Polished and complete.

⑧ **Syrah Kotsifali 2006** Lyrarakis (€11) Oenologist Myriam Abuzer and George Lyrarakis are on to something here in central Crete. Broad strokes of spicy warm fruit, yet silky wine. Brimming with terroir. One of the few Cretan addresses whose methodical approach has started to pay off.

⑨ **Savatiano 2007** Pappagianakos (€6) If you are flying into Athens airport and wonder what all those vines produce, you have the answer. And you will not find a more expressive variety than the Savatiano produced at this all-new, energy-efficient winery from vines more than 40 years old. Perhaps the most versatile food white wine now on the scene. Excellent value.

⑩ **Vardea 2006** Vertzamo (€6) From ungrafted high vines on the island of Lefkada, sadly now diminishing. Such an intricate racy florality on the nose, with a surprisingly elegant, rounded, harmonious palate. It tastes like a wine from a more northern-latitude region than this mountainous Ionian island.

Lebanon

Michael Karam

One could hardly consider 2007 to be Lebanon's finest hour.

MICHAEL KARAM

The continued downtown sit-in, a failed coup attempt, a gun battle at a Beirut university, three political assassinations, a summer terror campaign, and a farcical presidential crisis that threatened—and at time of writing, still threatens—to undermine Lebanon's highest office. The impasse could still drag Lebanon into the abyss, not to mention tempt the Syrian army back into Lebanon.

The macro-economy was understandably on the ropes. Lebanon's total debt stands at nearly US$40 billion (recording a staggering debt-to-GDP ratio of 200 percent). Still, there were grapes to be picked, wine to be made, and markets to reach. In 2007, Lebanon exported around 2.3 million bottles—a year-on-year increase of 14 percent—with the UK once again the biggest importer, giving refuge to roughly 25 percent of all Lebanese wine produced. All this was done with no government support (there was no government) and often with burdensome regulations designed, more than anything, to fill state coffers with little consideration for the sector.

Hochar steps down

Amid the national tensions came the news that Serge Hochar, the man who has done most since Bacchus to put Lebanese wine on the world map, was retiring and handing over day-to-day running of the operations to his eldest son, Gaston. Hochar will still be supervising the making

MICHAEL KARAM has lived in Lebanon since 1992. He is a business journalist and wine writer. His articles have appeared in *Decanter, Harpers Wine and Spirit Weekly*, and *The Spectator*. He is a contributor to *The Oxford Companion to Wine* (Oxford University Press). He is author of *Wines of Lebanon* (Saqi), which won the Gourmand award for the Best New World Wine Book, 2005; *Château Ksara: 150 Years of Wine Making 1957–2007*, and *Arak and Mezze: The Taste of Lebanon* (Saqi, 2007).

of his enigmatic flagship reds (released after seven years) but has said that he wants to devote more time to his writing and traveling to preach the Musar gospel.

Château Musar, founded in 1930, was "discovered" by wine writer Michael Broadbent MW at the 1979 Bristol Wine Fair. Rave reviews from luminaries such as Jancis Robinson MW, Auberon Waugh, and Broadbent himself helped cement a love affair between Hochar and the British, who love his claret-with-a-difference, Cabernet-led wines. In 1983, Hochar became *Decanter*'s first Man of the Year in recognition of his determination not to let Lebanon's civil war get in the way of his winemaking.

It remains unclear at the time of writing whether Hochar will remain as president of the Union Vinicole du Liban (UVL), Lebanon's association of wine producers, but what is not in question is Hochar's contribution, both as an ambassador for his country and as a producer of one of the world's great wines.

The battle for Britain

At the same time Serge Hochar entered semiretirement, it was announced that UK distributor Matthew Clark would be responsible for the on-trade distribution of Mosaic, a new Musar creation and, according to Hochar, a slight variant from his Cuvée Rouge. The announcement barely caused a ripple in the UK's multicultural and multibillion-pound wine sector, but it is surely an indication that Musar is responding to the challenge from other Lebanese producers in what Hochar had considered his own fiefdom.

Since 2004, three Lebanese producers in particular—châteaux Ksara and Kefraya, as well as Massaya, the achingly hip Franco-Lebanese partnership—have been flexing their export muscles. Ksara and Kefraya, Lebanon's two biggest producers in terms of volume, have both identified the UK as a promising market and have entrusted their fortunes to Halgarten and Enotria, respectively. Both are eyeing up the supermarket sector, while Massaya, in the capable hands of Thorman Hunt, has been carving out a burgeoning reputation, not to mention increasing sales, in independent wine merchants.

Grapevine

• **Alex, the flagship restaurant** in the Wynn resort in Las Vegas, has arguably the city's best wine list. Among its finest burgundies and bordeaux, one can find the only vertical selection of Musar in the world, starting from a venerable 1956 and culminating with the infant 1998. The '56—a wine basking in the mellowed fruits picked when Nasser took on the West—will cost the adventurous tippler over US$4,000.

AT LAST

Every edition of *Wine Report* has carried predictions of the establishment of a Lebanese National Wine Institute. Intended to be responsible for all areas of grape growing and wine production—viticulture, vinification, legal issues, commercial concerns, quality control, and analysis—as well as the eventual creation of a system similar to, and inspired by, the French Appellation d'Origine Contrôlée, it would protect and guarantee the name and quality of Lebanese wine.

But each prediction was met with a delay. There was the mind-boggling bureaucracy: individual ministries with their own agenda often delayed an initiative designed to enhance and guarantee the quality and reputation of Lebanon's most high-profile export.

This sorry state of affairs was not helped by the events of 2005, which saw the Cedar Revolution, the departure of Syrian troops from Lebanon, and the election of a government that promised a new sovereign and democratic dawn. The next year saw Lebanon caught in a war between Israel and Hezbollah and

nearly blown to kingdom come. But one month after the August ceasefire, Charles Ghostine, general manager of Château Ksara and the UVL representative tasked with lobbying the government, announced triumphantly that the file had reached the Cabinet. Having already been approved by the ministries of Economy, Agriculture, and Industry, it seemed that the hard work had been done. Then, at the 11th hour, it was decided that the Ministry of Social Affairs should have its say—effectively sending the file to the back of a very long line.

With the instability of 2007, which saw the government protected by soldiers behind razor wire, civil unrest, random political killings, and the very real threat of sectarian violence, there seemed little hope of success. But out of these ashes in late 2007 came the news from a Chamberlain-like Ghostine, file in hand, that the institute had been approved. Staff, a premises, and funding all have to be ironed out, but by the time *Wine Report 2009* is published, Lebanon's first national wine institute should be a reality.

Grapevine

- **Massaya** has once again been at the forefront of innovation. In mid-2007, the Tanail winery became the first to introduce screwcaps for the entry-level Classic range of red, white, and rosé wines. The move has reportedly gone down very well in the local market.

- **Lebanon's security situation** forced Château Ksara to abandon its plans for hosting international guests at its 150th birthday celebrations, but it has produced a limited-edition (30,000 bottles) celebratory wine,

Le Souverain, a blend of Arinarnoa and Cabernet Sauvignon.

- **Wines from Karam Winery,** south Lebanon's only producer, can now be found on the national carrier, Middle East Airlines (MEA), which also serves châteaux Ksara and Kefraya. Passengers can enjoy the aptly named Cloud Nine, made from Semillon and Muscat, grown in Jezzine, and St Jean, Habib Karam's flagship red made from Cabernet Sauvignon, Merlot, and Syrah, from the same area.

Opinion:
A sense of style

Too many Lebanese producers are making wines to be admired rather than drunk—high-alcohol, concentrated, heavily oaked reds in particular. This trend of using premium grapes—Cabernet Sauvignon, Merlot, and Syrah—and the best oak barrels has relegated other equally interesting varieties such as Cinsault, Grenache, Mourvèdre, and Carignan to the reserve team. There is very little variety among the top reds, most of which need at least seven years for the wood to disappear. There are exceptions, especially among the smaller producers, who probably cannot afford to stuff an entire oak tree in the bottle and who are making quality wines that can be drunk now without feeling one is chewing on a branch.

Leadership

As Lebanon descends into more political chaos and hovers on the cusp of economic meltdown, it is time for the UVL to show some teeth. There have been disappointments in recent years, notably the cancellation of the OIV conference and delays in establishing the national wine institute, and while these setbacks were not the fault of the UVL, the association still has to prove that it can genuinely represent all Lebanon's wine producers. Significantly, only half of Lebanon's wine producers are members. The war of summer 2006 did generate some short-term solidarity, but the UVL's new website has not been exploited to give Lebanese wine better exposure and to encourage nonmembers to join. A prolonged political crisis and the very real threat of inflationary bedlam if the lira goes under will not help Lebanon's cause. The UVL needs leadership and vision of the highest level if Lebanon is to retain its image of a small but perfectly formed wine nation.

Diverse terroir

While producers with wineries outside the Bekaa Valley still use Bekaa grapes, almost all have also planted in their local areas. When the vines are ready—probably around 2009—we will have wines made with grapes from Jezzine, Mount Lebanon, Kififane, Bhamdoun, Rashmaya, and the north. Lebanese wine should become very interesting with the taste of these new terroirs. Producers are also experimenting in the Bekaa, especially in Hermel, north of Baalbek, where the stony soil has produced interesting results. Time may prove that the western Bekaa, with its abundance of water, may not necessarily prove to be Lebanon's best grape-growing region.

Buy Lebanese!

Ultimately, promoting Lebanese wine promotes Lebanon. Chile, Argentina, and South Africa, once beyond the pale, now invoke images of rolling vineyards, summer dining, and beautiful people. Wine can wash away a lot of bad memories, and now is the time to launch an international generic campaign. Sadly, with no financing for such a venture, it probably remains a pipe dream. More viable would be a national marketing campaign emphasizing the quality of Lebanese wine, educating consumers on the health benefits of drinking wine over, say, whiskey or *arak*, and stressing the economic importance of buying Lebanese. It should also target the tourist. Posters for Lebanese or Bekaa wine should be among the first images visitors see when they arrive at Beirut airport.

A national strategy

The quality of Lebanese wine has improved dramatically since the mid-1990s. Producers are working with a wider range of grapes, including the so-called noble varieties, and they are discovering that the Bekaa's flat vineyards generally give grapes with low alcohol, low polyphenolic maturation, and high acidity, while the slopes tend to produce grapes with high alcohol, a high level of polyphenolic maturation, but low acidity. To produce grapes with lower alcohol and higher acidity that can reach full polyphenolic maturation, there should be UVL/government-sponsored strategic planting of clones and rootstock, selected according to the needs of the Bekaa's individual terroirs and, where necessary, irrigation. Such a program would involve a comprehensive study of all Lebanon's terroirs and the support of the future National Wine Institute but, if successfully executed, would paint a more detailed picture of Lebanon's viticultural potential and produce better results in the bottle.

Grapevine

- **Château Khoury,** the Zahleh microwinery established in 2004 by Raymond Khoury and his son Jean-Pierre, is finally releasing its wines—three reds, a white, and a dessert wine—into the local market. Khoury deliberately works with grapes not widely grown in Lebanon, such as Riesling, Gewurztraminer, and Pinot Noir. The winery uses only grapes grown on the 13-ha estate and is currently producing around 30,000 bottles each year.

- **Château Ka** was established in 2004 in the Bekaa village of Makseh, and was the first in Lebanon to use laser plantation for perfect alignment. It launched three wines in 2007: Château 2005, a blend of Cabernet Sauvignon, Merlot, and Syrah aged for 14 months in oak; Nuit Blanche 2005, a blend of Muscat and Chardonnay also aged for 14 months in oak; and Source Blanche 2006, an entry-level white.

Vintage Report

Advance report on the latest harvest
2007

So it was an unpredictable year. One producer called 2007 "microwave cooking." Winter saw 25 percent less rainfall, while spring was dry and cold. This normally augurs low but high-quality yields, but a searingly hot September accelerated the ripening, leaving behind any complexity that a slow burn might have achieved. This made selecting which parcels should be picked at what time all the more challenging. Consequently, each grape variety evolved in a different way. Determining factors may have been the hail and frost that hit the Bekaa Valley in April, affecting flowering. In the western Bekaa, Syrah, Cinsault, and Carignan did not develop as well as Cabernet Sauvignon, which by and large was unaffected by the unusual climatic conditions. Farther east, producers spoke of "astonishing" results from Mourvèdre and Syrah, with excellent aromas, but average results from Cabernet Sauvignon. Yields were down 10–20 percent, but the grapes were well balanced with low acidity and good tannins, giving what one producer has called a "masculine" wine. The whites had excellent acidity. Not a typical year, but one that might produce very interesting results.

Updates on the previous five vintages
2006

Vintage rating: *Red: 90, White: 85*

A very good homogeneous year for Lebanon's black grapes. The war, which began on July 12, came at the "best" time: it could have happened during the pruning and treatment seasons, which would have meant the loss of the entire crop. The August 14 ceasefire came just one day before producers wanted to start picking. The white grapes did not have a spectacular year; the consensus among Bekaa producers was that they would have been better suited to a cooler summer. However, farmers in the southern Lebanese town of Jezzine—altitude 4,265 ft (1,300 m)—said their Semillons and Muscats were the "best yet."

2005

Vintage rating: *Red: 80, White: 89*

A tough year, the most humid in nearly half a century. The winter was long and wet, so grapes took longer to ripen in the lower-lying areas of the Bekaa. In other areas, the grapes raced to maturity. The time span was phenomenal and reflected the performance of the various terroirs on the Bekaa plateau. However, any interesting results of this freakish summer were negated by excessive mildew, which especially affected black grapes. In contrast, it was a good year for whites, which had plenty of acidity and pleasant floral aromas. Black varieties had a mixed year. The traditional early ripeners—Cabernet Sauvignon, Merlot, and Syrah—all ripened well but were hit by mildew, while Cinsault and Grenache were helped by a cooler September that allowed them to compensate for the humidity. Indeed, they may prove to be the better grapes.

2004

Vintage rating: *Red: 90, White: 85*

A sudden heat wave two weeks into the harvest produced grapes with higher sugar and medium acidity. It was as though there were two harvests in the same year, and fermentation was affected accordingly. Generally, grapes picked in the first two weeks of the harvest were fruity, round, and mellow, with floral aromas, but Cabernet Sauvignon, one of the Bekaa staples, was different: it was powerful, intense, concentrated, and leathery, with red fruits. "Second-phase" grapes, especially Carignan and Cinsault, developed more of a red-fruit character in smell and taste, while smooth tannins became more obvious and the palate more velvety.

2003

Vintage rating: *Red: 91, White: 85*

A unique harvest came on the back of the wettest winter in 15 years and a 10-day heat wave in May, both of which contributed to a marvelous balance between acidity and sugar content and an exceptional concentration of phenol compounds due to dry weather in September. The whites were aromatic with high acidity, producing vivid gunflint notes, finishing with a pleasant, mild, and unctuous taste, while the reds produced intense color. They were more tannic than former vintages but with balanced, mellow tannins, supple, and not astringent. All the different varieties were exceptionally fragrant, producing full-bodied and powerful wines.

2002

Vintage rating: *Red: 91, White: 85*

After four successive years of drought, there was a long, cold, rainy winter, followed by a mild July and a hot August. The vines took longer to ripen their grapes and had high levels of sugar, acidity, and tannin. Grape maturity levels varied from vineyard to vineyard, forcing growers to be selective. Fermentation went perfectly but, against all the odds, was very slow—therefore much longer—and the wines have turned out to be much bigger, riper, and fuller than expected.

GREATEST WINE PRODUCERS

1. Château Musar
2. Château Ksara
3. Château Kefraya
4. Massaya
5. Domaine des Tourelles
6. Clos St Thomas
7. Domaine Wardy
8. Vin Nakad

FASTEST-IMPROVING PRODUCERS

1. Karam Winery
2. Domaine des Tourelles
3. Château Belle-Vue
4. Massaya
5. Clos St Thomas
6. Château Ksara
7. Cave Kouroum
8. Château Kefraya
9. Château Ka
10. Domaine Wardy

NEW UP-AND-COMING PRODUCERS

1. Karam Winery
2. Château Ka
3. Château Khoury
4. Château Belle-Vue
5. Kfifane Winery
6. Nabise Mont Liban

BEST-VALUE PRODUCERS

1. Heritage
2. Domaines des Tourelles
3. Clos St Thomas
4. Fakra
5. Château Ksara
6. Château Kefraya
7. Karam Winery
8. Domaine Wardy
9. Nabise Mont Liban

GREATEST-QUALITY WINES

1. **Château Musar 1988** (LL 150,000)
2. **Château Musar 1991** (LL 75,000)
3. **Château Musar 1995** (LL 53,000)
4. **Château Musar 1996** (LL 38,000)
5. **Château Musar White 1999** (LL 17,000)
6. **Reserve 2001** Massaya (LL 48,000)
7. **Comte de M 2001** Château Kefraya (LL 40,000)
8. **Marquis des Beys 2004** Domaine des Tourelles (LL 30,000)
9. **Château St Thomas 2002** Clos St Thomas (LL 30,000)
10. **Château Ksara 2002** (LL 20,000)

BEST BARGAINS

1. **Le Fleuron 2004** Heritage (LL 5,000)
2. **Reserve 2004** Massaya (LL 30,000)
3. **Perle du Château 2006** Domaine Wardy (LL 20,000)
4. **Marquis des Beys 2005** Domaine des Tourelles (LL 28,000)
5. **Cuvée de Printemps 2006** Château Ksara (LL 9,000)
6. **Rosé du Printemps 2004** Domaine Wardy (LL 8,000)
7. **Les Emirs 2005** Clos St Thomas (LL 12,300)
8. **Blanc de Blancs 2005** Heritage (LL 11,000)
9. **Domaine des Tourelles 2005** (LL 15,000)
10. **Cloud 9 2004** Karam Winery (LL 11,000)

MOST EXCITING OR UNUSUAL FINDS

1. **Domaine des Tourelles 2004** (LL 14,000) *Delicious and elegant Cabernet Sauvignon and Syrah! The find of 2007.*
2. **Cuvée Rouge 2003** Château Musar (LL 10,000) *Underrated member of the Musar stable. Great value. Fruity, excellent body, silky finish. Compares well with the Hochar Père & Fils at under half the price.*
3. **Arc en Ciel 2007** Karam Winery (LL 45,000) *Arguably Lebanon's best rosé; made from Cabernet Sauvignon and Syrah. Bubblegum and fruits with excellent acidity.*
4. **Les Breteches 2006** Château Kefraya (LL 8,500) *Beautifully balanced, full-bodied, and smooth; made from Cabernet Sauvignon, Cinsault, Carignan, Mourvèdre, Tempranillo, and Grenache.*
5. **Classic Red 2006** Massaya (LL 9,000). *A fruity favorite made from Cinsault, Cabernet, and Syrah.*
6. **Le Souverain 2003** Château Ksara (LL 52,000) *Cabernet Sauvignon and Arinarnoa aged for 18 months; only 30,000 bottles were produced to celebrate Ksara's 150th birthday.*
7. **St Michael 2007** St Michael Winery (LL 6,000) *One hundred percent Grenache and 100 percent delightful summer quaffing from this tiny winery in Masser el Chouf. Superb homemade organic wine—soft and supple.*
8. **La Renaissance 2003** Château Belle-Vue (LL 45,000) *A Cabernet and Merlot from Bhamdoun that is full-bodied, fruity, and mouth-filling.*
9. **Nouveau 2007** Heritage (LL 8,000) *Lebanon's most honest and most quaffable vin nouveau from one of its most honest producers. A wine that reeks of the sun, the soil, and the fruit. Should be drunk within two, maximum three, months of release, but its consistency should ensure that the 2008 is of a comparable standard.*
10. **Thouraya 2005** Karam Winery (LL 33,000) *Who said the Bekaa was Lebanon's only wine region?*

Grapevine

• **Another small producer** beginning to flex its modest muscles is Château Belle-Vue from Bhamdoun, which was established in 2000 by former Merrill Lynch executive Naji Boutros and his American wife Jill. The couple won a gold at 2007's International Wine & Spirit Competition in London for their La Renaissance 2003. The winery sells only to Château Belle-Vue club members. For further information, contact www.chateaubelle-vue.com.

Israel

Daniel Rogov

It seems that winemakers and wine growers have finally realized that in Israel's Mediterranean climate, grapes thrive far better at a high altitude, where the diurnal temperatures are more significant than on the plains.

DANIEL ROGOV

So the move to the hills is on. In the past three years, new vineyard plantings have increased by 15–20 percent annually, nearly all that expansion taking place in the mountainous regions of the Upper Galilee, on the Golan Heights, and in the Judean Hills. This phenomenon will probably also have an impact on the quality of the wines, both premium labels and entry-level wines. At the same time, there are changes in the varieties planted in those developing areas.

In addition to Cabernet Sauvignon, Merlot, Chardonnay, and Sauvignon Blanc, there are major increases in the number of vines of Syrah/Shiraz, Cabernet Franc, Petit Verdot, Malbec, Barbera, and Viognier. Less dramatic increases are found with Zinfandel, Gewurztraminer, and Riesling, and it seems that there will be less planting of Carignan, Pinot Noir, and Sauvignon Blanc in the near future.

Parker rates Israeli wines

For the first time, American wine critic Robert Parker and his team conducted a major tasting of Israeli wines. Tasting notes and scores for 94 wines were published in *The Wine Advocate* on December 21, 2007. The overall

DANIEL ROGOV is the wine and restaurant critic for the Israeli daily newspaper *Haaretz* as well as for the Israeli edition of the *International Herald Tribune*. He is the author of the annual *Rogov's Guide to Israeli Wines* and is a regular contributor to *Hugh Johnson's Pocket Wine Book*. Rogov also publishes wine and gastronomic reviews and articles on his website, Rogov's Ramblings (http://www.stratsplace.com/rogov/home.html).

results were very impressive: the wines scored highly and gave the Israeli wine industry yet more proof that it is now considered among the serious wine-producing regions of the world.

That's kosher

Hoping to boost their sales within Israel and abroad, an increasing number of small wineries are turning to entirely kosher production. That there is no contradiction whatever between the production of fine wine and the rules of *kashrut* has long been established, but the employment of Sabbath-observant additional workers and *kashrut* supervisors can add a hefty percentage to the cost of wine production, especially for small wineries. It is hoped that increased sales, especially abroad, will offset these costs.

Winemakers on the move

Two of the country's most talented winemakers, Lewis Pasco and Gil Shatzberg, both of whom trained at the University of California at Davis and worked in California, have made major job shifts. After being the senior winemaker of Recanati Winery since its founding in 2000, Pasco has moved into consulting to the wine industry. Shatzberg, the winemaker at Amphorae since its founding eight years ago, has moved into the slot as Recanati's senior winemaker. Amphorae has started marketing wines in the United States under the Marvah label, due to conflict with a California label.

Tabor expansion

Tabor Winery is more than tripling the area of its vineyards and is developing its winemaking facilities in the Galilee. The winery, whose first releases in 1999 were of 20,000 bottles, is already producing 750,000 bottles annually, and the move seems destined to take Tabor well beyond the 2 million mark within the next three or four years. This goes along with an increase in consumption within Israel of 11 percent during the past year.

Grapevine

• **The country's second** international wine exposition, Israwinexpo, took place in February 2008 in Tel Aviv. The exposition, sponsored largely by the Ministry of Agriculture, the Export Institute, and the Association of Grape Growers, was not the rousing success that had been hoped for, with only 36 wineries taking part and the exhibition open to local and foreign journalists and buyers for only one day.

• **At least two large wineries**—Zion and Teperberg (formerly Ephrat), which produced mostly sacramental wines—are now making table wines to appeal to a larger and somewhat more sophisticated audience.

Opinion:
Cheating the consumer

In some instances there is little control over what goes into a bottle of wine. Bottles labeled as Cabernet Sauvignon may appear remarkably similar to Carignan or Argaman wines. It seems (although it cannot at this stage be proven) that a few wineries are using table grapes and labeling their wines as those of noble varieties. The rumor that several small wineries buy bulk wine and bottle and label the wines as their own was substantiated recently by Danny Valero, CEO of Ella Valley Vineyards, who let it be known that his and several other wineries were selling finished bulk wine to some of the boutique and *garagiste* wineries.

Unification needed

There are currently six governmental or quasi-governmental agencies involved in the local wine trade: the Israeli Wine Institute, the Ministry of Agriculture, the Ministry of Trade and Industry, the Standards Institute, the Wine and Grape Board, and the Association of Grape Growers. Since they often work at cross-purposes and rarely communicate with each other, this situation almost guarantees that the industry has no central marketing arm, very limited control over labeling procedures, and no reliable source of data. What continues to be needed is a central body that will ensure proper standards, issue reliable data, and promote marketing both locally and abroad. An important step would be to establish a new wine institute that could function via full-fledged and enforceable new regulations.

Appellation system

The land area of Israel is a mere 7,992 square miles (20,700 sq km, or 5 percent of the land area of California), but due to its long north–south axis, it has a large variety of microclimates. In the north, weather conditions are comparable to Bordeaux and the northern Rhône Valley, yet a few hours away lies the Negev Desert, with a climate similar to that of North Africa. The country is currently divided into five broad vine-growing regions (Galilee, Shomron, Samson, Judean Hills, and the Negev), but these regions are not properly defined. The appellation system being developed by a joint effort of the wineries and faculty members of the Ben Gurion University in Be'er Sheva and the Hebrew University's Faculty of Agriculture in Rehovot aims to identify regional and subregional areas and to clarify labeling procedures.

Vintage Report

Advance report on the latest harvest

2007

A dry winter was followed by a cold spring and a warm, completely dry summer. The good weather continued until the end of October. A somewhat longer-than-usual harvest period of nearly 15 weeks gave lower-than-usual yields but a vintage of overall excellent quality, somewhat better for reds than whites.

Updates on the previous five vintages

2006

Vintage rating: *Red: 87, White: 85*
A low-yield harvest of not overly exciting quality. Probably better for reds than whites, but a year in which many of the top-of-the-line series and single-vineyard wines will not be released.

2005

Vintage rating: *Red: 90, White: 90*
One of the most promising years in the past decade, with a prolonged harvest of overall high quality, exceptionally good in many parts of the country for reds and whites alike. Wines have excellent balance, structure, and aging potential.

2004

Vintage rating: *Red: 89, White: 91*
A short and hectic harvest, but an excellent crop. Greatest strength is in whites, but reds have good concentration and intensity.

2003

Vintage rating: *Red: 90, White: 90*
An excellent vintage year for both reds and whites, with many intense and concentrated but elegant and ageworthy reds. The best whites are drinking nicely now and will cellar comfortably for another year or two.

2002

Vintage rating: *Red: 84, White: 80*

Prolonged heat spells made this a problematic year, both quality- and quantity-wise. Some good and even very good reds and whites, but nearly all are destined for early drinking.

GREATEST WINE PRODUCERS

1. Golan Heights Winery (Katzrin, Yarden, Gamla)
2. Margalit
3. Yatir
4. Castel
5. Clos de Gat
6. Flam
7. Chateau Golan
8. Carmel (Limited Edition, Single Vineyard, Appellation)
9. Galil Mountain
10. Pelter

FASTEST-IMPROVING PRODUCERS

1. Tabor
2. Odem Mountain
3. Tulip
4. Galil Mountain
5. Barkan
6. Dalton
7. Binyamina
8. Teperberg
9. Ben Hanna
10. Zion

NEW UP-AND-COMING PRODUCERS

1. Pelter
2. Vitkin
3. Assaf
4. Odem Mountain
5. Savion
6. Tulip
7. Agur
8. Ruth
9. Psagot
10. Avidan

BEST-VALUE PRODUCERS

1. Tabor
2. Golan Heights Winery (Gamla, Golan)
3. Galil Mountain
4. Dalton
5. Carmel (Appellation)
6. Recanati
7. Saslove
8. Barkan
9. Tishbi
10. Teperberg

Grapevine

• **For almost two years** it seemed that Baron Eric de Rothschild, who visited Israel on several occasions, was going to buy into the Yatir Winery, certainly one of the very best boutique wineries in the country (annual production currently about 120,000 bottles). Whatever negotiations were under way are now said to have come to nothing.

• **It is rumored** that, within the next year or two, the Golan Heights Winery is going to start up a fully independent boutique winery. It is also rumored that Shmuel Boxer, a senior partner in Barkan Winery, will be selling his shares in the winery and starting a boutique winery.

GREATEST-QUALITY WINES

1. **Yarden Cabernet Sauvignon El Rom Vineyard 2003** Golan Heights Winery (NIS 180)
2. **Limited Edition 2004** Carmel (NIS 180)
3. **Yatir Forest 2004** Yatir (NIS 150)
4. **Special Reserve 2004** Recanati (NIS 180)
5. **Cabernet Sauvignon Royal Reserve 2005** Chateau Golan (NIS 180)
6. **Sycra Syrah 2004** Clos de Gat (NIS 190)
7. **Cabernet Sauvignon Special Reserve 2005** Margalit (NIS 190)
8. **Grand Vin Castel 2005** Castel (NIS 180)
9. **Merlot Reserve 2005** Flam (NIS 150)
10. **Yiron 2004** Galil Mountain (NIS 140)

BEST BARGAINS

1. **Yarden Cabernet Sauvignon 2003** Golan Heights Winery (NIS 105)
2. **Med.Red 2005** Amphorae (NIS 70)
3. **Petite Sirah Shiraz Special Edition 2006** Recanati (NIS 75)
4. **Merlot Gamla 2005** Golan Heights Winery (NIS 50)
5. **Cabernet Sauvignon Aviv 2006** Saslove (NIS 62)
6. **Cabernet Sauvignon Terra Rossa 2005** Tabor (NIS 50)
7. **Shiraz 2006** Galil Mountain (NIS 45)
8. **Merlot Regional Upper Galilee 2005** Carmel (NIS 60)
9. **Tempranillo Reserve 2005** Barkan (NIS 61)
10. **Sauvignon Blanc 2006** Yatir (NIS 58)

MOST EXCITING OR UNUSUAL FINDS

1. **Carignan Old Vines Regional Zichron Ya'akov 2005** Carmel (NIS 70) *For many years Carignan had a bad name in Israel, so it took some courage to produce this wine. Thankfully, with the discovery that 30–40-year-old vines can produce excellent wines, this one shows fine balance between caressing tannins, spicy wood, and blackberry, cherry, and peppery chocolate aromas and flavors.*

2. **Viognier 2006** Galil Mountain (NIS 55) *Still a relatively new variety but, thanks in large part to this winery, rapidly gaining popularity. Lightly golden with greenish tinges; reveals enticing aromas and flavors of peaches, nectarines, pears, and apples, backed up by spring flowers and minerals, all complemented by hints of white pepper.*

3. **Geshem Royal Reserve 2005** Chateau Golan (NIS 100) *One of winemaker Uri Hetz's unusual (for Israel) blends. Medium-dark garnet, a blend of 70 percent Grenache and 30 percent Syrah, opens with a near-raspberry liquor nose, settling down to reveal oak-accented aromas and flavors of blackberries, cherries, and black pepper. Deep and long.*

4. **Zinfandel 2005** Dalton (NIS 55) *This dark royal-purple wine spent 12 months in new American oak. Full-bodied, with generous near-sweet tannins and smoky and vanilla oak, it opens on the palate to reveal black cherry, raspberry, and plum fruits backed up by hints of chocolate, vanilla, and espresso coffee. A generous and mouthfilling finish. Drink now to 2009.*

⑤ Chenin Blanc 2007 Sea Horse (NIS 70) *Made from 32-year-old Chenin Blanc vines, with drastic cutting back to concentrate the crop, fermented and still on its lees in three-year-old barriques. Rich, crisply dry, and well focused, with tangy mineral, chamomile, white peach, and nectarine aromas and flavors supported by hints of figs and ginger.*

⑥ Cabernet Franc 2005 Ella Valley Vineyards (NIS 80) *One of the first local releases of a varietal wine from this grape. Dark garnet, medium- to full-bodied wine with appealing vegetal aromas, opening to reveal gently spicy cedar wood, raspberries, and red currants with a hint of white chocolate on the long finish.*

⑦ Cabernet Franc 2005 Vitkin (NIS 65) *Deep garnet toward royal-purple, oak-aged for 16 months and blended with 12 percent Petit Verdot, the wine has generous tannins integrating nicely with the wood. Already showing an abundant array of spicy black cherries and currants, with overtones of green peppercorns, herbs, and smoked meat. Long and satisfying.*

⑧ Cabernet Franc Rosé 2005 Assaf (NIS 65) *Assaf Kedem may be the only winemaker in the country with the courage to make a rosé wine from Cabernet Franc. Medium-bodied, rose-petal pink wine; generous raspberry, strawberry, and black cherry fruits on a rich mineral background, all with just enough acidity to keep it lively.*

⑨ Petit Verdot La Mariée 2005 Ben Hanna (NIS 70) *The first varietal wine from this grape in the country and a rousing success, with its gently mouth-coating tannins and hints of spices and vanilla. Dark purple, with generous cherry and currant fruits and, on the long finish, a tantalizing hint of green olives.*

⑩ Gamay Nouveau Golan 2007 Golan Heights Winery (NIS 35) *Made, as are the wines of Beaujolais, entirely from Gamay grapes and by the process of carbonic maceration, this super-young wine, released only weeks after the harvest, offers up a generous dose of raspberry and grapey aromas and flavors. Dark black cherry toward purple in color, light, round, super-fruity, and fun. Destined for drinking in its youth.*

Grapevine

• **Sea Horse winery** is releasing its first varietal Chenin Blanc, and some (including this critic) are predicting that this will be the next white to become a true hit in Israel. An increasing number of fine releases of old-vine Carignan and even-older-vine Petite Sirah will also be seen in the local and foreign markets in the next year or two.

• **In recent years** I have been predicting that the proliferation of small, even minuscule, wineries was creating a bubble that was bound to burst and that many of these wineries would close or go bankrupt. I was wrong: the proliferation of these wineries continues, and only three or four of more than 150 have closed their doors.

South Africa

Cathy van Zyl MW & Tim James

Following some slippage in the performance of Kumala, the top South African brand in the UK, it was clear that action was needed.

CATHY VAN ZYL MW and TIM JAMES

What happened went deeper than market tinkering and was a surprise all around. Constellation, the owners of the Kumala brand, made a deal with Bruce Jack, the respected and dynamic owner of Flagstone. Flagstone itself is a winery that would seem as far from big branding as possible, given its 30 labels for a 60,000-odd annual case production. But Constellation bought Flagstone, with Jack taking overall viticultural and winemaking responsibility for the Kumala brand while continuing to lead the Flagstone team.

Constellation's new acquisition will serve as a basis for building a premium portfolio of South African wines to complement the volume-driven sector catered for by Kumala. The deal was reported as part of the company's strategy to increase its market share of South African wines in all its core markets, including the US and the EU. The company is confident that Bruce Jack is just the person for this "major destination marketing drive."

CATHY VAN ZYL MW and TIM JAMES both work on the Grape website (www. grape.co.za)—the descendant of the magazine they founded in 1999 to give an independent viewpoint on South African wine. Tim takes major editorial responsibility for the nonprofit, non-advertising site, and Cathy writes, among other things, a popular blog. Both also taste for the *Platter Wine Guide*, and Cathy frequently judges on the competition circuit and is also involved in wine education for the MW and other programs. In addition to Grape, Tim writes for various local and international publications, including *The World of Fine Wine*, and consults to *The World Atlas of Wine*.

Wine icons sought

There were many sighs of relief going into harvest 2008, with statistics showing a growth of sales in the major export markets over the previous year. After a year or two of slump, sales returned to the healthy state they had been in since the surpluses of the pre-1994 era were transformed into supermarket success. Conservative industry predictions are that new records for exports by volume will be consolidated, with at least 6 percent volume growth; also projected is that wine prices will increase by 3 percent annually until 2010.

Growth has been strong in Europe, particularly in Germany, and the negative trend of two years has been reversed in the UK (still the biggest buyer of Cape wine), where growth in the higher market segments is particularly encouraging.

But the US still seems to be where ambitious South African producers see the rainbow touching ground. Sales for 2007 were up by around 9 percent over the previous year (11 percent in Canada), and volumes are likely to increase with the marketing of Sebeka (see "Swartland gets the chicken" story). According to some industry strategists, establishing bigger brands is going to work best for the bigger national brands in the United States as well as in supermarket-dominated Europe. However, this is the Parkerized market that has spurred on those who think South Africa should have internationally recognized icons—smaller-scale wines of excellence and high price. They suggest (often invoking Australia's Grange or the 1976 Judgment of Paris) that such wines will lead to Cape wines being taken more seriously as a whole and will pull the reputation and price of others in their slipstream. Sometimes a producer can even intimate noble self-sacrifice when announcing the release of a stratospherically priced wine.

Grapevine

• **An unusual maiden release** came this year from generic marketing organization Wines of South Africa (WOSA). Fundi (pronounced "foon-dee"—the Zulu name means "learner," but the general connotation is "expert") is a high-priced red blend that will be put in the way of as many visiting tourists as possible (at hotels, for example, as well as retailers). The wine was put out to tender (as will be subsequent vintages), with the final choice made by experts from submitted samples. With heavy industry sponsorship, proceeds from Fundi will go to training black wine stewards, in line with WOSA's belief that service excellence (alas, not always prominent in South Africa) must be a vital part of Cape wine's growth.

The perceived need to create a stratum of exemplary "first growths" marked by price dates back a decade or two to Hamilton Russell's high price on the local market, followed by others. Now there are many that match that level, and a few more each year have leapfrogged it. Not all are plausible, but the goal remains a US$100+ wine.

Each year there are one or two more candidates, and while domestic sales for these generally low-volume, high-priced, and much-hyped wines are mostly good, the rhetoric remains the need for internationally recognized icons. But aspirational pricing is one thing; pleasing the critics is another.

So far, the greatest success in terms of all-important American point-scoring has come from wines that are very expensive by South African standards but less than the US$100 threshold—or the local equivalent of R750-some. While Ernie Els, Vergelegen V, and Waterford The Jem are around the higher level, for example, they don't have quite the cachet of Boekenhoutskloof Syrah, which has, to its enormous credit, remained at about R200 locally and under $50 in the US, despite being strenuously sought after in the home market and seldom easy to find. Nor (at time of writing) do the highest flyers have the glamour of Eben Sadie's Columella, which gave much satisfaction to many, including those who affect to despise the whole American 100-point business, when *Wine Spectator* gave the 2005 a score of 94, the highest yet for a Cape wine. Has national vinous respectability finally been attained?

Grapevine

• **The venerable Nederburg Auction** moved from fall to spring in 2007, muscling in on the October space of the Cape's other significant wine auction—that of the Cape Winemakers Guild (CWG). Comparison became easier, and the incomparably grander event suffered, with a fairly dismal sales performance, while upstart CWG prices were significantly higher this year: the price achieved per liter was three times that of Nederburg's and its total revenue not much less. The Nederburg Auction is perhaps more about publicity than revenue for owner Distell, but there will surely be a lot of head-scratching as a result. While things are more gratifying for the members of the CWG, the fact remains that in a situation where local wine sales and grape prices are generally stagnant, a few big spenders (particularly from the on-trade) are what made the difference on the day; let's not speak here about long-term growth or trends.

• **Stormhoek's huge success** through its innovative Internet viral marketing couldn't keep it from stormy waters when UK brand owners Orbital Wines went into administration. The business was taken over by Bernard Fontannez of Stellenbosch-based Origin Wine.

SWARTLAND GETS THE CHICKEN

The first wines were released in the US in 2007 in potentially the biggest deal yet for Cape wine in the country that is increasingly seen as the wine marketer's Holy Grail. Swartland Winery (one of the best known of the cooperatives-turned-companies) has an agreement to produce a South African range within the "international portfolio" of mega-winery E&J Gallo of California. The brand name is Sebeka—named after an orphaned cheetah cub that inspired a South African wildlife conservation movement some 50 years ago. Now available in supermarkets across the United States, the wines could mark a real breakthrough for the visibility and sales of Cape wine there.

NO GM YEAST FOR CAPE WINERIES

An application to be allowed to market a genetically enhanced malolactic yeast for commercial wine production has been turned down by the relevant government authorities. The bid came from a professor at the University of British Columbia's Wine Research Centre (though with a notably Afrikaans name—Hennie van Vuuren). It was formally opposed by Biowatch South Africa, a number of prominent local wineries, and the SA Wine Industry Council.

GETTING GREENER

With environmental concerns growing, Backsberg Estate in Paarl can now claim "to deliver a range of carbon-neutral fruit and wine." Following an exhaustive audit, it is planning to sequestrate its carbon emissions to gain carbon-neutral status—the first Cape winery to do so. Those who know owner Michael Back realize that this is no mere marketing ploy, but a statement of serious commitment. Some 10 percent of the property is now reserved for indigenous vegetation, within the Biodiversity & Wine Initiative. That initiative is growing in strength as a partnership between the wine industry and the conservation sector to protect ecosystems and the biodiversity that is an important part of the country's attraction for tourists (and now a focus of its generic wine marketing). By early 2008, well over 60,000 ha of wine-farm land had been set aside for conservation—equivalent to 65 percent of the vineyard footprint in the Cape winelands.

Grapevine

• **Threats of a lawsuit** against the wine industry in South Africa had, in early 2008, yet to lead to court action, but a war of words was taking place. The issue is the continuing scandal of widespread alcoholism, particularly in the Western Cape, and what many see as the inadequate response of the local wine industry—arguably historically responsible for the situation. The Black Association of the Wine and Spirit Industry, the small but vociferous grouping led by Nosey Pieterse, has demanded that an industry fund be established to deal with alcoholism and to set up an institution for the treatment of alcoholics, failing which it will proceed with a class action. The response from leaders of main industry institutions has thus far been disdain, irritation, and anger.

Opinion:
Let's reflect diversity on our labels

With all the wine-marketing concern about the Cape's great biodiversity ("Variety is in our nature," as the slogan has it), and with perhaps the most mature and rigorous appellation system in the New World, it is a pity that so few South African producers bother to indicate with precision the origins of their wines. It's a point that was made by map-conscious Jancis Robinson MW but is worth repeating here. With the Wine of Origin system, too many wines (whether for local consumption or export) declare a source in the Western Cape, which includes the vast majority of respectable vineyards, or Coastal Region—a slightly smaller but still large catch-all area.

While some of the wines lurking behind such blandness are indeed assembled from widely sourced fruit, a large proportion are not, though they may be from one or two different districts (Paarl and Stellenbosch, say). Until a few years ago, dual origins were not allowed, but now both names may be given. Also permitted now are wines vinified in a different appellation from those where the grapes were sourced. It is probably time to start allowing the same degree of latitude in reporting origins as applies to vintage and variety: bringing in up to 15 percent of grapes from elsewhere should not invalidate a single-appellation origin.

Grapevine

• **Squabbles over new appellations** are rarer in South Africa than in some other New World countries because the system is well established and perhaps because there is less at stake financially. But they do happen (and it is unlikely that the distinctive Helderberg area of Stellenbosch will easily attain ward status, given some blurred and disputed edges). Producers in the thriving Hemel-en-Aarde Valley, including famous ones such as Hamilton Russell, sought status as a ward, and after due process and scrutiny by the authorities, it was thought right to have three: Hemel-en-Aarde and Upper Hemel-en-Aarde were easy to name, but a delay in proclaiming the third, farthest-inland ward resulted from a dispute over whether it was entitled to invoke the valley's increasingly prestigious name at all.

• **Retief Goosen** has followed fellow local golfing pros Ernie Els and David Frost into wine. He has entered into a winemaking partnership in the tiny, far-flung, but interestingly cool-climate Upper Langkloof ward, high in the Outeniqua Mountains near George on the Eastern Cape coast. They've just released their maiden range (three reds and a Sauvignon) called—what else?—The Goose.

Lazy recourse to catch-all origins may be convenient for producers wanting to cut down on the paperwork they submit, but doesn't meet the desire of an increasing number of wine drinkers to know just where their wines are coming from. And it doesn't help the Cape's terroir-inspired image being promoted in foreign markets.

Ongoing concerns

Unusually, there's a spot or two of brightness with regard to previously raised problems. And the source of the light was the dynamic leadership of the SA Wine Council by Kader Asmal (who, unfortunately, resigned as chair in early 2008). The council has taken up the scandal of the name Riesling being officially conferred upon lowly Crouchen Blanc, while the real thing must bear the prefixed weight of "Weisser" or "Rhine" on the local market. Further investigation into the situation has been demanded of the relevant authorities. Disquiet has also been expressed about the way some distributors and wineries—particularly Distell—buy their way onto, and often dominate or monopolize, many restaurant wine lists. Official investigation into the matter is promised, including whether enormous Distell is infringing monopoly regulations.

Strategies for "black economic empowerment" in the wine industry increasingly focus on enriching a few rather than improving the (grim) conditions of the many.

Too many wine journalists have conflicts of interests, as consultants, entrepreneurs, public-relations practitioners, and the like.

Grapevine

• **The prospect of health warnings** on local labels has taken an ambiguous step forward. The Department of Health's announcement that mandatory warnings were to be phased in seemed clear enough. Yet the regulatory authority, the Wine and Spirit Board, seemed doubtful, amid rumors that the industry big players (read: Distell) were angered by the regulations. The board indicated that "the industry" was seeking legal advice on the issue. Months later it announced that, yes, the regulations were to come into force in February 2009. At that stage there was no further news of a legal challenge.

• **KWV's profits dropped** significantly for the year ended June 2007, mainly because of multimillion operating losses in its international markets, notably Germany and the UK. Some speculation about selloffs resulted, as did irritation from a major shareholder, who humiliated chair Danie de Wet at the subsequent AGM by blocking his election to the board. Some adroit maneuvering saw to it, however, that he retained his place. Soon after, there was talk about the desirability of a merger between KWV and the even larger Distell (if the competition authorities would allow it), but talks about talks were vigorously denied by KWV.

Vintage Report

Advance report on the latest harvest
2008

A difficult year to read: success seems to depend on location, location, location—as well as ultra-careful vineyard management. Winter was cold, which ensured proper dormancy and welcome rain. A cool summer lengthened the ripening period, preserved acid, let sugars and flavors pick up slowly, and allowed tannins to ripen without overripeness of fruit. But late summer rains increased the threats of powdery mildew and rot and of excessive vigor; green harvesting was often necessary.

Inland particularly, clever canopy management and fruit selection were critical; then many varieties ripened together, causing cellar congestion. Vineyard health in the coastal zones mostly benefited from a very active "Cape Doctor," the prevailing southeasterly wind. While rot did take its toll, many producers found much to celebrate. Some fruit is of exceptional quality, with good acidity, moderate sugar levels, and complex, intense flavors. Not all the rot was destructive: botrytis on the Chenin Blanc crop, especially in Stellenbosch, should only add richness. Crop size could be above average overall. Some areas, such as Constantia, saw a big decline, but the hot, irrigated Northern Cape's harvest should be up. So this is a vintage that it's hard to generalize about—and careful selection will no doubt be as necessary for the consumer as it was for the best producers.

Updates on the previous five vintages
2007

Vintage rating: *Red: 90, White: 90*
Quality-boosting factors included a cold winter with good rains, sufficient heat at the start of the ripening process, and then cooler weather countering the potential stress to the later-ripening varieties. Sauvignon Blanc and Chardonnay are most pleasing among the whites; smaller berry size on the black varieties has delivered wines with intense color and concentration.

2006

Vintage rating: *Red: 90, White: 95*

Several natural and other challenges (strong winds, excessive heat and runaway veld fires, rolling power cuts) besieged this vintage, yet it is one of the best of the 2000s. White wines, particularly Sauvignon and Chenin Blanc, are standout. With the exception of Shiraz, the biggest victim of the winds, red wines are fleshy with riper, rounder tannins.

2005

Vintage rating: *Red: 85, White: 85*

Early-season rain prompted mildew and excessive vigor in many vineyards; a heat wave sent sugar levels rising in others. Generalizations, therefore, are almost impossible, and cherry-picking is a necessity. Reds are concentrated, if alcoholic; whites mostly average.

2004

Vintage rating: *Red: 88, White: 88*

Despite uneven berry set (courtesy of unfavorable conditions during flowering but rectified by a large green harvest), this was a long and predominantly healthy harvest favoring Shiraz, Merlot, Chardonnay, and Sauvignon Blanc.

2003

Vintage rating: *Red: 95, White: 90*

Quantity and quality-wise, the vintage stands well above many in the past 25 years, with well-structured, generous reds and fine whites.

Grapevine

• **Top white blends** continue to attract acclaim locally and internationally in the context of the respective merits of the Cape's red and white wines generally, fueled by unflattering remarks about the reds made by a few prominent UK critics. Whether in the classic Semillon/Sauvignon pattern of Bordeaux or the autochthonous Chenin-based blends, there are more and more ambitious examples. This was the category of table wines that garnered most five-star ratings in the 2008 edition of the important *Platter Guide*—four out of 16 (there were an unprecedented five port-style winners), two of them maidens: Steenberg's Magna Carta and Sequillo White (made by Eben Sadie, who virtually invented the Chenin-based blend with his Palladius some years ago). We suggested in *Wine Report 2007* that this could well be the most exciting category of South African wine, and it seems an even more valid claim now. Watch out for more top-level white blends each year.

GREATEST WINE PRODUCERS

1. Boekenhoutskloof
2. Vergelegen
3. Sadie Family
4. Hamilton Russell Vineyards
5. Cape Point Vineyards
6. Rustenberg
7. Thelema
8. Kanonkop
9. De Trafford
10. Neil Ellis

FASTEST-IMPROVING PRODUCERS

1. Chamonix
2. Catherine Marshall Wines
3. Backsberg
4. La Motte
5. Diemersdal
6. Nederburg
7. Scali
8. Klein Constantia
9. Hartenberg
10. Meerlust

NEW UP-AND-COMING PRODUCERS

1. Oak Valley
2. Solms-Delta
3. The Foundry
4. Ataraxia
5. Vilafonté
6. South Hill
7. Belfield
8. Schonenberg
9. De Grendel
10. Edgebaston

BEST-VALUE PRODUCERS

1. Pecan Stream (Waterford)
2. Perdeberg Winery
3. Du Toitskloof
4. Paul Cluver
5. Little River (De Meye)

6. Guardian Peak (Ernie Els)
7. Grangehurst
8. Simonsig
9. Chamonix
10. Riebeek Cellars

GREATEST-QUALITY WINES

1. **Vergelegen White 2006** Vergelegen (R200)
2. **Columella 2005** Sadie Family (R480)
3. **Syrah 2005** Boekenhoutskloof (R200)
4. **Chardonnay 2006** Hamilton Russell Vineyards (R200)
5. **Tête du Cuvée Galpin Peak 2005** Bouchard Finlayson (R445)
6. **Morgenster 2004** Morgenster (R264)
7. **V 2004** Vergelegen (R750)
8. **The Jem 2004** Waterford (R680)
9. **CWG Auction Reserve Gravel Hill 2004** Hartenberg (R590)
10. **Isliedh 2006** Cape Point Vineyards (R150)

BEST BARGAINS

1. **Chenin Blanc 2007** Pecan Stream (Waterford) (R34)
2. **Cabernet Sauvignon 2005** Belfield (R42)
3. **Chenin Blanc 2007** Simonsig (R26)
4. **Shamrock Red 2006** Cloverfield (R25)
5. **Provenance Shiraz Rosé 2007** Saronsberg (R30)
6. **Sangiovese Socrate 2005** Monterosso (R35)
7. **Weisser Riesling 2007** Paul Cluver (R55)
8. **Paul de Villiers Reserve 2005** Landskroon (R49)
9. **Sauvignon Blanc 2007** Alexanderfontein (Ormonde) (R30)
10. **Rouge NV** Chamonix (R25)

MOST EXCITING OR UNUSUAL FINDS

1 The Jem 2004 Waterford (R680) *Confident, eight-way red blend—a marriage of Rhône and Bordeaux held in the lavish Helderberg (Stellenbosch) property owned by perfectionist winemaker Kevin Arnold and IT magnate Jeremy Ord. Jumps in at the top of the local price league.*

2 The Journeyman 2005 Boekenhoutskloof (R200) *Marc Kent of this Franschhoek winery, best known for his fine Syrah made from bought-in grapes, proves beyond doubt that his home appellation can produce red-wine excellence. Joining his varietal Cabernet is this first-class blend of Cabernet Franc, with Cabernet Sauvignon and Merlot as junior partners.*

3 Chenin Blanc 2006 Racetrack (R65) *Another demonstration of the virtues of the Cape's previously underrated and overcropped Cinderella grape. A first release from 60-year-old bush vines planted on unyielding ground on this Paarl farm (originally thought viticulturally useless because of the gravelly soil and given over to horse-racing).*

4 Koloni 2006 Solms-Delta (R93) *A partner to the red Africana, another wine made at this exciting, revivified Franschhoek property from vine-desiccated Riesling and Muscats de Frontignan and d'Alexandrie grapes, which yield a rich, round, ginger-seasoned delight.*

5 White 2006 Sequillo (R150) *From wine visionary Eben Sadie, a more modestly priced version of his fine Palladius; this Swartland blend of 60 percent Chenin, with Grenache Blanc, Viognier, and Roussanne, is forceful yet unforced, and it impresses with earthy tones, well-judged oak, and precise structure.*

6 Syrah 2006 Schonenberg (R150) *From biodynamically farmed grapes, fairly early picked and fermented with native yeasts, this first offering from a small Swartland estate is delicate and pure, unblurred by new oak, with modest 13.1 percent ABV.*

7 Cabernet Sauvignon 2005 Belfield (R65) *With its papal red cloak, delicate cassis aromas and flavors, poised acidity, and fine tannins, Mike Kreft's first bottling reflects the potential of the Elgin Valley's cool, long summers.*

8 Koetshuis Sauvignon Blanc 2007 De Grendel (R70) *Fans of Durbanville-grown Sauvignon note this as one of the best ever. Its asparagus and green-pea aroma and flavor nuances are overlaid with capsicum, scrub, and passion fruit—all tightly bound by a thrilling acid thread.*

9 Cape Tawny NV Boplaas (R65) *Good tawnies are much less common in South Africa than good vintage styles, but Carel Nel is a master. This one had 12 years in wood; from Tinta Barrocca, with opulent candied peel and caramel, this is sleek and complex.*

10 Pinotage 2005 Scali (R105) *This version, with 13 percent Syrah, from the lower slopes of the Perdeberg might surprise and satisfy many who disparage the grape: big, gorgeously fruit-sweet, succulent—but somehow with a refined air to it.*

California

Dan Berger

Dry Riesling and dry rosé have become the hottest of wines in the United States, although Pinot Noir remains most collectors' star wine.

DAN BERGER

Moreover, despite increasing sales of Chardonnay and Sauvignon Blanc, the quest by many American wine buyers for alternative whites like Viognier and even imports such as Austria's Grüner Veltliner indicates growing sophistication.

As US wine sales continue to rise on both a total volume and per capita basis, it's clear that wine is one of the fastest-growing of the beverage segments.

Evidence that it is growing broader comes from anecdotal tales of interest in Zinfandel, Cabernet Franc, and even Petite Sirah, Sangiovese, and Tempranillo.

Sluggish sales of Merlot and, surprisingly, Syrah have kept wine sales in the US still somewhat unpredictable. The most surprising aspect of the changes in wine-buying patterns is the interest in dry Rieslings and dry rosés, though this didn't initially show up on tax sales charts. The trends for both wines are up in tasting rooms and in sophisticated California restaurants but were transparent in non-California on-premise accounts or in supermarkets.

So powerful was the demand for dry Riesling that Chateau Ste. Michelle of Washington produced and sold 868,000 cases in 2006 and

DAN BERGER contributes a nationally distributed wine column weekly to Creators Syndicate; publishes his own weekly newsletter on wine, *Dan Berger's Vintage Experiences*; and writes trade-magazine articles for US magazines *Cheers*, *Beverage Dynamics*, and *Wines and Vines*, as well as *Off Licence News* and *Decanter* in London. He is a speaker at major wine symposiums around the world and is a judge at numerous wine competitions in the United States and abroad. He also coordinates the Riverside International and Long Beach wine competitions in southern California.

made about 950,000 cases in 2007. They would have produced more had the fruit been available.

Randall Grahm of Bonny Doon Vineyard fame spent millions building a 200,000-case wine facility dedicated solely to Riesling at Paterson, Washington, in the Columbia Valley, and an International Riesling Foundation was founded in late 2007 by two dozen wine companies to promote the variety and educate consumers about sweetness levels. Jim Trezise of the New York Wine and Grape Foundation heads the fledgling group, which has wide support in Europe and Australia, as well as other countries.

Meanwhile, rosé sales out of tasting rooms in California soared to new heights, although it was impossible to establish how great the actual demand was because most wineries made only scant amounts of rosé and sold them out quickly, so few had any real understanding of the actual demand. Interviews with dozens of winemakers showed that almost all were shocked that their initial efforts with dry pink wine were so successful.

The best story comes from Fetzer Vineyards, which for years made a Syrah rosé for Tesco stores in the UK. Each year, winemaker Dennis Martin would make more of the wine, hoping there would be enough for a US test. Each year, Tesco would happily take all he could make. In 2005, production of the wine topped 100,000 cases. In 2006, eager to see how it would do in the US market, Brown-Forman, the parent company, extracted 10,000 cases for the US market. Under the name Little Black Dress, the wine sold out in weeks.

Grapevine

• **The trend** by many wineries to use heavier bottles flies in the face of environmentalists, who say such bottles are much heavier and thus cost more fuel to ship. Now wine collectors are upset: they're finding that the 5-lb (2.3-kg) monsters are so fat they don't fit in traditional wine racks.

• **What goes up** must come down. California's soaring wine surplus seemed daunting in early 2005, but the sluggish US economy precipitated an 18-month plunge in the value of the dollar against the euro, edging out imported wines and encouraging California wine sales to grow both in the US and Europe.

• **An estimated 150,000 tons** (136,000 metric tons) of California wine grapes weren't harvested in 2006 and 2007 as a result of a significant amount of imported bulk wine being imported to the US. The vast surplus of wine in France and other European nations led some major wine companies to bring in bulk wine in tankers and bottle it here under familiar wine labels.

Opinion:
Hot topics

A bizarre phenomenon is occurring in the US. More people are buying refrigeration cabinets for the aging of red wines and are filling them with wines that, chances are, will not age much if at all. Indeed, aging of red wine appears to be a thing of the past with most of today's wine buyers, who have no clue what older wine is all about.

The hottest controversy on the fine-wine scene revolves around increasing alcohol levels. Internet wine bloggers were particularly eager to weigh in on the subject, many blaming critics of high-alcohol wines for ignoring the will of the people. And they argue that such wines may not age well, but "who cares? They'll all be consumed in a few years."

Others argued that higher alcohol robs a wine of its regional character ("terroir is the bonus you expect to get when you pay more for a wine with a delimited appellation"). And they added that high-alcohol wines don't work at all with meals.

On the latter side were supporters of AppellationAmerica.com. Taking a decidedly forceful stance in favor of bigness were those dedicated to such wines as high-end Napa Cabernets, powerful Rhône-style wines such as black-colored Syrahs, and notably members of the Zinfandel Advocates and Producers (ZAP, which stages a massive tasting annually in San Francisco), who blithely ignore the fact that some of these wines are higher in alcohol than sherry and compete with port.

Yet few are aware that high-alcohol wines typically have higher pH levels and consequently lower acids, which make for rapidly aging wines—and worse. Higher pH levels can lead to wines that are susceptible to spoilage elements. Caught in the middle of this are classicists among the retail and restaurant fraternities who admire better-structured wines but who have to sell what's in demand, and wines with high alcohol levels seem to score well, so that's what many younger consumers want.

Now comes the first sign of a possible alcohol backlash as sales of Syrah began to slide significantly late in 2007.

Grapevine

- **Sales of Pinot Noir** rocketed in 2007 with the release of the 2005 wines, from a vintage that, at least along coastal vineyards, was rated as very cool. The category was helped by the release three years earlier of the film *Sideways*. Pinot's success also relates to the greatness of the wines.

Vintage Report

Advance report on the latest harvest

2007

Scant rain in winter caused early budbreak, which led to most grapes ripening evenly. Though a few small heat spikes in summer created headaches for some growers, most heat spells were short-term, and the harvest began in mid-August, earlier than normal, but with sufficient time on the vine because of the early fruit set. The only problem was that in most north coastal areas, fruit all seemed to ripen at the same time. Suddenly in early September, cool weather arrived to slow things down. As a result, some Pinot Noir stayed on the vine for a few extra days. Low humidity prevented disease pressure and mostly healthy fruit was picked. Yields were down in most coastal areas, but even so, many growers left fruit unharvested because demand didn't meet fruit expectation.

Updates on the previous five vintages

2006

Vintage rating: 97

For the second year in a row, winter rains and a cool, rainy spring posed problems for growers, with the potential for early botrytis. Most of the summer was cool, but two weeks in late July and early August were so hot that many vines shut down. Cooler-than-usual weather followed, pushing harvest back nearly a month. Harvest was erratic, with some whites picked later than some black grapes. Pinot Noir, which suffered a tiny crop in 2005, rebounded to near-normal levels. Quality was rated as superb, with great natural acids.

2005

Vintage rating: 98

A cool, wet spring lasted until mid-June, leaving most of coastal northern California with severe mildew problems, necessitating drastic measures in some areas to prevent botrytis. A cool late spring and summer exacerbated the problems, but the cooler-than-normal weather led to a harvest that was topsy-turvy, with some black grapes (such as Pinot Noir) being picked before whites. Some coastal areas, such as Sonoma Coast and Russian River, suffered small crops, but larger tonnage was seen elsewhere. Most grapes had excellent acid levels, and overall quality was rated to be exceptional.

2004

Vintage rating: 94

A warm spring got vines off to a fast start. But two months of cooler weather followed, then two weeks of summer heat. That made for one of the earliest harvests in decades, running three to four weeks ahead of normal. The first grapes, for sparkling wine, were picked on July 23. Quality was rated as excellent. Tonnage declines of about 5 percent were reported in most Napa and Sonoma regions. The decrease followed nearly a decade of overproduction and low prices, both of which prompted growers to reduce acreage and slow new plantings.

2003

Vintage rating: 93

Early rains and late heat spikes contributed to lower overall yields. The result was a vintage of high quality, good color concentration, and intensity of flavor. Heat in March led to shatter, reducing crop size. Then a cold May left the crop a month behind schedule. Dramatic heat spikes in September moved the harvest forward closer to a normal schedule. There was a rush to get everything harvested, and much came in at the same time. Reds had high acid, high sugar, and low pH.

2002

Vintage rating: 90

No prolonged summer heat, just many short heat spells late in the season, resulting in excessively high sugars in many varieties. The heat spells occurred after a relatively cool summer, so sugars rose quickly. Some awkward reds; whites survived better, since the slightly cooler summer left Chardonnay, Sauvignon Blanc, and Pinot Gris with good acids.

Grapevine

• **Darrell Corti,** a respected Sacramento wine merchant, said that he would no longer stock wines that had more than 14.5 percent alcohol. Corti, perhaps the world's most knowledgeable wine and food buyer, said such wines do not work well with food. Weeks later, Napa winemaker Randy Dunn (Dunn Vineyards) called in a letter for "the current fad of higher alcohols [to] stop." The outrage from many bloggers who love huge red wines was evident for months.

• **Beam Wine Estates'** wine portfolio was acquired by Constellation Brands, giving it Clos du Bois, Geyser Peak, Gary Farrell, and Buena Vista, along with 1,200 acres of prime Sonoma County vineyard land. UK company Diageo acquired Rosenblum Cellars, a major Zinfandel specialist, in a $105 million deal.

GREATEST WINE PRODUCERS

1. Dutton-Goldfield
2. Navarro
3. Stag's Leap Wine Cellars
4. Morgan
5. Robert Sinskey
6. Iron Horse
7. Au Bon Climat
8. Chimney Rock
9. St Supery
10. Gundlach Bundschu

FASTEST-IMPROVING PRODUCERS

1. Sonoma Coast Vineyards
2. Lynmar
3. Sbragia
4. Charles Krug
5. Dry Creek
6. Eberle
7. LaZarre
8. Firestone/Curtis
9. Kenwood
10. Xtant

NEW UP-AND-COMING PRODUCERS

1. Kosta Browne
2. Halleck
3. Londer
4. Campion
5. Roar
6. Sapphire Hill
7. Shannon Ridge
8. Papapietro Perry
9. Foley
10. Goldschmidt

BEST-VALUE PRODUCERS

1. Sutter Home
2. Fetzer
3. Cycles Gladiator
4. Kendall-Jackson
5. McManis
6. Dancing Bull
7. Toad Hollow
8. Huntington
9. J Pedroncelli
10. Mirassou

GREATEST-QUALITY WINES

1. **Freestone Hill Vineyard Pinot Noir 2005** Dutton-Goldfield, Russian River Valley ($58)
2. **Rued Clone Chardonnay 2005** Iron Horse, Green Valley, Sonoma ($38)
3. **Tondre's Grapefield Pinot Noir 2005** Morgan, Santa Lucia Highlands ($55)
4. **Cherry Ridge Vineyard Syrah 2005** Dutton-Goldfield, Russian River Valley ($35)
5. **Sonoma County Selection Cabernet Sauvignon 2002** Gary Farrell, Sonoma County ($35)
6. **Cabernet Sauvignon Plus Alexander Valley 2005** Goldschmidt, Alexander Valley ($140)
7. **Balistreri Vineyard Pinot Noir 2005** Sonoma Coast Vineyards, Sonoma Coast ($100)
8. **Bancroft Ranch Merlot 2004** Beringer, Howell Mountain, Napa Valley ($90)
9. **Leras Vineyard Pinot Noir 2005** Papapietro Perry, Russian River Valley ($48)
10. **Highland Estates Syrah Alisos Hills 2004** Kendall-Jackson, Santa Barbara County ($35)

BEST BARGAINS

1. **French Colombard 2006** McNab Ridge, Niemi Ranch, Mendocino County ($12)
2. **Zinfandel Rosé 2006** J Pedroncelli, Dry Creek Valley ($10)
3. **Syrah 2005** Cycles Gladiator, Central Coast ($10)
4. **Chenin Blanc 2006** Dry Creek, Clarksburg ($12.75)
5. **Edelzwicker 2006** Navarro, Anderson Valley ($11)
6. **Pacific Rim Riesling 2006** Bonny Doon, America ($9)
7. **Rosé Table Wine 2006** Kenwood, California ($8)
8. **Meritage 2004** Kendall-Jackson, California ($12)
9. **Little Black Dress Syrah Rosé 2006** Fetzer, California ($10)
10. **Cabernet Franc 2005** Forest Glen, California ($10)

MOST EXCITING OR UNUSUAL FINDS

1. **Abraxas 2006** Robert Sinskey, Napa Valley ($30) *Exotic aroma of wild flowers and faint tropical fruit in this blend of Pinot Blanc, Pinot Gris, and Gewurztraminer. Succulent, but dry.*
2. **Barbera 2006** Shannon Ridge, Lake County ($20) *Fairly deep, concentrated red wine with excellent acidity.*
3. **Carignane 2005** Roshambo, Alexander Valley ($25) *Cranberry/ raspberry aroma, with traces of Beaujolais Nouveau; loads of mid-palate fruit.*
4. **Marcien 2004** Robert Sinskey, Carneros, Napa Valley ($65) *Startling aroma of red berry and spice, but with terrific structure (unlike so many Napa reds), so it will age.*
5. **Deviation NV** Quady, California ($25 per half-bottle) *Dessert wine flavored with rose geranium and Damiana, with orange Muscat as a base. Totally exotic and curious geranium-esque aroma. Hard to describe!*
6. **Albariño 2006** Tangent, Edna Valley ($17) *Tangerine and lime aroma; racy with a hint of white pepper.*
7. **Syrah 2004** Tolosa, Edna Valley ($20) *Black pepper, blueberry and blackberry fruit, and perfectly balanced acid.*
8. **Bungalow Red 2006** Casa Barranca, Santa Barbara County ($25) *A dramatic blend of 72 percent Syrah, 16 percent Grenache, 12 percent Mourvèdre, with racy acidity and a lot of early appeal.*
9. **Albariño 2006** York Mountain, Edna Valley ($16) *Floral/tropical aroma, with spice notes and notes of dried pear and apple. Great structural balance.*
10. **Vermentino 2006** Uvaggio, Lodi ($10) *Startlingly fresh aroma of white peaches and spiced blossoms. Just slightly off-dry.*

Grapevine

- **Tim Mondavi,** his sister Marcia, and his stepmother Margrit Biever announced that they have joined forces to make a super-premium Cabernet Sauvignon-based Napa Valley wine called Continuum, which will continue the Mondavi family legacy. Robert Mondavi, the elder statesman of the family, attended the announcement dinner but didn't participate. He has been confined to a wheelchair in recent years.

- **Ernest Gallo,** who dominated the California wine-marketing scene for half a century, died at the age of 97.

Pacific Northwest

Paul Gregutt

Though it began in California, the freeze placed on the granting of new AVAs by the Alcohol and Tobacco Tax and Trade Bureau (TTB) has spread into the Pacific Northwest.

PAUL GREGUTT

It was initially prompted by a spat between the petitioners for a Calistoga appellation and Calistoga Partners, the owners of Calistoga Cellars and Chateau Calistoga.

Calistoga Partners contested the application, arguing that neither of its Calistoga brands would qualify for the proposed Calistoga AVA, since the company sources grapes from throughout the state. When the initial Band-Aid suggested by the TTB failed to stick—an attempt to "grandfather in" such brands—the government brought down the big hammer and shut down the entire system.

"A comprehensive review of the AVA program is warranted in order to maintain the integrity of the program," the TTB announced in November 2007. "We are concerned that because the establishment of an AVA can limit the use of existing brand names, approval of an AVA can have a deleterious effect on established businesses, can limit competition, and can be used by petitioners to adversely affect a competitor's business.

"In addition, we note that over the years there has been an increase in the number of petitions for the establishment of new AVAs within already existing AVAs. Because the idea behind the recognition of an AVA is that

PAUL GREGUTT writes regularly on wine for *The Seattle Times*, the *Yakima Herald-Republic*, the *Walla Walla Union-Bulletin*, *The Spokane Spokesman-Review*, *Pacific Northwest* magazine, and *Wine Enthusiast* magazine. He is a member of the *Wine Enthusiast* tasting panel and the author of the critically acclaimed *Washington Wine & Wineries: The Essential Guide* (University of California Press, 2007). Online, you'll find him at paulgregutt.com.

it is a unique area for viticultural purposes with reference to what is outside it, we believe that preserving the integrity of the AVA program mandates clarifying the standards for AVAs to foster greater scrutiny on the establishment of new AVAs within existing AVAs."

The system suffers from myriad problems already, to which the TTB has now added a few more. This latest memo seems to indicate that the TTB will henceforth frown on applications that further define existing appellations. Fortunately for Oregon, the six new AVAs within the Willamette Valley were already approved. But Washington's future AVAs will almost certainly all lie within the vast Columbia Valley. Most would be further refinements of existing sub-AVAs such as Walla Walla Valley and Yakima Valley.

The first casualty of the TTB freeze is the proposed Lake Chelan AVA, which was nearing approval. That application is now on hold. In a developing wine region such as Washington State, where many new vineyards are being planted in areas once considered unsuitable for wine grapes, the refinement of the primary AVAs is ongoing and essential.

For example, new vineyard plantings in Walla Walla in recent years have moved farther south, east, and north, as well as to higher altitudes. In the process, they have defined at least four separate and quite distinct soil and climatic regions. It is difficult to see how the further evolution of Washington's vineyard sites can be accurately charted unless smaller and smaller subdivisions of existing AVAs are allowed.

Grapevine

• **Oregon consumers** may legally receive wine shipments from wineries both inside and outside the state, as of January 1, 2008. As in neighboring Washington, a direct-shipping permit is required, and all taxes must be paid. Wineries may ship up to two 9-liter cases of wine per month to Oregon residents who are at least 21 years old.

• **Chateau Ste. Michelle** has named Australia's Wendy Stuckey as its winemaker for white wines. Stuckey will report to head winemaker Bob Bertheau and will manage day-to-day operations at Chateau Ste. Michelle's white-wine cellar in Woodinville. For the past 15 years she has been the white-wine maker for Wolf Blass Winery (owned by Foster's), best known for its Gold Label Riesling. Both Bertheau and Stuckey began their careers at Chalk Hill Winery in Healdsburg, California, in 1993.

• **Vintage Wine Trust,** which invests exclusively in wine and vineyard properties, purchased the 700-acre Grandview Vineyards in the Yakima Valley for $12.4 million in September 2007. The sellers were the Den Hoed family. The property includes the Desert Hills vineyard, Andrew Den Hoed Farms, Foothill vineyard, and Rattlesnake vineyard. About 568 acres are planted to wine grapes, mostly Riesling, Chardonnay, and Merlot.

STE. MICHELLE MOVES SOUTH

Continuing a recent buying spree (Walla Walla's Spring Valley Vineyard, Oregon's Erath Winery), Ste. Michelle Wine Estates has purchased Napa's iconic Stag's Leap Wine Cellars.

The acquisition is a joint-venture partnership with Marchese Piero Antinori of Italy. For a reported $185 million, the partners acquired the Stag's Leap brand, the Napa Valley winery, and its oldest estate vineyards, SLV and Fay. The sellers—Warren Winiarski and family—will retain their Arcadia vineyard, which provides grapes for the Stag's Leap estate Chardonnay and Cabernet Sauvignon.

For CEO Ted Baseler and Piero Antinori, the purchase is a further extension of a partnership that also includes the $6 million Col Solare winery and vineyard atop Washington's Red Mountain and a broad distribution agreement for the Antinori wines in the United States.

RANDALL GRAHM MOVES NORTH

Billed as "a Northwest winery obsessed with Riesling," Pacific Rim crushed its first grapes in the fall of 2007 in West Richland, Washington. The Randall Grahm (Bonny Doon) project will make only white wines—a lot of white wines.

The first vintage produced 130,000 cases, almost entirely Riesling, made in a wide range of styles—dry, off-dry, single-vineyard, biodynamic, and cryogenic. Nicholas Quillé, formerly COO for Grahm's Bonny Doon winery, has been appointed general manager and winemaker at Pacific Rim.

UPDATED WINE-LABELING RULES FOR OREGON

The Oregon Winegrowers Association has succeeded in its efforts to update the state's labeling regulations, among the strictest in the country. The original guidelines, put into effect 30 years ago, were specifically designed to protect Oregon's growing reputation for Pinot Noir. They mandated a 90 percent requirement for varietal labeling of most grapes, the exception being the bordeaux varieties. Federal regulations, which apply throughout the country, require just 75 percent for varietal labeling.

In an October 2007 ruling, the Oregon Liquor Control Commission (OLCC) added 11 new varieties to the list of varieties exempted from the 90 percent rule. A 90 percent minimum requirement was retained for varietal labeling of the state's four leading grapes—Pinot Noir, Pinot Gris, Chardonnay, and Riesling—as well as 50 lesser varieties.

The other 18, which include Carmenère, Petite Sirah, Grenache, Marsanne, Mourvèdre, Roussanne, Sangiovese, Syrah, Tannat, Tempranillo, and Zinfandel, may be labeled varietally at just 75 percent. The changes are primarily a nod to the emerging interest in Mediterranean grapes, which are being widely grown in southern and eastern Oregon.

Opinion:
The 75 percent labeling rule

It is time to revise the law requiring that varietal wines should consist of at least 75 percent of the grape after which they are named. The TTB should follow Oregon's lead and make it 90 percent for leading varieties such as Pinot Noir, Cabernet Sauvignon, Chardonnay, and Riesling. This is especially true for Pinot Noir, where the consumer is often being misled.

Thanks to the popularity of the movie *Sideways*, which celebrated the pleasures of Pinot, sales have skyrocketed. Wineries large and small, but especially the corporate powerhouses, have scrambled to add Pinot Noir to their line-priced supermarket lineups. But what's actually in there?

If you find a cheap bottle of Pinot from California, the odds are pretty good it will have been based on overcropped, dilute plonk that's been beefed up with Petite Sirah, Zinfandel, and other dark, tannic black grapes. Some of these melange blends include up to half a dozen different grapes, yet still call themselves Pinot Noir. The situation is the same with California Merlot.

If wineries are going to use varietal labeling, it should mean that the wine in the bottle tastes like that variety. If they want to make something different, it should be labeled as a blend and/or tagged with a proprietary name. Surely we haven't run out of animals yet?

Charity wine auctions—enough already!

Why is it that the wine industry is expected to donate endlessly to charity auctions? There is not a day in the year that wineries don't receive requests to ship free wines to an auction benefiting one cause or another. Because this is an industry built upon talented and compassionate people, they meet far more of these requests than they reasonably should. The question is: are the benefits (to the charities named) commensurate with the time, talent, and dollars dedicated to orchestrating these glamorous and expensive fêtes?

The big charity wine events require full-time staff. They consume a tremendous amount of resources apart from just wines: committees to drum up donations, organize themed dinners and barrel tastings, create print and promotional materials, book the venues, and engage the (often costly) services of auctioneers, chefs, servers, and security staff.

The auctions themselves can be abusively loud, and bidding is usually dominated by a handful of well-heeled regulars. Many times I've seen excellent donations from less well-known wineries relegated to the darkest corners of the silent auction, where their lots, as often as not, are ignored or undervalued.

More worrisome are the demographics of the bidders, mostly baby boomers; charity wine auctions do not seem to be very popular with younger wine enthusiasts. Worse still, people of color are almost nonexistent in this rarefied universe. The whole charitable facade in which these auctions are shrink-wrapped is beginning to seem hypocritical at best, a sham at worst. A new paradigm is sorely needed. What that new paradigm might be is a good topic for discussion. But the days of the black tie, dinner, and wine auction are—or should be—numbered.

Time to overhaul the WSLCB

Washington State governor Christine Gregoire has asked the Washington State Liquor Control Board to provide her with an independent review and analysis of projected revenue growth, the impact of increased sales on public safety, operational and policy efficiencies, and possible organizational restructuring.

The laws governing the purchase, sale, and distribution of beer, wine, and spirits in Washington were set 75 years ago, and they are hopelessly out of date. The state is caught in the untenable position of having to both regulate and sell these products, opening it up to charges of being a state-run monopoly. It also finds itself trying to manage its thousands of stores profitably, while not appearing to promote the use of alcohol, which would be politically incorrect.

It has a burgeoning, multibillion-dollar wine industry under its supervision, yet state liquor stores cannot hold wine tastings, distribute educational materials, or even sell corkscrews!

Change the regulations

There are well over 500 wineries in Washington, close to 1,000 in the Pacific Northwest, double that number in California, and hundreds more scattered across the rest of the country. Almost none of them are benefiting from laws that make their products extremely difficult to market, distribute, ship, and sell.

Online shopping is here to stay. The current regulations are confusing, haphazardly applied, and often irrelevant. A complete and thorough overhaul of how to redesign the system to manage all these issues is a daunting task, but the current situation is jamming up the courts and making criminals of consumers who just want a glass of wine with their dinner.

Sink the ark!

The world needs more quality wines at everyday prices, not more wines named after critters, vehicles, and other gimmicks. Finding sound, flavorful wines in the lower price ranges is the hardest challenge any wine writer faces. Many frogs must be kissed (along with emus, roosters, kangaroos, jackaroos, crocodiles, cockatoos, swans, loons, penguins, fish, and koala bears) before you uncover a prince or princess.

Whether a wine is named after a critter, a river, a little black dress, or a tree stump matters little to me. What I want for my money is really quite simple. If a wine is labeled Chardonnay, it should taste like Chardonnay, not like microwave popcorn or vanilla syrup. If it is labeled Merlot, it should taste like something (with cheap Merlot you tend to be grateful for almost any flavor at all). If it is going to call itself Syrah or Shiraz or Cabernet, well, it had better be an honest representation of those grapes.

So, enough with the critter wines, O corporate marketing mavens! Instead of hunting for the next cute animal label, think what kind of success could occur if you spent the marketing money on improving the actual wine.

Grapevine

• **Mercer Estates Winery** opened its doors in Prosser, Washington, just in time for the 2007 crush. The $2 million project is a partnership between Mike Hogue (founder of Hogue Cellars, now part of Constellation Brands) and Bud and Rob Mercer, who planted some of Washington's first Cabernet Sauvignon grapes in the early 1970s (now called Champoux Vineyards). David Forsyth, previously winemaker for Hogue Cellars, will be winemaker and general manager.

• **An investment group** led by Allen Shoup, founder of Long Shadows Vintners and former CEO of Ste Michelle Wine Estates, has purchased Wallula Vineyards from the Den Hoed family, who first developed it a decade ago. The spectacular vineyard site is on the eastern edge of the Horse Heaven Hills AVA in Washington. Existing plantings total 650 acres, and Shoup's group has an option on a total of 1,500 acres, most of it with excellent vineyard potential.

• **Quilceda Creek Vintners** has purchased a 5-acre site adjacent to the Champoux vineyard in the Horse Heaven Hills. The new vineyard, previously known as Matador Ranch, will be renamed Palengat, the maiden name of Quilceda Creek cofounder Jeanette Golitzin. Paul Champoux will be the vineyard manager. The Golitzins have also purchased property adjoining their Snohomish (Washington) winery, and will be expanding that to meet growing capacity as new vineyards come online.

• **New winery openings** in Walla Walla are an everyday occurrence; much rarer is a winery closing. Colvin Vineyards, launched in 1999 by Mark and JoAnne Colvin, is one of the few recent casualties. Colvin was best known for its focus on red wines, particularly varietal Carmenère, the first to be made in Washington State. No reason for the closure was given.

Vintage Report

Advance report on the latest harvest
2007

Washington—The largest crop ever in Washington; 2007 featured an early and short budbreak; a cool, even ripening season with just a few heat spikes in July; and, for most wineries, a smooth and early harvest. September brought perfect picking conditions, but some late-ripening vineyards ran into mid-October rains. Across the state, berry size was small, giving dark, muscular red wines with concentrated fruit flavors. The white wines have plenty of natural acidity, freshness, and balance.

Oregon—Willamette Valley growers had a challenging vintage, with endless rain throughout harvest. Cool temperatures and strong winds kept most rot problems at bay. A lot of sorting was required prior to fermentation, but the best Pinot Noirs will have moderate alcohol and more burgundian, balanced flavors, with plenty of acid. White wines are more likely to be thin and green, especially from higher-elevation sites. In eastern and southern Oregon, a far better vintage.

Updates on the previous five vintages
2006

Vintage rating: *Washington—Red: 90, White: 88;*
Oregon—Red: 90, White: 88

Washington—Higher-acid wines than the 2005s; crop levels moderate. Crisp and fruity white wines, classic, ageworthy reds.

Oregon—Overall a very fine year, with both ripeness and depth. The Pinots are elegant and more burgundian than usual; the white wines, floral and nicely structured.

2005

Vintage rating: *Washington—Red: 94, White: 92;*
Oregon—Red: 90, White: 88

Washington—Whites are plump, juicy, and balanced. The reds are luscious, rich, and textural; yields are down, flavor concentration way up. The best vintage since 1999, and more accessible early on.

Oregon—The reds are light and fragrant, with plenty of natural acidity. For Pinot Noir the vintage marks a welcome return to finesse and elegance. Eastern Oregon sites in the Columbia Gorge and Walla Walla Valley AVAs had an exceptional vintage in line with Washington's.

2004

Vintage rating: *Washington—Red: 84, White: 78; Oregon—Red: 88, White: 84*

Washington—A severe January freeze wiped out most Walla Walla grapes. Many Walla Walla wines are atypical, sourced from Columbia Valley grapes. Quality can be very good, but it's producer-specific.

Oregon—A difficult start led to dramatically reduced yields. The best Pinots show ripeness, fine color, bright raspberry and mulberry fruit, and complex, elegant flavors.

2003

Vintage rating: *Washington—Red: 90, White: 88; Oregon—Red: 82, White: 84*

Washington—White wines are ripe and fruity, with forward, precocious flavors and lower acid levels. Merlot shows superb color, complexity, and balance. Cabernet Sauvignons are dark and concentrated; Syrahs are packed with juicy fruit.

Oregon—Red wines are deeply extracted, ripe, and tannic, but blocky and one-dimensional, with high levels of alcohol. Drink up!

2002

Vintage rating: *Washington—Red: 88, White: 90; Oregon—Red: 78, White: 86*

Washington—A record crop with high sugars, high acidity, and high extract. The white wines were juicy and crisp; the reds immediately accessible and loaded with bright, fresh fruit flavors. Should be drunk.

Oregon—A cold, wet year from beginning to end. Many Pinots are ungenerous and unyielding, with strong scents of tomato leaf and beet and earthy, hard tannins.

GREATEST WINE PRODUCERS

1. Quilceda Creek Vintners
2. Leonetti Cellar
3. Cayuse
4. Betz Family
5. Sineann
6. DeLille Cellars
7. Ken Wright
8. Andrew Will
9. Long Shadows
10. Woodward Canyon

NEW UP-AND-COMING PRODUCERS

1. Chateau Rollat
2. Fielding Hills
3. Raptor Ridge
4. Carabella
5. Abeja
6. Gorman Winery
7. Scott Paul
8. Mark Ryan
9. Stevens
10. Otis Kenyon

FASTEST-IMPROVING PRODUCERS

1. Leonetti Cellar
2. K Vintners
3. Buty
4. Torii Mor
5. Chehalem
6. Ponzi
7. Pepper Bridge
8. JLC
9. Nicholas Cole Cellars
10. Elk Cove

BEST-VALUE PRODUCERS

1. Columbia Crest (Two Vines)
2. Barnard Griffin
3. Amavi
4. Syncline
5. A to Z
6. Snoqualmie
7. Willamette Valley Vineyards
8. Robert Karl
9. Chateau Bianca
10. Kings Ridge

Grapevine

• **Idaho,** the odd scout among the better-known Pacific Northwest wine regions of Oregon, Washington, and British Columbia, has gained its first merit badge: the Snake River Valley has been designated an AVA. Though many of Idaho's best wineries still purchase grapes from neighboring Washington, this new AVA signals a commitment to raise the profile of homegrown fruit. Roughly half the size of Columbia Valley at 5.27 million acres, the Snake River Valley is larger than Connecticut and Delaware combined. In comparison, Oregon has 15 AVAs, and Washington has nine.

• **Oregon regulations** have been changed. Recognizing that consumers are more likely to recognize Pinot Grigio than Pinot Gris, the state's producers are now allowed to use either designation on wine labels. Until recently, only Pinot Gris was permitted. It has also amended an old rule that required wines to be 100 percent from a particular AVA to carry its designation. The new law allows up to 5 percent to come from outside the AVA, to accommodate such practices as topping off barrels.

• **A tiny Walla Walla startup** became Washington's 500th winery in May 2007. Sweet Valley Wines garnered a rush of publicity and quickly sold out of its first release—300 cases of a 2005 Merlot/Cabernet/Syrah blend named Double Barrel Red (the winery's owners also own a gun and pawn shop). By the end of 2007, the official count in Washington had topped 530 wineries, with no slowdown in sight.

GREATEST-QUALITY WINES

1. **Red Wine Reserve 2004** Leonetti Cellar ($110)
2. **Late Harvest White Riesling Ethos 2006** Chateau Ste Michelle ($40 per half-bottle)
3. **Pinot Noir Resonance Reserve 2006** Sineann ($72)
4. **Cabernet Sauvignon Galitzine Vineyard 2004** Quilceda Creek Vintners ($95)
5. **Syrah The Beautiful 2005** K Vintners ($50)
6. **Cabernet Sauvignon Widowmaker 2005** Cayuse ($65)
7. **Pinot Noir Abbott Claim Vineyard 2006** Ken Wright ($50)
8. **Chaleur Estate Blanc 2006** DeLille Cellars ($34)
9. **Riesling 2006** Poet's Leap ($20)
10. **Syrah La Serenne 2005** Betz Family ($50)

BEST BARGAINS

1. **Fumé Blanc 2005** Barnard Griffin ($9)
2. **Riesling 2006** Poet's Leap ($20)
3. **Gewurztraminer Oak Ridge Vineyard 2006** Phelps Creek ($15)
4. **67 percent Semillon/33 percent Sauvignon Blanc 2006** Buty ($25)
5. **Chardonnay INOX 2006** Chehalem ($19)
6. **Riesling Kungfu Girl 2006** Charles Smith Wines ($12)
7. **Merlot Two Vines 2003** Columbia Crest ($8)
8. **Pinot Gris 2006** Carabella ($16)
9. **Cabernet Franc 2005** Willow Crest ($16)
10. **Pinot Noir 2006** Eola Hills ($12)

MOST EXCITING OR UNUSUAL FINDS

1. **Red Wine Reserve 2004** Leonetti Cellar ($110) *This outstanding blend of Cabernet, Merlot, and Petit Verdot perfectly expresses the sleeker, less oaky, more vertically structured flavors that Chris Figgins is aiming for as he takes command of Washington's iconic Leonetti Cellar. More impressively, this was made in a year when few Walla Walla vineyards produced any fruit at all.*
2. **Cabernet Sauvignon Old Vines 2004** Woodward Canyon ($75) *Though friends and Walla Walla pioneers, Rick Small and Gary Figgins have not made wines in lockstep. But Woodward's 2004 Old Vines Cabernet Sauvignon is equally impressive in this difficult year. It's powerful and raw, hard and tight, but clearly ageworthy. Woodward Canyon has produced some of Washington's most exemplary Cabernets over the past three decades.*
3. **Pinot Noir Resonance Reserve 2006** Sineann ($72) *This is a limited release from some old-vine blocks in one of Oregon's greatest Pinot vineyards, now fully biodynamic. These intense flavors must come from the vines themselves; an amazingly detailed, impeccably nuanced mix of fruit, earth, and acid.*
4. **Syrah The Beautiful 2005** K Vintners ($50) *There are hundreds of different bottlings of Syrah now being made in Washington, but K's Charles Smith has shown, for the past five or six vintages, that no one can top him. This rare bottling has been made just twice, and both times it has proven to be a wine of immense charm and power, with a complexity rarely found outside France.*

⑤ Pinot Noir Les Dijonnais 2005
Brick House ($45) Doug Tunnell is one of the pioneers of organic and biodynamic viticulture in the Pacific Northwest, and with each new release his vines seem to deliver more concentration, grip, nuance, and power.

⑥ Cabernet Sauvignon Lewis Vineyard 2004 Dunham ($75) No one has done more to evangelize the Lewis vineyard than Eric Dunham. First with Syrah, and now with Merlot and Cabernet, he has showcased that vineyard's capacity for producing dense, intense, lush, and layered wines that seem to capture the essence of the variety and the terroir.

⑦ Red Wine 2005 Saggi ($45) This is the second vintage for Saggi, the newest Long Shadows collaboration, this one with Tuscany's Ambrogio and Giovanni Folonari. The blend is done in the Super-Tuscan mold: 45 percent Sangiovese, 35 percent Cabernet Sauvignon, and 20 percent Syrah.

⑧ Malbec 2005 Walla Walla Vintners ($30) There's very little varietal Malbec being made in Washington, but what there is can be very exciting. Here it is showcased as an unblended varietal, so inky it is literally black in color. The flavors echo the color, with amazing density. Black fruits, black olives, smoke, and spice are structured around thick tannins. Wines like this suggest that Malbec may be the next black grape (following Merlot and Syrah) that Washington wrestles from California's grasp.

⑨ Petit Verdot Meek Vineyard 2005 OS Winery ($42) Here is another 100 percent varietal red that is inky, tannic, and unyielding, yet it is done so well that it can indeed stand alone. Call it a steakhouse wine that can cut through the fattest, juiciest slab of beef you can toss at it.

⑩ Zinfandel Stone Tree Vineyard Reserve 2005 Columbia Crest ($30) The biggest winery in the Pacific Northwest has released its first-ever Zinfandel, a Washington version of the quintessential California grape. In Washington's hot Wahluke Slope AVA, the grape ripens well without turning into portlike jam. It is probably the terroir we should credit for creating this nicely balanced mix of berry, barrel, and crisp, palate-cleansing acid.

Grapevine

• **Oregon wine-grape crops** racked up sales of $46.7 million in 2006, an increase of 27.6 percent year on year, while wine-grape production was up by 25.6 percent. Southern Oregon's Umpqua Valley continues to show the most rapid growth, averaging 15–20 percent annually for the past three years, according to data from Oregon State University.

• **Echoing Washington's growth,** the number of Oregon wineries has tripled in the past decade, breaking the 300 mark in 2007. Counting brands as well as wineries, there are more than 400 distinct Oregon labels, almost all of them producing fewer than 5,000 cases a year.

Atlantic Northeast

Sandra Silfven

The long-awaited Riesling renaissance has arrived, with American wineries experiencing major double-digit growth in sales over the past five years.

SANDRA SILFVEN

Northeast vintners are turning Riesling into a franchise, as New York's Dr. Konstantin Frank, Hermann J. Wiemer, Heron Hill, and Standing Stone, along with Michigan's Chateau Grand Traverse, Shady Lane Cellars, and Black Star Farms, are all forging reputations on this variety.

This focus has raised interest in the World Riesling Cup competition, part of the International Eastern Wine Competition in New York, where submissions in 2007 were more than double the previous year's: 300 compared to 125. And though a wine from the northeast did not grab the crown in 2007, a Riesling from New Jersey's Alba Vineyards won in the semi-dry category—a first for any winery in that state.

Rieslings picked up traction from their exposure to world growers and writers at Chateau Ste. Michelle's first Riesling Rendezvous in Seattle in 2007, attended by producers from New York's Finger Lakes district, Michigan, the Pacific Northwest, California, Canada, Germany, Alsace, Australia, and New Zealand. Growers shared regional and style variations, as well as discussing ways to maintain world interest. Key issues were dryness levels and cork versus screwcap closures.

Jim Trezise, president of the New York Wine & Grape Foundation, used that momentum to organize the International Riesling Foundation at the end of 2007, with support from vintners attending the Rendezvous along

SANDRA SILFVEN lives in Dearborn, Michigan, and has worked in reporting and editing positions at *The Detroit News* for more than 35 years. She has written about wine for most of her career, and she produces the Michigan Wine Report for Detroit News Online (www.detnews.com/wine).

with California wine scribe Dan Berger, who writes the California section of *Wine Report*. Trezise argued in his speech at the 2007 International Riesling Symposium in Stuttgart that international standards should be established for sweetness levels in wines (dry, off-dry/semi-dry, sweet). The Riesling Foundation aims to address these points and to create an endowment fund for research.

Also, for the second year, Napa Valley vintner Scott Harvey purchased dry Riesling from the northeast for his Jana label, this time from Michigan's new Forty-Five North. It will carry the regional appellation, Leelanau, not American. The largest grower of Riesling in the region, Chateau Grand Traverse, also in Michigan, upped production of Riesling to 35,000 cases, all from Michigan grapes, in 2007 and placed the wines in Ralphs supermarkets, a subsidiary of Kroger, in Los Angeles.

New York's Fred Frank of Dr. Konstantin Frank, who sells wines in 30 states and produces 20,000 cases of Riesling in good years, says: "I think we are gaining credibility as a legitimate Riesling region in the United States."

Grapevine

• **Virginia said goodbye** to Juanita Swedenburg of Swedenburg Estate Vineyard in Middleburg. She was a feisty crusader, whether she was planting vinifera in the early 1980s when everyone else was planting hybrids, joining the male-dominated local cattleman's association, or suing the state of New York for the right to ship wine directly to customers there—a case that would lead to the US Supreme Court decision on interstate shipping in 2005. She died unexpectedly at her home on June 9, 2007, at the age of 82. The winery continues in the hands of her son, Marc Swedenburg, and his wife Elizabeth.

• **New York legend** Hermann J. Wiemer, who pioneered Riesling in the Finger Lakes, has sold his winery to his winemaker, Fred Merwarth, a Master of Wine student, who began making wine there in 2002. Wiemer will remain in an advisory role.

• **A new Ohio quality seal** sets wines apart for their quality and gives consumers an easy way to spot them. The Ohio Quality Wine Assurance Program issues special "Quality" neck tags and seals to wines that pass a rigorous sensory and chemical analysis. Program administrator Todd Steiner, oenologist at Ohio State University, says that, at minimum, these wines would be worthy of a silver medal. The wines must be made from 90 percent Ohio grapes.

• **Wine-and-food tourism centers** are multiplying in New York. In addition to the Finger Lakes' New York Wine & Culinary Center in Canandaigua, the Hudson Valley growers got a state grant to create a Hudson River Valley Wine & Culinary Center in Dutchess County; and to serve Long Island, the State University of New York at Stony Brook opened the Center for Wine, Food and Culture at its Southampton campus.

Shipping news: good, bad, ugly

Indiana consumers rejoiced over a US District Court ruling that allows out-of-state and local wineries to ship directly to residents without such hassles for customers as first making face-to-face contact with the winery. In New York, wineries were vexed by the red tape they have to go through to ship: three different permits and three tax filings. In Ohio, a new law restricts shipping rights to wineries producing fewer than 63,000 cases annually—a move that prevents many wineries from shipping to Ohio customers but protects Ohio wineries, none of which make more than that amount. Virginia wineries, which lost the right to self-distribute, saw some relief in the formation of a nonprofit, nonstock, state-administered "virtual" corporation, so they can deliver up to 3,000 cases annually.

Winemakers on the move

Virginia's Michael Shaps and King Family Vineyards parted ways; Shaps and partner Philip Stafford opened the Virginia Wine Works near Charlottesville. Though Shaps's wines are normally pricey, the new company makes $12 wines and offers custom-crush services. At King Family, the new winemaker is Frenchman Matthieu Finot, who last worked at Potomac Point Winery in Virginia. In Michigan, Leelanau Cellars hired Nichole C. Birdsall of Bonterra Vineyards in California, which makes her the first California vintner to take a job in Michigan. She replaced Shawn Walters, who left to head up Michigan's new Forty-Five North, owned by Indiana eye surgeon Steven Grossnickle. Michigan's two talented South African winemakers changed positions: Cornel Olivier left Brys Estate to open nearby Two Lads Winery with Chris Baldyga, and Coenrad Stassen quit Chateau Chantal to join Brys.

Grapevine

- **Pennsylvania wineries,** at the time of writing, were close to making their "Vintage 2012" initiative a reality. The aim of this five-year plan is to double the economic impact of the state's vineyards and wineries on agriculture, travel, and tourism (which in 2006 was a considerable $660 million), and it calls for a $2 million annual investment from the state budget. The money would go to the Pennsylvania Wine and Winegrape Development Foundation for marketing, research, and education, following the model of the New York Wine & Grape Foundation.

Opinion:
It's all in the blend

This time, I'm expressing optimism. It's an exciting time for wineries in the northeast, with several great vintages, more enlightened wine-growing and winemaking practices, smarter marketing, and less bickering. Vinifera wines are getting better and better, often because wineries think outside the box. Blending is a no-brainer to create more complex wines in an emerging wine region, but it has turned into an art form for some. New York's Christopher Tracy at Channing Daughters takes blending all the way to the vineyard with complantation—planting an array of varieties together to create field blends, micro-planting to the extent of changing varieties every fifth plant. He is achieving amazing flavors by harvesting, pressing, and fermenting a range of similar grape varieties together for wines like Mosaico and Sylvanus. At Bedell in New York, John Irving Levenberg, formerly of Paul Hobbs in Napa, found that ripe fruit and alcohol are not givens in the east. He employs blending and strict monitoring of fermentations (yeasts and pumpovers), in addition to aggressive vineyard practices, to eliminate "funky" flavors. Results are paying off, with beautiful wines such as Taste White, Taste Red, and Gallery. Even in an extremely tough growing area such as central-lower Michigan, Sandhill Crane has had success in blending vinifera and hybrids with fruit wines.

Aging is another issue with these wines—clearly the best wines, thanks to acidity, can age and should be aged. Barboursville in Virginia stunned judges at the 2007 Virginia Cup competition by submitting a 1998 Cabernet Sauvignon (still in supply at the winery) and winning the cup! In New York, Lenz, Wölffer, and Grapes of Roth can afford to hold back reds for five to six years before release, and what a difference it makes.

Alas, bad vineyard management, unclean cellars, and poor marketing choices, along with green tannins, silly names, too many sweet "tourist" wines, and stagnant websites, still plague the region. But their numbers are dwindling.

Vintage Report

Advance report on the latest harvest
2007

The "Easter massacre" frost in early April wiped out whites in parts of southern Ohio and central Virginia, and a freak hailstorm in June devastated the vineyards at Virginia's largest winery, Williamsburg, but overall it could be the best vintage since 1995. A hot, dry summer got relief in August, with enough rain to keep the leaves active through harvest. Picking of some varieties started three weeks early. Whites had softer acidity but higher sugar levels. Reds reached record levels of ripeness. Quantity was down a bit because of the drought or, in the case of New York, due to past winter damage.

Updates on the previous five vintages
2006

Vintage rating: *Red: 75, White: 87*

Stephen Barnard at Keswick in Virginia put it best: "It was an okay vintage," meaning it wasn't great, but not a loss. A cool August, cold September, but improved October throughout much of the region produced wines that were difficult in terms of balance. Nevertheless, whites showed good aromatics, acidity, and fruit expression, while reds needed some winemaking magic in the cellar.

Grapevine

• **West Virginia farm wineries,** at the time of writing, were expecting relief in the form of an exemption from paying a tax levied at 26 cents per liter if they produce no more than 20,000 gallons of wine. The proposed law would also allow wineries to self-distribute their wines and let out-of-state wineries sell directly to consumers.

• **Presque Isle** in Pennsylvania and Smoky Hill in Kansas are among the first to produce commercial crops of the new black hybrid Noiret. The Cornell-developed grape makes a hearty dry red with good tannic structure.

• **Vinny Aliperti,** winemaker at Atwater Estate Winery in New York, and his wife Kim have purchased Billsboro Winery on the west side of Seneca Lake, created in 2000 by the late noted viticultural researcher Dr. Bob Pool.

2005

Vintage rating: *Red: 92, White: 90*
One of the best vintages in the past 10–15 years. It was superb across the region because of the long, hot summer and fall. Whites were riper and richer than usual (atypical for the region); reds were a joy, with sugars higher than usual, wonderful tannic structure, and upfront fruit.

2004

Vintage rating: *Red: 85, White: 89*
In a smaller-than-average vintage with challenges from the weather, the whites are exciting, with bracing acidity and enough fruit to carry the day. Reds are on the lighter side.

2003

Vintage rating: *Red: 74, White: 88*
It was a small vintage that yielded some stunning crisp whites, but reds had low sugars, diluted acids, and light tannins. Many were declassified.

2002

Vintage rating: *Red: 90, White: 94*
Most regions, with the exception of Virginia and New York's Finger Lakes, were thrilled with the quality of all the whites and, almost uniformly in the northeast, the reds. Flavors are rich and intense for whites, concentrated with balanced acids for reds.

Grapevine

• **New Jersey** has gained a third appellation. The Outer Coastal Plain, in the southeast, is home to 20 wineries and commercial vineyards. The AVA is 2.25 million acres in size and covers the bottom third of the state.

• **Southern Ohio** had a thriving wine industry in the mid-19th century, but it was battered by black rot and then Prohibition. The area is experiencing a mini-comeback, with four wineries near or on the Ohio River east of Cincinnati: Kinkead Ridge, La Vigna, Harmony Hill, and Meranda-Nixon.

• **Maiolatesi's Wine Cellars** in northeastern Pennsylvania lost its entire winery—more than $1 million in inventory and equipment—in a fire in September 2007. Owner Sal Maiolatesi plans to rebuild.

GREATEST WINE PRODUCERS

1. Dr Konstantin Frank (New York)
2. Wölffer (New York)
3. Bedell (New York)
4. Lenz (New York)
5. Paumanok (New York)
6. Linden (Virginia)
7. Barboursville (Virginia)
8. Chaddsford (Pennsylvania)
9. L Mawby (Michigan)
10. Sakonnet (Rhode Island)

FASTEST-IMPROVING PRODUCERS

1. Heron Hill (New York)
2. Channing Daughters (New York)
3. Fox Run (New York)
4. Keswick (Virginia)
5. Thirsty Owl (New York)
6. Chateau Grand Traverse (Michigan)
7. Anthony Road (New York)
8. St Julian (Michigan)
9. Tomasello (New Jersey)
10. Shady Lane Cellars (Michigan)

NEW UP-AND-COMING PRODUCERS

1. Rooster Hill (New York)
2. Longview (Michigan)
3. Crossing (Pennsylvania)
4. White Springs (New York)
5. Left Foot Charley (Michigan)
6. Va La (Pennsylvania)
7. Hermes (Ohio)
8. Silver Decoy (New Jersey)
9. Paradocx (Pennsylvania)
10. Sugarloaf Mountain Vineyard (Maryland)

BEST-VALUE PRODUCERS

1. St Julian (Michigan)
2. Lakewood Vineyards (New York)
3. Firelands (Ohio)
4. Horton (Virginia)
5. Fenn Valley Vineyards (Michigan)
6. Ferrante (Ohio)
7. Debonne (Ohio)
8. Boordy (Maryland)
9. Swedish Hill (New York)
10. Glenora (New York)

GREATEST-QUALITY WINES

1. **Merlot 2002** Grapes of Roth, New York ($50)
2. **Reserve Merlot 2005** Bedell, New York ($48)
3. **Merlot Estate Selection 2003** Wölffer, New York ($35)
4. **Cabernet Sauvignon Old Vines 2001** Lenz, New York ($40)
5. **Assemblage 2005** Paumanok, New York ($40)
6. **Dry Riesling 2006** Dr Konstantin Frank, New York ($18)
7. **Merlot Reserve 2002** Breaux Vineyards, Virginia ($36)
8. **Hardscrabble Red 2005** Linden, Virginia ($38)
9. **Late Harvest Riesling Bunch Select 2006** Hermann J Wiemer, New York ($50)
10. **Due Rossi 2005** Chaddsford, Pennsylvania ($30)

BEST BARGAINS

1. **Dry Riesling 2006**
   Anthony Road, New York ($14)
2. **Vidal Blanc 2006**
   Boordy, Maryland ($11)
3. **Rustic White 2006** Longview, Michigan ($13)
4. **Traminette 2006** Rooster Hill, New York ($14)
5. **Keuka Village White 2006** Ravines, New York ($11)
6. **Ballet of Angels 2006** Sharpe Hill, Connecticut ($12)
7. **Gewurztraminer 2006** Firelands, Ohio ($10)
8. **Chambourcin Rosé 2006** Terra Cotta, Ohio ($10)
9. **Marechal Foch 2005** Flint Ridge, Ohio ($10)
10. **Vidal Blanc 2006** Sakonnet, Rhode Island ($11)

MOST EXCITING OR UNUSUAL FINDS

1. **Rkatsiteli 2006** Dr. Konstantin Frank, New York ($26) *Dr. Frank sets the standard for this unusual variety, and this vintage may be his best yet.*
2. **Riesling Reserve 2005** Fox Run, New York ($30) *A truckload of fruit, minerality, and crisp-tart acidity presses every sensory button in your head.*
3. **Pinot Blanc 2006** Left Foot Charley, Michigan ($18) *Is this succulent, intense Pinot Blanc the next variety for Michigan? Bryan Ulbrich, who makes world-class Gewurztraminer in the US, leads the way with this variety, too.*

4. **Riesling Reserve 2005**
   Heron Hill, New York ($30)
   Aromas, flavors, and body remind me of a Trocken Riesling from Schloss Vollrads.
5. **Sauvignon 2006** Channing Daughters, New York ($24) *A sturdy, layered, multidimensional Sauvignon Blanc ("Blanc" is deliberately omitted from the name), kicked up with a small component of Chardonnay.*
6. **Brut NV** Thibaut & Janisson, Virginia ($28) *This delicate, complex, finely balanced Blanc de Chardonnay is the result of two tried-and-true French champagne makers applying their standards and talent to Virginia fruit.*
7. **Riesling 2006** Standing Stone, New York ($14) *Jet-powered fruit, tartness, and minerality act as an amazing foil to the sweetness.*
8. **Petit Manseng 2006** Prince Michel, Virginia ($27) *Exotic, crisp, and dry, with twists and turns of intense floral, herbal, grapefruit strains.*
9. **Viognier Reserve 2006** Keswick, Virginia ($22) *Powerful and seductive, and able to manage the French oak.*
10. **Syrah 2005** Kinkead Ridge, Ohio ($20) *Ohio Syrah? Yes! Former Oregon grower Ron Barrett keeps proving the viability of the limestone soils along the Ohio River.*

Other US States

Doug Frost MW

Immigration reform, climate change, states' rights versus federal power, and corporate hegemony in the marketplace are shaping America's political landscape and have burst into the wine industry's staid chambers.

DOUG FROST MW

Each of these is not only roiling the presidential debates but also bubbling up through wine's seemingly placid surface. Immigration reform? Some wineries publicly worry about the issue, but few are willing to go on record about their use of Mexican migrant labor, and fewer still would be able to go on at all without it. News articles, magazine profiles, and op-ed columns rarely mention the effect of a disappearing migrant labor pool on viticulture; for the moment, lettuce pickers and orchard workers loom larger in the debate.

With the exception of certain municipalities, only Arizona has taken draconian steps to stifle illegal immigration. In mid-December 2007, a federal judge allowed a new Arizona law to go into effect: employers must demand iron-clad proof of US citizenship from their employees or face stiff fines and even the loss of their businesses.

Don't look for California to adopt these rules; Arizona politics are more brazen. Arizona agriculture (including viticulture) will suffer as a result, and the pain will be felt there long before it is felt in California's vast agricultural landscape.

But climate change was already providing a challenge to wineries and communities. A drought that has brought water levels to historic lows continued in 2007. The once-mighty Colorado River has been running at its lowest levels since measurements began 85 years ago. The river is a primary

DOUG FROST MW is the author of three wine books, including *On Wine* (Rizzoli International Publications, 2001). He is one of only three people in the world to hold the titles of both Master Sommelier and Master of Wine.

supplier of water to Colorado, Utah, New Mexico, Arizona, Nevada, Wyoming, and California. Lake Mead—Arizona and Nevada's water fountain and Las Vegas's primary water source—is only half full, and scientists broadly agree that its levels will only dip further in our lifetimes.

Perhaps this shouldn't come as a surprise. John Wesley Powell, a pioneering explorer, advised that water sources and river basins should determine the boundaries of future states. Instead, the system is set up for the states upriver to conflict with those downriver, and even Mexico is an unhappy partner in the complex arrangement of water sharing. The southwest and western states haven't seen the worst; exploding populations are expected to bring things to a boil in less than a decade.

The southeastern states have had it worse, and that's a shocking new development. The once-soggy region is, at least for the moment, battling for its life. North Carolina's Governor Michael Easley demanded that citizens use water only when "essential to public health and safety," albeit on a temporary basis. And he threatened to declare a state of emergency if volunteer efforts were not enough. In the Atlanta metro area of more than 4 million people, some experts are warning that the city's main source of water, Lake Lanier, could be drained dry in three or four months.

It all looks grim. But, surprisingly, the United States uses less water than it did 25 years ago, according to Peter Gleick, head of the Pacific Institute, a nonprofit organization based in Oakland, California. And vineyards use far less water than green peppers, lettuce fields, and fruit orchards. So vineyard owners ought to enjoy greater opportunities in the near future. The sticking point is that, due to their small numbers, they have far less political clout than other crop growers; they may get trampled underfoot in a rush for dwindling water sources.

At least vintners can take solace in their stronger footing in the ongoing legislative battle. With very few exceptions, direct shipping rules are tipping to wine producers' advantage. But the wholesalers are not done—not by a long shot. They will bloody the noses of any winery they can (and plenty of consumers) as they plummet from a market share of 100 percent to their new share of 99.5 percent. Pity the poor wholesalers. How have they fared in the past 12 months?

Two steps forward

Direct wine shipments to consumers topped $1 billion in 2006. It's no coincidence that new wineries are exploding throughout the US. The Midwest has 365 wineries, and the states between Pennsylvania and Arkansas have seen their industry grow from 69 wineries to nearly 600 since 1993.

In the past year, Arkansas has allowed small wineries to sell directly to its grocery stores. Arizona has opened the door for wineries to sell directly to retailers. Minnesota is now allowing consumers to order wine online. Colorado has dropped its requirement that out-of-state wine be purchased on-site. Kentucky has created licensing for small, out-of-state wineries to sell in the state.

Montana now allows wineries and customers to apply for licences to ship and receive wine. But at present no common carrier is willing to ship into the state, and wineries shipping more than 60 cases into the state must go through a wholesaler.

Three steps back

While shipping prohibitions are loosening, lots of silliness prevails. Iowa, Minnesota, and many other states prohibit online solicitations and ads for wine. South Dakota finally allows direct shipping but, confusingly, does not allow any common carriers to ship into the state. Tennessee and Utah are still, for the time being, felony states.

In 2007 alone, legislation prohibiting or limiting consumers' ability to purchase from out-of-state retailers was introduced or passed in Illinois, Missouri, Oregon, Florida, West Virginia, and Wisconsin. Craig Wolf, CEO of the Wine & Spirit Wholesalers Association, warned in an interview with *Wine & Spirits Daily*, "There are scores of thousands of retailers, and if the state allows retailers in addition to wineries to ship, how is it possible that they will ever be able to regulate those sales?" But wineries, not retailers, are the most common source of wine being shipped to consumers. The Specialty Wine Retailers Association, in a survey of shipping permits issued in New Hampshire, Nevada, North Dakota, Nebraska, Oregon, and Wyoming, found that retailers held fewer than 20 percent of the permits issued.

Grapevine

• **Retail giant Tesco** has entered the US market with its Fresh & Easy retail concept—but perhaps not as dramatically as it had intended. By early 2008 it had only one store each in the states of Arizona and Nevada (the rest are in southern California). Each state provides the barriers to entry so typical of US alcohol beverage retail: instead of a single liquor license, Nevada is requiring Tesco to apply for a new license for each subsequent store.

• **Is this fair?** Despite a somewhat hostile regulatory environment, both Oklahoma and Kansas now allow each state's wines to be marketed at state and county fairs.

• **Georgia** isn't making things any easier for its wineries. State law doesn't allow Georgia wineries to fortify wines, so Three Sisters Winery Port wasn't made at the winery. Instead it had to be sent to Shelton Vineyards in North Carolina to be fortified.

US wineries could be forgiven for believing that the new shipping law allows Illinois residents to receive wine shipments as they have done for years. But the new wine law permits only wineries (not retailers) to ship to consumers, and about one-third of US wine brands will also be blocked from the state's residents. Why? Illinois law defines a winery as a physical place, not a brand. So, unless a wine brand has a physical winery, that brand is no longer allowed to ship into Illinois. Need further proof that most legislatures are well stocked with crafty lawyers?

Roughly 40 percent of all wine produced in Illinois is made by two wineries: Galena Cellars and Lynfred Winery. The new wine law strips away their ability to sell directly to Illinois retailers, reserving that right for small wineries only.

Lots of states are implementing a production cap: the idea is that only small wineries will be able to ship directly, and large, well-known wineries will have to continue to distribute solely through wholesalers. Arkansas has passed a cap of 150,000 gallons a year, or just under 17,000 cases. Florida, the number-three US wine market, has a bill pending that calls for a cap of 105,000 cases a year. The Texas legislature continues to muddy their waters. A new 2007 law changes the shipping rules for Texas retailers in ways that can be explained only by inbred Texas attorneys.

While direct shipping to Florida residents has been legal since 2005, state regulators insist that taxes are not being properly collected and threaten to reinstate shipping prohibitions. Yet from July 2006 to January 2007, out-of-state wineries have self-reported shipping approximately 30,000 cases and have voluntarily paid more than $157,000 in state excise taxes. And according to retailer Tim Varan, "It's been, 'Don't ask, don't tell' for a long time." He's busy with Internet sales and jokes, "Let the wine cops come and get me."

Grapevine

• **Help is on the way** in many states: Oklahoma has hired Damon Smith as assistant professor and extension plant pathologist at OSU. A few states have realized that providing academic and practical support to their local vintners and growers is crucial to their current and future success. Idaho's 30 wineries have a new wine-quality testing service provided by the University of Idaho's Food Technology Center in Caldwell. Georgia wineries are involved in a fundraising effort to endow a professorship of oenology at the University of Georgia College of Agriculture and Environmental Sciences. But Illinois no longer has a full-time viticulturist employed by the state, and that has impacted research that could further the industry. Colorado continues to fund research and marketing, albeit on a limited basis, though budget shortages have necessitated cutbacks for research in most other middle-American states.

The Easter massacre

From April 5 to 9, 2007, the weather throughout much of the United States turned nasty; the temperature plummeted far below normal, and far below freezing. There's nothing unusual in that; the problem was that three to four weeks previously (again, depending on the region) the weather was bizarrely warm. It was so warm that vines from Nebraska to Texas, Illinois, Tennessee, North Carolina, and Georgia were already far into their spring growth.

Missourians saw the third-warmest March in 118 recorded years. Kentucky, three weeks before the freeze, had temperatures reaching 80°F (27°C). In Iowa, the freeze damage was most dramatic in the warmer south; again, it was the sunny weeks leading up to Easter that created the potential for damage, since the vines in the south were well on their way to flowering.

Worst of all for the vines, it was what meteorologists call an "advective" freeze. A cold polar air mass had arrived, accompanied by a stiff wind. Most freezes can be fought off with furnaces, smudge pots, windmills, and even sprinklers. But with advective freezes, not only does the wind quickly blow away any warmth generated by the vintner, evaporative cooling intensifies the rapidity of the temperature drop.

Across a swath of thousands of miles, the damage mounted. Grape-crop losses were at 95 percent in Missouri, 80–90 percent in North Carolina, 75 percent in Texas, and 60 percent in Kentucky. Oklahoma saw the nearly complete destruction of their Noiret, Chardonel, and Traminette crops. Iowa saw bud loss of 90 percent for Foch and 70 percent for Marquette.

US losses appear to exceed $1 billion; the state of Missouri alone may have lost almost $400 million. Among Missouri's many wine growers, I heard winery owner Tim Puchta's stark assessment echoed: "Even if you have a crop," Puchta says, "you're going to be asking yourself if it's even worth farming."

Grapevine

• **Wollersheim Winery** (Wisconsin) is making a habit of producing delicious icewine, helped in no small part by powerful December freezes. The 2006 is lovely, and the intense 2007 (both made from St. Pepin grapes) will be released in fall 2008.

• **Since 2000,** Colorado wineries have moved away from the state's vineyards in the west toward the more heavily touristed Front Range, which now hosts more than a third of Colorado's 65 wineries. The Front Range's share of the state's wine output has more than doubled in that time, and the number of wineries has tripled. Why? Tourist customers. "We're seeing 75 to 80 percent of our wine out the front door," said Tim Merrick, co-owner of Trail Ridge Winery.

Opinion:
Deep in the art of Texas

Maybe the reason Texas has yet to reach its long-promised potential is that its choice of grapes has been based more on perceived consumer preference than viticultural reality. Merlot, the most-planted grape, has increased in acreage by 47 percent since 2000. Sangiovese is the second most widely planted black grape. Without naming names, I have heard it posited many times that Sangiovese is a "warm-climate grape." Have these growers ever visited Tuscany? Sangiovese requires the low night-time temperatures provided by Tuscany's many hills and by its often bone-chilling morning harvests.

Chardonnay is Texas's number-two grape and has increased 28 percent in the past six years. Are vintners of the belief that Texas and Burgundy are viticultural twins? Hardly. But as so often happens with young wine industries, the tail is wagging the dog. Consumers buy and drink lots and lots of California Chardonnay; Texas responds by making so-so (at best) Chardonnay for familiarity and market share.

Cabernet Sauvignon acreage, barely behind Chardonnay and Sangiovese, has increased 23 percent since 2000. Almost equaling Cab are Sauvignon Blanc (41 percent increase in the same period), Riesling (why?), and Chenin Blanc, which is up 43 percent. But lest the state's vintners seem completely ham-fisted, wiser grape choices also prevail. Zinfandel, Syrah, Ruby Cabernet, and Black Spanish compete with these other misguided choices and roughly equal them in plantings. Texas's incipient star Muscat Canelli occupies the number-seven spot, and wineries such as Flat Creek, Cap Rock, Fall Creek, and Sister Creek have proved its quality.

Grapevine

• **Who threw cold water?** Alaska's shippers and consumers are supposed to differentiate "damp" communities, which allow limited shipping, from the 75 "dry" communities, to which it may be a felony to ship, but no one is quite certain of the rules. House Bill 34 would specifically allow in-state wineries to make direct shipments to the state's consumers; it has passed the Alaska House and sits in the Senate awaiting passage.

• **Nebraska's tiny wine industry** continues to claim attention, whether from James Arthur Vineyards' tasty Edelweiss bottling, Mac's Creek's pineapple-tinged Brianna wine, or the high-quality red Temparia (Tempranillo hybrid) from Cuthills Vineyards.

Vintage Report

Advance report on the latest harvest
2007

The Easter massacre destroyed or damaged crops from Nebraska to Texas to the Atlantic coast, but some areas bounced back better than others. For many the drought was a double whammy, but it did offer benefits to some vineyards in Georgia and the Carolinas, creating greater ripening in their tiny, freeze-damaged crops. Many had one-third of their normal crop; red wines fared best. Much of the Midwest did even worse: wineries will be buying a lot of fruit from the coasts. Texas, New Mexico, Arizona, and Colorado were greatly challenged by the drought; Texas also saw excessive rain before and during harvest. For all of them, the small harvests contain some pretty wines, especially reds. Idaho had a very good crop, though with less intensity and ripeness than in the past few years. But most believe the wines will have better balance as a result.

Updates on the previous five vintages
2006

It was a challenging year for many of the states in this survey. Missouri and Illinois had struggles with the weather, with insufficient ripeness. Like most of the Midwest, Wisconsin had rain problems; everything was perfect until the wet harvest. New Mexico was too wet, Arizona and Texas were too hot, but conditions in Colorado were good, and they were excellent in Idaho. The East Coast, too, was in better shape than some previous harvests; Georgia and the Carolinas had a good to great vintage.

2005

Missouri, Kansas, and Illinois saw rain in August, though reds did well. Wisconsin saw a good crop but with a lack of intensity. Most of Texas had one of the finest vintages in a decade. Arizona and New Mexico both had some bumper crops, and there was excellence on Colorado's Western Range. Idaho's vintage started out with 26 in (66 cm) of rain in June and July alone, but the season turned out far better than feared. Georgia and the Carolinas saw a cooperative harvest.

2004

Rain was the main story of the vintage, whether it's the trio of hurricanes to hit the southeastern states in rapid succession or the torrents that struck Texas, with rains of a remarkable 5 ft (1.5 m) in accumulation over the summer. Missouri experienced many of the moisture and mildew problems of other regions in the south and southeast. Colorado's vineyards saw significant losses due to the spring frost, and the same cold spell created problems in Nebraska. Idaho growers, however, were delighted with the vintage and Wisconsin growers were reasonably happy.

2003

The theme in most areas is spring damage. In central Texas, eastern Wisconsin, and Missouri, freeze and frost damage created very small crops—in some instances a third of the normal size. The wines, however, are often good. Missouri's whites are in short supply, but the reds are very good. Wisconsin's whites are excellent. Texas lost a lot of its crop, both reds and whites, but Colorado saw a very big and very high-quality crop. Idaho's wines were big and perhaps a bit too hard.

2002

Idaho's reds were slightly high in alcohol. Missouri's reds were intense and concentrated. In New Mexico, it was yet again a drought year, and the wines show good concentration as a result. Georgia and the Carolinas were victims of excessive rains. All vineyards were cooler than normal, and the wines a mixed bag. Texas saw cooler-than-normal temperatures and higher-than-normal precipitation.

GREATEST WINE PRODUCERS

1. Gruet Winery (New Mexico)
2. Stone Hill Winery (Missouri)
3. Augusta Winery (Missouri)
4. Callaghan Vineyards (Arizona)
5. Montelle Winery (Missouri)
6. Sutcliffe Vineyards (Colorado)
7. Ste. Chapelle Vineyards (Idaho)
8. Galena Cellars (Illinois)
9. Koenig Distillery & Winery (Idaho)
10. Carlson Vineyards (Colorado)

FASTEST-IMPROVING PRODUCERS

1. Childress Vineyards (North Carolina)
2. Bookcliff Vineyards (Colorado)
3. Holy-Field Vineyard & Winery (Kansas)
4. Pend d'Oreille (Idaho)
5. Flat Creek Estate (Texas)
6. S. Rhodes Vineyards (Colorado)
7. Alto Vineyards (Illinois)
8. Becker Vineyards (Texas)
9. Hell's Canyon Winery (Idaho)
10. Crown Valley Vineyards (Missouri)

NEW UP-AND-COMING PRODUCERS

1. Snake River Winery (Idaho)
2. Boulder Creek Winery (Colorado)
3. Coeur d'Alene Cellars (Idaho)
4. Garfield Estates (Colorado)
5. Williamson Vineyards (Idaho)
6. Frogtown Cellars (Georgia)
7. Ravissant Winery (Illinois)
8. Rockhouse Vineyards (North Carolina)
9. Fireside Vineyards (Iowa)
10. Spicewood Vineyards (Texas)

BEST-VALUE PRODUCERS

1. Wollersheim Winery (Wisconsin)
2. Les Bourgeois (Missouri)
3. St. James Winery (Missouri)
4. Adam Puchta Winery (Missouri)
5. Fall Creek Vineyards (Texas)
6. Stone Cottage Cellars (Colorado)
7. Sister Creek Vineyards (Texas)
8. Milagro Winery (New Mexico)
9. Cap Rock Winery (Texas)
10. Cedar Creek Winery (Wisconsin)

GREATEST-QUALITY WINES

1. **Late Harvest Vignoles 2006** Stone Hill Winery, Missouri ($30)
2. **Gilbert Gruet Grande Reserve 2000** Gruet Winery, New Mexico ($46)
3. **Syrah 2004** Boulder Creek Winery, Colorado ($20)
4. **Norton Port 2004** Stone Hill Winery, Missouri ($20)
5. **Syrah 2005** Gruet Winery, New Mexico ($18)
6. **Chambourcin NV** Holy-Field Vineyard & Winery, Kansas ($15)
7. **Vignoles NV** Adam Puchta Winery, Missouri ($18)
8. **Syrah Three Vineyard Cuvee 2005** Koenig Distillery & Winery, Snake River Valley, Idaho ($20)
9. **Claire's 2005** Callaghan Vineyards, Sonoita, Arizona ($28)
10. **Gewurztraminer 2006** Sutcliffe Vineyards, Colorado ($19)

BEST BARGAINS

1. **Traminette NV** Galena Cellars, Illinois ($12)
2. **Vidal Blanc NV** Cedar Creek Winery, America ($9)
3. **Prairie Fumé (Seyval Blanc) 2006** Wollersheim Winery, America ($8)
4. **Riesling 2006** Shelton Vineyards, Yadkin Valley, North Carolina ($12)
5. **Riesling Ice Wine Windridge Vineyard 2005** Koenig Distillery & Winery, Idaho ($20)
6. **Seyval Blanc 2005** Silver Coast, North Carolina ($14)
7. **Moscato Bianco 2005** Flat Creek Estate, Texas Hill Country ($16)
8. **Ambrosia (Traminette) NV** Somerset Ridge, Kansas ($22)
9. **Land's End Red NV** Reeder Mesa Vineyards, Grand Valley, Colorado ($17)
10. **Chambourcin 2004** Alto Vineyards, Illinois ($17)

MOST EXCITING OR UNUSUAL FINDS

1. **Traminette 2006** Stone Hill Winery, Missouri ($16) *A pretty version of a grape still in search of its proper style, Stone Hill's Traminette is less expressive than it is friendly. Floral in nature, because of its parent Gewurztraminer, Traminette can sometimes sprout into a garish caricature of Gewurz: bitter rosewater and potpourri. Instead, this is intent upon charm.*
2. **Syrah 2005** Garfield Estates, Grand Valley, Colorado ($21) *With a number of solid efforts with*

Syrah showing up from Colorado's western slopes, Garfield's Syrah is simply the one that seems likely to age more gracefully than some of the others that are either tinged with Brett or have been smacked by excessive amounts of new oak.

3 Berry Black NV Adam Puchta Winery, Missouri ($13) *Selecting this as a top Norton is likely to ignite a controversy, but is adding 2 percent blackberry juice to a Norton a less honest way to deal with the innate and fierce acidity and malic character of the Norton grape than, say, adding bags and bags of sugar and tartaric acid?*

4 Hearthstone NV Fireside Vineyards, Iowa ($12) *A blend of Chambourcin and Chancellor, this new Iowa wine was awarded the Dick Peterson Trophy at the Mid-American Wine Competition. It's a fruity, even simple wine, but it's a lot of fun to drink, and that hasn't been said much before about an Iowa wine.*

5 BodysGallen 2005 Sutcliffe Vineyards, Colorado ($25) *Most of Sutcliffe's red wines have a bit too much new oak for my pleasure, but it's hard not to enjoy Colorado's new-found ability to create thick, ripe wines from bordeaux varieties. About half of this wine is Merlot, about a quarter is Cabernet Franc, and the remainder is split between Cabernet Sauvignon and Petit Verdot.*

6 Late Harvest Chardonel 2005 St. James Winery, Missouri ($15) *A lot of people love this wine; I'm less persuaded. But, as a crowd pleaser, the wine is proven. Sure, it's a bit over the top and low on acid and balance, so it isn't going to last another three years. I don't*

think anyone will care that they have to drink this lush dessert wine sooner than that.

7 Petite Manseng Burton Blanc 2006 Tiger Mountain Vineyards, Georgia ($35) *Is Petite Manseng the right grape for Georgia's elevated vineyards in the northeast? Who the heck knows? But this is very, very interesting, balanced with honey, lemon, apples, and some ripe melon. And it's not the first delicious Petite Manseng the region has produced, just the best one this year.*

8 Chardonel Brut 2006 Crown Valley Vineyards, Missouri ($16) *A lot of us are still trying to figure out what Chardonel is supposed to be: a buttery, oak-laden Chardonnay wannabe? Crisp and tangy like unoaked New World Chardonnay? Here's yet another look at the grape's potential; this version is creamy, soft, textured, and quite pleasing.*

9 Touché 2004 Frogtown Cellars, Lumpkin County, Georgia ($30) *This might be considered a pleasing if somewhat ordinary Meritage-style wine, but what makes this wine notable is that Georgia has not previously shown a Meritage-style wine of this sort of power and intensity. Unlike some other Meritage wines from the southeast (or any other American region), Frogtown's version isn't overextracted or smothered by new oak barrels.*

10 Riesling Ice Wine Winemaker's Series 2005 Ste. Chapelle Vineyards, Idaho ($25) *Winemaker Chuck Devlin has produced a succession of fantastic icewines, and each and every one is offered at an absurdly low price. California, eat your heart out.*

Canada

Tony Aspler

Flying winemakers are so yesterday. Now there's a new Mr. Fix-It in town, and he's called the flying brandmaker.

TONY ASPLER

He is Bernie Hadley-Beauregard, head of the design and marketing company Brandever Strategies. One of his first clients was an Okanagan winery with an unpronounceable name: Prpich Hills. Hadley-Beauregard researched the history of the area, renamed the winery Blasted Church, doubled the price, and the wine has not stopped flying off the shelf.

In 1929, an old wooden church had to be dismantled and reassembled in Okanagan Falls. To loosen the wooden nails, the miners used four sticks of dynamite. They loosened the nails, but toppled the steeple. This story is now depicted on the winery's labels, along with other satirical images that poke gentle

TONY ASPLER was awarded the Order of Canada in 2007, the first wine writer to receive the country's highest honor. He has been writing about wine for 30 years. He was the wine columnist for *The Toronto Star* for 21 years and has authored 14 books on wine and food, including *The Wine Atlas of Canada, Vintage Canada, The Wine Lover's Companion, The Wine Lover Cooks,* and *Travels with My Corkscrew.* In February 2001, Tony cofounded a charitable foundation with Arlene Willis. Grapes for Humanity raises money through the wine community for the victims of landmines and children with disabilities (www.grapesforhumanity.com). Tony is the creator of the annual Ontario Wine Awards competition, an honorary governor of Cuvée, and a director of the Independent Wine & Spirit Trust. He is also a director of the Canadian Wine Library. At the Niagara Grape & Wine Festival 2000, Tony was presented with the Royal Bank Business Citizen of the Year award. Tony also writes fiction and is the author of nine novels. His latest series is a collection of wine murder mysteries featuring the itinerant wine writer/detective Ezra Brant: *Blood Is Thicker than Beaujolais, The Beast of Barbaresco,* and *Death on the Douro* (published by Warwick Publishing). He is currently working on *Nightmare in Napa Valley.*

fun at local wine writers and wine celebrities such as Robert Parker and *Wine Spectator* publisher Marvin Shanken. Thanks to Hadley-Beauregard, sales of Blasted Church wines jumped from 1,000 to 10,000 cases.

Since then, the flying brandmaker has redesigned the image and marketing strategy of wineries around the world. Another notable BC example is Dirty Laundry Vineyard, which was renamed from Scherzinger Vineyards after Hadley-Beauregard discovered a local Chinese laundry that fronted for a bordello in the early 1900s. The new label depicts a flatiron, and in the plume of rising steam you can make out several subliminal nudes. Then there is Megalomaniac, a small Ontario winery, whose labels have a Dada-like quality with names such as Son of a Bitch Pinot Noir, Pink Slip Rosé, Contrarian Sauvignon Blanc, and Coldhearted Icewine. The newest Ontario winery to receive the brandmaker's treatment is The Organized Crime Winery—not a Mafia-backed enterprise but a religious feud in the 1930s between two Mennonite communities in Ontario, one of whom stole the other's pipe organ and threw it in the river.

Chinese icewine

Brian Schmidt, president of Vineland Estates Winery in Ontario's Niagara Peninsula, has spent C$600,000 in legal fees in the past four years trying to protect his icewine in the Chinese market.

Although Schmidt has never sold a drop of Vineland Estate Icewine to the Chinese market, bottles with identical labels are turning up in department stores in China. The counterfeiters copied the label from the winery's website.

Schmidt is not alone; the VQA office has two dozen bottles of fake icewine under a variety of Ontario and British Columbia producers' labels. It is small consolation to Ontario's winemakers that Canadian icewine has become an icon product in East Asia. Unscrupulous entrepreneurs in Canada are shipping bogus icewine, made from fruit concentrate and honey, to China. According to the Ontario Wine Council, sales of genuine icewine have dropped 60 percent in the past five years as a result of the illegal wines.

Grapevine

• **British Columbia's winescape** has grown from 1,476 acres to 6,632 acres at the latest census in 2006. BC Agriculture Minister Pat Bell predicts that the industry in the Okanagan can grow by another 50 percent, but any remaining bare land beyond that will be unsuitable because of soil conditions and types. If he's right, that means the Okanagan will max out at about 9,000 acres.

JASON PRIESTLEY BUYS INTO BLACK HILLS

British Columbia–born actor Jason Priestley is now Jason Priestley, vintner. Priestley, best known for his role as Brandon Walsh in the 1990s soap *Beverly Hills, 90210*, bought a major chunk of the cult winery Black Hills Estate in the southern Okanagan in October 2007.

Priestley seemed the most obvious to make the first famous foray into the BC wine game. The North Vancouver native was already a lauded wine enthusiast, with an impressive 3,000-bottle cellar in his Los Angeles home. He was cohost of a lively reality wine program called *Hollywood & Vines* in 2006, and he remains a regular voice on a local wine-focused radio show called *The Tasting Room*.

MARK II

After a two-year wait, reports Julianna Hayes, the British Columbia government has announced new provincial standards and regulations for the wine industry, to be administered by the recently formed British Columbia Wine Authority.

Since the introduction of Vintners Quality Alliance (VQA) in 1990, there have been criticisms about the way it's run. Small producers protest about the 9-cents-a-liter fee; others accuse the system of being controlled by the larger producers. Many say the process is flawed because people affiliated with individual wineries sit on the tasting panel, sometimes assessing their own wines. All this led many producers to sidestep the program, since it wasn't mandatory. But there will be no opting out of the new standards, which are called Wines of Marked Quality. It seems, however, that the idea of a cohesive BC wine industry was a bit starry-eyed on the part of those pushing for the changes.

"They [the regulations] are an embarrassment," said Blue Mountain Vineyards proprietor Ian Mavety, who has been notoriously antiestablishment in the BC wine industry. "What they are forcing down our throats is basically the same old legislation that was never enforced and saying they are now going to enforce it. And we're all going to have to pay for it."

Wines meeting the standards will be identified as Wines of Marked Quality, but they have little to do with quality. They mostly regulate the alcohol, sugar, and acid levels, and address the thorny issue of labeling. For example, a label that reads "Product of British Columbia" has to be made from 100 percent BC grapes, as well as processed and bottled in BC.

REDUCING WASTE

Canada's largest liquor monopoly, the Liquor Control Board of Ontario, has launched an in-store environmental promotion program they call "Enviro Chic," in an effort to persuade their customers to reduce packaging waste.

"Consumers are increasingly looking to buy from companies that are socially and environmentally responsible," says Bob Peter, LCBO president and CEO. "In 2005, we called on our suppliers to help us eliminate 10 million kg [22 million lb] of waste every year through alternative packaging by 2009. The response has been overwhelming—introducing Tetra Pak cartons, PET plastic bottles, and aluminum containers helped us meet our waste-reduction goal two years ahead of schedule."

Opinion:

Paparazzi house wines

Dan Aykroyd, Mike Weir, fisherman Bob Izumi, Jason Priestley, and now hockey superstar Wayne Gretzky: each has his own wine label, and three of them will soon have their own wineries. What is it about celebrities that entices them to lend their names and images to wines instead of to the more conventional lines of clothing or fragrances?

This is not just a Canadian phenomenon. If you look around the world, you'll see growing numbers of movie stars, singers, sportsmen, chefs, and porn stars (!) whose names now adorn wine labels: Francis Ford Coppola, Greg Norman, Ernie Els, Nick Faldo, Gérard Depardieu, Olivia Newton-John, Sir Cliff Richard, Bob Dylan, Sting, former James Bond girl Carole Bouquet (perfect for a vintner), Madonna, Lorraine Bracco of *The Sopranos*, and adult movie star Savanna Samson, to name but a few.

But what effect are these wines with celebrity names having on the consuming public? Are we prepared to buy a bottle of Wayne Gretzky Chardonnay just because it has No. 99's name on it? We may do so once out of curiosity, but the wine has to be palatable for the price.

This tabloid approach to wine does have its benefits. Any ruse to get the public to buy a bottle of wine rather than a bottle of beer has got to be, in the words of Martha Stewart, a good thing. If novice wine drinkers are brought to the table because they are fans of Gretzky or want to fish like Bob Izumi or swing like Mike Weir, that's fine by me. They will get a taste for wine and will want to explore their palate preferences.

From the producers' point of view, the celebrity angle distinguishes their wines from the rest of the pack. In future, I predict we will see other wineries that eschew the celebrity route using fantasy names to individualize their Chardonnay or whatever without recourse to such empty phrases as "Winemaker's Select" or "Proprietor's Reserve." Flat Rock has already done it with its Rusty Shed Chardonnay.

Grapevine

- **Blomidon Estate** in Nova Scotia has been sold by the McCains to a local family, the Raimeys, who seem well financed and determined to do a good job. Bruce Ewart, former winemaker at Hawthorne Mountain and Summerhill in the Okanagan, will be winemaker. Ewart plans to open his own Acadia Vineyards in the next year or two.

Vintage Report

Advance report on the latest harvest
2007

Ontario—The 2007 vintage in Ontario has been hailed as the best in living memory. The warm, dry summer brought a slightly reduced crop with smaller berry size, so grapes have a lot of intensity of flavor and color and show great varietal characteristics. A mild winter and the absence of late frost preserved the vines and allowed them to continue regeneration after the challenging 2005 winter, when tonnages were reduced by some 60 percent. The variation of temperatures between the hot days and cool nights increased the concentration of aroma compounds in the berry skins and aromatic components in the black varieties. This promises to be a stellar year for reds, especially Pinot Noir and Cabernet Sauvignon, with good volumes for Chardonnay and Vidal for icewine.

British Columbia—The 2007 growing season was temperamental. A cold snap in November 2006, when the vines were not fully dormant, did considerable damage to Syrah, Sauvignon Blanc, and some Merlot in the south Okanagan, as well as to late-harvested varieties in the central part of the valley. Growing conditions were strong throughout the summer months in the Okanagan, Fraser Valley, and Gulf Islands regions, with temperatures about normal in the latter two areas, but higher in July and slightly cooler in August in the Okanagan/Similkameen. Harvest in the southern interior got off to an early start, beginning in the second week of September, but rain set in and temperatures cooled, slowing down the process. It was also damp and cooler on Vancouver and the Gulf Islands. Overall tonnage was down from the previous year. It was an excellent year for whites in BC, but less enthusiasm has been expressed for the reds due to the previous November's damage and the cooler, wet harvest.

Updates on the previous five vintages
2006

Vintage rating: *Ontario—Red: 89, White: 88;*
British Columbia—Red: 89, White: 91
Ontario—A long, hot summer meant good physiological ripeness and high sugars in the early- and mid-season varieties. Wet weather at harvest swelled the grapes, making cluster weights 50 percent larger than the

previous year. Some winemakers used reverse osmosis on bordeaux varieties, but Chardonnay and Pinot Noir performed well, making it something of a burgundian year in Ontario. However, 2006 augurs well for a perfect icewine vintage. Some wineries picked on December 6.

British Columbia—The 2006 grape-growing year was virtually seamless in BC. A warm, sunny summer brought on *véraison* in very good time, and an extended, generally sunny and warm fall allowed all varieties to reach full ripeness. An early-winter freeze in the last week of November permitted the daytime harvest of a larger-than-average icewine crop. Across the board, 2006 produced fruit of excellent quality, which will be reflected in generous amounts of high-quality wines.

2005

Vintage rating: *Ontario—Red: 93, White: 91; British Columbia—Red: 90, White: 92*

Ontario—Thanks to the hottest, driest growing season on record, 2005 produced the best fruit the wineries have ever seen, particularly for bordeaux varieties. But because of the horrendously cold winter and early spring, quantities were down drastically. It was the earliest harvest on record for table wines and icewine. Henry of Pelham picked on November 24.

British Columbia—A clement fall with mixed sun and a few brief showers allowed the grapes to reach full maturity over a period that extended to early November for the latest varieties. Another contributing factor to the favorable flavor profiles was a smaller crop, down anywhere from 10 to 30 percent. This is a vintage of well-balanced wines with fewer of the 15 and 16 percent alcohol readings that have popped up here and there in recent vintages.

2004

Vintage rating: *Ontario—Red: 85, White: 92; British Columbia—Red: 91, White: 92*

Ontario—A cool, elongated growing season began with so much rain that winemakers gloomily predicted another 1992. But Nature smiled in the fall; the sun shone and rescued the harvest. Tonnage was about normal after the previous year's disastrously low grape production. The earlier-ripening varieties showed better than the bordeaux varieties. This year is better for whites, with lively acidity.

British Columbia—Cool, moist conditions in late summer slowed ripening, but the cooler weather gave the vines the time they needed to pack the fruit with flavor and intensity without excess sugar and low acid; some outstanding white wines resulted. On the downside, the conditions caused some fungus problems. The return of warm, sunny conditions in late September continued into November, allowing black varieties to ripen, producing good-quality wines.

2003

Vintage rating: *Ontario—Red: 85, White: 90; British Columbia—Red: 94, White: 91*

Ontario—The Indian summer encouraged maximum ripeness, but it also woke up the ladybugs. The horrendously cold winter reduced the tonnage of grapes to below 50 percent of normal yields. Some varieties, such as Sauvignon Blanc and Merlot, were down to 25 percent of the 2002 harvest, but the quality of the fruit was good because of Nature's draconian thinning.

British Columbia—A record grape crop following the hottest and sunniest year ever. The 2003 red wines are potentially even better than the highly lauded 2002s. Bill Dyer at Burrowing Owl used extended maceration on his Cabernet Sauvignon for the first time.

2002

Vintage rating: *Ontario—Red: 86, White: 85; British Columbia—Red: 94, White: 94*

Ontario—Yields were slightly down from predicted levels, but the quality and concentration of fruit were excellent. Winemakers say that 2002 will be one of the best vintages on record, particularly for red wines.

British Columbia—It is likely that 2002 will go on record as being the best vintage yet, surpassing 1998 by having more moderate heat for further flavor development and allowing white wines to retain natural acid balance.

Grapevine

• **The Nova Scotia Liquor Commission** rolled back its markups on locally produced wines by as much as 70 percent in January 2008. This will be a huge boost to the potential of local wineries. It means that they can actually make a decent return on wines sold through the NSLC and can take advantage of the province-wide distribution system. It should encourage new plantings to meet growing demand and encourage new players to jump in.

• **Donald Ziraldo and Karl Kaiser,** cofounders of Inniskillin Wines, arguably put Canadian icewine on the global wine map when their Inniskillin Vidal Icewine 1989 won the Grand Prix d'Honneur at Vinexpo in 1991. Now retired, they have collaborated on a book entitled *Icewine: Extreme Winemaking.* Beautiful photographs complement more than 20 scrumptious recipes from Inniskillin's late resident chef Izabela Kalabis-Sacco, using icewine as a main ingredient.

GREATEST WINE PRODUCERS

1. Le Clos Jordanne (Ontario)
2. CedarCreek (British Columbia)
3. Jackson-Triggs Vintners (British Columbia)
4. Hidden Bench (Ontario)
5. Quails' Gate (British Columbia)
6. Burrowing Owl (British Columbia)
7. La Frenz (British Columbia)
8. Tawse (Ontario)
9. Stratus (Ontario)
10. Flat Rock Cellars (Ontario)

FASTEST-IMPROVING PRODUCERS

1. Daniel Lenko Estate (Ontario)
2. Thornhaven Estate (British Columbia)
3. Hillside Estate Winery (British Columbia)
4. Thirty Bench Vineyard & Winery (Ontario)
5. See Ya Later (British Columbia)
6. Orofino (British Columbia)
7. Hillebrand Estates (Ontario)
8. Creekside (Ontario)
9. Township 7 (British Columbia)
10. Coyote's Run (Ontario)

NEW UP-AND-COMING PRODUCERS

1. Norman Hardie (Ontario)
2. Le Vieux Pin (British Columbia)
3. Stoneboat (British Columbia)
4. Closson Chase (Ontario)
5. Niagara College Winery (Ontario)
6. Megalomaniac (Ontario)
7. Huff Estate (Ontario)
8. Seven Stones (British Columbia)
9. Tantalus (British Columbia)
10. Joie (British Columbia)

BEST-VALUE PRODUCERS

1. Colio Wines (Ontario)
2. Gehringer Brothers (British Columbia)
3. Jackson-Triggs Vintners (Ontario)
4. Lakeview Cellars (Ontario)
5. See Ya Later (British Columbia)
6. Jackson-Triggs Vintners (British Columbia)
7. Calona (British Columbia)
8. Sumac Ridge (British Columbia)
9. Magnotta Wines (Ontario)
10. Inniskillin Wines (Ontario)

GREATEST-QUALITY WINES

1. **Osoyoos Larose 2005** British Columbia (C$40)
2. **La Brunate 2005** (bordeaux blend) Hidden Bench, Ontario (C$70)
3. **Estate Select Syrah 2005** CedarCreek, British Columbia (C$34.99)
4. **The Iconoclast Chardonnay 2005** Closson Chase, Ontario (C$65)
5. **Cabernet Franc 2005** Burrowing Owl, British Columbia (C$33)
6. **Beamsville Chardonnay 2004** Tawse, Ontario (C$47)
7. **Merlot 2005** La Frenz, British Columbia (C$25)
8. **Vidal Icewine 2006** Château des Charmes, Ontario (C$44.95)
9. **Old Vines Riesling 2005** Tantalus, British Columbia (C$24.90)
10. **Apogee 2005** Le Vieux Pin, British Columbia (C$65)

BEST BARGAINS

1. **Aligoté 2006** Château des Charmes, Ontario (C$13.15)
2. **Pinot Noir 2005** See Ya Later, British Columbia (C$19.99)
3. **Cabernet/Merlot 2005** Henry of Pelham, Ontario (C$15.25)
4. **Baco Noir 2006** Sandbanks, Ontario (C$15.15)
5. **Merlot 2005** Hillside Estate Winery, British Columbia (C$18)
6. **Pinot Gris Special Reserve 2006** Magnotta Wines, Ontario (C$11.15)
7. **Trius Red 2005** Hillebrand Estates, Ontario (C$19.95)
8. **Dry Rock Sauvignon Blanc 2006** Gehringer Brothers, British Columbia (C$15.99)
9. **Vintners Reserve Muscat 2006** Domaine de Grand Pré, Nova Scotia (C$17.50)
10. **Cabernet Franc 2005** Sumac Ridge, British Columbia (C$19.99)

MOST EXCITING OR UNUSUAL FINDS

1. **Nuit Blanche White Meritage 2005** Hidden Bench, Ontario (C$40) *Medium straw color with a smoky, toasty, spicy nose; the flavor of fresh green plums backed by vanilla oak. Reminiscent of Domaine de Chevalier in style.*
2. **Carmenère 2005** Black Hills, British Columbia (C$26) *White pepper and bramble berries on the nose; on the palate, red currants, loganberries, and baker's chocolate, with a hint of spice. Medium-bodied with good structure and balanced acidity.*
3. **Charles Baker Picone Vineyard Riesling 2006** Stratus, Ontario (C$35) *Very pale color; honey and grapefruit nose with a floral note; lovely balance of lime and grapefruit flavors. Off-dry with a long finish.*
4. **Pinotage 2005** Stoneboat, British Columbia (C$24.90) *Rich cedar-box and cassis scents on the nose are complemented by soft strawberry-basket notes. Flavors of ripe plum, Bing cherry, and raspberry are finished with rich boysenberry and subtle black-pepper tones.*
5. **Semillon 2006** See Ya Later, British Columbia (C$22.99) *This is no wimpy wine—it's big and rich with ripe fruit flavors of citrus, kiwi, melon, and tangerine with hints of lemon grass and lanolin.*
6. **Vintners Reserve Ortega 2006** Domaine de Grand Pré, Nova Scotia (C$18.50) *Lush floral scents; ripe tropical and citrus fruit with subtle honeyed overtones. Ripe fruit, full-bodied, and almost fat on the palate. Subtle exotic fruits on the finish. Reminiscent of Viognier from a much warmer region.*
7. **Delaine Vineyard Pinot Noir 2005** Jackson-Triggs Vintners, Ontario (C$24.95) *Light ruby in color with a minerally, cherry nose, the wine gives a nod to Burgundy with its lightness and harmonious balance. Flavors of ripe cherries and raspberries fill the mouth, sustained by lively acidity. The tannic lift on the finish gives the wine a structural flourish.*
8. **Vaila 2006** Le Vieux Pin, British Columbia (C$25) *An elegant Pinot Noir rosé: bright strawberry, cranberry, and citrus fruit with beautifully balanced acidity.*
9. **Sage Grand Reserve 2006** Silver Sage, British Columbia (C$26.95) *Made from Gewurztraminer fermented with south Okanagan sage, this unique wine has a cult following and is very popular with turkey dinner.*
10. **Select Late Harvest Cabernet Sauvignon 2005** Cave Spring, Ontario (C$21.95 per half-bottle) *A delicious dessert wine, with flavors of wild strawberries and honey.*

Chile

Peter Richards

Behind the scenes in Chile, one man is causing much commotion. Pedro Parra is a forestry engineer turned terroir hunter.

PETER RICHARDS

A man who studied for his doctorate in both French and Chilean vineyards, and whose name translates literally as "Peter Vine," Parra has been encouraging Chilean wineries not only to explore but also to understand all aspects of their terroir. While his technical assistance is significant, it is perhaps his influence in challenging staid attitudes and inspiring a new generation of winemakers that is currently proving his most valuable contribution.

Forward-looking producers such as De Martino, Ventisquero, Concha y Toro, Cono Sur, and Montes have all undertaken detailed and groundbreaking projects studying terroir and its effects on wine. Ventisquero, for example, has developed a software program named Maya, which overlays constantly updated information—from soil analyses, to phenolic content in the final wines—on to a vineyard map in order to differentiate quality zones in the vineyard and help manage them accordingly. The ultimate aim, according to head winemaker Felipe Tosso, is "to define our vineyard, understand why it is how it is."

PETER RICHARDS is one of the UK's youngest award-winning wine writers. TV credits include *Saturday Kitchen* (BBC1), *Daily Cooks* (ITV1), *Taste* (Sky One), and UKTV Food's *Great Food Live* and *Food Uncut*. Peter has published two books on wine: *Wineries with Style* (Mitchell Beazley, 2004) and *The Wines of Chile* (Mitchell Beazley, 2006). His writing portfolio includes *The Guardian*, the *Daily Mail*, *Decanter*, and *Wine & Spirit*, and he also has a column in *The Liberal*. Chile is a specialty focus for Peter, who has lived and worked there and is now a regular visitor to the country, covering the region for many wine publications, as well as judging in wine competitions (in 2006 he became the youngest regional chairman—for Chile—at the *Decanter* World Wine Awards). Peter lives in London.

The price of success

What with record sales estimated at US$1.2 billion in 2007, up 30 percent on 2006, you'd expect the Chileans to be breaking open the bubbly, but the more they sell, the bigger the loss they make.

It's a curious paradox, and one due entirely to a brutal equation of cost and return. The weak dollar and strong peso situation is showing no sign of letting up, while costs (labor, energy, dry goods) have been rising. Result: wineries in the red.

While the big producers have been able to leverage their economies of scale and diversified portfolios, it's the smaller and medium-sized players (*pymes*) who have an unprofitable business with the dollar at 500 pesos. Given that some 80 percent of Chilean wineries are *pymes* with annual turnovers of under US$3 million, it's no wonder that the outlook could be construed as bleak.

Nonetheless, it's also true that in 2007 Chile managed to raise its average selling price of bottled wine by around 6 percent. Its big brands are finally starting to make headway in the more premium price categories that Chile has long been courting. The country wants to position itself as a premium supplier, moving away from its cheap-and-cheerful image, and it is starting to do so.

Grapevine

- **New sweet wines** are emerging from the likes of De Martino (a naturally botrytized late-harvest Semillon from Maipo) and Caliboro (a Vin Santo style made from 70-year-old Torontel vines whose fruit was dried in the winery and the wine aged with deliberate ullage in the barrel for a year).

- **Joy for Alvaro Espinoza** at being voted Personality of the Year at the International Wine Challenge 2007. Great to see Chile producing personalities on the world stage.

- **Notable ownership changes** of late have included, as predicted in *Wine Report 2008*, San Pedro buying its French partners Dassault out of their high-profile joint venture Altaïr. Meanwhile, the long-standing Canepa winery has quietly signed over its vineyards to Santa Rita and winery

and brands to Concha y Toro in what is reported to be a 10-year lease deal. Finally, Maule-based Via has continued its seemingly inexorable expansion with the acquisition of Colchagua producer Candelaria and its local co-op, Viñedos del Maule.

- **Chile's expansion abroad** continues, fueled by a strong peso. Veramonte is developing a project in Argentina in conjunction with Alvaro Espinoza and Carlos Pulenta of Finca Vistalba. Montes has bought new vineyards and a winery in Argentina for its Kaiken brand while also venturing into Paso Robles as part of its new US operation. Finally, a group of Chilean investors, including Montes cofounder Pedro Grand, is setting up a high-end sparkling winery named Cruzat in Argentina's Perdriel region at a reported cost of US$6 million.

TO PINOT OR NOT TO PINOT

That is the question. On the one hand, plantings of the Burgundian grape expand apace as its popularity among the Chilean winemaking community surges. Cono Sur has just finished planting 80 ha of Pinot in Leyda and Bío Bío and has ambitious aims to reach a total Pinot planting of 500–600 ha. On the other, however, there is respected De Martino winemaker Marcelo Retamal, who has just declared that he will not be making Chilean Pinot after the 2006 vintage, explaining, "Chile's just not able to produce world-class Pinot at the top price levels yet. And until I find the right spot to make it, I won't."

SQUEEZING GRAPES

The new, unified Chilean winery association, Vinos de Chile, has big plans. And its first chairman, Casa Tamaya's René Merino, is clearly not afraid to court controversy while setting out his stall.

Initially, Vinos de Chile will focus on three key areas: international and domestic promotion and research and development. Merino has outlined a number of aims, including promoting Chile's green and tourism credentials, as well as encouraging development of new yeasts to lower alcohol levels.

More controversial measures include proposals to raise funding by taxing grape producers—the same people who have been protesting of late over low grape prices. Merino's response? "If we can help raise the selling price for Chilean wine, everyone benefits, including the growers. They'll come around … with time and patience."

Then there's his lobbying to reduce the length of time that vine imports have to undergo quarantine (currently two years). While many industry players have long been calling for this, some remain unconvinced. "It's important to keep Chile phylloxera-free," says Miguel Torres. "We still don't really know why this is the case, so it's important we take all precautions until we do."

FIZZICAL GROWTH

More diversity beckons for the Chilean wine category, with several new sparkling wines ready to hit the market. Concha y Toro and Cono Sur are set to release new sparkling wines, both made by the tank method. The former's is made from Chardonnay grown in Limarí; the latter's, a Chardonnay/Pinot Noir/Riesling blend sourced from the other end of the country in Bío Bío. More are set to follow, mostly sourced from promising sites in the country's cool southerly climes and some made by the traditional method.

Grapevine

• **Although phylloxera has never been detected** in Chile, many new plantings are going in with rootstocks—partly a "just in case" mentality, partly to protect against nematodes and salinity and ensure vineyard homogeneity. De Martino's Marcelo Retamal is having none of it. "I want my vines in the earth. If I don't have phylloxera and have the opportunity, I will use the plant's own roots. Nothing distorts terroir more than rootstocks."

Opinion:
Changes for the future

By nature, Chileans are neither the most proactive innovators on the planet nor the finest stewards of the environment. This needs to change.

True, certain things are happening. Two wineries—Cono Sur and Ventisquero—have recently adopted carbon-offsetting programs, while the Córpora group has unveiled a new solar plant at its winery HQ in Cachapoal. Miguel Torres Chile finances a conservation project for the Andean condor.

Organic certification is also increasingly being undertaken. Previously, producers who cultivated in near-organic fashion were reluctant to certify due to costs and bureaucracy; there was also a perception that being organic would be disadvantageous with consumers. But this attitude seems to be changing, not least on the back of an increasing desire for premiumization in the industry as well as high-profile successes like Emiliana Orgánico.

But this is not enough. Chile needs to take a decisive and industry-wide lead on the green issue. It has significant and unique natural advantages as well, in Vinos de Chile, as a new strategic body to steer the campaign. At the same time, it should be wary of jumping on bandwagons.

For example, there have been serious and well-founded doubts aired about carbon-offsetting programs. Big business the world over has been eager to use such initiatives as handy corporate fig leaves, but these schemes are as yet largely unproven in efficacy, and Chilean wineries should be cautious about relying on this as a major point of difference.

Rather, there should be a profound revision of all stages of the wine-production process in Chile—from vineyard to point of sale—to maximize socially and environmentally responsible practices. This means achieving organic certification, implementing worker schemes, recycling, reducing packaging, and using renewable energy sources, among other measures.

In tandem with this, the new Vinos de Chile body needs to shout Chile's green credentials from the rooftops. ProChile needs to bin its uninspiring logo of "Chile: All Ways Surprising" in favor of a more naturally themed strapline ("Chile: The Natural Choice"?), which will benefit not only the country's wine but also the salmon, vegetable, fruit, and tourism industries. Serious money needs to be spent.

Chile wants an image. It wants to be premium. In the green issue it has the perfect opportunity to build a meaningful campaign and sell itself to the world. The time is ripe. If it does not seize this particular bull by the horns now, it risks losing a golden opportunity.

Vintage Report

Advance report on the latest harvest
2008

Early indications for 2008 point to another "game of two halves" vintage in Chile, though of a different kind to 2007. Where 2007 was divided in terms of timings—whites came in early, reds late—2008 looks like being the opposite (whites late, reds early), with a geographical split between the later-picked coastal areas and the early-picked warm interior regions. This could mean concentrated, expressive whites and coastal reds but warmer, perhaps simpler reds from the classic areas. Overall, the season got off to a very late start—budbreak was up to a month behind normal in some areas—due to the coldest winter in over half a century and a cool spring. Very dry conditions then persisted during the season, bringing average yields down by 10–20 percent. Whites were harvested up to two to three weeks late in coastal areas. But things then heated up in March, and by early April producers in Colchagua and Maipo were expecting harvest times to be either earlier or on a par with the 2007 vintage. The hot weather will, however, mean that sound vineyard management will be critical to deal with potential sunburn and berry dehydration.

Updates on the previous five vintages
2007

Vintage rating: *Red: 98, White: 94*

Winemakers are raving about 2007: "a perfect vintage," "outstanding," "the vintage of the decade." As ever, a bit of perspective is called for. Climatically, the 2007 vintage was a game of two halves: the first hot and wet, the second cool and dry. Thus, while Sauvignon Blanc was brought in up to two weeks early, some later black varieties were harvested two or even three weeks later than normal, with better-than-average natural acidity, color, and fresh fruit, plus low alcohols. Volumes were down by 15–30 percent over 2006. The upshot is that this vintage looks to be outstanding for mid-range reds and upward, as well as top whites.

2006

Vintage rating: *Red: 91, White: 92*

Cold, dry, and long was the summary of the 2006 vintage, with some of the best quality produced in aromatic whites, while reds generally show a fresh style. It was a moderately challenging year for growers, who had to be patient and judge their harvest times well to achieve quality. Overall crop size was about 10–15 percent up on 2005. The reds are not predicted to have quite the density and power of the 2005 vintage due to larger berry sizes this year, but in general quality seems good.

2005

Vintage rating: *Red: 96, White: 93*

Chile's most hyped vintages in recent times have been the odd years: 1999, 2001, 2003. While 2005 is no exception to this rule, it is different from its predecessors in character—this was not simply a hot, dry year but a long, moderate season that led to a late harvest and wines showing notable freshness, complexity, and natural balance. Reds fared best and are considered to offer good to outstanding quality; whites are good to very good.

2004

Vintage rating: *Red: 89, White: 86*

An uneven vintage that gave good, if variable, results. A hot summer and rainy fall meant that this was something of a pressurized harvest in which good vineyard management was crucial. Alcohol levels tend to be quite high, and while the wines generally show good concentration and often notably ripe character, this has resulted in some imbalance, especially in whites from coastal appellations such as Casablanca and San Antonio. One to drink sooner rather than later.

2003

Vintage rating: *Red: 93, White: 92*

Generally a very successful vintage, with concentrated, ripe reds and characterful whites. This was a warm year with a dry, long fall, and the wines tend to reflect this in their maturity and intensity. A classic warm Chilean vintage that gave consistent quality and good to excellent wines across the board.

GREATEST WINE PRODUCERS

1. Concha y Toro
2. Cono Sur
3. Montes
4. Almaviva
5. Emiliana Orgánico
6. De Martino
7. Errázuriz
8. Miguel Torres
9. Valdivieso
10. Neyen

FASTEST-IMPROVING PRODUCERS

1. Tabalí
2. La Reserva de Caliboro
3. Gillmore
4. Veramonte
5. Falernia
6. Córpora
7. Viña Casablanca
8. Carmen
9. Morandé
10. Botalcura

NEW UP-AND-COMING PRODUCERS

1. Loma Larga
2. Ventolera
3. Quintay
4. Kingston
5. O Fournier Chile
6. Intriga
7. Los Maquis
8. Amaral
9. Polkura
10. Viña Santa Cruz

BEST-VALUE PRODUCERS

1. Concha y Toro
2. Cono Sur
3. Viña Leyda
4. Emiliana Orgánico
5. GEO
6. Viñedos Emiliana
7. Tabalí
8. Casas del Bosque
9. Valdivieso
10. Ventisquero

GREATEST-QUALITY WINES

1. **20 Barrels Chardonnay 2006** Cono Sur, Casablanca (CLP 13,000)
2. **Syrah BK-BL 2005** Loma Larga, Casablanca (CLP 16,800)
3. **EQ Syrah 2005** Matetic, San Antonio (CLP 22,000)
4. **20 Barrels Sauvignon Blanc 2007** Cono Sur, Casablanca (CLP 13,000)
5. **Antiyal 2003** Antiyal, Maipo (CLP 33,000)
6. **SoldeSol Chardonnay 2003** Aquitania, Malleco (CLP 17,000)
7. **Neyen 2004** Neyen, Colchagua (CLP 39,000)
8. **Erasmo 2003** La Reserva de Caliboro, Maule (CLP 15,000)
9. **Single Vineyard Quebrada Seca Chardonnay 2006** De Martino, Limarí (CLP 9,900)
10. **Clos de Lolol 2003** Hacienda Araucano, Colchagua (CLP 8,500)

BEST BARGAINS

1. **Casillero del Diablo Shiraz 2006** Concha y Toro, Central Valley (CLP 3,500)
2. **Novas Chardonnay Marsanne Viognier 2006** Emiliana Orgánico, Casablanca (CLP 7,000)
3. **Shiraz Reserva 2005** Tabalí, Limarí (CLP 8,500)
4. **Garuma Sauvignon Blanc 2006** Viña Leyda, San Antonio (CLP 6,500)
5. **Falaris Hill Chardonnay 2006** Viña Leyda, San Antonio (CLP 8,000)
6. **Riesling Reserva 2007** Cono Sur, Bío Bío (CLP 5,000)
7. **Las Brisas Pinot Noir 2006** Viña Leyda, San Antonio (CLP 8,500)
8. **Sauvignon Blanc 2006** Quintay, Casablanca (CLP 6,000)
9. **Vendimia Tardía Riesling 2004** Miguel Torres, Curicó (CLP 8,500)
10. **Cuvée Carmenère 2005** Misiones de Rengo, Rapel (CLP 5,200)

MOST EXCITING OR UNUSUAL FINDS

1. **Lota 2004** Cousiño Macul, Maipo (CLP 60,000) *The new icon from a revamped Maipo stalwart is rounded, layered, and replete. Very classy, and great promise.*
2. **Ventolera Sauvignon Blanc 2006** Viña Litoral, San Antonio (CLP 8,000) *Scented, spicy, and food-friendly stuff from the new venture by Ignacio Recabarren in San Antonio.*
3. **Single Vineyard Carignan 2006** De Martino, Maule (CLP 9,900) *The terroir specialist Marcelo Retamal has hunted out some lovely rustic fruit with great earthy balance.*
4. **Nebbiolo 2005** Botalcura, Maule (CLP 25,000) *An extremely creditable (restrained and savory, red-fruited) effort from a difficult variety to grow well outside Piedmont.*
5. **Vertice Carmenère Syrah 2005** Ventisquero, Colchagua (CLP 19,000) *The team in Apalta has been doing excellent work getting to grips with the vines, and this rounded, spicy field blend shows why.*
6. **Hacedor de Mundos Cabernet Franc Reserva 2005** Gillmore, Maule (CLP 6,000) *Another crisp, balanced red from this dry-farming expert.*
7. **Maycas Chardonnay Reserva Especial 2006** Concha y Toro, Limarí (CLP 9,900) *In coastal Limarí, Chilean Chardonnay has found a home, as this nervy, intense version demonstrates.*
8. **Caballo Loco No 2 NV** Valdivieso, Central Valley (CLP 50,000) *Proving that Chilean icons can age. Based on the 1995 vintage, this is a claret-style red with tons of earthy dried fruit and juicy appeal.*
9. **Ocio Pinot Noir 2005** Cono Sur, Casablanca (CLP 35,000) *The standard of this top-rate Chilean Pinot keeps getting better by the vintage. This latest release manages to marry intense Pinot character with great elegance.*
10. **Pangea Syrah 2005** Ventisquero, Colchagua (CLP 29,000) *A step up from the excellent 2004 because of its increasingly elegant density.*

Argentina

Tim Atkin MW

The sound of American accents in the hotels of Mendoza, Neuquen, and San Juan has become commonplace over the past few years.

TIM ATKIN MW

Argentina's US success has attracted the country's top wine importers (if not necessarily its journalists, most of whom prefer to pontificate from afar) in increasing numbers.

In the past year, they have been joined by executives from some of Australia's largest wineries, attracted to Argentina by cheap land and labor, old vines, sizable quantities of bulk wine, and (the clincher) inexpensive and plentiful irrigation. If drought is a major headache Down Under, the proximity of the Andes means water will never run short in Argentina. That's why several major companies are said to be considering Argentina as a source for their bag-in-box and entry-level wines. These will be labeled clearly and should boost the standing of Argentina as a world player over the next 12 months.

The diversity of Argentina's vineyards—there are substantial plantings of 18 major grape varieties, including Malbec, Cabernet Sauvignon, Merlot, Syrah, Tempranillo, Chardonnay, Sauvignon Blanc, and Torrontés— is a major draw. Indeed, looking at the latest statistics from the Instituto Nacional de Vitivinicultura provides a snapshot of just how much Argentina has changed over the last 26 years.

TIM ATKIN MW is the wine correspondent of *The Observer* and wine editor at large of *OLN* and *Wine & Spirit*. He has won more than 20 awards for his wine writing, including five Glenfiddichs and four Lanson Wine Writer of the Year gongs. In 2007 he was named Communicator of the Year by the International Wine & Spirit Competition and Best Drink Writer in the Le Cordon Bleu World Food Media Awards. Tim first visited Argentina in 1994, since when he has returned to the country on nine occasions to taste its wines, dance the tango badly, and marvel at the thickness of its steaks. Tim judges wines all over the world and is co-chairman of the International Wine Challenge, the world's biggest blind-tasting competition.

There have been two major trends. The first is toward so-called high-quality varieties and away from basic Cereza and Criolla; the second is toward red wines. In 1990, only 36.2 percent of plantings were of premium varieties, compared with 61.1 percent today. The shift from "high-quality" white grapes to black has been even more dramatic. In 1990, whites made up 53.7 percent of the total, compared with only 29.6 percent in 2006. The biggest percentage increases (some of them from an admittedly small base) have all been for black grapes: Syrah (+1,704 percent), Tannat (+1,102 percent), Cabernet Sauvignon (+653 percent), and Cabernet Franc (+555 percent). The increase for Malbec has not been as marked, but that is partly because there was already a good deal of it planted in 1990. That said, Malbec is by far the most-planted high-quality variety in Argentina, with 24,379 ha under vine. Twenty-six years ago, Bonarda and Pedro Gimenez were both more important than the country's signature grape.

Way down south

Argentine wine producers are beginning to look beyond the traditional vineyard sources to develop new areas. Lawyer Fernando Muñoz de Toro is developing Pampas Estate, a 40-ha vineyard in Sierra de la Ventana, 350 miles (560 km) south of Buenos Aires, with the focus on dry-grown Pinot Gris and Sauvignon Blanc. The first releases will be the 2009s.

In the southern part of Patagonia, Cavas de Weinert has developed a 25-ha vineyard in the province of Chabut, close to El Bolsón. The winery, the most southerly in the Americas, is some 700 miles (1,120 km) south of Neuquen and Río Negro on the 42nd parallel. The first wines from Patagonian Wines will be released this year. There are five varieties on the farm: Merlot, Pinot Noir, Chardonnay, Riesling, and Gewurztraminer.

Grow your own

Fancy your own corner of viticultural Argentina? The Vines of Mendoza has created a Private Vineyard Estates project that gives investors the chance to invest in their own boutique wine production in Argentina. The American-Argentine company has bought 200 ha in the Uco Valley and has divided the land into plots of 1–4 ha. Yields are expected to be around 2,000 bottles per acre when the vines are in production. Prospective owners can be as hands on, or off, as they like, but advice is available from viticulturist Diego Reina and winemaker Santiago Achaval of Bodega Achaval Ferrer. They can then make the wine at the company's on-site winery or sell the grapes back to The Vines of Mendoza or any other *bodega*. Prices start at around US$200,000, with most of the interest so far coming from North America and Europe. See vinesofmendoza.com for further details.

Opinion:
Icon wines

"Is that one word or two?" runs the old joke about icon wines. Chile momentarily lost its way in the 1990s, producing a series of overpriced, overambitious wines that alienated critics and consumers alike before it came to the realization that you need to build a middle market before you can start charging $80 or more for a bottle of red. Even when the wines were good—and that wasn't always true by any means—too many of the icons looked like an expression of the owner's ego rather than a desire to make a genuinely world-class wine.

Is Argentina in the process of committing the same mistake at the start of the 21st century? As I traveled around Argentina recently, I lost count of the number of wineries that proudly presented me with a new icon wine. Even Trivento, best known for its value-for-money varietals, is about to release such a wine, called Eolo, made entirely from Malbec. The wine is pretty good, as it happens, but is it worth $100?

I suspect that several producers have looked at the success of wines such as Cobos, Achaval Ferrer's Altamira, Nicolas Catena Zapata, Val de Flores, and Noemía, all of which have track records stretching back over four or more vintages, and decided to copy their price tags without matching the quality of what's in the bottle. There's nothing wrong with producing high-end wines, but it shouldn't detract from what Argentina really needs to focus on: improving its mid-priced wines.

Grapevine

• **Spanish-owned** Bodegas O Fournier has developed a brand with Constellation, the world's largest wine producer, and Argentine producer Carlos Pulenta. The launch vintage of Diseño will be 2007, and will retail at around $11 in its American target market. The plan is to hit 5 million bottles within five years.

• **Familia Zuccardi** in Mendoza was awarded the international "innovative wine tourism experience" award in 2008 by the Great Wine Capitals of the World for its visitor center, vineyard and winery tours, art museum, and restaurant. See www.familiazuccardi.com and www.greatwinecapitals.com.

• **Is Bonarda,** one of Argentina's most-planted black varieties, with 17,200 ha under vine, the same grape that exists in Italy's Oltrepò Pavese and Colli Piacentini? According to a study carried out by Argentina's Universidad Nacional de Cuyo and the Trapiche winery, Argentine and Italian Bonarda are not related. The closest genetic match to the latter grape is the French variety Corbeau.

Time to talk about whites

As worldwide demand for Argentine Malbec continues to grow—underlined by the fact that the producers of Cahors have asked their South American counterparts to participate in events to promote the unique virtues of this high-quality variety—there is a danger that consumers will overlook one of the country's strongest viticultural suits—namely, its diversity. No country on earth can match Argentina's mix of French, Spanish, and Italian grapes.

Even people who are aware of this unique viticultural resource tend to regard Argentina as a red-wine-producing country. Very few of them realize that the best whites are a match for anything produced on the other side of the Andes. With the move to cooler, higher-altitude sites over the past decade, Argentina is in a position to make world-class Chardonnay and very good Sauvignon Blanc, as well as decent Viognier. The fact that Catena Zapata has released a 2005 Chardonnay (from Gualtallary in the Uco Valley) under its top Nicolas Catena Zapata label shows how far Chardonnay has come in Argentina.

Torrontés may not be a match for the finest Chardonnays, but there are signs that this adopted white variety is starting to emerge from the Argentine shadows. Previously regarded as a grapey, pleasant, but essentially one-dimensional grape, Torrontés is being taken much more seriously in its near-native land. Susana Balbo of Dominio del Plata thinks that the grape—or rather grapes, since there are three different types of Torrontés (Riojano, San Juanino, and Mendocino)—could become Argentina's "alternative flagship." Tasting a wine like the 2005 Felix Lavaque Torrontés Reserva, I am tempted to agree with her. This wine takes Torrontés to new levels of complexity. Let's hope it is an inspiration to other producers.

Grapevine

• **Humberto Canale in Patagonia** and Lagarde in Luján de Cuyo have made history by blending a wine from two demarcated regions and using their names on the label. The 2004 Dos Cielos is an equal blend of Merlot and Malbec and retails at AP 200.

• **Wines of Argentina's** new generic image will focus on the tango in its global campaigns. The decision to use the country's mournful dance routine to promote its wines was made as a result of a study by San Andres University in Buenos Aires, which discovered that tango, rather than football or gauchos, was what most consumers associated with Argentina.

• **Valle Perdido in Patagonia** has opened Argentina's first five-star wine resort and spa in Neuquen. Guests at the luxury 18-room hotel are surrounded by a working winery—laboratory, fermentation tanks, and all. Rooms start at US$200.

• **Bodega Catena Alta Malbec 2004** triumphed in the initial Malbec Made for Meat competition held in London in 2007. Catena also took second place with its 2004 Malbec. Third place went to the 2005 Doña Paula Malbec.

Vintage Report

Advance report on the latest harvest
2008

This will be remembered as a cold vintage marked by mixed weather patterns, including hailstorms, frost, strong winds, and unseasonable rains. Winter temperatures were some of the lowest on record, reaching 1.4°F (−17°C) in Patagonia, and spring was generally late across the country. By mid-February, some producers felt the vintage was heading for disaster, but it appears to have righted itself at the 11th hour, thanks to drier, sunnier conditions in late summer and fall. Quality is still likely to be mixed, however, depending on local conditions and the skill with which growers handled the adverse conditions earlier in the season. Looking on the bright side, the cooler day/night temperatures have produced red wines that are unusually deep in color, with thick skins, considerable polyphenolic concentration, and higher-than-normal levels of acidity. Overall crop levels are down by 20–35 percent, with most varieties affected, mainly because of spring frosts. Berry size and weight are both down. The higher levels of malic and tartaric acid have been beneficial for the crispness of the whites and the longevity of the reds.

Updates on the previous five vintages
2007

Vintage rating: *Red: 89, White: 88*

The overall growing season was characterized by warmer-than-usual daytime temperatures (3.2°F [1.8°C] above average) and colder nights (1.8°F [1°C] below average). Higher relative humidity helped prevent problems with sunburned bunches. On February 16, a particularly cold snap in Mendoza caused what Bodega Catena Zapata described as a "hormonal shock" in many vineyards, "significantly quickening the ripening process." As a result, picking was two to four weeks earlier than usual, depending on the region.

The vintage was marked by higher-than-average rainfall and a number of violent hailstorms. In San Rafael, 5,000 ha were hit by a storm at the end of January, while 3,000 ha in Mendoza lost between 50 and 100 percent of their grapes. Despite these challenges, quality levels were generally good to very good, if not as high as in 2006. As much as anything, this is a reflection of more modern viticultural practices. This was a winemakers' vintage.

2006

Vintage rating: *Red: 97, White: 92*

The 2006 vintage was one of the finest ever in Argentina, producing red wines with deep color, soft tannins, and intense flavors. The whites are also very good, especially from higher-altitude vineyards in areas such as the Uco Valley. In Mendoza, a cool, snowy winter was followed by warmer-than-average temperatures in spring and summer. Higher-than-normal levels of humidity meant that the vines did not suffer from heat stress. Pronounced diurnal temperature variation promoted slow grape maturation and well-balanced wines. In January, temperatures in Mendoza varied between 50°F and 90°F (10–32°C). On the minus side, Mendoza suffered from a large hailstorm on December 27, 2005, and a second, less damaging storm in March affected Medrano and the central-eastern region. Yields were up on 2005, with some wineries talking about an increase of 20 percent. Reacting to a potentially large crop, many leading producers used fruit thinning to reduce yields by as much as 50 percent.

2005

Vintage rating: *Red: 93, White: 90*

A cooler ripening season and a late harvest produced elegant, full-colored wines with intense fruit flavors and a slightly lower degree of alcohol than usual. January and February were cool. March was somewhat warmer, bringing on complete ripeness of the grapes, which were harvested in good condition and with no sign of dehydration. In San Juan, several producers rated 2005 as one of the best-ever vintages, with Syrah vines showing particularly well. The best Malbecs and Chardonnays are impressive in 2005, especially from high-altitude vineyards, where late fall was dry, sunny, yet comparatively cool.

2004

Vintage rating: *Red: 94, White: 92*

The winter of 2003 was particularly warm and dry and much affected by the Zonda, the warm wind from the mountains to the north, which causes humidity to drop dramatically. This led to irrigation starting earlier than usual, partly because of a lack of snow in the Andes. The summer was also hot and dry, with temperatures remaining high during the nights. Some rain fell at the end of January, leading to a rapid spurt in growth. In February, temperatures fell and there was a little more rain. The white wines are full of flavor, with crisp acidity, while the best reds are outstanding, with deep color, full tannins, and good aging potential, thanks to thicker skins and intense varietal character.

2003

Vintage rating: *Red: 95, White: 90*

The official word is that whites are "very good" and the reds "outstanding." Opinions are divided as to whether the wines are as good as those from the excellent 2002 vintage, but some vineyard managers think that 2003 outperformed 2002 in some vineyards. Cabernet Sauvignon was the star variety, though some of the high-altitude Malbecs are outstanding too.

GREATEST WINE PRODUCERS

1. Catena Zapata
2. Noemía
3. Pulenta Estate
4. Cheval des Andes
5. O Fournier
6. Norton
7. Val de Flores
8. Alta Vista
9. Fabre Montmayou
10. Achaval Ferrer

FASTEST-IMPROVING PRODUCERS

1. Chacra
2. Mendel
3. Humberto Canale
4. Valle Perdido
5. Tapiz
6. Trapiche
7. Finca Flichman
8. Familia Schroeder
9. Navarro Correas
10. Chakana

NEW UP-AND-COMING PRODUCERS

1. Belasco de Baquedano
2. Finca Decero
3. Carinae
4. Valle Perdido
5. Alma 4
6. Benvenuto de la Serna
7. RJ Viñedos (Pasión 4)
8. Melipal
9. Filus
10. Andeluna

BEST-VALUE PRODUCERS

1. Finca Flichman
2. Norton
3. Pascual Toso
4. Familia Zuccardi
5. Dominio del Plata
6. Callia
7. Argento Wine Company
8. Doña Paula
9. Trivento
10. Finca El Portillo

GREATEST-QUALITY WINES

1. **Malbec 2006**
   Noemía, Río Negro (AP 360)
2. **Malbec Argentino 2004**
   Catena Zapata, Mendoza (AP 240)
3. **Altamira 2005**
   Achaval Ferrer, Uco Valley (AP 330)
4. **Cheval des Andes 2004**
   Mendoza (AP 300)
5. **Alto 2005**
   Alta Vista, Mendoza (AP 210)
6. **Gernot Langes 2003**
   Norton, Mendoza (AP 330)
7. **Gran Corte 2005**
   Pulenta Estate, Mendoza (AP 105)
8. **Malbec 2005**
   Val de Flores, Uco Valley (AP 150)
9. **Malbec Viña Francisco Olivé 2005** Trapiche, Mendoza (AP 120)
10. **Alfa Crux Malbec 2005**
    O Fournier, Uco Valley (AP 120)

BEST BARGAINS

1. **Gestos Malbec 2007**
Finca Flichman, Mendoza (AP 36)
2. **Pinot Noir 2007**
Valle Perdido, Río Negro (AP 35)
3. **Malbec 2007** Finca El Portillo,
Uco Valley (AP 18)
4. **Malbec 2007**
Otra Vida, Mendoza (AP 15)
5. **Verdelho 2007** Don Cristóbal
1492, Luján de Cuyo (AP 18)
6. **Crios Torrontés 2007**
Susana Balbo, Salta (AP 30)
7. **Cabernet Sauvignon 2006**
Pascual Toso, Maipú (AP 30)
8. **Pasión 4 Bonarda 2006** RJ
Viñedos, San Rafael (AP 30)
9. **Privada 2005**
Norton, Mendoza (AP 60)
10. **Paisaje de Tupungato 2005**
Finca Flichman, Uco Valley (AP 60)

MOST EXCITING OR UNUSUAL FINDS

1. **Treinta y Dos Pinot Noir 2006**
Chacra, Río Negro (AP 360)
Easily the best (as well as the most expensive) Pinot Noir in South America, this classy, perfumed, tightly wound red wouldn't look out of place in Gevrey-Chambertin.
2. **Gran Cabernet Franc 2005**
Pulenta Estate, Agrelo (AP 105)
This could well be the most exciting red yet from this high-quality Mendoza operation. In a country where Cabernet Franc is rare, this silky first release is a standout.
3. **Malbec 2006** Mendel, Luján de Cuyo (AP 75) *By far the most impressive of the three releases to date from Roberto de la Mota's post-Terrazas project. Old-vine concentration and fine tannins are the hallmarks here.*
4. **Pinot Noir 2007** Canale Estate, Río Negro (AP 40) *The influence of consultants Susana Balbo and Pedro Marchevsky has been immediate on this Río Negro operation. A juicy, brilliant-value Pinot.*
5. **Malbec Remolinos Vineyard 2006** Finca Decero, Agrelo (AP 40) *After only three vintages, this Swiss-owned winery is producing a deeply colored, finely crafted Malbec that is better than a lot of wines at twice the price.*
6. **Torrontés Reserva 2005** Quara Lavaque, Salta (AP 60) *Torrontés rarely achieves real complexity (unless it's a late-harvest style), but this dry, partially barrel-fermented style from Salta is a revelation.*
7. **Urban Uco Tempranillo 2005** O Fournier, Uco Valley (AP 36) *Produced by the Spanish-owned O Fournier group, this well-priced, lightly oaked, raspberryish Tempranillo is sourced from 40-year-old vines in El Cepillo.*
8. **Innovación Touriga Nacional 2006** Familia Zuccardi, Maipú (AP 36) *One of a host of unusual varieties under examination at José Zuccardi's model winery, this is a soft, plummy, aromatic take on Portugal's best black grape.*
9. **Shiraz Viognier 2006** Doña Paula, Luján de Cuyo/ Tupungato (AP 66) *Not the only example of this Côte Rôtie–style blend in Argentina, but easily the best. This apricot and blackberry-like red benefits from co-fermentation with 3 percent Viognier.*
10. **Alma 4 Brut NV** Familia Zuccardi, Mendoza (Argentina, AP 70) *Sebastián Zuccardi has brought a much-needed youthful edge to the Argentine sparkling-wine scene, with varieties such as Bonarda. Frothy and fun.*

Australia

Huon Hooke

Carbon footprints have become a major concern of winemakers and grape growers, joining environmental initiatives as chief concerns of wine producers.

HUON HOOKE

Sniffing a marketing opportunity (or a negative image if they're not seen to be taking any action), wineries are busily getting their backyards in order and letting the world know what they are doing. British supermarkets are a major stimulus—with so much wine in the world, environmental issues have joined a long list of things that retailers must be able to check off in order to even consider letting the sales rep through the door.

Elgo Estate, in the Strathbogie Ranges of northeastern Victoria, is more serious than most. Its slogan is "Wines that don't cost the Earth." It has a 150-kW wind turbine that powers the winery and feeds excess electricity into the domestic power grid, enabling Elgo to boast that it is better than carbon-neutral—it's carbon-negative. It claims that this is an Australian and possibly a world first. The owners, the Taresch family, say the turbine's positioning, on a very windy hill, is crucial.

HUON HOOKE was coauthor of *The Penguin Good Australian Wine Guide*, the country's most respected buyer's guide, for 15 years, until 2007. He is a wine-marketing and production graduate of Roseworthy Agricultural College and has been a weekly columnist for the John Fairfax Group of newspapers since 1983. Huon writes columns in the Good Living section of the *Sydney Morning Herald* and the *Good Weekend* magazine of the *Herald* and Melbourne's *The Age*. He is also contributing editor of Australian *Gourmet Traveller Wine* magazine and writes for various other publications, such as *Decanter* and *The World of Fine Wine*. He has been judging in wine competitions since 1987 and judges eight to 10 shows a year in Australia and abroad. Huon has judged in New Zealand, South Africa, Chile, Belgium, Slovenia, Canada, the US, the UK, and Japan. He currently chairs several Australian competitions and is a senior judge at Adelaide and Sydney.

Grant Taresch says the turbine will save more than 400 tons of greenhouse gases annually, which offsets the emissions of 80 cars on the road and is the equivalent of planting 120 ha of trees. While the average household adds about 12 tons of carbon dioxide to the atmosphere every year, Elgo saves around 1 ton a day by producing enough energy not only to meet its own needs, but to feed enough power into the grid to run an additional 34 households a year. Elgo's other initiatives are grape-skin composting, "state-of-the-art" water management, using sheep to eat vineyard weeds, planting thousands of trees, and its own wildlife sanctuary.

Cullen, of Margaret River, was the first Australian winery to become carbon-neutral, in late 2006, with a tree-planting program to offset its carbon emissions. Others quickly followed.

The Winemakers' Federation of Australia has released what it claims is the world's first Carbon Footprint Calculation Tool. It can be downloaded from the WFA website (www.wfa.org.au) and can be used by anyone anywhere in the world.

Famine follows feast

If scarcity makes wine more desirable, Aussie wine should be in big demand. Following several years of oversupply, the short 2007 harvest turned a glut into a shortage. Drought, frost, bushfires, and savage cuts to irrigation water turned around the accumulated surplus in far less time than anyone imagined possible. Now Australia is facing another shortage from the 2008 harvest, which is estimated to be similar to 2007—that is, 29 percent down on what might be considered a normal year. Prices have inevitably risen as a result, and the cheap unlabeled bottles known as "cleanskins" are scarce. The Murray Valley (Riverland) has suffered most, with zero irrigation-water allocations for the 2007/08 summer, with the result that vines and fruit trees have simply died. The Riverina has fared better, while most wine-growing regions have had good rains during the season. At the other extreme, the Hunter Valley has had an unusually wet summer, with the worst bunch rot and other wet-harvest problems for many years.

Anti-Gunns movement

Tasmania's winemakers are up in arms over a proposal by the island's bad-guy timber and forestry company, Gunns Limited, to build a pulp mill on the Tamar River near several vineyards. Arguments are raging over pollutant levels expected in the water and sulfides in the air. Gunns, already unpopular because of its logging activities in a state with a great wealth of old-growth forests, is also a major player in Tasmania's wine industry. It owns Tamar Ridge and Rosevears Estate wineries and the brands Devil's Corner and Coombend, employs world-renowned viticulturist Richard Smart, and has planted vast new vineyards. A silent boycott has been imposed by some of the nation's top restaurants and bottle shops.

Biodynamics lowers alcohol

High alcohol levels of 15 and 16 percent in some Aussie reds are giving the wine industry a headache, but biodynamic viticulture may provide an answer. Vanya Cullen of the icon Margaret River winery Cullen says that one of the many benefits she's observed since converting her vineyards to biodynamics is that black grapes achieve phenolic ripeness earlier—that is, at lower sugar levels, which means less alcohol in the fermented wine. "Our Cabernet Sauvignon was never tannin-ripe before 13 degrees *Baumé*," she says. "Now the tannins are ripe at 11.5, which hopefully may mean that we have lower-alcohol wines with better balance. We have found the best balance—in terms of tannin, extract, and flavor— is around 13 percent alcohol." Ms Cullen is a strong advocate of biodynamics and has plenty to say, but the thrust of her findings is that both soils and vines are healthier, and wine pH is lower. "It is really just about having a good drink in a way that is good for the earth and ourselves," she says. "I believe these practices will keep the vineyard producing quality fruit for longer than any other method."

Grapevine

• **The number of wineries** continues to grow—by 6.9 percent in 2006/07—despite tough times in the wine business, according to the industry's bible, *The Australian and New Zealand Wine Industry Directory*. It shows that the number of Australian wine producers increased by 138, from 2,008 to 2,146. The directory was celebrating its 25th year; it began in 1983, when just 344 producers were listed. The state-by-state breakdown is: Victoria, 628 producers (up 7.7 percent); South Australia, 563 (up 12.2 percent); New South Wales and Australian Capital Territory, 432 (up 0.9 percent); Western Australia, 332 (up 6.4 percent); Queensland, 109 (up 3.8 percent); Tasmania, 81 (up 5.2 percent); and Northern Territory, 1 (no change).

Opinion:
Yalumba sets the standard

Yalumba has taken two bold stands on wine labeling in the past year, setting a standard of honesty in labeling where the wine laws are silent. The first is to do with claims of "old vines"; the second relates to the use of the word "reserve." Both have been abused, and neither is subject to any labeling law. Yalumba owner Robert Hill Smith and winemaking director Brian Walsh have drawn up charters for both, listing the standards they will adhere to. As part of the changes, Yalumba has renamed its 2-liter bag-in-box previously called Reserve Selection. Read more at www.yalumba.com.au ("Wine Information"). Other producers should bite the bullet and follow suit.

Clarify Riesling labeling

Bone-dry Riesling has become the Australian standard over the past 25 years—a situation that's been encouraged by the wine-show system, which is intolerant of medium-sweet Rieslings. In the past few years, several producers have begun trying their hand at a medium-sweet style akin to German Kabinett. In Tasmania, where natural acid is high and the style works well, Wellington and Frogmore Creek both label their medium-sweet Rieslings FGR, for Forty Grams Residual (or Effing Good Riesling, according to some!). This could catch on. We need a simple way to signal a sweeter style to the consumer. Bellarmine has a "Dry Riesling," while its wine labeled just "Riesling" is semisweet. Mr. Riggs has a dry "Watervale Riesling" and a sweeter style labeled "VOR-GS Riesling," whatever that means! Neither is satisfactory. The consumer must be quite mystified.

Pinot prejudice

Australian Pinot Noir has come of age in the 2005 and 2006 vintages, when regions such as Tasmania, Mornington Peninsula, Yarra Valley, Macedon Ranges, and Geelong have turned in a welter of superb wines. But Australian Pinot still suffers from the dismissive "Australia is too hot to produce great Pinot" attitude around the globe. The world is agog at Central Otago but ignores southern Australia. It's as though it cannot be imagined that Australia can produce great Shiraz, Semillon, Muscat, Riesling… and Pinot Noir. I have three words for you: taste the wines!

Rip-off magnums

Why are some magnums so much more than twice the price of two 75-cl bottles? It smells like a rip-off. Even if you accept that it costs more to purchase, fill, package, and handle oversize bottles when most wineries are set up for regular sizes, it doesn't adequately explain some prices. Penfolds Grange magnums have always sold at auction for a ridiculous premium, and you could argue that Penfolds encourages this by restricting supply. But the secondary market is one thing; first-release prices are another. A Sydney retailer charged 3.4 times the single-bottle price for 2005 Giaconda Shiraz: A$275 (single bottle: A$80). The 2006 Pinot Noir was almost as inflated at A$250 (A$77.50). If demand is what inflates prices, why don't they just bottle more magnums?

Grapevine

• **Pinot Gris/Grigio** is the next Sauvignon Blanc, by all indications. Australian plantings of Pinot Gris/ Grigio vines rose by 91 percent in 2006/07, according to *The Australian and New Zealand Wine Industry Directory*. Curiously, this growth excludes Western Australia, which hasn't a single PG on the market, to my knowledge. Planting has been slow in WA due to quarantine restrictions.

• **Australia continues to export strongly,** despite reduced returns caused by a strengthening Aussie dollar. Australia hit two new records in August 2007—for both value (A$3 billion) and volume (800 million liters). The milestones followed good growth in the year to July, of 10 percent in volume and 8 percent in value. The fact that high-quality bottled red wine was selling especially strongly was heartening news to the industry. Its volume rose by 30 million liters, and the average value rose by 10 percent.

• **A bottle** of Moss Wood Cabernet Sauvignon 1973 has set a new record for an Australian wine younger than 1970 at auction: A$1,726. It was the first release from Moss Wood, of Margaret River, now one of Australia's icon wineries. Collectors now treat rare old wine much as they do old coins or stamps: the first Penfolds Grange—1951— which is by all reports well past its use-by date, recently hit an auction peak of A$10,584.

• **In the wine world,** there's always an anniversary being celebrated somewhere. In 2008, Hunter Valley veterans Tyrrell's celebrated 150 years with, among other things, a reunion of all the winemakers who have worked there since the family began employing outsiders in the 1970s. And in Coonawarra, the Redman family celebrated 100 years since its first winemaking member, Bill Redman, bought land after coming to Coonawarra to work for pioneer John Riddoch.

Vintage Report

Advance report on the latest harvest

2008

Another hot, early vintage in many parts of Australia, with South Australia experiencing a 16-day heat wave in the heart of vintage, when temperatures stayed around 100°F (high 30s to 40°C) and night temperatures remained high, leading to some overripeness and desiccation. Southern Victoria and Tasmania have had a much better vintage—early but not excessively hot. Yields are up, following last year's paltry offering decimated by drought and frosts. Western Australia also had a hot summer. The exception was New South Wales: the Hunter Valley and Mudgee have had the worst vintage in living memory, with persistent rain following a cool summer; some whites will be good but it was a shocker for reds. Orange, Canberra, and Hilltops had an excellent harvest: summer also cool, but drier. The Australian Wine & Brandy Corporation's mid-harvest report predicted a harvest of 1.55–1.65 million tons. This is an increase on the pre-harvest estimate of 1.22 million and is on track to continue the restoration of the supply/demand balance that began with the very short 2007 harvest. It's still below the long-term average but an improvement on the frost-, drought-, and bushfire-affected 2007 vintage, which was 1.397 million tons.

Updates on the previous five vintages

2007

Vintage rating: *Red: 88, White: 87*

This was a less-than-average season for most Australian *vignerons*; while plenty of good wine was made, no region enjoyed a better-than-average harvest. Widespread drought, crippling frosts, and bushfires with their attendant smoke-taint problems all added up to overall yields slashed by 29 percent—the lowest for seven years. While catastrophic for many small growers, causing a cash-flow crisis, it helped bring the oversupply into balance. The vintage was so early—a month in places—that winemakers had an Easter vacation for the first time ever.

Quality is very variable: some hotter regions such as Riverland and Barossa Valley found the season too hot and dry, with reds being tough and tannic without much fruit, while cooler regions such as Tasmania and southern Victoria have some good to very good wine, but little of it.

Mornington Peninsula, Hunter Valley, and Margaret River look to have had the most successful vintages. White wines across the entire continent are forward, and while they offer attractive drinking while young, few will age very well, even in Tasmania. As usual in hotter years, reds are likely to be better, but no one is talking up their quality.

2006

Vintage rating: *Red: 93, White: 91*

The great paradox in this wide, brown land in 2006 was that in Western Australia it was one of the latest harvests on record, and in the eastern states one of the earliest. In the east, the hurried ripening was brought on by drought conditions and hotter summer-to-fall temperatures—generally good for red wines but not great for whites. In the west, the cool, overcast conditions delayed harvest, so that reds are very iffy but whites can be superb (some say the best ever in Margaret River). Most of the top wineries made some 2006 red but in much-reduced quantities.

One exception to the eastern states' white-wine rule was Clare and Eden Valley Rieslings, which are very good, although unlikely to live as long as the stellar 2005s and 2002s. Southern Victorian Pinot Noirs are superb. In most of Victoria, New South Wales, and South Australia, the 2005/06 season was the fourth successive season of drought, although the large size of the crop belied this fact. On average, a very good to excellent season.

2005

Vintage rating: *Red: 95, White: 96*

This is an excellent vintage—the best since 2002 and possibly 1998. It gave benchmark wines of all the classics: Rieslings in the Clare and Eden valleys, Semillons in the Hunter Valley, Shiraz in the Barossa, Cabernet in Coonawarra, and Pinot Noir in Tasmania and the Yarra Valley. The whites are tops, although the reds can also be exceptional, especially in South Australia, Victoria, New South Wales, and Tasmania. Western Australia is the only glitch: mid-vintage rain upset the pattern, and winemakers are less enthusiastic than elsewhere.

Production equaled the 2004 record, although high yields in the high-quality regions were not a problem as in 2004. Plentiful winter and spring rains in most parts of the country, except inland New South Wales, gave a vigorous start to the growing season, necessitating a lot of work in the vineyards. The summer was cooler than normal in most regions, giving the hot regions superior quality, while cooler regions had a long fall that—Western Australia aside—permitted the grapes to reach full ripeness.

2004

Vintage rating: *Red: 93, White: 86*

Initial expectations for the 2004 reds have been upgraded as the wines appear on the market, revealing 2004 as a very good red year, especially in South Australia. Early hopes were modest because of higher-than-normal yields, thanks to the best winter rains for years, which laid the foundations for high crops. Original estimates for a massive crop were trimmed after a combination of severe mid-February heat, especially in South Australia, and crop thinning, but it was still a record harvest. Picking was stop–start, due to alternating periods of heat and cool.

Southern Victoria had high yields and avoided temperature extremes. Yarra Valley quality is good, despite a wet end to the vintage: whites are very good, but lower yields would have made it a top red year, too. Coonawarra had big yields, and while quality is mostly good, overcropped vineyards struggled to ripen. Clare had a good vintage despite suffering in the February heat, and the Rieslings are good, if forward. McLaren Vale and the Barossa made excellent Shiraz, and the Adelaide Hills had a decent vintage overall. The Hunter made very good Semillon and Chardonnay, but reds are light.

2003

Vintage rating: *Red: 87, White: 83*

As assessments of the 2004s rose with more wines on the market, the 2003s continue to slip. Many of the reds already appear to be drying out, with unbalanced tannins and fading fruit. Universally, 2003 was a year of reduced yields caused by drought, with small bunches of small berries. Rain close to harvest resulted in berry split, further cutting yields in several regions, stretching from Tasmania to central Victoria to McLaren Vale, and smoke taint from January bushfires in northeast Victoria added insult to injury.

Some noted "big red" regions such as Heathcote, Barossa, and McLaren Vale struggled to attain flavor ripeness despite very high alcohols, because a hot summer abruptly turned into a cool late summer and fall. There are some reds with unripe tannins. The best wines are the Shirazes, with patches of excitement created by Eden Valley Riesling and the occasional Coonawarra Cabernet. Southern Victoria had quite a good vintage. Late rain spoiled the Tasmanian vintage and, to a lesser degree, the Great Southern in Western Australia; Margaret River was only middling.

GREATEST WINE PRODUCERS

The brands that qualify the umbrella company for inclusion are listed after the regions.

1. Giaconda (Beechworth)
2. Cullen (Margaret River)
3. Henschke (Eden Valley)
4. De Bortoli (Yarra Valley)
5. Balnaves (Coonawarra)
6. Kooyong (Mornington Peninsula)
7. Moss Wood (Margaret River)
8. Cape Mentelle (Margaret River)
9. Foster's (national) Penfolds, Seppelt, Wynns, Coldstream Hills, Devil's Lair
10. Hardys (national) Hardys, Houghton, Brookland Valley, Bay of Fires, Yarra Burn

FASTEST-IMPROVING PRODUCERS

1. Mountadam (Eden Valley)
2. Clairault (Margaret River)
3. Bannockburn (Geelong)
4. Wynns (Coonawarra)
5. De Iuliis (Hunter Valley)
6. Audrey Wilkinson (Hunter Valley)
7. Woodlands (Margaret River)
8. Capel Vale (Western Australia)
9. Coriole (McLaren Vale)
10. Fermoy Estate (Margaret River)

NEW UP-AND-COMING PRODUCERS

1. Collector (Canberra)
2. William Downie (Yarra Valley)
3. Luke Lambert (Yarra Valley)
4. Maverick (Barossa/Eden valleys)
5. Tar & Roses (Heathcote)
6. Punch (Yarra Valley)
7. Mandala (Yarra Valley)
8. Lethbridge (Geelong)
9. Home Hill (Tasmania)
10. Josef Chromy (Tasmania)

BEST-VALUE PRODUCERS

The brands that qualify the umbrella company for inclusion are listed after the regions.

1. De Bortoli (Riverina and Victoria) Windy Peak, Deen De Bortoli, Gulf Station, Sacred Hill
2. Westend (Riverina) Richland, Three Bridges
3. Trentham Estate (Murray Valley)
4. Hardys (national) Stepping Stone, Oomoo, Leasingham, Banrock Station
5. Foster's (national) Seppelt, Leo Buring, Saltram, Pepperjack, Wynns, Annie's Lane, Wolf Blass
6. Orlando Wyndham (national) Jacob's Creek, Jacob's Creek Reserve, Richmond Grove, Wyndham Estate
7. Peter Lehmann (Barossa Valley)
8. McWilliam's (national) Hanwood, Lillydale, Brand's, Barwang, Mount Pleasant
9. Yalumba (Barossa Valley) Y series, Barossa range, Pewsey Vale
10. Angove's (Riverland)

GREATEST-QUALITY WINES

1. **Block 42 Special Bin Cabernet Sauvignon 2004** Penfolds, Barossa Valley (A$450)
2. **Sangreal Pinot Noir 2005** By Farr, Geelong (A$60)
3. **Langi Shiraz 2004** Mount Langi Ghiran, Grampians (A$55)
4. **Yakka Shiraz 2006** Longview, Adelaide Hills (A$33)
5. **Steingarten Riesling 2005** Jacob's Creek, Eden Valley (A$32)
6. **Chardonnay 2006** Cape Mentelle, Margaret River (A$42)
7. **Susanne Semillon 2005** Drayton's, Hunter Valley (A$35)
8. **Braemore Vineyard Semillon 2007** Thomas, Hunter Valley (A$25)

⑨ **Sauvignon Blanc 2006**
Gembrook Hill, Yarra Valley (A$30)

⑩ **Arras Chardonnay Pinot Noir Brut 2002** Hardys, Tasmania (A$55)

BEST BARGAINS

① **Montage Chardonnay Semillon 2006** De Bortoli, Riverina (A$9)

② **Y Series Riesling 2007** Yalumba, South Australia (A$12)

③ **Reserve Shiraz 2006** Lindemans, Padthaway (A$14)

④ **Nine Vines Grenache Shiraz Rosé 2007** Angove's, Riverland (A$15)

⑤ **Red Dot Shiraz Viognier 2006** Penny's Hill, McLaren Vale (A$15)

⑥ **Watervale Riesling 2007** Jim Barry, Clare Valley (A$15)

⑦ **Verse One Shiraz 2006** Brookland Valley, Margaret River (A$16)

⑧ **Barossa Shiraz Viognier 2005** Yalumba, Barossa Valley (A$18)

⑨ **Clarry's Grenache Shiraz 2006** Kalleske, Barossa Valley (A$19)

⑩ **Pinot Noir Chardonnay Pinot Meunier Brut NV** Brown Brothers, King Valley (A$20)

MOST EXCITING OR UNUSUAL FINDS

① **Biodynamic Vineyard Semillon 2007** Krinklewood, Hunter Valley (A$20) *With just 10.2 percent alcohol, this is a traditional Hunter Semillon of great freshness with vibrant, high-intensity, tangy, citrus/ herby fruit. It should age superbly.*

② **Auslese Riesling 2007** Bellarmine, Pemberton (A$15) *At just 7.5 percent alcohol with lively acidity and understated sweetness, this is the kind of Mosel-inspired sweet wine very few in Australia can produce. Disarmingly fragrant, racy, and refined, it's an exciting wine that would encourage cellaring.*

③ **Fiano 2007** Coriole, McLaren Vale (A$25) *Coriole, Australia's first Sangiovese producer, continues to pioneer Italian grapes. This is a beautifully turned-out dry white smelling of fresh pear, apple, and a hint of passion fruit. The palate is soft, seamless, refined, and delicate—and beautifully flavored.*

Grapevine

• **Screwcaps** are now by far the preferred closure for Australian wine, and they are increasing their dominance for all wines except sparkling. In recent tastings, from a sample of about 600 wines, I found 81 percent screwcapped, 14 percent cork sealed, and 4.3 percent Diam sealed. The Diam "technical cork" enjoys a small but significant popularity among many leading boutique wineries in Victoria, such as Castagna, Bindi, Kooyong, Port Phillip Estate, Sergio Carlei, YarraLoch, Merricks Creek, Heathcote Estate, Yabby Lake, Prancing Horse, and Cobaw Ridge. And Domaine Chandon recently began using Diam for its sparkling wines.

④ Schomberger 2006 Barringwood Park, Tasmania ($A23) *This is a fragrant semisweet white from a left-field grape that could have a future in Tasmania. The combination of intense fruit, lively acidity, and liberal sweetness gives a jazzy mouthfeel. It's an arresting apéritif style, with appealing spicy passion fruit and tropical and black-currant aromas.*

⑤ Prestige Pinot Noir Chardonnay Brut 1995 Stefano Lubiana, Tasmania ($A138) *Aussie bubbly that can age for more than 12 years (over 10 on the lees, the label promises) and still be taut, delicate, and fresh is an exciting find indeed. High acid obviously helped. Undoubtedly dry and frisky, but layered with creamy/buttery, nutty, bready, and citrus flavors.*

⑥ Meslier Brut Royale NV Irvine, Eden Valley & Adelaide Hills ($A20) *Meslier is one of the grapes that fell out of favor in Champagne, but Jim Irvine has made it a specialty. It's more than novelty value: young, fruit-driven, and rather simple, for sure, but also distinctive and interesting. The floral, bath-bead, almost Muscat aromas are very different, and while somewhat short, it boasts a lot of fruit and charm.*

⑦ John Riddoch Cabernet Sauvignon 2005 Wynns, Coonawarra (A$77) *Definitive Coonawarra Cabernet, this is supremely elegant, with pinpoint ripeness (no hint of green or overripe characters); nor does it show overt oak, alcohol, or added tannin. All class.*

⑧ Nebbiolo 2006 Tar & Roses, Heathcote (A$45) *Tar & Roses signals the rebirth of ex-Mitchelton winemaker Don Lewis and his fascination with Italian and Spanish grapes. Floral, rose-petal, and earthy aromas carry a minty, aniseed high note, while ample but fluffy tannins flood the palate. Tight-packed; good with food.*

⑨ Durif 2006 The Bruiser, Rutherglen (A$20) *Durif (Petite Sirah) is a long-time resident of Rutherglen, as is winemaker Roland Kaval. This is not only a massive mouthful of sumptuous, fruit-sweet red wine, it's also great value. Blackstrap licorice, melted chocolate, liqueur cherry… Yum!*

⑩ 3 Amigos Shiraz Grenache Mataro 2005 McHenry Hohnen, Margaret River (A$27) *An unusual blend for this region, but 2005 was a hot, ripe year there. Beguiling spice, pepper, and meaty aromas; leather and licorice in the mouth; no obvious wood, but good fruit sweetness.*

Grapevine

• **Seppeltsfield,** the grand Barossa Valley property established by the Seppelt family in the 1850s, has an exciting new lease on life. It has been bought by the Clare Valley-based Kilikanoon syndicate, which is a successful exporter. It plans to take the great Seppeltsfield fortified wines (various sherry and port styles, Muscats, and Tokays) to the world— something the previous owners, Foster's and Southcorp, neglected.

New Zealand

Bob Campbell MW

New Zealand is almost completely screwed. Around 97 percent of all wine bottled in this country is sealed with a screwcap, and the switch from cork has proved to be particularly divisive for a normally cohesive industry.

BOB CAMPBELL MW

Cork-loyal labels tend to be small-production wines. In the past year, 93 percent of the New Zealand wines I've tasted have been sealed with a screwcap, while 4 percent have relied on traditional cork, and 3 percent on Diam. A statistically insignificant number of rebels chose technical cork and Zork (five wines).

When a handful of screwcap pioneers first made the break in 2001, they were regarded with a mixture of interest and pity—interest because the leaders were trialing an alternative to a troublesome closure; and pity because many didn't believe the market would accept screwcaps.

By 2003 a trickle of trialists had become a flood of fanatics. That's when the trouble started. As screwcap wines made their way onto an often skeptical export market, many thought that New Zealand's premium image would suffer. I recall having my chest prodded by a red-faced and moderately tipsy winery manager who thought my support for screwcaps would destroy the industry. Two years later, his company announced a move to screwcaps.

As their numbers dwindled, cork supporters used many arguments to defend their stance: the presence of rubbery reductive odors (a

BOB CAMPBELL MW lives in Auckland, where he is group wine editor for ACP Media and wine editor for four magazines within that publishing company. He writes for publications, including *Wine Spectator*, in seven countries, and has judged at wine competitions in eight countries. Bob established his own wine school in 1986, and more than 20,000 people have graduated from his wine diploma course.

preventable problem); greater carbon footprint (valid); damage to eagle habitat if cork forests disappear (emotive); and a claim that a compound used in screwcaps was an endocrine disruptor (false). All these claims have been used to discredit screwcaps.

Screwcap supporters initially attacked the shortcomings of cork but, as their numbers grew, switched to making claims about the benefits of screwcaps. Some of these claims are hard to substantiate, given the short history of screwcaps. At times the argument from both sides has been defensive, irrational, and vitriolic. It has driven a wedge between winemakers who once supported each other and has also created a chasm between the two wine critics who support cork and the rest who support screwcaps.

Judging jitters

Wine-show organizers appear to have gotten the jitters after the Wither Hills scandal last year, when differences between the wine entered and wine on retail shelves under the same label resulted in gold-medal awards being revoked.

At the Hawke's Bay A&P Awards, members of the media cried foul when they discovered Gunn Estate 2006 Skeetfield Chardonnay, champion wine of the show, was made by chief judge Tony Bish. Bish is winemaker of Sacred Hill and its associate company Gunn Estate.

Bish had avoided any conflict of interest by not entering Sacred Hill wines in the show after publicly declaring that no wine would be judged by the winemaker who produced it. The message didn't get through to Gunn Estate and, unknown to Bish, its wines were entered.

After protests in the press, Bish withdrew Gunn Estate 2006 Skeetfield Chardonnay from the show and said, "We have decided to withdraw the wine, even though technically no rules were broken, out of respect for the Hawke's Bay A&P Wine Awards." Bish was not on the panel that awarded the wine a gold medal, although he was involved in the trophy judging but didn't know Gunn Estate wines had been entered.

There are simply not enough competent non-winemaker judges in New Zealand to avoid winemakers occasionally having to judge their own wines. There are checks and balances in the judging process to reduce the risk of judging bias. It is unreasonable to expect wineries to boycott shows if they have a winemaker judging in it.

But wait, there's more. A couple of days after Bish withdrew his wine, the competition director announced that he'd made an error and that the overall winner was Vidal 2005 Reserve Syrah, not Gunn Estate 2006 Skeetfield Chardonnay. The admission is all the more extraordinary when you consider that the Vidal Syrah had already been announced as the natural successor when Gunn Chardonnay pulled out.

Anecdotal evidence suggests that consumer confidence in wine-show results has reached an all-time low.

Tough times at Te Kairanga

Martinborough winery Te Kairanga hit the headlines when it was revealed that an export order to Germany had been rejected after tests showed that it contained nearly three times the maximum allowable amount of copper. New Zealand Winegrowers chief executive Philip Gregan tried to make light of the incident, claiming that German officials were making a fuss about nothing. "They are just very pedantic about rules and regulations," said Gregan in a rather bizarre response to what was a significant breach of an EU regulation. The country's largest newspaper, *The New Zealand Herald*, suggested a link between increased copper use and the now widespread use of screwcaps, but analysis of a number of wines sealed with both screwcap and cork failed to support the suggestion. Te Kairanga agreed to take back the rejected wine.

Kiwi wine is best seller in Australia

Australian wine drinkers are proud of their country's wines and unashamedly parochial when it comes to choosing a bottle for their evening meal. New Zealand wine exporters have for years complained about the difficulties of breaking into the Australian market. What particularly rankles is the fact that around four out of every 10 bottles opened in New Zealand are labeled "Made in Australia."

But market-research company AC Nielsen recently announced that the top-selling white wine in Australia (by value) is Oyster Bay Marlborough Sauvignon Blanc. In fact, four New Zealand white wines found their way into Australia's top 10 white wines. Wine sales to Australia in 2008 were about one-third up on the previous year.

This is particularly cheering news to Kiwi winemakers, many of whom are attacking the Australian market with renewed zeal.

New CEO for Matariki

Talented ex-Vidal winemaker Rod Macdonald has been appointed as the new Matariki CEO. After leaving Vidal, Macdonald established a contract winemaking business and began developing his own brand, Broken Hills, as an outlet for grapes from his vineyard. Now the contract winemaking business has been integrated into Matariki and Rod's brand is on hold.

Opinion:

Pinot Gris: a leaky life preserver

The success of Marlborough Sauvignon Blanc distracts attention from the mediocre performance of the country's next two most widely grown grape varieties, Chardonnay and Riesling.

It's fair to say that the much-abused "brand Chardonnay" had it coming. A flood of cheap, bland Australian Chardonnay dulled the luster of one of the world's greatest white grape varieties. After a rapid rise, Chardonnay sales have begun to fall. The decline has been slowed by discounting—an action that has done little to lift Chardonnay's long-term image.

Riesling has, despite desperate cries of "the Riesling Renaissance is coming," simply never performed. That is a pity, because the best examples are truly world-class wines. New Zealand Riesling continues to be the country's best-value wine, although that's cold comfort to winemakers trying to sell it at a profit.

Just as things were starting to look a little grim for any winemaker not producing Marlborough Sauvignon Blanc, along came Pinot Gris. For many wine drinkers it was love at first sip, although I'm still not sure why. Some believe that Pinot Gris trades on the fashionable status of its close relative, Pinot Noir. I wonder whether it's popular simply because it's inoffensive.

Whatever the reason, Pinot Gris has become the new Sauvignon Blanc. Winemakers and wine growers have been furiously planting vineyards with an abandon that resembles the Sauvignon Blanc planting frenzy in Marlborough recently. The acreage of Pinot Gris more than doubled in 2006 and again in 2007.

Will Pinot Gris bring fame and fortune to the New Zealand wine industry? I don't think so. It's a second-division grape variety. New Zealand Pinot Gris is not significantly different from or superior to wines made in many other countries. The multitude of styles being made in New Zealand already frustrates many wine drinkers.

The love affair will soon be over. Grüner Veltliner, anyone?

Vintage Report

Advance report on the latest harvest
2008

Predictions that La Niña would bring hot, dry conditions during late summer and early fall were right on the nail—most New Zealanders enjoyed the best in memory.

Winemakers were equally happy. Before picking began, many claimed it would be an outstanding vintage. Rain in late February and early March dashed the hopes of growers in the most northerly regions, causing varying levels of botrytis pressure as far south as Marlborough.

Pre-vintage estimates put the likely harvest at 225,000–245,000 tons, considerably ahead of a record harvest of 205,000 tons the previous year. It now seems likely that the grape crop could exceed 245,000 tons. Growers, particularly in Marlborough, the country's largest region, have been surprised by the size of the harvest, which may be 15 percent above average. A large harvest has put pressure on processing capacity as well as dramatically reducing the price of Sauvignon Blanc grapes. Bulk wine that might have sold at between NZ$6.50 and NZ$7 per liter last year is being traded at NZ$4 per liter this year. Winemakers claim that Sauvignon Blanc quality is very good despite its being a large, hot, and botrytis-affected vintage. Pinot Noir quality is promising, particularly in Central Otago.

Grapevine

- **Seresin** is the first organic winery in Marlborough—officially. Seresin Estate's 2006 Marama Sauvignon Blanc and 2007 Memento Riesling are the region's first wines to show organic certification from BioGro on their labels. Seresin now has the largest area of fully certified organic vineyards in the country.

- **Collards** is throwing in the towel after 67 years of winemaking in West Auckland. The winery and a small 0.9-ha vineyard will be sold, although Collards plans to retain a 77-ha property north of Auckland and continue farming and grape growing. Urban pressure has finally raised land values to a point where the winery site has become uneconomic.

- **Brian Bicknell,** Seresin's ex-winemaker, has bought the Cellier le Brun winery. Bicknell will keep the winery and a small adjacent vineyard. Cloudy Bay purchased most of the vineyards while wine distributor Lion Nathan acquired the brand and wine stocks.

Updates on the previous five vintages

2007

Vintage rating: *North Island—Red: 86, White: 84;*
South Island—Red: 85, White: 93

A record vintage of 205,000 tons (up 11 percent on the previous year) may seem, on the face of it, to be pretty positive news, particularly with quality ranging from very good to outstanding. However, that figure disguises severe crop losses through frost and poor flowering in the relatively small regions of Martinborough and Waipara. Central Otago also experienced moderate losses through frost.

The grape varieties that experienced the biggest gains on the previous year were, in order, Pinot Gris and Chardonnay, while the largest falls in production were experienced by Riesling, Cabernet Sauvignon, and Pinot Noir. Sauvignon Blanc made a small (6 percent) gain on the previous year. Marlborough produced the region's finest examples of Sauvignon Blanc since 1991. Gisborne also had an outstanding vintage, with Hawke's Bay not too far behind.

2006

Vintage rating: *North Island—Red: 80, White: 86;*
South Island—Red: 86, White: 90

This was the largest-ever New Zealand vintage, thanks to an increase of 18 percent in vineyard area. The weather after flowering was near-perfect until late in March, when most regions experienced heavy rain. By that time, most white grape varieties had been harvested from Hawke's Bay and farther north. Winemakers in these regions then had to decide whether to harvest their first black grapes under pressure or to wait in the hope of a return to fine weather. Those who waited fared better.

Most South Island regions—in particular Central Otago—had an exceptionally early harvest. Marlborough's Sauvignon Blanc crop enjoyed very good ripening conditions and produced many exceptional wines. A long, dry fall throughout most of the country favored growers who were prepared to wait. A generally excellent vintage.

2005

Vintage rating: *North Island—Red: 86, White: 80;*
South Island—Red: 79, White: 87

The vintage was down on 2004 due to wet, cold weather during flowering. A long, dry Indian summer brought Auckland/Northland its best-ever harvest in quality terms. The Hawke's Bay vintage was dogged by rain.

There are deep colors and good flavors in red wines, but most wine-makers admit that whites were less successful. Martinborough suffered from rain, but the wines generally, and Sauvignon Blanc in particular, are very good indeed. Some Canterbury producers were affected by frost at the beginning of October and generally poor flowering. Quality is average to good. A below-average year for Central Otago Pinot Noir, with a few obvious exceptions.

2004

Vintage rating: *North Island—Red: 80, White: 78; South Island—Red: 72, White: 78 (except Sauvignon Blanc: 70)*
Generally a cool vintage with heavy February rain. Central Otago was hit by frost at the beginning and the end of the season. Marlborough Sauvignon Blanc is variable, with many diluted and high-acid wines. Warm, dry weather at the end of the vintage helped compensate for difficulties early in the season. Hawke's Bay has produced some excellent reds, although Cabernet Sauvignon struggled to ripen fully in some districts.

2003

Vintage rating: *North Island—Red: 60, White: 65; South Island—Red: 75, White: 80*
All regions except Central Otago and Nelson suffered frost damage, ranging from minor in Auckland to severe in Hawke's Bay. The North Island suffered from generally wet conditions, while the South Island was relatively dry, with drought in some areas. Many grape growers in frost-affected areas tried to recover some production by harvesting later-ripening grapes from "second set," but this often resulted in unsatisfactory wines with varying ripeness levels. The crop of Marlborough Sauvignon Blanc was significantly reduced by frost, although quality was good, with some outstanding wines made.

GREATEST WINE PRODUCERS

1. Neudorf
2. Craggy Range
3. Villa Maria Estate
4. Felton Road
5. Astrolabe
6. Ata Rangi
7. Cloudy Bay
8. Dry River
9. Herzog
10. Framingham

FASTEST-IMPROVING PRODUCERS

1. Church Road
2. Trinity Hill
3. Muddy Water
4. Pernod Ricard
5. Peregrine
6. Escarpment
7. Nautilus
8. Kaituna Valley
9. Seresin
10. Forrest Estate

NEW UP-AND-COMING PRODUCERS

1. Puriri Hills
2. Blake Family Vineyard
3. Blackenbrook Vineyard
4. Bell Hill
5. Greystone
6. Woollaston
7. Vinoptima
8. Delta
9. Passage Rock
10. Tresillian

BEST-VALUE PRODUCERS

1. Spy Valley
2. Mount Riley
3. Villa Maria Estate
4. Seifried Estate
5. Pernod Ricard
6. Morton Estate
7. Wither Hills
8. Coopers Creek
9. Mission Estate Winery
10. Oyster Bay

GREATEST-QUALITY WINES

1. **Long Gully Pinot Noir 2005** Mt Difficulty, Central Otago (NZ$80)
2. **Home Vineyard Pinot Noir 2005** Neudorf, Nelson (NZ$79)
3. **Mojo Pinot Noir 2005** Muddy Water, Waipara (NZ$50)
4. **Le Sol Syrah 2005** Craggy Range, Hawke's Bay (NZ$69.95)
5. **Homage Syrah 2006** Trinity Hill, Hawke's Bay (NZ$120)
6. **Reserve 2005** Puriri Hills, Clevedon (NZ$55)
7. **Tom 2002** Montana, Hawke's Bay (NZ$120)
8. **Chardonnay 2006** Dry River, Martinborough (NZ$45)
9. **Awatere Sauvignon Blanc 2007** Astrolabe, Marlborough (NZ$23)
10. **Select Riesling 2007** Framingham, Marlborough (NZ$29.90)

BEST BARGAINS

1. **Select Riesling 2007** Framingham, Marlborough (NZ$29.90)
2. **Sauvignon Blanc 2007** Astrolabe, Marlborough (NZ$19.95)
3. **Gewürztraminer 2007** Lawson's Dry Hills (NZ$21.95)
4. **Moutere Riesling 2007** Neudorf, Nelson (NZ$28)
5. **Manu Riesling 2006** Martinborough Vineyard, Martinborough (NZ$28)
6. **Chardonnay 2006** Escarpment, Martinborough (NZ$30)
7. **Clifford Bay Sauvignon Blanc 2007** Villa Maria Estate, Marlborough (NZ$24)
8. **Sauvignon Blanc 2007** Blackenbrook Vineyard, Nelson (NZ$19.90)
9. **Chardonnay 2005** Muddy Water, Waipara (NZ$27)
10. **Unplugged Riesling 2006** Muddy Water, Waipara (NZ$25)

MOST EXCITING OR UNUSUAL FINDS

1. **Retico 2003** Vin Alto, Clevedon (NZ$89) *Swiss-Italian Enzo Bettio and his wife Margaret have faithfully followed the Amarone process with technical help from Masi to make this big and impressively complex red wine. It's a triumph for a couple with great vision and determination.*
2. **La Collina Syrah 2005** Bilancia, Hawke's Bay (NZ$80) *A pocket-handkerchief hillside vineyard in the Gimblett Gravels district of Hawke's Bay produced this big, powerful wine. A tiny percentage of co-fermented Viognier exposes the wine's feminine side, adding complexity and a silkier texture.*

③ Ormond Gewurztraminer 2004
Vinoptima, Gisborne (NZ$54) *Nick Nobilo sold the shares in his family company and pursued a dream to make great Gewurztraminer. This wine must have put a smile on Nick's face as it does on mine. It takes NZ Gewurztraminer to a new level of quality.*

④ Sophia 2005 Craggy Range, Hawke's Bay (NZ$49.95)
This Merlot-dominant blend of bordeaux grape varieties offers a beacon of hope to other local producers of a style that is under siege. Intense red with a peacock's tail of ripe berry fruit flavors. Further proof that Merlot performs best in partnership.

⑤ Target Gully Riesling 2007
Mt. Difficulty, Central Otago (NZ$25)
Probably the best-ever example of a wine that hits the jackpot every year. Adjacent vineyards also make very good Riesling but none have quite the X factor of Target Gully. Central Otago must now be acknowledged as New Zealand's Riesling capital.

⑥ The Spirit of Marlborough Merlot Cabernet 2001 Herzog, Marlborough (NZ$56) *No one believed that Cabernet could ripen in Marlborough until Hans Herzog arrived and broke all the rules. Dense, deep red, with truly ripe flavors. It shows what can be done in a hot site using meticulous viticulture.*

⑦ Black Poplar Pinot Noir 2006
Pisa Range, Central Otago (NZ$38.95) *My top wine (equal with Felton Road) in an extensive tasting of wines from Central Otago's large 2006 vintage. It has more weight and complexity than most but retains the charm that was the hallmark of the vintage.*

⑧ Single Vineyard Omahu Gravels Viognier 2006 Villa Maria Estate, Hawke's Bay (NZ$35) *Best local Viognier I've yet tasted—and there have been many pretty creditable efforts to date. The wine shows ripe flavors in the apricot/tree-fruit spectrum, with an influence of yeast lees and subtle oak.*

⑨ Marlborough Cuvée Blanc de Blancs 2003 Deutz, Marlborough (NZ$38.95) *Montana, now Pernod Ricard NZ, raised a few eyebrows (mine included) when it released the first vintage (1994) of this restrained and powerful sparkler. Six vintages later it has grown in stature enormously to become my favorite New Zealand méthode.*

⑩ Te Muna Road Vineyard Sauvignon Blanc 2007 Craggy Range, Martinborough (NZ$25.95) *It's easy to miss the point of this tight, bone-dry, mineral-laced Sauvignon Blanc, but savor it with scampi or chargrilled snapper and you'll discover one of New Zealand's most food-friendly wines. Fine, steely wine with mountain-stream purity.*

Grapevine

• **Peter Hubscher,** Montana's ex-managing director, has joined Te Kairanga following the company's announcement of a NZ$2.17 million loss after a series of tough vintages. Hubscher was appointed as executive chairman and purchased 1 million shares for NZ$1 each. Montana (now Pernod Ricard NZ) prospered with Hubscher at the helm. The wine industry waits with bated breath to see whether Hubscher can steer Te Kairanga back into profit.

Asia

Denis Gastin

Momentum continues to build in the wine industry in Asia as the big industry stakeholders settle in to their ambitious strategies (see *Wine Report 2008*).

DENIS GASTIN

Even more new players are now arriving on the scene with plans to tap rapidly growing consumption trends, especially in the newer markets. But it's not just that the number of producers continues to grow and that their scale is expanding that excite. It's hard not to be impressed also by the energy and imagination that are now being applied to the experimentation with viticultural approaches that will work best in local conditions, as well as with winemaking formulations that will deliver wines that pitch to increasingly sophisticated local wine palates and harmonize best with local food customs.

More substance…

Global liquor giant Diageo is one of the more prominent of a growing number of foreign companies taking strategic positions in the wine industry in Asia. India is its first move into domestic production, where it is positioning to capture a substantial chunk of a market that is now growing in excess of 25 percent annually. It kicked off with the launch of some of its global wine brands early in 2007, then as the year ended it

DENIS GASTIN is a feature writer and Australian correspondent for Japan's liquor-industry newspaper *The Shuhan News* and for *Wine Review* magazine in Korea. He writes for *Australian & New Zealand Grapegrower & Winemaker* and contributes to various other journals and wine reference books, including *The Oxford Companion to Wine* and *The World Atlas of Wine*. His particular interests are the more unusual aspects of winemaking, the more remote and least understood regions of the wine world, and the groundbreaking work that some of the industry champions have been doing with exotic grape varieties and new wine styles.

released a range of domestically produced wines under the Nilaya label, targeting the popular end of the market with Bollywood flamboyance. The grapes are grown around Nashik, in Maharashtra State, headquarters of the Indian wine industry. The wine is made at the Mountain View, Renaissance, and Flamingo wineries, on contract to Diageo. The meaning of the word Nilaya is, literally, "blue heaven," and for Diageo it may well represent "blue sky": it had sold 2,000 cases of this alluringly packaged wine within 10 days of its launch in late 2007.

Pernod Ricard is also a very recent arrival on the Indian wine scene. Market observers were stunned when its Seagrams Nine Hills 2007 Cabernet Sauvignon, produced at its new Nashik winery, took the prize for best local red wine at the inaugural India Wine Challenge.

Another big-time new player is locally owned drinks conglomerate United Breweries. It kicked off its wine strategy in 2006, initially bottling imported bulk wine. In late 2007, it launched a range of competitively priced table wines under the Zinzy label and followed this in 2008 with the release of its Four Seasons "estate" range. Sparkling wines will be a major focus of the Four Seasons winery in Maharashtra's Baramati district: UB plans to produce 1 million bottles of sparkling wine each year from locally grown grapes.

… and style (*vive la différence*!)

A very pleasing aspect of the evolving wine scene in Asia is the expanding range of wine styles that can legitimately be called Asia's own. Some are wines made from grape varieties that are unique (in winemaking terms) to these countries; some are innovative style interpretations within this group; and some are unique local expressions of the more widely traveled classic varieties such as Merlot, Cabernet Sauvignon, Syrah, Chenin Blanc, Sauvignon Blanc, and Chardonnay.

In Japan, for example, there is now a phalanx of style interpretations with the local vinifera staple, Koshu. Traditionally it was most often made as a crisp, high-acid/lower-alcohol white wine. Then followed intense chaptalization, oak treatment, and extended *sur lie* maturation, when winemakers tried to defend their market share against imported French and New World Chardonnays. Now the move is back to the styles that best present this shy variety's naturally restrained fruitiness and its appealing minerality. Sparkling versions have also begun to appear recently. One step in a different direction is a Koshu fermented and matured in earthenware pots—the same as those used to make the local white spirit, *shochu*. Another very new interpretation is extended fermentation on the skins, which imparts some of the bronze to light purple tinge in this grape and, when bottled unfiltered, unexpected body and substance.

Other varieties increasingly appearing in similarly creative formulations in Japan are the hybrids Muscat Bailey A (often blended with Merlot), Kai Noir, Black Queen, and Campbell Early. Then there are the wines based on the quirky indigenous varieties (collectively known as Yamabudo) and the crossings of these with vinifera varieties, such as Seibel, Cabernet Sauvignon, and Pinot Blanc.

In China, extensive development work has been done in the established regions with Longyan and Cabernet Gernischt, and these varieties are increasingly appearing on retail shelves and winning local loyalties. Very recent appearances (in Yunnan province) are wines made from varieties known locally as Rose Honey, Crystal Dry, and French Wild, which are said to have been introduced by European missionaries in the 1800s. In Thailand, Malaga Blanc and Pokdum have become local staples. In India, the local Arkavati (white) and Arkeshyam (black) varieties are worth watching, having been admirably presented in contemporary styles by the Indage Group under its Vin Ballet label in blends, respectively, with Ugni Blanc and Gamay.

Grapevine

• **The tally** of Asia's wineries has just passed 800 (by my count) in 12 countries. Well over half of them are in China, in 26 provinces—virtually all of them established since the late 1970s and more than 100 of them less than 10 years old. Almost a quarter are in Japan, concentrated principally in Yamanashi and Nagano. Numbers are expanding rapidly in India, now with 50 wineries. Other Asian countries in which there is an established winemaking tradition are Thailand, Korea, Vietnam, and Indonesia. Fledgling operations can be found in Taiwan, Sri Lanka, Bhutan, Myanmar (Burma), and, most recently, Cambodia.

• **China's Grace Vineyard,** now under the operational direction of Australian *vigneron* and winemaker Ken Murchison, who took over from Frenchman Gerard Colin in 2005, continues to grow at a sizzling pace. Its first vines were planted in 1997 and its first vintage was in 2001. In the three years since Murchison took over, the area under vine has soared from 75 ha to 220 ha, and there

is much more on the way. New plantings of Riesling, Shiraz, Petit Verdot, and Marselan are delivering good results and will add attractive new dimensions to the Cabernet Sauvignon, Cabernet Franc, Merlot, and Chardonnay that have defined the label thus far. But Grace has finally given up on the small original plantings of Pinot Noir, and the vines have now been pulled.

• **Myanmar's first winery,** Aythaya Estate, kicked off in 1999 with trial plantings of 80 varieties in its vineyard at an altitude of 4,300 ft (1,300 m) in Shan State. So far, only Sauvignon Blanc, Chenin Blanc, Shiraz, Cabernet Sauvignon, and Muscat have made it to bottle. But founder Bert Morsbach says that Tempranillo and Dornfelder are on the way. He is not yet sure whether there will be enough for release as single varieties and they will probably first appear as a blend. Other varieties in the pipeline include Gewurztraminer, Chardonnay, Pinot Noir, and Barbera. A second winery is expected to open in Myanmar in 2009.

Opinion:
Action needed on integrity

Label integrity and formal industry winemaking standards remain compelling issues in Asia. Progressives in the industry understand that international standards must be met if broader consumer respect is to be won. But much of the traditional end of the industry still seems motivated by the convenience afforded by ambiguous production and labeling codes—and the practices of the few are damaging the status of the increasing number who are deadly serious. Government remains very much in the background.

A basic issue is origin. Some efforts are being made to reduce the scope for ambiguity by introducing regional AOC systems in parts of China and Japan. But a bigger issue is country of origin: labeling practices condone the use of imported bulk wine, imported grape must, and even imported grapes in "local" wine. Grape varieties are increasingly stated on labels, but most countries have no rules governing this or vintage declarations. Alcohol-content levels stated on labels are unreliable.

Change is on the way, though. China's decision to ban a local concoction known as "half-juice wine" from hijacking the name "wine" was commendable, especially since government action was urged by the industry itself. There was an industry-standards code promulgated at the end of 2006, but compliance is, and will remain, a big issue. In Myanmar (Burma), one of the newest wine countries in Asia, there is a determined effort to get it right at the outset, with a founding industry charter that has been written in collaboration with the relevant local ministry. But the benchmark has been set in Thailand, where the Thai Wine Association has set rigorous production and labeling standards and, critically, an equally rigorous audit process to ensure compliance.

Back to the vineyard

Another big constraint on producing good wine in Asia is the slow emergence of genuinely wine-focused viticultural practices. Most traditional grape growers are not yet confident enough to commit to the different viticultural practices required for good wine, and wineries are limited (by land-ownership laws, among other things) in the extent to which they can do this themselves. With heavy investment in modern winery equipment now behind them, the next challenge for most Asian winemakers lies in the vineyards, with yield management and ripeness the priority targets.

Vintage Report

Advance report on the latest harvest
2008

India—Maharashtra had its coldest winter in 50 years, followed by severe cold spells up to late January, so berries were developing slowly and most vineyards will be picking late. Whites are expected to be more complex this year, with attractive flavor definition and crisp acid support. Reds will also be more complex if the early favorable conditions continue through to harvest.

Thailand—After two very difficult vintages, this one is bringing considerable relief to winemakers. Very moderate rainfall from October through to late February, and virtually nothing in parts of Khao Yai, has averted losses due to fungal diseases and permitted even ripening of fruit. Yields are going to be greatly improved, and fruit quality looks even better than in 2005.

Updates on the previous five vintages
2007

China—In Shandong and Hebei, a cool summer and a lack of sunshine made it difficult to achieve desired sugar levels and satisfactory color in black varieties, but this is a perennial problem in these regions. Summer rains in Shanxi reduced usable yields and negatively impacted on wine quality. Farther west, in Ningxia, extended cloudy conditions slowed ripening and rain late in the season caused some losses of fruit. In far west Xingjiang it was an average result, but this is a high average.

Japan—It was a very good year in Nagano, where the early stages of ripening were helped by drier and warmer weather than usual and, although July brought extended cloudy weather, August and September were generally sunny and dry, providing good ripening conditions. Total sunshine hours were the lowest on record in Yamanashi, and this set back ripening and delayed vintage. Early-maturing varieties struggled to catch up, but later-ripening varieties generally finished in good condition.

India—Because of the 2006 vintage experience, some vineyards in Maharashtra pruned earlier than usual, bringing on harvests as early as Christmas Day. Conditions remained favorable through to the end of the vintage in late March, and most wineries achieved satisfactory yields with good fruit quality contributing to fuller-flavored wines. Farther south in

Bangalore, where harvests last through to May, lower yields resulted from drier-than-usual conditions, but good fruit concentration was achieved.

Thailand—This was another challenging vintage. Prolonged rainfall early in the season again delayed flowering and affected fruit set. Overall, yields were low—for some wineries even lower than the severely reduced levels of 2006. But colder-than-usual weather from mid-November to January slowed ripening, and relatively dry conditions in most regions from December to March allowed the vines to catch up and the grapes to develop good flavors.

2006

China—It was a good year in Shandong, with much less fungal disease than normal, and good fruit ripeness was generally achieved. Hebei got off to a good start with a mild winter, but heavy rainfall and prolonged humidity in spring and early summer caused some fungal disease and some loss of volume in the early-picked white varieties. Harvesting of black grapes was delayed by some weeks, resulting in better fruit flavors and colors, with reasonable yields. There were severe early frosts in Shanxi, so yields were down by up to 20 percent, but the rest of the season proceeded without setbacks and fruit was fully ripened.

Japan—A very cold spring complicated budburst in Yamanashi and parts of Nagano, and a long rainy season with less sunshine than usual didn't help. Yields were average, but fruit struggled to achieve moderate ripeness, as well as color for the black varieties. Nagano also experienced some losses due to fungal disease in September. But most of northern Honshu and Hokkaido achieved both good yields and quality fruit.

India—A monsoon of record severity and duration in Maharashtra delayed pruning. Yields were lower than usual, though adequate grape-sugar levels were ultimately achieved in most districts, while maintaining satisfactory acid levels. Farther south, in Bangalore, conditions were generally more favorable, with lower temperatures permitting slower bunch maturation and delivering strong aromas in white wines and good concentration in reds.

Thailand—Prolonged rain after pruning reduced flowering and affected fruit set. It also caused some early fungal disease. As a result, yields were down to as little as half 2005 levels in some vineyards, though the generally dry and cool weather from mid-December through to harvest and radical canopy and bunch management helped vineyards to ultimately deliver grapes with good color and flavors in most regions.

2005

China—For the second year running, Shandong province had heavy summer rains that caused widespread fungal disease and great difficulty reaching acceptable ripening. Combined with early frosts, yields were well down, forcing the larger wineries to look to other regions, especially in the west, for fruit. Hebei province fared much better, since it was spared the worst of the rains and enjoyed higher temperatures.

Japan—Overall, a difficult vintage, due principally to a shortage of sunshine days and generally lower temperatures, making it difficult to ripen fruit. Rain was less of a problem than usual late in the vintage—patchy recoveries were made and fungal damage was generally contained. In Yamanashi, Koshu didn't ripen well. Conditions were little better in Nagano: quality in Merlot varies among producers and Chardonnay was good rather than excellent.

India—Late monsoon rains affected early-pruned vineyards, causing lower yields, especially for Sauvignon Blanc. Later-pruned vineyards were unaffected and benefited from a cooler-than-normal ripening period.

Thailand—In Khao Yai, rain finished early after pruning in September, resulting in good fruit set and no disease. Mild weather throughout the vintage produced very good results in both early- and later-ripening varieties. It was an exceptional vintage in the Chao Phraya Delta region: very little rain, no disease, and mild weather from November through to harvest in February. Volume was low, but sugar levels were higher than usual. At Loei, in the north, Chenin Blanc was the best in 10 years.

2004

China—Heavy rains in July and August caused widespread mildew throughout the north and northeast, especially in Shandong and Hebei provinces, and much fruit was picked far too soon. Huailai was generally affected less by summer rains than other parts of Hebei. Conditions in Shanxi were much better, with good sugar and acid levels and few losses to disease. The northwest was, as usual, dry throughout, but yields were lower.

Japan—The year began well with prolonged warm, dry weather after *véraison*, which saw good early fruit development. But a blitz of typhoons late in the season caused many wineries to take fruit early. For others, fungal disease caused losses in quality and volume. As usual, the valleys fared worst, and the more elevated and inland locations did best.

India—A very good year for whites in Maharashtra and quite good for reds. Cool weather extended until mid-February, longer than usual, resulting in slower ripening and more complex flavors. Conditions were very favorable around Bangalore, adding to the region's growing reputation for consistency.

2003

China—Very wet conditions in Hebei and Shandong produced big berries with low sugar and acid levels in most white varieties, though late-maturing black grapes were generally of good quality. Fungal disease was a problem in most regions and was particularly devastating in parts of Shanxi province. Even in the west, where conditions are generally more amenable, colder and wetter weather than usual impacted adversely on quality. Overall, 2003 was not a good year.

Japan—Extensive summer rainfall severely dented yields and kept sugar levels low in all the major regions. A few of the later-picked varieties saw some recovery when rains eased late in the harvest in Yamanashi and the Komoro district of Nagano. But overall it was a poor year, and the wines generally suffer from suppressed natural flavors and colors.

India—Vintage was over early in Maharashtra. Warmer weather throughout the ripening period and a weaker monsoon saw fruit ripening early, relatively free of disease. Sauvignon Blanc and more aromatic wines are not as intense as in some years, but the reds have lots of flavor and color. In Bangalore, conditions were close to ideal.

Grapevine

• **Japan's Koshu variety** is attracting ever more collaborative interest from French winemakers. Bordeaux consultant Denis Dubourdieu has been working for some time with a number of wineries in Yamanashi Prefecture, the variety's spiritual homeland. More recently, Bernard Magrez of Château Pape Clément has teamed up with Yuji Aruga of Katsunuma Jozo Winery, and they have launched their first wine, Magrez-Aruga Isehara Vineyard Koshu.

• **Bali's pioneer winery,** Hatten Wines, has broken new ground with the launch of its first serious red wine—a Shiraz. Over the decade and a half since it began making wine in this intensely tropical environment (4° below the equator), the closest it had gotten to a red wine was the wine it called Aga Red, which is actually a cherry-colored rosé, made from Alphonse Lavallée grapes. The Shiraz vines were grafted over Alphonse Lavallée rootstock in 2005 and are trained over pergolas 6½ ft (2 m) high to provide some relief from the moist tropical conditions. They produce two vintages per year. The wine surprises, with quite pronounced varietal characteristics, despite the conditions. It is available in only very limited quantities at this early stage.

• **Southeast Asia's** largest wine producer, Thailand's Siam Winery, has swung its development focus to the southern coastal resort region, Hua Hin (12° north). Encouraged by results from its initial trial plantings, the vineyard area is being expanded to 80 ha by 2012. Siam's premium Colombard, Shiraz, White Shiraz (rosé), and Muscat now bear the regional tag of Hua Hin Hills, and a Chenin Blanc and a Sangiovese/Brunello are to be added soon. A visitor center opened at the vineyard in April 2008.

GREATEST WINE PRODUCERS

1. Château Mercian (Japan)
2. Dragon Seal (China)
3. Suntory (Japan)
4. Grace Wine (Japan)
5. Sapporo (Japan)
6. Great Wall (China)
7. Manns Wine (Japan)
8. Changyu (China)
9. Dynasty (China)
10. Château Indage (India)

FASTEST-IMPROVING PRODUCERS

1. Grover Vineyards (India)
2. Katsunuma Jozo (Japan)
3. Coco Farm & Winery (Japan)
4. Weilong (China)
5. Château Mars (Japan)
6. Siam Winery (Thailand)
7. Hayashi Noen (Japan)
8. Takahata (Japan)
9. Kizan (Japan)
10. Asahi Yoshu Soleil (Japan)

NEW UP-AND-COMING PRODUCERS

1. Suntime (China)
2. Sula Vineyards (India)
3. Domaine Sogga (Japan)
4. Tsuno Wine (Japan)
5. Grace Vineyard (China)
6. GranMonte (Thailand)
7. Yamazaki (Japan)
8. PB Valley (Thailand)
9. Yunnan Hong (China)
10. Shidax Château TS (Japan)

BEST-VALUE PRODUCERS

1. Dragon Seal (China)
2. Château Mercian (Japan)
3. Sula Vineyards (India)
4. Grace Wine (Japan)
5. Siam Winery (Thailand)
6. Tsuno Wine (Japan)

7. Weilong (China)
8. Grace Vineyard (China)
9. Marufuji Rubaiyat (Japan)
10. Izutsu (Japan)

GREATEST-QUALITY WINES

1. **Kikyogahara Signature Merlot 2004** Château Mercian, Japan (¥18,000)
2. **Chardonnay 2006** Ajimu Budoshu, Japan (¥2,433)
3. **Kikyogahara Merlot 2004** Hayashi Noen, Japan (¥5,250)
4. **Huailai Reserve Cabernet Sauvignon 2006** Dragon Seal, China (Rmb 140)
5. **Cuveé Misawa Private Reserve Koshu 2006** Grace Wine, Japan (¥3,000)
6. **Chairman's Reserve (Red) 2006** Grace Vineyard, China (Rmb 488)
7. **Hokushin Private Reserve Chardonnay 2006** Château Mercian, Japan (¥6,300)
8. **Dindori Reserve Shiraz 2006** Sula Vineyards, India (Rp 810)
9. **Primavera Unwooded Chenin Blanc/Colombard 2007** GranMonte, Thailand (THB 740)
10. **Marquise de Pompadour Brut NV** Château Indage, India (Rp 630)

BEST BARGAINS

1. **Momoiro Merlot 2006** Château Mercian, Japan (¥1,500)
2. **Monsoon Valley Colombard 2007** Siam Winery, Thailand (THB 500)
3. **Sparkling Campbell Early NV** Tsuno Wine, Japan (¥1,500)
4. **Koshu 2006** Grace Wine, Japan (¥1,890)
5. **Vineyard Chardonnay 2006** Grace Vineyard, China (Rmb 68)
6. **Toriibira Chardonnay 2006** Châteraise, Japan (¥2,800)

7 **Sauvignon Blanc 2007**
Sula Vineyards, India (Rp 570)

8 **Koshu 2006** Kizan, Japan (¥1,200)

9 **Petite Grand Polaire Koshu 2005** Sapporo, Japan (¥2,100)

10 **Müller-Thurgau 2006**
Matsubara Farm, Japan (¥1,600)

MOST EXCITING OR UNUSUAL FINDS

1 **Kusakabenne Muscat Bailey A 2006** Asahi Yoshu Soleil, Japan (¥1,890) *The best example of this variety I have seen so far. Carbonic maceration has highlighted the soft and spicy aromas and flavors that this local hybrid can deliver, and careful barrel-aging gives it substance and length.*

2 **Sparkling Red NV** Tsuno Wine, Japan (¥1,600) *Asia's first sparkling red. A local twist is the use of Muscat Bailey A as its base, with the more intense color and spicy aromas provided by a hefty portion of Shiraz. A fraction more residual sugar would add even more appeal.*

3 **Koshu FOS 2006** Coco Farm & Winery, Japan (¥3,600) *One of a suite of frontier styles at this intriguing winery in Tochigi Prefecture, this example presents Koshu well beyond established boundaries. Color has been extracted by fermenting on skins, and much greater body and definition are presented here than most would expect that this shy grape could deliver.*

4 **Viognier 2007** Sula Vineyards, India (Rp 294 per half-bottle) *One of only two Indian Viogniers, and Sula's first, with a light touch of residual sugar that underlines its fruity appeal. This is exotica at a very modest price.*

5 **Katsunuma no Awa Koshu Brut 2006** Château Mercian, Japan (¥1,800) *A stylish addition to the expanding spectrum of sparkling versions of this unique Japanese vinifera grape. Exceptional value as well.*

6 **Monsoon Valley White Shiraz 2007** Siam Winery, Thailand (THB 600) *A more substantial offering than most other local rosés and a first with Shiraz. Its pleasant musky aromas, with just the right amount of sweetness on the palate, make it a natural with spicy Thai food.*

7 **Vin Ballet Red Wine 2006** Château Indage, India (Rp 196) *A serious winemaking effort with the local Arkeshyam variety and a proportion of Gamay; represents extraordinary value.*

8 **YamaSauvignon 2006** Ikeda Winery, Japan (¥2,000) *A top example of this emerging variety, a cross of the indigenous Vitis coignetiae wild mountain grape with Cabernet Sauvignon. Despite a cool and wet vintage, it has achieved excellent color with rich, almost Pinotage-like, aromas and flavors.*

9 **Deep Blue 2006** Grace Vineyard, China (Rmb 288) *A new assemblage of the three black varieties that work best for this winery—equal proportions of Cabernet Sauvignon, Cabernet Franc, and Merlot.*

10 **Château des Brumes 2006** Village Farm Winery, Thailand (THB 740) *A stylish wine with a split personality. The 85 percent Shiraz component is from local fruit, but the 15 percent Cabernet Sauvignon, which firms up the structure, is from France.*

Organic & Biodynamic Wines

Monty Waldin

The New Zealand wine industry has finally dropped its ridiculously inappropriate tagline "The Riches of a Clean Green Land."

MONTY WALDIN

Bio wine growers and commentators were perplexed that New Zealand could pass off its wines as coming from land that was clean and green. Weedkiller use is still widespread—up to 70 percent in, for example, Marlborough's flagship Wairau Valley subregion, according to New Zealand's Soil & Health Association.

New Zealand Winegrowers' new tagline ("Pure Discovery") will remain equally meaningless unless more of its conventional growers stop acting like the sheep that once grazed some of the country's prime vineyard sites. Grove Mill scored an embarrassing own goal when it claimed to have become New Zealand's first carbon-neutral winery, all part of the Sustainable Winegrowing initiative (SWNZ) that New Zealand

MONTY WALDIN While working on a conventionally farmed Bordeaux château as a teenager, Monty Waldin realized that the more chemicals were applied to a vineyard, the more corrective treatments became necessary in the winery. When the opportunity arose to write about wine, he specialized in green issues. His first book, *The Organic Wine Guide* (Thorsons, 1999), has now been joined by *Biodynamic Wines* (Mitchell Beazley, 2004). This is the first guide dedicated to the world's biodynamic wine producers. Monty's interest in biodynamism was stimulated in 1999 by six months working on the Fetzer family's biodynamic Home Ranch vineyard in California's Mendocino County. Experience either living or working in Chile, Bordeaux, and Tuscany contributed to his other books: *Wines of South America* (Mitchell Beazley, 2003), *Discovering Wine Country: Bordeaux* (Mitchell Beazley, 2005), and *Discovering Wine Country: Tuscany* (Mitchell Beazley, 2006). Monty's attempt at making his first wine from biodynamically farmed grapes in Roussillon, France, in 2007 was filmed by British TV. He is now advising wine producers on biodynamic practices.

Winegrowers wants us to get behind. Visitors could be forgiven for wondering whether the scorched (weedkilled) earth under vines next to Grove Mill's winery had not only been sustainably weedkilled, but whether the carbon footprint created by whoever produced the weedkiller had been offset—perhaps by, er, planting some weeds somewhere else instead?

Now Grove Mill has started thinking for itself. The weedkilled plot is in official conversion to organics, a three- to five-year process. As New Zealand's biodynamic wine pioneer James Millton says, "The thing that certified organic wine growing brings is sincerity." In other words, organic growers work to a clear set of rules (no synthetic sprays or fertilizers or GMOs) and are regularly inspected by independently accredited third-party bodies.

Millton, like any other commentator with a genuine interest in our environmental future, has consistently supported the main goal of SWNZ. This is a reduction in—but not necessarily total abandonment of—the use of synthetic substances along the IPM (integrated pest management) model ("You can use the same synthetic sprays, just try to be a good wine grower and use a bit less next time").

IPM schemes like SWNZ have historically been viewed with suspicion by the organic community, especially when incentives for joining are provided by the government, the chemical industry, and conventional producer associations. Perhaps this is why SWNZ can't yet bring itself to do what the premier US organic wine producer, Fetzer Vineyards, did and set a date by which all its estate vineyards and grape growers would be third-party-certified organic. Initially Fetzer's target date was 2005, now it is 2010—yet Fetzer still farms, rents, or contracts from several times more certified organic vineyards than the whole of the New Zealand wine industry combined. However, New Zealand Winegrowers' chief executive Philip Gregan has said he wants every New Zealand vineyard and winery to be independently audited—either as certified organic, certified biodynamic, or certified "sustainable" as part of SWNZ by 2012.

Nobody expects the whole of the New Zealand wine industry to buy into organics overnight. But New Zealand's head honchos need to ditch their sniffy arrogance when legitimate concerns are raised about SWNZ's rulebook and accreditation system. Criticizing the Germans as being "sticklers for technical points" when some Kiwi Pinot Noir was pulled out of the German market in late 2007 for illegally high residues from copper fining is a case in point.

If New Zealand persists in retaining such a cavalier attitude to international norms, why should the international community believe SWNZ has the "audit structure that has integrity and rigor to comply with market expectations" that it boasts? Especially when the only audit structure that has a proven track record (in Europe anyway) is the clear set of rules and independent third-party inspections pertaining to organics (EU Norm 2092/91 and amendments). SWNZ will have to match this to gain the credibility it craves.

The big mental block that conventional New Zealand wine growers have is not the belief that organics is unsustainable environmentally, but that it is not sustainable economically. The main reason Wairau growers weedkill is frost (and thus yield) control. Although Cloudy Bay's viticulturist described organics to me as "dogma," other producers are finally seeing the light. Bell Hill, Ata Rangi, Fromm, Spy Valley, Babich, Alan Scott, Rippon, Kawarau, Burn Cottage, Pyramid Valley, Seresin, Vynfields, and Sunset Valley all now have some form of biodynamic composting program. Where SWNZ can play a role is to accept that its premium wines really do deserve nothing short of premium wine growing.

All those blue-chip and firmly bio Californians shut the door of the chemical cabinet for a reason: the lack of long-term sustainability they saw it causing their vineyards and thus the wine they were trying to sell. Converting to bio wine growing was not prompted by any need to live up to a ridiculous "Pure California" tagline, either. They did it because ultimately it was a question of pure economics.

Proposal to permit GM contamination

The EU is proposing to change EU organic regulation 2092/91 to allow 0.9 percent adventitious (or accidental) GM contamination of products that could still be labeled as organic. The use of GMOs is prohibited in organic farming. Organic lobby groups, including the UK's Soil Association, said that the proposed 0.9 percent limit is "unnecessarily high," since traces of GM organisms are detectable at only 0.1 percent.

To protect organic farmers, the Soil Association called for a strict coexistence regime, including legally enforceable separation distances between GM and non-GM crops; liability regulations to ensure the burden caused by GM contamination is not borne by organic farmers and consumers; and a limit of 0.1 percent contamination for all seed. Proponents of GM vines say that transgenic genes are detectable only in the vine itself (shoots, leaves) and the grape seeds, rather than in the juice or pulp from which wines are made. Opponents say that seeds can be crushed during pressing for white wine or can leach compounds into red wines during fermentation and/or postfermentation maceration.

CURRENT STATUS OF CERTIFIED ORGANIC VINEYARDS

Country or region	Hectares certified organic	Percentage of vineyards	Year	Comments
Europe (Western)	c. 80,000	2.5	2006	Italy has half of Europe's organic vineyard, despite recent falls. Growth remains steady in France and Spain, which battle for second place. Rises in über-green Austria and Germany seem to be speeding up again after a pause, encouraged now by market demand rather than subsidies. Of the smaller players, Luxembourg (6 ha/<0.3%) has fewer obvious climatic advantages than, say, Cyprus (<75 ha/0.4%), which is having to cope with drastic EU-imposed vineyard reform.
Europe (other)	<250	<0.5	2002–7	Demand for organic products within former Eastern Bloc countries is patchy, but NGOs are advising on organic standards and certification while EU subsidies are encouraging growers to convert. These are informed estimates of bio hectarages as a percentage of national vineyard: Albania 5 ha/<0.15%; Armenia <9 ha; Azerbaijan <72 ha/<1%; Bulgaria <500 ha/0.5%; Croatia <32 ha; Georgia <100 ha/<1%; Hungary: see separate entry; Republic of Macedonia <1%; Moldova: current official statistics lack any credibility, perhaps due to Moldova's dependence on/ dominance by the Russian market; Romania <96 ha (all belonging to Reh Kendermann of Germany)/0.1%; Slovakia <100 ha/<5%; Slovenia <150 ha/<0.6%; Turkey: mainly table grapes.
Argentina	<2,500	<2.0	2007	Argentina's organic vineyards are found in Mendoza (75%), La Rioja (20%), Salta province (3%), and Patagonia (2%).
Australia	<1,250	<0.6	2007	If severe drought, bushfires, and water restrictions really do force Australia's export vineyards to shift away from irrigation-dependent and regionally blended cheap wines to premium, regional (especially coastal) ones, we can expect more wineries to add the organic/biodynamic cherry to the upmarket mix; especially since humus levels in compost-rich, cover-cropped soils are increasingly seen as retaining moisture more easily than weedkilled or clear-cut ones.
Austria	1,766	3.5	2006	Around 200 of Austria's 469 bio grape growers sell their grapes to wine-producing colleagues. Although an Austrian (Rudolf Steiner) invented biodynamics, few of Austria's 24 biodynamic wine estates (188 ha) enjoy international renown, with the exception of Nikolaihof. Expect significantly more bio conversions from 2007.
Canada	200	2.1	2007	The main organic players are the part-Boisset-owned Le Clos Jordanne (Niagara, Ontario), with 50 ha of Pinot Noir and Chardonnay, Summerhill Pyramid Winery (Okanagan Valley, BC), with access to around 50 ha of organic grapes, and the emerging Southbrook Farms (Niagara, Ontario) with 25 ha. Frogpond Farm is Ontario's only wine producer with organic certification for both its vineyards (12 ha) and winery.
Chile	2,498	2.5	2.5	Chile boasts the world's biggest biodynamic player in the Alvaro Espinoza-inspired Emiliana Orgánico (around 500 ha already certified, plus 500 more in conversion). Other significant producers are the organic Cono Sur (255 ha and rising), La Fortuna (137 ha), and Casa Lapostolle (116 ha), plus the biodynamic Matetic/EQ. Santa Inés/De Martino uses

Country or region	Hectares certified organic	Percentage of vineyards	Year	Comments
				only one-sixth of its 300 ha of organic Maipo Valley vineyard for wines (the rest sells as grape juice), but is developing single-vineyard old-vine cuvées from organic growers in Maule and Cachapoal.
France	18,000	3.4	2006	France's organic vineyard expanded 9% between 2005 and 2006, but a tough growing season in Bordeaux, the Loire, Champagne, and Alsace (among others) in 2007 saw many estates embarking on their first year of bio conversion backtrack when it became hard to resist the urge to spray systemic antifungals. The overall trend in France is upward, especially among growers around the climatically less demanding Mediterranean basin.
France: Alsace				A wetter-than-usual summer meant mildew and oidium were especially prevalent. Jean-Paul Zusslin of the biodynamic Domaine Zusslin in Orschwihr said that organically approved copper and sulfur sprays became much more efficient when used in combination with teas made from yarrow flowers (Achillea millefolium) and willow (Salix alba). In July 2007, Alsace had 86 wine growers as certified organic/biodynamic or in conversion. Newly certified vineyards (or those nearing the end of the three-year conversion phase) include Jean-Baptiste Adam (Ammerschwihr, biodynamic) and Adam's affiliate Kuentz-Bas (Husseren les Châteaux, biodynamic), Laurent Bannwarth (Obermorschwihr, biodynamic), Laurent Barth (Bennwihr, organic), Jean-Pierre Bechtold (Dahlenheim, organic), René Fleith-Eschard (Ingersheim, biodynamic), and Maurice Barthelme/Albert Mann (Wettolsheim, biodynamic for some grand cru sites only); 5.6% of the Alsace vineyard is now organic. Almost one-third of Alsace's organic farmers are now wine growers.
France: Beaujolais				Among the latest Beaujolais estates to begin official organic conversion are Jean-Patrick Bourbon (cousin of the already organic Jean-Christophe Bourbon at Domaine des Barronières) in Oingt; Jean-Gilles Chasselay in Châtillon d'Azergues; Cathy and Jean-Luc Gauthier of Domaine du Cret de Ruyère, Marcel Lapierre, and Michel Guignier (in part), all in Villié-Morgon; Jean-Louis Dutraive in Fleurie; and Jean-Jacques Paire of Domaine Paire-Ronzières at Ternand.
France: Bordeaux				Heavy mildew pressure in 2007 made life especially difficult in Bordeaux for all wine growers, not just the organic/biodynamic ones. Bordeaux's biggest organic wine growers, the Raymond family (SCEA Raymond) in St-Laurent du Bois, with 105 ha of vines with full organic certification, have placed another 15 ha in organic conversion. Their brands include châteaux Haut-Planton, Joumes-Fillon, de Lagarde, Monereau, and Planton-Bellevue. Vineyards converting to or newly certified organic include Château La Maison Blanche (Montagne St-Emilion and Pomerol, part biodynamic), Château Vieux Pourret (St-Emilion, biodynamic), Château Grand-Corbin-Despagne (organic, St-Emilion), Château Haut-Brisson (St-Emilion, organic), Château La Marche Canon (Canon-Fronsac, organic), Château Poupille (Côtes de Castillon, organic), Château Fourton la Garenne (Entre Deux Mers, converting from organic to biodynamic), Clos de Grange Vieille (Médoc, organic), Château Morillon (Côtes de

Country or region	Hectares certified organic	Percentage of vineyards	Year	Comments
				Blaye, organic); Château La Salle (Entre Deux Mers, organic to biodynamic); Château Champ des Treilles (Ste-Foy, biodynamic); Clos de Mounisses (Premières Côtes, biodynamic); Château Lamery (St-Macaire, biodynamic); and Château Pontet-Canet (Pauillac, biodynamic).
France: Jura				Stéphane Tissot is now working two parcels in Arbois called Les Bruyères (Savagnin, Chardonnay) and Clos de la Tour de Curon (Chardonnay) with a team of three Comtois horses. The vines were planted by Tissot from 2002 at 12,000 vines/ha with only 3 ft 3 in (1 m) between vine rows and 2 ft 7 in (80 cm) between vines. Each vine is attached to its own post and without supporting wires. Here, biodynamic sprays are applied on foot using backpack sprayers.
France: Languedoc				Sylvain Fadat has put his 22-ha Domaine de l'Aupilhac in the Coteaux du Languedoc cru of Montpeyroux into organic certification with the aim of going biodynamic. Fadat's friend and near neighbor Bernard Bellahsen of the already biodynamic and 100% horse-powered Domaine de Fontedicto will advise, although Fadat is opting for an ATV rather than a horse for spraying herbal vineyard teas.
France: Loire				Eric Nicolas of Domaine de Bellivière in Jasnières/Coteaux du Loir is on course for having the most densely planted organic Chenin Blanc in the world, at 40,000 vines/hectare (although the plot covers only 0.07 ha). The domaine's other 12 ha began the three-year conversion to organic certification in 2005. Nicolas is being advised on the use of biodynamic compost and herbal teas by François Chidaine of Montlouis.
France: Rhône				Notable domaines in the Rhône in conversion to organics/biodynamics include Philippe Laurent's Domaine de Gramenon in Montbrison sur Lez (Demeter biodynamic), Daniel Boulle's Domaine Les Aphillanthes in Cairanne (biodynamic), Domaine Marcel Richaud in Cairanne (organic), and Hélène Thibon's Mas de Libian in St-Marcel d'Ardèche (biodynamic).
France: Roussillon				In 2007, the Pyrénées-Orientales département had a combined 936 ha of vines with organic certification or in conversion. The biggest players are Domaine Cazes (170 ha) and Domaine La Rourède (60 ha). Of the 54 wine growers, 13 were in conversion from 2007, the most notable of which were Sam Harrop MW, Tom Lubbe and Nathalie Gauby's Domaine Matassa, Jean Gardiés's eponymously named domaine, Claude Olivier's Château du Mas Deu, Jacques de Chancel's Domaine de l'Ausseil, Denis Ferrer's Domaine Ferrer Ribière, and Loïc Roure's Domaine du Possible.
France: Savoie				The most notable Savoie estate completing its three-year organic conversion in 2007 was the Michel Grisard-inspired 5.7-ha Domaine des Ardoisières in Cevins.
France: Southwest				Domaine Larrédya in Jurançon began official organic conversion for part of the 8.5-ha domaine. "The work we have done over the past few years—like loosening compacted soils by sowing deep-rooting winter cover crops, spreading compost, and use of biodynamic teas—vindicates our step-by-step approach to organics and has given us the platform to

Country or region	Hectares certified organic	Percentage of vineyards	Year	Comments
				apply for certification with confidence," says owner Jean-Marc Grussaute. Jean-Mary Le Bihan and his wife Catherine, who breed horses and grow organic cereals, have put their 16-ha vineyard, Domaine Mouthes Le Bihan, in Duras, created in 1997, into organic conversion.
Germany	<2,500	<2.5	2007	Germany's bio vineyards are concentrated in climatically benign southern regions like Baden-Württemberg and Pfalz. More than 10% (and rising) of Germany's bio vineyards belong to the Verband Deutscher Prädikats- und Qualitätsweingüter. VDP president Steffen Christmann sees the greening of Germany's vineyards as "no longer a flash in the pan, but a very widespread trend," perhaps because terroir-oriented bio farming makes the VDP's delineation of Grosse Gewächs ("Great Growths") vineyard sites worthwhile.
Greece	2,272	3.5	2006	Names to look for include Porto Carras (Thessaloniki) and Tsantalis (100 ha in various regions) for volume, and Gerovassiliou (Thessaloniki), Cosmetatos (Cephalonia), Hatzidakis (Santorini), and Moraitis (Paros) for quality.
Hungary	<1,000	<1.0	2006	Hungary's tradition of breeding disease-resistant grape varieties would appear to make it a potential Eastern European organic wine star. Austria's Franz Rheinhard Weniger's recently established project in Balf, near Sopron, comprises 22 ha of vineyards (biodynamic since 2006) and a smart new winery.
Italy	c. 35,000	<5.0	2005	Italy's organic vineyards are in freefall—from nearly 45,000 ha in 2001, to less than 32,000 in 2004. It seems growers who took subsidies for converting bailed out when faced with paying fees to maintain full organic certification after the three-year conversion process was over. However, from 2004 to 2005 organic hectarage increased by 8%.
New Zealand	<350	<2.5	2007	After several attempts, New Zealand's organic grape growers and winemakers finalized a set of organic standards in 2006. These give benchmarks for both grape growing and winemaking.
Portugal	<1,200	<0.6	2006	The Fladgate Partnership's release of its Fonseca Terra Prima premium ruby organic port in 2007 is a landmark event, partly because there are so few premium-brand organic wines worldwide outside France, but mainly because organic grape spirit distilled from certified organic grapes was used for fortification, even though there was no requirement to do this under EU organic rules.
South Africa	<500	<0.5	2007	Stellar Organics' continued expansion—in terms of the number of grape growers (more than 10) it is successfully encouraging to convert—and its range (now with brilliant unsulfited wines) and export sales should help allay the ingrained skepticism about the viability of organics in the Cape. The expanding environmentally and socially aware Reyneke, the reliable Laibach, super-premium Tulbagh Mountain Vineyard, offbeat Rozendal, and the idyllic Org de Rac are names to follow. Backsberg's (tiny) organic program is on hold.

Country or region	Hectares certified organic	Percentage of vineyards	Year	Comments
Spain	<20,000	<1.9	2006	*Cooperatives in La Mancha and estate wineries in Rioja and Penedès continue to drive Spain's organic wine scene. Organic sherry-style wines exist (from Bodegas Gabriel Gómez in Villaviciosa de Cordoba), as does organic sherry vinegar (Hidalgo)—but no organic sherry.*
Switzerland	<350	<2.5	2006	*More than 10% of Swiss farmland is certified organic, while 10% of Switzerland's biodynamic farms are vineyards (100 ha).*
United Kingdom	<30	<4.0	2007	*The UK's half-dozen certified organic vineyards are confined to England, but only Chevelswarde, Davenport, and Sedlescombe ferment and bottle their own wines. Ryedale Vineyard in Yorkshire is set to become Europe's most northerly wine producer with organic status from 2009.*
Uruguay	26	<0.3	2007	*Uruguay's first certified organic wine producer, Vinos de la Cruz, produces a slowly improving Cabernet Sauvignon from 4 ha of certified organic vines (part of a 26-ha portion) in Florida. Uruguay's oldest (but by no means best) winery, Los Cerros de San Juan in Colonia, is also developing an organic Cabernet.*
US: California	3,900	2.0	2008	*California's organic wine-grape vineyards account for 1.9% of the state's organic farm acreage (organic raisin, table, and juice grapes account for another 1.3%). Although only around 0.1% of California's wine vineyards have US Demeter Association biodynamic certification, this figure does include heavy hitters such as Bonterra's McNab and Butler Ranches, Benziger, Jimmy Fetzer's Ceago del Lago, Grgich, Quivira, and the pioneering, steadily improving Frey.*
US: Oregon	388	<7.0	2006	*The big player here is King Estate (174 ha), followed by Cooper Mountain (48 ha), Cornucopia (47 ha), Sokol Blosser (32 ha), Croft (18 ha), Brick House (11 ha), Bergström (9 ha), and Cattrall (9 ha).*

Grapevine

• **Vanya Cullen** of the eponymous Western Australian winery is now making her own biodynamic horn manure and trying to fulfill the biodynamic ideal of being as self-sufficient and polycultural as possible: food crops such as fava beans and Roma tomatoes are being grown between the vine rows.

• Winemaker **Mike Brown** of Gemtree Vineyards in South Australia's McLaren Vale, which has 10 ha dedicated to wetlands and 50 ha of vines under biodynamic management, says that "after a trip to see European distributors, we were convinced of the need for certification." Gemtree is now under official bio conversion with Australia's biggest bio certifier, NASAA.

• **Alessandro Barosi,** whose various careers span textiles, running Alpine refuges, and the Slow Food movement, now has all of his 5-ha Cascina Corte vineyard in Piedmont's Dolcetto di Dogliani subregion under organic certification. The oldest Dolcetto vines here date from 1947.

• **The Organic Trade Association** says that, in the US alone, retail sales of organic and biodynamic wines have more than doubled since 2002, reaching $90.4 million in 2006.

Opinion:
Less plowing, please

Organic rules rightly outlaw synthetic weedkillers. They contaminate groundwater and destroy the soil life that maintains healthy soil structure and helps prevent erosion. Weedkillers even disrupt the way vines grow, making them more disease-prone. But leaving weeds to grow too high increases the risk of spring frosts. Weeds also reduce grape yields by competing with vines for water and food. Weedkillers are the cheapest way of controlling weeds, which is why they remain popular.

You might think that burning weeds off with flamethrowers would be banned under the bio rulebook, but you'd be wrong. Although rarely practiced, the flamethrower option shows how being organic and being "green" (environmentally friendly) are two different things.

In terms of emissions, there is an even bigger culprit: plowing weeds by tractor. It takes three times longer than spot-spraying with weedkiller, burns more diesel, and causes more greenhouse-gas emissions, yet it's the most common way to control weeds organically. Over time, plowing can be just as erosive as weedkilling.

Organic growers who plow weeds off in the heat of summer, thinking that the vines will then benefit from rain, should think again. Often the rain water never reaches its intended target, since compacted topsoil blocks it. Soil compacts because plowing releases the soil microbes' main food source, carbon, into the atmosphere, contributing to climate change. "Every year we put back all that food plowing might inadvertently take from the soil, and more, with our compost," bio wine growers claim. Of course, compost from animal manure is a great source of fertility for vineyards, but the gastric gases cows, sheep, and pigs produce to make the manure are potentially big climate-change offenders. Far better to cut out the middleman and allow the animals into the vines over winter, so the manure goes directly onto the soil in manageable amounts. They won't eat the vines, because the grapes have been picked, but they will eat the weeds.

There is a braver option—especially for those few vineyards with balanced soil health: leave the weeds alone altogether. Chianti estate Terra d'Acoiris has done this for the past 20 years. No plowing, no mowing, nothing. One benefit of nonintervention is deeper vine roots, smaller grapes, more concentrated wines, and lower yields—all bonuses.

And leaving the soil alone also means less of the diesel and dust that fuel climate change.

GREATEST WINE PRODUCERS

1. Domaine Leroy (Burgundy, France)
2. Domaine Marcel Deiss (Alsace, France)
3. Domaine Zind Humbrecht (Alsace, France)
4. Ferme de la Sansonnière/ Marc Angeli (Loire, France)
5. Domaine Huet (Loire, France)
6. Nikolaihof (Wachau, Austria)
7. Domaine Leflaive (Burgundy, France)
8. Domaine des Epeneaux/Comte Armand (Burgundy, France)
9. Coturri (Sonoma Valley, California)
10. Emiliana Orgánico (Central Valley, Chile)

FASTEST-IMPROVING PRODUCERS

1. Santa Inés/De Martino (Maipo Valley, Chile)
2. Josmeyer (Alsace, France)
3. Château Franc la Fleur (Bordeaux, France)
4. Tulbagh Mountain Vineyard (Western Cape, South Africa)
5. Viña La Fortuna (Central Valley, Chile)
6. Domaine Bott-Geyl (Alsace, France)
7. Domaine Clusel-Roch (Rhône, France)
8. Château de Bellevue (Lussac St-Emilion, France)
9. Cullen (Margaret River, Australia)
10. Carl Rey Winery (Oprisor, Romania)

NEW UP-AND-COMING PRODUCERS

1. Domaine de Bellivière/Eric Nicolas (Loire, France)
2. Domaine d'Aupilhac (Languedoc, France)
3. Domaine Mouthes le Bihan (Southwest France)
4. Domaine Matassa (Roussillon, France)
5. Ryedale Vineyard (Yorkshire, England)
6. Laurent Barth (Alsace, France)
7. Gemtree (McLaren Vale, Australia)
8. Domaine des Trois Orris (Roussillon, France)
9. Domaine La Pépière/Marc Ollivier (Muscadet, France)
10. Cascina Corte (Piedmont, Italy)

BEST-VALUE PRODUCERS

1. Emiliana Orgánico (Central Valley, Chile)
2. La Riojana Cooperative (La Rioja, Argentina)
3. Stellar Organics (Western Cape, South Africa)
4. Domaine Huet (Loire, France)
5. Bodegas Bagordi (Rioja, Spain)
6. Domaine Zusslin (Alsace, France)
7. Mas de Libian (Ardèche, France)
8. Domaine Jean Bousquet (Tupungato, Mendoza, Argentina)
9. Perlage (Veneto, Italy)
10. Jacques Frélin (Midi, France)

GREATEST-QUALITY WINES

1. **Clos de la Roche 2000** Domaine Leroy, Burgundy, France (€415)
2. **Alsace Grand Cru Altenberg de Bergheim 2000** Domaine Marcel Deiss, Alsace, France (€61)
3. **Alsace Pinot Gris Clos Jebsal Trie Spéciale SGN 2002** Domaine Zind Humbrecht, Alsace, France (€93 per half-bottle)
4. **Zinfandel Estate Vineyards 2005** Coturri, Sonoma Valley, California (US$32)
5. **Steiner Hund Riesling Reserve 2001** Nikolaihof, Wachau, Austria (€40)
6. **The McNab 2003** Bonterra Vineyards, Mendocino, California (US$36.99)
7. **Chevalier-Montrachet 2000** Domaine Leflaive, Burgundy, France (€310)

⑧ G Colchagua Valley Tinto 2003 Emiliana Orgánico, Central Valley, Chile (CLP 48,500)

⑨ Fonseca Terra Prima Ruby Port NV Fladgate Partnership, Portugal (€13.80)

⑩ Alsace Riesling Grand Cru Pfingstberg 2006 Domaine Zusslin, Alsace, France (€26.50)

BEST BARGAINS

① Piave Rosso 2006 La Cantina Pizzolato, Veneto, Italy (€3.86)

② Malbec 2005 Caligiore, Luján de Cuyo, Argentina (AP 22)

③ Vouvray Clos du Bourg Demi-Sec 1996 Domaine Huet, Loire, France (€22)

④ Coteaux du Loir Blanc L'Effraie 2005 Domaine de Bellivière, Loire, France (€14)

⑤ Prosecco di Valdobbiadene Spumante Col di Manza NV Perlage, Veneto, Italy (€8.30)

⑥ Vin de Pays de l'Ardèche Rouge Vin de Pétanque 2006 Mas de Libian, Ardèche, France (€3)

⑦ Côte Rôtie 2003 Domaine Clusel-Roch, Rhône, France (€29)

⑧ Adobe Syrah Colchagua Valley 2005 Emiliana Orgánico, Central Valley, Chile (CLP 3,800)

⑨ Dão Rosado 2006 Casa de Mouraz, Dão, Portugal (€5)

⑩ Dolcetto di Dogliani 2006 Cascina Corte, Piedmont, Italy (€5)

MOST EXCITING OR UNUSUAL FINDS

① Alsace Pinot Gris Grand Cru Sonnenglanz 2004 Domaine Bott-Geyl, Alsace, France (€18.70) *Pinpoint picking provides perfect weight and sweetness. Soft pressing balances fruit and mineral flavors.*

② No Added Sulphur Cabernet Sauvignon 2007 Stellar Organics, Western Cape, South Africa (R22) *South Africa's first wine from certified organic, certified fair-trade grapes. No added sulfur dioxide.*

③ Malbec 2006 Domaine Jean Bousquet, Tupungato, Mendoza, Argentina (AP 25) *Whether it's the altitude of the vineyards or Jean Bousquet's French heritage, this Malbec is notably refined.*

④ Mount Barker Syrah 2005 Ngeringa, Australia (A$40) *The first estate-grown release from Erinn and Janet Klein's impeccably run, from-scratch biodynamic vineyard.*

⑤ Prosecco di Valdobbiadene Spumante Col di Manza NV Perlage, Veneto, Italy (€8.30) *Perlage is Italy's biggest producer of organic Prosecco. This one (19 g/l residual sugar) is its first from bio grapes.*

⑥ Neuburger Burggarten 2006 Nikolaihof, Wachau, Austria (€16) *Exotic peaches-and-cream flavors from the oddball Pinot Blanc x Silvaner crossing Neuburger.*

⑦ Malbec 2005 Caligiore, Luján de Cuyo, Argentina (AP 22) *Made from Malbec vineyards planted in Mendoza's prime Luján de Cuyo subregion (3,610 ft [1,100 m] high) in the 1930s, and organic by default (through lack of funds).*

⑧ Côtes de Castillon 2005 Château Franc la Fleur, Bordeaux, France (€10) *Refined, full-flavored red from low-yield (30 hl/ha), high-density (6,600 vines/ha) Merlot, Cabernet Franc, and Cabernet Sauvignon vineyards.*

⑨ Vin de Pays des Allobrogies Rouge 2006 Domaine des Ardoisières, Savoie, France (€18) *Fifty percent each of Mondeuse Rouge and (resurrected by Michel Grisard) Persan, destemmed and cool-fermented for extra smoothness.*

⑩ Côtes du Forez Rouge Mémoire de Madone 2006 Gilles Bonnefoy, Loire, France (€8.50) *Deceptively powerful Gamay planted in the 1940s on volcanic soil; 11.5 percent ABV, as unchaptalized.*

Wine & Health

Beverley Blanning MW

News of the positive health effects of wine consumption is increasingly overshadowed by reports of the very real dangers of binge drinking.

BEVERLEY BLANNING MW

This will be no surprise to regular readers of these pages, but the risks associated with excessive drinking, especially among the young, have given rise to widespread public concern. An indication of this concern in the UK was the formation of the Alcohol Health Alliance in November 2007. This organization of high-profile healthcare bodies aims to highlight the harmful effects of hazardous drinking and to increase taxation on alcoholic drinks. This change in attitudes does not mean that wine's health benefits have diminished. Rather, the shift in focus toward the negative health consequences of consuming alcohol highlights the most commonly reported research finding: the benefits of moderation.

Time and again, studies point to moderate alcohol consumption as offering the most positive outcome for a wide range of health conditions. The line between positive and negative consumption, however, is a fine one, even for responsible drinkers. It is here that the greatest confusion lies. As reported previously, there is widespread ignorance of what binge drinking means; most people assume a binge to be a heavier level of consumption than that defined by governments and researchers, although, maddeningly, there is no single agreed definition.

The definition of a unit, or a standard drink, also varies from country to country. With rising alcohol levels in wine, drinkers need to

BEVERLEY BLANNING MW is a wine writer based in London. She writes for a number of publications and tastes and travels widely. She also lectures, judges at international wine competitions, and organizes tasting events. Beverley became a Master of Wine in 2001, specializing for her dissertation on the effects of wine on cardiovascular health.

be increasingly vigilant if they wish to stay within recommended drinking limits. An added confusion is that wine producers have some flexibility in labeling the percentage of alcohol in their wine, and they will often understate the level of alcohol, either to avoid higher taxes or to attract the growing number of consumers who prefer wines with lower levels of alcohol. If one is interested in drinking moderately, it makes sense to search out wines with lower alcohol levels. Tightening regulations on labeling would help consumers to understand the potential effects of their drinking on their health, either positive or negative.

Post-heart-attack angina risk reduced

An American study by Buchanan et al. looked at the risk of angina following a heart attack. The researchers found that subjects who consumed moderate levels of alcohol (defined as one to four drinks per day) were 45 percent less likely to have angina in the year following their heart attack. Consuming more than four drinks per day was associated with an 81 percent greater risk of angina. These results were the same for men and women, except for binge drinkers (defined as those consuming six or more drinks on one occasion at least once a month). For male binge drinkers, the risk of angina was 34 percent higher than for non-bingers; for women, the equivalent figure was 55 percent, highlighting once again women's more fragile constitutions regarding alcohol consumption.

Postmenopausal benefits of moderate drinking

A study by Akesson et al. has provided a useful addition to the limited evidence that women, as well as men, derive cardio-protection from moderate alcohol consumption. The study followed healthy, post-menopausal women in Sweden over six years. A low-risk lifestyle—consuming 5 g or more of alcohol per day; eating a healthy, Mediterranean-style diet; not smoking; avoiding obesity; and engaging in daily exercise—was associated with a 92 percent reduction in risk of heart attack compared with women not pursuing this lifestyle. The research confirmed an earlier study of male health professionals in the US (reported here last year), which showed alcohol to be a key component of the combination of the five healthy lifestyle measures.

Grapevine

• **A pooled analysis** of 12 studies, covering half a million women and 230,000 men, showed that there is an association between moderate alcohol consumption and reduced risk of renal cell cancer. Consumption of at least 15 g of alcohol per day reduced risk, with no differences apparent by beverage type or between the sexes.

MODERATE ALCOHOL CONSUMPTION AND ENDOTHELIAL FUNCTION

A German study looked at the effect of alcohol on endothelial function on obese type 2 diabetics. Coronary disease is the leading cause of death among diabetics. The subjects were given two units of red wine daily for six weeks. At the end of the period, the patients showed a marked increase in flow-mediated dilation of the brachial artery (this is a standard measure of endothelial function). This would suggest a lower risk of coronary disease from moderate wine consumption.

Further support for the hypothesis that alcohol consumption is good for the functioning of the lining of the arteries has been provided by a multi-ethnic population study in New York. The Northern Manhattan Study showed that subjects consuming up to two drinks per day also had improved flow-mediated dilation of the brachial artery. There was no beneficial effect seen beyond two drinks per day.

ALCOHOL CAUSES SOME CANCERS—US REPORT

There is strengthening evidence that alcohol of any kind is a cause of various types of cancer. This is the view expressed in the second report of the World Cancer Research Fund and the American Institute for Cancer Research on the effects of diet on cancer. The report, which reviews research from around the world, concludes, "The evidence that alcoholic drinks are a cause of cancers of the mouth, pharynx and larynx, esophagus, colorectum (men), and breast is convincing."

Further evidence of breast cancer's link to alcohol was provided in a recent study by Klatsky et al., which showed that alcohol is associated with increased risk of breast cancer, regardless of the amount drunk or the type of alcohol consumed. The risk of subjects' developing breast cancer increased according to the amount drunk, rising from a 10 percent higher risk for one drink per day (compared with non-drinkers) to 30 percent for those consuming more than three drinks per day.

LIVER DISEASE: COULD J-SHAPED CURVE APPLY?

While it is widely known that excessive alcohol consumption can result in liver disease, the effect of low to moderate consumption has not been well understood. A study of Japanese men by Suzuki et al. showed that, while excessive alcohol consumption was associated with an increase in abnormal liver function tests, light to moderate drinking was associated with a decrease in the risk, compared to non-drinkers. If more studies back up these findings, there will be a case for saying that the J-shaped curve exists, contrary to expectations, for liver disease.

BENEFITS OF DRINKING WINE WITH FOOD

An American study by Brand-Miller et al. looked at the effect of alcohol consumption on blood glucose levels following a carbohydrate meal (in this case, bread). High blood glucose is associated with risk of diabetes and coronary heart disease. The authors found that blood glucose levels were up to 37 percent lower when beer, wine, or gin was served prior to or with the food. If alcohol was served an hour prior to eating, the greatest reduction in blood glucose was seen with beer; if alcohol was served with the meal, the greatest reduction was seen with wine.

In another study, this time with previously abstaining type 2 diabetics, Shai et al. found that those who were given one unit of alcohol to drink with their evening meal experienced lower levels of fasting blood glucose over a three-month period than those who drank no alcohol. The most beneficial effect was seen among participants with the most severe disease.

WINE AND DEMENTIA: POSITIVE NEWS

A study from the Department of Geriatrics in Bari, Italy, found that elderly subjects with mild cognitive impairment (MCI) experienced differing levels of cognitive decline according to whether or not they drank alcohol. Those who consumed one alcoholic drink per day developed dementia at an 85 percent slower rate than those who did not drink alcohol. Wine was the preferred choice of beverage for 85 percent of the participants. Those who consumed more than one drink per day developed dementia at a 53–56 percent slower rate compared with non-drinkers. The authors could offer no explanation for the findings but pointed out that there may be limitations to the study: wine drinkers tend to be more sociable and also follow a more Mediterranean diet, both of which are associated with slower mental decline.

WINE HEALTHIER THAN BEER OR LIQUOR

It has always proved difficult to compare the health effects of different alcoholic drinks accurately, since drinking preferences are often associated with socioeconomic status and other lifestyle factors. But a 29-year Finnish study has attempted to minimize these limiting factors by choosing as subjects a group of men with similar (high) social class and drinking habits. The men, age 40–55 in 1974, were studied for cardiovascular risk factors, mental health, and general health. The men who had stated they preferred wine experienced the lowest death rates due to lower cardiovascular mortality compared to those who preferred beer or liquor. The authors concluded that, for the group studied, wine preference was associated with better quality of life in old age.

Grapevine

• **Information on units of alcohol** and safe drinking levels will be carried by wine sold in the UK by the end of 2008. A voluntary agreement has been reached between the government and the drinks industry.

• **A California study** by Siu and colleagues concluded that moderate consumption of beer, wine, or liquor may assist lung function. The study found that, of 178,000 subjects questioned, those who consumed one or two drinks a day had the healthiest lung function. The researchers concluded that the protective effect of light to moderate drinking translates to around a 20 percent reduction in the risk of developing lung disease.

Opinion:
Current practices that should stop

- Sensationalist media reporting of issues relating to wine and health.
- Ban on ingredient labeling—of particular interest to vegetarians, buyers of organic food, and those with allergies.
- Misleading information on wine bottles relating to the health risks of wine.
- Producer flexibility on labeling alcohol by volume.

Things that should be happening

- Clearer dissemination of information on the meaning of moderate drinking and, especially, binge drinking; greater recognition of the differences between men's and women's health in relation to alcohol consumption.
- Up-to-date and unbiased reporting of the benefits of moderate wine consumption and what moderation means.
- International standardization of the definitions of a unit of alcohol and moderate consumption. Both vary enormously from country to country, causing consumer confusion over safe or desirable consumption levels.
- Unit labeling on bottles to indicate number of units per bottle, or number of grams of alcohol per bottle—an issue of growing importance as alcohol levels in wine continue to rise.
- A legal requirement for precise percentage alcohol measures on labels.
- Greater focus on research into the different effects of drinking on women's health.
- Greater focus on the effects of drinking on different age groups.
- More research distinguishing between wine and other drinks.
- More research that looks at patterns of consumption. Specifically, given the focus on the dangers of binge drinking, there is a need to understand how wine is now consumed compared to its traditional patterns.
- Research on the benefits of red versus white wine, and different types of red wine identified in research where possible.

Grapevine

- **An Australian study** by O'Callaghan et al. measured the attention, ability, and learning of a group of 14-year-old children. The researchers found no association between maternal intake of alcohol at less than one drink per day and adverse effects on the children. Some effects were seen at more than one drink per day, and unsurprisingly, the greatest likelihood of problems occurred among the children of binge-drinking mothers.

TOP WINE HEALTH BENEFITS

1 Increased longevity from regular, moderate consumption for men over 45 and postmenopausal women.

2 Significant protection from cardiovascular diseases (and consequently greater longevity) with moderate consumption for men over 40 and postmenopausal women.

3 Drinkers, especially wine drinkers, have lowered risk of many other diseases, including stress-related illnesses and the common cold.

TOP WINE HEALTH HYPES

1 Drinking is good for you— it always depends on individual circumstances.

2 The benefits of consumption are accrued equally by young and old, and men and women; research indicates the elderly benefit the most and premenopausal women seem to accrue few, if any, net health gains from drinking alcohol.

3 Resveratrol is the most important beneficial agent in wine.

4 Wine is necessarily a better option than beer or liquor—all alcoholic drinks can be beneficial.

5 Red wine is significantly better than white in providing health-related benefits.

6 The idea that regular, moderate consumption of wine is an acceptable substitute for improving health outcomes in place of changing diet and other lifestyle factors, such as regular exercise.

TOP WINE HEALTH DANGERS

1 Most dangers come from excessive consumption. Excessive will mean different things for different people. Risks include alcoholism; risk of accidents; violent crime; domestic violence; child abuse; suicide and depression; severe damage to every system in the body.

2 Increased risk of breast cancer, even at low levels of consumption. This is of greatest significance to young women, who have less to gain from the protective effects of alcohol against cardiovascular disease.

3 Increased risk of health problems for women drinkers at relatively low consumption levels.

4 Ignorance of sensible drinking levels, especially underestimating the dangers of excessive drinking and what constitutes a binge.

5 Increasing levels of dangerous consumption among the young, who appear to have little, if anything, to gain in terms of health benefits and much to lose.

TOP WINE HEALTH MYTHS

1 Drinking is bad for you.

2 Drinking is good for you.

3 Drinking any alcohol while pregnant significantly increases the risk of FAS.

Grapevine

• **Mukamal et al.** found, in a study of Americans over 65, a U-shaped relationship between alcohol use and risk of hip fracture, with those consuming up to 14 drinks a week experiencing a 20 percent lower risk of hip fracture. This is thought to be because alcohol increases bone mineral density through an increase in estrogen levels.

Grape Varieties

Dr. François Lefort

Grape-research hotspots, such as INRA Montpellier in France or Cornell University in Geneva, New York, continue to produce new varieties and rootstocks.

DR. FRANÇOIS LEFORT

INRA Montpellier is ready to release two new black wine-grape varieties and a new rootstock that is resistant to fanleaf disease. Alain Bouquet, one of the last French grape breeders, is excited about the 2008 release of two as-yet-unnamed wine-grape varieties.

Still labeled with its laboratory name, the first of these new varieties (Bdx 8381) was registered at Comité Technique Permanent de la Sélection (CTPS) in December 2007. A 1969 INRA cross between Merlot and Fer Servadou, it has been under testing for several years in southwestern France. Two of its characteristics are particularly interesting: it has good aromatic potential and high acidity, which make it a suitable grape for the higher summer temperatures that southern France is experiencing due to climate change.

The second variety, Mtp 68-11, will go for registration in December 2008. The result of a 1974 cross between Cabernet Sauvignon and Mourvèdre, it ripens later than Marselan but is comparable in aromatics, color, and tannin. Its advantages over Marselan are that it accumulates less sugar and produces wines weaker in alcohol. Sugar-accumulating varieties such as Marselan can easily reach 15 percent alcohol in hot summers.

These new INRA releases will be confined to *vin de pays* and *vin de table* areas, following the fate of all the excellent INRA creations over the past 40 years.

DR. FRANÇOIS LEFORT is a professor at the University of Applied Sciences of Western Switzerland in Geneva. He has been working on the diversity of grapevine varieties for many years. François is the creator of the Greek Vitis database and the coauthor of the Bulgarian Grapevine database. He is now more involved in describing new pathogens affecting grapevines and other plants.

Alain Bouquet is particularly proud of the new rootstock Mtp 3146-1-87, deposited in December 2007. This rootstock comes from a cross of a *Vitis vinifera* x *Muscadinia rotundifolia* F1 hybrid by the famous rootstock 140 Ruggeri (1987). Its main characteristic is its resistance to the nematode worm *Xiphinema index*, which gives a high resistance to grape fanleaf virus, responsible for fanleaf or *court-noué* disease. Large-scale trials, using an assortment of French varieties grafted on to the rootstock, were carried out in 2007 and 2008 in several vineyards (Alsace, Bordeaux, Beaujolais, Burgundy, Champagne, Côtes du Rhône, Languedoc-Roussillon, Midi-Pyrénées, and Val de Loire). Products resulting from classical breeding can still compete with GM products; in this case, the genetically modified rootstock for fanleaf disease resistance is not yet ready for use in vineyards.

Marselan makes progress

Marselan, a cross between Cabernet Sauvignon and Grenache Noir and the last wine-grape variety to be registered by INRA Montpellier, was listed in the ONIVINS catalog in 1997. Since then, it has increased to 1,350 ha in the southern region of Languedoc-Roussillon. It was number 11 in wine varieties sold in nurseries in 2005/06, with 3.5 million grafted shoots produced. That is a tremendous success for a variety limited to *vin de pays* and *vin de table* areas.

Three new varieties from Cornell University

Bruce Reisch, professor of grape breeding and genetics at Cornell University, has released three new wine-grape varieties—Noiret, Corot Noir, and Valvin Muscat—that have been bred for their suitability for the soils and cold climate of eastern American wine regions. They should provide consumers with wines superior to those traditionally produced in these regions. The new varieties are interspecific hybrids resulting from complex crosses carried out in Cornell more than 30 years ago—a benefit of the long experience of Cornell University, the leading grape-breeding institution in the United States.

Noiret is meant to be a midseason black wine grape and was obtained in 1973 from a cross between NY65.0467.08 (Chancellor x NY33277) and Steuben (Sheridan x Wayne). The complete pedigree is available at www.nysaes.cornell.edu/hort/faculty/reisch/bulletin/Noiret.pdf.

Corot Noir (NY70.0809.10) is a mid- to late-season black wine grape resulting from a 1970 cross between Seyve Villard 18-307 (Villard Blanc x Chancellor) and Steuben (Sheridan x Wayne). The complete pedigree is available at www.nysaes.cornell.edu/hort/faculty/reisch/bulletin/Corot_noir.pdf.

Wine trials were performed for several years by Professor Thomas Henick-Kling, professor of oenology at New York State Agricultural Experiment Station. Reisch and Henick-Kling claim that these varieties produce wines free of the hybrid aromas typical of many other black hybrid grapes and that Corot Noir can be used for varietal wine production or for blending.

The third interspecific variety, Valvin Muscat, is a midseason white-wine grape with a distinctive Muscat flavor and aroma, usable for blending or varietal wines. It resulted from a 1962 cross between Couderc 299-35 (= Muscat du Moulin) (Pedro Ximénez x Couderc 603 [= *Vitis rupestris* x Bourrisquou]) and Muscat Ottonel.

Wide range of grapes in UK

Grapevine nurseries in the UK offer a diverse range of grapevines, especially the remarkable Sunnybank Vine Nurseries run by Brian and Annie Edwards (vinenursery.netfirms.com), which has been granted the status of National Grape Vine Collection for the UK by the National Council for the Conservation of Plants and Gardens.

Most of the varieties are very rare, grown mainly in cold areas of the Northern Hemisphere and originating from French, German, Russian, Canadian, and American breeding programs in the 20th century. The nursery catalog recommends a number of varieties for red wines, white wines, and table grapes in the UK, but it also lists several little-known grapes. The main recommended varieties are listed below.

White varieties

Aurore: (Seibel 5279 = Aurora; hybrid of *Vitis lincecumii*, *Vitis rupestris*, and *Vitis vinifera*) An early-20th-century hybrid for wine or table grapes.

Bianca: (Eger 2 x Bouviertraube) A recent disease-resistant white hybrid variety for wine from Hungary; also being evaluated in Denmark.

Kanzler: (Müller-Thurgau x Silvaner = Alzey S.3983; cross from 1927) A German white-wine variety.

Madeleine Angevine: (Madeleine Royale x Précoce de Malingre, Vibert, 20th century) Early 20th-century white variety for wine or table grapes.

Phoenix: (= Geilweilerhof GA 49-22 = Bacchus x Villard Blanc; 1994) White hybrid suitable for wine or table grapes.

Seyval Blanc: (Seyve Villard 5-276 = Seibel 5656 x Seibel 4986) Wine or table grape; formerly Seyve-Villard 5/276. A disease-resistant and very productive white hybrid.

Solaris: (Merzling x GM 6493 [= Saperavi Severny x Muscat Ottonel]) A recent disease-resistant New German white-wine hybrid grape.

Zalagyongye: A new Hungarian white hybrid for wine or table grapes.

Black varieties

Brant: (Clinton x Black St. Peter, Ontario hybrid around 1869) Black grape variety suitable for wine or table grapes.

Gagarin Blue: Russian black variety suitable for wine or table grapes.

Kempsey Black: Dessert/wine grape. Mid-to-late, vigorous, disease-free hybrid. Large bunches of large grapes of excellent quality. No hybrid flavor. A new introduction, highly recommended.

Regent: (Gf 67-198-3; [Silvaner x Müller-Thurgau] x Chambourcin [= Joannes Seyve 26205]; BAFZ Geilweilerhof) Disease-resistant wine hybrid variety.

Rembrandt: (FMX633; Gary Taurick) Black variety for wine or table grapes.

Rondo: (= Geisenheim 6494-5; Saperavi Severnyi [= *Vitis amurensis* x Précoce de Malingre?] x St Laurent [= Pinot St Laurent], 1965, BAFZ Geilweilerhof) A *Vitis amurensis* hybrid wine variety.

Seibel 13053: (= Cascade) Disease-resistant hybrid wine variety.

Triomphe d'Alsace: (MG 101-14 x Knipperle = Kuhlmann 319-1) Hybrid wine variety.

***Vitis purpurea* (Spetchley Park):** Black variety for wine or table grapes.

Some 82 more white varieties and 58 more black varieties for wine and table grapes are available from the nursery, mostly interspecific hybrids from the US, France, Russia, Germany, or eastern European countries.

French classics in China

China's winemaking tradition stretches back at least to 138 BC, when Emperor Han-Wu established vineyards in Shaanxi province. Present Chinese wine production is steadily increasing at 12–15 percent per year, with 190,000 ha of vineyards. Until recently, all Chinese wine was consumed domestically, but the Chinese are beginning to export wine to neighboring Asian countries.

China now has well-established wineries, often advised by French oenologists and viticulturists. No surprise, then, that Chinese wine is mainly based on the French varieties traditionally enjoyed by Chinese urban wine connoisseurs: Cabernet Franc, Cabernet Sauvignon, Chardonnay, Gamay, Merlot, Pinot Noir, Syrah, and Riesling. Most prominent Chinese wineries (Changyu, Great Wall, Huadong, Dragon Seal, Imperial Court, Lou-Lan) result from collaborations during the past 20 years between French and Chinese companies.

An indication of the interest the Chinese are taking in developing their vineyards is the Sino-French demonstration vineyard supported by both governments. This experimental vineyard was established by the French organization ONIVINS on carefully chosen soils and will test about 30 French varieties thought to suit Chinese climatic and soil conditions.

Untapped resources in Turkey

Very little is known about viticulture in Turkey, although grapes are one of the main crops, covering 560,000 ha and producing about 3.5 million tons per year. The bulk of production is for table grapes or raisins, although wine production is increasing and now stands at 275 million liters per year. Turkey is quite rich in grapevine genetic resources, and ampelographic collections have about 1,200 varieties, of which very little is known. Only 40 are used for wine production. A single seedless variety, Sultana (known as Thompson Seedless in the United States), cultivated mainly for table grapes, is dominant over the entire country. A small proportion is used for white-wine production.

Since Anatolia was one of the cradles of domesticated grapevines, Turkish researchers think that wild grapevines in the region may provide favorable characteristics such as resistance to powdery mildew, downy mildew, and dead arm. There is an abundance of wild grapevines in the country in phylloxera-free areas. Breeding studies using the embryo rescue technique for the creation of hybrids produced new varieties in the 1990s.

Turkey is expanding its wine-production area and is basing its new plantings on successful French varieties such as Cinsault, Chardonnay, Cabernet Sauvignon, Grenache, Muscat, Semillon, and Riesling. Local grape varieties, unknown outside Turkey, are used to a lesser extent: Kalecik Karasi, Öküzgözü Bogazkere, Narince, and Emir. More than 90 percent of wine production is in the hands of two producers: the state-supported winery, Tekel; and the main private one, Doluca.

Variety in India

Although grapes have been cultivated since ancient times in India, with written evidence from 1200 BC, domesticated *Vitis vinifera* is thought to have been introduced by the Persians around 1400 AD. Previous to this, cultivated native varieties such as the Rangspay, Shonltu White, and Shonltu Red (all still cultivated) had been domesticated from *Vitis lanata* and *Vitis palmate*, which still grow wild in northwestern India. The Indian government encourages planting for table grapes, but wine production remains very low, with 10,000 tons (1 percent of annual production) of grapes devoted to wine. Varieties used for wine production include Bangalore Blue (a synonym of Isabella, mainly used for table grapes), Cabernet Sauvignon, Chenin Blanc, Chardonnay, Merlot, Pinot Noir, and Ugni Blanc.

LITTLE CHOICE IN THAILAND...

Thailand's grape production is small, with the main harvest used for juice and table grapes, as in neighboring Asian countries. Nevertheless, it produces rare Thai wines from the 2,600 tons devoted to wine production. The two main varieties used to make wine are Chenin Blanc and Syrah, although table grapes White Malaga and Cardinal are used to a lesser extent. All grape varieties are grafted on to a unique rootstock, Solonis x Othello 1613. It is used for its vigor and its resistance to nematodes, phylloxera, drought, and waterlogging.

...OR JAPAN

The situation in Japan is comparable to that in India and Thailand: about 27,700 tons (11 percent) of annual production is used for wine production, based on a limited choice of foreign grape varieties (Cabernet Sauvignon, Chardonnay, Merlot, Müller-Thurgau, Seibel) and a local domesticated vine, Yamabudo (*Vitis coignetiae*).

PRESERVING GRAPE HERITAGE

Grape conservatories are fashionable nowadays and are mushrooming, following consumers' increased interest in wine. Savvy consumers enjoy knowing more about the contents of their glasses. Details of two conservatories are given below.

Conservatoire de Chareil-Cintrat, 03140 Chareil-Cintrat, Allier, France Established in 2000 thanks to the tenacity of grapevine grower Jean Berthon, now a retired president of the Cooperative des Vignerons de St-Pourçain, the regional VDQS appellation. This conservatory is situated in the gardens of the castle of Chareil-Cintrat, close to St-Pourçain in central France.

It grows grape varieties used in making St-Pourçain today, as well as obsolete varieties. One of the oldest French vineyards and popular with the kings of France, St-Pourçain has been fighting for years to be classified as AOC. This is one of the rare places where you can see varieties such as St-Pierre Doré, a native white variety that was important historically but is no longer used in St-Pourçain, and Tressallier, another native white variety which gives typicality to the white wine of St-Pourçain.

Centre d'Ampélographie Alpine Pierre Galet, La Roche, 73370 Cevins, France This center of ampelography was named in honor of the famous and passionate French ampelographer Pierre Galet, now 86, who donated his archive. A principal objective of the center is to create a conservatory hosting alpine grape varieties cultivated in the French Alps, Jura, Switzerland, and Italy.

The first planting should begin in 2008 and will offer an opportunity to display varieties used in mountain or alpine viticulture, such as Jacquère, Altesse, Roussanne, Mondeuse Blanche, Persan, and Mondeuse Noire. The ampelographic center is hosted by the tiny vineyard of Cevins, one of the smallest *vin de pays* appellations, with a surface of 6 ha.

WANDERING CARMENERE

Chile offers a unique opportunity to taste varietal Carmenère wines. Chilean wines were, until recently, dominated by Merlot wines quite different from their French counterparts. Molecular profiling proved that most Merlot vineyards were in fact planted with an almost forgotten variety from the Bordeaux region: Carmenère (synonym Grande Vidure). It is estimated that over half of Chile's "Merlot" vines are actually Carmenère.

It has also been established that, just as Chile confused Carmenère with Merlot, northern Italy confused it with Cabernet Franc. It had been thought that much of Italy's Cabernet Franc was Merlot, but substantial plantings of this "Merlot" were in fact Carmenère. Carmenère is mainly grown in eastern Veneto and Friuli-Venezia Giulia. According to Alain Bouquet, Chilean Carmenère's popularity among French consumers has prompted some Bordeaux producers to think about replanting Carmenère and producing varietal wines.

Most widely cultivated white grape varieties
Global, wine grapes only.

Grape variety	Acres in 2007*	Main countries
1. Airén	756,320	Spain
2. Chardonnay	488,250	US, France, Italy
3. Ugni Blanc	372,970	France, Italy, Argentina
4. Rkatsiteli	264,840	Ukraine, Georgia, Moldova
5. Sauvignon Blanc	217,460	France, Moldova, US
6. Riesling	142,985	Germany, Ukraine
7. Macabeo	122,990	Spain, Argentina, Australia, Morocco
8. Muscat of Alexandria	114,735	Spain, Chile, Algeria
9. Welschriesling	113,670	Canada, Germany, US, Slovenia, Czech Republic
10. Muscat Blanc	110,210	Greece, Spain, Italy, France, Portugal, Australia, US

*Estimated. Source: Patrick W. Fegan, Chicago Wine School, 2008.

Most widely cultivated black grape varieties
Global, wine grapes only.

Grape variety	Acres in 2007*	Main countries
1. Cabernet Sauvignon	722,200	France, Chile, US
2. Merlot	718,900	France, Italy, US
3. Tempranillo	502,225	Spain, Argentina, Portugal
4. Grenache	497,190	Spain, France, Italy
5. Syrah	397,100	France, Australia
6. Carignan	257,890	France, China, Tunisia
7. Pinot Noir	223,750	France, US, Germany
8. Bobal	219,825	Spain
9. Sangiovese	187,825	Italy, Argentina, US
10. Monastrell/Mourvèdre	184,050	Spain, France, Australia

*Estimated. Source: Patrick W. Fegan, Chicago Wine School, 2008.

Most widely cultivated gray/rosé grape varieties
Global, wine grapes only.

Grape variety	Acres in 2007*	Main countries
1. Pinot Gris	74,765	Italy, Germany, US
2. Criolla Grande	57,425	Argentina
3. Cereza	44,810	Argentina
4. Gewurztraminer	40,830	Moldova, France, Ukraine
5. Grenache Gris	5,075	France
6. Roditis	2,470	Greece
7. Catawba	2,135	US
8. Grolleau Gris	1,165	France
9. Sauvignon Gris	450	France
10. Terret Gris	315	France

*Estimated. Source: Patrick W. Fegan, Chicago Wine School, 2008.

Fastest-growing white grape varieties
The greatest global increase in recent plantings of white (wine only) grape varieties.

Grape variety	Acres in 2006*	Acres in 2007*	% increase**
1. Viognier	17,000	21,540	27
2. Sauvignon Blanc	207,600	217,460	5
3. Chardonnay	473,640	488,250	3
4. White Riesling	139,450	142,985	3

*Estimated. **Some increases may reflect improved data collection rather than an actual increase in acreage. Source: Patrick W. Fegan, Chicago Wine School, 2008.

Fastest-growing black grape varieties
The greatest global increase in recent plantings of black (wine only) grape varieties.

Grape variety	Acres in 2006*	Acres in 2007*	% increase**
1. Petit Verdot	8,775	11,270	28
2. Malbec	78,800	84,250	7
3. Syrah	374,150	397,100	6
4. Merlot	700,380	718,900	3
5. Pinot Noir	219,335	223,750	2
6. Cabernet Sauvignon	709,530	722,200	2

*Estimated. **Some increases may reflect improved data collection rather than an actual increase in acreage. Source: Patrick W. Fegan, Chicago Wine School, 2008.

Fastest-growing gray/rosé grape variety
The greatest global increase in recent plantings of gray/rosé (wine only) grape varieties.

Grape variety	Acres in 2006*	Acres in 2007*	% increase**
Pinot Gris	67,650	74,765	11

*Estimated. **An increase may reflect improved data collection rather than an actual increase in acreage. Source: Patrick W. Fegan, Chicago Wine School, 2008.

BEST WINES FROM NEW VARIETIES OR NEW CLONES

1 Bernex Gamaret Garanoir 2004
Alexandre de Montmollin, Domaine de la République et Canton de Genève (SF 16) *Red wine (12.5 percent) made from Gamaret (Gamay x Reichensteiner [= Müller-Thurgau x (Madeleine Angevine x Weisser Calabreser)], Agroscope Changins, 1965) and Garanoir (Gamay x Reichensteiner [= Müller-Thurgau x (Madeleine Angevine x Weisser Calabreser)], Agroscope Changins, 1970).*

2 Nuits Rouges Gamaret 2006
Grégory Favre, Domaine d'En Bruaz, Meinier, Switzerland (SF 12) *Red wine (12.5 percent) from pure Gamaret (Gamay x Reichensteiner [= Müller-Thurgau x (Madeleine Angevine x Weisser Calabreser)], Agroscope Changins, 1965).*

3 Regent Auslese Trocken Pfalz 2003 Siebeldinger Mönchspfad, Institut für Rebenzüchtung, Geilweilerhof, Siebeldingen, Germany (€8.50 per 50-cl bottle) *Experimental red dry wine from Regent (Gf. 67-198-3; [Silvaner x Müller-Thurgau] x Chambourcin, BAFZ Geilweilerhof) in wood cask (14.5 percent). Bronze medal, Economic Chamber of Rheinland-Pfalz.*

4 Felicia Auslese Lieblich Pfalz 2005 Siebeldinger Mönchspfad, Institut für Rebenzüchtung, Geilweilerhof, Siebeldingen, Germany (€5.50) *Medium-sweet white wine (11.5 percent) from Felicia (Sirius x Vidal Blanc [= Ugni Blanc x Rayon d'Or], 1984; BAFZ Geilweilerhof).*

5 Vin de Pays d'Oc Rouge 2005
Domaine Faure, La Digne d'Aval, France (€5) *Red wine (12.5 percent) from Portan (= INRA 1508-25; Grenache Noir x Portugais Bleu, 1958, INRA Montpellier, Paul Truel) and Cabernet Franc.*

6 Vin de Pays des Bouches du Rhône Cuvée Prestige Van Gogh 2004 Le Mas de Rey, Trinquetaille, Arles, France (€4.50) *White wine (12.5 percent) from Chasan (= INRA 1527-78; Listan Blanc x Chardonnay Blanc, 1958, INRA Montpellier, Paul Truel), Gros Manseng, and Aranel (= INRA 1816-106; Grenache Gris x Saint Pierre Doré, 1961, INRA Montpellier, Paul Truel).*

7 Reserve Red 2005 Fulkerson Winery, New York (US$8.99) *A blend of Baco Noir and Corot Noir (= NY70.0809.10 = Seyve Villard 18-307 [Villard Blanc x Chancellor] x Steuben [Sheridan x Wayne]; 1970, New York).*

8 Corot Noir 2005 Davis Valley Winery, Virginia (US$19) *A red wine (14 percent) made from Corot Noir (see above).*

9 Triomphe d'Alsace Medium Dry Rosé 2005 Tas Valley Vineyard, Norwich, UK (£13.95) *Rosé wine made from Triomphe d'Alsace (MG 101-14 x Knipperlé = Kuhlmann 319-1).*

10 Valvin Muscat Finger Lake 2005 Knapp Winery, New York ($14.95) *White wine (11 percent) made from Valvin Muscat (Couderc 299-35 = Muscat du Moulin = [Pedro Ximénez x Couderc 603 (= Vitis rupestris x Bourrisquou)] x Muscat Ottonel).*

BEST WINES FROM UNUSUAL, OBSCURE, OR REDISCOVERED GRAPE VARIETIES

1 Malvasia Miliarakis 2007
Nikos & Takis Miliarakis, Minos Cretan Wines, Crete, Greece (€7.50) *White wine (12.5 percent) made from Malvasia di Candia, an ancient Cretan variety with a name recalling Candia, the old Italian name for Heraklion.*

2 Miliarakis Estate Bio 2004 Nikos & Takis Miliarakis, Minos Cretan Wines, Crete, Greece (€8.90) *Organic red wine (12.8 percent) using a blend of old Cretan varieties from the Heraklion area (80 percent Kotsifali, 20 percent Mandilari).*

3 Embruns Blancs Coteaux du Languedoc St-Georges d'Orques 2005 Domaine de la Prose, Pignan, France (€12) *Biodynamic white wine (13.5 percent) made from Vermentino, Grenache Blanc, and Roussanne, and matured for 10 months in oak casks.*

4 Los Pasos Carmenère 2006 Domaine Xpovin, Central Valley, Chile (SF 7 in Switzerland) *Red wine (14 percent) made from Carmenère, an old French variety from the Bordeaux region grown in Chile as "Merlot" for more than a century. Excellent value.*

5 Vin de Table Péchique 2002 Sylvain Saux, Domaine Péchigo, Lauraguel, France (€14) *Semi-dry organic white wine (12.5 percent) made from Mauzac Vert (synonym Blanquette).*

6 Vin de Table Cuvée Fié Gris 2006 Eric Chevalier, Domaine de l'Aujardière, St-Philbert de Grand Lieu, France (€4.80) *Table wine (11.5 percent) from pure Fié Gris, a west France variety that is almost extinct, though it was once widely grown in the Loire region.*

7 Touraine Le Brin de Chèvre 2002 Thierry & Jean-Marie Puzelat, Clos du Tue-Bœuf, Les Montils, France (€10.90) *Organic wine (12.5 percent) made from Menu Pineau (synonym Arbois).*

8 Vin de Table A Ferdinand Blanc 2005 Olivier Privat, Tresques, France (€10) *White wine (12.5 percent) from a blend of old local varieties: Clairette Rose and Blanche, Grenache Noir and Blanc, Cinsault, Bourboulenc, Picpoul, and Aubuns.*

9 Maury Plénitude Maccabeu 2006 Olivier Decelle, Domaine du Mas Amiel, Maury, France (€13.90 per half-bottle) *Passerillé wine (15.5 percent) made from Maccabeu (Spanish synonyms Alcanol, Maccabeo, Viura), an old variety grown in France and Spain (Catalunya).*

10 Vin de Table Vert de l'Or 2001 Domaine des Baumard, Rochefort-sur-Loire, France (€8) *Dry white wine (12.5 percent) from pure Verdelho (synonym Gouveio), a Portuguese variety from Madeira imported more than 200 years ago and extinct in France other than in this vineyard.*

Grapevine

- **The New York Wine Course and Reference** provides detailed information about viticulture in New York State. It includes a comprehensive list of all the wine varieties grown in the state, along with planted surfaces and locations. See www.newyorkwines.org/informationstation/newstouse/wine_course.pdf.

Classic Wine Vintage Guide

Serena Sutcliffe MW

What is classic wine? Apart from being a candidate term for Pseuds' Corner, it should deconstruct in an intelligible way. Classic usually means proven at a basic level, and this is a safe beginning.

SERENA SUTCLIFFE MW

A wine that has had a terrific reputation for a century or more, endorsed by consistent price levels, can be deemed classic, the absolute opposite of fly-by-night. The meaning should also tip over into intrinsic quality, linked to its benchmark taste for the particular region whence it comes. It should be representative and do honor to its zone, terroir, appellation, or equivalent. And it should have the depth and dimension to age with grace and added beauty.

There can be "new" classic wines that have emerged in past decades—wines such as Pingus and Harlan, Ornellaia and Masseto, the Guigal Côte Rôtie La-Las and Alois Kracher's sweet wines from Burgenland, to name but a few. One has to be able to do a vertical tasting of a wine and come out

SERENA SUTCLIFFE MW A Master of Wine and head of Sotheby's International Wine Department, Serena is considered one of the world's leading authorities on wine. A former chairman of the Institute of Masters of Wine, Serena was made a Chevalier dans l'Ordre des Arts et des Lettres by the French government in 1988. She was elected to the Académie Internationale du Vin in 1993, and in 2002 she received the New York Institute of Technology's Professional Excellence Award. In 2006, she received the Lifetime Achievement Award from the Society of Bacchus America, and was awarded the title of Chevalier dans l'Ordre National de la Légion d'Honneur for her seminal work in promoting and selling French wines. Serena is an internationally recognized wine writer and renowned taster, and she writes regularly for many international publications. Besides heading Sotheby's worldwide wine auctions, she is also a member of Sotheby's European Board and is a regular lecturer and broadcaster in Europe, the United States, and Asia. Her book *The Wines of Burgundy* appeared in its eighth edition in 2005.

at the other end saying, well, that was an experience, and I must cellar some of these wines myself as they are "worth it," to borrow a current catchphrase. A track record is essential to move into this classic category.

I think, however, there is another vital ingredient for a wine to merit the classic moniker—and that is personality. You can call it individuality or character, if you wish, but it comes down to a wine's ability to sing its own song, to be recognizably itself (on a good tasting day!), and to keep those traits down the years, come rain or come shine—literally, in the case of wine. I do not want a Nespresso type of wine, a capsule of boredom without an iota of an explosive bouquet nor a punch of a taste—and I speak as a coffee fanatic. I want the real thing, with the beans ground as I watch, when I am not doing it myself. Otherwise I would rather do without. Banality is the enemy of classic.

The best expression of sheer character in wines that I have looked at recently was at a *Gambero Rosso* tasting in London. It was a privilege to be joint commentator at a showing of 50 of Italy's finest and a revelation to see the fascinating diversity of the wines and their ebullient profile. Some of this originality comes, of course, from Italy's varied topography and geology, encompassing mountains, volcanoes, lakes, and maritime influences, but extra complexity and layers are then added when there is such a plethora of grape varieties—the latest count is 800, of which 400 are cataloged and "authorized." We did not sample them all, naturally, but reveled in the authenticity and vibrancy of Refosco and Pignolo, Pugnitello and Sagrantino, Aglianico and Uva di Troia, Nero d'Avola and Nerello Mascalese. What could be more classic than these ancient indigenous grape varieties?

PEAKING VINTAGES

RED BORDEAUX

1997 Provides lovely drinking now.

1994 Peaking.

1993 Peaking.

1992 Peaking (if you bothered at all).

1991 Peaking.

1987 Reds mostly dire, but Pavillon Blanc is marvelous!

1986 Right Bank wines should be in your glass.

1985 Peaking except for First Growths, top Seconds, and top Right Banks. Cos is magnificent.

1984 Mostly unpleasant, as well as past their best.

1983 Mostly at their peak, except for gems like Margaux, Palmer, Pichon-Lalande, and Figeac.

1982 Many have peaked, except for First Growths, Super-Seconds, top St-Emilions, and Pomerols. Gruaud-Larose excellent.

1981 Drink now.

1980 Mostly too old.

1979 Peak, but top wines still drinking well. Try Haut-Brion and Latour Haut-Brion.

1978 Peak, but top wines drinking well: Ausone, Lafite, Pichon-Lalande.

1977 Forget it, except for La Mission.

1976 Peaked. Lafite and Ausone still looking good.

1975 Mostly peaked. Exceptions include Pétrus, Latour, La Mission Haut-Brion, Pichon-Lalande, Cheval Blanc, Mouton, Trotanoy, and Figeac.

1974, 1973, and 1972 Enough said.

1971 Peaked. Top Pomerols still glorious, *viz* the heavenly "roasted" Pétrus and the riveting Trotanoy. La Mission Haut-Brion is excellent.

1970 Mostly peaked. Exceptions include Pétrus, Latour, La Mission Haut-Brion, Trotanoy, La Conseillante, Pichon-Lalande, Ducru-Beaucaillou, Palmer, Giscours, Beychevelle, and Figeac.

1969 & 1968 Don't even think about it.

1967 Peaked a long time ago. Pétrus still good.

1966 Mostly peaked. Exceptions include Latour, Cheval Blanc, Pétrus, Haut-Brion, La Mission Haut-Brion, Mouton.

1964 Mostly peaked. Exceptions include Pétrus, Latour, Haut-Brion, La Mission Haut-Brion. Cheval Blanc and Figeac are miraculous.

1962 Peaked, although the Firsts are still good. Mouton is glorious, and so is Trotanoy.

1961 Most wines still wonderful. That small crop gave the vital concentration. Cheval Blanc, Trotanoy, and Mouton dreamy.

1959 The top wines are still magic. Mouton, Cheval Blanc, and Figeac superlative.

RED BURGUNDY

2000 Lovely now at village level.

1997 Delicious drinking now, *viz* two Santenay La Comme *premiers crus* from Mestre-Michelot and Muzard.

1994 Drink now, because that dry finish will intensify.

1992 Delicious now, but hurry. Ponsot's Clos de la Roche Vieilles Vignes is superb.

1990 *Grands crus* have further to go, although Corton-Bressandes from Chandon de Briailles was outstanding recently.

1989 *Grands crus* have further to go, *premiers crus* lovely.

1988 The very top wines mostly have further to go.

1987 Should have been drunk.

1986 As above. Even Jayer is at its best.

1985 Mostly at, or over, its peak, except for top *grands crus*, such as Drouhin's Bonnes Mares, La Tâche, and all DRC and Jayer. Volnay Clos du Château des Ducs from Lafarge still youthful.

1984 Don't go there.

1983 A very few are hanging on.

1982 As above, for different reasons.

1981 Peaked.

1980 Past their peak, and even those brilliant Jayers should be drunk. La Tâche still amazing.

1979 Peaked.

1978 There are still some wonders at the top. They have a signature gaminess. DRC splendid.

1977 Treat them as though they were never there.

1976 Peaked a long time ago, with the odd, rare exception.

1975 Should not be mentioned in polite society.

1974 Unpleasant and old.

1973 Peaked a long time ago.

1972 One or two survivors, *viz* de Vogüé's Musigny Vieilles Vignes.

1971 Stay with DRC or similar here.

1970 It's all over now.

1969 Some survivors at *grand cru* level. Rousseau exceptional.

1966 A few still live gloriously on: Romanée-Conti is mind-blowing.

1964 A few terrific wines at *grand cru* level.

1962 A few top wines are still magnificent.

1961 As above.

1959 As above.

WHITE BURGUNDY

2000 Lovely now.

1999 Start on the lesser wines, which are quite soft.

1998 Many are ready.

1997 Very nice drinking now— Raveneau's Vaillons is wonderful, as is Ramonet's Chassagne Boudriotte.

1996 Some greats; some looking flat.

1994 Mostly at their peak, but Raveneau's Valmur *en pleine forme*.

1993 As above.

1992 As above—they matured faster than many believed.

1991 Mostly at their peak.

1990 Some top wines still have a bit to go; others are glowing right now.

1989 As above.

1988 Mostly at their peak or over it.

1987 Peaked.

1986 Mostly peaked. Some *grands crus* are lovely right now.

1985 Many of the top wines are so fat and full they will stay around for ages, such as the Bâtards of Ramonet and Niellon. I prefer it to 1986.

1984 Peaked a very long time ago.

1983 Some tremendous wines at the top. They seemed alcoholic and heavy when young, but, boy, are they marvelous now. Some of the greatest white burgundies of my life come from this vintage, such as Corton-Charlemagne from Latour and Bonneau de Martray.

1982 Virtually all peaked long ago.

1981 Peaked a long time ago.

1980 As above.

1979 Virtually all peaked some time ago.

1978 As above, but some gems live on, *viz* Chablis Les Clos from Drouhin, which now looks like a Côte d'Or wine.

1976 Peaked, but there are some stunners still about at *grand cru* level.

1973 Peaked, with the odd surprise at *grand cru* level.

1971 Peaked, with some stunners left.

1970 As above.

1969 As above.

1967 It starts getting esoteric from here, but the odd surprise.

1966 Mostly history, but DRC's Montrachet *makes* history.

1964 Peaked a long time ago, with a few exceptions hanging on.

1962 Peaked, of course, with a few marvelous exceptions.

1961 As above.

RED RHONE

2002 Drink quickly, if from the south.

1997 Drink from now.

1994 In my view, start drinking up.

1993 Peak.

1992 Peak.

1991 Peaked for the south; fine for the north.

1990 Excellent; the best will keep.

1989 As above.

1988 As above, especially Guigal's top Côte Rôties.

1987 Peaked, so drink now.

1986 As above.

1985 At peak, but the best will keep.

1984 Peaked.

1983 Peaked for the south, but the top wines from the north still have life in them.

1982 Peaked everywhere, although the north is better.

1981 Peaked for the north; a few good ones left in the south.

1980 Peaked.

1979 Peaked; the best still drinking well.

1978 At its peak, mostly, with some amazing wines at top level.

1976 Peaked some time ago, but Hermitage La Chapelle lives on to delight.

1972 As above.

1971 As above, but throw in Rayas, too, as well as Chave's glorious Hermitage.

1970 Peaked, but great Hermitage La Chapelle.

1969 Peaked: Glorious La Chapelle; Chave and Rayas still in there.

1967 Peaked, but tremendous La Chapelle.

1966 As above.

1964 As above.

1962 As above.

1961 The top wines are still out of this world (La Chapelle et al.).

1959 As above.

PORT

2000 Wonderful, but *keep*.

1997 Don't touch—too young.

1994 As above.

1992 As above.

1991 As above.

1985 Lovely drinking now, as evinced by Dow and Fonseca.

1983 As above, but a mite "patchy."

1982 Drinking well now and over the next few years.

1980 As above.

1978 Vargellas is still young.

1977 Drinking very well now, but the best will keep further.

1975 Drink up fast.

1970 Fabulous vintage; glorious now but will stay that way for ages.

1966 Excellent wines right now, but will keep, of course. The fruit is quite beautiful. Taylor's is magnificent.

1963 Huge, powerful wines, for drinking or keeping.

1960 Beautiful now.

1958 Mostly peaked, but don't say that to Noval Nacional! Extraordinary wine.

1955 Superb now, and not about to fall off the perch. Fonseca marvelous.

1950 Drink up, but the Nacional is eternal.

1948 Great now. Taylor is stunning.

1947 Drink now.

1945 Still there, after all these years. Mammoth. Graham is great, and so is Taylor.

GERMANY

2000 For early drinking.

1999 Drink up at the bottom end.

1997 Lovely at Kabinett level, *viz* Eitelsbacher Karthäuserhofberg Riesling.

1996 Broach and enjoy.

1995 Broach and enjoy, especially Von Schubert's Maximin Grünhäuser Herrenberg Riesling Spätlese.

1994 Peak.

1993 Approaching peak, but the best will mature in splendid fashion.

1992 Peak.

1991 Peak.

1990 Excellent, and the best will age beautifully.

1989 As above. Egon Müller's Scharzhofberger Riesling Beerenauslese surreally beautiful.

1988 As above.

1987 Peaked.

1986 Mostly peaked.

1985 Mostly at peak.

1984 Dreadful vintage.

1983 Mostly peaked, but some wines beautifully present.

1982 Peaked a long time ago.

1981 As above.

1980 Forget it.

1979 A very few survivors.

1976 Tremendous. A plethora of fantastic sweet wines vie for top honors.

1975 As above, especially for the Mosel.

1971 The tops and still magnificent in the upper echelons.

1967 Peaked some time ago, but a few stunning survivors at TBA level.

1959 At peak—and glorious too.

1953 Peaked, with a few beauties left.

GREATEST-QUALITY AUCTION WINES

❶ **Moët & Chandon 1921** *This is here because it is one of the most magical wines of my life. In the cellars at Moët, with chef de cave Benoît Gouez, who is far too young* to have made it. A scent of broom in the sun, truffles and wild mushrooms on the palate, and the 1921 signature spicy rich taste and mythical vanillin texture.

2 **Marqués de Murrieta Ygay Reserva 1912** Unbelievably, we had forgotten this in our cellar. Glorious scent of undergrowth and old laurels with mineral saltiness. Incredible taste of salt, chocolate, and rosemary. American oak seasoned in Spain. Spellbinding, finishing with a flavor of the sea and plums.

3 **Château Figeac 1947** The start of Thierry Manoncourt's uninterrupted era here, and drunk to celebrate his 90th birthday. Amazingly spicy, aromatic, and rich on the nose; unbelievably sweet, but so pure. Finish of violet creams. Such attack and absolute clarity of taste.

4 **Château Figeac 1959** Absolutely no apologies for this, given the occasion, at Taillevent in Paris, to mark Thierry's milestone. Wonderful, deep, intense nose. Cassis and violets. Cloves and red cabbage. Such a fantastic, nostalgic taste of the past—will we see it again? Extraordinary allspice and gingerbread finish. Stunning.

5 **Château Mouton Rothschild 1959** I don't know about Mary, but there is something about 1959. At a country house with a deep cellar. Compared with the 1961, I veer between the two, but there is a riveting minty, eucalyptus bouquet here, with a voluptuous, rich taste that is a hedonist's delight. Burnt cassis berries, licorice plus coffee beans at the end.

6 **Château Trotanoy 1962** At a breathtaking Trotanoy vertical with the Moueix team. I might equally have chosen the 1961 (both from half-bottles)—this was pure seduction, the 1961 multilayered and grandiose. The '62 has a sweet, concentrated bouquet, and in the mouth it is heady, succulent, and opulent—enivrant, if I am really honest.

7 **Colgin Cariad 2001** At a Bacchus Society California dinner at Craft in New York, this really beat the (considerable) competition—it was just classier: 54 percent Cabernet Sauvignon, 32 percent Merlot, 7 percent Cabernet Franc, and 7 percent Petit Verdot, all from the Madrona Ranch. Okay, it had a "bordeaux" bouquet, but it had real breed, a chocolaty taste, and a silky texture—really beautiful, in fact.

8 **Château d'Yquem 1975** At a Bipin Desai extravaganza in Los Angeles, where Wolfgang Puck at Spago again got the food just right. The source was the château itself. This could have been top of the list, but we must give the others a chance! And one could have gone older (the 1945 was amazing pomegranates), but this 1975 was unputdownable, overconcentrated grapes delivering extraordinary purity, sweetness, and balance.

9 **Château Cheval Blanc 1949** I really give up on a logical order here—this could head the list (as could the 1948). At the same LA bacchanal as above and château-sourced, increasingly important in these tricky days. The high-temperature, dry summer gave only 25 hl/ha and a miraculously low 12.4 percent alcohol—oh, joy! Roasted berries nose, pure bliss on the palate—liquid cocoa. Everlasting in its total beauty.

10 **Taylor 1945** Only here on the list because it is "the end of the meal," and it could also have been the totally violetty 1948, or the Fonseca black-cherries 1948 for

that matter. At The Great Wine Seminar in West Palm Beach, with Alistair Robertson, always an amusing experience, and this wine is always a knockout, all cherry kernels and nuts—pure liquid Christmas cake. How I wish it was in my Christmas stocking!

MOST EXCITING OR UNUSUAL AUCTION FINDS

① Château Ducru-Beaucaillou 1970 This château is certainly not "unusual," but it is exciting, right at the top of the 1970 ladder and a badge of honor for the late Jean-Eugène Borie. Luxurious, luscious, with absolutely juicy blueberries in the mouth and a concentrated cassis finish. Still so fresh, fruity, and immediate—miss it at your peril.

② Savennières Clos du Papillon 2000 Domaine des Baumard Nose of fresh grass, greengages, and quince. Lovely fresh, mineral taste with delicacy and length and a finish of ripe crab apples and grapefruit. Perfect with rainbow trout and new potatoes. One of France's most intriguing appellations.

③ Cabernet Sauvignon Harvest Selection 1974 Mirassou A Monterey County winery that always gave value but was never for label collectors. We discovered it in New York 30 years ago, and it became an iconic memory until we happened upon a bottle in a cellar reorganization. It has kept its cassis allure and is full of tannin, fruit, and acidity. Glossy, opulent, and exciting, as it always was.

④ Vat 5 Winemaker's Selection Hunter River Dry Red 1977 Tyrrell's Sun-kissed Shiraz from that magician Murray Tyrrell and in a brown bottle. Earthy, sweet, and leathery, full of fruity, clovelike aromatics. Utterly soft and yet full of flavor. Damsons, cloves, and aniseed. Simply fascinating with cold wild duck and, at last, a wine for our wedding anniversary!

⑤ First Harvest Cabernet Sauvignon 1975 Firestone A real blast of the past! Winkled out of our early California cellar, since this was when we were "discovering" the area and buying to find out whether the wines would last. This has, magnificently, and at only 12 percent alcohol. Lots of fresh, ripe, plummy fruit. Utterly gulpable, almost sweet—1975 was a very good year here. Quite a feat, because this was never expensive.

⑥ Alfred Gratien 1979 Drunk on Christmas Eve. Dark colored now, with an incredible, almost sweet, bready nose. Resemblance to old Bolly—both are fermented in small oak barrels. Very "salty" taste, stunning with Iranian Imperial Ossetra caviar. Full, rich/marine, and briochy. A huge, mature mouthful.

⑦ Alpha Estate Unfiltered 2004 Fourteen percent alcohol and made from ungrafted Xinomavro, Syrah, and Merlot grapes in the Amyndeon region of northern Greece. Dark-hued, with a bouquet of warm wild herbs and wild cherries and layers of hedonistic sweet, ripe fruit on the palate, with the bite of that Greek grape variety to give extra pizzazz.

⑧ Mirafiore Barbaresco 1959 Fontanafredda Amazing, cakelike porty sediment and a bouquet of the maquis in sunlight. Utterly melting in the mouth, with gummy licorice and walnut flavors and a typical tarry finish. Probably tough when young, but what a treat now.

⑨ Château Talbot Caillou Blanc 2003 Almost no one knows this unexpected white from a favorite

St-Julien, but it always elicits cries of rapture. Drunk from magnum, and a miracle from this very hot year. Wonderful lemon and lanolin nose and a rich, enveloping taste that stays fresh. Equally good with linguine, fresh salmon, and dill as with spaghetti, anchovies, and tomatoes!

🔟 **Stony Hill Chardonnay 1991**
The kind of Chardonnay that is not usual in the Napa, but it is grown 600 ft (180 m) above the valley floor. It has personality, minerality, and that amazing bone-dry but "sweet" finish that is its signature. Stony Hill has never fallen into the banality of some Cal Chard.

BEST AUCTION BARGAINS (hammer price)

1️⃣ **Mazis Chambertin 1999** Armand Rousseau; at the London December 2007 sale (12 bottles: £460) How this slipped through I will never know. Everyone's favorite burgundy producer and a great year, but Mazis is often overlooked.

2️⃣ **Château Duhart-Milon-Rothschild 1990**; at the London January 2007 sale (12 bottles: £320) A Fourth Growth, a super year, and the wine is owned and made by the Lafite team—what more could you want? Somehow, few have "caught on."

3️⃣ **Gewurztraminer Vendange Tardive Sélection de Grains Nobles 1976** Hugel; at the New York May 2007 sale (5 bottles: US$475) These drops of gold usually go for fiendish prices, with good reason, given the tiny quantities, so this was a red-letter day for the buyer.

4️⃣ **Vouvray Moelleux Cuvée Constance 1989** Huet; at the New York May 2007 sale (6 bottles: US$500) Evidently there was a dearth of sweet-toothed clients at this sale, because this fabulous liquid orange cream of a wine went to a watchful connoisseur for a ludicrous price.

5️⃣ **Vieux Château Certan 2001**; at the London April 2007 sale (12 bottles: £360) Clearly those present had not woken up to the fact that Pomerol 2001s are outstanding, and VCC is a gem of a property, making wines of real finesse.

6️⃣ **Graham 1983**; at the London April 2007 sale (12 bottles: £280) Port continues to be a source of great buys if you know where to look, and this very pretty, beautifully made wine melts in the mouth.

7️⃣ **Bonnes Mares 1997 Comte Georges de Vogüé**; at the New York Warren Stephens November 2007 sale (12 bottles: US$1,700) There were not many bargains in this single-owner sale, but 1997s remain misunderstood, and this voluptuous, spicy wine, for once, became almost accessible in price.

8️⃣ **Château Sociando-Mallet 2003**; at the London November 2007 sale (12 magnums: £360) What a gift! The ideal format, a superb cru, and in a year when the northern Médoc made such exciting wine. Wish I could have joined in.

9️⃣ **Pavillon Rouge du Château Margaux 1995**; at the London November 2007 sale (12 bottles: £420) The second wine of the First Growth in a lovely year, ready to drink and delivering delicious fruit and a touch of breed as well.

🔟 **Château Laville Haut-Brion 1999**; at the New York December 2007 sale (12 bottles: US$650) Incomprehensible really, because this is stunning stuff, all creamy limes and butter and set for a long future. I admit to jealousy here.

Wine Auctions & Investment

Anthony Rose

The New World marches on, Mediterranean regions feature increasingly strongly, Bordeaux struggles—on the high street, that is. In the more rarefied world of wine investment, the opposite is the case.

ANTHONY ROSE

Bordeaux continues to dominate the auction scene by such a broad margin that predictions of a new investment order with the rise of Burgundy, the Rhône, Spain, Italy, and the New World are proving, at least for now, wide of the mark. True, the likes of Harlan and Screaming Eagle do well enough in California and Grange in Australia. But these markets are essentially parochial, and as the global market expands to include a young, moneyed clientele in China, Russia, Malaysia, India, Brazil, and North America, the tried and tested *crus classés* of Bordeaux, First Growths especially, take greater pride of place in the secondary auctions and investment market than ever.

According to the fine-wine exchange Liv-ex, the value of top bordeaux increased by more than 90 percent, with fine wine second only to oil as an investment. An in-depth look at Sotheby's 2007 US sales reveals that First Growths represented 37 percent of the total lots sold by value. If you factor in Cheval Blanc and Pétrus, the total rises to 50 percent. Pétrus alone represented 10 percent of the lots sold by value. Until the slowdown in the latter half of the year caused by the subprime crisis in the US, extravagant prices were obtained not just for large formats and rare, older vintages, but

ANTHONY ROSE is the award-winning wine correspondent for *The Independent*, and he also writes for a number of other publications, including *Wine & Spirit* magazine and *Harpers Wine and Spirit Weekly*. He specializes in the auction scene, writing a monthly column on the subject for *Decanter* and contributing to *The Oxford Companion to Wine* on auction and investment. Anthony is married to an Australian wine photographer and lives in London.

for younger vintages too. The burgeoning economy, the entry of so many rich new players, and the fact that Bordeaux can claim three good to great vintages in the first six years of the millennium—2000, 2003, and 2005—have given the investment market a massive boost.

But a new order of sorts has begun to emerge. Until quite recently, First Growth châteaux Margaux and Latour had performed consistently well among the top five of the Médoc and Graves, but Rothschild is in the ascendant. Thanks to a reputedly monumental 2006, Mouton Rothschild saw its stock rise to an average price increase of 50 percent for the year and the highest level of trading on the Liv-ex exchange at 13.2 percent, ahead of Lafite Rothschild, where a strong revival is also under way. There was an almost exact parallel at Sotheby's in the US, where Mouton was the leading First Growth (13 percent by value), followed by Lafite (9 percent).

A number of other top Bordeaux châteaux are also jostling for high honors, most notably Château Ausone, joint top of the St-Emilion tree with Cheval Blanc, yet, until Alain Vauthier took over recently, it was failing to live up to its potential.

Before even hitting the auction rooms, the 2005 bordeaux vintage, in part thanks to the spectacular performances of Le Pin and Ausone, showed a big increase on the secondary market in the 18 months since its offer *en primeur* in the spring of 2006 and the end of 2007. Next to it, 1986, 1996, and 1990 have also been highly successful vintages, while 2003 and 2000 have performed the strongest. Among top performers, the 2003 Montrose rose by 64 percent to reach $3,000 a case, 2003 Margaux moved from $6,550 to $10,290 per case over the year, and Léoville-Poyferré registered one of the more impressive gains with an increase of $710 to $1,480.

What of the market beyond Bordeaux? Certainly, a select number of burgundies continue to outperform the rest, most notably the extraordinary Domaine de la Romanée-Conti, whose wines represented 9 percent of all lots sold by value at Sotheby's US over the year. The great vintages of 1959, 1962, 1971, 1978, 1985, and 1990 are also in strong demand, particularly from producers such as Henri Jayer, Leroy, Comte Georges de Vogüé, Coche-Dury, Leflaive, and Lafon, while Roumier's Bonnes Mares, Rousseau's Chambertin, and Mugnier's Musigny grow in stature. In the Rhône, the 1961 Hermitage La Chapelle outperformed the market, and the names of Guigal, Chave, and top Châteauneufs continue to do well, while in Champagne, Roederer Cristal, Dom Pérignon, and Krug remain on fizzing form. Outside France, Italy's Sassicaia and Spain's Vega Sicilia command international respect, although cult California and Australia don't quite cut it yet in the mainstream global investment market.

ALL WINNERS,
NO LOSERS

Of course, like Janus, auction houses face both ways. If a vintage, château, or style goes off the boil, they tell you what great value it's become for the drinker. So what goes down in the investment broker's esteem may well go up among those who enjoy drinking wine. What's flopped, then, from an investment point of view? Primarily vintage port, which has barely moved—so much so that it's no longer a sound investment, except in the most exceptional circumstances. In Bordeaux, the fact that trophy vintages have done so well points, in Christie's David Elswood's view, to the value of "lesser" vintages such as 1983, 1985, 1988, 1995, and 2001, not forgetting 1997 and 1999. The 1982 vintage continues to do well, but with falls in value for 1982 Lynch-Bages and Léoville Barton, some Super-Seconds may have peaked, while garage bordeaux such as Valandraud and Mondotte has been shown to be wine's answer to the emperor's new clothes.

Despite the 18-month boom that preceded the credit crunch, it was almost inevitable that there would be a slowdown of some sort. By the turn of the year, however, there was a resumption of strong demand, especially from the hypersensitive emerging Asian countries. The outlook for the market, however, remains uncertain.

WIZARDS OF OZ

Penfolds Grange dominated the 2007 wine-auction list compiled by leading Australian auctioneer Langton's. With its top sale a bottle of 1951 Bin 1 for A$50,854 ($43,900), Grange registered all top 10 prices, 15 of the top 20, and 48 of the top 100 during the year. The 1951 was the first but experimental vintage made by Max Schubert and was so derided in its early years he had to conceal the fact that he was still making Grange, then known as Grange Hermitage, from the Penfolds board.

The next-highest price was A$14,950 ($13,200) for the 1957 Bin 113 Grange, while a 1962 Bin 60A Penfolds Coonawarra Cabernet/Barossa Shiraz recorded the 11th-highest price of A$3,106 ($2,720). Moss Wood, one of the founding wineries of Margaret River, posted a record price for a post-1970 bottle of Australian wine with A$2,301 ($2,010) paid for a 1973 Cabernet Sauvignon, the 14th-highest price of the year, while a 1974 Moss Wood Cabernet Sauvignon fetched A$1,726 ($1,520). A 1955 Wynn's Coonawarra Estate Michael Shiraz sold for A$1,588 ($1,390) and a 1965 Lindemans Bin 3100 Hunter Valley for A$1,398 ($1,220). Overall, Barossa Shiraz emerged as the strongest regional performer.

THE AUCTIONEERS

The major auction houses realized some $333 million in 2007, up from the previous year's $242 million. At the forefront of the international wine auction market, Christie's International Wine Department reported its best year ever, with a global total of $71.7 million. In the US, NY Wines/ Christie's realized a grand total of $27.2 million, while in Europe, Christie's grossed £22.3 million ($44.4 million) in 29 sales, up from £15.4 million ($30.7 million) in 2006. Christie's King Street's top lot of the year was a 12-bottle case of 1961 Hermitage La Chapelle, which sold at London King Street for £123,750 ($247,747), setting a new world auction record for a case of Rhône and for any case sold in Europe. American auctions included "Rarities from the Cellars of Mähler-Besse" in New York and "The Quintessential Modern Cellar" in Los Angeles, while "Grands Crus Part II: Finest and Rarest Wines from the Superlative Collection of Christen Sveaas" was a highlight, raising £3.3 million ($6.8 million).

Sotheby's International Wine Department sold $49.3 million worth of wine globally, surpassing its 2006 figure of $37.3 million by some distance. The top lot of the year was a jeroboam of 1945 Mouton Rothschild, which sold for $310,700 in New York. UK revenues totaled £10.4 million ($20.9 million), a 23 percent growth over £9.2 million ($17 million) in 2006. The sums included income from five successful single-owner sales, including "Treasures from the Private Cellar of Baroness Philippine" ($2.2 million/£1.1 million), "Magnificent Wines from the Warren A Stephens Collection" ($3.8 million/£1.9 million), "The Cellar of Thomas O. Ryder" ($1.7 million/£840,000),

"The Adrian Bowden Cellar Part II," and "The Great Bordeaux Cellar." Aulden Cellars/Sotheby's edged out its rival NY Wines/Christie's in North America, with $28.4 million in sales.

Acker Merrall & Condit again dominated the North American market, with 24 auctions bringing in $60 million. Zachys, which held Las Vegas's first-ever commercial wine auction in February 2008, grossed $52.5 million from 13 auctions, exceeding its 2006 total of $34.7 million, while Chicago's rising star, Hart Davis Hart, held seven auctions totaling $26.9 million in just its third year. In San Francisco/ Los Angeles, Bonhams & Butterfields' simulcast sales achieved $7.3 million from six sales. Morrell & Company realized $6.1 million; Edward Roberts International, a Chicago boutique, $1.7 million; while, in its debut year, Skinner, a Boston house, managed $300,000. The growing attraction of the Internet was illustrated by California-based WineBid.com's tally of $26 million.

Langton's Top 10 Wines

1	1951 Penfolds Bin 1 Grange Hermitage: A$50,854 (US$43,840)
2	1957 Penfolds Bin 113 Grange Hermitage: A$14,950 (US$12,650)
3	1958 Penfolds Bin 47 Grange Hermitage: A$12,995 (US$11,205)
4	1953 Penfolds Bin 2 Grange Hermitage: A$12,651 (US$10,906)
5	1953 Penfolds Bin 9 Grange Cabernet: A$12,650 (US$10,905)
6=	1952 Penfolds Bin 4 Grange Hermitage: A$10,926 (US$8,876)
6=	1954 Penfolds Bin 11 Grange Hermitage: A$10,926 (US$8,876)
8	1956 Penfolds Bin 14 Grange Hermitage: A$9,205 (US$7,935)
9	1952 Penfolds Bin 9B Grange Cabernet: A$7,935 (US$6,840)
10	1955 Penfolds Bin 95 Grange Shiraz: A$3,451 (US$2,975)

Conversion rate: US$1=A$1.16

KOCH AND BULL STORY?

The saga involving the American über-collector Bill Koch, his nemesis the German *bon viveur* and dealer Hardy Rodenstock, and several controversial bottles said to have belonged to former US president Thomas Jefferson continues. The fabled 1787 "Jefferson Lafite," engraved with the initials "Th.J.," was, at $206,830, the most expensive bottle ever sold at auction, but doubts later surfaced as to its authenticity. Similar doubts were raised over a number of "Jefferson" bottles sold to Koch that the German collector Hardy Rodenstock claimed to have discovered behind a bricked-up wall in Paris. After Rodenstock was sued by Koch, who alleged that four Rodenstock-sourced bottles attributed to Thomas Jefferson were fakes, Judge Barbara S. Jones, a federal judge in New York City, dismissed Koch's fraud lawsuit, ruling that the court lacked "personal jurisdiction."

Koch, along with collector Russell H. Frye, has vowed to continue his pursuit of the German dealer, while federal authorities have launched an investigation into wine counterfeiting. The US Department of Justice is working with the FBI, gathering evidence about allegations of counterfeit bottles being sold, while Zachys in New York and Christie's in London are also both cooperating with the authorities. Koch says that experts who examined the 35,000 bottles in his cellar discovered a number of fakes, almost all purchased at auction, that hadn't been detected earlier. The interest provoked by counterfeiting has spread to Hollywood, where the movie rights to a book on the case, *The Billionaire's Vinegar* by Benjamin Wallace, have been bought by a consortium including actor Will Smith, while the rights to a *New Yorker* article on the subject have been snapped up by HBO Films.

THE 147TH HOSPICES DE BEAUNE

Inaugurating a new era of virtual bidding in November 2007 with the 147th Hospices de Beaune auction of red and white burgundy, 469 barrels of red wine and 138 barrels of white wine were sold for a total of €4.65 million ($6.56 million), including premium, representing an increase of 27 percent, and for red burgundy of 38 percent. Overall, the Domaine des Hospices de Beaune was offering a smaller amount of wine for sale: 607 barrels, compared to 680 last year (down 10.7 percent) because of stringent sorting and further, rigorous sifting of vineyard plots. A new red *cuvée* was offered this year, the Corton Clos du Roi Cuvée Baronne du Baÿ, bringing the sale to a total of 30 *cuvées* of red wine and 12 of white.

With international demand for burgundy strong and production down compared to 2006, record prices were established for Corton-Vergennes, Clos de la Roche, and Mazis-Chambertin. The seven barrels of the new Cuvée Corton Clos du Roi were bid up to record levels for a Corton at Hospices de Beaune, averaging €12,000 ($16,925) per barrel (excluding premium). For the third year in a row, private individuals were able to participate and buy barrels of different *cuvées* under the hammers of François Curiel, chairman of Christie's Europe, and Emmanuelle Vidal-Delagneau of Christie's France.

CHRISTIE'S AND SOTHEBY'S GLOBAL TOP 10s

In US dollar order, and estimates do not include buyer's premium.

Christie's

1. 30 dozen bottles of 1986 Château Mouton Rothschild: *US$288,000 (£137,799) on estimate US$240,000–360,000 (£115,000–172,000)*

2. 12 bottles of 1990 Romanée-Conti, DRC: *US$252,000 (£122,927) on estimate US$100,000–150,000 (£48,800–73,100)*

3. Ditto

4. 12 bottles of 1961 Hermitage La Chapelle Jaboulet: *US$252,000 (£120,574) on estimate US$80,000–120,000 (£38,300–57,400) (US$ world auction record for a case of Rhône)*

5. 12 bottles of 1961 Hermitage La Chapelle Jaboulet: *US$247,747 (£123,750) on estimate £40,000–50,000 (US$80,000–100,100) (European auction record for a case of wine)*

6. 12 bottles of 1985 Romanée-Conti DRC: *US$240,000 (£117,073) on estimate US$100,000–150,000 (£48,800–73,100)*

7. Ditto: *US$237,000 (£119,697) on estimate US$100,000–150,000 (£50,500–75,800)*

8. 12 bottles of 1961 Hermitage La Chapelle Jaboulet: *US$225,225 (£112,500) on estimate £40,000–50,000 (US$80,000–100,100)*

9. 12 bottles 1990 Romanée-Conti DRC: *US$216,000 (£104,348) on estimate US$100,000–150,000 (£48,300–72,500)*

10. 12 bottles of 1945 Château Mouton Rothschild: *US$204,000 (£98,551); no estimate given*

Sotheby's

1. 1 jeroboam of 1945 Château Mouton Rothschild: *US$310,700 (£158,457) on estimate US$80,000–150,000 (£40,800–51,000)*

2. 12 bottles of 1990 Romanée-Conti DRC: *US$262,900 (£128,821) on estimate US$120,000–200,000 (£58,800–98,000)*

3. 12 bottles of 1947 Château Cheval Blanc: *US$146,429 (£71,300) on estimate £40,000–60,000 (US$82,100–123,200)*

4. 12 bottles of 1989 Romanée-Conti DRC: *US$143,400 (£70,266) on estimate US$100,000–150,000 (£49,000–73,500)*

5. 84-bottle 2000 Great Growth Superlot: *US$143,400 (£70,266) on estimate US$70,000–100,000 (£34,300–49,000)*

6. 12 bottles 1967 Romanée-Conti DRC: *US$119,587 (£58,650) on estimate £15,000–20,000 (US$30,600–40,800)*

7. 1 nebuchadnezzar 2000 Château Mouton Rothschild: *US$119,500 (£60,945) on estimate US$15,000–25,000 (£7,650–12,750)*

8. 10 bottles 1961 Château Pétrus: *US$117,435 (£59,800) on estimate £25,000–30,000 (US$49,100–58,900)*

9. 24 bottles 2000 Right Bank Horizontal Lot: *US$95,600 (£46,844) on estimate US$50,000–70,000 (£24,500–34,300)*

10. 6 magnums 1982 Château Pétrus: *US$94,852 (£48,300) on estimate £22,000–28,000 (US$43,200–55,000)*

Prices may vary due to the fluctuation of currencies, most notably the US dollar, throughout the year.

Exceptional growth 1999–2007

Position '08 '07 '06 '05	Vintage	Wine	1999	2004	2005	2006	2007	% growth[1]	% growth[2] annualized
1 1 – 3	1978	La Tâche	5,136	15,860	N/S	30,360[4]	41,455	707	29.81
2 2 8 8	1982	Lafleur	5,532	10,260	9,340	23,000[5]	36,800	565	26.71
3 8 7 5	2000	Mouton[3]	N/A	4,370	3,110	4,140	9,600	500	25.1
4 9 2 7	1982	Pétrus	7,800	14,690	20,900	15,870	43,700	460	24.02
5 5 4 4	2000	Margaux[3]	N/A	4,570	3,400	5,520	8,400	425	23.02
6 4 6 10	1989	Pétrus	6,156	8,640	12,870	23,000	32,200	423	22.96
7 – 1 2	1998	Le Pin	2,900	9,180	6,230	N/S	13,340	360	21
8 3 1 1	1961	Latour	7,920	29,020	22,600	31,900	33,200	319	19.6
9 6 5 9	1982	Le Pin	11,550	18,380	24,500	39,720[6]	33,650	191	14.29
10 7 – 6	1978	Gugal Côte Rôtie La Landonne	2,736	5,440	N/S	9,000	5,660	107	9.51

Prices in GBP per case of 12 bottles (best hammer price achieved in year indicated).

Sources: Christie's, Sotheby's.

1 Percentage growth between July 1, 1999 and June 30, 2007.
2 Annualized growth between July 1, 1999 and June 30, 2007.
3 £1,600 en primeur in 2001.
4 £2,530 a bottle.
5 Magnums.
6 £6,620 per magnum.

Blue-chip growth: 1998 vintage

Position '08 '07 '06 '05 '04 '03	Wine	1999[1]	2002[2]	2003[2]	2004[2]	2005[2]	2006[2]	2007[2]	% growth[3]	% growth[4] annualized
1 1 1 2 3 3	Pétrus	3,800	7,520	6,460	7,260	9,680	15,870	19,550	415	22.7
2 3 6 6 7 5	Lafite	800	1,150	1,035	1,060	1,245	2,100	3,795	374	21.47
3 N/A 2 1 1 4	Le Pin	2,900	6,540	7,590	9,180	6,230	N/S	13,340	360	21
4 2 3 3 4 4	Cheval Blanc	1,150	2,110	1,840	1,725	2,430	4,140	4,485	290	18.53
5 9 10 10 5 7	Ausone	1,150	1,420	1,725	935	1,300	1,210	4,025	250	16.94
6 8 5 5 6 6	Haut-Brion	875	1,090	1,230	1,210	1,470	1,200	2,530	189	14.18
7 5 4 4 2 2	Trotanoy	800	1,740	1,550	1,210	1,470	1,550	2,070	159	12.61
8= 6 9 9 8 9	Margaux	780	830	860	750	1,010	1,270	1,840	136	11.32
8= 4 7 7 9 8	Mouton	780	910	800	940	1,130	1,550	1,840	136	11.32
10 7 8 8 10 10	Latour	780	780	710	665	1,020	1,250	1,670	114	9.98

© Anthony Rose 2008

Prices in GBP per case of 12 bottles.

Sources: En primeur prices (excluding VAT) Wine Society in bond.

1 En primeur price July 1, 1999.
2 Best auction price in year indicated.
3 Percentage growth over July 1, 1999 to June 30, 2007.
4 Annualized growth over July 1, 1999 to June 30, 2007.

Blue-chip growth: 1999 vintage

Position '08	'07	'06	'05	'04	Wine	2000[1]	2003[2]	2004[2]	2005[2]	2006[2]	2007[2]	% growth[3]	% annualized growth[4]
1	1=	4	2	2	Lafite	775	1,092	1,040	825	1,270	2,415	212	17.62
2	1=	2	3=	5	Margaux	775	912	960	858	1,270	2,400	210	17.52
3	6	6	6	4	Mouton	775	936	780	748	1,090	2,100	171	15.3
4	4	1		6	Latour	775	900	1,080	880	1,210	2,070	167	15.06
5	N/A	N/A	10	8	Ausone	1,146	1,044	N/S	N/S	N/S	2,990	161	14.68
6	1=	3	5	3	Pétrus	3,650	5,076	3,680	3,960	6,000	7,360	102	10.53
7	8	5	3=	1	Haut-Brion	775	1,476	960	770	940	1,430	85	9.14
8	5	N/A	7	10	Le Pin	3,300	N/S	3,330	N/S	5,060	4,370	32	4.1
9	9	7	8	7	Cheval Blanc	1,146	1,272	960	1,020	1,130	1,320	15	2.04
10	7	N/A	9	9	Trotanoy	550	408	410	N/S	700	460	–16	–2.52

© Anthony Rose 2008

Prices in GBP per case of 12 bottles.

Sources: En primeur prices (excluding VAT) Wine Society in bond.

1 En primeur price July 1, 2000.
2 Best auction price in year indicated.
3 Percentage growth over July 1, 2000 to June 30, 2007.
4 Annualized growth over July 1, 2000 to June 30, 2007.

Blue-chip growth: 2000 vintage

Position '08	'07	'06	'05	Wine	2001[1]	2002[2]	2003[2]	2004[2]	2005[2]	2006[2]	2007[2]	% growth[3]	% annualized growth[4]
1	1	1	N/A	Le Pin	2,640	N/S	N/S	N/S	20,300	17,940	19,000	620	38.93
2	6	3	5	Latour	1,600	2,375	3,450	3,280	3,680	5,060	10,580	561	36.98
3	10	5	2	Mouton	1,600	1,850	2,990	4,370	3,110	4,140	9,600	500	34.78
4	3=	8	3	Lafite	1,600	2,050	3,220	4,200	2,690	5,520	9,100	469	33.59
5	3=	4	1	Margaux	1,600	2,400	3,910	4,570	3,400	5,520	8,400	425	31.82
6	2	2	6	Pétrus	5,500	N/S	8,370	10,580	15,280	21,850	25,300	360	28.95
7	7	10	8	Ausone	2,400	N/S	N/S	4,180	3,250	7,200	10,350	331	27.57
8	5	7	4	Las-Cases	780	N/S	1,640	1,680	1,430	2,530	2,250	189	19.3
9	8	9	9	Cheval Blanc	2,500	N/S	5,290	3,900	3,820	7,480	7,200	188	19.27
10	9	6	7	Haut-Brion	1,600	2,095	2,990	3,000	2,970	4,600	4,370	173	18.22

© Anthony Rose 2008

Prices in GBP per case of 12 bottles.

Sources: En primeur prices (excluding VAT) Wine Society in bond.

1 En primeur price July 1, 2001.
2 Best auction price in year indicated.
3 Percentage growth over July 1, 2001 to June 30, 2007.
4 Annualized growth over July 1, 2001 to June 30, 2007.

Viticulture

Dr. Richard Smart & Dr. Caroline Gilby MW

Carbon-neutral wineries—every country has one. Forgive the pun, but carbon-neutral wineries seem to be "flavor of the month."

DR. RICHARD SMART   DR. CAROLINE GILBY MW

Is there a wine-producing country that is not claiming a first in this area? Perhaps one of the first is the New Zealand Wine Company in Marlborough. The company claims to have estimated its carbon emissions and has reduced them where possible, offsetting the balance through regeneration of native forest. The program was certified by the New Zealand program of Land Care. One wonders how these programs would fare without forestry offsets.

DR. RICHARD SMART BScAgr, MSc, PhD, DScAgr, termed by some "the flying vine-doctor," is an Australian vineyard consultant with clients in 28 countries. He is now resident in Tasmania, Australia, where Tamar Ridge Estates is his principal client. He began his career in viticulture research in Australia, spanning Israel, the US, France, and New Zealand. Richard is the principal author of *Sunlight into Wine* (Winetitles, 1991) and is considered an authority on canopy management of grapevines. He has regular columns in trade journals *The Australian and New Zealand Wine Industry Journal* and California's *Practical Winery & Vineyard*, is published widely in scientific and other journals, and was viticulture editor for three volumes of Jancis Robinson's *Oxford Companion to Wine*.

DR. CAROLINE GILBY MW is a freelance writer specializing in Eastern Europe and viticulture. She contributed to *The Oxford Companion to Wine* and Dorling Kindersley's *Wines of the World* and has been published in *Decanter*, *Harpers Wine and Spirit Weekly*, *Off Licence News*, and *New Scientist*. She is on the editorial board of the *Journal of Wine Research*. She has a PhD in plant sciences but left science to become senior wine buyer for a major UK retail chain. She lectures for the WSET Diploma on tasting technique, vinification, and wine handling, and she judges at international wine shows, as well as working as a consultant to the wine trade.

Using DNA to build better Chardonnay

Claims by molecular biologists that they are about to improve wine quality abound in the popular press. One of the more recent has been from two professors of the University of British Columbia, Stephen Lund and Joerg Bohlmann, who are studying volatile organic compounds that give wines their flavor. Their aim is to understand how berry flavors are determined by the interplay of grapes' genetic makeup with environmental factors such as light, water, and nutrients. In other words, they seek God's understanding.

They hope to come up with handheld tools that could be taken into the vineyard and used to detect the presence of certain proteins in the grapes. Unlike some of their colleagues in molecular biology, they have been careful not to raise expectations about what they can achieve. They also claim to be aware of consumer concerns about genetically modified grapes.

New vine pests threaten California

As if the glassy-winged sharpshooter and concern over Pierce's disease weren't enough, Napa's wine industry is now on the lookout for the western grapeleaf skeletonizer moth. An adult male was found in a trap on Mount Veeder Road in August, and further traps have been set to see whether this was an isolated incident or a wider problem. The insect is already established in other parts of California and causes damage by consuming leaves and fruit, which allows secondary infections.

In March 2007, the presence of the light-brown apple moth (LBAM), *Epiphyas postvittana*, was confirmed in California by the USDA. This is the first time this pest has been detected in the continental United States. Since then, the insect has been found in nine counties throughout the state, including Napa Valley. Strict quarantine regulations have been imposed, and $15 million has been pledged to help fight this class A pest. The insect is a leafroller-type moth, native to Australia, where it is generally considered the most significant insect pest in Australian vineyards and a major threat to the wine industry.

Grapevine

• **The grapevine genome** has been sequenced by a joint French-Italian project—only the fourth plant species to be sequenced, and the first for a fruit crop. The grapevine was selected because of its important place in the cultural heritage of humanity, dating back to the Neolithic period, and its economic importance as the world's most valuable horticultural crop.

Go higher, go cool!

One company taking the threat of climate change seriously is Torres in Spain. Torres decided to grow cool-climate grapes such as Pinot Noir in the foothills of the Pyrenees, the mountains that divide Spain and France, and the first vineyards have been planted near the town of Tremp. Now Torres is wondering about this region's potential in the context of climate change.

Another Spanish company, Pago del Vicario of Ciudad Real, has also recently invested in high-altitude, cool-climate vineyards in the Sierra Nevada mountains south of Granada. These could be the highest vineyards in Europe. Again, the initial planting will be to cool-climate grapes, but who knows what might happen in the future?

Smoke gets in your eyes—and your wine

Over the past few seasons, Australian vintners have struggled with bushfires, which some commentators say are a feature of climate change. There is no doubt that the present drought in parts of Australia is exceptionally severe. Drought is linked to bushfires, particularly in the northeast of Victoria, and some vineyards were covered in smoke haze for several months.

The resulting wines were tainted, and scientists from the Australian Wine Research Institute have identified the responsible compounds in smoke. Further studies are needed to determine the concentration of these compounds in smoke and critical times during the year when smoke can taint the vines. One aspect of this is that vintners are becoming more nervous about industrial developments in wine regions.

Ladybug, ladybug, fly away home!

Asian lady beetles may yet cause wine problems in Europe. Over the past five years, the insects have been found in Ontario and parts of the northeastern United States, where they caused problems by tainting wine with a peanut-butter-like aroma. The bugs exude methoxypyrazines when disturbed, tainting the grape juice and, subsequently, the wine.

This pest is also in Europe and has spread to the UK. In the Vaud region of western Switzerland near Lake Geneva, two major Asian lady beetle infestations were discovered, prompting fears for the region's wine harvest.

Phytoplasma blues

The first case of grapevine yellows disease Bois Noir has been discovered in Canada in a batch of imported Grenache vines from France. The infected vines have been destroyed and the industry put on a state of high alert.

In Austria, *Scaphoideus titanus* was recently recorded. This leafhopper can carry the phytoplasma that causes Flavescence Dorée, though as yet it is not a vector of the disease. Researchers are concerned that there is no climatic limitation on disease spread into south Germany and north Austria, with South Styria particularly at risk.

Phylloxera in Australia

To date, 83 different genotypes of phylloxera have been found in Australian vineyards, and the Phylloxera Board wants more vines planted on resistant rootstocks to prevent potential devastation. However, with over 20 different rootstocks available to Australian growers, it is vital to assess performance against different strains of the pest; research is beginning to look at this.

In one trial, the impact of three phylloxera lineages was assessed under glasshouse conditions on two rootstocks (Ramsey and Schwarzmann) and compared with self-grafted *Vitis vinifera*, which unsurprisingly showed least resistance to phylloxera genotypes. The G4 strain was significantly more virulent on *Vitis vinifera* than the G20 strain after 10 weeks of infestation, while both rootstocks performed equally well. A new control area in Victoria has been declared to protect the viticulture industry in the Bendigo/Heathcote region from the pest. Phylloxera has also now been found in Martinborough in New Zealand's North Island, where around 25 percent of the vines are on own roots and will have to be replanted.

Eucalyptus taint in Australian red wines

In a paper presented to the Australian Wine Industry Technical Conference in August 2007 by a team of French and Australian scientists, it was argued that the presence of eucalyptus trees near vineyards was the cause of eucalyptus flavor taints in wine. The offending compound is 1,8 cineole, known as eucalyptol. Experiments have shown its presence in wine from vineyards with eucalyptus trees nearby. Such an effect has long been rumored in California, where eucalyptus trees are also abundant.

Nitrogen and TDN

It seems that increased levels of nitrogen fertilization lead to lower levels of TDN (trimethyl-dihydronaphthalene, an important component of the kerosene-like aroma in Riesling), according to German research looking at various fertilizer treatments carried out over several vintages. Other aromatic compounds, including actinidol (important in aged bouquet) and ß-damascenone (intensely fruity), tended to increase with increasing fertilization. Increasing nitrogen fertilization also increased the likelihood for wines to exhibit UTA (untypical aging off-flavors), and this was related to increased aminoacetophenone concentrations, which have been identified as playing a causal role.

Opinion:
The effects of climate change

"Wine styles are defined by regions and variety." Such a simple statement, but it lies at the heart of the contemporary world wine sector. These factors essentially define the geographical origin of wine and its sense of place, so important in marketing and wine appreciation.

The principal defining effect of region is that of climate, especially temperature. Differences in temperature conditions determine wine-style differences between regions—an effect far greater and more universal than, for example, soils. To give an analogy, if Burgundy had the temperature conditions of Bordeaux, it could not grow quality Pinot Noir and would be well suited to ultra-premium Cabernet Sauvignon production.

By this example I mean to emphasize that grape composition and wine style are greatly affected by temperature conditions in the region where the grapes are grown. This has led to the geographical spread of wine regions and variety use around the world. Even a casual glance at a map of the world's wine regions will show these as discrete, and many have reputations for wine excellence for certain varieties.

Over the past two years there has been an extraordinary shift in public awareness about the issue of climate change. This has largely been due to the efforts of Al Gore and the International Panel for Climate Change, both rewarded with the Nobel Peace Prize in 2007. The climate-change issue was a major factor in deciding a government change in Australia's

Grapevine

• **In January 2007,** the EU and INRA launched GrapeGen06, a Europe-wide program that will run until December 2010. Seventeen countries are participating in the research, which is aimed at long-term preservation of *Vitis* genetic resources for future generations. It will particularly seek to protect old, rare, or neglected autochthonous (indigenous) grape varieties, as well as germplasm from wild *Vitis sylvestris*.

• **Climate change** in Burgundy since the 14th century has been tracked in research published in leading science journal *Nature*. The researchers used village records to study harvest dates from 1370 to 2003. Parallels have been found for the warm summers of the 1990s in periods around the 1520s, and also from the 1630s to the 1680s. However, the exceptional heat of 2003 seems to be unique.

November 2007 elections. And now, finally, parts of the wine business are taking notice. At some meetings, winemakers with little awareness of the gravity of the situation give reassuring words: one even suggested that "canopy management and rootstock change can overcome global warming." Sorry—this is nonsense!

I recall giving a paper at the 1988 OIV Congress in Luxembourg on impacts of climate change. Some members of the audience laughed when I suggested that in the future Grenache may be the preferred variety in Bordeaux, but we may yet see that by 2050.

Given the projected increase in temperature, the wine world as we know it will be exceedingly disrupted. In a nutshell, the present reputations that regions have for wine style and variety will inexorably change. No doubt this gradual change will be denied by many, but as time progresses and summer temperatures continue to rise on average, even the most determined diehard will be forced to admit that things have changed, and are changing. Cold regions will become cool; cool regions will become warm; warm regions will become hot; and hot regions will become very hot and may even cease to exist as wine-producing regions.

There are more implications beyond wine style and quality. Pests and diseases will change, some with dramatic implications. Already the deadly phytoplasma disease Bois Noir is moving northward into south Germany and north Austria, as warmer temperatures encourage the migration of the insect that spreads the disease. Pierce's disease in North America is known to be contained in places by temperature, so its impact will spread. Some scientists predict an increase in summer rainfall in some regions, which will cause more fungal disease. There are also predictions of increased drought. Australia is presently suffering the most serious drought in recorded history since European occupation, with dramatic effects on wine production.

My fear is principally for European producers. They have generally failed to realize that their strict regulations have inhibited their ability to compete with the New World and have thus lost market share; in a similar way, their inflexibility may inhibit their opportunity to respond to climate change. Clever wine regions should now be developing production and marketing strategies for 25, 50, and 75 years down the track. The old adage of turning a challenge into an opportunity is appropriate here.

Some wine regions will be more affected than others. Europe will fare badly compared to the Southern Hemisphere because there is more ocean in the southern hemisphere. Iberia and southern France will be most affected, and Tasmania, southwest Australia, New Zealand, and Chile/Argentina will be least affected. Chile is the best-located country of all to combat climate change; water supply will generally be unaffected, and vineyards can be easily relocated to the west, near cool, ocean-current coastal influences, to the east up the Andes foothills, and to the south away from the equator.

Those of you who are lucky enough to have extensive wine collections may well see them change in value. I wonder how long it will be before wine commentators start to classify wine-production periods as "classic," "post-classic," and "new style." Will wines from famous regions in the 1980s be regarded as more precious because they are more like the wine styles that made the regions famous over the past 150 years or so? How many covet the 2003 French vintage as typical? That hot vintage in France was a taste of the future.

To finish on a political note, wine lovers should be foremost in our societies in urging governments to begin the process of combating climate change. For those of us who love our wines as they are, this may be our best hope—and based on the results of the 2007 Bali conference, it is apparent that American wine lovers have the most work to do.

Grapevine

• **Botrytis bunch rot** continues to cause significant crop losses, especially in humid regions, so researchers at Cornell University are studying its biology and control. It seems that humid conditions at flowering can cause latent infections that may develop later in the season, particularly on humid soils. Experiments on Pinot Noir found that more open bunches (deliberately pruned to be similar to the Mariafeld clone) are important in helping air circulation and avoiding disease development, implying that bunch form is a key factor in disease resistance.

• **INRA researchers** have developed techniques for detecting aroma precursors in grapes before harvest. These odorless compounds are difficult to detect in the field but are essential because they are transformed into varietal aromas during winemaking. The technique uses infrared spectroscopy to detect glycosides and has been tested on four varieties (Chardonnay, Muscadet, Riesling, and Gewurztraminer). This should allow growers to make better decisions on picking time.

• **Leaf plucking** has almost become a mantra in the pursuit of full ripeness, but it seems that fruit quality may be at risk when fruit is overexposed to sunlight or when too many leaves are removed from the fruit zone. Sparser canopies can leave sensitive varieties like Cabernet Sauvignon, Grenache, Merlot, and Sangiovese vulnerable to sunburn. Research shows that only 10 percent of full sunlight is required for full color development in the fruit, while higher exposure to solar radiation brings the risk of fruit heating up and loss of anthocyanins.

Wine Science

Dr. Ronald Jackson

A compound that apparently gives Shiraz (Syrah) its varietal flavor has been discovered.

DR. RONALD JACKSON

The peppery aroma appears to come from the presence of rotundone. Although it occurs only in trace amounts, it can be detected in parts per billion. The compound is a quaiane type of sesquiterpene. Those recognizing the term "sesquiterpene" might feel some discomfort, since most sesquiterpenes generate unpleasant, musty odors. For example, sesquiterpenes produced by *Penicillium* generate moldy odors, whereas those produced by actinomycetes generate the odor that typifies soil.

Rotundone is not new to science, having been isolated from several Asian sedges and trees used medicinally. Like many of the aromatics currently being isolated from wine, it occurs (and is aromatically detectable) in minute quantities. However, this is the first report of rotundone being of sensory significance, at least in wine. It is currently unclear whether rotundone is synthesized in grapes or is generated from a grape precursor during fermentation. At least one fungus, a *Penicillium*, can produce rotundone. *Penicillium* gained international renown in the 1940s as the source of penicillin.

Once more is known about the origin of rotundone, it will be easier to assess the practical significance of its discovery. If rotundone is produced in grapes, it may be possible to adjust vineyard activities to influence its synthesis favorably. Too much may be undesirable, as with another group of trace aromatics, the methoxypyrazines, found in Cabernet and related

DR. RONALD JACKSON is the author of *Wine Science* (3rd edition, Academic Press, 2008), *Wine Tasting* (2nd edition, Academic Press, 2009), and *Conserve Water, Drink Wine* (Haworth Press, 1997), and he has contributed several chapters to other texts and encyclopedias. He has retired from active university participation and enjoys the relaxed life of a writer in Bic, Quebec, Canada.

varieties. However, if it is generated during fermentation, adjustments during winemaking may be more significant in influencing its sensory impact. Either way, rotundone may provide a new chemical indicator in the production of quality wine. One sad aspect is that many people are unable to detect its presence at the concentrations that occur in wine.

Rotten aroma

Until recently, it seemed fairly clear which chemicals gave botrytized wines their distinctive fragrance. Terpenes, such as sotolon, and several mushroom alcohols seemed to be critical. A study of Sauternes by Sarrazin and coworkers has put this in doubt. Their research suggests that elevated levels of other compounds with complex chemical names distinguish the flavor of botrytized wines.

In these studies, researchers used extremely sophisticated analytical equipment. However, all instruments have their limitations, as do the people who interpret the data. It is not without reason that most scientists use an abundance of conditionals in their writing. It would be nice to know absolute truth. At the moment, we know only partial truths.

Fungus guards cellar

Anyone who has visited an old European wine cellar must have wondered about the mold that covers the damp walls. Recently, Tribe and coworkers reviewed studies of this unique fungus and decided that its correct name should be *Racodium cellare*. Of more general interest is its possible function in removing volatile pollutants from the cellar atmosphere. These could contaminate wine with off-odors, which is a particular problem in damp, poorly ventilated cellars. The fungus is known to consume alcohols and esters that escape into the cellar air.

Grapevine

• **Consumers prefer corks:** Since the use of synthetic corks and screwcaps is now commonplace in most wine regions and many expensive wines are now being closed without cork, one might assume that consumer opinion would be neutral about closure type. Not yet in Oregon—at least as assessed in a study by Martin and coworkers. They found that use of natural cork is still correlated in the minds of consumers with higher quality. This perception existed despite consumers showing similar preferences and quality ratings if the bottle closure type was concealed. It may take decades for ingrained prejudices to die out. What else is new?

OXYGEN AND CORK

The relative merits of cork versus alternative closures will probably remain unsettled for decades. However, the debate has had a beneficial effect on research into bottle closures. The latest in a slew of recent studies has investigated how oxygen enters wine in stoppered bottles and the dynamics of the process. Lopes and coworkers have discovered that most of the oxygen that enters wine closed with natural cork does so during the first month. Subsequently, ingress falls sharply, becoming negligible after a year. By comparison, technical cork (composed of cork particles) is far superior in limiting oxygen uptake, whereas synthetic cork is considerably worse.

Why does oxygen ingress vary so much over time with natural cork? Scientists cannot as yet give a definitive answer, but a major factor probably involves the oxygen contained within the cellular structure of cork. Cork consists of multiple layers of empty cells that act like miniature gas pockets. A cork of average length consists of a series of cells about 500 cells deep. When the stopper is compressed for insertion into the bottle, pressure on the air in each cell increases. This either diffuses outward into the surrounding air or is absorbed by the wine. Because air contains about 23 percent oxygen, this can contribute several milliliters of oxygen to the wine. In contrast, technical cork is made from cork particles and glue compressed together in a mold. That means that some of the oxygen in the cork cells is forced out during production. In addition, technical cork is less resilient than natural cork and is compressed less prior to insertion into the bottle. The greater oxygen permeability of artificial (synthetic) corks is undoubtedly explained by the slow but continual ingress of oxygen through the stopper.

Only with time, experience, and controlled study will the benefit/deficit consequences of limited oxygen ingress on wine development become clear. There is no perfect bottle closure, just options with different consequences—some good, some bad, some indifferent. In the past, we experienced only the consequences associated with quality variations in natural cork. The wine world is much more complex today, with closure options now encompassing not only natural cork, but also hybrid cork, technical cork, a diversity of synthetic corks, glass stoppers, crown caps, and screwcaps. As the famous oenologist Vernon Singleton said years ago, "Wine is, and must remain, I feel, one of the few products with almost unlimited diversity… keeping the consumer forever intrigued, amused, pleased, and never bored."

ZAPPING HYDROGEN SULFIDE

Off-odor development is one of a winemaker's worst nightmares. Prominent among these is the rotten-egg smell of hydrogen sulfide. Even at concentrations where this revolting odor is not evident, hydrogen sulfide can mask a wine's aromatic finesse. Hydrogen sulfide is usually present at some stage in the production of all wines. However, white wines are more susceptible to its sensory influence, partly due to their more subtle fragrance and the fact that most are bottled early, which provides little time for hydrogen sulfide to escape (volatilize) or oxidize prior to bottling.

Oenologists have long been looking for effective ways to solve the problem. There are remedial solutions, but these have potentially undesirable side effects or are inconsistently effective. Consequently, researchers were on the lookout for yeast strains that produced minimal or no detectable hydrogen sulfide. Although some strains generate low levels of hydrogen sulfide, none produced undetectable levels. For the breeder, the conundrum has been the central role of hydrogen sulfide in the metabolism of the sulfur-containing amino acids required for yeast growth. Recently, however, knockout mutations have permitted Sweiger and coworkers to make strains producing no detectable hydrogen sulfide. These will become commercially available in 2008.

WHITE GRAPES ADD COLOR TO RED WINES

It is an old tradition in some regions to add a small amount of white juice to the must of black grapes prior to fermentation—for example, in the formula developed by Baron Ricasoli in 1874 for Chianti. The formula consists principally of Sangiovese must, with small amounts of Canaiolo and Colorino, plus up to 15 percent from white varieties Trebbiano and Malvasia. Recently this formula has been rejected by several famous Chianti producers; it was viewed simply as a means of speeding maturation at the expense of the integrity of the wine. However, recent studies have given support to

the value of the tradition. Studies on the formation of red pigments during and shortly after fermentation show that the juice from white grapes can enhance the density and stability of a wine's red color. The benefits are most evident with black varieties low in hydroxycinnamic acids and white varieties with high levels of the acids. Because hydroxycinnamic acid derivatives are readily soluble, they are rapidly extracted with the juice during pressing, in marked contrast to the delayed release of anthocyanins and the slow liberation of tannins. It can take days or weeks for them to be extracted from the seeds and skins.

During and after fermentation, hydroxycinnamic acid derivatives react with anthocyanins. These complexes, termed pyranoanthocyanins, are more intensely colored and stable than free anthocyanins. This means that the wine retains a richer color considerably longer than otherwise. Hydroxycinnamic acid derivatives also protect wines from the oxidative loss of the fragrance generated by fruit esters and floral-smelling terpenes.

Studies by Morata and coworkers have added a new dimension to the story. They have shown that different yeast strains can influence the development of pyranoanthocyanins. This apparently depends on their relative abilities to convert native hydroxycinnamic acids to the derivatives that react with anthocyanins.

Since color intensity strongly influences quality perception, winemakers are now in a better position to produce wines that appeal to critics and consumers.

BOTRYTIS INHIBITS FOAM

In the production of sparkling wine, grapes are traditionally harvested manually and transported to the winery with minimal grape rupture. This permits whole grape clusters to be pressed, minimizing pigment and flavor release (especially important in producing champagne from black grapes). Since fungal infection disrupts grape development and typically generates a moldy odor, infected grapes have to be removed manually. In the case of one of the more common pathogens, *Botrytis cinerea*, the fungus was also suspected of affecting the wine's foaming qualities. This suspicion has been confirmed by Clindre and coworkers. Typically, the foaming qualities of sparkling wine have been ascribed to cell-wall mannoproteins released by yeast cells after the second, in-bottle fermentation. However, Clindre's work shows that botrytis directly affects foaming quality. Thus, the tradition of selectively removing infected grapes before pressing has received both confirmation and additional explanation.

FIZZICAL PROPERTIES

It is a popular belief that wines make themselves, winemakers simply acting as midwives. Nothing could be further from the truth. Winemaking skill is crucial in the production of the quality wine consumers deserve and have come to expect. Among these expectations is the production of perfectly clear, stable wines that retain the regional, varietal, and vintage attributes of the grapes.

In sparkling wines, crystal clarity is essential for the unobstructed appreciation of the wine's lively effervescence. Unfortunately, clarity and effervescence are inherently opposed attributes. Crystal clarity requires that haze-generating elements in the wine be reduced to a minimum. This is typically achieved in the production of sparkling wines by the riddling process: riddlers agitate champagne bottles, progressively moving dead yeast cells in the bottle toward the cork. Subsequently, the sediment is ejected in a plug of frozen wine prior to insertion of the traditional cork stopper. However, to facilitate settling of the yeasts during riddling, a fining agent called bentonite (a clay) is added before the second, in-bottle fermentation. Unfortunately, bentonite also removes yeast-wall proteins that are foam stabilizers. These help generate the slow, steady release of bubbles and the formation of a collar of effervescence around the flute/wine interface.

Recent studies by Vanrell and coworkers have confirmed laboratory studies showing that bentonite also removes these foam stabilizers under winery conditions. Thus, the addition of bentonite must be kept to a minimum. However, since bentonite has traditionally been used as the fining agent of choice, the removal of some of these yeast-wall proteins may be beneficial. Consumers would be dismayed if their champagne developed a "head" like beer.

A ROSE BY
ANY OTHER NAME

Table-wine producers have no
easier time than their sparkling-wine
colleagues. Filtering has popularly been
viewed as removing the essence of a
wine's individuality. However, avoiding
it risks the wine becoming cloudy.
Connoisseurs accept sediment in old
wines, incorrectly thinking that it is
an indicator of quality. Tight filtration
(removing all residual microbes and
sediment particles) has often been
viewed as unnecessary—the wine's
alcohol content, acidity, lack of oxygen,
presence of sulfur dioxide, and low
nutrient status being thought sufficient
to assure microbial stability. Results
from Renouf and coworkers have
shown that faith to be ill founded.

Using a variety of techniques, they
were able to enumerate and identify
yeasts and bacteria in bottled wine. They
found surprisingly large numbers of
viable microorganisms in the bordeaux
wines they were studying. Even a wine
bottled in 1909 contained more than
2,000 viable yeast cells per milliliter.
Their study also noted that some wines
showed a marked increase in the
presence of volatile phenols. These can
donate spicy, smoky, pharmaceutical to
stablelike odors. These were probably
generated by the potent spoilage yeast
Brettanomyces, which can survive in
mildly filtered or nonfiltered wine for
years. Viable acetic acid bacteria were
also isolated from many of the wines.

These findings are disconcerting,
especially in light of new data on the
oxygen permeability of cork. It makes
one wonder if some of the bouquet so
eulogized in old wines is not spoilage
under another name.

PRIMARY TCA SOURCE

Since its discovery in the early 1980s,
the moldy off-odor of TCA has been a
major concern of the wine industry.
Considerable success has been achieved
in removing TCA from commercial cork
supplies, and the use of synthetic corks
and screwcaps prevents its occurrence.
Nevertheless, there is still the nagging
question about the origin of TCA.
Without this knowledge, measures
to eliminate it will remain curative
rather than preventive.

Simpson and Sefton conclude from
their review that the primary source
of contamination occurs in the forests
where cork oak is grown. The most
likely culprit is PCP, a biocide used
extensively since the 1930s. One of the
techniques microbes use to detoxify
PCP involves adding methyl groups
to the compound. The unfortunate
by-product is the generation of TCA,
with its intense moldy odor at
infinitesimally small concentrations.
Since the current use of PCP is much
reduced, if not eliminated, and the
harvest cycle for cork removal is
normally nine years, maybe we can
hope that within 10 to 20 years,
the incidence of TCA off-odor will
diminish, even if cork is not treated to
remove the compound.

Opinion:
Finish

The duration and attributes of a wine's fragrance are often considered a central component of its quality. Its duration has been codified in terms of a unit called the caudalie. A finish lasting 20 seconds would be defined as having a caudalie of 20. Regrettably, the origin of this phenomenon is still shrouded in mystery. All that can be done is to hypothesize, based on data gleaned from autonomous studies. Its explanation probably involves changes in alcohol content and shifts in the equilibrium between the bound, dissolved, and volatile states of a wine's aromatic constituents. For example, dilution of a wine's alcohol content (as occurs in the mouth) markedly enhances the escape of aromatic compounds from the wine. This is particularly noticeable with fruit esters, which give young white wines their primary fruity attributes. These esters are most volatile (escape into the air) at about 2 percent alcohol. There is also anecdotal evidence that slight variation in the alcohol content of wine in the glass can significantly influence its fragrance.

In addition, and as a consequence of bottle opening, changes in the equilibrium between the various states of the wine's aromatic compounds undoubtedly affect the finish. Many (if not most) aromatic compounds in wine are weakly "fixed" in nonvolatile complexes with other wine constituents. As dissolved molecules escape into the air, bound forms dissociate and release their constituents into the wine. These are now free to escape into the air. The best-known compounds that bind wine aromatics are mannoproteins, the breakdown products of yeast cell walls. Dilution in the mouth probably disrupts bound complexes, facilitating the release of aromatic constituents into the air. These reach the nose via the back of the throat. Enzymes in the saliva may also promote the degradation of bound complexes, selectively releasing particular aromatics.

Off-odors

When discussing off-odors, it is as if one were discussing incorrect grammar. The difference is that, whereas accepted grammar texts exist, there are no equivalents for wine off-odors. What is considered an off-odor often depends on its vinous context. I have seen renowned Sauternes, spoiled by the nail-polish-remover odor of ethyl acetate, lauded for its quality, and prestigious Rhône wines praised for their wonderful terroir when spoiled by the manure smell of ethylphenols.

Even sherry is so oxidized (in a complex way) that it is considered one of its principal quality attributes. If experts have problems separating off-odors from contextual issues, what hope does the average consumer have? Years ago, before "corked" became the safe expression to use when rejecting wine, "vinegary" was commonly used—that is, unless you wanted to be more sophisticated, in which case "oxidized" was preferable. This is intended not to poke fun at experts or consumers but to highlight the legitimate problem of defining what a wine fault is, to whom, and under what conditions.

A valuable study would be for returned wine to be assessed by qualified tasters as well as chemically analyzed. It would be useful to know what correlation exists between the stated reason for rejection and any fault detected. My suspicion is that there would be little correlation. If so, this is a lamentable situation. How can winemakers improve their efforts to produce faultless wines if what the clientele objects to cannot be correctly identified?

Genie in the bottle

Influencing opinion is one of the goals of all journalists and certainly of most wine writers. For me, if the genie in the bottle would grant me one wish, it would be to promote the production of wines using unique techniques and from superb but little-known grape varieties. Standard varieties such as Cabernet Sauvignon, Sangiovese, Tempranillo, Pinot Noir, Chardonnay, Riesling, Gewurztraminer, and Sauvignon Blanc are superb. However, how many variations on a theme can any range of vineyard and winemaker generate without their products becoming essentially indistinguishable and somewhat hackneyed?

Unfortunately, my genie would have to work several major miracles. The first would be to produce a new crop of grape growers and winemakers willing to break from the staid traditions of their forebears and take the risk of producing something new. Next, there would have to be a mind shift in most wine critics, as well as wine merchants and restaurateurs. Most are incredibly tradition-bound and thoroughly habituated to standard tastes and quality perceptions. Finally, there are the fickle and timid wine buyers. If the label is not one they immediately recognize, or the wine from a familiar producer or country, there is little chance of the wine's purchase. Most consumers are amazingly loath to try something new, unless already sanctified by some authority. How could the genie shake people out of their comfortable ruts? I suspect my genie would say I had asked for too much.

Wine on the Web

Tom Cannavan

Are you part of the YouTube generation? YouTube.com allows anyone to upload a short film and lets anyone else watch it.

TOM CANNAVAN

A phenomenal success, YouTube has grabbed a huge audience, and wine is well represented among the millions of video clips to be found there. A search for the keywords "wine tasting" finds no fewer than 1,500 different clips of wine tasting—from Matt Skinner tasting with Gordon Ramsay, to Borat's infamous tasting with the "Knights of the Vine" in Mississippi.

Some switched-on winemakers and retailers have cottoned on quickly to this free and relatively easy route into "viral marketing" by creating their own YouTube showcases. Berry Bros. & Rudd has a whole virtual wine school, with a series of high-quality educational films, while London merchant Bibendum Wines has put up a fun and offbeat timeline of the company's history for your entertainment.

With a barrage of wine-related blogs, podcasts, and video clips out there, the wine world has certainly not been slow to embrace the possibilities of online multimedia.

TOM CANNAVAN has published wine-pages.com since 1995, making it one of the world's longest-established and most popular online wine magazines. He also publishes beer-pages.com and whisky-pages.com. According to Jancis Robinson MW, "wine-pages.com should be of interest to any wine lover seeking independent advice" (*Financial Times*). In Richard Ehrlich's opinion, "if all sites were this good, we'd spend more time surfing than drinking" (*The Independent on Sunday*), and Robert Parker finds wine-pages.com a "superb site. All-inclusive, friendly, easily navigated, with plenty of bells and whistles" (*The Wine Buyer's Guide*).

Crushpad

At crushpadwine.com, anyone can become a winemaker without necessarily leaving their armchair. Run by a combination of wine-industry veterans and technology-industry boffins, Crushpad is a San Francisco winemaking facility that sources grapes from nearby Napa and Sonoma and will make wine to order for customers anywhere in the world.

Proving popular with both individuals and groups, the site allows clients to interact with the winemaking team by email and the Web to participate in decision-making through all stages of the winemaking process—from choosing which grapes to vinify, to deciding on the label for the bottles. Costs vary, depending on the source of grapes and style of wine, with a minimum outrun of one barrel (25 cases) ranging in price from $4,500 to $9,900 before shipping charges.

While many customers are making wine for their own interest and enjoyment, Crushpad also offers a low-cost and low-risk first step into commercial winemaking: Crushpad Commerce will help you establish your own brand, market it, and even sell and deliver the wines to your customers for a set fee.

And all that from the comfort of your own PC.

Grapevine

• **Internet technology** is playing an increasingly important role in winemaking. Winemakers can now monitor the weather in their vineyards or the temperature of their tanks via the Internet. They can even set wheels in motion to deal with problems with a few mouse clicks.

• **The popularity of wine tourism** has inspired several sites dedicated to the subject. Extremely good online guides to 45 regions of France are provided by www.winetravelguides.com. Each comes with interactive maps and itinerary planners and costs $15, but a $100 annual subscription grants access to everything on the site.

• **Drinkrhone.com,** the website of acclaimed Rhône expert and author John Livingstone-Learmonth, was launched recently. A subscription of $75 per year provides full access to in-depth tasting notes, estate profiles, and feature articles.

• **www.thewinegang.com** is a new twist—an independent collaboration involving five of the UK's best-known wine critics, Tim Atkin MW, Joanna Simon, Anthony Rose, Olly Smith, and this writer. The site presents a monthly look at 200 wines on UK retail shelves chosen by the wine gang, with a database that can be searched by retailer, price, wine style, and the wine gang's own scoring system. An annual subscription costs £19.95 (about $40).

• **Further evidence** that finding a niche for online wine retailing is one route to success, Peter Sidebotham has recently launched Hand Picked Burgundy Wines at hpb-wines.com. He sells mature bottles of burgundy (and some Pinot Noir from other locations) by the single bottle, bringing rare access to this most esoteric of wine regions to anyone with an Internet connection.

Opinion:
The growth in online wine retail

I have been a commentator on the wine e-tailing scene for more than a decade now, and in that time scores of online wine retailers have come and gone, as have just as many theories on how to make a success of this tricky but potentially lucrative business model.

In the early days, the mantra was "content is king," with big players spending fortunes on adding extensive editorial to their sites. Mostly this ploy failed because the basic proposition was flawed: the first choice for anyone seeking fact and unbiased opinion will never be those trying to sell them something.

These days, having an online store that is well organized, easy to use, and reliable is taken for granted. But that is not enough to really crack this tough nut. My advice has always been the same: to sell wine successfully on the Web, you need to create a genuinely interesting shopping experience. That is a much harder challenge.

Yet successful wine e-tailing is possible, as illustrated by four wine retailers of very different hues.

Majestic is one of the UK's brightest wine-retailing stars, and its online store at majestic.co.uk has been a huge success, with sales of around £18 million in 2007 representing 7.5 percent of total sales. Commercial director Jeremy Palmer says, "We offer improved search and navigation, as well as a personalized experience for each customer, based on their preferences and purchase history. This lets us recommend more esoteric wines from our range, which are among our most interesting and best-value offerings."

So, personalizing the experience is working for Majestic and can even help broaden customers' drinking habits. Is that the same for example number two, the UK's biggest multiple grocer, Tesco?

Nick Jackman is commercial category manager of the hugely successful tesco.com/winestore. "Online wine sales continue to play a key part in the overall growth of wine within Tesco," he says. "Our customer research has defined clear types of online-consumer behavior—ranging from the bargain hunters to those who are keen to experiment more and widen their own product knowledge. Our Wine Club members are willing to spend more on the average bottle of wine." Jackman also points to the very large range of wines available online—more than 1,200—and plenty of mixed-case deals as keys to success.

At the other end of the market, case study three is a small startup wine business that has weathered the storm of dot-com uncertainty. Jonny Gibson, who runs Wine Discoveries, says, "It was clear to us when we launched that we had to have an online shop window. Today, www.winediscoveries.co.uk accounts for 20 percent of our monthly sales." The site allows customers to read about "secret discoveries" from Gibson's small family producers. Jonny comments, "We have worked hard, constantly trying new ideas and measuring what works."

The final case study for successful wine e-tailing is an interesting one: Adrian Bentham is wine director for the UK's most successful direct-selling wine business, Laithwaites (laithwaites.co.uk). He says, "Laithwaites currently does about 20 percent of business on the Web, and Web sales grew by 34 percent last year." Laithwaites built its business through mail order and wine clubs and embraced the Internet at quite a late stage. Has it been a challenge? "The Internet changed the retail landscape considerably, giving customers far more control. It requires different thinking but also represents a fantastic opportunity for anyone with a great product who can provide a really good service."

That comment sums up quite succinctly the current position for selling wine on the Web: the successful breed of online wine retailers reaches wine lovers everywhere, and they are helping bring greater choice and diversity to our drinking.

Grapevine

• **Quality websites** created by genuine, slightly obsessive amateurs were the foundation of modern-day cyberspace. Check out some independent wine enthusiasts continuing the tradition, such as Swedish Alsace-lover Per Warfvinge's alsace-wine.net or Brit Peter May's self-explanatory pinotage.org.

• **Even the slowest-witted** of the world's print publications have cottoned on to the fact that the Web has grown up and needs to be taken seriously. Many more resources are being directed toward online editions of established wine magazines, such as harpers.co.uk, wine-spirit.com, and www.finewinemag.com.

• **Wine and food writer** Natasha Hughes has launched a blog that looks at her specialty subjects from an unusual angle: that of someone who is fighting a battle with weight and finding ways to cope with her diet while acknowledging a love of food and wine. As Natasha says: "I no longer fit into my regular clothes, [and] my 'fat clothes' are becoming a tight squeeze too. This year, though, I'm going to do something about it—and I'll be recording my triumphs and tribulations on this blog." Follow her progress at 3littlewords.net.

Alexa ratings

Since the first edition of *Wine Report* I've included a snapshot of the world's 10 most popular wine websites, as suggested by Alexa.com. Partnered by Google, Alexa tracks the surfing behavior of 10 million people, building up a picture of which websites they visit. This theoretically allows Alexa to compile popularity rankings for hundreds of thousands of websites, broken down into categories. The reliability of the statistics must be in some doubt, however. For example, Alexa lists a total of 4,300 websites in the category "wine." Apparently, the third most visited wine site in the world is that of Frankland Estate, a small winery in Australia. Still, some people may find this top 10 of all wine sites listed by Alexa.com useful.

Alexa's top 10 most-visited wine websites

1. www.winespectator.com
2. www.foodandwine.com
3. www.franklandestate.com.au
4. www.erobertparker.com
5. www.localwineevents.com
6. www.wine-pages.com
7. www.vinakoper.si
8. www.biltmore.com
9. www.penley.com.au
10. www.domaine-wardy.com

Best Internet wine sites

[S] = paid subscription required for some/all content
[R] = no paid subscription, but registration required for some/all content
[E] = non-English-language site, but with English-language version

Editor's note: I asked Tom Cannavan not to include his own site, wine-pages.com, in any of the lists he compiled because, inevitably, he would either be accused of self-promotion or (more in line with his character) he would not rate his site highly enough. However, I would place wine-pages.com at number two under Best Wine Sites and number one under Best Wine Forums. Although I have a small corner at wine-pages.com, I receive no payment. TS

BEST WINE SITES

1. www.wine-searcher.com [S]
2. www.erobertparker.com [S]
3. www.winespectator.com [S]
4. www.cellartracker.com [S]
5. www.bbr.com
6. www.jancisrobinson.com [S]
7. www.wineloverspage.com
8. www.decanter.com [R]
9. www.wineanorak.com
10. www.burgundy-report.com

BEST WINE FORUMS

1. www.ukwineforum.com
2. www.erobertparker.com [S]
3. forum.auswine.com.au
4. groups.msn.com/bordeauxwineenthusiasts
5. www.enemyvessel.com/forum
6. www.westcoastwine.net
7. forums.egullet.com
8. www.wldg.com
9. www.vinocellar.com/wineforums.aspx
10. www.wineweb.com/fusetalk/forum/index.cfm

BEST WINE RETAILERS ON THE WEB

1. www.bbr.com (UK)
2. www.wine.com (USA)
3. www.oddbins.com (UK)
4. www.majestic.co.uk (UK)
5. www.bevmo.com (USA)
6. www.wineaccess.com (USA)
7. www.auswine.com.au (AUS)
8. www.winecommune.com (USA)
9. www.finewinelist.net (UK)
10. www.bibendumwine.co.uk (UK)

BEST SMALLER INDEPENDENTS SPECIALIZING IN REGIONS

1. www.yapp.co.uk (Rhône and Loire)
2. www.domainedirect.co.uk (Burgundy)
3. www.rogerharriswines.co.uk (Beaujolais)
4. www.nzhouseofwine.com (New Zealand)
5. www.dvino.co.uk (Italy)
6. www.lasbodegas.co.uk (Argentina)
7. www.lsfinewines.co.uk (South of France)
8. www.australianwinesonline.co.uk (Australia)
9. www.englishwine.co.uk (England)
10. www.nickdobsonwines.co.uk (Austria, Switzerland)

BEST REGIONAL WINE SITES

Sites in national language. Those with an English-language version are marked [E].

Argentina
www.winesofargentina.org [E]

Australia
www.wineaustralia.com
www.winestate.com.au

Austria
www.austrian.wine.co.at [E]
www.weinserver.at

Belgium
www.boschberg.be [E]

Brazil
www.brazilian-wines.com/en [E]

Bulgaria
www.bulgarianwine.com/pages/bulg.htm [E]

Canada
www.canwine.com
www.winesofcanada.com

   British Columbia
   www.bcwine.com

   Ontario
   www.winesofontario.org

Chile
www.winesofchile.org [E]

China
www.winechina.com/en/ [E]
www.wineeducation.org/chinadet.html

Croatia
www.bluedanubewine.com/croatia.html [E]

Cyprus
www.cyprus-wine.com [E]
www.wine-pages.com/guests/contrib/nncyprus.htm

Czech Republic
www.znovin.cz [E]
www.czecot.cz/?id_tema=16 [E]

Denmark
www.vinbladet.dk/uk/ [E]
www.vinavl.dk

France
www.frenchwinesfood.com [E]
www.terroir-france.com [E]
www.abrege.com/lpv

Alsace
www.alsacewine.com [E]
www.alsace-route-des-vins.com [E]

Bordeaux
www.bordeaux.com [E]
www.medoc.org [E]
www.sauternes.com

Burgundy
www.bivb.com [E]
www.burgundy-report.com

Champagne
www.champagne.fr [E]
www.champagnemagic.com [E]

Corsica
www.corsicanwines.com [E]

Jura
www.jura-vins.com [E]

Languedoc-Roussillon
www.languedoc-wines.com [E]
www.coteaux-languedoc.com [E]
www.vinsduroussillon.com

Loire
www.interloire.com
www.loirevalleywine.com [E]

Provence
www.provenceweb.fr/e/mag/terroir/vin [E]

Rhône
www.vins-rhone.com [E]

Southwest France
www.vins-gaillac.com [E]

Georgia
www.gws.ge [E]

Germany
www.winepage.de [E]
www.germanwine.de/english [E]

Greece
www.allaboutgreekwine.com [E]
www.greekwinemakers.com [E]

Macedonia
www.macedonian-heritage.gr/wine [E]

Hungary
www.winesofhungary.com [E]

Indonesia
www.hattenwines.com [E]

Israel
www.israelwines.co.il [E]
www.stratsplace.com/rogov/israel [E]

Italy
www.italianmade.com/wines/home.cfm [E]
www.italianwineguide.com [E]

Piedmont
www.italianmade.com/regions/region2.cfm [E]

Tuscany
www.chianticlassico.com [E]
www.wine-toscana.com [E]

Japan
www.kizan.co.jp/eng/japanwine_e.html [E]

Latvia
www.doynabeer.com/wine [E]

Lebanon
www.chateaumusar.com.lb [E]
www.chateaukefraya.com [E]

Luxembourg
www.luxvin.lu [E]

Malta
www.marsovinwinery.com [E]

Mexico
mexicanwines.homestead.com [E]

Moldova
www.turism.md/eng/wine [E]

Morocco
www.lescelliersdemeknes.net [E]

New Zealand
www.nzwine.com
www.wineoftheweek.com

Peru
www.easy-wine.net/peru-wine.htm [E]
www.tacama.com [E]

Portugal
www.portugal-info.net/wines/general.htm [E]
www.vinhos.online.pt

Madeira
www.madeirawineguide.com [E]
www.madeirawinecompany.com [E]

Port
www.ivp.pt [E]
www.portwine.com [E]

Romania
www.aromawine.com/wines.htm [E]

Russia
www.russiawines.com [E]

Slovenia
www.matkurja.com/projects/wine [E]

South Africa
www.wosa.co.za

www.wine.co.za

Spain
www.jrnet.com/vino [E]
www.verema.com/en [E]

> **Ribera del Duero**
> www.riberadelduero.es [E]
>
> **Rioja**
> www.riojawine.com [E]
>
> **Sherry**
> www.sherry.org [E]

Switzerland
www.wine.ch [E]

Tunisia
www.tourismtunisia.com/eatingout/
wines.html [E]

United Kingdom
www.englishwineproducers.com
www.english-wine.com

United States
www.allamericanwineries.com

> **California**
> www.napavintners.com
> www.wineinstitute.org
>
> **New York**
> www.fingerlakeswinecountry.com
>
> **Oregon**
> www.oregonwine.org
>
> **Texas**
> www.texaswines.org
>
> **Washington**
> www.washingtonwine.org
> www.columbiavalleywine.com

Uruguay
www.winesofuruguay.com [E]

BEST WINE-SITE LINKS

www.winelinks.ch
www.bluewine.com

BEST VINTAGE-CHART SITE

www.erobertparker.com/info/
vintagechart1.asp

BEST TASTING-NOTES SITES

www.erobertparker.com [S]
www.finewinediary.com

www.winemega.com [E]
www.stratsplace.com/rogov
www.yakshaya.com
www.thewinedoctor.com
www.metawines.com
www.gangofpour.com

BEST WINE-EDUCATION SITES

www.wset.co.uk
www.wineeducation.org
www.wineeducators.com
wine.gurus.com
www.rac.ac.uk/?_id=1512

BEST VITICULTURE SITES

www.crcv.com.au
winegrapes.tamu.edu

BEST OENOLOGY SITE

en.wikipedia.org/wiki/winemaking

BEST GRAPE-VARIETIES SITE

www.wine-lovers-page.com/wineguest/
wgg.html

BEST SITES FOR FOOD-AND-WINE PAIRING

www.matchingfoodandwine.com
www.forkandbottle.com

THE FAR SIDE OF WINE

www.soundofwine.net
www.justwinepoints.com
www.wineloversmeet.com
www.dibbukbox.com
www.valentinomonticello.com
www.rupissed.com
www.winespirit.org
www.winelabels.org
www.gmon.com/tech/stng.shtml
www.howstuffworks.com/question603.
htm

The 100 Most Exciting Wine Finds

A number of these wines will be available on certain markets, but many are so new, restricted in production, or downright obscure that the only way to get hold of them would be to visit the producer— if he or she has not already sold out.

The entire *raison d'être* of this section is to bring to the attention of serious wine enthusiasts the different and most surprising wines being developed in classic areas, the best wines from emerging regions, and other cutting-edge stuff. The prices are retail per bottle in the local currency of the country of origin (see About This Guide, p.5). My tasting note follows the contributor's own note, for comparison or contrast, or simply a different take.

Riesling Vin de Glace 2006 Alice Hartmann (Luxembourg, €68 per half-bottle) *This* aïswein *is yet another in a string of winemaker Hans Jörg Befort's ever-expanding arsenal of fine wines— be it from Burgundy, Luxembourg, or his native German Mosel. A harbinger of things to come from a Europe with fewer barriers?* David Furer
Stunning. Electrifying. Like Mosel Spätlese Eiswein used to be before it was stupidly outlawed. Tom Stevenson

Pure Brut Nature NV Pol Roger (Champagne, €34) *A skillful blend of freshness with some softly aged components and lovely acids, underscored by a silky mousse. This* cuvée *achieves an unprecedented level of instant class and finesse.* TS

Estate Select Syrah 2005 CedarCreek, British Columbia (Canada, C$34.99) *Voted Wine of the Year by Canadian Wine Awards judges in 2007. Winemaker Tom DiBello brings a California ethos to this rich, voluptuous wine, redolent with flavors of black cherry, black raspberry, and smoked meat. A plush, sexy wine with whispers of oak, soft tannins, and a spicy, peppery finish.* Tony Aspler
I shall discard all the superlatives I wrote while tasting this wine and replace them with a confession: this is the most gorgeous Syrah I have ever tasted. It might not be the most complex (although it does have complexity), but its fruit is so seductive that I drank the bottle, opened the backup bottle, drank that, and tried to order three cases from CedarCreek, but they had run out! TS

Antique Oloroso Rey Fernando de Castilla (Sherry, €28) *Small shippers often do not go in for the official VOS and VORS classifications owing to the*

cost and red tape, but if they did, this would certainly qualify for VOS. It is a beautifully aged wine, by oloroso standards relatively light, dry, deeply impressive, and very long. It is a bargain, too. I am not surprised that Jan Petersen ran out of some of his wines this year. Julian Jeffs QC
Very pale in color, with a searchlight brightness and clarity, but the aroma is so deceptively light and delicate that I was completely surprised and blown away by the great purity and intensity of flavor on the palate. The finish is endless, marked with laserlike precision and great finesse. TS

Solera P∆P Palo Cortado Osborne
(Sherry, €150) *This is my idea of a perfect dessert wine. Being a palo cortado, it is not too heavy and has just the right degree of sweetness to smooth the edges. Its age gives it a fascinating complexity. It is a wine that reveals itself with every sip, and every sip calls for another.* Julian Jeffs QC
I usually prefer genuinely dry palo cortado, but the distinct touch of sweetness in this wine has a haunting quality. Very special. TS

Cockburn's 20 Year Old Tawny Port
(Port & Madeira, €16 per half-bottle) *Pale amber tawny; lifted dried fruit and Christmas cake on the nose; quite full, rich yet supremely elegant and seductive. Soft, silky length. Serve chilled in the summer months.* Richard Mayson
Perfectly poised sweetness. Great class. TS

Yatir Forest 2004 Yatir (Israel,
NIS 150) *Almost inky in its deep garnet color, this blend of 80 percent Cabernet Sauvignon, 14 percent Merlot, and 6 percent Syrah is showing elegant, full-bodied, and solid, with soft tannins, smoky wood, and vanilla all in fine balance with*

ripe blueberry, black currant, and plum flavors. Look as well for an appealing, earthy undercurrent leading to a long, deep, broad, and generous finish. Drink now–2014. Daniel Rogov
Quite simply the classiest Israeli wine I have ever tasted. TS

Gran Cabernet Franc 2005 Pulenta
Estate, Agrelo (Argentina, AP 105) *Pulenta's first release of a stand-alone Cabernet Franc is well up to the outstanding quality of its other reds. This is seductively oaked, with fine, medium-weight tannins, elegant green-pepper and cassis notes, and a finish that lasts for minutes.* Tim Atkin MW
Shades of Loire fruit bush on the nose, but nothing raw. Ripe and delicious fruit on the palate. Long and beautifully balanced. TS

Cuvée Luitmar Trocken Barrique
Aged 2005 Philipp Kuhn, Pfalz
(Germany, €19.20) *Kuhn sets a high standard of European harmony with this blend of Blaufränkisch, Cabernet Sauvignon, St Laurent, and Sangiovese. Pronounced aromas of fruits of the forest are ably supported by delicate notes of coffee and chocolate. A mere suggestion of pepper and spice lends a touch of elegance. An ample presence of ripe tannins gives the wine a youthful edge and the promise of longevity.* Michael Schmidt
To tell the truth, I would not have been bowled over by the thought of blending these varieties, but I was bowled over by the wine, which is beautiful now, yet promises even more to come. TS

John Riddoch Cabernet Sauvignon
2005 Wynns, Coonawarra (Australia,
A$77) *A far cry from the oaky, tannic blockbusters of the 1990s, this is the reinvented John Riddoch, courtesy of winemaker Sue Hodder. A thoroughly delicious wine and a welcome change*

of direction, which began with the 2004. Huon Hooke
You're right, Huon—the new John Riddoch has downsized. But it has retained its gravitas. TS

Blanc de Blancs Brut 2002

Palmer (Champagne, €24.90) *From a cooperative currently on top form, this very fresh and crisp, yet lovely and smooth blanc de blancs contains 75 percent Trépail (eastern Montagne).* TS

Sycra Syrah 2004 Clos de Gat (Israel, NIS 190) *The flavors and aromas in this firm, dense wine seem to shift and change every few moments. Opens with cherries and currants, goes to grapes and pepper, sage and anise, and then on to freshly ground Arabica coffee. On the superbly long and tannic finish, the cherries and currants rise again. Well focused and intense. Drink now–2012.* Daniel Rogov
A stunner, Rogov! Lovely, lip-smacking, juicy fruit, with refreshing acidity and café crème finish. TS

Brunello di Montalcino Poggio al Vento Riserva 1999 Col d'Orcia,

Tuscany (Central & Southern Italy, €65) *Lively, brilliant ruby hue. Nose fresh, elegant, floral; slight wild-fruit hints. Magnificent structure, full flavor, velvety, full, warm, but without anything in excess; great length and persistence, perfect fusion between tannins, acidity, and fruit. A noble wine of great elegance.* Franco Ziliani
An inspired choice, Franco: not big or in your face; just elegant, restrained, and classy. TS

Muscat Tradition 2006 J-M & F Bernhard (Alsace, €6) *This delicious, flowery, off-dry wine with orange-flower on the finish is the best 2006 Alsace Muscat I have come across.* TS

Salento IGT Rosato Magilda 2006
Barsento, Puglia (Central & Southern Italy, €10) *Full, bright, light ruby color; perfume of mature fruit. Structured, rich, and complex on the palate, with plenty of body and vibrancy. Long, while still managing a surprising freshness and drinkability.* Franco Ziliani
Not a particularly complex wine, but absolutely satisfying, with delightful fruit and a long finish. TS

Ventolera Sauvignon Blanc 2006
Viña Litoral, San Antonio (Chile, CLP 8,000) *Though full-flavored and intense, this coastal Sauvignon develops in the glass, becoming more subtle and food-friendly over time. Very promising signs for a new venture from Sauvignon specialist Ignacio Recabarren.* Peter Richards
Wet-pebble nose, very sharp fruit, and really quite exhilarating. TS

Riesling Reserve 2005 Fox Run, New York (Atlantic Northeast, US$30) *Floral, herbal, green, zingy aromas are magnified on the palate against lime zest, grapefruit, nectarines, and minerality. Winemaker Peter Bell's passion is red wine, but even he was wowed by the whites that the 2005 vintage produced.* Sandra Silfven
It is the elegance, freshness, and purity of Riesling fruit that make this wine stand out. Superb! TS

Single Vineyard Quebrada Seca Chardonnay 2006 De Martino, Limarí

(Chile, CLP 9,900) *It's the tangy, nervy acidities in Limarí's new breed of coastal Chardonnays that are catching the eye, and this one marries the freshness well with plenty of nutty, savory oak depth.* Peter Richards
Crisp, lime-dominated citrus fruits, with barely discernible oak. Extraordinary minerality for Chardonnay. Lovely, Peter! TS

Cabernet Sauvignon Old Vines 2004
Woodward Canyon (Pacific Northwest, US$75) *This is a super-sappy, rich, ripe, dense, and saturated wine made in the currently fashionable high-octane mode. Thick, chocolaty, and young, it is powerful and almost over the top, but delivers such juicy, sappy, vibrant fruit flavors that it holds itself in balance and should reward another decade or more of cellaring.* Paul Gregutt
Rich, powerfully constructed, and with a highly complex and satisfying finish, this is a meal in a glass. TS

Noé Pedro Ximénez Muy Viejo
VORS González Byass (Sherry, €36) *This is a classic aged Pedro Ximénez, with a wonderful nose—powerfully concentrated and very sweet, but showing its great age with a dry sting on the finish.* Julian Jeffs QC
It's that dry sting in the tail that stops me pouring it over vanilla ice cream! This nectar should be sipped. TS

Laški Rizling Ledeno Vino 2005
PraVino, Slovenia (Eastern & Southeastern Europe, €120) *The Čurin family have always been passionate about their sweet wines, and it's not hard to see why. This icewine is definitely the best Laški Rizling I've ever tasted, with incredible weight and intensity, yet it's ultra-clean and lingering, too.* Dr. Caroline Gilby MW
The most extraordinary thing about this wine (apart from its being delicious) is how it can be this sweet and have such low VA. Canadian icewine-makers, take note! TS

Carignane 2005
Roshambo, Alexander Valley (California, US$25) *Cranberry/raspberry aroma, with traces of Beaujolais Nouveau; loads of mid-palate fruit reminiscent of old California reds. A tad rustic/earthy, but with great polish and finesse.* Dan Berger
Soft and creamy fruit, with a touch of oak and class. TS

Unplugged Riesling 2006
Muddy Water, Waipara (New Zealand, NZ$25) *Luscious wine that's been made from hand-selected bunches to maximize the influence of botrytis. There's a strong and pure honeyed influence counterbalanced by fresh acidity that prevents any suggestion of cloying. A restrained sticky—better as an aperitif than as a match with sweet desserts.* Bob Campbell MW
Elegant, light Auslese style, ideal for sipping on a balmy evening. TS

Sacromonte 15 Year Old Oloroso Seco
Valdivia (Sherry, €33.50) *Everything about this wine is exactly what it ought to be: color, nose, and mouthfeel. Its age gives complexity, and it has admirable length. It is just the right age at which to drink an oloroso, with all the nuances of maturity without those intimations of immortality that call for tiny sips and deep thoughts.* Julian Jeffs QC
The aromatics are so powerful, complex, and hypnotic that I would have been happy inhaling them all night without ever getting around to drinking this wine. But I'm glad I did. Rich, polished, and totally dry. TS

Coteaux du Languedoc 2005
Mas des Dames (Languedoc-Roussillon, €6.30) *From a new estate outside St-Chinian. I love its spicy, undemanding fruit.* Rosemary George MW
Owners Aad and Lidewij Kuijper must be natural winemaking geniuses to produce such a polished and silky wine. I want to buy three cases! TS

Château Séguin Pessac-Léognan 2005
(Bordeaux, €16.50) *Shows rich, juicy fruit with vibrant extrovert character. Still quite tight tannins, but*

there is plenty of lovely fruit and elegance to provide a fine future. David Peppercorn MW
Refreshing, crunchy red-currant fruit supported by fine oak. Drink now or in 10 years. TS

Alentejano Alicante Bouschet 2005 Paulo Laureano Vinus (Portugal, €58) *Dense, inky, treacly wine, packed with mulberry and blackberry fruit and high in both alcohol and acidity. Aromas are smoky and rich, and the length berry and rhubarb.* Charles Metcalfe
I've always been fascinated by this teinturier grape, and this is the classiest example I've ever encountered. Thank you, Charles. TS

Bairrada FLP 2005 Luís & Filipa Pato (Portugal, €16 per 50-cl bottle) *A blend of Bical, Sercealinho, and Maria Gomes, the juice is treated by cryoextraction to give a richer must than normal. Aromas are honeyed, with notes of hay and toast, and the acidity is high. It will be interesting to see how it ages…* Charles Metcalfe
I'm not a fan of cryoextraction, but it can produce some interesting results, and this is perfectly pitched between sweetness and crisp acidity. Is it the reduction effect or one of the grapes that gives this wine its almost petrolly, terpene-like mineral notes? TS

Vin de Pays des Coteaux d'Enserune Cuvée d'en Auger 2005 Domaine de Perdiguier (Vins de Pays & Vins de Table, €9) *I think this is one of the best Cabernet/Merlot blends of the Midi, especially for the price. I hope you agree.* Rosemary George MW
The fruit is soft and sensual in the mouth, yet it has the structure to take food. Absolutely delightful—and amazing value. TS

Yarden Cabernet Sauvignon El Rom Vineyard 2003 Golan Heights Winery (Israel, NIS 180) *Intensely dark ruby toward royal purple; full-bodied, with caressing tannins and a moderate oak influence. Opens with black currants, blackberries, and minerals; goes to meaty, earthy, and herbal aromas and flavors, and then to spices and a long and elegant fruity finish. Firmly structured with excellent grip and complexity. Best 2010–20.* Daniel Rogov
Long, elegant, and beautifully structured, with powerful, spicy fruit. TS

Tokaji Mylitta Alma 2005 Dobogó Winery, Hungary (Eastern & Southeastern Europe, HUF 13,300) *A really lovely, elegant example of modern late-harvest Tokaji. It's intense and luscious, yet very fresh and pure. Honeyed, with notes of peach, citrus zest, and orange blossom, and great acid lift on the finish.* Dr. Caroline Gilby MW
I'm an avid fan of modern-style Tokaji, and stunning examples like this make me wonder why anyone would want the old oxidative stuff. TS

Limited Edition 2004 Carmel (Israel, NIS 180) *This blend of 65 percent Cabernet Sauvignon, 20 percent Petit Verdot, and 15 percent Merlot shows soft tannins and generous but gentle wood, those in fine balance with currant, blackberry, and black-cherry fruits, all melding together with light hints of pepper, anise, and cigar-box aromas and flavors. Round and caressing, elegant and long. Best 2009–13.* Daniel Rogov
Softness on the nose belies the richness and power on the palate, combining for extraordinary elegance. TS

The Journeyman 2005 Boekenhoutskloof (South Africa, R200) *Delicate herbaceousness and subtle florality proclaim Cab Franc as the*

senior component, but there's also cassis—although fruitiness is not what this wine is about. Tannins are ripe, elegant, and tucked away (making for easy early drinking), and there's a fresh savoriness. Typical Boekenhoutskloof understatement, and local rather than blandly international in character. Tim James
Greater than the sum of its parts. TS

Reserve Merlot 2005 Bedell, New York (Atlantic Northeast, US$48) *Like a fine essence of Merlot, with tons of ripe plums, sweet blueberries, fine chocolate, and vanilla, braced by supple tannins and acidity. An amazing wine by John Irving Levenberg.* Sandra Silfven
On the one hand I get a sense of something too soft and polished, while on the other it is very long and elegant. I could mark this down as being too crafted, a showpiece. But instead I've given it the benefit of the doubt, marked it up, and will take another look at it in a couple of years. TS

Vin de Pays d'Oc Réserve 2004 Domaine de Nizas (Vins de Pays & Vins de Table, €25) *A new wine from Domaine de Nizas; the blend includes a large dollop of Petit Verdot as well as Cabernet and Syrah.* Rosemary George MW
Deep, lip-smacking fruit and chalky tannins. Elegant. TS

Gewurztraminer 2004 Vinoptima, Gisborne (New Zealand, NZ$54) *Big, intense wine with an almost chewy, oily texture. Very complex, with layers of floral and exotic spice characters. Very powerful indeed and still remarkably fresh. A truly class act.* Bob Campbell MW
Luscious and intense, with passerillage of an Indian summer concentrating the fruit. Definitely exotic, but I cannot get much spice, and it is much drier

than expected for 20 g residual sugar. Anyone crazy enough to invest millions in a specialist Gewurztraminer vineyard and winery gets my vote. TS

Arlanza Varietales 2004 Buezo (Spain, €13) *Cabernet black currant perfume is prominent on the nose, as is the French-oak character. On the palate the wine has a firm, tannic structure with some background richness. The finish has more than a hint of elegance. Will keep.* John Radford
The oak is a bit too showy, but it is well balanced with the plush fruit. A polished wine for the price. TS

Gaia S 2006 Gaia Wines (Greece, €18) *Estate-grown on their hillside Nemea-Koutsi limestone vineyard. Aghiorghitiko 70 percent and Syrah 30 percent. A floral, classy, complex, burgundian aroma. Fleshy, soft flavors of black cherries. Layered. Has structure for aging up to five to seven years. A seductive wine.* Nico Manessis
The oak is noticeable, but it has lovely fleshy fruit. TS

Fitzrovia Rosé Sparkling 2004 RidgeView Estate (Great Britain, £19.95) *This is a classy, elegant wine, with subtle fruit and none of the confected fruit you get from champagne. Their best to date.* Stephen Skelton MW
Fresh and elegant, with a perfectly balanced dosage. TS

Graham's Crusted Port (bottled 2001) (Port & Madeira, €20) *Deep, youthful vintage-port color; ripe and opulent with violets and mint on the nose; full and plummy with tannic grip, solid structure, and good length. Drink now or keep 10 years. This is poor man's vintage port!* Richard Mayson
Modern-style crusted port, if that doesn't sound like a contradiction in terms! TS

Clarry's Grenache Shiraz 2006
Kalleske, Barossa Valley (Australia,
A$19) *Kalleske's cheapest wine is
a great buy: deep and sapid; earth
and dry-spice aromas; sweetly ripe
on palate, but not unctuous or syrupy
like some of its peers. Very drinkable.*
Huon Hooke
*Definitely not unctuous or syrupy. Lovely
and creamy, slips down a treat.* TS

**Côtes du Lubéron Grand Deffand
2003** Château La Verrerie (Rhône
Valley, €30) *Deep nose with fresh fruit
and spice flavors, with a nice touch of
oak. On the palate, the wine is well
balanced, complex, and fresh, like a
great Côte-Rôtie.* Olivier Poels
*First bottle corked, but second fine
and silky, with violetty fruit.* TS

Las Brisas Pinot Noir 2006 Viña
Leyda, San Antonio (Chile, CLP 8,500)
*Pitched at a very acceptable price, this
Leyda Pinot shows the attractive
combination of intensity and elegance
that characterizes this region and
producer.* Peter Richards
*The oak shows, but the oak is good,
and this Pinot needs the oak.* TS

Gelber Muskateller Klassik 2006
Daniel Jaunegg, South Styria (Austria,
€7) *What wonderful freshness! This is
the ideal aperitif wine: cool, fragrant,
animating, with delicate notes of lilac
and jasmine. Summer in a glass—
fresh, long, and elegant.* Philipp Blom
*Fresh, crisp, and floral, this makes the
ideal alternative to Sauvignon Blanc
when accompanying asparagus.* TS

Minervois 2005 Domaine St Jacques
d'Albas (Languedoc-Roussillon, €5)
*I liked this wine for its lack of oak,
preferring it to the oaked Château St
Jacques d'Albas. Firm, dry, spicy fruit
that reminds you of the wild Minervois
countryside.* Paul Strang

*Deliciously sweet fruit, with instant
smoky complexity. Mellow tannins on
the finish make this a great guzzler.* TS

Barbaresco Basarin 2004 Adriano
Marco & Vittorio, Piedmont (Northern
Italy, €20) *Aged in 25-hl botte, no
barrique, this wine of exemplary
purity, enjoyability, and elegance has a
fresh bouquet. It is lively, chewy, and
full of juicy fruit, the mouthfeel velvety
and the tannins firm but not
aggressive.* Franco Ziliani
*I found the tannins almost gritty, yet
not at all rough, and strangely it is the
tannins that make this wine.* TS

Grüner Veltliner Tradition 2005
Schloss Gobelsburg, Kamptal (Austria,
€14) *I simply cannot resist this wine.
Marvelous complexity, perfect Veltliner
notes with creamy structure—a wine
that breathes generosity despite its
perfectly judged focus. This is all
balance and expression, at once fresh
and ageless.* Philipp Blom
*For those who prefer a not-too-dry,
fatter-styled Grüner Veltliner.* TS

Special Reserve 2004 Recanati
(Israel, NIS 180) *A blend of 92 percent
Cabernet Sauvignon and 8 percent
Merlot, with generous but not
exaggerated toasty oak and soft
tannins, those integrating nicely and
opening to reveal a rich array of
currant, blackberry, and black-cherry
fruits, with gentle overlays of mint and
chocolate. As the wine develops, look
for a hint of cigar tobacco on the long
finish. Drink now–2012.* Daniel Rogov
*A big, big wine that is softened on the
finish by elevated fruit.* TS

The Jem 2004 Waterford (South Africa,
R680) *Aromas of scrub, fresh herbs,
and ripe black berries, with hints of
menthol and oak vanillin. Though
aiming at expensive iconhood, this*

seamless blend of mostly bordeaux and Rhône varieties is unshowy, elegant, and refreshing, but with plenty of sweet fruit. Long, fine tannins; good length. Cathy van Zyl MW
It's that sense of seamlessness that makes this wine refreshingly light, long, and fine. TS

Carolina Bela 2004 Jakončič, Slovenia (Eastern & Southeastern Europe, €20) *Cooler conditions in 2004 mean this blend of Chardonnay with Rebula works really well. The two varieties are seamless, with lovely texture and harmony, and ample balancing acidity. Great to see a well-made wine with a sense of place, too.* Dr. Caroline Gilby MW
Soft, rich, and creamy, with cashew notes in the fruit and sweet, creamy oak on the finish. TS

Touraine Sauvignon 2007 Jacky Marteau, Domaine de la Bergerie (Loire Valley, €4.20) *One of the stars of the Touraine, Jacky makes wonderful Sauvignons that go way beyond that simplistic "gooseberry and lime" cliché. This has the richness of ripe grapes and the classic citrus aromas of Sauvignon, backed up with an almost sweet-fruit palate that adds weight to this totally dry white. Sancerre, eat your heart out—this is a Loire Sauvignon that screams value!* Charles Sydney
Citrus verging on passion fruit, without any of the sweaty armpits that can blight Marlborough Sauvignon when it goes out on this particular limb. Real structure and depth. Excellent. TS

Cabernet Franc 2005 Burrowing Owl, British Columbia (Canada, C$33) *This is like no other Cabernet Franc I've tasted. It's massive. Dense ruby color with a swashbuckling flourish of blackberries, black currants, and dark chocolate on the nose. Richly extracted fruit flavors on the palate echo the bouquet with like flavors; fleshy and almost chunky on the palate, but for all its Rubenesque sensuality it keeps its balance.* Tony Aspler
Rich and complex aromatics, including good telltale fruit-bush notes, followed by very dense fruit, with pulsating alcohol and acidity to help keep everything lively. TS

Mercurey Blanc 2006 Château de Chamirey (Burgundy, €8) *Supple and fruity. Easy to drink. Unexpectedly stylish. Excellent value.* Clive Coates MW
Lovely lemony Chardonnay fruit supported by nicely understated oak. Remarkable value, and it will still improve. TS

Bourgogne Blanc 2006 Guy Roulot (Burgundy, €10) *Crisp and pure and harmonious. Very elegant indeed for a generic wine.* Clive Coates MW
Tasted after returning from a burgundy tasting, and I found this to be delightfully not toasty or oaky. Delightful, in fact. TS

Arbois Savagnin Vendange de Novembre 2005 Domaine Jacques Tissot (Jura & Savoie, €17.50 per half-bottle) *From late-harvested 50-year-old Savagnin vines, this has an attractive spicy and ripe nose, which leads on to a delicate palate with balanced sweetness and that spiciness coming through again. Delicious and far removed from the oxidative Savagnin that is traditional to the Jura and, I know, disliked by Tom!* Wink Lorch
Yes, indeed, there is some spiciness—more than might be expected for the supposedly nonaromatic white Savagnin (sure it's not pink at harvest time?), and it is not at all oxidative. A distinctive wine—thank you, Wink. TS

Pinot Noir Resonance Reserve 2006
Sineann (Pacific Northwest, US$72)
*Amazingly detailed and nuanced, this
brings a cornucopia of fruits—berries
and cherries, figs and prunes. The
acids are perfectly balanced and the
barrel notes so well integrated that
you cannot separate them out, but
they add streaks of coffee, smoke,
chocolate, bourbon, and caramel. The
finish just keeps on going.* Paul Gregutt
*I just wish this wine had a tad less
oak and alcohol, but I cannot deny
the seductiveness of its silky, sensual
blackberry fruit.* TS

St-Joseph Les Granits 2005 Michel
Chapoutier (Rhône Valley, €50) *Mineral,
with a fabulous nose of blackberry,
herbs, and smoke. This full-bodied
wine has great intensity and a pure
finish.* Olivier Poels
*No heaviness, has finesse, and will age
gracefully.* TS

VDQS St-Pourçain Pinot Noir 2006
Union des Vignerons de St-Pourçain
(Loire Valley, €3.90) *Young Jacques
Vigier and his team in St-Pourçain
have turned up trumps with what
has to be one of France's best-value
Pinot Noirs. Light and easy to drink,
its classic (and pretty!) Pinot Noir
red-currant-and-spice nose follows
through on its surprisingly intense
palate and appetizingly fresh finish.
I'd serve it coolish and drink it with
anything, though maybe a glass would
be best!* Charles Sydney
*First bottle spoiled by slight spritz;
second bottle perfect. Although light-
bodied, this wine doesn't need to be
chilled, since it has surprising length
and intensity for its weight, and
chilling will only dumb this down.
The price is mad!* TS

**Mandelberg Sangiovese Trocken
Barrique Aged 2005** Philipp Kuhn,
Pfalz (Germany, €32) *Pronounced
aromas of cherries, cassis, and prunes
on the nose are supported by notes of
herbs, Christmas spices (Lebkuchen),
and white pepper on the palate.
Twenty months' aging in partly new
French oak gives the wine a firm
backbone and good aging potential.
The price reflects rarity as well as
class.* Michael Schmidt
*Too oaky, but good creamy-spiced fruit.
A great wine to serve blind and win a
few bucks from your guests!* TS

**Riesling Wormeldange Koeppchen
*** 2006** Alice Hartmann
(Luxembourg, €14) *As good as any
top German dry Riesling from a light-
to medium-bodied vintage at a
comparable, if not better, price.*
David Furer
Classy. TS

Pinot Noir 2005 Judith Beck,
Burgenland (Austria, €20) *Delicate
and deep, a walk through an autumn
forest with leaves, mushrooms, and
red berries. The balance is right, the
fruit is clear yet playful, tannins are
fine and ripe, and the wood is fully
integrated. Yum!* Philipp Blom
Classic cherry varietal aroma. TS

Sauvignon 2006 Channing Daughters,
New York (Atlantic Northeast, US$24)
*"Blanc" is omitted on purpose. This
wine, in name and composition, is an
expression of winemaker Christopher
Tracy's whimsy and passion. It's mostly
Sauvignon Blanc, with a complement
of Chardonnay, fermented both in
oak and stainless steel. It has huge
aromas and flavors—from grass,
citrus, herbs, and minerality, to
butterscotch and smoky oak. It has
weight and texture and a powerful
finish.* Sandra Silfven
*Extremely refined and thankfully
not overoaked.* TS

Faugères Les Collines 2006
Domaine Ollier-Taillefer (Languedoc-Roussillon, €5.50) *Their basic Faugères cuvée—and none the worse for that. It tastes of the warmth of the Midi.* Rosemary George MW
I get that warmth, too, which gives the wine a definite sense of place. Yet there's elegance with the warmth. TS

Vin de Pays d'Oc Viognier 2006
Domaine de Gourgazaud (Vins de Pays & Vins de Table, €7.80) *Some lovely peachy fruit with a hint of oak and excellent varietal character. From one of the pioneering Minervois estates. I first went there in 1978!* Paul Strang
Very soft, floral Viognier, but with a refreshingly assertive finish. TS

Malbec 2006
Domaine Jean Bousquet, Tupungato, Mendoza, Argentina (Organic & Biodynamic Wines, AP 25) *Another ripe, rather than overripe or simply jammy, version of Argentine Malbec, with a surprising lightness of touch.* Monty Waldin
I agree, Monty: there's a lightness and drinkability seldom seen in top Argentine Malbec. TS

Saint-Romain Blanc 2006
Domaine Alain Gras (Burgundy, €10) *Lean in the best sense. Clean and ripe and refreshing.* Clive Coates MW
Yes, lean, but rich. And it will age a few years. TS

Chenin Blanc 2006
Racetrack (South Africa, R65) *Medium yellow, it brims with passion-fruit, papaya, and bruised-apple aromas and flavors. The oak component is barely noticeable—just a light spiciness on the nose and palate. The palate is rich and balanced; refreshed by brilliant Chenin acidity.* Cathy van Zyl MW
Heavily oaked Chardonnay-style Chenin… TS

Chambourcin NV
Holy-Field Vineyard & Winery, Kansas (Other US States, US$15) *Simple and fruity is more or less the good news with most Chambourcin, but there is also some sweet coffee-laden toast here, along with bursts of ripe raspberry and strawberry. The hints of its hybrid parentage are hiding in the aromas and finish, but the harmoniousness of the wine allows the taster to look beyond that.* Doug Frost MW
Does it rain in Kansas, Doug? Because that's the only excuse I've heard for planting this "waterproof" hybrid grape. This is the richest, most serious Chambourcin I've tasted. Acid-bright fruit. TS

Domaine des Tourelles 2004
(Lebanon, LL 14,000) *Delicious! This year's find. Cabernet Sauvignon/Syrah. A nose of morello cherries. In the mouth, strawberries and mild spices are underpinned by the silkiest of tannins. Simply one of the most elegant Lebanese reds I have ever tasted.* Michael Karam
Easy-drinking, light-bodied red, with sweet chocolate and berries on the palate. TS

Biodynamic Vineyard Semillon 2007
Krinklewood, Hunter Valley (Australia, A$20) *Biodynamism is catching on slowly in Australia, but both the viticulturist and the winemaker at Krinklewood claim to have seen major changes in grape quality since converting. The wine is certainly outstanding, partly thanks to talented contract winemaker Jim Chatto.* Huon Hooke
An unusual, slow-developing Semillon that needs 4–5 years' bottle-age. TS

Blaufränkisch Cupido 2004
J Heinrich, Middle Burgenland (Austria, €40) *A marvelous wine from a*

difficult vintage. Nutmeg and berries, a wine of great elegance and depth. A salty touch, ripe tannins, and sophisticated use of wood but lively fruit dominates. Lovely. Philipp Blom
Big, oaky, and rich. TS

Ribera del Duero Astrales 2005

Los Astrales (Spain, €24) *The nose has a wonderful, big, fresh raspberry/ strawberry perfume, and the palate marries massive fruit with huge but soft tannins. It needs time but will be magnificent: a new classic in the making.* John Radford
Substantial and satisfying, yet capable of development. Drying tannins on the finish need food to help achieve the balance that will come in time from the richness of the underlying fruit. TS

Sierras de Málaga Ariyanas Tinto 2006 Bentomiz (Spain, €12.50)

Big, spicy, almost Syrah-like pepper on the nose (although there's no Syrah in it—the local Romé gives it that characteristic) and lots of warmth and ripeness on the mid-palate, with a soft, gentle finish belying its 14 percent ABV. John Radford
Good, guzzling, creamy fruit. TS

Vin de Pays Charentais Colombard 2006 Les Hauts de Talmont (Vins de Pays & Vins de Table, €6.75)

A new estate from the Charente where no vines have been planted before. Lovely fresh, pithy fruit. Rosemary George MW
Fresh, generous fruit, highlighted by green notes, with an off-dry finish. TS

Terrazze Retiche di Sondrio Pignola 2004 Triacca-Marchiopolo,

Valtellina (Northern Italy, €35) *Lively, luminous ruby/garnet hue. Complex aroma, mineral with notes of raspberry, dog rose, and black currant; also graphite, leather, hints of white truffle and pepper. Perfectly balanced on the palate, mineral, nervy, with crunchy fruit nicely balanced by firm acidity. Great wealth of flavor; tannic but not aggressively so.* Franco Ziliani
Very fresh and light in the mouth for 13 percent alcohol. Crunchy fruit, crisp tannins. TS

Franciacorta Brut Blanc de Blancs Collezione 2001 Cavalleri, Franciacorta

(Northern Italy, €35) *Straw yellow, of notable brilliance and good perlage. Fragrant bouquet, fresh but very complex, with hints of chocolate, white flowers, bread crust, and spice. In the mouth, the attack is lively, articulate, nervy, of great purity and marvelous freshness. Great length, very agreeable.* Franco Ziliani
Soft mousse supporting creamy-biscuity fruit with excellent acidity. TS

Monterrei Godello 2006 Crego e Monaguillo (Spain, €9.50)

The Godello has the most beguiling aroma of hazelnuts, which follows through on to the palate. The acidity is fresh but gentle, and the fruit subtle and almost musky. The finish is astonishingly long and elegantly subtle. Delicious. John Radford
Is this soft, fresh tapas wine waiting for Godello? TS

Dão Primus Branco Reserva 2006

Quinta da Pellada (Portugal, €26) *Lean and citrous, with toasty perfume; hints of pineapple and passion fruit on the palate. Ascetic overall, but with toasty, candied length.* Charles Metcalfe
It would have been impossible to find such a fresh, full and gently rich white wine like this in Portugal 10 years ago. Even five years ago, it would have been a struggle. TS

Vin de Pays du Lot Rouge 2006

Domaine de Sully (Southwest France, €16) *Dark garnet color still purple*

throughout. Slightly spirity nose gives way to abundant fruit on the palate, well balanced with soft tannins and fair acidity. Some length, needs a year or two. Unusual blend of Malbec, Merlot, and Mansois. Paul Strang
You're right, Paul: it is an unusual blend, and it has an unusual, somewhat high-toned elegance, with a long finish maintained by soft tannins. Scores well for individuality. TS

Les Breteches 2006 Château Kefraya (Lebanon, LL 8,500) *With a new winemaker, this Kefraya stalwart is much improved. Made from Cabernet Sauvignon, Cinsault, Carignan, Mourvèdre, Tempranillo, and Grenache, it is beautifully balanced, full-bodied, and smooth. Great cherry nose. In the mouth, berry fruits and peppers. Good tannins. A terrific example of modern Lebanese wine.* Michael Karam
Carbonic maceration lifting the nose? Too soft for my taste, but that will be why some people will buy it. TS

Vin de Pays des Côtes de Gascogne Moelleux 2005 Domaine Lauroux (Southwest France, €7) *Pale gold. A minerally, even flinty nose introduces unexpected citrus and pineapple flavors on the palate. The kind of aperitif that d'Artagnan's mother would have drunk and even kept to accompany her foie gras. Satisfyingly half sweet and not cloying. Highly affordable, too.* Paul Strang
First bottle oxidized; second bottle fine. Light and fresh; tangy, sweet finish. TS

Adoli Ghis 2007 Antonopoulos (Greece, €11) *From high Achaia (altitude 650 m [2,130 ft]). A unique blend of Lagorthi (60 percent) and other delicate and insistent white grapes under the umbrella term of Asproudes. Lemon-blossom aroma and freshly pressed apples and pears followed by a*

lovely extract on the finish. Impeccable balance to help it evolve over the next three to four years. Nico Manessis
A fresh, crisp lemony flavor. Ideal sidewalk-café wine. TS

Target Gully Riesling 2007 Mt. Difficulty, Central Otago (New Zealand, NZ$25) *Lovely wine with great purity of mineral and orange-blossom flavors. Although relatively sweet (40 g/l), it is exquisitely balanced by gently assertive acidity. Subtly powerful Riesling.* Bob Campbell MW
What the Aussies call an FGR. TS

Malvasia Miliarakis 2007 Nikos & Takis Miliarakis, Minos Cretan Wines, Crete, Greece (Grape Varieties, €7.50) *Vigorous citrus and peach aromas, round in the mouth with sufficient acidity and a long finish.* Dr. François Lefort
Fresh, clean, and deceptively easy-drinking, with good acidity helping intensify the finish. TS

VDQS Entraygues-le-Fel La Pauca 2005 Domaine Laurent Mousset (Southwest France, €8) *Deep brilliant ruby with rich curranty nose from 50 percent Mansois (Fer Servadou) and 50 percent Cabernet Franc. Weightier than most wines of this region but still easy to drink. The Cabernet is aged in old barrels for eight months, the Mansois in tank.* Paul Strang
Very curranty, but also very smoky and very dry, with an intense finish. TS

Vallée d'Aoste Petite Arvine Vigne Champorette 2006 Les Crêtes, Aosta Valley (Northern Italy, €13) *Pale straw, brilliant and translucent. Lively nose, stony, with notes of sage, citrus, and white flowers. Direct, incisive attack, ample, broad consistency, with great elegance and good nerve, full of freshness. Still very young, with good*

aging prospects. Franco Ziliani
First bottle corked; second bottle fine. Fresh and floral, with green notes. TS

Kékfrankos Spern Steiner Selection
2004 Weninger & Gere, Hungary (Eastern & Southeastern Europe, HUF 5,600) *Franz Weninger (junior) is an impressively thoughtful and committed winemaker. The Spern Steiner vineyard in Sopron has a great location overlooking the lake and elderly 40-year-old vines. Kékfrankos is not usually well regarded in Hungary and is often thin and mean, but Franz's secret is to treat it like Pinot Noir to coax the best out of it. This is a revelation—Kékfrankos taken to a higher level.* Dr. Caroline Gilby MW
Although currently a bit rustic, there is also an underlying silkiness, suggesting that it could grow into a much finer, more elegant wine. TS

No Added Sulphur Cabernet Sauvignon 2007 Stellar Organics,
Western Cape, South Africa (Organic & Biodynamic Wines, R22) *The brightness of color and incredible clarity of the smooth fruit flavors here belie South Africa's historic reputation for somewhat tough-tasting reds.* Monty Waldin
Franc-like fruit-bush aroma, with plenty of acid to keep the fresh currant fruit bright. TS

Müller-Thurgau 2006 Schlossgut
Bachtobel, Ottoberg (Switzerland, SF 15) *Pure freshness. Light in color and weight, this is an ultra-crisp wine with intense freshness, lots of natural, well-integrated acidity, and a citric backbone. Energetic finish.* Chandra Kurt
Very rich nose giving an impression of sweetness, followed by medium-sweet fruit on the palate and surprising minerality on the finish. TS

Vin de Pays des Côtes Catalanes
Trigone 2006 Domaine Le Soula (Vins de Pays & Vins de Table, €9) *The second wine of Le Soula. Rather cheaper and from younger vines. Mainly Macabeu. A touch of oak gives some extra backbone to some herbal flavors. Good acidity.* Paul Strang
Rich and oily with green fig fruit and a slight spritz. TS

Heida Spätlese 2005 Mario Chanton,
Chanton Weine, Visp (Switzerland, SF 35 per half-bottle) *Dark golden in color, and oily texture. Intense aromatics of lime marmalade, fleur de sel, and liquid honey. Even with such opulent aromas, the wine shows an overall balance.* Chandra Kurt
Although the nose is too oaky for me, and the thought of rich apple fruit with oaky notes does not appeal, somehow it works, and the oak dissipates the longer the finish goes on. TS

Muscadet Sèvre & Maine Sur Lie Clos des Montys Vieilles Vignes
1914 2006 Jérémie Huchet (Loire Valley, €6.50) *The pleasure with most Muscadet is immediate: young wines with loads of zip, just begging to be drunk. Here we've got really ancient vines giving minerality, fresh concentration, and a character that's moved from simple fruit to a more rewarding complexity. To me, this is just a great, understated wine to be drunk for sheer pleasure.* Charles Sydney
I used to age Muscadet as serious as this, but experience has taught me to enjoy it young. TS

Louwberg Maastricht Riesling
2006 Apostelhoeve, Netherlands (Belgium, Netherlands & Scandinavia, €9) *Well-made Riesling. Open, pure, nice and flowery; pear, lemony in the nose, elegant and fresh; nice acidity, some apple, a hint of*

sweetness, but dry enough on the finish. Ronald de Groot
Surprisingly soft and ripe for its origins, this wine needs at least 12 months bottle-age to bring out the terpenes. TS

Château La Prade Côtes de Francs 2004 (Bordeaux, €17) *On the nose, vivid fruit allied to a lovely purity and freshness. The palate shows intense fruit amplified by oak. Ripe tannins will need a little time to mellow. Drink 2009–12.* David Peppercorn MW
I found the tannins outweighed the fruit, although it worked well with food. However, I came across a bottle of the 2003, which you had originally wanted to submit, and found that to be absolutely delicious and amazingly fresh for the vintage. TS

Torrontés Reserva 2005 Quara Lavaque, Salta (Argentina, AP 60) *Barrel fermentation and time on lees have given this intriguing white wine a toasty, creamy dimension to add to the honeyed spice of top-notch Salta Torrontés.* Tim Atkin MW
Soft and typically perfumed, but extraordinarily rich. TS

Vin de Savoie Chignin Bergeron Cuvée Noé 2006 Pascal & Annick Quenard (Jura & Savoie, €11) *A bright green-gold color leads on to an almost herbal, minerally nose with rich yellow fruit. This Roussanne is properly dry with really crisp acidity and a slight touch of CO_2. The spicy yellow fruits build in the mouth to a really long finish. Supremely balanced, the wine is amazingly versatile with food— anything from foie gras, to dried ham, cheese, or creamy sauces.* Wink Lorch
Soft and floral from start to finish. TS

Crémant Rosé Brut 2005 Caves St Martin (Luxembourg, €5) *Does it deserve all the fuss made over it by*

Telecran magazine and its judges? Very good value, to be sure, but let's have Mr. Bubbles decide. David Furer
No, it doesn't deserve any fuss at all. There is nothing wrong with this wine, but it is just a respectable, good-value fizz, and Marc Gales produces other (better) crémants. TS

Vinho Verde Espumante Côto de Mamoelas Alvarinho Brut 2005 PROVAM (Portugal, €11) *This fits the criteria for good bubbly: high acidity and relatively neutral flavors (although it is made from aromatic Alvarinho and full of character). It's bottle-fermented, with 12 months on the lees. And it works—nearly bone-dry, with rich, stone-fruit perfume, a hint of toast, and a vigorous mousse.* Charles Metcalfe
The nose is a bit reductive, but that should go with time. I like the idea of a fully sparkling Vinho Verde, but they need to experiment with different base wines and tweak the dosage. TS

Hommage Vin de Mousseux NV Cep d'Or (Luxembourg, €7) *Having tasted an Elbling Sekt just across the river in Germany's Nittel, disgorged 12 years later from its 1989 vintage, I knew this ignoble grape could have wonders worked with it elsewhere, and Johnny Vesque has done just that.* David Furer
This has more potential than actual quality. Johnny needs to work on the base wine he uses for the dosage, so that it brings out more fruit on the nose and palate. TS

Grillette Brut Absolu G Méthode Traditionnelle NV Grillette Domaine de Cressier, Cressier (Switzerland, SF 26) *An ultra-dry, crisp sparkling wine, with delicate mousse and good length. Seductive minerality on the finish.* Chandra Kurt
Firm, good acidity. Will gain finesse with nine months in bottle. TS

Index

Abbona, Ernesto, 109
Acadia Vineyards, 286
Achaval, Santiago, 301
Achaval Ferrer, Bodega, 301
Acker Merrall & Condit, 376
Aegean islands, 215
Agroscope Changins-Wädenswil
  (ACW), 186
l'Aigle, Dom. de, 83
Airén grape, 107
AIS (Associazione Italiana
  Sommeliers), 109
Alaska, 278
Alba Vineyards, 265
Albert, Marcellin, 83
Alcohol and Tobacco Tax and Trade
  Bureau (TTB), 254–5, 257
alcohol
  alcoholism in South Africa, 240
  health effects of rising levels,
    349–50
  levels in biodynamic wines, 310
  levels increase, 249, 251, 310
  see also vinification
Alentejo, 145
Alex, Las Vegas, 222
Alexa, 400
Alfrocheiro grape, 146
Alicante Bouschet grape, 145
Aliperti, Vinny, 269
Alphonse Lavallée grape, 335
Alsace, 38–46
  bottles, 39
  certified organic vineyards, 342
  competition awards, 43, 46
  failure to try screwcaps, 40
  rejection of physiological
    ripeness, 38–40
  sugar levels, 41
  vintage reports, 42–4
  websites, 402
Altair, 293
Altesse grape, 63, 360
Alvarinho grape, 146
Aly Duhr, Mme, 177
Amarone, 107
Amphorae, 231
Angélus, Ch., 11
Anjou, labels, 50
Antinori, Marchese Piero, 256
Apostelhoeve, 169
Aragonez grape, 145, 146
Argentina, 293, 300–7
  Australian investment in, 300
  certified organic vineyards, 341
  climate change, 386–7
  diversity of vineyards, 300–1

Argentina (cont.)
  icon wines, 302
  investment in boutique wine
    production, 301
  Malbec, 74
  new wine areas, 301
  tango used to promote wines,
    303
  vintage reports, 304–6
  website, 401
  white wines, 303
Argiolas, Antonio, 121
Argüeso, Bodegas, 141
Arinto grape, 146
Arizona, 273, 275
Arkansas, 275, 276
Arkavati grape, 330
Arkeshyam grape, 330
Arlaud, Dom., 21
Armagnac, white, 73
Aruga, Yuji, 335
Asia, 328–37
  domestic wine production,
    328–9
  labeling problems, 331
  vintage reports, 332–5
  viticultural practices, 331
  wine styles, 329–30
  see also individual countries
Asmal, Kader, 242
Assyrtiko grape, 215
Athiri grape, 215
Atkin, Tim, 397
Atlantic Northeast, 265–72
  aging wines, 268
  blends, 268
  competition awards, 268
  direct-shipping permits, 267
  expansion of Ohio wine
    industry, 270
  new AVA, 270
  Ohio quality seal, 266
  pests, 383
  Riesling renaissance, 265–6
  tax relief for West Virginia farm
    wineries, 269
  vintage reports, 269–70
  wine-and-food tourism centres,
    266
Atwater Estate Winery, 269
auctions and investment, 373–80
  auction house profits, 375–6
  Australia, 312, 375
  best bargains, 372
  Bordeaux, 373–4, 375
  boutique wine production in
    Argentina, 301

auctions and investment (cont.)
  champagne, 35
  charity auctions, 257–8
  counterfeit wines, 377
  greatest-quality wines, 369–71
  Hospices de Beaune, 377
  "Jefferson" bottles, 377
  most exciting finds, 371–2
  Nederburg Auction, 239
  port, 375
  price tables, 379–80
Aurore grape, 357
Ausone, Ch., 11, 12, 374
Australia, 308–18
  alcohol levels in biodynamic
    wines, 310
  auctions and investment,
    312, 375
  bush fires, 383
  climate change, 385–6
  drought, 309, 383, 386
  environmental initiatives, 308–9
  eucalyptus taint, 384
  exports grow, 312
  growth in number of wineries,
    310
  increased plantings of Pinot
    Gris/Grigio, 312
  investment in Argentina, 300
  labeling standards, 311
  medium-sweet Rieslings, 311
  New Zealand wine imports, 321
  objections to proposed
    Tasmanian pulp mill, 310
  organic and biodynamic wines,
    341, 345
  pests, 382
  phylloxera, 384
  Pinot Noir, 311
  prices of magnums, 312
  screwcaps, 317
  shortages, 309
  vintage reports, 313–15
  websites, 401
Austria, 192–9
  Blaufränkisch grape, 192–3
  DAC system, 193, 194
  organic and biodynamic wines,
    194, 341
  pests, 383–4
  Pinot Noir production, 192
  quality control, 194
  return to old vines and
    methods, 194
  Viennese wines, 193
  vintage reports, 195–7
  websites, 401

Auxerrois grape, 74, 177
awards see wine competitions
    and awards
Aykroyd, Dan, 286
Aythaya Estate, 330

Bacchus grape, 170
Bach, Johann Sebastian, 102
Back, Michael, 240
Backsberg Estate, 240
Bairrada, 146
Balaniuk, Willi, 193
Balbo, Susana, 303
Baldyga, Chris, 267
Balearic Islands, 129
Bali, 335
Bangalore Blue grape, 359
Banyuls, 92
Barbera grape, 230, 330
Barbieri, Paolo, 112
Barboursville, 268
Barkan Winery, 234
Barosi, Alessandro, 345
Baseler, Ted, 256
Bastardo grape, 153
Bastian, Mathis, 177, 183
Beam Wine Estates, 251
Beaujolais
    Beaujolais Nouveau, 19
    certified organic vineyards, 342
Beaulieu, Ch. de, 74
Beck, Judith, 194
Bedell, 268
Befort, Hans-Jörg, 178
Bekaa Valley, 224, 225
Belgium, 168–9, 171–6
    festivals, 176
    overuse of oak, 171
    sparkling wines, 169
    vintage reports, 172–4
    website, 401
Bellarmine, 311
Belle-Vue, Ch. (Lebanon), 229
Bellevue, Ch. (St-Emilion), 18
Belvedere, 206
Ben Gurion University, 232
Bentham, Adrian, 399
Bento Dos Santos, José, 57
Berardo, Joe, 154
Berger, Dan, 266
Bernard-Massard, Caves, 182
Berry Bros. & Rudd, 396
Bertheau, Bob, 255
Berthon, Jean, 360
Bertrand, Gérard, 83
best bargains
    Alsace, 45–6
    Argentina, 307
    Asia, 336–7
    Atlantic Northeast, 272
    Australia, 317
    Austria, 198–9
    Belgium, 175
    Bordeaux, 18
    Burgundy, 27–8

best bargains (cont.)
    California, 253
    Canada, 291
    Central & Southern Italy,
        126–7
    Champagne, 36
    Chile, 299
    Eastern & Southeastern
        Europe, 211
    Germany, 105
    Great Britain, 167
    Greece, 219
    Israel, 235
    Jura, 70
    Languedoc-Roussillon, 88
    Lebanon, 229
    Loire Valley, 54
    Luxembourg, 184
    madeira, 159
    Netherlands, 175
    New Zealand, 326
    Northern Italy, 118
    organic and biodynamic
        wines, 348
    other US states, 281
    Pacific Northwest, 263
    port, 159
    Portugal, 150
    Rhône Valley, 60–1
    Savoie, 70
    sherry, 143
    South Africa, 245
    Southwest France, 79
    Spain, 135
    Switzerland, 190–1
    vins de pays and vins de
        table, 95
best-value producers
    Alsace, 45
    Argentina, 306
    Asia, 336
    Atlantic Northeast, 271
    Australia, 316
    Austria, 198
    Belgium, 174–5
    Bordeaux, 17
    Burgundy, 27
    California, 252
    Canada, 290
    Central & Southern Italy, 126
    Champagne, 36
    Chile, 298
    Eastern & Southeastern
        Europe, 210
    Germany, 105
    Great Britain, 167
    Greece, 219
    Israel, 234
    Jura, 69
    Languedoc-Roussillon, 87
    Lebanon, 228
    Loire Valley, 53
    Luxembourg, 183
    madeira, 158
    Netherlands, 174–5

best-value producers (cont.)
    New Zealand, 326
    Northern Italy, 118
    organic and biodynamic
        wines, 347
    other US states, 281
    Pacific Northwest, 262
    port, 158
    Portugal, 150
    Rhône Valley, 60
    Savoie, 69
    sherry, 142
    South Africa, 245
    Southwest France, 78
    Spain, 135
    Switzerland, 190
    vins de pays and vins de
        table, 94
Bhutan, 330
Bianca grape, 357
Bicknell, Brian, 323
Billsboro Winery, 269
biodynamic wines see organic
    and biodynamic wines
Biowatch South Africa, 240
Birdsall, Nichole C, 267
Bish, Tony, 320
Black Association of the Wine
    and Spirit Industry (South
    Africa), 240
Black Hills Estate, 285
Black Queen grape, 330
Black Spanish grape, 278
Black Star Farms, 265
Blasted Church Winery, 283–4
Blauer Zweigelt grape, 99
Blaufränkisch grape
    Austria, 192–3
    Switzerland, 185, 187
Blaxa Vineyard, 170
Blomidon Estate, 286
Bodenstein grape, 194
Boekenhoutskloof, 239
Bohlmann, Joerg, 382
Bojanowski, John, 91
Bonarda grape, 301, 302
Bonhams & Butterfield, 376
Bonnes Mares, 374
Bonny Doon Vineyard, 248
Bordeaux, 10–18
    auctions and investment,
        373–4, 375
    certified organic vineyards,
        342–3
    Chinese purchase, 12
    guide to classic vintages,
        366–7
    Liv-ex ranking, 10–11
    market, 13
    price differentials, 11–12
    reclassification, 12
    vintage reports, 14–16
    websites, 402
Botrytis cinerea, inhibiting
    foam, 392

botrytis and late-harvest wines
Chile, 293
source of flavors, 389
vins de pays and *vins de table*,
92–3
bottles *see* wine bottles
Bouquet, Alain, 355–6, 361
Boutros, Naji, 229
Bouzeron, 20
Boxer, Shmuel, 234
Brandever Strategies, 283
brandy, white Armagnac, 73
Brant grape, 358
Brazil, website, 401
Bridge, Adrian, 152–3, 155
Britain *see* Great Britain
British Columbia
expansion of vineyards, 284
vintage reports, 287–9
website, 401
Wines of Marked Quality
regulations, 285
Broadbent, Michael, 222
Broken Hills, 321
Brown, Mike, 345
Brown-Forman, 248
Bründlmayer, Willi, 192
Brunello di Montalcino, 121, 122
Brunello grape, 335
Brys, 267
Bugey, Vins de, 64
Bulgaria, 207
EU subsidies, 202
rakia, 204
vintage reports, 205, 207–10
website, 401
Burgundy, 19–28
Beaujolais Nouveau, 19
climate change, 385
Côte Chalonnaise, 20
Fondation Pinot Noir, 21
future prospects, 22
guide to classic vintages, 367–8
price rises, 21
vintage reports, 23–6
websites, 402
Burma *see* Myanmar
Buxy, 20
Buzzard Valley, 164

C Comme Champagne,
Epernay, 35
Cabardès, 84
Cabernet Dorsat grape, 185
Cabernet Franc grape
Argentina, 301
California, 247
China, 358
Greece, 218
Israel, 230
Sweden, 170
Cabernet Gernischt grape, 330
Cabernet Sauvignon grape
Argentina, 300, 301
Australia, 310

Cabernet Sauvignon grape (*cont.*)
California, 249, 253
China, 358
Germany, 100
India, 359
Israel, 230
Italy, 110
Japan, 330, 360
leaf plucking, 387
Lebanon, 224
Myanmar, 330
new crosses, 355
Pacific Northwest, 257
Spain, 132
Texas, 278
trace aromatics, 388–9
Turkey, 359
vins de pays, 90
Cabrières, 80
Cahors, 303
Auxerrois grape becomes
Malbec, 74
blackness of wines, 75
and "French paradox," 72–3
Calatayud, 131
Caliboro, 293
California, 247–53
aging of red wines, 249
biodynamic vineyards, 340
bulk wine imports, 248
certified organic vineyards, 345
eucalyptus taint, 384
grapes unharvested, 248
high-alcohol wines, 249, 251
pests, 382
popularity of Riesling and dry
rosés, 247–8
websites, 403
wine surplus, 248
Calistoga, 254
Cambodia, 330
Camel Valley, 163
Camp Galhan, Dom., 92
Campbell Early grape, 330
Canada, 283–91
celebrity wine labels, 286
certified organic vineyards, 341
competition awards, 289
counterfeit icewine, 284
diseases, 383
"flying brandmaker," 283–4
icewine, 289
increasing vineyards in British
Columbia, 284
new regulations in British
Columbia, 285
reduction of Nova Scotia Liquor
Commission markups, 289
reduction of packaging
waste, 285
vintage reports, 287–9
websites, 401
Canaiolo grape, 391
Canale, Humberto, 303
Candelaria, 293

Canepa Winery, 293
Cap Rock Winery, 278
Cape Winemakers Guild (CWG),
239
Caprai, Marco, 110
Capurso, Nunzio, 121
Cardinal grape, 360
Carignan grape
Israel, 236
Languedoc-Roussillon, 84
Lebanon, 224
vins de pays and *vins de
table*, 91
Carmenère grape
Chile, 361
Pacific Northwest, 256, 259
Carnuntum, 194
Carrefour, 187
Carruades de Lafite, 11
Casa do Douro, 154, 155
Catena Alta Malbec, Bodega,
303
Catena Zapata, 303
Cava, 129
Cavas de Weinert, 301
Caves de la Loire, 47
Cazes Frères, 93
Cazottes family, 74
Cellier le Brun, 323
Centre d'Ampélographie Alpine
Pierre Galet, 360
Cereza grape, 301
Chainer, Pierre, 374
Chamarré, 90
Chambertin, 374
Champagne, 29–37
auctions and investment,
35, 374
competition awards, 35
Perlage system, 35
prices, 31
proposed expansion, 29–31
riddling, 392
sugar levels, 32
vintage reports, 33–5
websites, 402
Champoux, Paul, 259
Chandon, Dom., 317
Channing Daughters, 268
Chanson Père & Fils, 21
Chantal, Ch., 267
Chapel Down, 161, 162
Chapoutier, Michel, 57, 61
Chardonel grape, 277
Chardonnay, 94
Argentina, 300, 301, 303
Belgium, 168, 169, 171
California, 247
Chile, 294
China, 358
DNA analysis, 382
Great Britain, 163
India, 359
Israel, 230
Italy, 110

Chardonnay (cont.)
Japan, 360
Myanmar, 330
New Zealand, 322
Pacific Northwest, 256, 257
Slovenia, 202
Spain, 132
Sweden, 170
Texas, 278
Turkey, 359
vins de pays, 90, 92
Chasselas grape, 63
Switzerland, 185, 186, 187
Château see individual châteaux
Château-Chalon, 64
Châteauneuf-du-Pape, 374
Chave, 374
Chenin Blanc grape
India, 359
Israel, 236
Myanmar, 330
Texas, 278
Thailand, 335, 360
Chenonceaux, 48
Cheval Blanc, Ch., 11, 12, 373
Chianti
adding white grape juice to
black grape must, 391
Consorzio del Vino Chianti,
120–1
fraud, 107
global warming and, 122
weed control, 346
Chile, 292–9
absence of phylloxera, 294
carbon offset programs, 295
effects of climate change, 386
grape varieties, 361
organic vineyards, 295, 341–2
Pinot Noir plantings, 294
planting on rootstocks, 294
solar-powered winery, 295
sparkling wines, 294
sweet wines, 293
terroir research, 292
unprofitable sales, 293
Vinos de Chile, 294, 295
vintage reports, 296–7
website, 401
China, 330
AOC system, 331
counterfeit wine, 284
grape varieties, 330, 358–9
"half-juice wine" banned, 331
purchase in Bordeaux, 12
vintage reports, 332–5
websites, 401
Chivite, Bodegas, 130
Christie's, 375–6, 378
Christmann, Steffen, 100
Churchill Graham, 154
Cinsault grape
Languedoc-Roussillon, 84
Lebanon, 224
Turkey, 359

Cinzano, Count Francesco
Marone, 121
La Clape, 80
Clark, Matthew, 222
classic vintage guide, 365–72
climate and weather
extremes in US, 277
Israel, 232
monitoring on Internet, 397
see also vintage reports
climate change
Australian initiatives, 308–9
Burgundy, 385
bush fires, 383
carbon-neutral wineries,
240, 381
carbon offset programs in
Chile, 295
CO_2 emissions reduction, 178
droughts, 273–4, 309, 386
effects of, 385–7
and Italian vineyards, 122
New Zealand initiatives, 338–9
Spain, 383
weed control and, 346
Clos des Agaises, 168
Clos d'Ambonnay, 31, 37
Clos de Gravillas, 91
Clos Mon Vieux Moulin, 177
Clos d'Opleeuw, 168
Clos des Rochers, 179
Clos des Terrasses, 73
Clos de Thorey, 21
Cloudy Bay, 323, 340
Coche-Dury, 374
Cockburn's, 153, 155
Colemont, Peter, 168
Collards, 323
Colli Berici, 113
Colombard grape, 93, 335
la Colombette, Dom. de, 95
Colorado, 275, 277
Colorado River, 273–4
Colorino grape, 391
Columbia Valley, 255
Colvin Vineyards, 259
competitions see wine
competitions and awards
Concha y Toro, 292, 293, 294
Cono Sur, 292, 294, 295
Conservatoire de Chareil-Cintrat,
360
Constellation, 237, 251, 302
Coonawarra, 312
cooperatives
Greece, 213
Languedoc-Roussillon, 82
Corbeau grape, 302
Corbières, 81
Corder, Roger, 72–3
Corino, Carlo, 122
corks
consumer preference for, 389
Diam "technical cork,"
317, 319

corks (cont.)
Italy, 109
oxygen and, 390
TCA contamination, 393
see also screwcaps and non-
cork closures
Cornas, 57
Cornell University, 356–7, 387
Corot Noir grape, 356–7
Córpora group, 295
Corsica
organic vineyards, 82
website, 402
Corti, Darrell, 251
Cos d'Estournel, 11, 12
Cosse, Mathieu, 73
La Coste, Ch., 73
Costières de Nîmes, proposed
power station, 83
Côte Chalonnaise, 20
Coteaux du Languedoc, 80–2
Côtes de Gascogne, 93
Côtes de Provence, 83
Côtes du Roussillon, 81
Côtes du Roussillon Blanc, 82
counterfeit wine, 107, 284
Courtellier grape, 101
crémants, Luxembourg, 179
Criolla grape, 301
Croatia
EU accession negotiations, 202
vintage reports, 206, 208, 209
website, 401
Crouchen Blanc grape, 242
crushpadwine.com, 397
Cruzat Winery, 293
Cullen, Vanya, 310, 345
Cullen Winery, 309, 310
Cuthills Vineyards, 278
Cuvelier family, 16
Cyprus
domestic wine consumption,
204
EU funds for, 202, 212
vintage reports, 206–10
websites, 401
Czech Republic
EU funds for, 202
vintage reports, 207, 208, 209
websites, 401

Dassault, 293
De Martino, 292, 293, 294
de Wet, Danie, 242
Decanter magazine
Man of the Year, 222
World Wine Awards, 35, 43,
201–2
Decker, Charles, 183
Den Hoed family, 255, 259
Denbies, 161
Denmark, 170
websites, 401
dessert wines see botrytis and
late-harvest wines

Diageo, 251, 328–9
Dirty Laundry Vineyard, 284
diseases see pests and diseases
Distell, 242
DNA
  flavor and, 382
  testing, 62–3, 112, 218
Dolcetto di Dogliani, 345
Doluca, 359
Dom Pérignon, 374
Dom Pérignon Rosé, 35
Domaine see individual domaines
Domecq, 141
Domina grape, 170
Dornfelder grape
  Germany, 99, 100
  Myanmar, 330
Douro, 146, 152–3, 154, 155
Dow, 153
Dubourdieu, Denis, 335
Ducru-Beaucaillou, Ch., 11
Duhr, Abi, 183
Dunn, Randy, 251
Duque, Pedro, 139
Dveri Pax, 207
Dworkin, Marc, 206

Easley, Michael, 274
Easter massacre (US), 277
Eastern & Southeastern Europe,
  200–12
  hygiene problems, 203–4
  old oak barrels still in use,
    203–4
  vintage reports, 205–10
  Western supermarkets in, 204
Ecard, Maurice, 21
Edward Roberts International, 376
Eiswein see icewine
Eivissa, 129
Elbling grape, 187
Elgo Estate, 308–9
Ella Valley Vineyards, 232
Elswood, David, 375
Emiliano Orgánico, 295
Emir grape, 359
l'Engarran, Dom. de, 92
Ephrat Winery, 231
Erste Gewächs, 101
Erste Lagen, 100, 101
Escapades, 214
Espinoza, Alvaro, 293
Estévez, José, 138
Estournelles, Domaines des, 21
Estremadura, 145
European Court of Justice, 187
European Union
  assistance in Madeira, 153
  certified organic vineyards, 341
  and Eastern & Southeastern
    European countries, 202
  enrichment allowance, 161
  funds for Cyprus, 212
  GM contamination permitted
    in organic wines, 340

European Union (cont.)
  overproduction, 164
  planting ban, 161
  proposed chaptalization
    ban, 176
  see also individual countries
Eurovinq, 186
Ewart, Bruce, 286

Fairs see festivals and fairs
Faiveley, Maison, 21
Fall Creek Winery, 278
Familia Zuccardi, 302
Fanti, Fillippo Baldassare, 121
fastest-improving producers
  Alsace, 45
  Argentina, 306
  Asia, 336
  Atlantic Northeast, 271
  Australia, 316
  Austria, 198
  Belgium, 174
  Bordeaux, 17
  Burgundy, 27
  California, 252
  Canada, 290
  Central & Southern Italy, 126
  Champagne, 36
  Chile, 298
  Eastern & Southeastern
    Europe, 210
  Germany, 104
  Great Britain, 167
  Greece, 219
  Israel, 234
  Jura, 69
  Languedoc-Roussillon, 86
  Lebanon, 228
  Loire Valley, 53
  Luxembourg, 183
  madeira, 158
  Netherlands, 174
  New Zealand, 325
  Northern Italy, 118
  organic and biodynamic
    wines, 347
  other US states, 280
  Pacific Northwest, 262
  port, 158
  Portugal, 149
  Rhône Valley, 60
  Savoie, 69
  sherry, 142
  South Africa, 245
  Southwest France, 78
  Spain, 134
  Switzerland, 190
  vins de pays and vins de
    table, 94
Faugères, 80
Federación Español del Vino
  (FEV), 129
Federvini, 109
Fenouillèdes, 93
Fer Servadou grape, 355

festivals and fairs
  Belgian Wine Fair, 176
  Festival Vins & Crémants, 183
  Fête du Vieux Carignan, 91
  Israel, 231
  Millésime Bio, 82
  MiWine, 112
  Oklahoma and Kansas reach
    reciprocal agreement, 275
  Vinitaly, 112
Fetzer Vineyards, 248, 339
Filtrox company, 187
Finca Vistalba, 293
Fine Wines Board (Portugal),
  144–5
Finger Lakes, 266
Finot, Matthieu, 267
Fladgate Partnership, 152,
  153, 154
Flagstone Winery, 237
Flat Creek Winery, 278
Flat Rock Winery, 286
La Fleur-Pétrus, Ch., 11
Florida, 276
Florido, Gaspar, 138
Foch grape, 277
Fondation Pinot Noir, 21
Fonseca, Alvaro Moreira da, 155
Fontannez, Bernard, 239
food and wine
  health benefits, 351–2
  websites, 403
Forbes, Mac, 194
Formentera, 129
Forsyth, David, 259
Les Forts de Latour, 11
Fortune, 153
Forty-Five North, 267
Foster's, 94
Fournier, Bodegas O, 302
France
  certified organic vineyards,
    342–4
  and Chinese winemaking,
    358–9
  climate change, 386
  vins de pays and vins de table,
    89–96
  websites, 401–2
  wine tourism, 397
  see also individual regions
François, Claude, 178
Frank, Fred, 266
Frank, Dr. Konstantin, 265, 266
Franke family, 102
Fregoni, Marco, 112
Friuli-Venezia Giulia, 113
Frogmore Creek, 311
Front Range, Colorado, 277
Fronton, 74
Frühburgunder grape, 183
Furmint grape, 63

Gagarin Blue grape, 358
Gaja, Angelo, 110

Galena Cellars, 276
Gales, Marc, 178
Galet, Pierre, 63, 360
Galilee, 232
Gallo, E&J, 113, 240
Gallo, Ernest, 253
Gamay grape
  China, 358
  India, 330
  Switzerland, 186
García, Eduardo, 131
García, Mariano, 131
Gardrat, Lionel, 93
Garnacha grape, 107, 131
Garvey, 141
Gaujal de Saint Bon, Dom., 92–3
Gebelshuber grape, 194
Gelderland, 169, 171, 176
Gemtree Vineyards, 345
genetics
  DNA testing, 62–3, 112, 218
  flavor and, 382
  grapevine genome sequenced, 382
  preservation of genetic resources, 385
Genoels-Elderen, 168, 176
Georgia
  Russia bans wine from, 200, 201, 203
  super-premium Saperavi, 207
  vintage reports, 205, 207–9
  website, 402
Georgia (US), 275
Germany, 97–106
  certified organic vineyards, 344
  eastern regions, 97–9
  guide to classic vintages, 369
  most northerly wine estate, 102
  ungrafted vines, 101
  VDP classification, 100–1
  vintage reports, 102–4
  websites, 402
  see also individual regions
Gerovassiliou, Evangelos, 214
Gewürztraminer grape
  Argentina, 301
  Israel, 230
  Lebanon, 225
  Myanmar, 330
Gibson, Jonny, 399
Gil Luque, 138
Ginestet, 91
Givry, 20
Gleick, Peter, 274
global warming see climate change
Gobelsburg, 194
Golan Heights Winery, 234
Goldriesling grape, 101
Golitzin, Jeanette, 259
Goosen, Retief, 241
Gouais Blanc grape, 63
Grace Vineyard, 330
Grahm, Randall, 248, 256

Gran Cruz, 154
Grand, Pedro, 293
Grand Traverse, Ch., 265, 266
Grandes Pagos de España, 130
Grands Chais de France, 47–8
Grandview Vineyards, 255
grape varieties, 355–64
  best wines from new varieties/clones, 363
  best wines from unusual varieties, 364
  Chile, 361
  China, 358–9
  DNA testing, 62–3, 112, 218, 382
  fastest-growing varieties, 362
  "French paradox," 72–3
  grape conservatories, 360
  India, 359
  Japan, 360
  Marselan, 356
  most-cultivated varieties, 361–2
  new black varieties, 355–6
  new varieties from Cornell University, 356–7
  New York, 364
  Thailand, 360
  Turkey, 359
  UK national collection, 357–8
  website, 403
  see also hybrid grapes and individual grape varieties
Grapes of Roth, 268
Grassa, Yves, 73
Grauer Burgunder grape, 99
Gravegeal, Jacques, 90
Graves, 374
Great Britain, 160–7
  certified organic vineyards, 345
  increase in vine-planting, 160–1
  national collection of grapevines, 357–8
  sparkling wines, 160–1, 162, 163
  vintage reports, 165–6
  websites, 403
greatest-quality wines
  Alsace, 45
  Argentina, 306
  Asia, 336
  Atlantic Northeast, 271
  Australia, 316–17
  Austria, 198
  Belgium, 175
  Bordeaux, 17
  Burgundy, 27
  California, 252
  Canada, 290
  Central & Southern Italy, 126
  Champagne, 36
  Chile, 298
  Eastern & Southeastern Europe, 211

greatest-quality wines (cont.)
  Germany, 105
  Great Britain, 167
  Greece, 219
  Israel, 235
  Jura, 69
  Languedoc-Roussillon, 87
  Lebanon, 228
  Loire Valley, 53–4
  Luxembourg, 184
  madeira, 158
  Netherlands, 175
  New Zealand, 326
  Northern Italy, 118
  organic and biodynamic wines, 347–8
  Pacific Northwest, 263
  port, 158
  Portugal, 150
  Rhône Valley, 60
  Savoie, 70
  sherry, 142
  South Africa, 245
  Southwest France, 78
  Spain, 135
  Switzerland, 190
  vins de pays and vins de table, 95
greatest wine producers
  Alsace, 45
  Argentina, 306
  Asia, 336
  Atlantic Northeast, 271
  Australia, 316
  Austria, 198
  Belgium, 174
  Bordeaux, 17
  Burgundy, 27
  California, 252
  Canada, 290
  Central & Southern Italy, 126
  Champagne, 36
  Chile, 298
  Eastern & Southeastern Europe, 210
  Germany, 104
  Great Britain, 166
  Greece, 219
  Israel, 234
  Jura, 69
  Languedoc-Roussillon, 86
  Lebanon, 228
  Loire Valley, 53
  Luxembourg, 183
  madeira, 158
  Netherlands, 174
  New Zealand, 325
  Northern Italy, 117
  organic and biodynamic wines, 347
  other US states, 280, 281
  Pacific Northwest, 262
  port, 158
  Portugal, 149
  Rhône Valley, 59

greatest wine producers (*cont.*)
  Savoie, 69
  sherry, 142
  South Africa, 245
  Southwest France, 78
  Spain, 134
  Switzerland, 189
  vins de pays and *vins de table*, 94
Greece, 213–20
  certified organic vineyards, 344
  cooperatives, 213
  domestic market, 214
  poor treatment of wine, 215
  vintage reports, 216–18
  websites, 402
Gregan, Philip, 321, 339
Gregoire, Christine, 258
Grenache grape
  and climate change, 386
  diseases, 383
  Languedoc-Roussillon, 84
  leaf plucking, 387
  Lebanon, 224
  Pacific Northwest, 256
  Turkey, 359
Grenache Blanc, 92
Grenache Gris, 92
Grenache Noir, 80–1, 92
Le Grenelle de l'Environment, 49
Grès de Montpellier, 80
Gretzky, Wayne, 286
Gringet grape, 63
Gros, Dom. Anne, 20, 22
Große Gewächse, 100
Grossnickle, Steven, 267
Grove Mill, 338–9
Grüner Veltliner grape, 247
Guedes, Salvador, 154
Guelbenzu, Bodegas, 131
Guigal, 57, 374
La Guita, 141
Gundersen, Jens Michael, 170
Gunn Estate, 320–1
Gunns Limited, 310
Gutevin AB, 170
Gutswein trocken, 101

Hadley-Beauregard, Bernie, 283–4
Händel, Georg Friedrich, 102
Harmony Hill Winery, 270
Hart Davis Hart, 376
Hartmann, Alice, 178
Hartmann, Laurens, 218
harvests *see* vintage reports
Harvey, Scott, 266
Hasselbach, Agnes and Fritz, 97
Hatten Wines, 335
Haut-Brion, Ch., 11
health issues *see* wine and health
Hebrew University, 232
Helderberg area, 241
Hemel-en-Aarde Valley, 241
Henick-Kling, Thomas, 357

Henkell & Söhnlein, 202
Henrys, Dom. des, 92
Hermitage La Chapelle, 374
Heron Hill, 265
Herrick, James, 94
Hespanhol, Manuel Pinto, 155
Heuvelland, 169, 171
Hill Smith, Robert, 311
Hitler, Adolf, 37
Hochar, Serge, 221
Hof van Twente, 169
Hogue, Mike, 259
Horse Heaven Hills, 259
Hospices de Beaune, 377
Hubscher, Peter, 327
Hudson Valley, 266
Hughes, Natasha, 399
Humagne Rouge grape, 186
Hungary
  certified organic vineyards, 344
  domestic market, 204
  EU funds for, 202
  vintage reports, 205, 206–10
  website, 402
  wine levy, 207
Hunter Valley, 309, 312
hybrid grapes
  embryo rescue technique, 359
  see also individual grape varieties

Icewine
  Canadian, 289
  counterfeit, 284
  Norwegian *Eiswein*, 170
  Slovenia, 201–2
  Sweden, 170
  US, 277
Idaho, 262, 276
Illinois, 276
INAO
  agrément procedure, 56
  proposed expansion of Champagne, 29–31
Indage Group, 330
India
  domestic wine production, 328–9
  grape varieties, 330, 359
  sparkling wines, 329
  vintage reports, 332–5
Indiana, direct-shipping permits, 267
Indonesia, 330
  website, 402
Infalt, Constant, 183
INRA (Institut National de la Recherche Agronomique), 355–6, 387
Institut des Vins du Jura, 63
Interloire, 50
International Eastern Wine Competition, New York, 265
International Riesling Foundation, 265–6

Internet, 396–403
  Alexa ratings, 400
  food-and-wine pairing, 403
  grape varieties site, 403
  making wine to order, 397
  monitoring weather, 397
  oenology site, 403
  online magazines, 399
  online wine retailing, 397, 398–9, 401
  regional wine sites, 401–3
  smaller independents, 401
  tasting-note sites, 403
  vintage-chart sites, 403
  viticulture sites, 403
  wine-education sites, 403
  wine forums, 401
  wine-site links, 403
  wine tastings on YouTube, 396
  wine tourism, 397
investment *see* auctions and investment
Iowa, 275, 277
Isabella grape, 359
Israel, 230–6
  bulk wine sold as wineries' own, 232
  development of appellation system, 232
  expansion of vineyards, 230, 231
  kosher wines, 231
  Parker rates wines, 230–1
  proliferation of small wineries, 236
  vine-growing regions, 232
  vintage reports, 233–4
  weather, 232
  websites, 402
  wine festivals, 231
  wine institute needed, 232
Israwinexpo, 231
Italy, 107–27
  auctions and investment, 374
  certified organic vineyards, 344
  classic vintages, 366
  fraud, 107
  growth in exports, 108
  IGT Italia, 110
  price increases, 108
  screwcaps vs. corks, 109
  websites, 402
  see also Italy, Central & Southern; Italy, Northern
Italy, Central & Southern, 120–7
  climate change and, 122
  new DOCs, 122
  vintage reports, 123–5
Italy, Northern, 111–19
  branded wines, 113
  festivals, 112
  Piedmontese identity, 114
  traceability of wine, 111–12
  vintage reports, 115–17
Izumi, Bob, 286

Jaboulet Aîné, 56
Jack, Bruce, 237
Jackman, Nick, 398
Jacquère grape, 63, 360
James Arthur Vineyards, 278
Japan, 330
 AOC system, 331
 grape varieties, 360
 Koshu grape, 335
 vintage reports, 332–5
 website, 402
 wine styles, 329–30
Jayer, Henri, 374
Jefferson, Thomas, 377
Jestin, Hervé, 37
Johanitter grape, 185
Jordan estate, 100
Judean Hills, 232
Jura, 62–71
 AOC reforms, 65
 falling sales, 64
 "natural" wines, 66
 organic vineyards, 66, 343
 vin jaune, 63, 66
 vintage reports, 67–9
 website, 402

Ka, Ch., 225
Kai Noir grape, 330
Kaiser, Karl, 289
Kalecik Karasi grape, 359
Kansas, 275
Kanzler grape, 357
Karam Winery, 223
Karanika Wines, 218
Katazyna Winery, 206
Katsunuma Jozo Winery, 335
Kefraya, Ch., 222, 223
Keller, Klaus Peter, 170
Kempsey Black grape, 358
Kentucky, 275, 277
Khoury, Ch., 225
Kilikanoon syndicate, 318
King Family Vineyards, 267
Kinkead Ridge Winery, 270
Kleine Schorre, 169
Kloster Pforta, 98, 99
Koch, Bill, 377
Korea, 330
Koshu grape, 329, 335
Kracher, Alois, 193
Krier, Guy, 178, 179
Kristančič, Ales, 202
Krug, 31, 374
Ksara, Ch., 222, 223
Kuijper, Lidewej, 81
Kumala, 237
KWV, 242

Labels
 British Columbia, 285
 health warnings, 242
 problems in Asia, 331
 South African wines, 241–2
 standards in Australia, 311

Lafite Rothschild, Ch., 11, 374
Lafleur, Ch., 11
Lafon, 374
Lagarde, 303
Lageder, Alois, 215
Laithwaite, Tony, 163
Laithwaites, 399
Lake Chelan, 255
Langton's, 375, 376
Languedoc-Roussillon, 80–8
 AOC Languedoc, 81
 certified organic vineyards, 343
 Coteaux du Languedoc, 80–2
 Millésime Bio, 82
 organic wines, 82–3
 overproduction, 83
 use of oak, 84
 village cooperatives, 82
 vins doux naturels, 92
 vintage reports, 84, 85–6
 websites, 402
Laroche, Michel, 96
late-harvest wines see botrytis
 and late-harvest wines
Latour, Ch., 10, 374
Latour-Laguens, Ch., 12
Latvia, website, 402
Lavrenčič, Primoz, 202
Lazio, 122
Lebanon, 221–9
 exports increase, 221
 lack of variety in red wines, 224
 marketing campaign needed,
  225
 national strategy needed, 225
 new terroirs, 224
 political problems, 221,
  223, 224
 use of screwcaps, 223
 vintage reports, 226–8
 websites, 402
 wine institute necessary, 223
Leelanau Cellars, 267
Lefkada grape, 212
Leflaive, 374
legislation, drink-driving, 183
Leithaberg, 194
Lenz, 268
Léon Millot grape, 170
Léoville Barton, Ch., 11, 375
Léoville-Las-Cases, Ch., 11
Léoville-Poyferré, Ch., 11, 374
Leroy, Dom., 374
Lésineau, Jacques, 84
Levenberg, John Irving, 268
Lignier, Dom. Hubert, 22
Limburg, 169, 171
Lindo, Sam, 163
Lion Nathan, 323
Lippe, Prinz zu, 99
Liquor Control Board of Ontario,
 285
Lisboa, 145
Listrão grape, 153
Liv-ex, 10–11, 373

Livingstone-Learmonth, John, 397
Loimer, Fred, 194
Loire Valley, 47–55
 blind tastings, 47
 certified organic vineyards, 343
 chaptalization and
  cryoextraction, 49–50
 esca fungus, 50
 Interloire, 50
 takeovers, 47–8
 vins de pays, 50
 vintage reports, 51–2
 websites, 402
Long Island, 266
Longhai International, 12
Longyan grape, 330
Lorrand, Andrew, 194
Lötschberg wine bars, 186
Lund, Stephen, 382
Luther, Martin, 102
Luxembourg, 177–84
 blind tasting, 178
 crémants, 179
 drink-driving laws, 183
 export promotion, 177
 festivals, 183
 German and French wines
  made in, 178
 vintage reports, 180–2
 website, 402
 yields limited, 179
LVMH, 12
Lyddon, Jonathan, 182
Lynch-Bages, Ch., 11, 375
Lynfred Winery, 276

Macabeu grape, 82, 93
Macdonald, Rod, 321
Macedonia
 EU funds for, 202
 vintage reports, 208, 210
 website, 402
McLaren Vale, 345
Mac's Creek, 278
Mád, 206
madeira, 152–9
 EU assistance, 153
 vintage reports, 156–8
 websites, 402
Madeleine Angevine grape, 357
Madiran grape, 74
 and "French paradox," 72–3
Magrez, Bernard, 335
Maiolatesi's Wine Cellars, 270
Maison du Vin de Savoie, 64
Majestic, 398
Malaga Blanc grape, 330
Malagousia grape, 214
Malbec grape
 Argentina, 74, 300–3
 Israel, 230
 Southwest France, 73, 74, 75
Mallorca, 129
Malta, website, 402
Malvasia Cândida grape, 153

Malvasia grape, 156, 157, 391
Malvasia Roxa grape, 153
Malvoisie de Roussillon grape, 82
La Mancha, 131
Maratheftiko grape, 212
Marchesi di Barolo, 109
Margaux, Ch., 10, 374
Marguet, Benoît, 37
Marlborough, 322, 338
Marqués del Real Tesoro, 141
Marquette grape, 277
Marsanne grape, 82, 256
Marselan grape, 330, 355, 356
Martin, Dennis, 248
Martinborough, 384
Mas des Dames, 81
Massaya, 222, 223
Matador Ranch, 259
Matariki, 321
Mathier, Diego, 187
Mavety, Ian, 285
May, Peter, 399
Mayer am Pfarrplatz, 193
Mediterra Winery, 218
Médoc, 13, 16, 374
Megalomaniac Winery, 284
Menorca, 129
Meranda-Nixon Winery, 270
Mercer, Bud and Rob, 259
Mercer Estates Winery, 259
Mercurey, 20
Merino, René, 294
Merlot grape, 259
  Argentina, 300, 301, 303
  California, 247, 257
  Chile, 361
  China, 358
  Germany, 100
  India, 359
  Israel, 230
  Italy, 110
  Japan, 360
  leaf plucking, 387
  Lebanon, 224
  new crosses, 355
  Sweden, 170
  Texas, 278
Merrick, Tim, 277
Merwarth, Fred, 266
Merzling grape, 171
Messias, 153
Mexico, website, 402
Meyer, Detlev, 97
Mezzacorona, 113
Miesbauer, Fritz, 193
Miguel Torres Chile, 295
Millton, James, 339
Minervois, 81
Minnesota, 275
La Mission Haut-Brion, Ch., 11
Missouri, 277
MiWine, 112
Moesgaard, Sven, 170
Moldova
  contaminated wine, 203

Moldova (cont.)
  dependence on Russia,
    200–1, 203
  vintage reports, 205, 207–9
  vodka consumption, 204
  website, 402
Molette grape, 63
Mondavi, Robert, 253
Mondavi, Tim, 253
Mondeuse Blanche grape,
  62, 360
Mondeuse Noire grape, 62, 360
La Mondotte, Ch., 375
Montagny, 20
Montana, 275
Montes, 292
Montrose, Ch., 11, 12, 374
Morocco, website, 402
Morrell & Company, 376
Morsbach, Bert, 330
Mosaico grape, 268
Mosel, 100
Moss Wood, 312, 375
most exciting or unusual finds
  Alsace, 46
  Argentina, 307
  Asia, 337
  Atlantic Northeast, 272
  Australia, 317–18
  Austria, 199
  Belgium, 175–6
  Bordeaux, 18
  Burgundy, 28
  California, 253
  Canada, 291
  Central & Southern Italy, 127
  Champagne, 37
  Chile, 299
  Eastern & Southeastern
    Europe, 211–12
  Germany, 106
  Great Britain, 167
  Greece, 219–20
  Israel, 235–6
  Jura, 70–1
  Languedoc-Roussillon, 88
  Lebanon, 229
  Loire Valley, 54–5
  Luxembourg, 184
  madeira, 159
  Netherlands, 175–6
  New Zealand, 326–7
  Northern Italy, 119
  organic and biodynamic
    wines, 348
  other US states, 281–2
  Pacific Northwest, 263–4
  port, 159
  Portugal, 150–1
  Rhône Valley, 61
  Savoie, 70–1
  sherry, 143
  South Africa, 246
  Southwest France, 79
  Spain, 135–6

most exciting… (cont.)
  Switzerland, 191
  vins de pays and vins de
    table, 96
La Motte vineyard, 94
Mourvèdre grape
  Languedoc-Roussillon,
    80–1, 84
  Lebanon, 224
  new crosses, 355
  Pacific Northwest, 256
Mouton Rothschild, Ch.,
  11, 374
Mtsvane grape, 201
Müller-Thurgau grape
  Germany, 98, 99
  Japan, 360
  Switzerland, 185
Muñoz de Toro, Fernando, 301
Murchison, Ken, 330
Murray Valley, 309
Musar, Ch., 222
Muscat grape
  Greece, 214
  Myanmar, 330
  Thailand, 335
  Turkey, 359
  vins de pays, 92, 93
Muscat Bailey A grape, 330
Muscat Canelli grape, 278
Musigny, 374
Myanmar (Burma)
  first winery, 330
  labeling regulations, 331

Napa Valley, 249, 253, 256,
  382
Narince grape, 359
Nashik winery, 329
Navarra, 130–1
Nebraska, 278
Nederburg Auction, 239
Negev Desert, 232
Négrette grape, 74
Netherlands, 171–6
  competition awards, 176
  expansion of vineyards, 169
  proposed EU chaptalization
    ban, 176
  vintage reports, 172–4
Neusiedlersee-Hügelland, 194
Nevada, 275
New Jersey, 270
new up-and-coming producers
  Alsace, 45
  Argentina, 306
  Asia, 336
  Atlantic Northeast, 271
  Australia, 316
  Austria, 198
  Belgium, 174
  Bordeaux, 17
  Burgundy, 27
  California, 252
  Canada, 290

new up-and-coming… *(cont.)*
Central & Southern Italy, 126
Champagne, 36
Chile, 298
Eastern & Southeastern Europe, 210
Germany, 105
Great Britain, 167
Greece, 219
Israel, 234
Jura, 69
Languedoc-Roussillon, 87
Lebanon, 228
Loire Valley, 53
Luxembourg, 183
madeira, 158
Netherlands, 174
New Zealand, 326
Northern Italy, 118
organic and biodynamic wines, 347
other US states, 281
Pacific Northwest, 262
port, 158
Portugal, 149–50
Rhône Valley, 60
Savoie, 69
sherry, 142
South Africa, 245
Southwest France, 78
Spain, 135
Switzerland, 190
vins de pays and *vins de table*, 94
New York
direct-shipping permits, 267
website, 403
New York Wine Course and Reference, 364
New Zealand, 319–27
climate change, 386
excess copper found in wine, 321, 339
exports to Australia, 321
organic wines, 323, 338–40, 344
phylloxera, 384
Pinot Gris planting frenzy, 322
screwcaps, 319–20, 321
vintage reports, 323–5
websites, 402
wine competitions, 320–1
New Zealand Wine Company, 381
Newman family, 153
Niederberger, Joachim, 100
Niepoort, Dirk, 154
Niersteiner Pettenthal, 97
Nilaya, 329
Nittnaus, John, 194
Noiret grape, 269, 277, 356–7
Nordlund winery, 170
North Carolina, 277
Norway, 170
Nova Scotia Liquor Commission, 289
Nuits-St-Georges, 21

NY Wines/Christie's, 375
Nyetimber, 161, 162, 163

Oak
Belgium, 171
old barrels used in Eastern & Southeastern Europe, 203–4
Rioja bans staves, 129
use in Switzerland, 187
vins de pays, 90
wines from Languedoc-Roussillon, 84
Ohio
direct-shipping permits, 267
expansion of wine industry, 270
Ohio Quality Wine Assurance Program, 266
Okanagan, 283–4, 285
Oklahoma, 275, 276, 277
Öküzgözü Bogazkere grape, 359
Olivier, Cornel, 267
Oltrepò Pavese Metodo Classico, 113
Onivins, 90
Ontario
"flying brandmaker," 284
pests, 383
vintage reports, 287–9
website, 401
Opus One, 66
Opus Vinum, Dom., 66
Orbital Wines, 239
Oregon
certified organic vineyards, 345
direct-shipping permits, 255
increase in wineries, 264
increased sales, 264
website, 403
wine labels, 256, 262
Oregon Winegrowers Association, 256
organic and biodynamic wines, 338–48
alcohol levels, 310
Australia, 345
Austria, 194
California, 340
Chile, 295
current status of certified vineyards, 341–5
GM contamination permitted in EU, 340
Jura, 66
Languedoc-Roussillon, 82–3
Millésime Bio, 82
Netherlands, 169
New Zealand, 323, 338–40
Spain, 131
US, 345
weed control, 346
Organic Trade Association, 345
Organisation Commune du Marché Vitivinicole (OCM-Vin), 129, 132
The Organized Crime Winery, 284

Origin Wine, 239
Orion grape, 170
Orviel, Dom., 92
Osborne, 141
other US states, 273–82
academic support for wineries, 276
Alaska shipping regulations, 278
direct-shipping legislation, 274–6
drought, 273–4
expansion of new wineries, 274–5
extreme weather conditions, 277
fortification laws, 275
grape choices in Texas, 278
icewine, 277
migrant labor, 273
production cap, 276
Tesco enters market, 275
vintage reports, 279–80
wine fairs, 275
Ott, Bernhard, 194
overproduction
European Union, 164
Languedoc-Roussillon, 83
Oyster Bay, 321

Paarl, 241
Pacific Northwest, 254–64
charity auctions, 257–8
direct-shipping permits, 255
freeze on granting of new AVAs, 254–5
increase in Oregon wineries, 264
increased sales in Oregon, 264
naming wines, 259
new AVAs, 262
Oregon wine labels, 256, 262
reform of Washington alcohol laws needed, 258
varietal wine laws, 257
vintage reports, 260–1
Pacific Rim Winery, 256
Pago del Vicario, 383
Pajotin, Valerie, 90
Palencia, 131
Palengat, 259
Palmer, Ch., 11
Palmer, Jeremy, 398
Pampas Estate, 301
Pape Clément, Ch., 11, 335
Parker, Robert, 77, 230–1, 284
Parra, Pedro, 292
Pasco, Lewis, 231
Patagonian Wines, 301
Pato, Filipa, 146
Pato, Luis, 146
Pauqué, Ch., 183
Pavie, Ch., 11
Pavie Macquin, Ch., 11
Pavillon Blanc, 11
Penfolds Grange, 312, 375
Pennautier, Ch., 84, 92

Pennsylvania, "Vintage 2012" initiative, 267
Perez Marín, 138
Perlage system, 35
Pernod Ricard, 329
Persan grape, 360
Peru, websites, 402
pests and diseases
    Asian ladybugs, 186, 383
    Bois Noir, 383, 386
    botrytis, 392
    botrytis bunch rot, 387
    climate change and, 386
    esca fungus, 50
    fanleaf disease, 356
    light-brown apple moth, 382
    nematodes, 356
    phylloxera, 294, 384
    Pierce's disease, 386
    resistance in wild grapevines, 359
    Scaphoideus titanus, 383–4
    western grapeleaf skeletonizer moth, 382
Peter, Bob, 285
Petit Verdot grape, 230, 330
Petite Arvine grape, 186
Petite Sirah grape
    California, 247
    Israel, 236
    Pacific Northwest, 256, 257
Petre-Rose, Dom., 81
Pétrus, Ch., 11, 12, 373
Pézenas, 80, 81
Phipps and Company, 154
Phoenix grape, 357
phylloxera
    absence in Chile, 294
    in Australia, 384
Pichard, Dom., 74
Pichon-Baron, Ch., 11
Pichon-Lalande, Ch., 11
Picpoul, 92
Piedmont
    loss of identity, 114
    website, 402
Pieterse, Nosey, 240
Le Pin, Ch., 10, 374
Pinault, François, 12
Pinot Blanc grape
    Japan, 330
    Switzerland, 186
Pinot Gris/Grigio grape, 107
    Argentina, 301
    Australia, 312
    Italy, 110
    Luxembourg, 177, 178, 179
    New Zealand, 322
    Pacific Northwest, 256, 262
Pinot Meunier grape, 100, 101
Pinot Nero grape, 113
Pinot Noir grape
    Argentina, 301
    Australia, 311
    Austria, 192

Pinot Noir grape (cont.)
    Belgium, 169
    botrytis bunch rot, 387
    California, 249
    Chile, 294
    China, 330, 358
    early harvesting, 39
    Hungary, 207
    India, 359
    Israel, 230
    Lebanon, 225
    Luxembourg, 183
    Myanmar, 330
    Pacific Northwest, 256, 257
    Slovenia, 202
    Spain, 383
    Switzerland, 186, 187
    vins de pays, 90
Pithon, Jo and Isabelle, 48
Platter Guide, 244
Plumpton College, 161, 164
Pokdum grape, 330
Pool, Dr. Bob, 269
port, 152–9
    auctions and investment, 375
    beneficio system, 152–3, 155
    fortification in Georgia, 275
    guide to classic vintages, 369
    shippers, 154
    vintage reports, 156–8
    websites, 402
Porter, Michael, 144
Portugal, 144–51
    certified organic vineyards, 344
    exports to US, 144–5
    growth in the Alentejo, 145
    hotels in port region, 154
    local grapes, 146
    vintage reports, 147–9
    VR Lisboa, 145
    websites, 402
    see also madeira; port
Potel, Nicky, 20
Powell, John Wesley, 274
Prager grape, 194
Preisinger, Claus, 192
Presque Isle, 269
Priestley, Jason, 285, 286
Private Vineyards Estate, 301
Prosecco, 107
Provence, website, 402
Prpich Hills Winery, 283
Puchta, Tim, 277
Pulenta, Carlos, 293, 302
Pyrenees, 383

Quatourze, 80
Quilceda Creek Vintners, 259
Quillé, Nicholas, 256
Quinta do Cachão, 153
Quinta da Eira Velha, 153
Quinta do Zimbro, 155

Raimey family, 286
Rangspay grape, 359

Recanati Winery, 231
Redman family, 312
Regent grape, 171, 358
Reina, Diego, 301
Reisch, Bruce, 356–7
religion, sacramental wines, 231
Rembrandt grape, 358
Retamal, Marcelo, 294
Rheingau, 101
Rheinhessen, 97
Rhône Valley, 56–61
    agrément procedure, 56
    certified organic vineyards, 343
    guide to classic vintages, 368–9
    off-odors, 394
    vintage reports, 58–9
    website, 402
    "zero-sulfite" debate, 57
Ribatejo, 145
Ribera del Duero, 129
    website, 403
Ricasoli, Baron, 391
Richaud, Marcel, 56
Riddoch, John, 312
RidgeView Estate, 162, 163
Riesling grape
    Argentina, 301
    Atlantic Northeast, 265–6
    Australia, 311
    California, 247–8
    China, 330, 358
    early harvesting, 38–40
    Germany, 99, 100
    Lebanon, 225
    Luxembourg, 177, 178, 179
    New Zealand, 322
    Norway, 170
    Pacific Northwest, 256, 257
    South Africa, 242
    Texas, 278
    Turkey, 359
    World Riesling Competition, 46
    World Riesling Cup, 265
Riggs, Mr., 311
Rioja, 129
    website, 403
Riverina, 309
Roberts, Mike, 160, 162
Robinson, Jancis, 161, 241
Rodenstock, Hardy, 377
Roederer Cristal, 374
Rolland, Michel, 206
la Romanée-Conti, Dom. de, 374
Romania, 73
    domestic market, 204
    EU funds for, 202
    problems with Moldovan wine, 203
    vintage reports, 205, 207–10
    website, 402
Romero, Pedro, 138
Rondo grape, 171, 358
La Roque, Ch., 83
Rose, Anthony, 397
rosé wines, California, 247, 248

Rosenblum Cellars, 251
Rosevears Estate Winery, 310
Roter Gutedel, 102
Roter Riesling, 101
Rothschild, Baron Eric de, 234
Roussanne grape
    grape conservatories, 360
    Languedoc-Roussillon, 82
    Pacific Northwest, 256
    vins de pays, 92
Roussillon *see* Languedoc-
    Roussillon
Ruby Cabernet grape, 278
Rully, 20
Ruppert, Henri, 178, 179
Russell, Hamilton, 239, 241
Russia
    bans wine from Georgia and
      Moldova, 200–1, 203
    vintage reports, 207, 209
    website, 402

Saale-Unstrut, 97–9
Sachsen, 97–9, 102
sacramental wines, 231
Sadie, Eben, 239, 244
St-Chinian, 80, 81
St-Emilion, 12, 374
St Lannes, Dom. de, 93
St Laurent grape, 178
St Martin, Dom., 178
Ste Michelle, Ch., 247–8, 255,
    256, 265
St. Pepin grape, 277
St-Pierre Doré grape, 360
St-Pourçain, 360
St-Saturnin, 80
Sala Ogival, Lisbon, 145
Salgesch, 186
Samos Muscat, 214
Samson, 232
San Pedro, 293
Sandhill Crane, 268
Sangiovese grape, 107
    California, 247
    Chianti, 391
    leaf plucking, 387
    Pacific Northwest, 256
    Texas, 278
    Thailand, 335
Santa Rita, 293
Santameriana grape, 214
Saperavi grape, 201, 207
Sardinia, 121
Sarkozy, Nicolas, 90
Sartori, Andrea, 108
Sassicaia, 374
Sauternes, 389, 394
Sauvignon Blanc grape
    Argentina, 300, 301, 303
    California, 247
    Israel, 230
    Myanmar, 330
    Texas, 278
    vins de pays, 89–90, 92

Savagnin grape, 63
Savoie, 62–71
    certified organic vineyards, 343
    DNA testing of grapes, 62–3
    falling sales, 64
    vintage reports, 67–9
    wine tastings, 66
    wine tourism, 65–6
Scandinavia, 170
    see also individual countries
Schenk, 113
Schloss Gobelsburg, 192
Schloss Proschwitz, 99
Schloss Wackerbarth, 98, 99
Schmid, Hans, 193
Schmidt, Brian, 284
Schubert, Max, 375
Schulte, Robert and Agnes, 74
Schwarzriesling, 100, 101
science *see* wine science
screwcaps and non-cork closures
    Alsace, 40
    Australia, 317
    Italy, 109
    Lebanon, 223
    New Zealand, 319–20, 321
    see also corks
Sea Horse Winery, 236
Sebeka, 238, 240
Seibel grape, 330, 358, 360
Semillon grape, 359
Señorío de Arínzano, 130
Seppeltsfield, 318
Sercial grape, 153
Seresin Estate, 323
Seyval Blanc grape, 357
Shady Lane Cellars, 265
Shanken, Marvin, 284
Shaps, Michael, 267
Sharpham Vineyard, 161
Shatzberg, Gil, 231
Shelton Vineyards, 275
sherry, 137–43
    age-dated wines, 138
    alcohol prices, 139
    classification, 141
    consolidation, 138
    cupo, 141
    future prospects, 139
    health benefits, 141
    increasing sales, 137–8
    off-odors, 395
    satellite-based vineyard-control
      system, 139
    sherry vinegar, 138, 139
    vintage reports, 140–1
    website, 403
Shiraz grape
    Bali, 335
    China, 330
    Cyprus, 212
    Myanmar, 330
    Thailand, 335
    trace aromatics, 388–9
    see also Syrah

Shomron, 232
Shonltu Red grape, 359
Shonltu White grape, 359
Shoup, Allen, 259
Siam Winery, 335
Sidebotham, Peter, 397
Siena, 122
Sierra Nevada, 383
Silvaner grape, 99
Simčič, Aleks, 202
Simon, Joanna, 397
Singleton, Vernon, 390
Sister Creek Winery, 278
Skaersoegaard, 170
Skinner, 376
Slovakia
    vintage reports, 207, 209
Slovenia, 207
    competition awards, 201–2
    domestic market, 204
    vintage reports, 205, 206,
      208–10
    website, 402
Smart, Richard, 310
Smith, Damon, 276
Smith, Olly, 397
Smoky Hill, 269
Snake River Valley, 262
Snohomish Winery, 259
Sogrape, 154
Soil Association, 340
Solaris grape, 171, 357
Soldatos, Takis, 214
Sonoma County, 251
Soria, Marlène, 81
Sotheby's, 373, 374, 376, 378
South Africa, 237–46
    alcoholism, 240
    appellation system, 241
    auctions, 239
    certified organic vineyards, 344
    competition awards, 244
    Constellation increases market
      share, 237
    exports increase, 238
    genetically enhanced yeast, 240
    labeling problems, 241–2
    monopoly regulations
      infringed, 242
    Riesling naming problems, 242
    vintage reports, 243–4
    websites, 402–3
    wine icons, 238–9
South African Wine Council,
    240, 242
South Dakota, 275
Southwest France, 72–9
    blackness of Cahors wines, 75
    certified organic vineyards,
      343–4
    "French paradox," 72–3
    Fronton and the Nègrette
      grape, 74
    vintage reports, 76–7
    website, 402

Spain, 128–36
 auctions and investment, 374
 climate change, 383
 independent producers share
  marketing, 130
 OCM proposals, 129, 132
 organic and biodynamic wines,
  131, 345
 pagos, 130
 planting-rights legislation, 132
 Rioja bans staves, 129
 Viñedos de España
  classification, 110, 128–9
 vintage reports, 133–4
 websites, 403
 wine classification, 129
 see also sherry
sparkling wines
 Belgium, 169
 botrytis inhibits foaming
  quality, 392
 in Chile, 294
 clarity, 392
 Great Britain, 160–1, 162, 163
 India, 329
 Luxembourg, 178, 179
 Spain, 131
 Ukraine, 202
 see also Champagne
Spätburgunder grape, 99, 100
 see also Pinot Noir
Specialty Wine Retailers
 Association, 275
Sri Lanka, 330
Stafford, Philip, 267
Stag's Leap Wine Cellars, 256
Standing Stone, 265
Stassen, Coenrad, 267
Steenberg, 244
Steiner, Todd, 266
Stellenbosch, 241
Stift Göttweig, 193
Stony, Ch. de, 93
Stormhoek, 239
straw wine, 100
Stuckey, Wendy, 255
Sud de France brand, 83
Sultana grape, 359
Sunnen-Hoffman winery, 178
Sunnybank Vine Nurseries, 357–8
Suyrot, Fabrice de, 73
Swartland Winery, 240
Sweden, 170
Swedenburg, Juanita, 266
Sweet Valley Wines, 262
sweet wines see botrytis and
 late-harvest wines
Switzerland, 185–91
 Asian ladybug infestations, 186
 certified organic vineyards, 345
 loss of export subsidies, 187
 new grape varieties, 185
 older rootstocks, 186
 pests, 383
 use of oak chips, 187

Switzerland (cont.)
 vintage reports, 188–9
 website, 403
Sylvanus grape, 268
Symington, Rupert, 153
Symington family, 155
Syrah grape
 Argentina, 300, 301
 California, 247, 248, 249
 China, 358
 Israel, 230
 Languedoc-Roussillon, 80–1, 84
 Lebanon, 224
 Pacific Northwest, 256
 Portugal, 145
 Rhône Valley, 62
 Switzerland, 186
 Texas, 278
 Thailand, 360
 vins de pays, 90
 see also Shiraz
Szepsy, István, 206

T abor Winery, 231
Tafelwein Trocken, 101
Taiwan, 330
Tamar Ridge Winery, 310
Tannat grape
 Argentina, 301
 Pacific Northwest, 256
 Southwest France, 73
Tapp, Hermann, 183
Taresch family, 308–9
Taricco, Mino, 114
Tariquet, Dom. de, 93
Tasmania
 climate change, 386
 medium-sweet Riesling, 311
 proposed pulp mill near
  vineyards, 310
tastings
 dessert wines, 92
 Luxembourg wines, 178
 Salon des Vins de Loire, 47
 Savoie, 66
 websites, 403
 on YouTube, 396
Te Kairanga, 321, 327
Tekel, 359
Telish Wine Cellars, 206
Temaria grape, 278
Tempranillo grape
 California, 247
 Argentina, 300
 Myanmar, 330
 Pacific Northwest, 256
Tennessee, 275
Teperberg Winery, 231
Terra d'Acoiris, 346
Terrantez grape, 153
Terrasses du Larzac, 80, 81
terroir
 Portugal, 146
 research in Chile, 292
Tesco, 248, 275, 398

Tetramythos, 215
Texas
 choice of grapes, 278
 direct-shipping permits, 276
 Easter massacre, 277
 website, 403
Thailand, 330
 expansion of vineyards, 335
 grape varieties, 330, 360
 labeling regulations, 331
 vintage reports, 332–4
Three Sisters Winery, 275
Tocai Friulano, 113
Tokaj, 206
Torontel grape, 293
Torres, 383
Torrontés grape, 300, 303
Tosso, Felipe, 292
La Tour du Pin Figeac, Ch., 16
Touraine, 50
Touriga Franca grape, 146
Touriga Nacional grape, 145, 146
tourism see wine tourism
Tracy, Christopher, 268
Trail Ridge Winery, 277
Traminer grape, 63, 99
Traminette grape, 277
Trebbiano grape, 391
Trentino-Alto Adige, 113
Tressallier grape, 360
Trezise, Jim, 248, 265–6
Tribaie machine harvester, 16
Trimbach, Maison, 43
Trincadeira grape, 145
Triomphe d'Alsace grape, 358
Trittenheimer Apotheke, 178
Trivento, 302
Troplong Mondot, Ch., 11
Tsabournakos grape, 218
Tsaktsarlis, Vasilis, 214
Tukker family, 162
Tunisia, website, 403
Turkey
 grape varieties, 359
 international marketing, 212
 vintage reports, 208
Tuscany, 278
 websites, 402
Two Lads Winery, 267
Tyrrell, 312
Tzvetanov, Ognyan, 206

U co Valley, 301
Ugni Blanc grape
 India, 330, 359
 vins de pays and vins de table, 93
UIV (Unione Italiana Vini), 109
Ukraine, 202
Umpqua Valley, 264
United Breweries, 329
United Kingdom see Great Britain
United States of America
 certified organic vineyards, 345
 drought, 273–4
 increasing sales, 247

United States of America (cont.)
pests and diseases, 386
Portuguese wine imports,
144–5
South African exports to, 238–9
websites, 403
see also Atlantic Northeast;
California; other US states;
Pacific Northwest
Upper Langkloof, 241
Uruguay
certified organic vineyards, 345
website, 403
Utah, 275
Uzunashvili, Lado, 207

Vaccari, Carmela, 111–12
Val, Ch. de, 207
Valandraud, 375
Valdespino, Bodegas, 138
Valdivia, Bodegas, 141
Valery, Danny, 232
Valle Perdido, 303
Valvin Muscat grape, 356–7
van Vuuren, Hennie, 240
Varan, Tim, 276
Vardea grape, 214
Vaud, 383
Vauthier, Alain, 374
VDP, 100–1
Vega Sicilia, 374
Velich, Roland, 193
Velich grape, 194
Ventisquero, 292, 295
Veramonte, 293
Verdelho grape, 153
Vermentino grape, 82
Vertzami grape, 214
Verus Estate, 207
Veyder-Malberg, Peter, 193
Via, 293
Vidaigne, 168
Vidal grape, 170, 185, 320–1
Viennese wines, 193
Vietnam, 330
Vieux Château Certan, 11
La Vigna Winery, 270
Villaine, Aubert de, 21
Vin de Pays Charentais, 93
Vin de Pays d'Oc, 92, 93
vin jaune, 63, 66
Viñedos de España, 110, 128
Viñedos del Maule, 293
vinegar, sherry, 138, 139
Vineland Estates Winery, 284
The Vines of Mendoza, 301
vinification
adding white juice to red
wines, 391
aging wines in Atlantic
Northeast, 268
alcohol levels in biodynamic
wines, 310
alcohol levels increase, 249,
251, 310

vinification (cont.)
alcohol prices for fortified
wines, 139
carbon-neutral winery, 240
chaptalization, 49–50, 129,
161
cryoextraction, 50
drought in US, 273–4
genetically enhanced yeast,
240
kosher wines, 231
new yeasts, 186
preventing hydrogen sulfide,
390–1
proposed EU chaptalization
ban, 176
removing sediment, 392, 393
sugar levels, 32, 41
trichloranisole filter, 187
website, 403
"zero-sulfite" debate, 57, 66
see also oak
ViniPortugal, 145
Vinisud, 61
Vino Nobile di Montepulciano,
122
Vinos de Chile, 294, 295
Vinos Singulares de Pagos
Andaluces (VSPA), 130
vins de pays and vins de table,
89–96
competition awards, 95
dessert wines, 92–3
festivals, 91
from sherry grapes, 139
Italy, 110
Loire Valley, 50
Vin de Pays de l'Atlantique,
90–1
Vin de Pays des Gaules, 90–1
Vin de Pays de Méditerranée,
91
Vin de Pays d'Oc, 90
Vin de Pays du Val de Loire, 91
Vin de Pays des Vignobles de
France, 89–91, 110, 128
Viñedos de España, 110, 128
yields, 96
vins doux naturels, 92
Vinsmoselle, 183
vintage reports
Alsace, 42–4
Argentina, 304–6
Asia, 332–5
Atlantic Northeast, 269–70
Australia, 313–15
Austria, 195–7
Belgium, 172–4
Bordeaux, 14–16
Burgundy, 23–6
California, 250–1
Canada, 287–9
Central & Southern Italy,
123–5
Champagne, 33–5

vintage reports (cont.)
Chile, 296–7
Eastern & Southeastern
Europe, 205–10
Germany, 102–4
Great Britain, 165–6
Greece, 216–18
Israel, 233–4
Jura, 67–9
Languedoc-Roussillon, 84, 85–6
Lebanon, 226–8
Loire Valley, 51–2
Luxembourg, 180–2
madeira, 156–8
Netherlands, 172–4
New Zealand, 323–5
Northern Italy, 115–17
other US states, 279–80
Pacific Northwest, 260–1
port, 156–8
Portugal, 147–9
Rhône Valley, 58–9
sherry, 140–1
South Africa, 243–4
Southwest France, 76–7
Spain, 133–4
Switzerland, 188–9
Vintage Wine Trust, 255
vintages
website, 403
see also classic vintage guide;
vintage reports
Viognier grape
Argentina, 303
California, 247
Israel, 230
Portugal, 145
Rhône Valley, 62
vins de pays, 92
Virginia, direct-shipping permits,
267
Virginia Wine Works, 267
viticulture, 381–7
in Asia, 331
biodynamics, 49
bush fires, 383
carbon-neutral wineries, 381
complantation, 268
detecting aroma precursors,
387
DNA analysis, 62–3, 112,
218, 382
early harvesting, 38–40
effects of climate change, 383,
385–7
eucalyptus taint, 384
grapevine genome sequenced,
382
high-altitude vineyards, 383
leaf plucking, 387
migrant labor, 273
"natural" wines, 66
nitrogen fertilization and
aromatic compounds, 384
older rootstocks, 186

viticulture (cont.)
preservation of genetic resources, 385
rejection of physiological ripeness, 38–40
satellite-based vineyard-control system, 139
soil compaction, 346
terroir research in Chile, 292
ungrafted vines, 101
very low temperatures in US, 277
websites, 403
weed control, 346
see also organic and biodynamic wines; pests and diseases
Vitis coignetiae, 360
Vitis lanata, 359
Vitis palmata, 359
Vitis purpurea, 358
Vitis sylvestris, 385
Vitis vinifera, 359
Vlassides, Sophocles, 212
Voguë, Comte Georges de, 374
Volg Winery, 187
Vouillamoz, Dr. José, 62–3

Wachau, 194
Wädenswil wine university, 187
Wairau Valley, 338, 340
Walla Walla Valley, 255, 259, 262
Wallula Vineyards, 259
Walsh, Brian, 311
Walters, Shawn, 267
Warfvinge, Per, 399
Washington
AVA reform, 255
websites, 403
Washington State Liquor Control Board, 258
water shortages, US, 273–4
weather see climate and weather
websites see Internet
Weinviertel, 194
Weir, Mike, 286
Weisser Burgunder grape, 99
Weisser Gutedel grape, 102
Weisser Riesling grape, 101
Wellenstein, 183
Wellington, 311
Weninger, Franz, 194
Weninger & Gere Winery, 207
White Malaga grape, 360
Wiemer, Hermann J., 265, 266
Wikingsson, Fredrick, 37
Willamette Valley, 255
The Wine Advocate, 230–1
wine and health, 349–54
benefits of drinking after menopause, 350
benefits of drinking wine with food, 351–2
benefits to lining of arteries, 351

wine and health (cont.)
binge drinking, 349–50
breast cancer, 351
cancer, 351
dementia, 352
"French paradox," 72–3
hip fractures, 354
liver disease, 351
lung function, 352
maternal intake of alcohol, 353
post-heart-attack angina risk reduced, 350
reduction of renal cancer, 350
rising alcohol levels, 349–50
sherry and, 141
units of alcohol, 349, 352
warnings on labels, 242
wine compared to beer and spirits, 352
wine bottles
Flûte d'Alsace, 39
heavier bottles, 248
magnums, 312
see also corks; screwcaps and non-cork closures
wine competitions and awards
Decanter Man of the Year, 222
Decanter World Wine Awards, 35, 43, 201–2
Dutch Wine Selection, 176
Effervescents du Monde, 163
Fine Wines Board (Portugal), 144–5
Hawke's Bay A&P Awards, 320–1
India Wine Challenge, 329
International Wine and Spirit Competition (IWSC), 161
International Wine Challenge (IWC), 161, 293
Malbec Made for Meat, 303
Platter Guide, 244
Salon des Vins de Loire blind tasting, 47
South East Vineyards Association, 164
Top 100 Vins de Pays, 95
UK Vineyards Association, 163
Vinexpo, 289
Virginia Cup, 268
World Riesling Cup, 265
World Riesling Competition, 46
wine courses, Plumpton College, 161
Wine Discoveries, 399
wine-education websites, 403
wine labels
Oregon, 256, 262
varietal wines, 257
wine science, 388–95
adding white juice to red wines, 391
botrytis inhibits foaming quality, 392
botrytized wines, 389

wine science (cont.)
DNA analysis, 382
finish, 394
fungus in cellars, 389
microorganisms in bottled wine, 393
off-odors, 394–5
oxygen and corks, 390
preventing hydrogen sulfide, 390–1
role of bentonite, 392
rotundone in Shiraz, 388–9
source of TCA, 393
Wine Spectator, 239, 284
wine tourism
Internet and, 397
Savoie, 65–6
WineBid.com, 376
Wines of South Africa (WOSA), 238
Winiarski, Warren, 256
Wither Hills, 320
Wolf, Craig, 275
Wolf Blass Winery, 255
Wölffer, 268
Wollersheim Winery, 277

Yakima Valley, 255
Yalumba, 311
Yamabudo grape, 360
Yatir Winery, 234
Yearlstone Vineyard, 164
yeasts
filtering wines, 393
genetically enhanced, 240
new yeasts, 186
preventing hydrogen sulfide, 391
removing sediment, 392
yields
Luxembourg, 179
vins de pays and *vins de table*, 96
YouTube, 396
Yquem, Ch. d', 11

Zachys, 376, 377
Zalagyonge grape, 357
Zanella, Maurizio, 110
Zeeland, 169
Zinfandel grape
California, 247
Israel, 230
Pacific Northwest, 256, 257
Texas, 278
Zinfandel Advocates and Producers (ZAP), 249
Zion Winery, 231
Ziraldo, Donald, 289
Zitsa Wine Cooperative, 213
Zoinos, 213

Index compiled by Hilary Bird